RICHARD K. DEBO is a member of the Department of History at Simon Fraser University

This is a highly readable and absorbing account of Bolshevik foreign policy during Lenin's first year in power. In tracing the development of that policy, the book considers both the impact it had on a world torn by war and the effect it had on the Bolsheviks themselves, now no longer engaged in clandestine struggle but in effective state control.

The book explores Lenin's relationship with the various elements of the party – his fruitful, but frequently discordant, relationship with Trotsky in particular – and the way he sought and obtained support for his policies in the tumultuous political circumstances of 1917 and 1918. It studies Lenin's political style as well, in an attempt to explain the shift from his utopianism of 1917 to his hard-headed political realism of 1918.

The analysis focuses on the fundamental questions of how the Soviet state, lacking significant military forces in the midst of a world war, succeeded in surviving the first year of the revolution, and how it survived the new threat of the changed political situation at the end of the war.

Revolution and Survival is the first history of Lenin's foreign policy during this crucial period, and Richard Debo has fused insight with style in a fascinating and authoritative book.

RICHARD K. DEBO

Revolution and survival: the foreign policy of Soviet Russia, 1917-18

UNIVERSITY OF TORONTO PRESS
Toronto and Buffalo

© University of Toronto Press 1979
Toronto   Buffalo   London
Printed in Canada

Library of Congress Cataloging in Publication Data

Debo, Richard K   1938–
  Revolution and survival.

  Bibliography: p.
  Includes index.
  1. Russia – Foreign relations – 1917–1945.   I. Title.
  DK265.D35   327.47   78-9671
  ISBN 0-8020-5411-0

TO JANIE, TONI, AND NATASHA

Preface

This work emerged from an early interest in Russia, graduate seminars in the history of international relations, and a dissertation on the life of Georgii V. Chicherin. It was subsequently reshaped and brought to focus on the critical year from the Bolshevik revolution to the end of the First World War.

Many scholars have contributed to this development. Albin T. Anderson of the University of Nebraska provided initial stimulation, patient guidance, and continuous encouragement. More than any other individual he aroused my interest in Russia, its people, language, literature, and history. I have been very fortunate in never lacking encouragement. Special mention is due Rex Wade, Michael and Anita Fellman, Michael Carley, John Hutchinson, and Phyllis Auty. Successive chairpersons of the Department of History at Simon Fraser University have aided me in countless ways.

The staff of Love Library, University of Nebraska; the Missouri State Historical Society; the Hoover Institution; the National Archives of the United States; the Library of Congress; the New York Public Library; Butler Library, Columbia University; Houghton Library, Harvard University; the International Institute of Social History, Amsterdam; the British Museum; New College Library, Oxford University; the University of British Columbia Library; the Public Record Office, London; the Archives of the French Foreign Ministry, Paris; and the Archives of the French Ministry of War, Vincennes, have all given me their full cooperation in obtaining materials necessary to complete this study. Special thanks are due the staff of the Simon Fraser University Library, especially Helen Gray whose assistance has been indispensable.

The research for this work could not have been completed without generous grants received from the United States Educational Institution in the Netherlands; the President's Research Grant Committee, Simon Fraser University; and, especially, the Canada Council. Philip Amos undertook the arduous task of reading my proof-sheets and, together with Norma Boutillier and Janie Debo, helped prepare the index. The cost of indexing was paid by a special grant from the President's Research Grant Committee, Simon Fraser University.

This book has been published with the help of a grant from the Social Science Federation of Canada, using funds provided by the Social Sciences and Humanities Research Council of Canada, and a grant to the University of Toronto Press from the Andrew W. Mellon Foundation.

All dates in this work are given according to the Gregorian or Western calendar. Transliteration from Russian is based on the Library of Congress system but diacritical marks have been omitted.

Richard K. Debo
Simon Fraser University
29 March 1978

Contents

x Contents

Introduction

Shortly after the death of Lenin, in a brief memoir of the deceased leader, Georgii V. Chicherin wrote: 'The time has not yet come to give an account of the harmonious foreign policy system of Vladimir Il'ich.'[1] This, he said, would be the task of future historians. In 1924, Chicherin still served as foreign commissar of the Soviet Union and although he was not a contender for the mantle of Lenin he was caught up in the rough and tumble struggle for power which followed the leader's death. Thus, he had good reason to avoid a thorough analysis of Lenin's foreign policy and to describe it in only the most general terms. A more detailed examination of that policy would have involved him in controversy with virtually every surviving founder of the Soviet state. It need not be assumed, however, that his hesitation to write about Lenin's work was motivated by simple political expedience, for the foreign commissar, as a trained historian, was undoubtedly aware that he was much too close to the subject to obtain a clear perspective. More than fifty years have passed since then, however, and the time has now come to attempt a thorough analysis of Lenin's work in foreign policy, at least in so far as it relates to the first year of the Bolshevik revolution.

Other historians, of course, have written on this subject. The works of J.W. Wheeler-Bennett and E.H. Carr are classics in the field and served to open it for further study.[2] These works, however, were written at a time when few primary sources were available, and their authors had to base them primarily on newspapers, memoirs, and the small number of docu-

1 G.V. Chicherin, *Stat'i i Rechi po Voprosam Mezhdunarodnoi Politiki* (Moscow, 1961) 276
2 J.W. Wheeler-Bennett, *Brest-Litovsk: The Forgotten Peace. March 1918* (London, 1938);
   E.H. Carr, *The Bolshevik Revolution, 1917-1923.* Three vols. (London, 1950-3) vol. III

ments published by various governments prior to the opening of their archives. Recently, substantially greater documentation on the subject has become available as the archives of the United States, Germany, Great Britain and, finally, France have been opened to historical research. Although the Soviet government has not yet chosen to open its archives for this period to western scholars, it has sanctioned the publication of an increasing number of important documentary collections which cast much light on the subject. These documents, especially those drawn from the western archives, have led to the publication of a number of interesting and important studies of the policies pursued by western governments in Russia at the time of the revolution. These have provided an exposition and analysis of many of the reasons why the British, American, and German governments acted as they did in Russia at that time.[3] Unfortunately, none of these studies tells us much about the development of *Soviet* foreign policy or the reasons why it developed in the way it did. It is possible, however, using the rich archival resources of Washington, London, Paris, and Bonn, plus the continuing flow of Soviet documentation on the early years of the Bolshevik revolution, to focus on the development of Soviet foreign policy itself rather than viewing it simply as a foil against which other governments pursued their interests in Russia. Such is the aim of this work.

This study will seek to examine the origins and developments of Bolshevik foreign policy as it emerged from the revolutionary struggle for power in Russia to be given concrete form in the acts of the new Soviet state. It will examine not only the manner in which this policy was formulated, executed, and received in a world torn by the last year of the Great War, but also the impact which this policy, and the circumstances surrounding it, had on the Bolsheviks themselves as they underwent the transition from a revolutionary party accustomed to clandestine struggle in conditions of illegality to a government effectively exercising state power. Such an examination requires a close study of the relationship among the various elements which composed the Bolshevik party and, in particular, the fruitful, but frequently discordant, relationship between Lenin and Leon Trotsky during the first critical year of the revolution in Russia. It also requires an equally close study of the nature of Lenin's influence within the Bolshevik party and Soviet state, especially the manner in which the Bolshevik leader sought and obtained support for his

3 G.F. Kennan, *Russia Leaves the War* (Princeton, New Jersey, 1956), and the *Decision to Intervene* (Princeton, New Jersey, 1958); Richard H. Ullman, *Intervention and the War* (Princeton, New Jersey, 1961); Winfried Baumgart, *Deutsche Ostpolitik 1918* (Munich, 1966)

policies in the tumultuous political circumstances of 1917 and 1918. Such a study involves an analysis of Lenin's special style of politics, developed in the struggle for power in Russia but projected with telling effect on the international scene in 1918. How can his utopianism of 1917 be reconciled with the hard-headed political realism which he displayed to such great advantage in the following year? To what extent were his policies based on ideology, opportunism, raw emotion, cold calculation, and political acumen?

In examining the events of the stormy year between the Bolshevik seizure of power and the end of the Great War in Europe the reader is consistently struck by the frequency with which the fall of the Soviet government was predicted. Hardly a day passed without some leading political figure inside or out of Russia proclaiming that the days of the Bolshevik regime were numbered. Even the Bolsheviks shared this view, and Lenin himself consistently draped the future of his government in the darkest of colours. How then did the Soviet government, bereft of significant military force in the midst of what was until then mankind's most destructive war, succeed in surviving the first year of the revolution? During 1918 the Soviet government was forced to conclude two of the most extortionate political agreements in the annals of international relations. The Treaty of Brest-Litovsk and the later supplementary agreements to this treaty deprived the Soviet state of vast stretches of territory, immense economic resources, and a large part of its political freedom of action. Yet the Bolsheviks not only survived these treaties but were able to draw strength from their hostile pages. How was this possible? How were these devastating treaties used to safeguard the Bolshevik regime in Russia and provide a defence behind which Lenin and his associates were able to entrench themselves in power? With the end of the Great War, of course, the entire political situation in Europe changed once again, and the existence of Soviet Russia was once more imperilled. How did the Soviet government view this threat and seek to defend itself in the perilous circumstances of November 1918? As far as possible this work will seek to provide at least partial answers to these questions.

REVOLUTION AND SURVIVAL

Vulpinari cum vulpibus

1
The genesis of a
revolutionary foreign policy

... if the Russian revolution were to pass from impotent and pitiful yearning for peace to a forthright peace offer coupled with the publication and annulment of secret treaties, etc., there are ninety-nine chances in a hundred that peace would quickly follow, that the capitalists would be unable to stand in the way of peace. Lenin, September 1917

What diplomatic work are we apt to have now? I will issue a few revolutionary proclamations to the peoples of the world and then shut up shop. Trotsky, November 1917

In March 1917, tsarist Russia collapsed, a victim of internal instability and the world war then in its third year. From the wreckage, suddenly liberated from years of repression, emerged all the highly diverse political tendencies in the ramshackle empire. While gunfire still echoed along the streets of Petrograd, monarchists and democrats, aristocrats and socialists began to scramble for the authority fallen from the hands of Nicholas II. In place of the autocracy rose two competing institutions: the Provisional Government, self-appointed ministers drawn primarily from the privileged classes represented in the old State Duma; and the Petrograd Soviet of Workers' and Soldiers' Deputies, a heterogeneous mixture of socialists hastily elected from the factories and regiments of the capital. The two cooperated badly, each viewing the other with suspicion and agreeing only on the necessity of preventing a restoration of the autocracy. Vital problems demanded solution, but the two authorities paralyzed each other.

This was especially true in foreign affairs. The Provisional Government, inspired by its foreign minister Pavel Miliukov, wished to continue the war in concert with its western allies. Not only did it wish to honour the obligation undertaken by the tsarist regime not to conclude a separate peace with the central powers, it also wanted Britain, France, and Italy to reaffirm the treaties guaranteeing Russia the right to annex Constantinople, Galicia, and other enemy territory. For Miliukov the revolution meant that Russia had an opportunity to wage war effectively rather than in the slipshod manner tolerated under Nicholas II. With memories of the heroic transformation of France wrought by the great revolution of the eighteenth century the Provisional Government called for a continuation of war to a victorious conclusion. The socialists sitting in the Soviet viewed the situation much differently. Although badly divided on other issues they united behind the leadership of Irakli Tsereteli, a Georgian Menshevik, to demand an end to the conflict. For them the war was an abomination, a struggle conducted by rapacious capitalists for booty and plunder to be won at the expense of popular suffering. Pavel 'Dardanel'skii' might want Constantinople, but they sought peace. True, the revolution had to defend itself: the central powers could not be allowed to crush it under foot; a separate peace with Berlin was unthinkable. But the foreign policy of revolutionary Russia had to be re-oriented toward the negotiation of a general peace of no annexations and no indemnities. Tsereteli's 'revolutionary defencism' quickly became the rival of Miliukov's war to a victorious conclusion.

The first great clash between the Provisional Government and Soviet came over just this issue, and its outcome, the resignation of Miliukov, illuminated the realities of power in revolutionary Russia. Yet it was one thing to drive Miliukov from office and another to secure peace. A general peace required the cooperation of Russia's allies, and, in the third year of war, with the United States having just entered the conflict, London and Paris were hardly in a mood to consider a peace of no annexations and no indemnities. Nevertheless, a campaign was mounted on two levels: the Russian foreign ministry, now entrusted to M.I. Tereshchenko, assaulted the allied chancelleries while the Soviet urged entente socialists to support a peace conference based on the principles enunciated in Petrograd. This campaign smashed on the rocks of allied intransigence and the lack of interest displayed by socialists in Great Britain and France. When it failed the moderate socialists were left without a credible foreign policy. Alexander Kerensky, Tereshchenko, and other members of the Provisional Government who, at best, only weakly supported the peace initiative of the Soviet, were free to pursue a policy of procrastination, gambling that allied victory would come before their own collapse.[1]

---

1 On the foreign policy of the Provisional Government see Rex Wade, *The Russian Search for Peace: February-October 1917* (Stanford, California, 1969)

The odds against Kerensky were very long. To succeed, his government had to restrain the centrifugal forces loosed by the revolution and hold back the Germans until the western allies forced Berlin to sue for peace. But such a possibility receded further into the background as summer lengthened into fall. Freed from the grip of autocracy Russian society began to disintegrate. As existing organs of adjudication lost their legitimacy, sheer power became the decisive answer to all disputes. In the countryside, peasants seized the land; in the cities, the proletariat took control of the factories; and in the borderlands, dissident nationalities prepared to declare their independence. At the front, the Russian armies began to dissolve as millions deserted the trenches to return home. To stem this tide Kerensky had only rhetorical weapons, and in the chaos of late 1917, words counted for little.

Kerensky's problems were magnified and rendered unmanageable by the violent attack launched against his government by V.I. Lenin and the Bolshevik faction of the Russian Social Democratic Labour party. In the weeks immediately following the fall of Nicholas II, the Bolsheviks had joined with the other socialist parties in the Soviet to support Tsereteli's policy of 'revolutionary defencism,' but, on his return from exile in April, Lenin put an end to this collaboration. Instead of helping to unite Russia in defence of the March revolution, Lenin urged all dissident elements in the former empire to press their claims against society as it was then constituted. The overthrow of the autocracy, he said, represented only the triumph of the bourgeoisie; the workers and peasants had to move on to the socialist revolution. Nothing less than a transfer of power from the Provisional Government to the Soviets would satisfy him. Without the overthrow of the privileged classes 'revolutionary defencism' was a sham and, in Lenin's eyes, a crime against international socialism. Although these views shocked even his closest associates they followed logically from the position he had adopted at the outbreak of the Great War.

As early as 1907 he had distinguished himself by insisting that in the event of a general Europeon conflict 'the essential thing' would be 'to utilize the crisis created by war in order to hasten the overthrow of the bourgeoisie.'[2] Other socialists might argue over ways to avert war, but Lenin was not interested in the debate. Instead, he was already considering the ways in which a general war could be utilized to destroy the social-economic system which would generate it. When war came in August 1914, he moved decisively in this direction. While other socialists strug-

2 V.I. Lenin, *Polnoe Sobranie Sochinenii,* 5th ed., 55 vols. (Moscow, 1958–) vol. XVI, 72. This edition of Lenin's collected works will hereafter be cited as Lenin, PSS

gled ineffectively to prevent war and then turned to support their governments Lenin denounced the conflict and called for a 'ruthless and all-out struggle against Great Russian and monarchist chauvinism.' 'From the viewpoint of the working class and the masses of all the peoples of Russia,' he wrote, 'the defeat of the tsarist monarchy and its army ... would be the lesser evil by far.'[3] But tsarism, *per se*, was not the primary enemy. For Lenin it was only the weary spearbearer of an antiquated social-economic system which had to be moved from the historical stage before battle could be joined with his chief adversary, bourgeois capitalism in its imperialist stage of development. In the months following the outbreak of war he began to elaborate his views, producing an analysis of the conflict and a political program which would form the basis of Bolshevik policy in 1917.

According to this analysis, the world war was not a national conflict such as had characterized the wars of the previous century. Instead it was an imperialist war fought by states in the last stage of capitalist development. National wars had marked the destruction of feudalism and had been a necessary step in the liberation of the bourgeoisie from feudal society. Now capitalism had reached its final stage, exporting capital rather than commodities and extending its control over the entire world; everything which could be accomplished under capitalism had been accomplished. National boundaries had already proved too limited for it, and the great powers, driven forward by their bourgeois masters, had seized the remainder of the world for economic exploitation. Dissatisfied with this division the capitalists of each state were desperately seeking a new division which would permit them to dominate their rivals in other countries. In this situation revolutionary socialists could not, as in the previous era, support the aspirations of their national bourgeoisie. Such support was counter-revolutionary and opportunist in nature, counter-revolutionary as it retarded the transformation of society from a capitalist to a socialist base, opportunist as it had no foundations in Marxist principles and advanced the interests of individuals rather than the proletariat. Socialists who supported the war had ceased to be social democrats and become social chauvinists, socialists in word but chauvinist in deed. For these renegades Lenin reserved a special place in the innermost circle of his political inferno. They had become the class enemies of the proletariat, for they utilized the familiar rhetoric of socialism to advance the aims of the ruling classes.[4] This was intolerable. Revolutionary socialists in each state

---

3 Lenin, PSS, vol. XXVI, 6
4 *Ibid.*, vol. XXXIV, 98-9

had to work for the defeat of their own government and the transformation of the imperialist war of nation against nation into civil wars of class against class. To those socialists who argued that they were only defending their state against foreign aggression he responded: 'Neither group of belligerents is inferior to the other in spoliation, atrocities, and the boundless brutality of war.'[5] The Marxist laws of social-economic development functioned in war as in peace, and the aims of socialism could not be advanced without a ruthless struggle against opportunism, social chauvinism, defencism, and imperialism. Revolutionary socialists could not falter at the possibility of their own country's defeat. Defeat could only benefit the revolution, for it would disorganize the army, weaken the government, heighten social tension and hasten the coming of civil war.[6]

Lenin was thinking primarily of Russia, yet believed his views were universally valid. The key element of his policy was that enunciated in 1907: the utilization of the crisis created by war for the overthrow of the bourgeoisie. Like Clausewitz, whom he admired,[7] Lenin believed war to be the extension of politics by other means. War hastened the process of historical development, accelerating the decline of antiquated institutions while stimulating the rise of movements meeting the demands of new historical forces. Thus, Lenin had no use for pacifists who opposed war on humanitarian grounds. They simply obfuscated the issue and led the simple-minded to believe that peace could be restored without the overthrow of the ruling classes. Peace without revolution would be worse than no peace at all, for it would allow the ruling classes to consolidate their hold on society. Always the politician, Lenin thought in terms of how the war would stimulate revolution. When asked in 1915 what he would do if the Bolsheviks suddenly came to power, he chose to emphasize the international significance of such a victory. A revolution in Russia, he said, would 'fan the flames of the "left" movement in Germany a hundredfold. If we defeated tsarism completely we would propose peace to all the warring Powers on democratic conditions, and, if they were rejected, we would conduct a *revolutionary* war.'[8] As Lenin defined 'democratic conditions' in a way which no existing government could accept, including the liberation of all colonies and dependent nationalities, he was pledging his party, once in power, to wage revolutionary war against world capitalism.

5 *Ibid.*, vol. XXVI, 16-17
6 *Ibid.*, 166
7 See John Erickson, 'Lenin as Tactician.' In Leonard Schapiro and Peter Reddaway (eds.), *Lenin: The Man, the Theorist, the Leader* (New York, 1967) 182, n.1
8 Lenin, PSS, vol. XLIX, 133. Emphasis in original

Peace without victory held just as little attraction for him as it did for bourgeois generals and politicians; he simply defined his object in different terms and approached it from a different direction. In 1915, however, the possibility of implementing his policy seemed remote even to Lenin. Consequently it remained at an immature stage of development, unrefined and unelaborated, a concept rather than a plan, but a concept, as Lenin would show, capable of the most subtle and elaborate embellishment.[9]

The March revolution signaled the beginning of this process. The long awaited revolution had materialized, but it was necessary to act quickly if the brilliant opportunity created by the fall of the autocracy was not to be lost in the intoxication of the moment. The first news from Petrograd distressed Lenin greatly. The tsar was gone, but the Provisional Government represented the capitalists and landowners of Russia. In its first proclamation it had not even mentioned 'the basic issue of the time, peace.' Lenin concluded that the Provisional Government, like all other capitalist regimes, intended to conceal its war aims with patriotic slogans and delude the workers. For him this meant that 'the working class must ... continue its fight for socialism and peace utilizing for this purpose the new situation.'[10] But what were his comrades doing to unseat the bourgeois ministers? Nothing. Instead the Bolsheviks in Petrograd seemed to be joining with the other socialist parties to support the Provisional Government.

Within a week Lenin launched his attack against both the Provisional Government and those socialists, his own associates included, who would tolerate its policies. In *Letters from Afar* he presented his own analysis of the political situation in Russia and guidelines for Bolshevik policy. In the fourth of these letters he examined the problem of the war, elaborating on

9 The literature on proletarian internationalism is quite extensive. The two classics are Merle Fainsod, *International Socialism and the World War* (Cambridge, Massachusetts, 1935) and Olga Gankin and H.H. Fisher (eds.), *The Bolsheviks and the World War: The Origin of the Third International* (Stanford, California, 1940). In recent years much new work has been added. See: Julius Braunthal, *History of the International, 1914-1943* (London, 1967); Georges Haupt, *Socialism and the Great War: The Collapse of the Second International* (Oxford, 1972); Jules Humbert-Droz, *Der Krieg und die Internationale* (Vienna, 1964); N.E. Korolev, *Lenin i Mezhdunarodnoe Rabochee Dvizhenie, 1914-1918* (Moscow, 1968); Horst Lademacher, *Die Zimmerwalder Bewegung*, 2 vols. (The Hague, 1967); Arnold Reisberg, *Lenin und die Zimmerwalder Bewegung* (Berlin, 1966); Alfred Erich Senn, *The Russian Revolution in Switzerland, 1914-1917* (Madison, Wisconsin, 1971); and two works by Ia.G. Temkin, *Tsimmerval'd-Kiental'* (Moscow, 1967) and *Lenin i Mezhdunarodnaia Sotsial-Demokratiia, 1914-1917* (Moscow, 1968)
10 Lenin, pss, vol. xxxi, 2

his earlier views and ridiculing the idea that the new government could serve the cause of peace. 'To urge that government to conclude a democratic peace,' he wrote, 'is like preaching to brothel keepers.' Guchkov, Miliukov, and L'vov were little better than pimps pandering to the interests of capital. As the imperialists wanted to redivide the colonial and dependent areas of the world a democratic peace concluded by imperialist regimes was impossible. Talking peace to a bourgeois government was nothing less than fraud, just another variety of opportunism to be exposed, attacked, and destroyed. Only a transfer of power to the proletariat could end the war. The German workers had no more reason to trust Miliukov than they had to trust Nicholas II; a bellicose monarchy had simply been replaced by a bellicose republic. The workers, therefore, had to take power, publish the treaties binding Russia to the entente, renounce the claims contained in them, call for an immediate armistice and sponsor peace terms based on the liberation of all colonial, dependent, and oppressed nations. Since bourgeois governments could not accept such terms they had to be overthrown. The Russian proletariat would have to call upon the workers of all nations to establish soviets and wage revolutionary war against imperialism. Only then would peace be restored and imperialism crushed.[11] Such was Lenin's analysis of the revolutionary situation in Russia and its relationship to the Great War two weeks after the fall of Nicholas II. Although his views were transmitted to his associates in Petrograd, they made little impact. Lenin was still in Switzerland, and the Bolshevik leaders in Petrograd felt that he had become divorced from Russian realities. They ignored his letters and continued to cooperate with the other socialist parties in providing limited support of the Provisional Government.

Outraged by the inaction of his associates Lenin sought desperately to return to Russia. With the entire continent aflame a thousand obstacles stood in his way. Finding all other channels blocked, Lenin asked the German government for permission to travel through its territory. He specified, however, that no political strings be attached to the agreement. The Germans, who had kept close tabs on Lenin, agreed willingly, and, in early April, the Bolshevik leader and thirty-one other Russian exiles crossed Germany in a special train. The German authorities, fearing Lenin's influence on their own increasingly volatile population, allowed no contact between the revolutionaries and German citizens. In effect the train enjoyed extraterritorial immunity, and its passengers were not sub-

11 *Ibid.*, 48-54

ject to passport control or baggage inspection. These circumstances later gave substance to the charge that Lenin was a German agent smuggled into Russia. Instead, Berlin was gambling that Lenin, motivated by his own political aspirations, would create chaos in Petrograd, thus forcing Russia from the war and splitting the allied coalition. Lenin passed quietly through Germany, reached Sweden and, on 16 April, arrived in Petrograd.[12] A new phase in the Russian revolution had begun.

In the weeks following his return to Russia Lenin regained ascendancy over the Bolshevik movement, reversed the policies pursued in his absence and had his views endorsed by a special party conference. While doing this he introduced a new element to his evaluation of the international situation and subtly began to change the emphasis in his desiderata for world revolution. Where before he had talked primarily in international terms he now began to assign an ever larger role to Russia in hastening the revolution. At the Seventh All-Russian Conference of Bolsheviks he announced this new theme, bluntly asserting that 'the Russian bourgeois-democratic revolution is now not only a prologue to, but an indivisible and integral part of the socialist revolution in the west.'[13] Russia, he claimed, had emerged as the standard-bearer of the revolutionary future. The Russian revolution, as it progressed from a bourgeois-democratic to socialist stage, would ignite similar revolutions elsewhere. Yet he was also forced to admit that the workers' revolution in the west would not materialize as it had in Russia. 'They have no half-wits there like Nicholas and Rasputin,' he said, 'there the best men of their class are at the head of government.'[14] This meant that all the more responsibility fell on Russia to assist in the birth of revolution in the west. The world revolution had to be driven forward by accelerating the revolution in Russia and taking power in the name of proletarian internationalism. It enraged him that weeks were slipping past while nothing was done to implement a genuinely revolutionary foreign policy. He dismissed the efforts of the moderate socialists as merely an 'impotent and pitiful yearning for peace.' The situation demanded direct peace proposals and the exposure of the predatory nature of the war. If this was done by a genuinely revolutionary government, he claimed, there were 'ninety-nine chances in a hundred that

12 For Lenin's return to Russia see Werner Hahlweg, *Lenins Rückkehr nach Russland 1917* (Leiden, 1957) and Senn, *The Russian Revolution in Switzerland*
13 Lenin, PSS, vol. XXXI, 403-44
14 *Ibid.*, vol. XXXII, 97

peace would come soon, that the capitalists would not be able to stand in the way of peace.'[15]

These seemed to be good odds, but not even his own supporters were eager to accept them. When he first returned he was nearly alone in demanding the overthrow of the Provisional Government and a confrontation with imperialism. Although he succeeded in gaining the reluctant concurrence of his followers the newly energized Bolsheviks found themselves isolated in their refurbished radicalism.[16] In early May, however, another revolutionary leader, Leon Trotsky, returned from exile and promptly lined up along the mark drawn by Lenin. Trotsky, in fact, had independently arrived at the same conclusions as the Bolshevik leader. In New York at the time of the March revolution he had hastily left for home only to be detained at Halifax by British authorities who wished to stop him reaching Russia. Before embarking for Petrograd, however, he had written a series of articles for *Novy Mir*, a Russian newspaper published in New York City, which show the similarity of his views to those then being developed in Switzerland by Lenin.

In these articles Trotsky, like Lenin, took aim at the failure of the Provisional Government to address itself to the question of peace, highlighted the imperialist aspirations of the new bourgeois ministers and denounced defencism. It was insufficient merely to guard against a restoration of the autocracy; it was necessary 'to sweep out the monarchic and feudal rubbish to the last corner.'[17] Nor was he afraid of forcing the revolutionary pace, provoking civil war and establishing a regime dedicated to setting the world afire. In his view the Russian proletariat had to unite with the peasantry, overthrow the regime of capitalists and landowners, socialize the means of production and pursue a revolutionary foreign policy.[18] The revolutionary parties could not accept the foreign policy of the new government; to do so 'would be a terrible blow to our colleagues, the revolutionary socialists of Germany,' allowing the Hohenzollerns 'to raise the patriotic spirit and restore the "national unity" of the German people.' The new Russia had to show its 'irreconcilable hostility not only to the dynastic aristocratic reaction but to liberal imperialism.'[19] Drawing on his theory of 'permanent revolution' first expounded during the revo-

15 *Ibid.*, vol. xxxiv, 148-9
16 Alexander Rabinowitch, *Prelude to Revolution* (Bloomington, Indiana, 1968) 36-53
17 Leon Trotsky, *Sochineniia* (Moscow, 1925-7), vol. iii, part i, 19
18 *Ibid.*, 15
19 *Ibid.*, 15-16

lution of 1905 he proclaimed the dynamic role of the Russian revolution even before Lenin. Thus, while the Bolshevik leader did not fully develop this interpretation until April, Trotsky on 16 March wrote: 'At the head of the popular masses the Russian revolutionary proletariat will fulfill its historic task; it will drive out the monarchical and aristocratic reaction from all its refuges and stretch out its hand to the proletariat of Germany and all Europe.'[20] He also addressed himself to the question of what should be done if, despite appeals from a revolutionary government for an end to the slaughter, the ruling classes of the belligerent states refused to negotiate a general and democratic peace. His answer paralleled that of Lenin: 'The revolutionary workers' government would wage war against the Hohenzollerns, summoning the brother proletariat of Germany to rise against the common enemy.' Reverting again to his concept of 'permanent revolution' he further asserted: 'war conducted by a proletarian government would be only an armed revolution. It would be a question not of the "defence of the government," but of the defence of the revolution, and its transplantation into other countries.'[21] Thus, unknowingly, even before leaving New York, Trotsky had planted himself firmly beside Lenin in the struggle for control of Russia.

Yet there were differences, subtle and unarticulated, but differences nonetheless. Although reaching very similar conclusions the two men arrived at common ground by way of different routes. Trotsky's approach was that of the virtuoso, improvising upon his earlier theory of 'permanent revolution.' First developed with the aid of Alexander Helphand during the revolution of 1905, this theory asserted that the Russian proletariat possessed the potential, in a revolutionary situation, to inflame the Russian peasantry and, with their assistance, to carry the torch of revolution throughout the world. Disappointed in 1905, Trotsky viewed the events of 1917 as a second and vastly improved opportunity to justify his earlier commitment. His early views on the Russian revolution clearly revolve around his treasured theory. Brilliant as these views were, they represented a very doctrinaire approach to the problems of Russia in 1917. Lenin's approach was different. Although Lenin could be classed as both virtuoso and theoretician, intellectually he was less inclined than Trotsky to allow his theories to obscure his perception of reality. More cautious in

20 *Ibid.*, 7. The earliest development of Trotsky's theory of permanent revolution is dealt with by Isaac Deutscher, *The Prophet Armed: Trotsky, 1879-1921* (New York, 1954) 144-74. Also see Alain Brossat, *Aux origines de la révolution permanente: la pensée politique du jeune Trotsky* (Paris, 1974)
21 Trotsky, *Sochineniia*, vol. III, part I, 20

formulating his ideas, he was also more willing to dispose of them when they had ceased to be useful. These differences can be attributed in part to the different roles which the two men played in the Russian revolutionary movement. Trotsky was a free-lance revolutionary; Lenin stood at the head of a party structure extending to the far corners of the Russian empire. Thus Lenin found it necessary to attune his senses more keenly to the necessities of the moment, making tactics rather than theory and action rather than rationalization his chief stock in trade. The constant factor in all his decisions was the effort to draw a maximum of political advantage from any situation. In the first days after the overthrow of the autocracy the two men came to adopt very similar policies, but the manner in which they did so was pregnant with meaning for the future. Trotsky, again mounted astride his favorite theoretical formulation, would find it difficult to adjust to changes in the political environment and prove reluctant to abandon his cherished 'permanent revolution.' Lenin would remain highly attuned to the political environment, not only willing, but eager, to make whatever tactical alterations necessity imposed upon him, always a theoretician, but an even greater realist.

From these differences stemmed another. Trotsky, with his intellectual and emotional commitment to 'permanent revolution,' ascribed special significance to the spread of revolution to Germany. Without a revolutionary victory in the heart of the continent he found it difficult to believe that a revolutionary regime could long survive in Russia. This emphasis is absent from Lenin's writing. For him, Germany was important but not crucial; he did not feel that the fate of the revolution in Russia necessarily turned on the immediate fate of the revolution in Germany. For Lenin the range of revolutionary possibilities extended far beyond Unter den Linden; the high road of revolution might well run through Berlin, but the side roads were also worth investigation. These differences were not immediately apparent in the summer of 1917 when Trotsky returned to Petrograd, discovered the close proximity of his views with those of Lenin and joined forces with the Bolsheviks. Nevertheless, subtle as they seem, they were to play a significant role in the events following the Bolshevik seizure of power.

The Bolsheviks, however, were not eager to stake their entire future on the success or failure of a *coup d'état.* Only with difficulty had Lenin shifted his party from a policy of cooperation to one of confrontation with the moderate socialists in the Soviet. He found it even more difficult to convince his colleagues, including Trotsky, to seize power. Following the abortive Kornilov *putsch* Lenin decided the revolutionary situation had ripened sufficiently to justify the overthrow of the Provisional Government and the assumption of power by the Bolsheviks. These views frightened his followers who, also fearing to oppose Lenin's will, found a thousand excuses for postponing, rather than rejecting outright, the prospect of an uprising. They procrastinated, and Lenin, on the very eve of the revolution, found it necessary to rake them with scorn and sarcasm. To the fainthearted he addressed a blistering letter denouncing all those who would delay the seizure of power. 'We should reason,' he wrote, 'like the Scheidemanns and Renaudels, that it is most prudent not to revolt, for if we are shot then the world will lose such excellent, reasonable, ideal internationalists!'[22] Seeking to shame his colleagues Lenin declared that for six months the Bolsheviks had been free to spread propaganda, publish their newspapers and speak in the Soviet. They had gained the upper hand in the two capitals, won over the Baltic fleet and the army in Finland yet they still had not called for an insurrection. If the Bolsheviks did not seize power at once, Lenin exclaimed, it would be a betrayal of international socialism greater than that of the social chauvinists in Germany, France, and Great Britain.[23]

Urging his followers forward, Lenin also had to defend himself against the charge that he was a German agent seeking to destroy Russia. Such accusations were given substance by the circumstances of his return from exile and the uncompromising stand he had taken on the war. Lenin found these charges scandalous as they totally distorted his aspirations and attempted to force the interpretation of his program back into the national chauvinist mold which he was seeking to smash. For him the Germans, like the western allies, were simply 'robber imperialists,' and he asserted time and again that it was 'ridiculous' to charge the Bolsheviks with wanting a separate peace with Germany. It was, he said, the diplomats of the capitalist states who were seeking a separate peace to avoid revolution; the Bolsheviks wanted a general peace brought about by the world workers' revolution. In *War and Revolution* he asserted:

To end the war which is being waged by the capitalists of all the wealthiest powers, a war stemming from the decade-long history of economic development, by one-sided withdrawal from military operations is such a stupid idea that it would be absurd even to refute it. ... The war which the capitalists of all countries are waging cannot be ended without a workers' revolution against these capitalists.[24]

22 Lenin, PSS, vol. XXXIV, 408
23 *Ibid.*, 385-7
24 *Ibid.*, vol. XXXII, 97

On the eve of his seizure of power, therefore, Lenin had prepared the foreign policy of his government. Once established it would call for an armistice, a peace conference and a peace of no annexations and no indemnifications. To expose the imperialist nature of the war the Bolsheviks would publish the secret treaties of the allied powers. In these circumstances Lenin believed the peoples of the world would force their governments to make peace. He was ready, however, for the one chance in one hundred that the war would continue. 'If the least probable case should happen,' he wrote, 'then a revolution in Europe would come a hundred times nearer.' The Bolshevik government would then place itself at the head of an army of workers and peasants and wage revolutionary war in alliance with the proletariat of the rest of the world.[25] On 7 November 1917, the Bolsheviks seized power and on the following day began to implement their revolutionary foreign policy.

The Bolshevik *coup* coincided with the opening of the Second All-Russian Congress of Soviets. Although the Bolsheviks and their ally, the left Socialist Revolutionary party, enjoyed a very substantial majority of the deputies elected to the Congress, that majority was composed of untried revolutionaries drawn from the four corners of the empire. Lenin feared that in the excitement of the moment they might easily go whoring after false idols, and to avert this possibility he wanted to confront the Congress with a *fait accompli*. His colleagues, however, still resisted his demand for a seizure of power, and, as an outlaw, he could not even appear safely in public. These circumstances forced Lenin from hiding, and, on the eve of the Congress, having disguised himself by shaving his beard and donning wig and spectacles, he proceeded to Smolny Institute, the headquarters of the Military Revolutionary Committee, where he overcame the last resistance to an immediate seizure of power.[26] The Committee, firmly in Bolshevik control, ordered its military and naval units into action, seized all vital centres in the city and laid seige to the Winter Palace. On the evening of the seventh, with the insurrection in full swing, the members of the Second All-Russian Congress of Soviets assembled in the Smolny Institute. With his own subordinates preparing to arrest the Provisional Government Lenin was free to appear at the Congress.

The Congress first debated the revolutionary propriety of the seizure of power then taking place in the capital. A minority denounced the *coup* as a conspiracy, but Trotsky, in the name of the Bolshevik Central Committee,

25 *Ibid.*, vol. xxxiv, 148-9
26 Robert V. Daniels, *Red October* (New York, 1968) 132-64

best expressed the sentiment of the majority when he characterized the seizure of power as a popular insurrection and read out of the Congress all those who rejected this interpretation. 'Go where you belong from now on,' he told them, 'into the rubbish can of history.'[27] The Congress then proceeded to endorse the action of the Military Revolutionary Committee, pronounce the Provisional Government deposed, and authorize the formation of a new government dedicated to ending the world war.

Late the next evening Lenin appeared at the Congress to introduce his new government. As its first official act the Council of People's Commissars (Sovnarkom) presented the Congress with a decree on peace. Written by Lenin and addressed to 'all warring peoples and their governments,' it summarized Bolshevik doctrine while foreshadowing the policies which would guide the new government in its early management of foreign affairs. As a summation, the decree unequivocally put forward the demand for an 'immediate peace without annexations and with indemnifications,' stressing the application of this doctrine to all parts of the world regardless of the time, place, or circumstances in which a given people had been forcibly incorporated in the political structure of another state. Lenin demanded an immediate end to the war, proposing as the first step a three-month armistice during which time a conference could meet to negotiate peace. For its part, the Soviet government proclaimed the abolition of secret diplomacy and the abrogation of all agreements and treaties 'having for their object the securing of benefits and privileges to the Russian landlords and capitalists.' It promised to publish the secret treaties of former Russian governments to prove that the war was simply being waged to divide the weak nationalities among the powerful states of the world.

Up to this point Lenin was simply fulfilling a 'campaign promise.' Like the decree on land, issued the same day, the decree on peace represented an act of good faith. The Bolsheviks had promised land reform and peace if they came to power, and, having formed a government based on the Soviets, they had to make good their promises. The worker and soldier deputies who had just cheered Trotsky's consignment of the moderate socialists to the 'rubbish can of history' would have deposited the Bolsheviks in the same container if they had shown any sign of hesitation. Unfortunately, the actual conclusion of peace could not be realized by decree. The peasantry could be relied upon to seize the land for themselves, but the warring states of Europe were unlikely to heed the writ of a revolu-

27 Leon Trotsky, *The History of the Russian Revolution.* Three vols. (Ann Arbor, Michigan, 1961) vol. II, 311

tionary assembly. Lenin, therefore, included more than popular sentiment in his decree. He also declared that his government did not regard its conditions of peace as an 'ultimatum.' It was prepared to consider any other conditions provided only that such alternatives were submitted promptly and 'in the clearest terms, without ambiguity or secrecy.'[28] This was not mere rhetoric; it was an integral part of Lenin's strategy. Thus, he quickly spurned the suggestion of one deputy who moved to have the decree put forward as an ultimatum. Lenin objected that this would make it too easy for the belligerent states to reject; they would be able to 'conceal the whole truth from the people, to hide the truth behind our irreconcilability.'[29] Alternate proposals would have to be considered, he said, but probably with a sly twinkle in his eye added, 'consideration does not necessarily mean acceptance.'

Lenin was doing two things. In part, he was expanding his area of maneuver, recognizing that as head of a functioning government he needed time to consolidate his position and ready the defences of the new state. Never a man to stake all his rubles on one card, Lenin was seeking other options in case his expectations did not materialize. Inherent in his rejection of an ultimative character for the decree on peace was a recognition that he might have to take one step backward so that later he could take two steps forward. The bulk of the Russian revolutionary movement had now embraced his theses on the imperialist war, but Lenin was already moving off in a somewhat different direction. 'The future disagreements of Brest-Litovsk,' wrote Trotsky, 'gleam out for a moment already in this episode.'[30]

On the day of triumph, however, this was merely contingency planning. In insisting upon the non-ultimative character of the decree Lenin primarily was setting the stage for his attempt to spread the revolution beyond Russia. Lenin could not expect the warring powers to accept his peace proposals. It was another instance of preaching to brothel keepers. As he could be virtually certain that his decree would be rejected, how could it be presented to advance the cause of revolution? The people of the world had to be shown proof of the imperialist nature of the war; therefore, the decree had to be structured in such a way as to provide this evidence. Lenin, as a consequence, insisted on the inclusion of the section soliciting alternative proposals, because he did not want the decree to be

28 James Bunyan and H.H. Fisher (eds.), *The Bolshevik Revolution, 1917-1918: Documents and Materials* (Stanford, California, 1934) 125-8
29 Trotsky, *History of the Russian Revolution*, vol. II, 326
30 *Ibid.*

buried in a conspiracy of silence. He wanted it to elicit some proposal which could be used for propaganda purposes inside and outside Russia. Inside Russia a counter-proposal could be used to show the necessity of a revolutionary war against rapacious imperialism; abroad, it could assist internationalist groups in the struggle against their own imperialist regimes. A counter-proposal, hopefully replete with the most piratical demands, would provide Lenin with exactly the evidence he needed to convince peoples everywhere that the only way to escape from the world war was through world revolution. Lenin was handing his adversaries a substantial length of rope in the hope that they would hang themselves. While not appreciating Lenin's subtlety the Congress unanimously accepted the decree on peace. The Bolsheviks, only vaguely understanding where Lenin was leading them, were launched on the stormy sea which would carry them to Brest-Litovsk and beyond.

Who would conduct the revolutionary foreign policy of the new regime? The Bolshevik Central Committee chose Leon Trotsky. As one of the architects of victory and the earliest exponent of a revolutionary foreign policy he was well qualified for the position. Forceful, dynamic and articulate, he could popularize the peace program and defend it against distortion. If a peace conference actually materialized, he would make an eloquent spokesman for the revolutionary cause; if a peace conference did not materialize he could serve with equal distinction as chief of staff for the spread of revolution. Trotsky, however, did not want the assignment and seemed even more sanguine than Lenin about the prospects of world revolution. 'What diplomatic work are we apt to have now?' he is reported to have said, 'I will issue a few revolutionary proclamations to the peoples of the world and then shut up shop.'[31] Here again the psychological chasm separating him from Lenin appeared through the smoke of the revolution. Nevertheless, Lenin insisted that he take the position, and on the day following the Bolshevik seizure of power Trotsky assumed responsibility for the foreign affairs of the Soviet Republic. In accordance with the decision to discard the old titles of 'minister' and 'ministry,' Trotsky became a 'people's commissar' (Narkom), his portfolio being known as the People's Commissariat of Foreign Affairs (Narkomindel).

For nearly two weeks the determined resistance of officials in the foreign ministry made Trotsky a commissar without a commissariat. Among the bureaucrats of Petrograd those of the foreign ministry possessed the

31 Leon Trotsky, *My Life* (New York, 1930) 341

least understanding of the revolution. Their minds still dwelt in the past, and the significance of the March, let alone the November, revolution escaped them completely. As late as the summer of 1917 a modest proposal to employ women in the ministry had 'evoked a storm of indignation' and led one of its highest officers to declare that 'it had been proved as early as the Middle Ages that woman was in close connection with the devil, and it would, therefore, be against the laws of both God and man to admit her into the Ministry.'[32] Men such as these would never reconcile themselves to the revolution. Together with the *sanovniki* of other ministries they decided to deny the state apparatus to the Bolsheviks. In late September the Union of Civil Servants had declared they would not serve a government formed by a single party. As the Bolsheviks had now formed a government, the strike notice of the civil servants became operative and, in the cold, dreary days of November, the bureaucrats of Petrograd initiated a campaign of passive resistance against the new regime.[33]

The confrontation between revolutionary power and recalcitrant bureaucracy was not long delayed. The Bolsheviks had pledged to publish the secret treaties of former Russian governments, and on the day following the seizure of power they sent a special commissar to the foreign ministry to take charge of this work. The old officials received him coldly, refused to cooperate and rudely showed him the door. Frustrated in this first attempt to take control of the foreign ministry the Military Revolutionary Committee dispatched Ivan Zalkind to overcome the resistance of the *sanovniki*. An old Bolshevik, a doctor of the Sorbonne and the alumnus of seventeen assorted prisons, Zalkind went armed not only with the credentials of the Soviet government but also with a long-barrelled Mauser lodged in his belt. His normally abrasive personality was made all the more unpleasant by the contempt in which he held the recalcitrant bureaucrats. When they refused to cooperate he summoned the Red Guard and ordered the arrest of all those who had organized the strike. Subjected to intense psychological pressure the old officials broke down and provided Zalkind with the information he wanted. Taking him on a guided tour of the archives, they explained how they were organized and where the most interesting documents were located. The Bolsheviks made a big production of their triumph. Reporters from all newspapers were summoned to the foreign ministry, and Zalkind announced that publication of the docu-

32 Vladimir Korostovetz, *Seed and Harvest* (London, 1931) 205
33 *Ibid.*, 298-307

ments would begin at once. Four days later the first collection of documents rolled from the press.[34]

After these events the Bolsheviks could not trust the old officials of the foreign ministry and, with a few exceptions, they were discharged. Zalkind filled their ranks with reliable party members who set to work publishing the documents culled from the foreign ministry archives and preparing propaganda for distribution among German and Austrian troops at the front. Until January 1918, however, the centre of Soviet foreign policy remained at Smolny. Trotsky rarely visited the Narkomindel, leaving Zalkind to carry out the routine activities of the commissariat.[35] The Bolsheviks had no contact with the foreign representatives of the former Russian governments. Not only did these representatives refuse to recognize Lenin's government, they also ignored Trotsky's telegrams removing them from office. They remained at their posts awaiting the overthrow of the Bolshevik regime.[36]

While these events delayed the unfolding of Soviet foreign policy, armed opposition to the revolution also prevented the prompt implementation of the decree on peace. Only after the new government had repulsed Kerensky's counter-attack, established its authority in Moscow and extended its control to other major cities could it presume to act with any credibility in the name of all Russia. The consolidation of power consumed the energy of the new government for nearly two weeks. During that time it was unable to give serious attention to its foreign policy, and, consequently, many critics, like those of the moderate socialists in the summer months,[37] began to complain that it was doing nothing to advance the cause of peace. Worse yet, voices of alarm began to assert that the Bolsheviks had erred in their assessment of the international situation. Opponents on the right said that the Bolsheviks had lied when they claimed that they could end the war, while those whom Lenin would soon brand as 'infantile leftists' proclaimed that the time had already come for a

34 Ivan Zalkind, 'Iz pervykh mestiatsev NKID.' *Mezhdunarodnaia Zhisn*, no. 15 (133) (7 November 1922) 55-61. See also Zalkind, 'NKID v semnadtsam godu.' *Mezhdunarodnaia Zhisn'*, no. 10 (1927) 15-25; M. Sonkin, *Kliuchi ot Bronirovannykh Komnat* (Moscow, 1966) 10-41; Trotsky, *Sochineniia*, vol. III, part II, 97-9; Korostovetz, *Seed and Harvest* 307-9; and B. Kantarovich, 'Organizatsionnoe razvitie NKID.' *Mezhdunarodnaia Zhisn'*, no. 15 (133) (7 November 1922) 51-5
35 Zalkind, 'NKID v semnadtsam godu,' 20-25; Trotsky, *Sochineniia*, vol. III, part II, 97-9
36 Zalkind, 'Iz pervykh mestiatsev NKID,' 55-61; Kantarovich, 'Organizatsionnoe razvitie NKID,' 51-5. See also John M. Thompson, *Russia, Bolshevism and the Versailles Peace* (Princeton, New Jersey, 1966) 67
37 Wade, *The Russian Search for Peace*, 64

revolutionary war against world capitalism.[38] Lenin had little patience with those who made these charges, telling them 'it is highly naive to think that peace can be easily attained and that the bourgeoisie will hand it to us on a platter as soon as we mention it. Those who ascribed this view to the Bolsheviks were cheating.'[39]

Cheating or not, the charges had to be answered. Lenin's first reaction was defensive, saying on 17 November that 'we never promised that the war would be ended at one stroke, by driving bayonets into the ground.'[40] But this was not good enough. The same day, at a meeting of the All-Russian Central Executive Committee, he was bitterly attacked by those who were disappointed that the Russian revolution had not yet produced any discernible effect in western Europe. 'The west,' exclaimed one left Socialist Revolutionary, 'is disgracefully silent!' Lenin met this attack head-on. 'No internationalist,' he sneered, could even think such a thing. 'Only the blind' could fail to see the ferment at work in the west. Revolution was 'inevitable,' he said, but patience was needed, for revolutions could not 'be made to order.' Well aware that patience was in short supply Lenin was careful to conclude on a positive note, asserting that if 'we can not decree a revolution ... we can help it along.'[41] But Lenin had been warned; if he wished to retain his revolutionary following it was time to act rather than talk and to initiate the process of converting the war of state against state into civil conflicts of class against class.

How could this be done? Although the decree on peace had been broadcast to the world it had produced no response. The war continued, and other states, particularly the allied powers, appeared intent on ignoring the Bolshevik regime. The strategic problem was to secure the attention of the belligerent states and involve them in peace negotiations, doing so in such a way as to build support for the Soviet regime within Russia and the embryonic revolutionary movements abroad. The imperialist states had to be forced to reveal their predatory ambitions and practices. To attract attention Lenin decided to confront the belligerent powers with a *fait accompli*, a unilateral initiation of peace negotiations without preliminary formalities.

The Soviet government took the first step in this direction on the evening of 20 November when it ordered General Dukhonin, the Russian commander-in-chief, to initiate negotiations with the German military

38 Robert V. Daniels, *The Conscience of the Revolution* (Cambridge, Massachusetts, 1960) 71
39 Lenin, pss, vol. xxxv, 116-17
40 *Ibid.*, 62
41 *Ibid.*, 60-1

authorities for an armistice on all fronts of the war.[42] The next day Trotsky addressed his first official communication to the allied governments. In notes sent to each western embassy he announced the formation of the Soviet government, its desire for a 'democratic peace' and the intention of seeking an 'armistice on all fronts.' Trotsky could have done this in an unprovocative manner, but he chose to be as irritating as possible. To mobilize public support it was necessary to assume a firm and revolutionary posture when addressing the allied powers. He also had to draw the allied ambassadors from the veil of silence behind which they had hidden since the Bolshevik seizure of power. Trotsky, therefore, ostentatiously informed them that although they were being informed of the proposed armistice this proposal was being made 'simultaneously to all the belligerent nations and their governments.' Mocking traditional diplomatic usage and taking a deep bow toward the revolutionary proletariat he hastened to express 'the profound respect of the Soviet government for the people' of the allied states while carefully avoiding any mention of their governments.[43] Trotsky could be certain that his message would be favourably received in the factories and barracks of Petrograd while forcing the western governments to react in some way to this manifestation of Soviet power.

The notes received a hostile reception in the allied embassies. Neither Sir George Buchanan, the British ambassador, nor Joseph Noulens, his French colleague, would consider the Soviet proposal. Believing that Russia's continued participation in the war was essential for allied victory they had worked diligently to reinforce the sagging eastern front. They were the sworn enemies of Bolshevism and viewed Lenin's seizure of power as a disaster. Nor had the events of November shaken their basic convictions; instead they had turned them against their Russian allies. Buchanan reacted to Krasnov's defeat atop the Pulkovo Heights by saying that 'Kerensky has again failed us,'[44] while Noulens gave up all hope that a civil government could hold Russia together.[45] The ambassadors and their governments had lost faith in Russian politicians in general and Russian

42 Ministervo Inostrannykh Del SSSR, *Dokumenty Vneshnei Politiki SSSR*. 18 vols. (Moscow, 1959–) vol. I, 15-16. Hereafter cited as DVP
43 *Ibid.*, 16-17
44 Sir George Buchanan, *My Mission to Russia and other Diplomatic Memories*. Two vols. (London, 1923) vol. II, 212-13
45 France. Archives du Ministère des Affaires Etrangères, Quai d'Orsay. La Guerre de 1914-1918. Russie, vol. 18, 167. Hereafter cited as MAE, followed by collection title, volume number, and page

socialists in particular. Another Kerensky-style government might be more co-operative than the Soviet regime, but it could hardly contribute much to the allied war effort. 'Chernoff, Tsereteli and the rest of them are all equally useless for our purposes,' wrote Lord Robert Cecil to the British foreign secretary. 'Nothing but a strong military government offers the slightest hope for the Allied cause.'[46]

Noulens, in fact, had already called upon his government to dispatch an expeditionary force to restore 'order' in Russia.[47] More intense, excitable, and violent than his British colleague, the French ambassador became a permanent focus of anti-Soviet conspiracy, his counter-revolutionary activities continuing long after the Great War had ended.[48] Although less volatile than Noulens, Buchanan was more experienced. His long years of diplomatic service had taught him the frequently devious ways of bringing his government's influence to bear on foreign powers. Seemingly more flexible than the French ambassador he projected an image of moderation and common sense. Behind this image, however, was an iron determination to hold Russia in the war. When the two ambassadors met to discuss Trotsky's note, therefore, they had little difficulty in deciding on a common policy. Noulens readily accepted Buchanan's proposal that they ignore the Soviet government and address themselves directly to the commander-in-chief of the Russian armies. Buchanan was already in contact with Dukhonin, and by turning to the general instead of Trotsky the ambassadors could avoid contact with the Soviet government while bringing pressure to bear on all anti-Bolshevik forces to intensify their efforts to crush the revolution.[49] The other allied ambassadors endorsed this plan, and, on 24 November, their representatives at Stavka delivered identical notes to Dukhonin protesting the violation of the treaty of 5 September 1914 and warning that it would 'entail the gravest consequences for Russia.'[50]

Dukhonin agreed with the allied ambassadors but was unable to offer significant resistance to the Soviet government. Isolated at Mogilev and surrounded by the mounting Bolshevik tide he was, in fact, already preparing to flee. Short days before, while fighting continued in Petrograd, the situation had been different. Dukhonin had assumed the functions of

46 British Museum, London. Balfour Papers, Add. Mss. 49738. Lord Robert Cecil to Balfour, 28 Nov. 1917
47 MAE, Guerre, Russie, 18/114
48 Joseph Noulens, *Mon Ambassade en Russie Sovietique, 1917-1919.* Two vols. (Paris, 1933) *passim*
49 MAE, Guerre, Russie, 18/88; 26/235
50 Bunyan and Fisher, *The Bolshevik Revolution,* 245. Also see 249-50

generalissimo and assured allied representatives that, in so far as it was in his power, Russia would continue the struggle against Germany. In return, he pleaded with them 'not to abandon Russia to its fate.'[51] Presumably this message prompted Buchanan to file his protest against an armistice with Stavka rather than Smolny; it also explains the reference to the 'gravest consequences for Russia' if her government elected to negotiate with Germany.[52] But in the third week of November, the situation had changed completely. With the Bolsheviks triumphant and his army hypnotized by the possibility of peace, Dukhonin could not even answer for his own safety. His orders were no longer obeyed by the Russian army.

Convinced that he no longer possessed sufficient authority to confront the Bolsheviks directly Dukhonin sought refuge in passive resistance. Instead of rejecting the order to open armistice negotiations, he simply ignored it; and, twenty-four hours later, when the commissar of war, Nikolai V. Krylenko, telegraphed Stavka demanding to know why the order had not been obeyed, Dukhonin replied evasively. The order was unclear, he said, and needed clarification. Lenin, who was with Krylenko at the Petrograd end of the direct wire, reacted angrily. The order, he replied, was 'clear and precise;' he would not tolerate further delay. Dukhonin, however, continued to equivocate. An armistice, he said, could not be negotiated in the manner demanded by the Soviet government. 'Only a government ... supported by the army and the country can have sufficient weight to impress the enemy.' But Lenin had heard enough; not having received a clear answer from the general he dismissed him from his post.[53] 'It was clear to us,' Lenin told the All-Russian Central Executive Committee, 'that we were dealing with an opponent of the people's will and an enemy of the revolution.' Dukhonin had 'stolen at least one full day' from 'the vital matter of peace.'[54] Lenin appointed Krylenko as the new commander-in-chief of the Russian armies. As a consequence, when Dukhonin received the allied protest he was no longer even nominally in command of the Russian armies and entirely powerless to prevent Russia from withdrawing from the war. The Bolsheviks had effectively met the first allied challenge to their foreign policy.

---

51 MAE, Guerre, Russie, 26/163-4. Also see Oliver H. Radkey, *The Sickle under the Hammer* (New York, 1963) 73ff

52 MAE, Guerre, Russie, 18/88. In explaining his proposal to Noulens, Buchanan had echoed Dukhonin's words: 'if Russia should make a separate armistice she will be abandoned to her fate ...'

53 DVP, vol. I, 17-19

54 Lenin, PSS, vol. XXXV, 85-6

Nor did Lenin stop with merely dismissing Dukhonin. Instead, he placed the Bolshevik propaganda machine into high gear, issuing a proclamation giving his version of the day's events and instructing front line regiments to open negotiations with the Germans. 'Soldiers,' he wrote, 'the cause of peace rests in your hands! You will not permit counter-revolutionary generals to frustrate the great cause of peace.'[55] On the same day the first group of 'secret treaties' drawn from the archives of the foreign ministry were published in the Petrograd papers. This collection was soon followed by many others, all designed, as Trotsky said, to provide 'documentary evidence of the plans with which the financiers and industrialists together with their parliamentary and diplomatic agents were secretly plotting.'[56] Trotsky took advantage of the publicity surrounding the publication of these documents to circularize the embassies of the neutral states in Petrograd officially informing them of the Bolshevik peace initiative and asking them to bring it to the attention of their peoples.[57] In this way the Bolsheviks hoped to mobilize public opinion against the war and provide propaganda for the nascent revolutionary movements in the west. Lenin explained: 'We can contact Paris by wireless and when the peace treaty is drawn up, we shall be able to inform the French people that ... it is up to them to have the armistice concluded within two hours. Let's see what Clemenceau will have to say then.'[58]

The notes delivered by the allied representatives at Stavka permitted the Bolsheviks to intensify their propaganda campaign. Dukhonin had published the allied warning, and when word of it reached Petrograd the Bolsheviks turned it to their own advantage. Invoking xenophobia,

55 DVP, vol. I, 19-20
56 Ibid., vol. I, 21
57 Ibid., vol. I, 22-3. Apart from William Oudendijk of the Netherlands, all the neutral ministers acknowledged this note. With the exception of the Spanish minister, however, these replies were non-commital and did not excite much attention. The reply from the Spanish minister, however, was so cordial that, with great fanfare, the Bolsheviks splashed it across the pages of their newspapers, and the French government, fearing that the cordiality reflected Spanish policy, protested sharply to Madrid. The French need not have worried. The Spanish minister, much less his government, had no sympathy for the Bolsheviks; instead, the minister, who was about to leave Petrograd, had his heart set on receiving the accustomed state decoration awarded departing diplomats. In fact, he received his coveted award, Zalkind offering him a choice of decorations from a large box of such trinkets which he kept in his desk! The French also received satisfaction, as shortly after this incident the Spanish minister left Petrograd. See Zalkind, 'NKID v semnadtsam godu,' and 'Iz pervykh mestiatsev NKID.' Also see MAE, Guerre, Russie, 26/256 and 27/85
58 Lenin, PSS, vol. XXXV, 85-6

Trotsky branded the allied action as 'a flagrant interference in the domestic affairs of our country,' and hastened to orchestrate this theme by appealing to the war-weariness and class-consciousness of his audience. 'Your Soviet government,' he asserted, 'will not allow the foreign bourgeoisie to wield a club over your head and drive you into the slaughter again.' The developing revolution in Europe, he predicted, would shield the Russian people from again becoming 'cannon fodder for the allied imperialists.'[59]

Confidence and revolutionary bravado were necessary when addressing the masses. They provided comfort for the faithful, reassurance for the uncertain, and inspiration for the uncommitted. But meanwhile the moment of truth was fast approaching when actual armistice negotiations would begin. The talks could be conducted in the absence of the allied powers, but a general, rather than a separate armistice, remained the objective of Soviet foreign policy. Even Trotsky did not relish the thought of facing the Germans alone, and, in terms of revolutionary strategy, a meeting of all belligerents promised a much better forum for Bolshevik propaganda than a solitary confrontation with the stern-faced generals from Potsdam.

These circumstances dictated a second approach to the allied powers, and despite the Soviet denunciation of secret diplomacy, Trotsky chose to make it in private. Not only was it not publicized at the time, but the note which Trotsky addressed to the allied military representatives on 26 November is still omitted from Soviet documentary collections. Although the foreign commissar used terse, almost peremptory, language his note was not designed to generate propaganda for public consumption and was immediately recognized by its recipients as a 'testimony of the ardent desire of Trotsky to enter into *de facto* relations with the allied governments.'[60] It set forth Soviet intentions very clearly, conveying Trotsky's determination to negotiate an armistice. If this led to a separate agreement with Germany, said Trotsky, the responsibility would 'fall completely upon the allied governments.' For its part, the Soviet government was prepared 'at any moment' and 'with any representatives of the Allies to conduct negotiations on the ways and means to adopt so as to arrive at an armistice in the most rapid possible way.' While Trotsky inquired if the allied governments would support the Soviet peace initiative he also asked if they had other proposals to make, and, if so, what they might be.

59 DVP, vol. I, 23-4
60 MAE, Guerre, Russie, 26/250

If the Soviet government did not receive a satisfactory answer, he warned, it intended to 'appeal to the peoples against their governments.'[61]

Negotiations with the Germans did not await a reply from the allies. In response to Lenin's appeal Soviet agitators had begun to fraternize with German troops while Russian planes showered the German lines with leaflets calling for a general armistice. To control the situation Lenin dispatched his newly breveted commander-in-chief to take charge of the negotiations. Krylenko made his way south to Dvinsk where he assumed personal command of the Russian Fifth Army. On the afternoon of 26 November he sent representatives across no-man's land to the German trenches. Preceded by a bugler and a large white flag the delegation was met by a German officer who led them behind his lines.[62] This was the day for which the German high command had long waited. For weeks they had watched the confused struggle for power in Russia never quite knowing exactly what was happening;[63] now plenipotentiaries bearing credentials from the Soviet government had arrived at the command post of a German divisional commander. 'Is it possible to negotiate with these people?' asked General Ludendorff from Spa. 'Yes, it is possible,' replied General von Hoffmann, chief-of-staff of the German army in Russia. 'Your Excellency needs troops and this is the easiest way to get them.'[64] Hoffmann ordered the negotiations to begin, and early on the morning of 27 November the two sides agreed to meet five days later at Brest-Litovsk, general headquarters of the German army in Russia.[65] The decisive step to ending the war in eastern Europe had been taken.

A Russo-German armistice, by itself, however, was not the aim of Bolshevik policy; at best, it was only a beginning. The Bolsheviks wanted a people's peace, not one negotiated by existing governments. Therefore, to place additional pressure on the allies, to provide inspiration for anti-war militants everywhere and to build their own prestige within Russia, Lenin and Trotsky promptly prepared a proclamation to the peoples of all bellig-

61 United States Department of State, *Papers Relating to the Foreign Relations of the United States, 1918, Russia.* Three vols. (Washington, 1931) vol. I, 250. Hereafter cited as FRUS, *1918, Russia*
62 Sonkin, *Kliuchi*, 72ff. Also see V.V. Kutuzov, 'Dokumenty o Bratanii.' Sovetskoe Arkhivy, no. 4 (1968) 98-101
63 Wolfgang Steglich, *Die Friedenspolitik der Mittelmächte, 1917-1918* (Wiesbaden, 1964) 232-43
64 General Max von Hoffmann, *War Diaries and other Papers.* Two vols. (London, 1929) vol. II, 190
65 DVP, vol. I, 26-7

erent states informing them of the impending negotiations and demanding to know if their governments intended to participate in these talks. Unlike the note delivered to the allied military representatives this was a revolutionary tract descanting on Soviet virtue and capitalist vice.[66] In so far as it was directed to the western governments it was designed to force them to take a public stand on the question of the armistice negotiations.

Krylenko's success greatly embarrassed the allied representatives in Petrograd. Their attempt to outflank Smolny by appealing to Stavka had failed, and they were now confronted with yet another *fait acompli*. Not knowing what to do, the ambassadors asked their governments for new instructions, suggesting that the allied powers should draft a joint response to the Bolshevik demand for an immediate armistice and peace conference. At the end of November, when the allied leaders met in Paris to discuss the Russian question, they rejected this suggestion as they were unable to agree on the wording of such a response and were particularly baffled by how to respond to the Bolshevik call for a peace without annexations or indemnities. They decided instead to instruct their representatives in Russia to publicize allied policy in an informal manner, taking every opportunity to inform Russian public opinion that when a 'responsible' (read: pro-allied) government had been formed the allied powers were prepared to discuss with it questions concerning war aims and the conditions of a just and lasting peace. With or without Russia the western allies intended to continue the war against Germany.[67]

The allied governments also sent new instructions to their military representatives in Russia, Clemenceau's order being an unambiguous answer to Lenin's question of how the French premier would respond to peace negotiations. The head of the French military mission in Russia was directed 'to lend all possible assistance to groups opposing the "criminal" action of the Bolsheviks.'[68] In London the war cabinet decided 'to support any responsible body in Russia that would actively oppose the Maximalist movement and at the same time give money freely, within reason, to such bodies as were prepared to help the allied cause.'[69] In both countries, generals began to unroll maps of Russia. The French general staff proposed

---

66 *Ibid.*, 28-30
67 Richard H. Ullman, *Intervention and the War* (Princeton, New Jersey, 1961) 25-7; George F. Kennan, *Russia Leaves the War* (Princeton, New Jersey, 1956) 131-8; MAE, Guerre, Russie 27/57
68 MAE, Guerre, Russie, 26/191, 263-4
69 Great Britain. Public Record Office, London. Minutes of the War Cabinet. Cabinet 23/4/222. Hereafter cited as PRO *Cab*

that a line from Vladivostok to Moscow be placed under allied control; the British war office concurred but also expressed an interest in seizing Archangel as a naval base.[70] The first steps toward intervention in Russia had been taken.

Unaware of these decisions, but conscious that, in Lenin's words, 'international imperialism is mobilizing all its forces against us,'[71] the Bolsheviks hastened to strengthen their military and political position. Dukhonin had again become a problem, the general not only issuing an anti-Soviet manifesto[72] but also remaining in contact with the allied embassies. If an armistice was to be negotiated, he claimed, then he should conduct these talks as only he possessed sufficient prestige to assure the Germans that an armistice would be honoured by the Russian army.[73] Fearful that the Germans might accept this logic and wishing to shatter any illusion the allies might have concerning the authority of the former commander-in-chief, the Sovnarkom decided to send Krylenko on a new mission. The commissar of war proceeded south to arrest Dukhonin. On 3 December, he arrived in Mogilev and assumed command of army headquarters. When it was learned that Dukhonin had released Kornilov, Denikin, and other generals known as enemies of the revolution, an outraged mob of soldiers surrounded Krylenko's train and demanded that their former commander be surrendered to them. The commissar of war, either unable or unwilling to intervene, stood aside while the angry troops lynched his predecessor.[74]

While this grisly scene unfolded at Stavka armistice negotiations had gotten under way at Brest-Litovsk. Heading the Soviet delegation was Adolph A. Ioffe, a protégé of Trotsky and a member of the Bolshevik Central Committee. Assisting him were Lev B. Kamenev, Grigorii Sokol'nikov, and Lev Karakhan. To this political centre were attached decorative symbols of the revolution personified in a peasant, a proletarian, a soldier, and a sailor; military experts drawn from the ranks of the Russian armed forces; and Anastasia Bitsenko, a relic of the terrorist past representing the left Socialist Revolutionaries. Opposite this motley group sat a pride of bemedalled officers representing the armed forces of the central powers. It was an incongruous assembly in which all the participants felt ill at ease.

70 MAE, Guerre, Russie, 26/191, 263-4; PRO *Cab* 23/4/222
71 Lenin, PSS, vol. XXXV, 86
72 Bunyan and Fisher, *The Bolshevik Revolution,* 253-4
73 MAE, Guerre, Russie, 26/251
74 George Stewart, *The White Armies of Russia* (New York, 1933) 25-6; Bunyan and Fisher, *The Bolshevik Revolution,* 266-8

The two sides approached the negotiations with widely divergent aspirations. For the central powers the talks were an end in themselves, a formality to be completed as quickly as possible. Russia was defeated, but the western allies still had to be dealt with. German divisions tied down in the east were badly needed in France. Hoffmann had already begun to transfer his divisions to the western front, one having been sent in October, ten more in November, and another twelve scheduled to leave in December.[75] He wanted nothing to interfere with this schedule and, consequently, was prepared to offer what he considered to be generous terms. As his army was entrenched deep inside Russia and the Russian army was disintegrating he was satisfied with the *status quo*. He proposed, therefore, that the existing military situation be maintained and hostilities end. All other questions would be reserved for the peace conference.[76]

The Soviets viewed the negotiations differently. For them the talks were a prelude to revolution and a platform from which to speak to the world. Ioffe demanded that the negotiations be public and sought to entangle Hoffmann in a political debate. The general, who held a very low opinion of revolutionaries, agreed that the negotiations should be publicized but was unwilling to talk politics. The chief difficulty arose, however, when Ioffe asserted that he was empowered to sign only a general armistice. Hoffmann responded by asking if the Soviet delegation had authority to negotiate in the name of all the allied powers. Ioffe had to admit that he held no such mandate, but that the Sovnarkom had not authorized him to accept an armistice limited to the eastern front. An impasse had been reached, and Ioffe suggested a recess permitting him to return to Petrograd for new instructions. He also proposed that the talks be moved to Pskov, saying that the Russian city offered freer access to the world press than the fortress at Brest-Litovsk. Hoffmann, having no desire to place himself at the mercy of a revolutionary mob, rejected this suggestion, but agreed to recess the negotiations for a week. In the interval the two sides would invite all belligerents to take part in the negotiations.[77]

Ioffe left Brest-Litovsk on 5 December. His return to Petrograd forced the Soviet leaders to decide if they would accept an armistice limited to the eastern front. The arguments in favour of such an armistice strongly outweighed those against it. The mass of the population was no less war-weary

75 Institut für Deutsche Militärgeschichte, *Militarismus gegen Sowjetmacht 1917 bis 1919* (Berlin, 1967) 44

76 Erich von Ludendorff, *The General Staff and its Problems.* Two vols. (London, 1920) vol. II, 517

77 A.O. Chubar'ian, *Brestskii Mir* (Moscow, 1964) 90

in December than in November and what remained of the Russian army was rapidly demobilizing itself. More important, the distribution of propaganda in the German trenches had only begun. *Die Fackel,* a newspaper designed to bring revolutionary enlightenment to the German fighting man, had just begun to roll from the presses, and Bolshevik agitators needed time to spread it throughout the German army. Against such political, military and revolutionary imperatives no serious case could be made for rejecting a separate armistice with Germany.

Yet the Bolsheviks still hesitated. Before reaching a decision Lenin and Trotsky again invited the allied powers to join the negotiations at Brest-Litovsk.[78] They received no direct answer. Instead, the allied embassies issued a press release which reflected the political decisions reached in Paris at the end of November.[79] The Bolsheviks correctly assumed that this would be the only answer which they would receive and drew the logical conclusion that the allies would not join them in the negotiation of an armistice. Two days later Lenin authorized Ioffe to proceed with a separate armistice.[80] Trotsky fired a last round at the allied governments on 13 December when, in a press release of his own, he denounced the western refusal to join the negotiations and warned them that a separate armistice was not a separate peace, but it was the first step in that direction.[81]

Ioffe's new instructions allowed the negotiations to proceed rapidly, and within three days of his return to Brest-Litovsk a final accord was reached. It provided for a twenty-eight day armistice, automatically renewable at the end of that time. After the twenty-first day the armistice could, with seven days' notice, be terminated by either side. The existing fighting front served as the line of demarcation between the two armies; Germany, as a consequence, retained control of all Russian territory occupied during the war. The Germans accepted a Bolshevik demand that a prohibition be placed on the movement of troops during the armistice but added a modifying clause to the agreement which exempted those transfers which 'had already been begun at the moment of the signing of the armistice.' Hoffmann could accept this compromise quite willingly as he had already prepared orders for the movement of no less than one-third of the entire German army in Russia to the western front.[82] The Bolsheviks were adamant on the question of fraternization. They insisted that soldiers

---

78 DVP, vol. I, 42-3
79 Buchanan, *My Mission to Russia* vol. II, 233-7
80 D.V. Oznobishin, *Ot Bresta do Iur'eva* (Moscow, 1966) 47
81 Trotsky, *Sochineniia,* vol. III, part II, 194-5
82 Steglich, *Die Friedenspolitik der Mittelmächte,* 248

of the two armies be allowed to meet during the armistice, and the Germans rather reluctantly agreed. Although such meetings were to be limited to groups of twenty-five soldiers or less and be supervised by German officers the Bolsheviks were satisfied that they could find ways to spread their propaganda inside the enemy lines. On 15 December, the armistice was signed,[83] and two days later all fighting on the eastern front came to an end.

The armistice represented the first tangible success of Soviet foreign policy. To those critics who asked what they had done for the cause of peace the Bolsheviks could answer that within five weeks of seizing power they had brought an end to the fighting along the eastern front. In place of war to the bitter end they had substituted their policy of a 'people's peace,' and, in the teeth of allied opposition, had taken the first steps toward its realization. For the overwhelming mass of war-weary Russians this was sufficient, but for those who recalled that the Bolsheviks had promised a general, rather than localized, end to the fighting the Soviet government could respond that by agreeing to a separate armistice they had purchased the time and circumstances needed to spread the revolution beyond Russia.

Nevertheless, this success was sufficiently tarnished to make it lose much of its lustre. A separate armistice had undeniable implications and, as Trotsky had said, it was the first step in the direction of a separate peace. How far could Soviet Russia travel down that path without seriously endangering its revolutionary integrity? If a separate armistice could be justified by impelling political, military, and revolutionary circumstances, why not a separate peace? And despite Lenin's denial, the west was 'disgracefully silent.' What could the Bolsheviks do if revolution failed to materialize beyond the borders of Russia? Lenin and Trotsky could talk bravely of a revolutionary war, but who would march off to fight its battles? Significantly, Lenin had already stopped talking about such a possibility. With the peace conference due to begin in seven days the stage was set to determine the political future of eastern and central Europe.

2

The establishment of unofficial relations with the western powers

The revolutionary democracy cannot accept the position that worthy heroes languish in concentration camps in England while counter-revolutionary British citizens suffer no restraint on the territory of the Russian Republic. Trotsky to Buchanan, 26 November 1917

To give you a visa we must consult with Comrade Chicherin; no Chicherin, no visa! Zalkind to British subjects seeking to leave Russia, 29 November 1917

... I am clearly of the opinion that it is to our advantage to avoid, as long as possible, an open breach with this crazy system. Balfour, 9 December 1917

The armistice with the central powers revealed a serious imbalance in Soviet foreign policy. It had been easy enough to draw Germany into peace negotiations, but Smolny found it impossible even to communicate with the western powers. This had forced the Soviet government into a lopsided development of its revolutionary strategy, concentrating increasingly on what might be called 'the German gambit.' Trotsky found this intolerable, not because he coveted western recognition, but because the allied tactic of treating the Bolsheviks as more of an irritant than a legitimate government did in fact offer them a certain degree of protection against the revolutionary strategy of the Soviet government. As long as London and Paris did not recognize the existence of the Soviet government they could not be entangled in negotiations which, by their very nature, could have revolutionary consequences. Moreover, since Lenin and Trotsky assumed the existence of widespread popular unrest in western Europe they wished to establish contact with internationalist circles in allied countries. A means was needed, therefore, to break the 'conspiracy of silence' with which the allied powers had surrounded the Russian revolution.

It did not take long to find ways to loosen allied tongues. Effectively possessing power in the large cities of Russia, the Bolsheviks had within their grasp a sizeable community of allied citizens who could be exploited for this purpose. During late 1917, therefore, the Soviet government subjected this community to a carefully considered campaign of harassment and inconvenience. George Kennan has come to a different conclusion about the 'severe difficulties and embarrassments' suffered by allied citizens in Russia at this time. 'One has the impression,' he has written, 'that once the decision was made to proceed independently with the peace talks [with Germany], the men in Smolny Institute saw no reason why they should continue to observe any particular restraint with regard to the Allied representatives.'[1] This view, implying a certain uncaring malevolence on the part of the Soviet authorities, misses the whole point of Bolshevik policy. Once the Soviet government had decided to negotiate separately with Germany, their need for countervailing relations with the allied powers was greater than before. It was simply too dangerous to be left absolutely alone with the Germans. If the Germans believed the Bolsheviks could talk only to them their arrogance would be completely without check. Conversely, if the allies were permitted to ignore Smolny they would develop their policy in Russia without any reference to the Soviet government. Therefore, it was vital to open channels of communication with the western powers. The Bolsheviks could not do this in a polite way. Lenin and Trotsky had too frequently denounced 'secret diplomacy' to be caught going hat in hand to the allied ambassadors. Instead, for the sake of their political image, they had to deliver a swift kick to allied posteriors while at the same time conveying the impression that they wished to negotiate. To do this Trotsky launched a studied campaign of coercion against allied citizens and representatives in Russia.

Trotsky did not have to look far to find a suitable pretext. In September, two Russian Social Democrats, Peter Petrov and Georgii V. Chicherin, had been imprisoned in Great Britain. Charged with pro-German and anti-ally activities they had been sentenced to indeterminate detention pending the conclusion of the war. Neither were Bolsheviks, but both had been active in the internationalist cause and were deemed

1 Kennan, *Russia Leaves the War*, 154

worthy of Soviet protection.[2] Chicherin was of special interest as he had earlier served in the tsarist foreign ministry and would be a valuable addition to the fledgling Narkomindel. Most important, a demand for their liberation, backed by pressure on the allied community in Russia, would force the British government to break its silence. Once negotiations had begun concerning these men the talks could be expanded to include more significant topics. Accordingly, on 26 November, Trotsky sent a note to the British ambassador demanding the release of Chicherin and Petrov. 'The revolutionary democracy,' he said, 'cannot accept the position that worthy heroes languish in concentration camps in England while counter-revolutionary British citizens suffer no restraint on the territory of the Russian Republic.'[3]

The British government understood the significance of Trotsky's message. Although junior officers in the foreign office were inclined to comply with the Soviet demand, Lord Robert Cecil, the acting foreign secretary, thought otherwise. He brought the Soviet demand to the attention of the war cabinet which discussed it at their meetings of 29 and 30 November. They agreed with Cecil 'that to release [Petrov and Chicherin] at Trotsky's bidding would greatly add to his prestige and would be tantamount to a recognition of his Government.'[4] They also felt that 'to give way to these demands ... would form but a precedent for further demands of the same nature.'[5] As a consequence, the foreign office instructed Buchanan to ignore Trotsky's note. 'It would be impossible for His Majesty's Government,' said Lord Robert, 'to take any notice of a demand of that kind.'[6]

At Petrograd events had already raced ahead of the British cabinet. Having received no response to his demand for the liberation of Petrov and Chicherin, Trotsky decided to increase the pressure on Buchanan. On 29 November, British subjects seeking to leave Russia were told that no further exit visas would be issued until London had complied with the Soviet demand. 'To give you a visa,' they were told, 'we must consult with Comrade Chicherin; no Chicherin, no visa!'[7] This had the desired effect,

2 Richard Kent Debo, 'The making of a Bolshevik: Georgii Chicherin in England, 1914-1918.' *Slavic Review* XXV, no. 4, (Dec. 1966) 651-62
3 Great Britain. Public Record Office, London. Foreign office papers, record group 371, vol. 3019, doc. 226627. Foreign office papers will henceforth be cited as PRO FO followed by the record group, volume, and document numbers
4 PRO *Cab* 23/4/211-12
5 *Ibid.*, 23/4/218
6 PRO FO 371/3019/226627
7 Zalkind, 'NKID v semnadtsam godu,' 18

for that same day Buchanan decided on his own initiative to send the British consul to contact Trotsky. The foreign commissar received him angrily, saying that when he sent a message he expected an answer and that unless his demands were met he would intern British subjects suspected of spreading anti-revolutionary propaganda. Nor was that all. The Petrograd garrison, said the foreign commissar, was equally tired of the British attitude, and since 'feeling ran high among the soldiers, he could not answer for the consequences if the interned Russians were not let out.'[8]

Trotsky's tirade impressed the British ambassador, and he decided that further talks were necessary. Despite his instructions from London he believed that it was impossible to continue a policy of ignoring the Soviet authorities. Indicating that he had taken Trotsky's warning to heart he reported that the 'Red Guards and Sailors are getting out of hand' and that he did 'not want to see public opinion excited against our subjects.' To avoid a possible tragedy, he advised London to authorize unofficial talks with Trotsky, suggesting that the British government 'should try to arrive at some *modus vivendi*' with the Soviet authorities.[9]

Buchanan's proposal was not well received in London. Whitehall shared his concern for the safety of British subjects in Russia but found it difficult to agree to negotiations with Trotsky. His message, however, did generate further consideration of the problem. Cecil, who knew nothing of Chicerin and Petrov except that Trotsky wanted them released, wrote plaintively: '*Please*, let me know who these two men are and what they have done.' No one in the foreign office knew, and it was necessary to ask the home office. When the home office replied that the charges against the two were rather nebulous and stated that it had no objection to their deportation, sentiment quickly crystalized in favour of getting the two Russians out of Britain as fast as possible. The two offices agreed that Chicherin and Petrov 'would be less prominent among their fellow Bolsheviks in Petrograd ... and they would not be quite such "heroes of revolution" when they have to compete for the front row with all the other "heroes" in Petrograd.'[10]

The war cabinet, however, would not reverse its earlier decision. Crippled by the absence of the prime minister, it postponed a decision until his return. Buchanan was left without instruction and forced to rely on his

8 PRO FO 371/3019/227713
9 *Ibid.*
10 PRO FO 371/3019/233595. Emphasis in original

own judgment. Having received no reply to his telegram he felt compelled to 'make an effort to relieve the present intolerable situation' and sent his aide, Captain Smith, to open unofficial talks with Trotsky.[11]

Trotsky, having administered a swift kick to the British backside, now had to make them understand that the purpose of his rudeness had been to get their attention. Thus, he received Smith in a very cordial manner and, as Buchanan was at pains to report, 'was perfectly courteous throughout' the meeting. Trotsky set the tone for the conversation by denying that he was attempting to deal in threats and blackmail. His object, he said, was to emphasize the difference between the treatment accorded Russian citizens in Great Britain and British subjects in Russia. Smith then suggested that if Trotsky would lift his ban on British subjects leaving Russia that Buchanan would advise London to reconsider the cases of Petrov and Chicherin. The foreign commissar agreed that this was a reasonable solution, but, having his revolutionary credibility in mind, proposed that the order of events be reversed. He promised that if the British government announced its willingness to reconsider the cases of the two men, the Narkomindel would again issue exit visas to British subjects. Having disposed of this problem in a conciliatory fashion, not to mention one which would enhance his revolutionary image, Trotsky turned to the primary purpose of the entire exercise. Telling Smith that he harbored 'no ill will for the British people' he assured him that the question of Chicherin and Petrov was of a decidedly 'secondary' nature. 'It was folly to prolong such disputes at a time when vast international questions had to be settled.'[12] His message delivered, Trotsky could only wait to see if he had been understood in London.

London understood, and the wheels of British policy-making began to turn. Lloyd George and his leading ministers had just returned from France, and having sifted recent reports from Russia they picked up the scent left by Trotsky. The foreign secretary attached special significance to Smith's meeting with Trotsky. 'The situation,' wrote Balfour, 'has certainly been changed by Buchanan's telegram.'[13] On 7 December the war cabinet had rejected any idea of negotiating with the Bolsheviks, but three days later, with Lloyd George in the chair, it again debated the Russian question. In front of them was a memorandum from the foreign secretary calling for nothing less than a fundamental change in British policy. Bal-

11 PRO *Cab* 23/4/224; PRO FO 371/3019/232832
12 PRO FO 371/3019/232832
13 *Ibid.*, 800/206/219

four argued that it was advantageous to avoid as long as possible an open breach with what he called 'this crazy system.' The Bolsheviks, he said, were no more ill-disposed to the British empire than any other existing state. They were 'fanatics to whom the constitution of every state, whether monarchical or republican, is equally odious.' This being the case he saw no purpose in driving them into the German camp.

Russia, however incapable of fighting, [he wrote] is not easily overrun. Except with the active goodwill of the Russians themselves, German troops (even if there were German troops to spare) are not going to penetrate many hundreds of miles into that vast country. A mere armistice between Russia and Germany may not for very many months promote in any important fashion the supply of German needs from Russian sources. It must be our business to make that period as long as possible by every means in our power, and no policy would be more fatal than to give the Russians a motive for welcoming into their midst German officials and German soldiers as friends and deliverers.

Although a number of ministers continued to argue that any 'traffic with the Bolsheviks' was dangerous and that it was inconsistent to negotiate with the Bolsheviks while aiding their enemies, the cabinet, led by Lloyd George, endorsed Balfour's policy. Assistance to anti-Soviet forces, they decided, 'was directed against the Germans and not the Bolsheviks.' They also accepted Balfour's contention that the question of the interned Russians was of a secondary nature, subordinate to the broader concerns of general policy. As the case against the two men 'was not a very strong one,' and since 'by continuing to intern Tritchirine [sic] and Petroff [sic] the lives of thousands of British subjects were being endangered,' the war cabinet authorized Balfour and the home secretary to dispose of the two Russians as they saw fit.[14]

In short, the British government had abandoned its policy of ignoring the Bolshevik regime. Unwilling to let central Russia fall by default to the Germans the war cabinet decided to investigate Trotsky's hint that the Bolsheviks wished to discuss 'vast international questions' with Great Britain. Naturally, Balfour wished to do this on his own terms and directed his policy not toward agreement with 'this crazy system' but toward the opportunity which unofficial relations with the Bolsheviks might offer to strike at the Germans in Russia. Trotsky, of course, approached the British in the same way, hoping to find in unofficial relations with them some

14 PRO *Cab* 23/4/239-42

one-sided advantage for the Soviet policy of converting the 'imperialist' war into the desired conflict of class against class. In many ways it resembled two confidence men each trying to defraud the other.

Nevertheless, the British decision removed the immediate cause of tension between London and Petrograd. The foreign commissar expressed his pleasure at this decision and promised to lift his embargo on British subjects leaving Russia. In fact he did, but Trotsky already had another contentious issue to raise. Diplomatic couriers, he now told Smith, would not be allowed to enter or leave Russia unless a similar privilege was extended to messengers employed by the Soviet government.[15] This demand had a two-fold purpose. It would keep alive negotiations with Britain, and, if successfully pressed, it would open a direct channel of communication with the internationalists of western Europe. As Balfour had decided not to break with the Bolsheviks it quickly became obvious that he would have to satisfy their new demand.

It was difficult to argue with Trotsky's logic. He contended that if he could not send couriers to London because Whitehall did not recognize the Soviet regime then he had an equal right to stop British couriers from entering Russia. The British ambassador, he pointed out, was 'accredited by a government which did not recognize the Bolsheviks to a government which is no longer existent.' Buchanan recognized that Trotsky had a 'certain amount of truth' in his argument and suggested that the question be discussed with him 'on the basis that he should give us an assurance that his messengers would go to England only in that capacity and should not carry Socialist or Pacifist propaganda.' The foreign office concurred, although Balfour's private secretary observed that it would 'be difficult to credit Trotsky's word that he will send no hooligans here.'[16] The French government also found the prospect of Bolshevik couriers distasteful and urged London to reject Trotsky's demand. The Bolsheviks, said Paris, were a 'perjured and non-recognized government' while their messengers could be expected to be 'sources of impudent propaganda and disorder.'[17]

Trotsky, however, had the whip hand, and when he turned back the first British diplomatic courier Balfour instructed Buchanan to negotiate a settlement of the problem. Nevertheless, the foreign secretary still sought to equivocate. 'Until the Bolsheviks have authorized representatives abroad,' Balfour told Buchanan, 'it will not be easy for them to find an

15 PRO FO 371/3020/237030
16 *Ibid.*
17 *Ibid.*, 371/3020/233970

excuse for a diplomatic messenger.'[18] His idea, of course, was to concede the principle of reciprocity, thus insuring the British right to send couriers, while using a technicality to prevent Bolshevik messengers from entering Great Britain.

This ploy led to another confrontation with the Bolsheviks. On hearing the assertion that the Bolsheviks had no 'authorized representatives' in western Europe an unidentified Soviet official[19] lost his patience and issued a statement declaring: 'The pretension that a "non-recognized" Government can not have diplomatic couriers is without foundation as the Soviet consider diplomatic relations to be necessary not only with Governments but also with Socialist revolutionary parties who are striving to overthrow existing governments.'[20] This 'extraordinary message,' as Buchanan described it, upset the allied diplomatic community. Buchanan called a meeting of his colleagues where it was decided to inform Trotsky 'unofficially' that such pretentions were unacceptable.[21] The incident placed the foreign commissar in a difficult position. The militant declaration was a true statement of Soviet intentions, but obviously he could not endorse it and expect in return to receive the right to send his couriers abroad. Consequently, he adopted a defensive posture, denying personal responsibility for the statement and explaining that it had been 'written in a moment of irritation.' Primarily, however, he relied on half-truth and a casuistry derived from two decades of experience in the Russian revolutionary movement. 'It was not his intention,' he asserted, 'to foment revolutionary movements in foreign countries'; instead, he claimed only the right for his representatives to 'have relations with whomever they pleased.' His assertion, it should be noted, corresponded with the Bolshevik view of revolutionary politics. They did not believe they or their agents had to foment revolution. The revolutionary situation already existed, and the revolution in the west would arise from the very nature of bourgeois society in its imperialist stage of development. Soviet agents might assist western revolutionaries, but they would not be the cause of such revolutions. Trotsky, therefore, could declare with a reasonably straight face that he did not intend 'to foment revolutionary movements in foreign countries,' and add that Soviet couriers would be bound by the

18 *Ibid.*
19 The official is identified obscurely first as the 'Secretary of the Council of People's Commissaries' and then later as 'Secretary to the Council of the Commissary of the (?rights) of the People.' PRO FO 371/3020/241960
20 *Ibid.*
21 PRO FO 371/3020/238012

laws of the countries which they entered. Upon the delivery of their bags they 'could no longer claim any diplomatic immunity and would be subject to arrest in the event of engaging in any anti-government campaign.' This declaration, together with his statement that he wished 'to get this question settled with the least possible delay' produced a favourable impression in the foreign office. Lord Hardinge, the permanent under-secretary of state, still blissfully ignorant of the subtlety of the Bolshevik mind, minuted 'this places us in a strong position to deal with revolutionary propagandists.'[22]

Nevertheless, the foreign office still hesitated to grant reciprocity, and it required yet another outburst from the foreign commissar to clear the way for this decision. The flare-up occurred on 22 December, when Trotsky angrily told Smith that the British 'were purposely making difficulties' and that none of their couriers would pass until the issue was settled. He also noted that Chicherin and Petrov were still imprisoned, adding that if they were not promptly released he would again stop British subjects from leaving Russia.[23] This brought an immediate response from London authorizing Buchanan to visa the passports of Soviet couriers and to inform Trotsky 'officially' that Petrov and Chicherin would leave for Norway on the next admiralty steamer.[24] Chicherin and Petrov left Britain two weeks later, and on 1 January 1918, the first Soviet courier departed for western Europe having received a visa from both Buchanan and Noulens.[25] Much against its will Paris had agreed to allow the Soviet courier to enter France.[26] In explaining this action to an outraged associate the French foreign minister explained that his 'hand had been forced' by the British. To refuse the visa, he said, would not only expose French citizens to reprisals but would also 'separate us from our ally, creating for us the gravest of difficulties.'[27] Trotsky, therefore, had succeeded in forcing concessions not only from Britain but also France which found it necessary to follow the lead of its ally.

France also found it necessary to follow the British lead in establishing unofficial relations with the Bolsheviks. London had already decided that the existing means of communication with the Soviet government were inadequate and, in mid-December, sought French agreement for ex-

22 *Ibid.*, 371/3020/241647
23 *Ibid.*, 371/3020/242028
24 *Ibid.*
25 *Ibid.*, 371/3296/834
26 MAE, Guerre, Russie, 27/171
27 *Ibid.*, 27/192

panded contacts with the Bolsheviks. In a meeting held in Paris on 23 December 1917, ministers of the two governments decided they 'should at once get into relations with the Bolsheviks through unofficial agents, each country as seems best to it.'[28] The British decided to send a special agent, Bruce Lockhart, their former consul-general in Moscow; they also subsequently agreed to recognize Maxim Litvinov as the unofficial representative of the Soviet government in London. The French who had only reluctantly agreed to the British proposal, instructed their military mission in Russia to establish unofficial ties with Trotsky. Only if the Bolsheviks resumed the war against Germany would Paris genuinely want to talk with them, and, in such a case, their military mission seemed the most appropriate agency to conduct these talks. Nevertheless, in the last days of 1917, the first lines of communication between Smolny and the western capitals had been opened.[29]

Trotsky also succeeded in forcing the American ambassador David Francis to establish a form of relationship with the Soviet government. Just as Chicherin and Petrov had provided a pretext for bringing Buchanan under fire, the activities of Andrew Kalpashnikov, a Russian in the employ of the American Red Cross, gave him an opportunity to turn his guns on the American embassy. Kalpashnikov, who had attempted to send a trainload of ambulances to south Russia at a time when such an action could easily be interpreted as aiding the counter-revolutionary movement forming in that part of the country, had quickly attracted Soviet attention. It is immaterial whether Kalpashnikov was guilty or not of the charges brought against him; what is important is the manner in which Trotsky used these charges to loosen the tongue of the American ambassador. Thus, on 21 December, Kalpashnikov was arrested and charged with participating in a counter-revolutionary conspiracy. The same evening Trotsky appeared before a large public meeting and launched a vicious verbal assault against Francis, whom he claimed to be implicated in the conspiracy. Having read his audience a number of telegrams which appeared to compromise the American ambassador he proclaimed: 'This Sir Francis will have to break his golden silence which has remained unbroken since the Revolution ... these documents will force him to unloose his eloquence against the calumnies which are being set up against him.' Then in a manner designed to excite the already feverish crowd he re-

28 PRO *Cab* 23/4/278
29 Richard Kent Debo, 'Litvinov and Kamenev – Ambassadors extraordinary: the problem of Soviet representation abroad.' *Slavic Review* XXXIV, no. 3 (Sept. 1975) 463-82

called how the British embassy had been taught a lesson. 'Let them understand [he cried] that from the moment that they interfere in our internal strife they cease to be diplomatic representatives – they are private counter-revolutionist adventurers and the heavy hand of the Revolution will fall upon their heads!' The audience jumped to its feet screaming 'Arrest Francis! Hang him! Shoot him!'[30] Trotsky had whipped his audience into a frenzy with the object of bringing pressure on the American ambassador.

Trotsky's tactic worked spectacularly. Francis, who feared that a mob would lynch him, sent at once for 'Colonel' Raymond Robins, the director of the American Red Cross in Russia. The ambassador asked Robins, who had established a cordial relationship with Trotsky, to visit Smolny and clear the embassy of the charges brought against it. This was not an easy request to make, because Francis did not get along well with the 'Colonel' and, earlier, had even asked the state department to forbid Robins from seeing Trotsky. Washington had complied, but Francis now brushed this prohibition aside, assuring Robins that he would take full responsibility for doing so. The same day Francis also broke his 'golden silence,' publishing a refutation of the charges brought against him. Trotsky had succeeded again, for the link with Robins which had previously been limited to Red Cross affairs, was now expanded to include questions of general political importance. For the next five months Robins was to serve as the Soviet channel of communication with the United States government.[31]

In short, through the liberal application of coercion, demonstrating that the Soviet government did exercise effective control over the centre of the old Russian empire, Trotsky had succeeded in establishing unofficial relations with the western powers. He could now communicate directly with the western governments, and, as a consequence, the Bolsheviks were not quite as isolated as before. But only in the case of Great Britain had a genuine change in policy taken place. France and the United States had merely been forced to recognize effective power and make minimal accommodations. Even in the British case the change in policy was one of means not ends, Whitehall only seeking a more effective way of coming to grips with Germany in Russia. The extent to which Russia had become an object in the struggle between the allied and central powers can be seen in the agreement reached between Britain and France at the same time they agreed to 'get into relations with the Bolsheviks.' Thus, they had also

30 Kennan, *Russia Leaves the War*, 209-10
31 *Ibid.*, 191-218. Kennan examines the Kalpashnikov affair in depth

decided to divide Russia into 'spheres of activity,' suspiciously resembling spheres of influence, in which each would assist groups willing to continue the war against Germany. France took the Ukraine for its 'sphere of activity' while Great Britain chose south-eastern Russia and the Caucasus. In addition to financial support the two decided that they would also send 'agents and officers to advise and support the Provisional Governments and Armies' formed in these areas.[32] Trotsky had broken the 'conspiracy of silence' against the Russian revolution, but the allied powers had also decided to launch themselves into the holocaust of the Russian civil war. The basis for intervention had been laid.

32 PRO *Cab* 23/4/278-9

3

On s'engage et puis on voit

... any territory shall be deemed to be annexed whose population, over the last few decades (since the second half of the 19th century) has expressed dissatisfaction with the integration of its territory into another state, or its status in the state ... Soviet definition of annexation, 10 December 1917

The Russian government ... takes cognizance of the decisions expressing the will of the peoples inhabiting Poland, Lithuania, Courland, and portions of Estonia and Livonia demanding full state independence and separation from the Russian Federation. German formula for the achievement of self-determination, 27 December 1917

The armistice of 15 December provided that a peace conference would open in Brest-Litovsk one week later. The Bolsheviks would then have to sit down at the conference table, not with Karl Liebknecht and Rosa Luxemburg, but with the representatives of the German ruling classes. This realization made the weakness of the 'German gambit' only too painfully apparent; if the revolution did not spread to Germany, Soviet Russia would be left alone to face German imperialism. While seeking to undermine the morale of the German army, therefore, the Bolsheviks also redoubled their efforts to open channels of communication with the allied powers.

Trotsky pursued this objective in two ways. Conforming to Bolshevik practice he addressed another appeal 'to the toiling, oppressed and exhausted peoples of Europe' again exhorting them to join the struggle against the war.[1] More unusual, but in keeping with his effort to bring

---

1 Trotsky, *Sochineniia*, vol. III, part II, 206-9

direct pressure on the allied governments, he also decided to pay a personal call on the French ambassador. This, it should be noted, was not his idea, but that of Captain Jacques Sadoul, a member of the French military mission in Petrograd. Sadoul, like Raymond Robins, believed that the Soviet government might still contribute to the allied war effort against Germany, and had established contact with Smolny in the hope of influencing the Bolsheviks. For some time he had sought to arrange a meeting between Trotsky and Noulens, but he had failed, since neither man was eager to be seen in the company of the other. With the peace conference only four days in the future, however, he finally convinced Trotsky that if Ioffe could go to Brest-Litovsk to meet with the Germans, the foreign commissar could stroll down the street to speak with the French ambassador. But how would Noulens receive Trotsky? Not wishing to give the ambassador an opportunity to avoid the meeting, Sadoul waited until the last minute to inform Noulens of the visit. A refusal to receive the foreign commissar, he said, would have 'the most unfortunate results.' Sadoul hinted darkly that if Noulens slammed the door in Trotsky's face the Soviet government would expel all French officers from Russia.[2] 'I did not wish to risk an immediate rupture by refusing to see the people's commissar,' wrote Noulens, 'so I resolved to receive him.'[3] Despite these circumstances, perhaps because of them, the meeting was relatively cordial. The two men discussed many topics but talked primarily about war and peace. Predictably, Noulens wished to talk of war while Trotsky wanted to discuss peace. Moreover, they were left with different impressions of what had been said, Trotsky declaring that Noulens had shown 'an inclination to move toward peace negotiations,'[4] while Noulens said he had insisted that France would continue the war until Germany was finally defeated.[5]

This difference probably arose from the unwillingness of either man to press the other too forcefully. A cordial conversation between two such opinionated individuals as Trotsky and Noulens was unlikely to be one of frankness and candor. Thus, Sadoul said of the conversation that there was 'nothing definite, no irreparable words spoken,'[6] while Noulens noted that Trotsky had avoided topics likely to lead to an argument.[7] Neither man wished to push the other too far. Trotsky still hoped to draw the allied

2 Jacques Sadoul, *Notes sur la Revolution Bolchevique* (Paris, 1920) 158-61
3 Noulens, *Mon Ambassade*, vol. I, 170-1
4 Trotsky, *Sochineniia*, vol. III, part II, 217
5 MAE, Guerre, Russie, 27/161-5
6 Sadoul, *Notes*, 158
7 Noulens, *Mon Ambassade*, vol. I, 175

powers into the peace negotiations, and Noulens did not wish to endanger his already precarious position in Petrograd.[8] Both men used the meeting to evaluate the other and interpreted the conversation to suit their own purposes. Trotsky, in particular, wishing to preserve the illusion that a general, rather than a separate peace was possible, appears to have distorted the substance of the conversation.

By the third week in December, however, the possibility of a general peace was fading rapidly into the mist, and Trotsky, through his dealings with the allies, knew it. What was to be done? A separate peace with Germany or a revolutionary war appeared to be the only alternatives to a general peace. As no international socialist had seriously adumbrated the first possibility, a revolutionary war seemed the only alternative. Trotsky, in fact, had already begun to think in terms of such a conflict. As early as 15 December he had begun to talk of rebuilding the Russian army,[9] and his interest in Sadoul and the French military mission was not limited solely to the channel of communication which they provided with the French government. Instead, Trotsky had to ponder ways in which the young Soviet state could defend itself while still advancing the cause of revolutionary socialism. In a speech delivered on the eve of the peace conference he seemed, as I. Deutscher has pointed out,[10] to be debating with himself the possibilities of this course. In the midst of his address, Trotsky suddenly halted, and, referring to the lack of revolutionary support from the European proletariat, declared bluntly: '... if it should turn out that we had been mistaken, if this dead silence were to reign in Europe much longer, if this silence were to give the Kaiser the chance to attack us and to dictate terms insulting to the revolutionary dignity of our country then I do not know whether – with this disrupted economy and universal chaos entailed by war and internal convulsions – whether we could go on fighting.' Having shocked his audience he then reversed himself, asserting, 'Yes we could,' and developed the argument for fighting a revolutionary war in which the weary and the old would step aside and a 'powerful army of soldiers and Red Guards strong with revolutionary enthusiasm' would conduct a 'holy war against the militarists of all countries.'[11]

There was, of course, nothing new in the assertion that the proletariat *could* wage a revolutionary war against capitalism. The novelty lay in the

8 MAE, Guerre, Russie, 27/161-5
9 Sadoul, *Notes*, 154-5
10 Deutscher, *The Prophet Armed*, 357
11 Trotsky, *Sochineniia*, vol. III, part II, 211-7

suggestion that the western proletariat might fail their Russian brothers, that the 'one chance in a hundred' might materialize and that Soviet Russia would *actually have to fight* a revolutionary war. Trotsky's audience, composed of revolutionary militants, received his words with enthusiasm, but it was very significant that Lenin said nothing. The breach, already visible in retrospect on 8 November, was now widening. Unobserved at the time, it was nonetheless marked by Lenin's silence.

If Lenin and Trotsky had begun to differ on future contingencies they were united in believing that the peace conference had to be used as a forum to incite social unrest throughout Europe. Lenin had already prepared his instructions for the Bolshevik delegation at the peace conference, and although these instructions were innocently entitled an 'Outline Program for Peace Negotiations' they amounted to nothing less than a program for the bolshevization of Europe. Lenin called for a peace based on no annexations, no indemnities, and the self-determination of all peoples, packing the revolutionary dynamite of his program in the definition of annexation and the means by which self-determination was to be secured. To start, he rejected any definition of annexation which related only to lands integrated into another state since the start of the world war. Instead, he proclaimed:

any territory shall be deemed to be annexed whose population, over the last few decades (since the second half of the 19th century) has expressed dissatisfaction with the integration of its territory into another state, or its status in the state, regardless of whether such dissatisfaction has been expressed in writings, decisions of meetings, assemblies, municipal councils and similar institutions, in state and diplomatic acts, arising from the national movement in these territories, in national friction, clashes, disturbances, etc.

The people of such areas were to be given the right to self-determination 'through a referendum of the whole population of the territory' in question. Before such a referendum, however, it would be necessary to establish 'preliminary conditions, guaranteeing ... free self-determination.' These included the withdrawal of troops, the return of refugees, the creation of a democratically elected caretaker administration and the 'establishment under the caretaker administration of commissions of the contracting parties with the right of reciprocal control.' All expenses were to be paid by the 'occupying party.'[12]

12 Lenin, pss, vol. xxxv, 121-2

Lenin's peace proposals must rank as one of the most revolutionary documents of all time. If implemented, they would have opened every political sore on the continent, encouraged every group with a grievance to race forward with it, and established conditions for the collapse of government authority everywhere. Without even considering its application elsewhere in the world, it is sufficient to recall the tangled mass of conflicting national claims which afflicted Europe to understand that this program would have led to anarchy pure and simple. Where in the previous seventy years had individuals claiming to represent the people of one area or another not 'expressed dissatisfaction with the integration of their territory into another state'? On the basis of Lenin's program regionalist movements and other groups under the guise of regionalism could take power everywhere. In place of two warring coalitions a hundred regions, all with their petty claims against one another, would have emerged in a truly Hobbesian *bellum omnium in omnes.* The anarchy which had brought the Bolsheviks to power in Russia would have spread to the rest of Europe creating the circumstances needed by Lenin for the success of his revolutionary policies. Just as Lenin had studied the ways in which a general war could be utilized to destroy the existing social-economic system he had now turned his attention to the way in which a general peace could be made to serve the same purpose. Faithfully following Clausewitz, Lenin saw war and peace as two closely related aspects of the same process,[13] only in this instance he reversed the dictum of his mentor; for him peace was a continuation of war by other means. He wanted a 'people's peace,' by which he meant a peace totally destroying existing social, political, and economic relationships, a peace which would leave him with a set of building blocks with which to construct his ideal society. He had no more than a sketch for such a society, but before he could prepare more detailed drawings he needed the raw materials at his feet. Lenin, like Napoleon, firmly believed that *on s'engage et puis on voit.*

Armed with Lenin's 'Outline Program' and little else, Ioffe and Kamenev returned to Brest-Litovsk. This time, however, they went to meet the political leaders of the 'quadruple alliance' and travelled not as petitioners but as political warriors intent on sowing havoc in the lands of their enemy. It was to be a strange meeting held in an isolated fortress set

---

13 See Werner Hahlweg, 'Lenin und Clausewitz. Ein Beitrag zur politischen Ideegeschichte des 20. Jahrhunderts.' *Archiv für Kulturgeschichte* xxxvi, 20-59 and 357-87. Lenin's notebooks on Clausewitz are reproduced in *Leninskii Sbornik,* 36 vols. (Moscow, 1924-59) vol. xii, 387-452

in a devastated countryside. The diplomats of half a continent had gathered there, and the fortress became a focal point of international attention. There were no journalists to badger the diplomats as they filed in and out of their meetings, but stenographers recorded every word spoken around the conference table. The Bolsheviks had insisted upon this innovation and released a verbatim account of each meeting to the waiting world.

Considering the political chasm which separated the two sides their relations at first took on an almost festive air; blue-blooded aristocrats, bemedaled soldiers, and veteran revolutionaries exchanged pleasantries and rubbed shoulders in a very congenial fashion. There were, however, awkward moments when the veneer of hypocrisy was stripped from the raw emotions just beneath the surface. There was, for example, the shock of realization when Prince Leopold of Bavaria discovered that he had just shaken hands with an assassin; there was also the excruciating moment when Ioffe in a 'kind, almost imploring tone' informed the Austrian foreign minister that 'I hope we may yet be able to raise the revolution in your country too.'[14] Two worlds met at Brest-Litovsk and neither was comfortable in the presence of the other. When the first plenary meeting convened it was the Bolshevik turn to be especially uncomfortable, for they were seated in such a manner as to be nearly surrounded by the representatives of Germany, Austria-Hungary, Turkey, and Bulgaria. On 22 December the great engagement began.

When the conference opened, only the Soviet delegation had a clear policy. Their opponents were badly divided among themselves. The Turks and the Bulgarians wished to annex as much territory as possible; the Austrians, their empire already collapsing about them, simply wanted peace; while the Germans, the senior partners in the alliance, were suffering badly from political schizophrenia. A German crown council held at Kreuznach on 19 December had failed to reach agreement on a policy to be followed at Brest-Litovsk. The army high command, represented by Hindenburg and Ludendorff, had sponsored an iron fisted policy of annexations, demanding that Poland and the Baltic provinces be joined to the Reich. Richard von Kühlmann, the foreign secretary, had opposed the blatantly annexationist policy of the military 'demigods.' An advocate of *Mitteleuropa*, a disciple of German economic and political domination of Europe, Kühlmann was not an opponent of imperialism. Quite to the contrary, he might best be described as an ultra-imperialist with ambitions

14 Count Ottokar Czernin, *In the World War* (London, 1919), 220-1

bounding far in advance of the plodding generals. At Kreuznach he had argued that the time had come for Germany to seek a general, rather than a separate peace. With her enemies in disarray, Germany could dominate a peace conference and emerge from the negotiations stronger than ever. German strength was so great that Kühlmann doubted that the entente would agree to negotiate. But for exactly that reason, Germany should project an image of reasonableness, moderation, and idealism by ostentatiously embracing the principles of the Soviet peace program. If, as seemed likely, the allies rejected these principles, Germany could then turn on Russia with specific territorial demands disguised as a defence of self-determination; Courland, Lithuania, and Poland could be snatched from Russia with the tantalizing possibility of also 'liberating' Finland, the Ukraine, and the Caucasus should the chaos generated by the Bolshevik revolution lead to the total disintegration of the Russian empire. Once 'free' of Russia these areas would easily fall under German domination. Such a policy, he believed, could be pursued without arousing implacable political opposition at home; the German Social Democrats could be convinced to look through their fingers at this camouflaged imperialism. The generals found this approach to the negotiations distasteful, but the Kaiser vacillated, and the foreign secretary, while not having his policy adopted, arrived at Brest-Litovsk with a relatively free hand.[15] How long he would enjoy such freedom was problematical, for he could be certain that Hindenburg and Ludendorff would work industriously to have their own policy adopted by Wilhelm.

The disarray among the central powers became apparent at the first meeting of the peace conference. Formalities and platitudes having been exhausted, the Soviet delegation presented a six-point program calling for a peace of no annexations, no indemnities, and self-determination of peoples. Although the central powers had known what to expect they had to ask for a recess to consider their reply. As Ioffe was playing for as much time as possible he willingly agreed and waited patiently while the recess dragged on for three days. During this interval Kühlmann feverishly sought to have his colleagues accept the proposals which he had outlined at Kreuznach. The Austrian foreign minister, Count Czernin, did not object to this strategy,[16] but the Turks and Bulgarians, who thought only of

15 See Wheeler-Bennett, *Brest-Litovsk*, 107ff; Fritz Fischer, *Germany's Aims in the First World War* (New York, 1967), 475ff; and Richard von Kühlmann, *Erinnerungen* (Heidelberg, 1948)
16 Czernin, *In the World War*, 222

annexations, could not understand how Kühlmann could seriously suggest that they accept the Soviet peace program. They were finally convinced that this was only a game, but Kühlmann also had to obtain the sanction of General Hoffmann, the representative of the army high command at the peace conference. Although Hoffmann disliked the charade, he agreed to play it out. On Christmas Day, therefore, with hypocritical remarks about 'peace on earth' and the 'spirit of the season' the central powers responded to the Soviet peace proposal. With great surprise[17] the Soviet delegation heard Czernin declare that the representatives of the 'quadruple alliance' wished 'to conclude a just and general peace as soon as possible ... and are of the opinion that the principles laid down by the Russian delegation form the basis for the discussion of such a peace.' Czernin made two reservations. The Russian principles, he said, could be accepted only if 'all belligerents without exception pledge themselves to accept by a certain time and without reservations the terms as binding on all nations.' Moreover, the central powers could not accept the Soviet claim of self-determination for nationalities not then enjoying political independence. Self-determination for such peoples had to 'be solved by each state ... in accordance with the constitution of that state.' He concluded by suggesting that the negotiation of questions concerning only Russia and the 'quadruple alliance' begin at once.[18]

Ioffe received his 'Christmas present' with obvious satisfaction. Although Czernin had specifically rejected the Bolshevik definition of self-determination he seemed to have accepted the remainder of the Soviet peace program. In response, Ioffe stressed this acceptance and dealt only incidentally with the problem of self-determination. The question of national minorities, he said, would have to be dealt with in the final treaty, but agreement in principle had been reached for the conclusion of a just peace. He suggested a ten-day recess during which the allied powers could be informed of this agreement and again invited to participate in the conference. While awaiting their response Russia and the 'quadruple alliance' could discuss issues which concerned them alone.[19] After the meeting Ioffe jubilantly informed Petrograd of the surprising turn of events.

Ioffe should have been more cautious. Why, for example, had Czernin placed so much emphasis on allied acceptance of the Soviet principles?

17 A.A. Ioffe, 'Brest-Litovsk: Vospominaniia,' Novy Mir (June 1927), 140
18 Bunyan and Fisher, The Bolshevik Revolution, 479-81
19 Ibid., 481-2. See also D.G. Fokke, 'Na Stsene i za Kulisami Brestskoi Tragikomedii,' Arkhiv' Russkoi Revoliutsii xx, 103-7, 118

What had he meant when he said that the central powers wanted 'guarantees that the allies ... will honestly and without reservation live up to these conditions in regard to the quadruple alliance?' And in agreeing to evacuate occupied Russian territory why had Czernin added that the conditions for evacuation were 'to be determined by the peace treaty unless some understanding is reached before that time to remove the troops from certain places?' Ioffe should have asked for clarification of these details, but instead he seems to have taken the Germans at their word; he was, in the words of one Russian observer, 'sincerely naive.'[20] The Soviet delegation believed that the Germans had accepted its proposals, and, in private talks with the representatives of the central powers, showed that it had completely misunderstood the intent of Czernin's statement.[21] Thus, in the two days following Christmas, a strange atmosphere settled over Brest-Litovsk, with the Russians enjoying a false sense of euphoria and the Germans left with the nagging impression that their deception had proved too successful.

Not only had the Russians been deceived, public opinion in Germany had also been misled. Reading of Kühlmann's supposed renunciation of conquests in the east, German annexationists exploded in a burst of outrage. Ludendorff angrily informed the government that under no circumstances would the army evacuate Russian territory it had seized during the war, and the chancellor, somewhat confused himself, telegraphed the foreign secretary inquiring what exactly was happening at the peace conference.[22] Caught in a storm of his own making, the German foreign secretary sought shelter. While Hoffmann tried to calm Ludendorff, Kühlmann spelled out his policy to the chancellor. Only if the French were to renounce Alsace-Lorraine; the Italians, the Trentino; and the Japanese, Kiautschou would Germany be bound to accept the Russian program. 'In as much as it is almost out of the question [he wrote] that in existing circumstances the entente will negotiate on such a basis, then, on the

20 Fokke, 'Brestskoi Tragikomedii,' 118
21 *Ibid.*, 108-9
22 Ministerium fur Auswärtige Angelegenheiten der DDR und Ministerium fur Auswärtige Angelegenheiten der UdSSR, *Deutsche-Sowjetische Beziehungen von den Verhandlungen in Brest-Litowsk bis zum Abschluss des Rapallovertrages.* Two vols. (Berlin, 1967-71) I, 198. Hereafter cited as DSB. The same institutions have published these volumes in the Russian language as well. They appear as Ministerstvo Inostrannykh Del SSSR i Ministerstvo Inostrannykh Del GDR, *Sovetsko-Germanskie Otnosheniia ot peregovorov v Brest-Litovske do podpisaniia rapall'skogo dogovora.* Two vols. (Moscow, 1968-71). When using Soviet documents I will make use of the Russian language volumes and cite them hereafter as SGO.

expiration of the indicated time limit we will be completely free to change the fundamental points of negotiation not only in relation to the other enemies, but also in relation to Russia.'[23] Nevertheless, Kühlmann decided it was too dangerous to allow the Soviet delegation to remain in ignorance of Germany's real intentions; it was time, he felt, that they were informed of the facts of life in eastern Europe.

Kühlmann had no taste for such honesty and left the task to General Hoffmann who, with the bluntness of his profession, found the assignment more congenial than the parlour games in which he had participated in the first meetings of the conference. On 27 December, the general informed Ioffe of the German interpretation of 'self-determination.' This concept, he said, was a constituent part of the German peace program and, consequently, the central powers drew great satisfaction from the emphasis which Soviet Russia placed on it, especially the willingness, repeatedly expressed, to allow the withdrawal from the Russian empire of all peoples desiring independence. Poland, Lithuania, and Courland, he noted, had already expressed this desire, and Germany recognized these peoples to be independent of Russia. When Ioffe exclaimed that these areas were presently under German occupation and that their peoples could not be said to have expressed their views freely Hoffmann brushed his objections aside. He added that if at some future date the peoples of these areas, as well as those of Livonia and Estonia, who seemed ready to express a similar persuasion, should seek union with Germany their application would be given favourable attention. Such a voluntary union could not, he said, be considered annexation; it would be the triumph of 'self-determination.' As Hoffmann reports it, Ioffe 'looked as if he had received a blow on the head.'[24]

Ioffe, of course, could not be certain that the general spoke for the 'quadruple alliance.' To test Hoffmann's authority he prepared a draft proposal on the future of occupied territories, which he presented that evening to the peace conference. The meeting was short and decisive, devoid of all the pleasantries which had characterized earlier sessions. Ioffe began by proposing the evacuation of all territories occupied by foreign armies since the beginning of the war. Citing the principles of self-determination, Soviet style, he specified that the populations of all occupied districts were to be 'given the opportunity at a definite time in the near future of deciding freely the question of their union with one or another state or of forming independent states.' These plebiscites were to

23 DSB, vol. I, 201
24 Hoffmann, *War Diaries*, vol. II, 209-11

be held in accordance with the terms laid down in Lenin's instructions of 10 December.[25] The Germans immediately replied with their version of 'self-determination' calling upon the Soviet government to take 'cognizance of the decisions expressing the will of the peoples inhabiting Poland, Lithuania, Courland and portions of Estonia and Livonia, demanding full state independence and separation from the Russian federation,' and 'recognize that in the present circumstances the above decisions must be regarded as the expression of the will of the people.'[26] This made the German position only too clear, but if Ioffe required further clarification he received it when Kühlmann inquired if the Russians were prepared to evacuate the remainder of Livonia and Estonia 'to give the local population, the possibility without military pressure ... to declare their repeatedly expressed wish to unite with their fellow-countrymen now living in the occupied regions.'[27] Even more alarming were German questions about the exact status of Finland and the Ukraine. The sharp edge of self-determination designed by Lenin for capitalist throats was now ruthlessly drawn across the jugular vein of Soviet Russia. Forty minutes after it had begun, the meeting adjourned, and the Soviet delegation raced to the telegraph office to 'bombard' Smolny with reports of what had just happened.[28]

The German demands had shattered the self-confidence of the Soviet delegation. Ioffe was stunned, and that evening asked for a ten-day recess. Kühlmann agreed, but stipulated that the period in which the western allies could join the negotiations would expire ten days from the day on which Germany had accepted the Soviet peace program. Thus, although the conference would not resume until 9 January 1918, the allies would be required to give their answer no later than 4 January. The first euphoric phase of the peace negotiations was at an end.

The abrupt turn of events at Brest-Litovsk seriously embarrassed the Soviet government. The German declaration of 25 December had badly misled Bolshevik leaders, causing them to give it wide publicity and even order a victory parade to celebrate this 'triumph of Soviet diplomacy.' Worse yet, Trotsky had publicly gloated over this 'huge success.' In a report to the Central Executive Committee, delivered that same fateful evening of 27 December, the foreign commissar even claimed that the

25 Bunyan and Fisher, *The Bolshevik Revolution*, 483
26 *Ibid.*, 484
27 Fokke, 'Brestskoi Tragikomedii,' 118
28 *Ibid.*, 119

Congress of Soviets had 'dictated' the terms which Germany had been forced to accept. When asked to explain the meaning of the reservation attached by the Germans to their acceptance of the Soviet formula for peace he displayed the same naiveté as Ioffe. 'The reservation,' he asserted, 'does not permit two interpretations ... This means that if Russia concludes a separate peace with Germany that the obligations of Germany in relation to our allies does not extend to a future peace with them. ... German diplomacy can not say to us: if France will not take part in the negotiations, then we will not return Courland and Lithuania to Russia.'[29] Unfortunately, the reservation *did* permit two interpretations, which was a lesson in diplomacy that Kühlmann was just then teaching Ioffe; however, Trotsky, buoyant in his ignorance, was blissfully unaware of this. He was, in fact, already composing his ultimatum to the allies. Asserting that, as a consequence of the German acceptance of the Soviet peace program, the allies could no longer claim to be waging war to liberate oppressed peoples, he called upon them to join the negotiations for a general peace. This, he said, was their 'last chance;' if the allied governments persisted in their stubbornness they would have to suffer the 'consequences.'[30] The threat of a separate peace with Germany at the expense of the entente was clear and unmistakable. Trotsky's omnipotent exuberance was of brief duration, for within hours of addressing the Central Executive Committee he received the crushing news that the German acceptance of the Soviet peace program had been meant only as a fig leaf to conceal their annexationist intentions. How nauseated he must have felt at that moment! Several months later he could still convey a measure of this feeling when he wrote that the Soviet leaders 'found the abyss separating the true proposals of German imperialism from that formula which was presented to us on 25 December to be truly inconceivable ... Such shamelessness we did not expect.'[31]

So inconceivable was the German maneuver that it briefly paralyzed the Soviet government. Until then Lenin and Trotsky had held the initiative, forcing their adversaries to react to policies prepared in Petrograd. Now the initiative passed to the Germans. The transition occurred so quickly that the Bolshevik leaders found it momentarily impossible to adjust to this change. Thus, Trotsky's ultimatum, although nothing but an empty bombshell, was sent to the allies, and the 'victory parade,' now a

29 Trotsky, *Sochineniia*, vol. III, part II, 225-9
30 DVP, vol. I, 67-70
31 Trotsky, *Sochineniia*, vol. III, part II, 325

grotesque anachronism, was allowed to proceed on schedule. At the last moment the Soviet leaders did regain sufficient presence of mind to shift its emphasis from that of a proletarian 'triumph' to a proletarian show of strength.[32]

Reports of the debacle at Brest-Litovsk unleashed a wave of anger and indignation in Petrograd. The left Socialist Revolutionaries, who, in the words of Oliver Radkey, reacted as 'idealists who felt themselves to have been wickedly deceived,' demanded a struggle to the end against German imperialism.[33] Many Bolsheviks felt the same. Thus, Karl Radek, 'breathing war of arms and propaganda,' swore that 'the Bolsheviks would fight ... because they would perish if they did not.'[34] The spontaneity of this response caught Lenin unprepared, and, similar to his experience during the July days of the previous summer, he found it necessary to swim with the tide of revolutionary militancy, all the while seeking to regain control of the situation. Lenin had to project an image of dynamic leadership in sympathy with the prevailing emotions in Petrograd without committing his government to a policy which it did not have the resources to sustain. On 31 December he presented the Sovnarkom with a program based on these desiderata. Very moderate in scope, it was tricked out in revolutionary symbols to appeal to the left Socialist Revolutionaries and the radical wing of the Bolsheviks. In substance it called for the prolongation of negotiations at Brest-Litovsk and a new emphasis on defence. To give the revolution in Germany time to materialize he called for an intensification of propaganda against German imperialism, the allocation of additional funds for this purpose and an effort to move the peace conference to Stockholm where he believed greater influence could be exerted over events in Germany. Everyone agreed that the Russian army was unprepared to fight Germany, and to remedy this situation Lenin proposed new steps to reorganize the armed forces, urgent measures to safeguard Petrograd, and propaganda explaining the 'necessity for a revolutionary war.'[35] The proposals sounded sufficiently militant to satisfy the Sovnarkom, and, on the next day a much less explicit program was ratified by the Central Executive Committee.[36] In a press conference held on 2

32 Kennan, *Russia Leaves the War*, 224
33 Radkey, *Sickle under the Hammer*, 151
34 Edgar Sisson, *One Hundred Red Days: A Personal Chronicle of the Bolshevik Revolution* (New Haven, Connecticut, 1931) 189
35 Lenin, PSS, vol. xxxv, 181
36 Jane Degras (ed.), *Soviet Documents on Foreign Policy*. Three vols. (Oxford, 1951) vol. I, 24-6

January, Trotsky could once again sound an optimistic note, declaring: 'We shall continue the negotiations on the basis of the principles proclaimed by the Russian revolution. We shall do all we can to bring the results of these negotiations to the notice of the popular masses of all European countries ... We do not doubt that the negotiations themselves will make us stronger, and the imperialist Governments of all countries weaker.'[37] Lenin, significantly, said nothing.

On the surface it appeared as if the Bolshevik leaders had regained their equilibrium and put together a program to meet the German challenge. A closer examination reveals a much different situation. With one exception, none of the measures adopted on 31 December could be described as an imaginative approach to the problem. Instead they were a simple rehash of existing policies flung together in a single container and garnished with appropriately revolutionary symbols. The only exception was the call for propaganda explaining the 'necessity for a revolutionary war,' and even this was based on hoary Bolshevik tradition. Moreover, dangling at the end of the program, barely supported by the measures designed to enhance Russian military strength, it gives the impression of having been added at the last moment, perhaps after a meeting of Trotsky with Lenin. As is frequently the case, unanimity in a moment of crisis concealed diversity of opinion.

This diversity becomes particularly evident when the activities of Lenin and Trotsky in the days following the debacle of Brest-Litovsk are examined. Trotsky, who already subscribed to the possibility of a revolutionary war, began to cast about for allies in such a conflict. He turned at once to the western powers, completely disregarding the absurd light which this threw on the ultimatum which he had just sent them. The foreign commissar had to be extraordinarily discreet in making these inquiries, for in approaching the allies he was treading on very dangerous ground. If revolutionary war was suddenly popular in Petrograd, the entente was not; even a hint of cooperation with the allies was political dynamite. Nevertheless, for some time he had been sounding Sadoul on the possibility of renewed French military assistance for Russia, and now he informed him that 'German duplicity' had enraged the Bolsheviks and 'more than ever they were considering the possibility of resuming the war.' He also turned to Robins with the same story, explaining the military measures being taken to defend the revolution and asking what the United States would do if the peace negotiations failed. Robins, who had been waiting for just

37 *Ibid.*, vol. I, 26-8

such an opening, rushed to Francis and secured a written statement from him pledging that he would urge Washington to 'render all aid and assistance possible' to the Soviet government just as soon as hostilities had actually resumed between Russia and Germany.[38] Sadoul was unable to obtain a similar pledge from Noulens but left Trotsky in little doubt that France would support anyone, even the Bolsheviks, who took up arms against Germany.

Lenin followed a different line of inquiry. The prospect of allied assistance did not appeal to him. Such aid would bring with it unwanted political advice, and the last thing he wanted was Buchanan, Noulens, or Francis whispering in his ear about the delights of a *union sacrée* uniting all parties in a patriotic war against the Germans. Even worse than allied ambassadors whispering in *his* ear, he could, in the event of renewed hostilities with Germany, anticipate those same ambassadors murmuring in the ears of his colleagues. If Lenin was certain he could resist such blandishments and that Trotsky would find them scandalous, then what guarantee did he have that individuals such as Kamenev or Zinoviev, men whom he had recently denounced as revolutionary strike-breakers, might not find them attractive? More to the point, in the event of a complete reversal of policy, what guarantee did he have that his colleagues might not find his continued presence at the head of government an embarrassment? But even if the allies were willing to provide military assistance without any strings attached, how valuable would this aid be? Allied assistance in the past had not prevented Russian defeat, and the combat potential of the Russian army had declined even further since the Bolshevik seizure of power. Trotsky could talk bravely of a 'powerful army of soldiers and Red Guards strong with revolutionary enthusiasm,' but, in the event of the 'holy war' which the foreign commissar advocated, just who would fight for the Soviet government? This was the question which Lenin asked. Before he led the Soviet state off to war he wanted to know who would follow. While Trotsky sought foreign assistance which might or might not materialize, Lenin was busy investigating how many Russians would actually return to the trenches to fight the Germans.

To answer his question Lenin turned to the Congress on the Demobilization of the Army which had just assembled in Petrograd. Summoned to devise a rational method of disbanding the old army it was hoped that the congress would significantly retard the process of 'spontaneous demobilization' which was threatening to spread anarchy throughout Russia.

38 Kennan, *Russia Leaves the War*, 233-41

With good reason Lenin believed that the delegates to this congress could provide him with the information he wanted. Not only were the delegates drawn from every part of the armed forces, but as a majority were Bolsheviks, they could also be counted upon to be well-tempered with revolutionary militancy. On 30 December Lenin circulated a questionnaire among the delegates asking them to give him their views on the existing military situation. He specifically asked if the army could retreat in good order should the Germans resume their offensive and if the delegates thought it more desirable to drag out peace negotiations at Brest-Litovsk or 'to break them off immediately in revolutionary fashion.' Most important, he inquired: 'if the army could vote, would it be in favour of immediate peace on annexationist (loss of the occupied regions) and economically very harsh terms for Russia or would it favour the maximum effort for a revolutionary war?'[39]

The delegates' response painted an appalling picture of the Russian army. In the event of renewed hostilities, they said, the best for which the Soviet government could hope would be for the army to retreat in good order. In doing so, however, it would lose its artillery and the incidence of 'spontaneous demobilization' would increase. A majority of the delegates said that the army could provide no serious opposition to a German offensive and, in the event of such an attack, Petrograd would fall to the enemy. The delegates urged the Soviet government to make the most strenuous efforts to drag out the peace negotiations and, in case of necessity, to secure 'peace at any price.'[40]

Lenin could draw only one logical conclusion from these answers: it was impossible for Soviet Russia to resume the war against Germany. In early December he had observed: 'It was quite easy to drive out a band of nitwits like Romanov and Rasputin, but it is immensely more difficult to fight against the organized and strong clique of German imperialists, both crowned and uncrowned.'[41] Without a revolution in Germany and without an army he could not fight at all, therefore, it was necessary to make peace. A revolutionary war without an army was an absurdity, and Lenin was not accustomed to dealing in that commodity. In the days and weeks following the poll of the delegates, he advised all advocates of revolutionary war to speak with those who would have to do the fighting if the conflict with Germany resumed. 'Go and take a walk,' he would tell them,

39 Lenin, pss, vol. xxxv, 179-80
40 E.N. Gorodetskii, 'Demobilizatsiia Armii v 1917-1918 gg.' *Istoriia SSSR*, no. 1 (1958) 15-19
41 Lenin, pss, vol. xxxv, 116-17

'hear what the soldiers say in the streets.'[42] Nevertheless, Lenin had to proceed cautiously. The handwriting was already on the wall, but Lenin knew it was still dangerous to give a reading of this inscription. In the past he had spoken too favourably of revolutionary war suddenly to reverse himself and argue against it. Too many of his associates and followers believed this a viable alternative, and Trotsky, his closest collaborator, had already proclaimed himself the champion of such a course. Moreover, a separate and annexationist peace might still be avoided. Germany had not yet delivered an ultimatum, and the demand for vast tracts of Russian territory might be only a bluff. Germany required peace, and Trotsky's talk of revolutionary war might frighten Berlin sufficiently to force it to make concessions to the Soviet position. The German revolution might yet burst out in the same way that the March revolution had overthrown the Romanovs. Given such uncertainty, Lenin chose to remain silent and allow the complicated political situation to develop further.

To gain time it was necessary to drag out the negotiations at Brest-Litovsk. Ioffe had not shown himself particularly adept at negotiating with the Germans so it was necessary to choose another chairman of the Soviet delegation. Who better than Trotsky? 'To delay negotiations,' said Lenin, 'there must be some one to do the delaying,' and he nominated Trotsky to lead the delegation.[43] But more was involved than Lenin's desire to delay the negotiations. What better way to get Trotsky out of the way than to send him to Brest-Litovsk? Trotsky emphasizes in his memoirs that he did not volunteer to head the delegation; Lenin insisted that he go. In doing so Lenin assured himself that German difficulties would be maximized while his own would be minimized. The significance of this subtle maneuver seems completely to have escaped Trotsky. Not only did he agree to go to Brest-Litovsk, he also invited Karl Radek, another advocate of revolutionary war and the most able journalist among the Bolsheviks, to go with him. Lenin was left in control of Petrograd politics. In retrospect it can be seen that this maneuver foreshadowed the departure of Trotsky from the foreign commissariat. Lenin, who wished to exercise decisive control over foreign affairs, was beginning to find Trotsky difficult to handle.

For the moment, however, Lenin had contained the advocates of revolutionary war. With Trotsky's departure for Brest-Litovsk, Lenin could give careful consideration to his own position. Since November he had

42 Nadezhda Krupskaia, *Reminiscences of Lenin* (New York, 1970) 444-5
43 Trotsky, *My Life*, 363

been forced to cope with one emergency after another, and this activity had left him no opportunity to re-evaluate his fundamental policies. Krupskaia, in recalling those days, has written that: 'the work was more than strenuous, it was work at high pressure that absorbed all of one's energies and strained one's nerves to the breaking point.' During that time Lenin had found little time to rest, and, when he did, 'he would talk business in his sleep.'[44] Now he needed to think. His silence of late December and his cautious advocacy of delay had been occasioned not only by political discretion but also genuine uncertainty. Events since the Bolshevik seizure of power had made nonsense of his original foreign policy; but what should be put in its place? As soon as Trotsky was safely out of town Lenin left for a short holiday in Finland, ostensibly to rest but in reality to reconsider the very foundations of his foreign policy.

Lenin spent the next four days in thought, arranging his priorities and deciding on the policies which he wished to follow. 'As a holiday,' wrote Krupskaia, 'it wasn't much of a success ... Ilyich's mind was occupied, and he spent much time writing.'[45] During these days he wrote several essays and a list of themes upon which he intended to elaborate at a later date. Entitled 'From the Diary of a Publicist' these themes are very important, for they allow us to peer into Lenin's mind as he attempted to define his new policy. Much like Trotsky as he groped toward a policy of revolutionary war Lenin now seemed to be debating with himself. 'A separate peace, its danger, and its possible significance,' he wrote; 'Would a separate peace be an agreement with the imperialists?' The next theme indicated that Lenin answered this question in the negative, for here he has already accepted the inevitability of such an agreement and passed on to the topic of 'a separate peace and our duty to the international proletariat.' Succeeding themes dealt with the justification for a separate peace listing in order 'stages in the revolution,' 'calculation of class strength,' the desire of the imperialists to 'smother the Soviet Republic' and the apprehended allied desire to make peace 'at the expense of Russia.' He then left this problem, but some time later, as if realizing that his justifications, good as they might be, would be insufficient to convince his colleagues, returned to ponder it again, this time putting on paper his primary reason for seeking peace with Germany. As theme twenty-eight in this 'Diary of a Publicist' Lenin wrote: 'At first to vanquish the bourgeoisie in Russia, then to fight with the bourgeoisie abroad.'[46]

44 Krupskaia, *Reminiscences*, 415
45 *Ibid.*, 425-6
46 Lenin, PSS, vol. XXXV, 168-9

The crucial significance of this last theme becomes apparent when it is seen in relation to one of the essays Lenin wrote during his 'holiday' in Finland. 'Fear of the Collapse of the Old and the Fight for the New,' a composition never published during Lenin's lifetime and a work which might best be described as a *cri de coeur*, or an *aide-mémoire* from Lenin's id to his super-ego, vividly explained what he meant by vanquishing the bourgeoisie in Russia. In so doing it makes perfectly clear why he would not tolerate the adventure of a revolutionary war against Germany. It also demonstrates the truth of Krupskaia's view that 'Ilyich was anything but coldly rational, a sort of calculating chess player. He felt things intensely ...'[47] for in this essay he displays the intense emotions which governed his great intellect. It is an essay of almost demonic fury illuminating Lenin's hatred of the bourgeoisie and glorifying civil war as 'class struggle at its highest pitch ... the only war that is legitimate, just, and sacred.' Civil war, he believed, would be a school in which the proletariat would learn to destroy their exploiters. Thus, he railed against all those who would stay the hand of the revolution. 'The grasping, malicious, frenzied, filthy avidity of the moneybags; the cowed servility of their hangers-on is the true social source of the present wail raised by the spineless intellectuals ... against violence on the part of the proletariat and the revolutionary peasantry. Such is the objective meaning of their howls, their pathetic speeches, their clownish cries of "freedom" (freedom for the capitalists to oppress the people).' The resistance of the bourgeoisie, he wrote, 'must really be *broken*, and it *will* be broken ... by systematic application of *coercion* to an entire class and its accomplices.'[48] With plans such as these Lenin had no time to waste on Germany. First he had to destroy the Russian bourgeoisie, then he could turn to their class cousins in other parts of Europe. His deepest emotions and instincts drove him in this direction leading him to reject the arguments of those who would turn the sword of the revolution against the foreign enemies before drenching the soil of Russia with the blood of the indigenous 'moneybags' and their 'accomplices.' Lenin had launched the seizure of power in November, confident in the belief that his revolution would inaugurate the world workers' revolution and promptly sweep aside the existing social and political structure of the entire planet. Frustrated in this ambition, he now turned inward on Russia, temporarily lowering his sights and deciding to concentrate on driving the revolution in Russia to its logical extreme. In

47 Krupskaia, *Reminiscences*, 443
48 Lenin, PSS, vol. XXXV, 191-4. Emphasis in original

scaling down his objectives, however, he lost none of his emotional commitment to the revolution, and, indeed, confined to narrower limits, it burned with a white-hot fire new even to Lenin. It is no wonder that Krupskaia reported Lenin's deep pre-occupation with his own thoughts during this short 'holiday' and that sometimes 'Ilyich ... even dropped his voice while speaking, the way we used to do when we were in hiding.' During those few short days in Finland, Lenin had completely reorganized his political agenda, recognizing the failure of one of his fundamental policies and constructing another to take its place. Having arranged his priorities Lenin returned to Petrograd to be on hand as the conference at Brest-Litovsk entered its second phase.

The first phase of the peace conference had been marked by pomp and circumstance, a certain strained conviviality and illusory hopes. The second round bore no such character. Trotsky arrived still smarting from the German duplicity which had made him appear such a fool in his speech of 27 December, and he came prepared to instruct the Germans in the ways of revolutionary diplomacy. Several weeks earlier he had promised that the peace negotiations would resemble a trial in which the imperialists would be in the dock and the Soviet delegation would act as prosecutor.[49] Ioffe had failed in this role, but Trotsky had resolved that he would not be found wanting. On his way to the conference he had stopped at many points to rally the faltering morale of the Russian army. Everywhere his message was the same: 'The Russian revolution will not bow its head before German imperialism. The Russian peasantry, soldiers and workers did not throw off the yoke of the tsar in order to take on their shoulders ... the yoke of the German imperialists and bourgeoisie. In the full certainty of your support, comrades, we will only sign an honourable peace.'[50] But what disappointment! Instead of revolutionary enthusiasm he found despair. 'The trenches were almost empty,' he later wrote, 'and no one ventured to speak even conditionally of a continuation of the war.' 'Peace, peace at any price!' came the cry from the front line troops.[51] The weariness which he found at the front quickly cooled his enthusiasm for revolutionary war; the demoralized soldiers made him realize that a holy war could not be waged without an army. Yet he still would not sign the peace demanded by Kühlmann. While turning away from the chimera of revolutionary war, he arrived at Brest-Litovsk determined to impress the

49 Trotsky, *Sochineniia*, vol. III, part II, 178
50 Fokke, 'Brestskoi Tragikomedii,' 128
51 Leon Trotsky, *Lenin* (London, 1925) 103-4

Germans with the revolutionary seriousness of his mission. His arrival, in fact, was like a cold wintry blast from the north. 'The wind,' said Czernin, 'seems to be in a very different quarter now from what it was.'[52] As a start Trotsky put an end to the courtesies exchanged during the first phase of the conference while Karl Radek set the tone for the new meetings by distributing revolutionary leaflets to German soldiers as the Soviet train pulled into the station at Brest-Litovsk.

The Germans also arrived in a different mood. Although wishing to continue the masquerade of a peace conference attended by supposedly equal states they were no longer willing to humour what they considered the ideological fantasies of the Soviet government. They had already rejected the Soviet proposal to transfer the negotiations from Brest-Litovsk to Stockholm[53] and had lost no time informing Smolny that the ten days allotted the western allies to join the peace conference had expired.[54] In effect, they had said that they were no longer bound by their Christmas declaration and were free to advance new proposals if they wished. Indeed, during the recess the German appetite had grown. Informed by the Ukrainian Rada that it wished to join the peace negotiations the German authorities had invited Kiev to send a delegation to Brest-Litovsk. Kühlmann had already hinted at such a maneuver on 27 December when he had addressed his pointed question to Ioffe concerning the relationship between Petrograd and Kiev. Now the threat materialized. Although the appearance of a Ukrainian delegation at the peace conference would embarrass Austria, the Germans were convinced the Rada would discomfit Trotsky even more. Kühlmann, in fact, had written the chancellor that 'if [the Ukrainians] agree to a separate peace with us ... then our position in relation to Trotsky would become immeasurably stronger and we could, with equanimity, rupture negotiations with him if, as I suspect, he should attempt to delay the negotiations.'[55]

How was Trotsky to deal with this wild card which the Germans had suddenly slipped into the diplomatic game? Although he had nothing but contempt for the Rada delegation, styling them as a 'Ukrainian variety of Kerenskyism' only 'more provincial,' and later asserting that 'they were never intended by nature for any other fate than to be led by the nose by any capitalist diplomatist,' he also realized, again in his words, that these

---

52 Czernin, *In the World War*, 232
53 DSB, vol. I, 299
54 Trotsky, *Sochineniia*, XVII, part I, 616-17
55 A.A. Akhtamazian, 'O Brest-Litovskikh peregovorakh 1918 goda.' *Voprosi Istorii* no.11 (1966) 34

'democratic simpletons' were the 'trump card' in the German hand.[56] Trotsky, therefore, tried to finesse the 'trump' by reaching an agreement with the Ukrainians before the conference resumed. In exchange for Trotsky's pledge that he would publicly reaffirm the right of the Ukraine to self-determination and acknowledge the Rada delegation as fully empowered to represent the Ukraine, the Ukrainians agreed to form a united front against German annexationist demands and consult with the Soviet delegation on all major issues.[57] In temporarily neutralizing the Ukrainian delegation, however, Trotsky had weakened his own position. A trump can not be finessed without another trump, and, in trying to do so, Trotsky had given away an ace. Once admitted to the conference, the Rada delegation could adopt any policy it wished and prior agreements with Trotsky would be meaningless. This was especially true since the agreement had been made under false pretenses, Trotsky having led the Rada delegation to believe that Soviet recognition constituted a safeguard for Ukrainian independence and that he genuinely intended to negotiate peace with the Germans. Once they discovered that the foreign commissar was interested only in sparring with Kühlmann while awaiting the revolution in central Europe and that the Kharkov Soviet intended to destroy the Rada, they threw themselves into the arms of Germany. At the time, however, Trotsky had little choice. If he had refused to recognize the right of the Rada to represent the Ukraine he would have made a mockery of the Soviet declaration of the right of all peoples to self-determination, forced the Germans to take sides in the Russian-Ukrainian conflict and possibly have exploded the entire peace conference. As Trotsky had been sent to Breat-Litovsk to play for time he was forced to accept the presence of the Ukrainians.

The central powers, however, were growing weary of Soviet delaying tactics. Czernin in particular was frantic to conclude peace, and the German general staff was eager to conclude the war in eastern Europe so it could devote its full attention to the western front. Kühlmann, who believed that the Bolsheviks needed peace even more than the central powers, was in no hurry, but he finally agreed to a strategy which Czernin and Hoffmann hoped would move the conference forward at a faster pace. The three men decided to present Trotsky with an ultimatum, demanding that he agree at once to continue the talks at Brest-Litovsk, to negotiate an avowedly separate peace and to form a number of commissions to expe-

56 Trotsky, *My Life*, 376
57 Fokke, 'Brestskoi Tragikomedii,' 129

dite the work of the conference. At their first meeting with Trotsky on 9 January, Kühlmann and Czernin presented these propositions and asked if the foreign commissar would accept them. Trotsky, who listened silently, showed no inclination to be helpful; instead he asked for a recess to prepare his answer. The game of delay had begun.[58]

But much more was involved than simply delaying the negotiations. Trotsky had come to the meeting ready to unburden himself of a lengthy polemic,[59] but having been presented with an ultimatum he decided to give further thought to his inaugural address. Clearly revolutionary rhetoric alone would be insufficient, for once he had discharged his last verbal salvo he would still be faced by the dour representatives of the central powers demanding answers to their peremptory questions. Trotsky needed a gimmick which would permit him to disorient his adversaries and give him time to elaborate his indictment of imperialism.

The next day the foreign commissar was ready to assume his role of prosecuting attorney. From beginning to end he subjected the representatives of the 'quadruple alliance' to a withering barrage of revolutionary invective, attacking their peace proposals, governments, and social structures. The diplomatic offensive of the central powers collapsed before Trotsky's response. Step by step he answered their questions, but his answers simply left the situation more confused than ever and presented the central powers with a dilemma on which they would hang for the next four weeks. Soviet Russia, he said, could not accept any of the proposals made by Kühlmann and Czernin. It could approve neither the continuation of the negotiations at Brest-Litovsk, the negotiation of a separate peace nor the suggested structure of commissions to work out the details of a peace treaty. Least of all could it accept the German definition of self-determination advanced at the end of the previous session of the peace conference. The German repudiation of the agreement of 25 December had left the conference without any generally accepted principles on which peace could be based, and until such agreement was reached, there could be no talk of deciding on the details of a final treaty. Having rejected the entire German program Trotsky then abruptly announced that he was prepared to remain at Brest-Litovsk and continue the negotiations. But it was an announcement from which Kühlmann, Czernin, and Hoffmann could draw little satisfaction, for in his next breath he con-

58 Kühlmann, *Erinnerungen*, 532; Czernin, *In the World War*, 234. Also see Werner Hahlweg (ed.), *Der Friede von Brest-Litowsk* (Düsseldorf, 1971), 229-34
59 Fokke, 'Brestskoi Tragikomedii,' 138

cluded his presentation by saying; 'Our government has placed at the head of its program the word "Peace," but it has engaged itself at the same time before its people to sign only a democratic and just peace.'[60] The central powers had attempted to force Trotsky to say 'yes' or 'no' to peace; he had now turned the tables on them and was forcing them to say 'yes' or 'no' to the continuation of negotiations.

Here then, in essence, was Trotsky's later formula of 'no war, no peace' presented in the less extreme form of 'no agreement but no rupture.' The later formula would grow logically from the first declaration of the foreign commissar at Brest-Litovsk, but this first version presented the Germans with no less a problem. If anything, this conundrum was more difficult to solve than the later more spectacular one, for its very nebulousness defied solution. At this point the Germans could still hope that Trotsky was simply putting on a show for his proletarian constituents and that once he had shown himself to be a worthy defender of Bolshevik ideals he would sign the documents placed before him. Kühlmann, in particular, believed this and, as a consequence, the conference continued day after day tying itself into rhetorical knots as Trotsky and the German foreign secretary debated an endless number of politically academic questions, testing their forensic skills on one another. Kühlmann also allowed this dialogue to continue, for he had come to realize the danger of Bolshevism and the threat which it posed to the realization of his own aspirations. He had developed a grudging respect for Trotsky whom he characterized as 'being cut from a very different wood than Ioffe'[61] and believed that if the accusations of the foreign commissar were left unanswered they would shake the political stability of Germany. Thus, he rose to the challenge of Trotsky's 'open diplomacy' and through the application of verbal 'thumbscrews' sought to compel the foreign commissar to admit that Bolshevism was based on force, terrorism, and dictatorship. When Trotsky acknowledged that the Soviet government did not rest upon democratic principles but on armed force Kühlmann considered it 'one of the greatest triumphs of the discussion.'[62] The peace conference then truly became a courtroom in which Kühlmann and Trotsky laboured to impeach each other and the different social systems which they represented. Yet in another sense the two men were collaborators, each assisting the other to

60 Trotsky, *Sochineniia*, vol. XVII, part I, 3-11. Also see Hahlweg, *Der Friede von Brest-Litowsk*, 241-51
61 Kühlmann, *Erinnerungen*, 529
62 *Ibid.*, 524. Also see Hahlweg, *Der Friede von Brest-Litowsk*, 255-71, 277-83, 284-7, 294-301, 327-37, 342-51, 351-9

delay proceedings and advance their separate aims. Trotsky was later to remark ironically that in dragging out the conference he could 'claim no credit ... my partners helped me as best they could.'[63]

But this international debating society could not long endure. The German high command grew increasingly angry, and, on 18 January, Kühlmann, who knew he could not test Ludendorff's patience any further, agreed that Hoffmann should present the German demands to Trotsky. He did so with the aid of a large map marked with a heavy blue line extending from Brest-Litovsk to the Baltic Sea. This line represented the proposed Russian frontier and would require the Soviet government to renounce Poland, Lithuania, and most of Latvia. Trotsky observed that the line halted at Brest-Litovsk and inquired about the disposition of territory to the south of the city. Hoffmann replied that the future of that territory would be settled with the Ukrainian delegation. When Trotsky shot back that such a settlement would depend upon a previous arrangement between Russia and the Ukraine the general menacingly switched the subject to Russia's relationship with the peoples of the Caucasus.[64] The implication was quite clear: if Trotsky objected too strenuously to the German demands they would again expand the scope of the conference. Hoffmann had put the German trump on the table. After nine days of masterly delaying tactics the foreign commissar realized that the game was nearly at an end and that his opponent had the winning cards. What was to be done?

Trotsky's ever-fertile imagination had already provided an answer. A few days earlier he had written Lenin informing him that the negotiations could not be dragged out indefinitely and that the Germans would soon demand a final answer to their peace proposals. 'We can not sign their peace,' he wrote; 'My plan is this: We announce the termination of the war and demobilization without signing any peace. We declare we cannot participate in the brigands' peace of the Central Powers, nor can we sign a brigands' peace. Poland's, Lithuania's and Courland's fate we place upon the responsibility of the German working people.' Internal conditions in Germany, he said, would make it impossible for her to attack Soviet Russia. Most German political parties, he claimed, were demanding an understanding with Russia, internal strife was demoralizing the government, and bitter controversy was raging in the press. Even if Germany was able to resume the war, he asserted, 'our position will be no worse than now ...'

63 Trotsky, *My Life*, 329
64 Hahlweg, *Der Friede von Brest-Litowsk*, 373-82

Having canvassed the other delegates and received their support he sought Lenin's sanction for the immediate implementation of his scheme. Stressing that the situation was urgent he concluded his letter with a postscript saying 'Answer direct by wire: "I agree to your plan" or "I don't agree."'[65]

Lenin refused to make a snap decision. He already believed it necessary to sign the 'brigands' peace' but was not yet prepared to announce this publicly. Moreover, with Trotsky at Brest-Litovsk, beyond effective control, he had to tread carefully lest the foreign commissar implement his scheme without further consultation. Thus, on 16 January, he replied non-committally: 'I think your plan is worth discussing. Can its final implementation be somewhat deferred, and the final decision taken after a special Central Executive Committee meeting over here?' Later in the day he repeated his message in firmer language[66] and, it would seem, did so again on the eighteenth.[67] Trotsky was left to draw his own conclusions and decided to ask for an adjournment of the peace conference.

Three other considerations led him in this direction. Word had at last arrived that food riots had broken out in Vienna and that similar disturbances were occurring in other cities of the Habsburg empire. The long-expected revolution in central Europe, therefore, seemed to be at hand and a further delay in the peace conference might result in a vastly altered situation when the talks resumed. In addition, civil war had broken out in the Ukraine and the Red Guards were advancing rapidly from Kharkov to Kiev. Within a week the Rada might be gone and with it the German trump. Finally, the Constituent Assembly was scheduled to convene in Petrograd on the eighteenth, and Trotsky wished to be present when it began its deliberations.

With these considerations in mind and with Hoffmann's map thrust under his nose, Trotsky took the opportunity to seek an adjournment. While vilifying the rapacity of German imperialism he praised the general's honesty and declared that this clear statement of the German position made it necessary for him to consult his government. Implying that he would return with a definitive answer to the peace proposals of the central powers he secured the assent of Kühlmann and Czernin to another ten-day recess.[68] That night he left Brest-Litovsk bound for the

65 Wheeler-Bennett, *Brest-Litovsk*, 185-6
66 Lenin, pss, vol. xxxv, 225
67 Chubar'ian, *Brestskii Mir*, 129
68 Trotsky, *Sochineniia*, vol. xvii, part i, 51-3. Also see Hahlweg, *Der Friede von Brest-Litowsk*, 384-9

greatest crisis yet to be faced by the Soviet government. The German intentions were clear and Trotsky knew how he wished to respond to their challenge. The Soviet government now had to decide what it was going to do.

4
War or peace:
revolutionary foreign policy in transition

Germany is only pregnant with revolution, in our country we already have a very healthy baby – the Socialist Republic – which we will murder by resuming the war. Lenin, 24 January 1918

We will fight against them, and they cannot scare us by their threats of an offensive ... And if German imperialism attempts to crush us on the wheel of its military machine, then we as Ostap to his father will cry out to our brothers in the west: 'Do you hear?' And the international proletariat will answer, this firmly we believe: 'I hear!' Trotsky, 26 January 1918

Before devoting its attention to the threat of German imperialism the Soviet government first had to contend with a more immediate danger. The long-promised Constituent Assembly had finally been elected, and, in January, its members had begun to assemble in Petrograd. Although the Bolsheviks had polled nearly ten million votes and, with their left SR allies, had elected over two hundred deputies, the right SRs had obtained an absolute majority of the votes cast and would control the Assembly. Only with great reluctance had Lenin agreed to allow the elections to be held in the first place, and now his government was faced with the dilemma of how to deal with this rival. If allowed to proceed unhindered the Assembly was sure to claim plenary legislative and executive power, but if the Soviet government used force to disperse it the SRs were certain to declare civil war. As the latter prospect held no terror for Lenin, who looked forward to such a conflict as the crucible in which the dictatorship of the proletariat would take shape, he decided to dissolve the Assembly and press forward with his own revolution. Remembering that the Bolsheviks had seized power on the eve of the Second All-Russian Congress of

Soviets Lenin took no chances that the SRs would follow his example and use the Constituent Assembly to legitimize a *coup d'état*. Instead, he summoned reliable regiments to defend the capital, issued a call for a Third All-Russian Congress of Soviets to endorse the dissolution of the rival legislative body and proceeded to rid himself of what he described as this 'ghost from the past.' The Assembly was called to order on 18 January, and, with Lenin present, the Bolsheviks allowed the SRs to elect Victor Chernov as chairman and reject the motions placed before them by the Soviet government. Early the next morning the Assembly was dispersed. Although Lenin wrote that during the meeting he felt that he was in the company of 'corpses and lifeless mummies,'[1] he nevertheless had gone to the meeting armed with a revolver and was prepared to shoot his way out of the hall if necessary.[2]

Such precautions proved unnecessary but not unwarranted. The right SRs had been planning an insurrection in support of the Constituent Assembly,[3] and only the timely show of Bolshevik military strength had averted a *coup*. Nor in the aftermath of this triumph did Lenin show any inclination toward moderation. In an address to the Central Executive Committee on 19 January he gave full expression to the hard line on which he had settled during his short vacation in Finland. The socialist revolution, he said, 'will inevitably be accompanied by civil war, sabotage and resistance ... Those who assert the contrary are either liars or cowards.' Promising to crush those who opposed the revolution he proclaimed that 'nothing in the world will make us give up Soviet power.'[4]

Lenin's words were also pregnant with meaning for the future of Soviet foreign policy. In the speech he stressed the relationship between war and revolution, asserting that 'the fire of revolution broke out solely because of the indescribable sufferings of Russia and because of the conditions created by the war.' This had 'inexorably faced the working people with the alternative of taking a bold, desperate and fearless step or of perishing, of dying from starvation' as a consequence of the conflict.[5] As he spoke he

1 Lenin, PSS, vol. XXXV, 214
2 Krupskaia, *Reminiscences*, 434. Four days earlier there had been an attempt on Lenin's life when unknown assailants had fired on the car in which he was riding. This may have influenced his decision to go armed to the meeting of the Constituent Assembly. See Institut Marksizma-Leninizma pri TsK KPSS, *Vladimir Il'ich Lenin: Biograficheskaia Khronika, 1870-1924.* 7 vols. (Moscow, 1970-6) vol. V, 170-1
3 MAE, Guerre, Russie, 22/35; Radkey, *Sickle under the Hammer*, 364-5
4 Lenin, PSS, vol. XXXV, 240-2
5 *Ibid.*, 239

was undoubtedly thinking of the Germans as well as the SRs. If the revolution was to survive, be believed it necessary to fight one enemy at a time, and he had already decided to destroy his opponents inside Russia before embarking on any foreign adventure. For the moment he left these thoughts unvoiced, but reading the speech in the context of his then unpublished manuscripts the meaning of his words is clear.

The time for concealment was rapidly coming to an end, for sentiment within the party had begun to crystallize in a manner unfavourable to Lenin. The Moscow Regional Bureau in particular had become very truculent, demanding an immediate revolutionary war against Germany. Other party organizations had also taken up this refrain, and, as the delegates to the Third All-Russian Congress of Soviets arrived in Petrograd the left Communists, as the advocates of revolutionary war would soon be known, began to organize their forces. The Muscovites provided the staff, and Nikolai Bukharin, one of the party's leading theoreticians, became the chief apostle of the bellicose creed. *Pravda* and *Izvestiia*, dutifully churning out heated polemics against German rapacity, added fuel to the fire, and before Lenin could extinguish the blaze he was confronted with a widely based movement demanding revolutionary war in defence of proletarian internationalism.[6]

Lenin either had to take a firm stand or watch while Bukharin and his followers plunged the country into a war which it could not win. Knowing the very existence of the Soviet state was in the balance he chose to meet Bukharin head on, throwing his entire intellectual and political capital into the struggle against an immediate revolutionary war. For the moment, however, a tactical retreat was necessary, and he bought a few more days to prepare for the struggle by inviting his adversaries to an enlarged meeting of the Bolshevik Central Committee to discuss the negotiations at Brest-Litovsk. Taking advantage of the presence of party leaders from all parts of Russia who had come to Petrograd to attend the Congress of Soviets Lenin summoned nearly fifty provincial chiefs to give their views on the issues involved.

Prior to the meeting of the Central Committee the problem of the peace negotiations was aired in the Sovnarkom.[7] Trotsky presented his report and presumably also gave his colleagues a first-hand account of the political situation in Warsaw which he had visited on his way back to Pet-

---

6 Stephen F. Cohen, *Bukharin and the Bolshevik Revolution* (New York, 1973) 61ff. Also see Daniels, *Conscience of the Revolution*, 71
7 M.I. Trush, *Vneshnepoliticheskaia Deiatel'nost' V.I. Lenina, 1917-1920* (Moscow, 1963) 89

rograd. News from the Polish capital was nearly as bad as that from Brest-Litovsk,[8] and neither report could have sparked much hope in the hearts of the commissars. Although the minutes of this meeting have not yet been published it would be fair to assume that the Sovnarkom adjourned on a note of gloomy pessimism. If Lenin had any reservations about advocating acceptance of the German peace terms he abandoned them that afternoon. He went from the meeting straight to his study where he prepared one of the most important documents of his political career, entitling it bluntly 'Theses on the Question of the Immediate Conclusion of a Separate and Annexationist Peace.' It was this work which he read to the enlarged meeting of the Central Committee the next day and which served as the foundation of his position throughout the crisis of the following month. Here, in twenty-one crisply worded theses, he set forth his reasons for opposing a revolutionary war and favouring the formerly unthinkable alternative of an annexationist peace with Germany.

In preparing this document Lenin drew freely on the themes he had noted in his 'Diary of a Publicist,' and, in places, the wording of the two is identical. Here, however, he emphasized the success of the socialist revolution in Russia, the additional time needed to consolidate its power and the intolerable risk that the Soviet government would take if it were 'to formulate its policy on the supposition that within the next six months (or thereabouts) there will be a European, to be more specific, a German socialist revolution.' Any attempt to predict the outbreak of that revolution was nothing but a 'blind gamble.' Instead of taking such an 'adventurous' risk Lenin submitted the novel and momentous proposition that 'the situation in which the socialist revolution in Russia finds itself' should be 'taken as the point of departure for every definition of the international task confronting the new Soviet government.' Viewed in this light, he argued, the only rational policy was to accept the German demands. Poland, Lithuania, and Courland would be lost, but the socialist revolution would gain the time it needed to crush the bourgeoisie and 'make social-

---

8 Civil unrest in Warsaw had been growing throughout January, and, in mid-month, the municipal employees had gone on strike. This gave the socialist parties in the city an opportunity to fan the flames of unrest, and they scheduled a general strike to begin on 19 January. It is unclear if this was arranged to coincide with Trotsky's visit, but, in any case, the general strike failed to materialize, the socialist parties proved to be badly organized and the German authorities found little cause for alarm. See Akademiia Nauk SSSR, Institut Slavianovedeniia i Pol'skaia Akademiia Nauk, Sektor Istorii Pol'sko-Sovetskikh Otnoshenii, *Dokumenty i Materialy po Istorii Sovetsko-Polskikh Otnoshenii.* Six vols. (Moscow, 1963-9) vol. I, 244-51. Hereafter cited as DiM SPO

ism unconquerable in Russia.' In five hard-hitting theses he swept aside the arguments advanced against his proposal. It was not true, he said, that a separate peace would be a betrayal of proletarian internationalism, the German Social Democrats and the promises made by the Bolsheviks. The socialist revolution in Russia had done everything possible to advance the cause of proletarian internationalism. It had seized power from the bourgeoisie, published the secret treaties, initiated peace negotiations and prolonged those negotiations for nearly two months in order to give the other socialist parties in Europe an opportunity to strike at their own imperialists. None of these measures had precipitated revolution in western Europe. The German internationalists had not yet succeeded in organizing a revolution nor were they even able to hazard a guess when they might be able to do so. Nor would a revolutionary war launched by the socialist revolution in Russia assist them. It could end only in failure as the old Russian army was too weary and the new Red army was too weak to take the field against German imperialism.

Having used brutal fact to bludgeon the arguments that a separate peace would be a betrayal of proletarian internationalism Lenin found it necessary to stretch the truth in order to escape the charge that peace would betray Bolshevik promises. Despite all *his* earlier statements on the subject[9] Lenin now asserted quite disingenuously that the *Bolsheviks* had never promised to wage an immediate revolutionary war against imperialism. Instead, displaying a casuistry worthy of a seventeenth century Jesuit, he claimed that the *Party* had only promised 'to prepare to wage' a revolutionary war. With seemingly outraged innocence he added that 'we never assumed the obligation to wage a revolutionary war regardless of whether time and conditions were favourable for such a war.' Indeed this was true, the Bolshevik *Party* had officially assumed only the obligation 'to prepare to wage' a revolutionary war, but official spokesmen for the party and Lenin himself had spoken so frequently of revolutionary war as the automatic response to a failure to obtain a democratic peace that his adversaries can be forgiven their confusion. In the heroic days of 1917 there had been no mention of any limitation placed on this doctrine; the faithful had simply been led to believe that in any circumstances the revolution would roll forward from one victory to another. Now that this myth had become counter-productive and potentially lethal Lenin found it necessary to jettison it in this unceremonious manner. Like so many other myths which had outlived their usefulness this one was simply abandoned in the trash can of history.

9 See above, chap. 1

With greater regard for truth Lenin disposed of the argument that 'by concluding peace we become agents of German imperialism.' If the socialist revolution in Russia became an agent of German imperialism by signing peace, he pointed out, it was equally true that it would become an agent of British and French imperialism by not signing peace. 'No matter which way we turn,' he said, 'we cannot wholly escape this or that imperialist group. That is impossible without the complete destruction of world imperialism.' Lenin believed a socialist foreign policy could not be based on such considerations. Instead, enunciating what was to become one of the fundamental principles of his foreign policy he asserted: 'from the time a socialist government is established in any one country, questions must be determined not with reference to the preferability of any one imperialist group but solely from the point of view of what is best for the development and the consolidation of the socialist revolution which has already begun.' He then made use of his favourite polemical technique, challenging the revolutionary credentials of his opponents. They had, he charged, placed the principle of self-determination above the interests of socialism. The Soviet government was 'doing everything possible to give real self-determination' to the peoples of the former Russian empire, but this could not be pursued to the point of endangering the safety of the Socialist Republic. He branded his opponents as men 'who crave the romantic and beautiful' but who had lost all contact with reality. Even if the Soviet government could sign a peace with Germany guaranteeing self-determination for Poland, Lithuania, and Courland, 'it would be none the less a peace with annexationists and with the German imperialists.' It would be a 'patriotic peace from the Russian point of view,' but no less shameful and humiliating from the standpoint of proletarian internationalism. In the circumstances of the moment it was simply folly to reject the terms offered by Germany. If the Soviet government refused to make peace then the peasants would overthrow it and a new government, probably 'some kind of coalition between the bourgeois Rada and the followers of Chernov' would be forced to sign an even worse treaty. The only way out of the existing situation was to conclude a separate and annexationist peace with Germany, thus: 'ridding ourselves as far as present circumstances permit of both imperialist groups fighting each other. We can take advantage of their strife, which makes it difficult for them to reach an agreement at our expense, and use that period when our hands are free to develop and strengthen the Socialist Revolution.'[10]

10 Lenin, PSS, vol. XXXV, 243-51

Here in a nutshell was the foreign policy developed by Lenin to replace that of permanent revolution. The key note was defence and the underlying theme was one of caution. The socialist revolution, triumphant in Russia, could not be endangered by hurling itself onto the bayonets of German imperialism. Instead the revolution was to ransom itself at the expense of Poland, Lithuania, and Courland, insulate Russia against the belligerent coalitions and consolidate its hold over the country. Under such conditions wrote Lenin: 'A Socialist Soviet Republic in Russia will be a model for all other peoples and excellent material for propaganda purposes. On the one side there will be the bourgeois system engaged in a strife between two coalitions of confessed plunderers, and on the other side a Socialist Soviet Republic living in peace.'[11] It was an eminently reasonable policy synthesizing Bolshevik aspirations and harsh reality, preserving and strengthening a centre of revolutionary socialism, but not a policy which found prompt support among other Bolshevik leaders. It came as too much of a surprise, requiring them to re-orient their thinking too quickly to be readily acceptable. No protocols of the enlarged meeting of the Central Committee held on 21 January were kept, but the skimpy evidence available shows that Lenin's theses did not receive a warm welcome. They were sharply attacked; Lenin was reproached as a revolutionary defeatist; the left Bolsheviks continued to insist on revolutionary war; and Trotsky came forward with his own policy of 'no war, no peace.' At the end of the meeting the proposal to launch an immediate revolutionary war garnered thirty-two votes against sixteen for Trotsky's scheme and fifteen for the signing of an annexationist peace with Germany.[12] Having heard the verdict Lenin turned to Krupskaia and in an 'unutterably weary and bitter tone' said, 'Ah well, let's go!'[13]

Lenin did not intend to leave matters stand this way. He believed his opponents were wrong and after the meeting wrote: 'Objectively ... the majority of the Party functionaries, proceeding from the very best revolutionary motives and the best Party traditions allow themselves to be carried away by a 'flash' slogan and *do not grasp the new* socio-economic and political situation, do not take into consideration *the change in the conditions* that demand a speedy and abrupt change in tactics.'[14] If they would not listen to reason, he would have to outmaneuver them politically. Al-

11 *Ibid.*
12 *Leninskii Sbornik*, vol. xi, 42-4; Lenin, pss, vol. xxxv, 255
13 Krupskaia, *Reminiscences*, 448
14 Lenin, pss, vol. xxxv, 253-4. Emphasis in original

though the vote in the expanded Central Committee had gone against him it was not binding on the party. Only the Central Committee could make such decisions, and in the smaller circle of his colleagues he stood a better chance of enforcing his will. Nevertheless, he could not overcome the opposition alone, and if he was to prevail he needed an ally. In the circumstances this could only be Trotsky, and, at some point before the Central Committee meeting of 24 January, Lenin and his foreign commissar sat down for an important discussion.

The accounts of this conversation, unfortunately, are not comprehensive or exact. That of Trotsky, given in *My Life* and *Lenin*, is really the only substantial account available. In both works he recalls how he had argued with Lenin over the question of accepting the German peace terms, Lenin insisting that 'before everything else we must save the revolution.' Trotsky adhered to his formula of 'no war, no peace' and argued that there was 'pedagogical' value in forcing the Germans to decide if the war was to resume. Given their domestic and international difficulties they might well decide to end the war without Soviet Russia signing a definitive peace. If they did resume the war their army, demoralized by Bolshevik propaganda, might refuse to fight, and even if the German army took the field that blatant act of violence might be sufficient to touch off the revolution in Germany. In the worst of cases, Trotsky asserted, his plan would force the Germans to unmask themselves revealing that they were interested only in plunder. He also argued that 'if the Central Committee decides to sign the German peace only under the pressure of a verbal ultimatum we risk a split in the Party.' The advocates of revolutionary war would have to be shown the irresponsibility of their position, and the only way to do this was to let them see the Germans advancing unopposed across the Russian landscape. Only when they realized that defence was impossible would they agree to peace. Lenin was not impressed with these arguments and insisted that the danger involved was not worth the supposed benefit of such a demonstration. 'This beast springs suddenly,' he kept repeating, and argued that the Germans, once having resumed their offensive, might not give the Bolsheviks a second chance to sign a peace treaty. Trotsky, however, remained adamant, and Lenin either had to accept the foreign commissar's scheme or see the left Bolsheviks unleash a war which could end only in disaster. But what would Trotsky do if his plan failed? Would he then support a revolutionary war? 'Under no circumstances,' replied the foreign commissar. This opened the door to an alliance between the two men. Trotsky, holding the balance between Lenin and the left Bolsheviks, would have his way, and the policy of 'no war, no peace' would be given a trial. If it failed, the foreign commissar, while not necessarily supporting capitulation, would not oppose Lenin's policy. Lenin anticipated that Trotsky's plan would fail and that this would cost the Socialist Republic additional territory, but, according to the foreign commissar, declared that 'for the sake of a good peace with Trotsky, Latvia and Estonia are worth losing.'[15]

Lenin referred to this bargain only once, confirming its existence but providing almost no information about it. He did so in March 1918 at the Seventh Party Congress: 'it was agreed between us [he said] that we would hold out until the Germans presented an ultimatum, and then we would give way ... Trotsky's tactics were correct as long as they were aimed at delaying matters; they became incorrect when it was announced that the state of war had been terminated, but peace had not been concluded. I proposed quite definitely that peace be concluded.'[16] Soviet historians have claimed that this statement proves Trotsky had double-crossed Lenin and even acted contrary to the decisions of the Central Committee.[17] This is untrue. As shall be seen, the Central Committee accepted Trotsky's proposals, and although Lenin believed the policy to be in error and 'proposed quite definitely that peace be concluded' he had no authority to overrule his colleagues or reason to expect that the foreign commissar would pursue any policy other than that of the Central Committee. What this passage does reflect is a certain ambiguity in the agreement which, in the circumstances, would have been quite understandable. Lenin was determined to end the war at the least possible cost; Trotsky was concerned with the 'pedagogical' and demonstrative effect of the way in which the war was terminated. Lenin, therefore, would have interpreted the word 'ultimatum' very broadly to mean almost any threat which the Germans made to secure Soviet agreement to a peace treaty; Trotsky, on the other hand, understood the term in its narrowest possible construction, meaning an actual resumption of hostilities. Lenin undoubtedly knew this, but also knew that Trotsky would not abandon his definition. For the moment he needed Trotsky to defeat the advocates of revolutionary war; therefore, he could not be too fussy about the meaning of words, even important words such as 'ultimatum.' Moreover, circumstances could change with remarkable swiftness in early 1918, and, as a consequence, Lenin would not have wanted to tie himself explicitly to Trotsky's

15 Trotsky, *My Life*, 382-4; *idem, Lenin,* 106-10
16 Lenin, PSS, vol. XXXVI, 30
17 See for example, Chubar'ian, *Brestskii Mir*, 139; and Oznobishin, *Ot Bresta do Iur'eva*, 69

definition; it was better for him to leave the term undefined and await events. As it turned out this worked temporarily in Trotsky's favour, but Lenin had very little option but to follow this rather tortuous path. Certainly in March at the Seventh Party Congress he showed no inclination to pursue the topic further, simply noting at the end of his short statement about the agreement that 'since history has swept that away it is not worth recalling.'[18] If Lenin had been double-crossed he would have found a great deal worth recalling; in fact, he had simply been outmaneuvered and forced to make the best of a bad situation. Even so, he had Trotsky's political IOU available for future use.

But how durable was the agreement between Lenin and Trotsky? Tenuous at best, it could be rendered meaningless by some unexpected turn of events. Nor did the foreign commissar merely wait for the wheel of fortune to turn; in the interval between 21 and 24 January he exploited his unofficial contacts among the allied missions to determine if a more militant policy offered any hope of success. An indignant Trotsky shoved Hoffmann's map into the hands of Sadoul telling him to show it to Noulens and asserting rather cryptically that the 'moment had come for the allies to decide!'[19] He also conferred with Robins inquiring pointedly if the United States was prepared to provide assistance if Russia resumed the war with Germany.[20] These inquiries excited Robins and Sadoul but did not generate any concrete pledge of assistance. Sadoul's lament summarized the situation rather well. 'What are the allies going to do?' he wrote, 'Alas! I fear more and more that they will do nothing.'[21] This impression, which Sadoul must have conveyed to Trotsky, figured large in the foreign commissar's calculations. Although Trotsky wanted a confrontation with Germany he realized that he could not challenge Hoffman's army without allied assistance. Having received little reason to believe the Bolsheviks would receive western aid he had to shelve his hopes for a more militant policy. When the Central Committee met on 24 January, therefore, Trotsky had little choice but to honour his pledge to Lenin and seek approval for his policy of 'no war, no peace.'

This meeting provided a first test of the agreement between Lenin and Trotsky. Three days before, a majority at the expanded session of the Central Committee had voted for war, but the actual members of the

18 Lenin, PSS, vol. XXXVI, 30
19 Sadoul, *Notes*, 204
20 Kennan, *Russia Leaves the War*, 398-401
21 Sadoul, *Notes*, 204

Committee were known to be more reluctant to place the fate of the revolution in the hands of the German proletariat. The left Bolsheviks, however, had not been inactive and had continued their campaign for an immediate declaration of revolutionary war. The question, therefore, remained whether Trotsky and his supporters would insist on their policy of 'no war, no peace' or join with the left in plunging Russia into a new war against Germany. The debate was intense and all sides advanced their arguments vigorously. Lenin, in particular, hammered away at his fundamental contention that the revolution in Russia should not be sacrificed for the mere possibility of accelerating the pace of events in Germany. 'Germany is only pregnant with revolution,' he said, coining what were to become the most famous words of the debate, 'in our country we already have a very healthy baby – the Socialist Republic – which we will murder by resuming the war.' He strained every nerve to prevent his colleagues from yielding to the absurd contention that infanticide was sound revolutionary doctrine but had his arguments rejected by a majority of the Committee. Many of his closest associates spoke against him, most charging that he had placed the interests of Russia ahead of international revolution. In vain he protested that it was the socialist revolution in Russia, not Russia itself, to which he gave priority, a valid statement of his position but not one made more defensible by the words of those who ostensibly supported him. Completely misunderstanding the subtlety of Lenin's argument, Stalin spoke sneeringly of the revolutionary movement outside Russia while Zinoviev tended to write it off as unimportant. Lenin had to disassociate himself from the unsophisticated statements of his lieutenants, probably thinking to himself that with friends such as these he really had no need of enemies. Lenin relied on Trotsky to save the day. Although he described Trotsky's policy as an 'international political demonstration' he did not attack it as sharply as he did the concept of revolutionary war and was well aware that if Trotsky's plan was adopted the revolution would not be committed irrevocably to an unequal contest with German imperialism. The wave of bellicose enthusiasm, in fact, did break against Trotsky's insistence that his policy be given a chance to prove itself. Bukharin realized that whatever his strength among the party functionaries he did not command a majority in the Central Committee, and, like Lenin, agreed to Trotsky's middle position as a way of keeping the question open. If Trotsky's scheme worked, honour would be saved and no compact would be signed with the devil; if it failed, he would have another opportunity to argue for war. In any event, his only alternative was to split the party, and, unlike Lenin, he was manifestly unprepared to take this step. To wage revolutionary war Bukharin required a reasonably unified party; to sign a capitulationist peace Lenin needed much less. Lenin, therefore, could contemplate a ruinous struggle dividing the party over the issue of war and peace; Bukharin had to be much more careful. When the debate was over, Bukharin and enough of his supporters voted with Trotsky to give the formula 'no war, no peace' a majority. Rather than present a motion which was sure to fail Lenin did not bring forward his proposal to sign an annexationist peace. Instead, he introduced another motion simply calling for the Soviet delegation to drag out the negotiations for as long as possible. In the context of the Bolshevik Central Committee this was equivalent to a vote in favour of motherhood, and it promptly passed with only Zinoviev opposed.[22] Having tied each other in knots for nearly a week the Bolshevik leaders decided in essence to prolong their agony. Trotsky would return to Brest-Litovsk, send up more revolutionary fireworks and when the Germans called a halt to his pyrotechnic display he would explode a firecracker marked 'no war, no peace.' If the Germans were impressed, no further debate was necessary; if not, the whole painful process would be repeated, only in more desperate circumstances. Unable to settle on a policy, the Bolsheviks agreed to disagree.

All that remained was to translate the decisions of the Bolshevik Central Committee into the policy of the Soviet government. This was done at a meeting with the central committee of the left SRs where the resolutions of Lenin and Trotsky were adopted and made binding on the Sovnarkom. Needless to say, these decisions were not publicized, and when Trotsky reported to the Third All-Russian Congress of Soviets on the twenty-sixth, he confined his remarks to a summary of the peace negotiations and a hortatory conclusion which only hinted at the policy which he intended to follow. 'We make no triumphant boasts ... [he said] ... but we will fight together with you for an honest democratic peace ... And if German imperialism attempts to crush us on the wheel of its military machine, then we as Ostap to his father will cry out to our brothers in the west: "Do you hear?" And the international proletariat will answer, this we firmly believe: "I hear!"'[23] How Lenin must have suffered! The reference to Gogol's famous tale must certainly have made him wince, for despite the impression which Trotsky sought to convey, the story of Ostap and his

22 Institut Lenin pri TsK VKP (b), *Protokoly Tsentral'nogo Komiteta RSDRP (b): Avgust 1917 g. – Fevral' 1918 g* (Moscow, 1929) 199-207. Hereafter cited as *Protokoly Tsk*
23 Trotsky, *Sochineniia,* vol. XVII, part I, 65

father had not ended happily. Indeed, in *Taras Bulba*, Ostap, having been taken prisoner by the Poles, had been broken on the wheel and had died an agonizing death, while his tempestuous father, thirsting for revenge, had led his army to disaster and had himself perished, nailed to a tree and burned alive. Was this the fate which Trotsky foresaw for the revolution! Such indeed was the gloomy future apprehended by Lenin if the Soviet government did not mend its ways, but it was hardly proper to summon this spectre from the tribune of a revolutionary assembly! Whatever his thoughts, Lenin said nothing, nor did anyone else, and the Congress dutifully approved Trotsky's report. It also passed a series of vague resolutions which endorsed the manner in which the Soviet delegation had conducted the negotiations at Brest-Litovsk and directed it to 'insist on principles of peace based on the program of the Russian Revolution.'[24] Trotsky left the next day for Brest-Litovsk.

The struggle for control of Soviet foreign policy, however, was just beginning. The intense debate in the Bolshevik Central Committee had been only the opening skirmish of a political battle which would drag on through most of 1918. The left Bolsheviks, vastly dissatisfied with the results of the meetings, immediately took their case to the party at large, demanding that a conference be summoned to decide the issue. Lenin, in turn, raised the stakes, arguing that a conference could not make decisions binding the Central Committee and calling for a party congress to resolve the question.[25] The Central Committee agreed with Lenin and summoned a congress to meet three weeks later. This gave Lenin time to influence the choice of delegates, and he set to work at once to undermine the position of the left Bolsheviks.

In the last days of January, Lenin began to prepare the party and the masses for the abrupt shift in foreign policy which he wished to execute. In his address to the Third All-Russian Congress of Soviets, for instance, he compared the Soviet state with the Paris Commune and contended that the socialist revolution in Russia had survived longer than the first proletarian government in France because of the alliance of the Russian workers with the peasantry. Only through the continuation of this alliance, he said, could the Soviet state hope to survive.[26] Two days later he skilfully wove additional arguments from his twenty-one theses into a speech to the All-Russian Congress of Railwaymen. Russia, he said, had taken

24 *Ibid.*, 66
25 Lenin, PSS, vol. XXXV, 318-20
26 *Ibid.*, 261-79

the lead in the world workers' revolution. The world wide victory of socialism was certain, but, he added, 'we don't know how long it will take for the socialist revolution to break out in other countries – it might take a long time.' Until the proletariat in other countries could seize power it was necessary for the revolution in Russia to remain strong.[27] He went no further at this point, but it was clear that with each passing day the gulf separating him from those who would speculate adventurously on the fate of the revolution was widening.

A political storm of the first magnitude was about to break, and if Lenin emerged victoriously from this struggle he would require a new foreign commissar. Whereas before Trotsky had been an asset, he was now becoming a liability. The events of January had shown that the foreign commissar could seriously impair Lenin's ability to control foreign affairs. Trotsky was a colleague and a peer, and, as such, a man with whom Lenin had to negotiate as an equal. Lenin's remark that 'for the sake of a good peace with Trotsky, Latvia and Estonia are worth losing' is especially instructive. Lenin was not a man to whom compromise came easily, and, in this instance, while implying that Lenin had lightly accepted the necessity of losing two provinces for the sake of a questionable policy, Trotsky also noted that Lenin spoke almost wistfully of the progress which socialism was making in Estonia and his sadness that it would be crushed as a consequence of the agreement which he had just made.[28] Lenin had been forced to don the unaccustomed mask of genial compromiser, but behind the banter he was almost certainly grinding his teeth in anger.

Lenin simply could not trust Trotsky with the foreign commissariat. Nothing about his foremost colleague would dispose him to pursue a defensive foreign policy, and, instead of seeking shelter in the international storm which was then breaking over Russia, he would want to stand and fight. Lenin prized this quality in Trotsky, especially since there would be more than enough fighting before the revolution in Russia was reasonably secure, but in January it was clear that the Narkomindel was not the post for his pugnacious associate. In that office he was a menace, for Lenin could never be certain what promises he might make to the French or what provocation he might offer the Germans. At the Narkomindel Lenin needed a subordinate not a peer, a lieutenant rather than a general and a man who could organize and direct a genuine foreign ministry to replace the propaganda mill then functioning under the inaccurate title of

27 *Ibid.*, 292-305
28 Trotsky, *Lenin*, 109

foreign commissariat. Above all he needed a reliable individual who would act as *his* foreign minister in balancing the entente against the central powers while the Soviet state consolidated its power in Russia.

But where would Lenin find such a man? His desiderata excluded almost every available candidate; political considerations eliminated most of his colleagues while the skills required for the position ruled out lesser members of the hierarchy. Nor could he make an appointment from among those already at the foreign commissariat. Ioffe was too closely tied to Trotsky; Radek was a great propagandist, but, his political views aside, too volatile even to imagine as foreign commissar; Zalkind, for reasons which will shortly become clear, was not suited for the position. In surveying the possible successors to Trotsky, Lenin must have felt nearly as disheartened as when he pondered the views of his colleagues.

Fortunately, there was another candidate available. This was Georgii Vasilevich Chicherin who, having been released from Brixton gaol, was already on his way to Petrograd.[29] A descendant of an old aristocratic family, Chicherin had been educated to enter the tsarist foreign ministry and had worked there for eight years before throwing in his lot with the revolutionary movement and emigrating to western Europe. During the war he had become an outspoken internationalist, played a key role in nurturing anti-war sentiment in Britain and distinguished himself as a leader of the Russian emigré community in London.[30] Combining a diplomatic background with proletarian internationalism, an unparalleled knowledge of languages with a love of polemics, and an interest in world affairs with a near legendary capacity for hard work Chicherin was well qualified to assume a responsible position in the Narkomindel.

In other respects Chicherin's *vita* was blotted. He was not a Bolshevik and, worse yet, had spent most of his revolutionary career in close association with the Mensheviks. Moreover, in the years prior to the war he had lost no opportunity to discredit the Bolsheviks and, in the ever-fluid political life of the revolutionary emigrés, had consistently aligned himself against Lenin and his party. Few Bolsheviks were likely to view him sympathetically or forget the trouble which he had previously caused them.

Lenin was one Bolshevik who could afford to overlook Chicherin's past. In terms of his requirements, in fact, the negative reaction which Chicherin was sure to trigger within the party could well be a positive asset, for such hostility would effectively insulate him from the influence

29 See above, 34-41
30 Debo, 'The making of a Bolshevik,' 656-62

of other Bolshevik leaders and tie him all the more closely to his patron. For Lenin the important question was how Chicherin would relate to the struggle for control of Soviet foreign policy. If he would accept a defensive foreign policy then Lenin could make good use of his services. Chicherin would bear watching, and his appointment to a responsible position in the Narkomindel would provide the best opportunity for such observation. But how could this be arranged? Fortunately, during the negotiations for Chicherin's release from British imprisonment Trotsky had announced that he intended to employ him at the Narkomindel, and, whether this was a true statement or merely rhetoric, Lenin took the foreign commissar at his word. Even before Chicherin arrived in Petrograd Lenin sent a message to Brest-Litovsk asking Trotsky to 'send an official telegram to the Sovnarkom with a request to name Chicherin as your deputy.'[31] It is unknown how Trotsky reacted to this request, but three days later, on 21 January, Lenin officially appointed Chicherin to the post of Deputy People's Commissar of Foreign Affairs.[32]

What were Chicherin's views when he arrived in Petrograd? From the available evidence it is clear that his credentials as an internationalist were impeccable. It is also evident that he had broken with the Mensheviks and was prepared to throw in his lot with the Bolsheviks.[33] On the crucial question of war or peace, however, the story was different. Just prior to his expulsion from Great Britain, a Rumanian diplomat was allowed to speak with him, and from their conversation it is clear that Chicherin held views more closely akin to those of Trotsky or the advocates of revolutionary war than Lenin. When asked if he did not believe that the Germans could take Petrograd whenever they wished Chicherin replied, 'So what? What good would it do them? The time has passed when one conquers territory. And then would the German soldiers let them do it?' The ideas of the Russian revolution, he declared, would destroy the Kaiser's army.[34] Three weeks later, when he finally reached Russia, he continued to voice the same optimistic sentiments.[35]

It would be interesting to know Lenin's first reactions to Chicherin, but they are unfortunately not available. Engrossed by the struggle in the Cen-

31 Leninskii *Sbornik*, vol. XI, 19
32 Trush, *Vneshnepolitcheskaia Deiatel'nost V.I. Lenina*, 90
33 Debo, 'The making of a Bolshevik,' 659-62
34 PRO FO 371/3310/6596. Also see *The Weekly Dispatch* (London, 6 Jan. 1918)
35 *Tretii Vserossiskii S''ezd' Sovetov' Rabochikh', Soldatskikh i Krest'ianskikh Deputatov* (Petrograd, 1918) 7-9. Also see I. Gorokhov, L. Zamiatin, and I. Zemskov, *G.V. Chicherin – Diplomat Leninskoi Shkoly* (Moscow, 1966) 29

tral Committee, Lenin probably had little time to devote to the new *zam-narkom* (deputy commissar) and, in any case, was not yet prepared to discuss questions of high policy with him. The dispute over foreign policy was still confined to the highest echelons of the party, and, in accordance with his bargain with Trotsky, it was necessary to play out the foreign commissar's policy before he could come into the open with his own extraordinary proposals. A discussion of this issue with Chicherin had to be postponed until later. In the meanwhile, however, the *zamnarkom* was immediately plunged into the work of the foreign commissariat.

The situation there had begun to deteriorate during the negotiations at Brest-Litovsk, and the need for a responsible deputy to act in Trotsky's absence had become apparent. Not only did Trotsky's other responsibilities prevent him from exercising sufficient supervision of the commissariat, but Ivan Zalkind had proved unsatisfactory as his deputy. Though a man of considerable education Zalkind had brought with him to the Narkomindel an attitude of coarseness and brutatility which later caused a German diplomat to observe that 'his manners, even for a Bolshevik, are horrible.'[36] This rough exterior had served him well when he had commanded a unit of the Red Guards defending Petrograd and even during his first days at the foreign commissariat, but in the changing circumstances of early 1918 he was no longer qualified to remain at the Narkomindel. The time had come when the Soviet government needed a genuine diplomat rather than a gunman at the Dvortsovaia.

An incident involving Zalkind highlighted this situation. Shortly before Chicherin arrived at the Narkomindel, an anarchist meeting had threatened to 'take energetic measures' against the United States embassy if the American government did not free certain anarchists it had arrested. The meeting had drafted a resolution to this effect and sent it to the foreign commissariat for delivery to the American ambassador. Zalkind did as requested, passing the threatening note to Francis without comment and without promise of protection. This enraged the Americans who protested at once to Lenin. Robins in particular was most explicit in his condemnation of Trotsky's deputy. Lenin responded quickly, ordering the anarchist demonstration suppressed and informing Robins that Zalkind was being removed from the foreign commissariat and sent abroad, probably to Bern. Robin's reaction to this news epitomized the sentiments felt gen-

36 Germany. Auswärtiges Amt. Politisches Archiv. Russland 87: 'Die diplomatische Vertretung Russlands im Auslande.' Band 19. St. Antony's College microfilm collection, reel no. 141. German Minister in Stockholm to Reichskanzler (Stockholm, 12 March 1918)

erally in the diplomatic community about Zalkind. 'Thank you, Mr. Lenin,' he said, 'As I can't send the son of a bitch to hell, "burn" is the next best thing you can do with him.'[37] Zalkind later wrote of this incident: '... I caught hell about it from Vladimir Il'ich: "Don't go scaring the ambassadors," he said, "for nothing at all." '[38] This incident had nothing to do with Zalkind's removal, he had already been reassigned to revolutionary work more suitable to his talents, but it does illustrate why Lenin was happy to see the change at the Narkomindel. Chicherin's appointment had the desired effect. A few days later Jacques Sadoul wrote: 'Chicherin replaces ... Zalkind. The latter is a nervous, an impulsive, often a brutal man. Chicherin is a man who is well bred, intelligent and cultured ... He is a gentleman in every respect of the word ... Relations with him will be easier.'[39]

Chicherin had much to do. While everyone's attention had been focused on the confrontation at Brest-Litovsk other states had been busy undermining what was left of the old Russian empire. The allied powers, groping for a way to restore the eastern front, had already divided Russia into potential spheres of influence; the Rumanians had seized Bessarabia; the Japanese were casting covetous glances at the maritime provinces and newly independent Finland had given notice that it claimed a substantial portion of the Soviet north. Soviet Russia's international position was deteriorating with each passing day, and the Narkomindel had few resources to reverse the trend.

When Chicherin arrived at the Dvortsovaia he found about one hundred individuals engaged more in the preparation of propaganda than anything else. Having begun this activity with the publication of the secret documents of former Russian governments, the Narkomindel had expanded its scope to include the production of propaganda for distribution at the front and in the camps holding large numbers of German and Austro-Hungarian prisoners of war. This concentration on propaganda had come about partly by chance and partly by design. A government dedicated to encouraging social upheaval in other lands necessarily had decided to devote considerable resources to this activity, but the refusal of other governments to recognize the Soviet regime had intensified this natural tendency. Walled off from the normal channels of international communication, possessing only a handful of unrecognized representatives

37 Sir Robert H. Bruce Lockhart, *British Agent* (Garden City, New York, 1933) 228
38 Zalkind, 'NKID v semnadtsam godu,' 18. Also see Kennan, *Russia Leaves the War,* 401-5
39 Sadoul, *Notes,* 215-16. For a more sympathetic description of Zalkind see Louis Bryant, *Six Red Months in Russia* (New York, 1918), 200-1

abroad, severely limited in the extent of reliable information at its disposal, the foreign commissariat, half-blind and nearly deaf, had had little choice but to accomplish what it could by appealing to the peoples of the world over the heads of their governments.

Chicherin's arrival at the Narkomindel marked the first step in reversing this expedient. Under his direction and with Lenin's approval, revolutionary propaganda gradually lost its former importance in Soviet foreign policy, and the Narkomindel underwent a complete reform designed to restore its function as a foreign office. Within two months of his arrival the apparatus for the fabrication and circulation of Soviet propaganda was removed from the foreign commissariat while an administrative machine very similar to that which had existed in the old foreign ministry took its place.[40]

These steps were indicative of Chicherin's desire to make the Narkomindel a more effective instrument of Soviet state power. So also was the interest he took in the draft treaty which the Germans had presented as a basis for negotiation at Brest-Litovsk. Alarmed by what he found, particularly among the economic proposals, Chicherin telegraphed Trotsky suggesting that the Soviet delegation should seek to modify these clauses, because they contained 'demands which cannot be met.'[41] Chicherin's initiative represented a considerably different approach to the problem of the peace negotiations than that taken by Trotsky. The foreign commissar had consistently followed a policy of seeking to breathe life into the expected German revolution; his newly appointed deputy was striking out in an entirely different direction, implying at least that the Soviet delegation should view the negotiations as a process which might lead to an agreement rather than merely a stage from which to address the masses. This was a startling departure from previous form, and not one which could have been too pleasing for Trotsky. On the other hand, it was a step which Lenin could applaud and may well have been suggested by him as a way of determining whether or not the *zamnarkom* would be of use in administering the new foreign policy which he had in mind. The time was fast approaching when Lenin would have to put him to the final test. With Trotsky having returned to Brest-Litovsk time was running out at the peace conference, and a final crisis could not long be delayed.

40 Carr, *The Bolshevik Revolution*, vol. III, 72. Also see S.Iu. Vygodskii, *U Istokov Sovetskoi Diplomatii* (Moscow, 1965) 32-3

41 Sisson, *One Hundred Red Days*, 324-5. The document in question is not included in the notorious 'Sisson Documents.' See George F. Kennan, 'The Sisson Documents,' *Journal of Modern History*, vol. XXVIII, no. 2 (June, 1958) 130-54

5

'No war, no peace'

You know our standpoint; it has lately been confirmed ... Lenin and Stalin to Trotsky, 10 February 1918

We are going out of the war, but we feel ourselves compelled to refuse to sign the peace treaty. Trotsky, 10 February 1918

Unerhört! General Hoffmann, 10 February 1918

The peace conference reconvened on 30 January. As Trotsky had anticipated, the revolutionary pulse of Europe had quickened during the recess, and, superficially at least, he returned to Brest-Litovsk with a stronger bargaining position than when he had left. Wherever he looked the old order was crumbling. Civil unrest had spread from the Habsburg empire to Germany where strikes and demonstrations had swept through München, Hamburg, Essen, and Berlin, with four hundred thousand workers downing tools in the German capital to demand an end to the war, improved food deliveries, and responsible government. Meanwhile, Bolshevism had moved from victory to victory, dispersing the Constituent Assembly, gaining strength in Finland, and roughly shouldering aside the Rada in the Ukraine. The Red Guard of Antonov-Ovseenko was drawing ever closer to Kiev. The days of the Rada were clearly numbered, and with its fall the Germans would lose their trump card in the peace negotiations. Summarizing these circumstances Kühlmann wrote the German chancellor that on his return to Brest-Litovsk he had found the Bolsheviks 'even more arrogant than before and still less inclined to compromise.'[1]

1 DSB, vol. I, 339-42

This was certainly the image which Trotsky wished to project, and the foreign commissar did his best to convey the impression that the wheel of history was about to take a sharp turn in his favour. 'It is evident ...' wrote Czernin, 'they [the Russians] positively expect the outbreak of a world revolution within the next few weeks.'[2] While the issue in Germany remained in doubt Trotsky gained a psychological advantage over his adversaries. Czernin was deeply shaken, and at the height of the crisis, Kühlmann telegraphed Hertling asking if the internal situation in Germany required a change of policy at the peace conference.[3]

Was the long-expected German revolution about to begin? Trotsky would have liked to think so, but he was too wise in the ways of revolution to be misled by the events in Germany. He was nearly as depressed as Kühlmann, because he doubted that the unrest would transcend spontaneous indignation and be transformed into a movement capable of smashing the foundations of German society. Reading *Vorwärts* he could see that the German majority socialists, rather than leading the demonstrations, were seeking to restrain the newly generated revolutionary enthusiasm of the masses. 'The leaders of the Social Democracy,' he later wrote, 'voluntarily chained themselves to Austro-German capital and were helping their governments forcibly to chain the Russian revolution.'[4] While Trotsky swaggered around Brest-Litovsk sowing fear in the hearts of German diplomats he did not hide the truth from himself. On 31 January, he sadly informed Petrograd that although events in Germany appeared promising there was no basis to assume that they signified an imminent revolution.[5] With regard to the Ukraine, where a genuine revolution was under way, the foreign commissar was more confident. On his return to Brest-Litovsk he brought with him two representatives of the Kharkov regime whom he intended to introduce as the authentic voice of the Ukraine; they would provide a stumbling block to the German plan of concluding a separate peace with Kiev.

The question of the Ukraine, in fact, was to dominate the third phase of the negotiations at Brest-Litovsk. Politically and strategically it was the key to the remainder of the conference and would largely determine the relationship of the participants after peace was finally concluded. If the

2 Czernin, *In the World War*, 245
3 DSB, vol. I, 344
4 Trotsky, *My Life*, 364
5 Chubar'ian, *Brestskii Mir*, 140

Soviet government could establish its authority in the Ukraine it would foil the German policy of divide-and-rule in eastern Europe. Instead of facing a crazy quilt of petty, mutually hostile and easily influenced states, Germany would confront a single great power generating far-reaching political influence in Europe. With her exposed eastern frontier Germany would be especially vulnerable to this influence. On the other hand, if Germany succeeded in detaching the Ukraine from the rest of Russia, Petrograd rather than Berlin would be vulnerable, for an independent Ukraine beholden to Germany would outflank Russia, separate her from the Black Sea, encourage further separatism, and represent a perpetual danger to the Soviet regime.

Equally important, whoever walked off with the Ukraine would take with them its immense natural resources. Germany wanted these resources, and Austria coveted the rich granaries of the Ukraine, but the demand for southern foodstuffs was greatest in Petrograd. Even while the Bolshevik conquest of the Ukraine was under way Lenin sent a steady stream of telegrams to Kharkov ordering Antonov-Ovseenko and Ordzhonikidze to requisition grain for Petrograd. On 28 January, in the most emphatic of these, Lenin demanded: 'For the sake of God, take all the most energetic and revolutionary measures to send *bread, bread* and *bread*!!! Otherwise Petrograd may die. Special trains and detachments. Collect and dispatch. See the trains off. Inform us daily. For the sake of God!'[6] These frantic messages brought results, Ordzhonikidze requisitioning all freight cars loaded with grain and redirecting them to Petrograd,[7] but Lenin took no chances on losing the Ukraine. He remained in close contact with his plenipotentiaries in the south, provided them with constant advice and sent them large sums of money to support their government.[8] Along with the currency, the value of which was falling with every passing day, went additional detachments of the Red Guards needed to conquer and hold the treasure house of Russia.

Ironically, Bolshevik success in the Ukraine was not without benefit for Kühlmann. As soon as he received word from Berlin that the disturbances in Germany were not serious enough to require any change of

6 Lenin, PSS, vol. L, 30. Emphasis in original
7 Institut istorii partii TsK KP Ukrainy – filial instituta Marksizma-Leninizma pri TsK KPSS and Arkhivnoe Upravlenie UKSSR, *Bol'shevistskie organizatsii Ukrainy v period ustanovleniia i ukrepleniia sovetskoi vlasti (Noiabr' 1917– Aprel' 1918 gg.)* (Kiev, 1962) 41-2. Hereafter cited as BOU
8 Lenin, PSS, vol. L, 34-5

policy at Brest-Litovsk[9] he made good use of the Rada's misfortune. 'As before,' he informed Hertling, 'we must attempt to keep the Bolsheviks in suspense until it is possible to come to an agreement with Kiev, but then proceed to an energetic discussion [with Trotsky].' The Rada, he believed, 'because of its failure should be more inclined to agreement and to the promptest conclusion of peace,' while Czernin, who was counting on peace with the Ukraine to provide the starving cities of the Habsburg empire with food, should also prove more flexible.[10] Prior to the recess negotiations with the Rada had bogged down in disputes over the district of Cholm, which the Ukrainians wished to annex, and the status of Ukrainians in the Habsburg empire. Kühlmann anticipated that Czernin would now be willing to let the Ukrainians have the portion of Poland which they wanted and agree to allow the Ruthenians in Austria to establish a separate crownland within the Empire. With the very existence of the two states hanging in the balance Kühlmann confidently looked forward to a satisfactory compromise. Austria would pay the price of peace, and Germany would collect the benefits. Then he could turn to Trotsky for what he euphemistically called 'an energetic discussion' and what, in fact, would amount to an ultimatum.

What would be the result of this 'discussion'? Kühlmann was far from certain. In late January he warned Berlin that a rupture of the negotiations might soon occur and that a campaign should be launched to prepare public opinion for this eventuality. The press, he said, should be instructed 'to create strong dissatisfaction in Germany over the long delay in conducting the negotiations' at Brest-Litovsk so that when the time was right he could break off the talks in such a way as to make it appear that it was being done 'under the pressure of public opinion.'[11] German propaganda agencies accordingly began to generate the desired pressure and also to collect horror stories from Russia with which to fill the newspapers. The *Auswärtiges Amt* wanted the German press to paint 'a terrifying picture of Russia' both to discredit the Soviet regime and also to 'counteract ... the strikes' which were then taking place in Germany.[12] Kühlmann had thus completed his preparations for a final showdown with Trotsky.

Simply from reading the German newspapers Trotsky was able to determine the basic outline of Kühlmann's plans. But what could he do to

9 DSB, vol. I, 344
10 *Ibid.*, 339-42
11 Akhtamazian, 'O Brest-Litovskikh peregovorakh,' 36
12 DSB, vol. I, 345

counter them? His strongest weapon was the growing strength of Bolshevism in the Ukraine, but as the peace conference resumed, the issue at Kiev remained in doubt, and no one knew exactly what was happening. 'Everywhere fighting is in progress,' Kühlmann wrote, 'without it being possible to distinguish for or against whom the various detachments are fighting.'[13] Trotsky continually sought new information which would allow him to impeach the credentials of the Rada, but the vital report that Kiev had fallen to the Red Guards did not arrive until too late. Trotsky also took note of the German press campaign to discredit Bolshevik *bona fides* in the negotiations at Brest-Litovsk. 'The German press,' he wrote Lenin, 'has started to blare out that we allegedly do not want peace at all, but are only concerned with spreading the revolution in other countries.' His answer to this press campaign was to suggest a propaganda line which Petrograd could use to counter the accusations. 'These asses,' he wrote, 'can not appreciate that it is precisely from the angle of the European development of the revolution that peace at the earliest possible moment is of such enormous importance to us.'[14] Reading this message Lenin must have nodded his head in agreement, wishing that his foreign commissar intended to act in this spirit rather than the manner decided by the Central Committee on 24 January. Unfortunately, he knew what Trotsky had in mind.

Much to his consternation Trotsky discovered that the German press also knew. When he opened the newspapers on 31 January he found several which carried stories from Stockholm reporting an account contained in *Politiken* relating in detail the dispute within the Bolshevik Central Committee and his own plan to refuse to sign a definite peace treaty. Since *Politiken* was the journal of Karl Höglund who was known to have close friends among Bolshevik leaders Trotsky feared that the Germans would take this report seriously and begin to ask embarrassing questions. To put them off the track the foreign commissar sent an *en clair* telegram to Petrograd ridiculing the story as 'monstrous nonsense.'[15] As it happened, Trotsky did not need to worry, for the Germans paid no attention to the story. It was simply too incredible and, in the snowstorm of countless other rumours, was ignored. Thus, when Trotsky did, in fact, bring the conference to an end with his dramatic announcement Kühlmann and all the representatives of the central powers were caught completely by surprise.

13 *Ibid.*, 339
14 Jan M. Meijer (ed.), *The Trotsky Papers* (The Hague, 1964) 13
15 Trotsky, *My Life*, 385

There were, however, no surprises when the conference reconvened. Everything proceeded as expected. Trotsky called upon the conference to recognize the delegates from Kharkov as entitled to speak for the Ukraine, and the central powers refused. Only when the full Rada delegation had returned from Kiev, said Kühlmann, could the conference settle this problem. He noted, however, that three weeks before Trotsky had agreed that the Rada could speak in the name of the Ukrainian people. Trotsky replied that when the matter had been discussed previously the Workers' and Peasants' Government had not existed in the Ukraine, but now that it had been organized and was driving the Rada from power it alone was entitled to speak for the Ukraine. If the Germans wished, he said, the Rada could be represented at the conference, but the central powers should not delude themselves by believing that any government other than that of Kharkov exercised effective authority in the Ukraine; hence, it was the only regime with which a binding international agreement could be signed. 'How triumphantly Trotsky announced that the existence of the Rada could only be measured in hours,' wrote Kühlmann.[16] The German foreign secretary, however, had a reply for Trotsky, and skilfully combining a well-aimed propaganda barb with a veiled threat, he asserted: 'According to the communication which the Chairman of the Russian delegation made to us earlier, the government now existing in Russia bases itself on force and, therefore, the question arises which of the two organizations which at the present time consider they have the right to speak in the name of the Free Ukrainian Republic has preponderance and armed might on its side.' At this point the meeting collapsed in name calling and mutual recrimination.[17]

Kühlmann was obviously not eager for serious negotiations at this time and simply let the meetings drift in a wash of acrimonious and inconclusive debate. It was now Trotsky's turn to complain that the Germans were attempting to delay the conference,[18] but it was clear that the German foreign secretary would not proceed further until his own position improved. The telegram from Hertling informing Kühlmann that he could proceed with the negotiations without reference to internal circumstances in the Reich[19] heralded this improvement, and when the Rada delegation reached Brest-Litovsk the stage was set for a settlement of the Ukrainian question.

16 DSB, vol. I, 345
17 Fokke, 'Brestskoi Tragikomedii,' 177ff
18 Meijer, *The Trotsky Papers*, 13
19 DSB, vol. I, 344

The showdown came on 1 February. The central powers, wishing to win a propaganda victory, discredit the Bolsheviks and build as strong a case as possible for their support of a faltering regime, left nothing to chance. Czernin took the Rada delegation aside and coached them on what they should say. When the conference convened that afternoon Kühlmann asked the chairman of the Rada delegation to present the case for his government's right to represent the Ukraine. The diatribe which followed exceeded even Czernin's expectations: 'I have succeeded almost too well,' he confided to his diary.[20] By this he meant that Lyubynski, who spoke for the Rada, had minced no words and had utilized rhetoric drawn straight from the rough and tumble political world of the Russian revolution where no charge was too heinous or slander too vile to go unused against one's enemies. In his address Lyubynski had ripped into the Bolsheviks scattering accusations in every direction, characterizing Lenin's government as one based on the bayonet and terrorism and attacking the Soviet regime at Kharkov as nothing but an insignificant minority generating violence and oppression. Against these allegedly odious regimes he set his own government, which he said had been elected by the overwhelming majority of the Ukrainian people and had the unchallengable right to speak in their name.[21] Before he concluded, Lyubynski had tarred the Soviet regime with every infamy imaginable and, in so doing, played an important role in the German effort to dispel the democratic mystique in which Lenin and Trotsky had wrapped themselves. The representatives of the central powers, who had grown weary of the abuse heaped upon them by Trotsky, enjoyed every minute of Lyubynski's presentation. Hoffmann described the speech as 'excellent'[22] while Czernin wrote gleefully that the 'insults hurled by the Ukrainians ... were simply grotesque.'[23] Trotsky was understandably of a different opinion, writing that 'Kühlmann, Czernin, Hoffmann and the rest were breathing heavily like gamblers at a racecourse who had placed bets on the winning horse.' Lyubynski, he wrote, had merely 'heaped rudeness on arrogance' for the benefit of the central powers.[24] Nevertheless, the foreign commissar was visibly affected and even he admits that the scene was 'most distressing.' Czernin who de-

20 Czernin, *In the World War*, 246
21 A.A. Ioffe (ed.), *Mirnye Peregovory v Brest-Litovske* (Moscow, 1920) 136-43. Hereafter cited as *Mirnye Peregovory*. Also see Hahlweg, *Der Friede von Brest-Litowsk*, 462-75
22 Hoffmann, *War Diaries*, vol. II, 212
23 Czernin, *In the World War*, 246
24 Trotsky, *My Life*, 376

scribes Trotsky as being 'perfectly pale' and staring 'fixedly before him, drawing nervously on his blotting paper' attributed this distress to the foreign commissar 'being abused by his fellow-citizen in the presence of the enemy.'[25] Trotsky, on the other hand, shrugged off his discomfort as being caused by the 'frantic self-humiliation' and 'grandiloquent baseness ... of these miserable national democrats who for a moment had been touched with power.'[26] In either case the effect was the same, a humiliation made even worse when Czernin speaking for the central powers not only recognized the Rada as having the right to speak in the name of the Ukraine but also as a sovereign power capable of concluding international treaties. Although Trotsky protested against the recognition of the Rada's sovereignty asserting that it could not alter 'the juridical status of the Ukraine as an integral part of the Russian Federation,' much less existing circumstances in the Ukraine,[27] the central powers closed ranks behind the Rada. For them it was now only a question of reaching a satisfactory accord with Kiev.

Negotiations with Lyubynski proceeded rapidly. While the peace conference marked time the central powers met with the Rada delegation to hammer out a separate agreement. Not that Kühlmann or anyone else believed that Kiev could honour its signature. 'Given the strongly shaken position of the Rada,' wrote Kühlmann, 'it is impossible to build great illusions concerning the real value of such an agreement.' In fact, the Germans already assumed that the Rada would appeal for help against the Bolsheviks, and when they did, wrote Kühlmann, 'it would be necessary to consider their request seriously.'[28] Although he described such a step as being 'very dangerous,' General Hoffmann was already preparing to go to the rescue of the Rada. It made no difference to him or the other representatives of the central powers that, as Trotsky told them, 'they were treating with the delegation of a government whose entire territory was confined to Brest-Litovsk.'[29] This difficulty, Hoffmann wrote, was 'transitory in so far as at any time we could support this Government with arms and establish it again.'[30] With good reason Trotsky observed that 'the diplomacy of the Central Powers was merely drawing up a passport for their

25 Czernin, *In the World War*, 246
26 Trotsky, *My Life*, 377
27 Meijer, *The Trotsky Papers*, 21-3
28 DSB, vol. I, 345-6
29 Trotsky, *My Life*, 378
30 Hoffmann, *War Diaries*, vol. II, 216-17

admission' to the Ukraine.[31] German arms would guarantee a German peace well calculated to benefit the Reich.

Within a week the treaty with the Rada was ready. The time, therefore, had come to have the 'energetic discussion' which Kühlmann had promised Hertling, and on 7 February, the foreign secretary telegraphed Berlin that circumstances now allowed him 'to speak with Trotsky in a more categorical and threatening language.'[32] This did not mean that he intended to turn on Trotsky without warning; instead he decided to try some behind-the-scenes bargaining. The first step in this direction was taken by Dr Schüller of the Austrian ministry of commerce, who on 6 February, visited Trotsky seeking to determine if a compromise was possible. It is a measure of the changed circumstances that Trotsky, who had previously insisted on open diplomacy, now agreed to negotiate behind closed doors. Feeling the pressure of the impending crisis he was in a rather quarrelsome mood, but ready to talk. His major complaint was with Kühlmann who, he said, wanted Germany to be able to annex everything while hypocritically shielding this theft under the fig-leaf of self-determination. He simply would not sign such a treaty. When the Austrian bureaucrat suggested that Trotsky was too concerned with external forms the foreign commissar explained that it was precisely those forms which interested him, for he was convinced that the substance of any treaty concluded at Brest-Litovsk would soon be swept away by the anticipated world revolution. 'It would be possible for me to conclude a peace by which Russia would be violated,' Trotsky told Schüller, 'but in that case this intention would have to be openly acknowledged by the other side. We cannot be asked for a moral testimonial as well.'[33] Here then was the basis for a possible compromise. Trotsky with his sights carefully set on stimulating revolution in Germany was willing to exchange territory for a treaty which would allow him to arraign the German government before public opinion as a blatantly imperialist and annexationist regime. Would the Germans accept such a bargain? It was hardly a compromise which would appeal to Kühlmann who had devoted so much time and effort seeking to avoid such an indictment and who, in his own words, was determined 'to avoid anything which might provide [Trotsky] with material for agitation among

31 Trotsky, *My Life*, 378
32 DSB, vol. I, 375-6
33 Gustav Gratz and Richard Schüller, *The Economic Policy of Austria-Hungary during the War* (New Haven, Connecticut, 1928) 103-4

the German socialists.'[34] Nevertheless, it was a longer step toward actual negotiations than Trotsky had ever previously taken, and Czernin was eager to discuss the matter further with the foreign commissar. After some hesitation on the part of Kühlmann and against the advice of Hoffmann, Czernin was allowed to proceed.

The next evening Czernin and Dr Gratz, a high official of the Austrian foreign ministry, called on Trotsky. Conjuring with the bellicose image of General Hoffmann, they attempted to convince him that the war would be resumed if he did not promptly reach an agreement with Kühlmann. Trotsky reiterated his arguments of the day before making them yet more emphatic by declaring that 'even if his refusal were to cause the collapse of the new regime in Russia' he could not sign the type of treaty demanded by Kühlmann. Gratz then observed that if the foreign commissar did not feel he could provide a 'testimonial' for what he considered an annexationist peace then he could not demand that Germany 'recognize as an annexation that which she regarded as no annexation.' This led Trotsky to cut straight through to the heart of the matter declaring that 'it is not necessary that Germany should acknowledge in the treaty that she is making annexations, but I must reserve the right to describe Germany's activities as annexations.' The Austrians immediately saw this as a way out of the impasse. A neutral formula could be devised, they said, which would provide for the territorial changes demanded by Germany while leaving both sides free to interpret the agreement as they saw fit.[35]

Trotsky agreed that such a course could be followed, but suddenly changing the subject, he objected to the extent of the German demands. For all his talk of not being concerned about the substance of the treaty he left no doubt that he was vitally interested in that subject. Why this sudden change by Trotsky? Judging from what is known of his objectives, he was probably attempting to determine how much of the former Russian empire could be saved if he did agree to sign a treaty with the central powers. He was fully prepared, and even eager, to proceed with his 'no war, no peace' gambit, but his mind was too supple and his imagination too fertile to plod myopically toward that objective heedless of all other considerations. Moreover, even Trotsky might have had second thoughts about his strategy. Was it not possible that the element of risk involved in his plan might be too great? Might not everything be lost if he proceeded

34 Kühlmann, *Erinnerungen*, 530
35 Czernin, *In the World War*, 246-7; Gratz and Schüller, *The Economic Policy of Austria-Hungary during the War*, 104

with his intended demonstration? Not that he expected or even wanted to save the entire Russian empire. Far from it, for the sake of revolutionary propaganda it was absolutely essential that Germany be seen to be blatantly plundering the Russian empire, trampling on the right of self-determination, brutally oppressing numerous peoples and generally acting with the rapacity which Bolshevik propaganda depicted as typical of an imperialist power. Inverting the old canon of English common law Trotsky believed that it was imperative not only that injustice be done, but that it be seen to be done. But there was a limit beyond which German annexation of Russian territory would become counter-productive. Germany must be encouraged to gorge itself on Poland and Lithuania but not eviscerate Soviet Russia by consuming the economically and strategically important parts of the former empire. Short of immediate revolution in Germany the best of all possible worlds for Trotsky was a treaty signed under suitable duress assigning vast but comparatively unimportant parts of Russia to Germany. He could then have had his anti-imperialist propaganda and the vital regions of Russia at the same time. To this politically advantageous arrangement he now turned his attention demanding from Czernin and Gratz that the Moon Islands, Riga, and a strategically important part of Lithuania all be returned to Russia. There was, he hastened to add, also the question of the Ukraine. If he was to accept a neutral formula to describe the other German annexations, the central powers would have to give up their plan of a separate accord with the Rada. That regime, he said, was a phantom government, and an agreement with it would be nothing but a disguised form of intervention in the internal affairs of Russia.[36] Having listened to Trotsky, the Austrians retired to consult their German allies.

The Germans found Trotsky's proposals entirely unacceptable. Hoffmann, in particular, would not hear of surrendering the territory demanded by Trotsky. As for the treaty with the Ukraine, negotiations had gone too far to turn back. It was, in fact, ready for signature and would be signed that very night. Both Kühlmann and Hoffmann informed Czernin, who was desperately seeking to mediate between Russia and Germany, that Trotsky would have to be satisfied with a neutral formula describing the annexations; he would receive nothing more. Either he would accept the single concession and do it promptly or hostilities would resume at once. Confident in the knowledge that the Soviets no longer

---

36 Czernin, *In the World War*, 248; Gratz and Schüller, *The Economic Policy of Austria-Hungary during the War*, 104-6

had an army with which to fight, the Germans expected that Trotsky, with bad grace to be sure, would give in and sign the treaty.[37]

Trotsky's response to this informal ultimatum seemed to justify German confidence. Although the 'lion' roared that 'a treaty with the Ukraine must be regarded by Russia as an unfriendly act and would make peace impossible' he did not break off negotiations. Much to the contrary, he insisted that, Ukrainian peace or not, the peace conference should continue and Czernin's proposals be explored further.[38] When Kühlmann heard this he was almost certain that Trotsky would capitulate. Not even imagining the incredible spectacle which Trotsky was preparing he believed that the foreign commissar was simply going to fight to the last ditch and then strike his colours. Instead, Trotsky, by insisting that the conference continue, was simply safeguarding the stage on which he intended to play his last and most spectacular role at Brest-Litovsk.

The treaty with the Ukraine was signed early on the morning of 9 February. It provided for the cession of Cholm to the Ukraine, the creation of a separate Ruthenian crownland in Austria and an economic agreement by which the Ukraine would deliver large quantities of food to the central powers in exchange for manufactured goods. The tenuous nature of the agreement is reflected in Czernin's diary. 'I wonder,' he wrote, 'if the Rada is still really sitting at Kieff?'[39] It was not, but, with Hoffmann's legions waiting in the wings, that detail was irrelevant. Kühlmann had his treaty, and he now intended to speak 'in a more categorical and threatening language' to Trotsky.

The German foreign secretary moved quickly to press his advantage. When the conference met late the same afternoon he informed Trotsky of the treaty with the Ukraine and told him that it was 'impossible to drag on endlessly negotiations which did not promise any successful outcome.' 'Circumstances,' he said, 'force us to reach some specific decisions as quickly as possible.' To permit such an acceleration Kühlmann proposed that the contentious question of self-determination be dropped in favour of a simple statement specifying the territorial changes which would result from the treaty. The new Russian frontier would be established by a territorial sub-committee which would report to the full political commission on the following day.[40] This was 'energetic negotiation' with a vengeance,

---

37 Gratz and Schüller, *The Economic Policy of Austria-Hungary during the War*, 106-7
38 *Ibid.* 107
39 Czernin, *In the World War*, 249
40 *Mirnye Peregovory*, 177-87. Also see Hahlweg, *Der Friede von Brest-Litowsk*, 509-20

and Kühlmann, staring at Trotsky across from him, believed that the foreign commissar would gladly have brought the 'unsympathetic negotiations to an abrupt and final end by hurling a few hand grenades over the green table.'[41] In a sense this was exactly what Trotsky was planning, but he had to wait one more day before he could strike his great coup. The Germans had not yet presented an ultimatum, and, with the territorial question still unsettled, there were aspects of the situation yet to be investigated. While offering token resistance, therefore, Trotsky agreed to study Kühlmann's proposals. Thus Kühlmann had every right to believe that his master plan was proceeding according to schedule and that the next day would bring decisive results.

Triumph for the German foreign secretary seemed so close. Then suddenly the teleprinter began to beat out a message which promised disaster. Kühlmann, it turned out, was not the only politician to seize on the Ukrainian peace to advance his own interests. Ludendorff had also done so, turning to the emperor with a demand that the negotiations with Russia be brought to a prompt end. Wilhelm had followed Ludendorff's advice, and, in his message, directed Kühlmann to present Trotsky with an ultimatum giving him until eight o'clock the following evening to sign a treaty not merely accepting the peace conditions already presented, but one which would require the Russians to evacuate all of Livonia and Estonia up to a line running through Narva, Pskov, and Dvinsk. Any delay was to be met with an immediate rupture of the negotiations.[42] This telegram was waiting for Kühlmann when he returned from his triumphant meeting with Trotsky. When he read it he must have felt as if he had been hit by a sledgehammer, for if he did as he was told he would smash the labour of months exactly at the moment when his persistent efforts seemed about to achieve spectacular results.

His answer reflected the despair with which he greeted his Sovereign's command. Kühlmann told Wilhelm that to comply with his order would destroy the alliance with Austria-Hungary, for Czernin had informed him that it was incompatible with the instructions which he had received from Vienna. The Austrians wanted peace and were not prepared to throw it away for the sake of Livonia and Estonia. If Wilhelm insisted on putting forward new demands Czernin was certain to continue negotiations with Trotsky on the basis of the conditions previously agreed upon by the cen-

41 Kühlmann, *Erinnerungen*, 530
42 DBS, vol. I, 390-1. Also see Steglich, *Die Friedenspolitik der Mittelmächte*, 556

tral powers and, in so doing, would effectively rupture the alliance of the two empires. Kühlmann implored the Kaiser to reconsider his decision, explaining that he expected decisive results within a very short time. Failing such results, he would be able to rupture the negotiations according to a plan already arranged with Czernin. If Wilhelm insisted on the new policy then Kühlmann declared that he would not be responsible for its implementation. In effect, therefore, he tendered his resignation effective at the moment the emperor confirmed his order. Wilhelm would then have to find someone else to present his ultimatum.[43]

Kühlmann immediately sought to enlist the support of the chancellor, informing him that he would 'not bear the responsibility for, nor participate in, a departure from the line of diplomatic action which has long been prepared and carried out.'[44] Hertling responded by drafting a telegram to the Kaiser expressing his own despair at the orders issued the previous day. He asked the sovereign to reconsider these orders, keeping in mind particularly the consequences of his actions. If implemented, he wrote, they would have both international and internal consequences leading almost certainly to a rupture of the alliance with Austria, the isolation of Germany, the 'most disastrous effect' on the world's few remaining neutral countries and the outbreak of further strikes and unrest in Germany. If Wilhelm insisted on this policy, the chancellor said, he personally had no other choice but to tender his resignation effective at once.[45]

Here then was a direct challenge to the military 'demi-gods' and their hold over the easily influenced emperor. As it turned out, however, the chancellor did not have to weigh in at Homburg. Kühlmann's threatened resignation and the possibility of a rupture in the alliance with Austria-Hungary proved sufficient to give Wilhelm pause, and he decided to withdraw his demands until he had received news of the afternoon meeting at Brest-Litovsk. Learning of this, Hertling withheld his original telegram but sent another, no less emphatic, message, informing the emperor that he fully shared the viewpoint of the foreign secretary and could not take responsibility for a change in policy. He asked the emperor to await his advice before reaching a final decision.[46] In the interval, with a difficult decision in the offing, all eyes turned toward Brest-Litovsk.

43 DSB, vol. I, 391-2
44 Ibid., 388-90
45 Ibid., 393-5
46 Ibid., 396

While these dramatic telegrams were being exchanged the territorial sub-committee struck at the meeting of 9 February was at work. Chaired by Gustav Gratz its task was to establish the future Russian frontier between the Baltic Sea and Brest-Litovsk. Russia was represented by the historian Mikhail Pokrovskii who had been instructed to demand the return of Riga and the Moon Islands. Pokrovskii also claimed all territory occupied by a predominantly Latvian population arguing that the Latvian people should not be divided by artificial boundaries. The German representative, Frederic von Rosenberg, rejected this motion declaring that 'ethnographic considerations had to give way to demands of a military character,' but suggested that if Russia wished to avoid dividing the Latvians into two groups it could evacuate Livonia and Estonia thus permitting the Baltic peoples to decide their own fate. This was the closest the German delegation came to obeying Wilhelm's order to liberate the Baltic provinces from Soviet control, but Rosenberg put it forward not as a peremptory demand but as a simple suggestion. Needless to say, Pokrovskii had little use for this proposal and quickly fell back on Riga and the Moon Islands. The only purpose Germany could have for retaining them, he said, was to threaten Petrograd. Rosenberg shrugged off the Soviet objection, and the sub-committee found itself tied in knots. 'Agreement not reached' wrote Gratz in the protocols of the meeting.[47]

Having failed to reach an agreement with Pokrovskii, Rosenberg consulted Kühlmann and then called on Trotsky. The same ground was covered again, but the foreign commissar proved to be just as stubborn as his deputy. Before abandoning the discussion, however, Rosenberg, acting on instructions from Kühlmann, inquired if Trotsky would put in writing his willingness to negotiate a settlement if Riga and the Moon Islands were returned to Russia.[48] What was the purpose of this maneuver? Kühlmann, as he testifies in his memoirs, knew that the general staff would not agree to return these areas to Russia.[49] Was he simply trying to trick Trotsky? As these areas were Latvian rather than Russian such a document would certainly have provided valuable ammunition against the Bolsheviks if the Soviet government chose to continue its propaganda war against Germany. Or, for the sake of a treaty with Russia, was Kühlmann prepared to risk the wrath of Hindenburg and Luden-

47 *Mirnye Peregovory*, 200ff
48 Hoffmann, *War Diaries*, vol. II, 218
49 Kühlmann, *Erinnerungen*, 544

dorff, hoping to brazen out his impetuous act with the aid of public opinion once the war in the east was at an end? Or, perhaps, he had some compromise in mind whereby he would recognize Russia's claim to Riga and the Islands while reserving the right of German occupation until the conclusion of a general peace with the western allies? Kühlmann, who played his cards very close to his chest, did not say, and, therefore, we do not know. Trotsky, fearing a trap, refused to commit himself to paper, and this whole maneuver, whatever its purpose, failed. The question of the Russian frontier was left to be settled by the political commission.

Another question left for the political commission was Russia's relationship to the treaty which the central powers had just signed with the Rada. Trotsky had repeatedly stated that he would not recognize this document, yet if he agreed to peace on the basis of a frontier extending from the Baltic Sea to Brest-Litovsk he would, by implication, recognize the demise of Russian sovereignty in the Ukraine and, indirectly, the treaty signed by the Rada. Would Trotsky then refuse to sign a peace treaty with the central powers? Fearing that he might, Czernin, sometime on 10 February, sent Schüller to discuss the problem with him. The foreign commissar was still angry about the Ukrainian treaty and accused the central powers of planning to use the Rada as a pretext for continuing the war against Russia. 'If that were the intention,' said Schüller, 'the advance would be on Petrograd, not on Kiev. If we had concluded peace with the Ukraine in order to proceed against Russia, there would be no sense in our trying to conclude peace with you now.'[50] But Trotsky continued to argue, pointing out time and again that the Rada had been deposed. He even offered to allow Germany or Austria to send an officer to Kiev in order to confirm this fact. This did not interest Schüller who had called upon Trotsky to find a way to reconcile the Soviet desire for the Ukraine with the central powers' need of raw materials and grain. He was not concerned with discovering if the Rada still sat in Kiev. He promptly explained himself, pointing out that any international agreement was only as effective as the authority of the government which concluded it. Dropping a broad hint, he added that 'the peace with the Ukraine is so favourable that, in given circumstances, you will be glad to take it over.'[51] In short, if the Rada had fallen and the Bolsheviks exercised power in the Ukraine then the whole problem could be settled by the Ukrainian Soviet endorsing the treaty signed by its predecessor. The central powers could then

50 Gratz and Schüller, *The Economic Policy of Austria-Hungary during the War*, 111
51 *Ibid.*

have the grain and raw materials which they required, and Soviet Russia could have the Ukraine. Here was a way out of the impasse, but it was not one which appealed to Trotsky. He correctly observed that 'by the Ukrainian peace you wish to secure yourself supplies of grain, but we too draw grain supplies from the Ukraine,' meaning that it would be difficult for two hungry thieves to plunder the same breadbasket. Yet if Trotsky had genuinely desired peace he would have jumped into this opening and investigated Schüller's suggestion. He did not, and the opportunity of a *modus vivendi* was lost. Although such an arrangement would have left Soviet Russia an enormous base on which to develop its power and immense scope to swindle its unwanted partners these considerations did not interest the foreign commissar. He continued to view the struggle against German imperialism within a virtually eschatological framework and could not yet conceive of the conflict as a protracted contest in which maneuver and compromise would play a worthwhile role. Intent on precipitating a dramatic confrontation with the central powers, Trotsky chose to ignore their final effort to negotiate a compromise.

To what extent did Trotsky inform Lenin of these last minute negotiations? From a telegram sent by Lenin and Stalin to Trotsky at six-thirty on the evening of 10 February, it would seem that the foreign commissar had not mentioned these talks at all. Lenin and Stalin wrote: 'We repeat; nothing remains of the Kiev Rada, and the Germans will have to recognize the fact, *if they have not done so already*.'[52] Moreover, if Lenin had been informed that the Germans were prepared to negotiate about the Ukraine he almost certainly would have pressed even harder for a settlement with Kühlmann, and Soviet authors, eager to prove that Trotsky had disobeyed Lenin and betrayed the revolution, would have triumphantly produced these messages as evidence of the crime. As it is, they have published excerpts of a telegram sent from Brest-Litovsk on 9 February in which Ioffe wrote: 'Our press is impossibly exaggerating events in Germany; there is no revolution in Germany, there is only a sharp turn, a displacement, the beginning of a revolution and only that.'[53] Presumably Trotsky had approved this message, and it is produced as evidence to support the contention that 'Trotsky knew the state of affairs in Germany and Austria-Hungary did not offer a basis for revolution, but he did not wish to take this into consideration.'[54] Quite true, but Trotsky was not counting

52 Lenin, PSS, vol. XXXV, 332. Emphasis added
53 Chubar'ian, *Brestskii Mir*, 140
54 *Ibid.*, 140-1

on an immediate revolution in central Europe, only sufficient unrest to force the Kaiser to accept his 'no war, no peace' solution. The revolution, he believed, would materialize later; in the meanwhile Russia would remain ideologically uncontaminated by signing an agreement with the imperialists and preserve its moral integrity for the great struggle to come. Ioffe's telegram was probably intended to provide ammunition against the advocates of immediate revolutionary war.

In Petrograd, Lenin had continued his campaign in favour of peace. In the privacy of the Central Committee he began to assert that an immediate peace, rather than retarding the development of revolution in Germany, would accelerate it, arguing that 'by concluding peace we could at once have an exchange of prisoners of war, thereby sending to Germany a great mass of people who had seen our revolution in action and had been schooled by it.'[55] In public he still avoided all reference to this subject continuing instead to focus attention on internal affairs. The topic of civil war was always on his lips, Lenin consistently harping on the idea that socialism would be molded in the crucible of civil war and that the time was ripe, while the capitalist states were tearing each other apart, to devote the resources of the Soviet state to the utter annihilation of the Russian bourgeoisie.[56] On 3 February, the Central Committee again debated foreign policy, but on this occasion Lenin drew up the list of individuals from outside the inner circle who were invited to speak. Although all shades of opinion were represented, some were better represented than others, and it is not surprising that in preparing his list Lenin proved more adept at distinguishing shades of opinion among those who stood close to him than he did in differentiating among those who differed slightly with Bukharin. The results of this meeting were much more satisfactory for Lenin than the gathering of 21 January, where a majority had voted in favour of revolutionary war. The majority at this meeting now agreed with Lenin that if the existence of the Soviet state was seriously threatened it would be possible to conclude an annexationist peace with Germany. On the question of whether it was possible to sign an annexationist peace at once Lenin was still in a minority, but he had nevertheless succeeded in showing his colleagues that he was not alone in believing that it was folly to sacrifice the revolution in Russia for a possible revolution in Germany.[57]

55 Lenin, pss, vol. xxxv, 318-20
56 *Ibid.*, vol. xxxv, 323-7
57 *Protokoly TsK*, 190-1; Lenin, pss, vol. xxxv, 318-20, 484-5

The results of this meeting, of course, did not, as Soviet historians have claimed,[58] alter the earlier decision of the Central Committee. As in the case of the meeting of 21 January, non-committee members had voted, and the results were not considered binding. Lenin knew this and also knew that for the moment he had no chance to reverse the decision of 24 January. In the undiluted meetings of the Central Committee which followed he made no attempt to overturn the earlier decision. Rather than seek decisive results at an unpropitious moment he sought to prepare for the next round of political warfare which would follow the end of negotiations at Brest-Litovsk. Lenin clung tenaciously to his conviction that for the moment the revolution in Russia could not expect any assistance from the west, and not even the unrest in Germany at the end of January caused him to change his mind. The only concession which he made to his critics during the upheaval in Germany was a codicil, added as point twenty-two, to his earlier twenty-one theses that the events in Germany gave Soviet Russia a further opportunity to drag out the negotiations at Brest-Litovsk.[59] Thus, it is not surprising that on 10 February when Trotsky sent a last telegram asking rhetorically 'What further is to be done?' Lenin and Stalin wired back immediately: 'You know our standpoint; it has lately been confirmed, especially after Ioffe's letter.'[60] Trotsky, however, had already decided on his course of action. This, together with the rhetorical nature of his question, is shown in the remainder of his last telegram. 'Today,' he wrote, 'near six o'clock we will give our final answer. It is necessary that its substance become known to all the world. Take all necessary measures.'[61] The curtain was going up on the last and most spectacular scene at Brest-Litovsk.

At 5:58 p.m. Kühlmann brought the political commission to order. Intent on getting quick results, he disposed of all ceremony and went right to work. 'In view of the serious nature of today's meeting,' he said, 'all polemics should be avoided' and he asked that attention be focused strictly on 'the consideration of questions giving us the possibility of reaching specific practical results.' With that he turned to Gratz and asked for the report of the territorial sub-committee. When the Austrian replied that the sub-committee was deadlocked the German foreign secretary looked

58 Chubar'ian, *Brestskii Mir*, 139
59 Lenin, PSS, vol. XXXV, 252
60 *Ibid.*, 332. 'Ioffe's letter' apparently refers to the message of 9 February indicating that there was no immediate hope of revolution in Germany.
61 Chubar'ian, *Brestskii Mir*, 141

across the table at Trotsky and asked if he had anything to contribute which 'would aid us in satisfactorily resolving this question.'

The crisis had come. Kühlmann would now discover if all his careful preparations had been in vain or if Trotsky, faced with the choice of war or peace, would capitulate. The last ditch had been reached, and Kühlmann waited impatiently for the foreign commissar to strike his flag. As Trotsky began to speak this appeared to be what was happening. Although he lashed out bitterly against German imperialism, incongruously lumping the Moon Islands with Belgium, Serbia, Poland, Rumania, and Lithuania as objects of German greed he quickly struck a different note and proclaimed:

We no longer wish to take part in this purely imperialist war where the claims of the possessing classes are paid for completely by the blood of mankind. We are equally irreconcilable to the imperialism of both camps and we will no longer agree to spill the blood of our soldiers in defence of the interests of one camp of imperialists against the others. In expectation of that near hour which we anticipate when the oppressed labouring classes of all countries will take power in their own hands just as the toiling peoples of Russia have already done, we are withdrawing our armies from the war.

Kühlmann, Czernin, and Hoffmann all breathed easier. Trotsky seemed on the verge of repeating his performance of 10 January; he would follow a roaring propaganda blast with surrender. He continued: 'We are going out of the war. We inform all peoples and their governments of this fact. We are giving the order for a general demobilization of all our armies opposed at the present to the troops of Germany, Austria-Hungary, Turkey and Bulgaria. We are waiting in the firm belief that other peoples will soon follow our example.' But then came the bombshell exploded with the skill of the true platform orator:

At the same time, we declare that the conditions as submitted to us by the Governments of Germany and Austria-Hungary are opposed in principle to the interests of all peoples ... We cannot place the signatures of the Russian Revolution under these conditions which bring with them oppression, misery and hate to millions of human beings. The governments of Germany and Austria-Hungary are determined to seize lands and peoples by violence. Let them do so openly. We cannot approve violence. We are going out of the war, but we feel ourselves compelled to refuse to sign the peace treaty.[62]

62 *Mirnye Peregovory,* 207-8. Also see Hahlweg, *Der Friede von Brest-Litowsk,* 537-43

'The declaration,' wrote Colonel Fokke, 'came like a clap of thunder in a clear sky.'[63] For a moment total silence reigned in the conference hall, only Pokrovskii reporting that he had heard Hoffmann exclaim under his breath *'unerhört!'*[64] It was 10 January all over again, complete with the implacable dilemma on which Trotsky impaled his opponents. Kühlmann was the first to recover, but as he himself has admitted, he did not know what to say and spoke only because he was chairman and had to say something.[65] In the circumstances he did the only thing he could, asking Trotsky for time to study the Russian statement. When it became apparent that Trotsky, who was already preparing to leave, was not going to give him time to study the extraordinary statement, Kühlmann began to threaten the foreign commissar reminding him that the central powers remained in a state of war with Russia. 'On the basis of the armistice agreement,' he said, 'military activity has temporarily been suspended. At the time this agreement is annulled military activity automatically is resumed. The fact that one side or the other demobilizes its army does not alter that situation either in fact or in law.' Then, as Trotsky remained unimpressed and continued his preparations to leave, Kühlmann, somewhat more frantically, asked how Russia intended to regulate its relations with the central powers. Where did Russia intend to locate its boundaries? Did Russia plan to renew consular, economic, and legal connections with the central powers? Trotsky paused long enough to respond, his voice dripping with irony, that at the moment it was impossible to find any juridical formula which would describe the relations between Russia and the central powers. Kühlmann asked for a meeting on the following day at which time the central powers would respond to the Russian declaration, but Trotsky just shook his head and proceeded to leave the room. As he reached the door Kühlmann called after him, asking how the two sides could communicate in the future. Trotsky turned, shrugged his shoulders and replied that the radio had served very well prior to the beginning of the peace conference and it could once again be used. Having said that, Trotsky led the entire Russian delegation from the hall leaving those of the central powers to stare at each other in amazement.[66] A new, if somewhat short, chapter in international law had just been written.

63 Fokke, 'Brestskoi Tragikomedii,' 206
64 *Ibid.*, 207
65 Kühlmann, *Erinnerungen*, 544
66 Fokke, 'Brestskoi Tragikomedii,' 206-7

The Russian delegation hurriedly packed their bags, sent several tele-grams announcing the end of hostilities and ordered their train readied for departure. Only Ioffe was left behind to settle minor details. Early on the morning of 11 February Trotsky left Brest-Litovsk believing that his great coup had been successful. The entire delegation was in a jovial mood be-lieving that the war had been ended without having to sign Kühlmann's obscene treaty. Pokrovskii, in particular, kept everyone amused as he moved about the platform giving his imitation of General Hoffmann hiss-ing '*unerhört!*' at the conclusion of Trotsky's peroration. Considering the consternation which had been created among the delegates of the central powers and Kühlmann's almost imploring tone in asking Trotsky to con-tinue the negotiations, the Soviet delegation can be forgiven their error. The third and decisive phase of the peace negotiations had come to an end.

6
This beast springs quickly

Let Kühlmann go back to Germany and show the workers his peace and explain to them why our signatures are not there. Trotsky, 15 February 1918

... on 18 February at twelve o'clock the armistice concluded with the Russian Republic will end and a state of war will again be resumed. General Hoffmann to Soviet Government, 16 February 1918

The trial is a failure. Hoffmann will and can fight. To delay is impossible; they have already taken five days from us that I counted on. And this beast springs quickly. Lenin to Trotsky, 16 February 1918

Trotsky had scored a brilliant tactical success. He had taken the central powers completely by surprise and left their representatives speechless with his incredible announcement. How quickly could they regain their equilibrium, calculate the damage which had been done and regain the initiative? Totally unprepared for Trotsky's *coup de théâtre* each of the major representatives of the central powers reacted differently. Johannes Kriege, chief of the legal division of the *Auswärtiges Amt*, sought some precedent for this extraordinary situation; Czernin hastened to inform Vienna that the war was at an end; Hoffmann calculated the number of divisions he had ready for action while Kühlmann shrewdly began to mull over the implications of Trotsky's statement. Late that night they met to conduct a post-mortem on the conference.

What was to be done? Although Kriege reported that he had found a precedent in ancient history for Trotsky's declaration the other representatives of the central powers showed little interest in his discovery. Hoffmann quickly let everyone know his views; the diplomats had failed, and it was time for him to 'clarify' the situation. The Bolsheviks appreciated only superior force, and, sword in hand, he would negotiate with them in the idiom which they understood. Czernin spoke against the resumption of war. Austria needed peace, and, if Trotsky's formula excluded a classic treaty, it provided the next best thing, a *de facto* cessation of hostilities and the demobilization of the Russian army.

Kühlmann listened to these arguments and several others before presenting his own. His subtle mind had quickly grasped the essential weakness of Trotsky's declaration, and he now explained to his rather startled listeners that he was of the opinion that 'in general, nothing could be more favourable for the central powers than Trotsky's decision.' At one stroke the foreign commissar had renounced all the rights of a belligerent state while ostentatiously refusing to accept those of a state at peace with its neighbors. Had Trotsky signed the peace treaty the central powers would have had to make numerous concessions and grant Soviet Russia all the prerogatives of a sovereign state. This was no longer necessary, and, in terms of international law, Russia could be treated as simply nonexistent. The central powers, therefore, could regulate the affairs of eastern Europe in any manner they saw fit.

Kühlmann rejected Hoffmann's proposal to resume the war. Reminding the general that war was simply the continuation of politics by other means he asked what policy would be pursued by resuming the war with Russia. A search for 'clarity' in the east? An effort to force the Bolsheviks to accept 'in black and white' the terms dictated by Berlin? These policies could no longer be pursued by military means. 'A higher goal than the annihilation of enemy strength cannot be exceeded by waging war,' he said, and that had already been attained. Even if the Bolsheviks were forced to sign a peace treaty they would seize the first opportunity to violate it. More to the point, a German offensive was likely to lead either to the overthrow of Lenin and Trotsky by those dependent on the allies or the withdrawal of the Soviet government into the depths of Russia. Then, said Kühlmann, we might well 'march through all of Russia, a sword in our right hand and a pen in our left without accomplishing the slightest thing.' Rather than embark on an adventurous policy, the end of which could not be foreseen, he favoured doing absolutely nothing at all, allowing the juridical state of war to continue, the armistice to remain in force and leaving Trotsky's declaration unanswered. 'In diplomacy,' he asserted, 'all that is not absolutely necessary is to be omitted,' and he proposed to follow this maxim to the letter. In this way eastern Europe could be reorganized as the central powers wished, political peace could be maintained in Germany and the army, having left a corporal's guard in Russia, could shift the bulk of its divisions to the west. Trotsky, hoist by his own petard, could be left to contemplate the folly of his ways. Eventually the Bolsheviks would come begging to make some kind of more satisfactory arrangement.[1] The diplomats endorsed Kühlmann's views, but Hoffmann refused to subscribe to this policy of malignant neglect. Kühlmann's policy might satisfy politicians accustomed to dealing in uncertainties, but he and his army required 'clarity.'[2] The stage was set for yet another confrontation between the German civil and military authorities over the enduring question of which elite group would control the destinies of the Reich.

The civil authorities of Germany were at an immense disadvantage. Possessing neither the prestige nor the self-confidence of the generals they lacked a response to the argument that in wartime all other considerations had to give way to military necessity. Since the generals could always find compelling military reasons why the outcome of the war hinged on any given decision the politicians had consistently been forced to defer to the military. Nevertheless, the war within a war continued with the object being the control of the Kaiser in whose hands ultimate authority rested. Weak-willed, indecisive, and vulnerable to emotional arguments based on sentiment or flattery, the Kaiser was the storm-centre around which the battle raged. Inclined to listen to the military 'demigods' rather than his civilian ministers the Kaiser always gave way when Ludendorff threatened resignation.

In this confrontation Ludendorff did not even have to resort to his ultimate weapons. He had prepared his position well in advance and knew that victory required only a minimum of effort. Already he had impressed the Kaiser with the urgent necessity of securing 'clarification' of the military situation in eastern Europe, excited him to demand additional annexations in the Baltic and nearly succeeded in disrupting Kühlmann's strategy at Brest-Litovsk. He had forced Kühlmann and Hertling to make the most far-reaching promises of almost immediate success, and now that they had failed he was in an excellent position to press for the acceptance of his more violent solution to the Russian problem.

1 DSB, vol. I, 402-3; Werner Hahlweg, *Der diktatfrieden von Brest-Litowsk 1918 und die bolschewistische Weltrevolution* (Münster, 1960) 65-73; Kühlmann, *Erinnerungen*, 545-6; Gratz and Schüller, *The Economic Policy of Austria-Hungary during the War*, 113
2 Hoffmann, *War Diaries*, vol. II, 219

A crown council met at the imperial residence of Homburg on 13 February to determine future German policy in Russia. The meeting had become necessary when an exchange of telegrams between army and government leaders had failed to resolve the differences between them.[3] Hindenburg, Ludendorff, and Holtzendorff represented the armed forces while Hertling, Kühlmann, and Payer, the vice-chancellor, spoke for the government. Wilhelm, who in the absence of an agreement would have to render his decision, took the chair, but quickly absented himself from the meeting to allow his highest advisors to seek a compromise without his august presence to distract them.

The meeting lasted throughout the morning and thoroughly rehashed all the old arguments concerning German policy in Russia. Kühlmann and Payer did most of the talking for the government, the foreign secretary recapitulating the views he had already expressed at Brest-Litovsk. A resumption of the war, he added, threatened to inflame nationalism in Russia and create a worse, rather than better, situation in eastern Europe. Worse yet, the loss of Livonia and Estonia would permanently alienate Russia from Germany. He steadfastly adhered to his point of view that Germany's best course of action was to do nothing 'until necessity forces us to act.' Payer served as a strong second to the foreign secretary, explaining that the internal situation in Germany would be adversely affected by a resumption of the war. Only if the Bolsheviks took up arms, he said, would the German people understand the need for a new war. The people, he stressed, wanted peace, not war, and the Reichstag was sure to create troubles for the government if an offensive was launched against Russia. It was difficult enough, he added, to convince the Social Democrats of the need to launch a new offensive in the west, and it might be impossible to do so if the army resumed the war in the east.

Hindenburg and Ludendorff said very little. They rested their case firmly on military necessity, asserting that the numerous divisions still tied down in Russia were needed in the west and could not be moved until the political situation in eastern Europe had been clarified. They also argued that as long as a stable peace had not been secured in the east the allied powers would continue to seek ways of bringing Russia back into the war. The British, they said, planned to establish themselves in Estonia and use that province as a base from which to attack Germany. Ludendorff simply brushed aside Payer's arguments about the German people wishing peace, asserting that the army wished the same thing, but that to secure

3 DSB, Vol. I, 397-9

peace it was first necessary to wage war to a successful conclusion. For the most part, however, the 'demi-gods' awaited the return of the emperor who they knew would support them.

When Wilhelm formally took the chair late in the morning the rather sluggish meeting took on new life. He was in a bellicose mood and left no doubt where his sympathies lay. He also brushed aside Payer's argument that the Reichstag and the German people would not tolerate a resumption of the war in eastern Europe. He reproached the vice-chancellor for even implying that the Reichstag could meddle in military affairs, for that, in his estimation, would mean that Germany had become a republic. 'What do you wish, Excellency?' he asked Payer, 'I am a Dynast!'[4] Payer retreated, saying that the Reichstag did not wish to interfere in military operations, but it had a constitutional role to play in making political decisions. 'What is political about this question?' Wilhelm exclaimed, brilliantly illuminating that state of mind which in nine months time would lead the last Hohenzollern emperor into exile. The Bolsheviks in his view were only seeking to stir up trouble in Germany, and in doing this, they were being supported by the entente. Spurred on by Ludendorff he launched into a long harangue against the Bolsheviks, denouncing Petrograd as the 'Great Eastern Lodge of International Jewry' and the centre of revolutionary contagion. It was necessary, he said, to help Russia rid herself of the terrible Bolsheviks. Ludendorff quickly chimed in saying that one of the consequences of resumed military activity in the east *might* be the overthrow of the Bolsheviks and the establishment of a more desirable form of government in Russia. Such a change in government would undercut the British plan of establishing themselves in the Baltic. This led the emperor to declare solemnly that he could not assume the responsibility for permitting the 'anglicanization' of Russia, and, therefore, the Bolsheviks had to go.

This extraordinary duet sung to the identical tune as the anti-Bolshevik ballads then popular in London and Paris horrified Hertling. He had been very quiet up to this point, but as it seemed that Wilhelm and the army were about to march off on a crusade against the Bolsheviks he intervened to call a halt to this dangerous trend of the meeting. Emphatically opposed to this policy he threatened to resign if it should be adopted. Wilhelm, however, continued to rage against the Bolsheviks, loudly contending that they were part of an international conspiracy of Jews and Freemasons cen-

4 Winfried Baumgart, *Deutsche Ostpolitik 1918* (München, 1966) 25, n.53

tred in Paris and dedicated to enslaving the world to their evil will.[5] Germany, he argued, should be 'magnanimous' and deliver the Russian people from 'the revenge of the Jews.' When the meeting adjourned for lunch no agreement had been reached.

Food and drink seem to have had a soothing effect on the German elite, for when they returned from lunch they had worked out the basis for what had the appearance of a compromise. Although Kühlmann still opposed any military action and Hertling asserted that he would not sanction a new offensive in the east, the chancellor now said he would agree to the dispatch of a 'gendarme corps' to the Baltic. In short order this was expanded to include the Ukraine, and the meeting decided that a 'police action' designed to restore peace and order in the areas adjacent to the territories occupied by the German army would begin as soon as possible. As if to substantiate Voltaire's dictum that history is a 'story agreed upon' the generals and politicians then prepared their version of what was about to happen. They decided that Trotsky's 'no war, no peace' declaration would be interpreted as a Russian repudiation of the armistice of 15 December; that, as a consequence, the seven-day grace period required by the armistice agreement before the resumption of hostilities would elapse on 17 February; and that Operation *Faustschlage*, as Ludendorff styled the 'police action,' would begin on the following day. 'Appeals for help' would reach Berlin from the Baltic and the Ukraine no later than 18 February, and the operation would be billed in the German press as a humanitarian rescue mission designed to save innocent peoples from the ravages of Bolshevik tyranny.[6]

Ludendorff had skilfully outmaneuvered his civilian opponents. In urging a resumption of hostilities on the eastern front he had very limited

---

5 Wilhelm, of course, was not the only major figure to cherish such absurd ideas. Leaders elsewhere shared his belief in an 'international Jewish conspiracy.' Thus, a report submitted to the British foreign office by a Captain Alexander Proctor, purporting to demonstrate by 'reason and logic' that 'Trotsky, Lenin and Company' were, in fact, German agents, was dismissed by John Duncan Gregory, who handled Russian affairs in the foreign office, in the following way: 'There is nothing new in all this,' he wrote, 'Captain Proctor is as intently convinced that Lenin and Trotsky are German agents as Mr Lockhart is that they are the reverse. They are probably both wrong. Trotsky is mainly the agent of the Jewish conspirary of Eastern Europe whose chief aim is to destroy European civilization at all costs and by any means, German, Allied, Socialist or any other.' All the mandarins of the foreign office, up to and including Lord Hardinge, initialled this minute without adding a word of protest or comment! PRO FO 371/3299/64858

6 DSB, vol. I, 403-11; Baumgart, *Deutsche Ostpolitik*, 25-6; Erich von Ludendorff, *Meine Kriegserinnerungen* (Berlin, 1919) 446-9; George Alexander von Müller, *Regierte der Kaiser?* (Göttingen, 1959) 354-6

objectives – the seizure of Livonia and Estonia, the establishment of a more defensible military frontier and the restoration of the Rada in the Ukraine – yet in the course of the meeting he had pandered to the emperor's prejudices and stressed that the campaign which he wished to launch *might* lead to the overthrow of the Soviet government. Could Ludendorff, with his spring offensive on the western front hardly a month away, seriously have contemplated a crusade against Bolshevism? It seems unlikely. As much as he disagreed with Kühlmann he would have been hard pressed to reject his contention that it was impossible to foresee how an advance into the heart of Russia might end. Ludendorff consistently stressed that he wanted 'clarity,' and, for him, this meant circumstances and conditions of his own making. Given the limited objectives eventually adopted by the crown council, Ludendorff could, in fact, look forward to securing his desired 'clarity' in a short period of time and with a minimum expenditure of effort. Given the disintegration of the Russian army a defensive line running from Narva to Dvinsk was easily within his grasp. Given the same circumstances the rest of Russia was beyond his command, for as Kühlmann had stressed it would be possible to march through all of Russia without accomplishing anything. And who needed it? Certainly not Ludendorff on the eve of launching a campaign in the west which he described as 'the most colossal military problem which has ever been set to any army.'[7] Then why all the talk about overthrowing the Soviet government and his encouragement of Wilhelm to rage like a wild man against the Bolsheviks? Ludendorff, employing one of the oldest political games in existence, needed a foil for use against the civilian authorities. Wilhelm served this purpose admirably. In contrast to the emperor, Ludendorff appeared absolutely moderate, and having terrified Hertling with Wilhelm's extreme measures the general could turn to the chancellor and suggest a 'compromise' which, of course, contained what he had wanted in the first place. Hertling was only too happy to accept the general's offer and banish the terrible apparition conjured up by the emperor that morning. Hertling, having accepted the 'compromise' of his own free will, could then be counted upon to return to Berlin and loyally do his best to secure the acceptance of this policy by the various parties in the Reichstag. Ludendorff's only disappointment was that Kühlmann, who had obstinately refused to endorse the agreement, had not resigned as foreign secretary.[8] That, however, could wait; for the moment the gen-

7 Ludendorff, *The General Staff and its Problems,* 548
8 Ludendorff, *Kriegserinnerungen,* 449

eral had received all he really wanted. Given a 'compromise' of this nature it is easy to understand the contempt Ludendorff felt for the civilian authorities, and why, in the framework of Wilhelmine Germany, the government stood no chance of exercising effective control over the army.

While Ludendorff was setting the stage for the resumption of hostilities, Russia was celebrating the end of the war. Before leaving Brest-Litovsk Trotsky had sent telegrams to the war commissariat, Stavka, and Krylenko declaring that the war was over and demobilization of the Russian army should begin at once. The foreign commissar had not bothered to elaborate on what had happened at that day's meeting of the peace conference, and, consequently, as no one outside the Bolshevik Central Committee knew of the audacious plan to issue a declaration of 'no war, no peace,' his telegrams were generally interpreted to mean that a peace treaty had been signed and the long war was at an end. Across the telegram received at Stavka some exuberant soul had written in large capital letters: 'Peace has come!' On receiving his telegram early on the morning of 11 February, Krylenko did as he was told and ordered immediate and general demobilization. 'Peace!' his order began, 'War is ended. Russia will fight no more.' The news raced through the army, and by mid-day what was left of Russia's fighting forces began to leave the trenches. Spontaneous demobilization was now given official sanction.[9] But not for long. Krylenko had issued his order without consulting Petrograd, and when Lenin awoke on the morning of 11 February to discover what Trotsky and Krylenko had done, he desperately sought to countermand their orders.[10] He was too late. The contradictory orders only served to demoralize the army further, and the commanders in the field informed Lenin that there was nothing they could tell their troops which would convince them that the war was not at an end.[11]

In Petrograd, the 'end of the war' was received with the same enthusiasm as in the trenches. The people thronged the streets in celebration, and if they became somewhat subdued when they learned that peace had not actually been signed, they quickly regained their buoyancy when the more politically minded among them explained how Trotsky had 'outwitted' the Germans. That same day the Petrograd Soviet officially approved Trotsky's policy with Zinoviev solemnly declaring that 'our delegation has

9 A.L. Fraiman, *Revoliutsionnaia Zashchita Petrograda v Fevrale-Marte 1918 g* (Moscow, 1964) 58; Oznobishin, *Ot Bresta do Iur'eva*, 76-7
10 Lenin, PSS, vol. L, 364
11 Fraiman, *Revoliutsionnaia Zashchita Petrograda*, 59

found the only correct way out of the situation.'[12] The other socialist parties joined the Bolsheviks in congratulating Trotsky on his 'successful' handling of the negotiations. The allied representatives, on the other hand, were thunderstruck. 'I could not believe it,' wrote Jacques Sadoul, 'I still cannot believe it.'[13] Another Frenchman was more explicit. 'Only a Slav mentality could have thought up this bastard combination of an intermediary state between peace and war. If German divisions march into Petrograd gun in hand it will still be war, no matter how Trotsky may describe this action.'[14]

The same thought haunted Lenin who asked pointedly: 'Won't they deceive us?' Trotsky thought not. Before leaving Brest-Litovsk he had talked to German troops stationed at the fortress, and not only soldiers but officers as well had told him 'we are not bandits. It is impossible for us to attack Russia.' 'Very well,' replied Lenin, 'If it is so, so much the better. We have kept our face, and we are out of the war.'[15] But he still doubted if Soviet Russia would escape so easily. Sadoul probably had Lenin in mind when he wrote about the Bolshevik leadership: 'Some are excited, others are stupified. Some crying, they are the wise ones. Like me they think that the gesture is very romantic, that it is so pure that it will exceed the understanding of the pan-Germanists, that an immense peal of laughter will ring throughout Germany, that tomorrow the regiments will resume the offensive with an ardour increased by the agreeable perspective of easy and fruitful conquests.'[16] In any case, Lenin said nothing in public about the negotiations. It was Trotsky's policy and he would have to assume responsibility for its consequences.

On 14 February, Trotsky appeared before the Central Executive Committee. He was still confident that his policy would succeed, but he warned that 'an attack cannot be excluded from consideration in all circumstances.' In fact, his entire address was a rather curious amalgam of ebullient optimism and more thoughtful circumspection. In many ways this was a speech much like that of 21 December where the foreign commissar had debated with himself the virtues of revolutionary war. Once again, in rather veiled form, the possibility of a great revolutionary conflagration appeared time and again in his speech, serving more as a backdrop against which he developed his ideas than a specific and identifiable part of the

12 Trotsky, *My Life*, 385
13 Sadoul, *Notes*, 237
14 Louis de Robien, *Journal d'un diplomate en Russie, 1917-1918* (Paris, 1967) 220
15 Trotsky, *Lenin*, 111; *idem, Sochineniia*, vol. XVII, part I, 107
16 Sadoul, *Notes*, 237-8

address. Thus, while declaring that nothing had diminished the force of those factors originally impelling Germany to engage in peace negotiations with Russia, he also asserted that 'we know that the Kaiser can always find five or six corps of crack troops and with their aid organize an attack.' What should be done if that attack materialized? He did not address himself directly to this question, making instead repeated oblique references to the underlying purpose of his policy at Brest-Litovsk. That policy, designed to awake the German proletariat, was in his view the best defence against a resumption of hostilities. A German attack, he said, would serve to 'strike the coverings from the eyes of the German proletariat' and cause them to act in defence of the revolution in Russia. Nor was this the extent of his reliance upon proletarian internationalism. He also unveiled an aspect of his thinking which would be of the greatest importance in evaluating his conduct in the coming weeks. This was a mutation of an old theme in Bolshevik paranoia, the fear that the imperialist powers would unite to crush the revolution. There was, he said, a danger that the belligerent coalitions were conspiring to make peace at Russia's expense, agreeing to allow Germany to expand in the east in exchange for crushing the revolution in Russia. In that event the Germans would reject the *de facto* peace offered them at Brest-Litovsk and resume the war. There was no military defence against such an attack; Russia no longer had an army with which to fight. Instead it would have to trust that the European proletariat would not allow the revolution in Russia to be destroyed. Saying that his method of negotiating peace had been the best defence against a resumption of the war he asserted that 'by way of our tactics at Brest-Litovsk we have maintained and reinforced our connection with our natural allies – the workers of France, England, Germany, Austria and America.'[17]

When he addressed the Petrograd Soviet on the following evening he spoke in a more concrete manner. Here he flatly stated that 'I consider a German attack to be in the highest degree improbable' and calculated that there was a ninety per-cent chance against such a possibility. The Germans, he said, 'had to have the stamp of the Russian workers and peasants to show their own workers that we had signed their peace.' Gloating over his refusal to attach his seal to the German treaty he continued: 'Let Kühlmann go back to Germany and show his workers his peace and explain to them why our signatures are not there.' This in itself, he claimed, would create immense difficulties for the German government, but if it was to hurl those 'five or six corps of crack troops' against Russia, this

17 Trotsky, *Sochineniia*, vol. XVII, part I, 107-10

would 'create a powerful revolutionary protest in Germany.' Such a protest 'at the given moment is our best means for the protection of our country.' In conclusion he summarized his policy as succinctly as it has ever been stated: 'Listen! we are telling them – we are leaving the war. But if the German militarists succeed in moving their counter-revolutionary detachments against us, if the German annexationists attempt to strike a blow at our revolution, then we place all responsibility on the German Social Democrats who must exert all their efforts, all their influence to prevent the imperialists from strangling us.'[18]

On this basis Trotsky rested his case. It harmonized perfectly with the tenets of proletarian internationalism and was in accord with the dominant current of opinion within the Bolshevik party. In the exultation of the moment few seemed to care that it flew in the face of harsh reality, that it required a truly remarkable suspension of critical judgment to accept its postulates and that it placed the safety of the Russian revolution in the hands of men who had shown very little concern for the fate of that movement. Trotsky's faith is all the more remarkable when it is remembered that he was later to write: 'At the most difficult stages of the Brest-Litovsk negotiations when Lenin or I would come across a copy of the Berlin *Vorwärts* or the Vienna *Arbeiterzeitung*, we would silently point out to each other the lines underscored with a colored pencil, lift our eyes to one another for a moment, and then turn away with an inordinate sense of shame for the men who, only the day before, had been our comrades in the International.'[19] If Trotsky had known how deeply the German Social Democrats were committed to the support of the German government he would have felt more than shame, he would have well and truly known the meaning of terror. On the same day as the foreign commissar so heedlessly commended the soul of the Russian revolution to the German Social Democrats the German government was told by Ernst Heilmann, one of the leading journalists and political leaders of that party, that the SPD would go 'hand in hand' with the government and would not cause any difficulty over the decision to resume the offensive against Russia.[20] Ludendorff knew his Social Democrats very well; German nationalism had again triumphed over the principles of proletarian internationalism. If the tender neck of the Russian revolution was to be saved from the rope of German imperialism it would not be the German Social Democrats who

18 *Ibid.*, 111-16
19 Trotsky, *My Life*, 364
20 DSB, vol. I, 411-13

stayed the hand of the hangman. Having built the gallows and prepared the noose they were dutifully holding the coat of the executioner.

None of this was known in Petrograd where official celebration remained the order of the day. Lenin remained strangely silent, but no one seemed to notice. Only the elite of party and state knew Lenin's views on the subject and they, as well as Lenin, were bound to silence by the requirements of democratic centralism. The party had committed itself to Trotsky's policy; he had carried it out; and on 14 February, the Central Executive Committee put its stamp of approval on his daring strategy. No less a personage than Iakov Sverdlov, speaking on behalf of the Bolsheviks, moved a resolution of confidence, fulsomely declaring that the Central Executive Committee was 'deeply convinced that the worker-socialists of all countries together with the working class of Russia recognize the full correctness of that policy which in the course of the entire period of negotiations was conducted at Brest by the delegation of the Russian socialist revolution.' Like an echo, the resolution repeated Trotsky's words, commending the safety of the Russian revolution to the vigilance of the European proletariat and expressing the 'certainty that the workers of all countries would protect Soviet Russia from the ravages of world imperialism.'[21] The resolution passed without opposition, and all Russia settled down, somewhat uncomfortably, to see if the war was in fact at an end.

Russia did not have long to wait. On 16 February, less than forty-eight hours after the Central Executive Committee had solemnly endorsed Trotsky's policy, the Germans informed the Soviet government that 'on 18 February, at twelve o'clock, the armistice concluded with the Russian Republic will end, and a state of war will again be resumed.'[22] Lenin and Trotsky were meeting with their left Socialist Revolutionary allies when the telegram arrived, and, after reading it, Lenin passed it to the foreign commissar without comment. 'I remember his look,' wrote Trotsky, 'which made me feel at once that the telegram contained important and unfavourable news.' Lenin hastily finished the conversation with the left SRs in order to consider the new situation.[23]

What was to be done? Lenin wanted to ask the Germans if it was still possible to sign the peace treaty, but Trotsky would not hear of it. He still did not believe that Ludendorff could blatantly launch a new offensive against Russia and escape the revolutionary consequences in Germany. A

21 Trotsky, *Sochineniia*, vol. XVII, part I, 655-6, n.98
22 DVP, vol. I, 105
23 Trotsky, *Lenin*, 111-12

resumption of the war meant 'new sacrifices,' he said, 'but they are necessary so that the German soldier enters Soviet territory in actual fighting. They are necessary so that the German workman on one hand and the French and English workmen on the other may understand.' 'No,' said Lenin emphatically, 'there is not an hour to lose. The trial is a failure. Hoffmann will and can fight. To delay is impossible; they have already taken five days from us that I counted on. And this beast springs quickly.' [24] With Lenin and Trotsky at loggerheads the question was submitted to the Central Committee where on 17 February a coalition of left Bolsheviks and Trotsky, by a vote of seven to six, decided in favour of the foreign commissar. Rather than capitulating as Lenin desired, the Committee decided to send a message of inquiry.[25] This message was dispatched that day, and, for propaganda purposes, was phrased in a rather naive and innocent manner. 'The government of the Russian Republic,' wrote Trotsky, 'presumes that the telegram received by us does not in fact originate with those who signed it, and has a provocative character, in as much as even if it is granted that Germany has decided to terminate the armistice, warning of this, according to the conditions of the armistice, must be given seven days, not two, prior to its expiration. We ask for clarification of this misunderstanding by radio.'[26]

'Clarification' arrived promptly but not by radio. On the following morning, exactly as promised, Operation *Faustschlage* began, General Hoffmann unleashing his army and advancing unhindered toward Petrograd and Kiev. Nor was this an attack by 'five or six corps of crack troops.' Far from it, for Hoffmann had at his disposal only *Landwehr* divisions of over-age reservists and men wholly unfit for service elsewhere. The Russian armies, however, were in even worse condition. They were mere skeletons reduced to one regiment per division. Troop strength was approximately twenty per-cent of its pre-revolutionary level, and the number of men in a German infantry company was about equal to that in a Russian regiment. Spontaneous demobilization had totally destroyed the fighting capacity of the Russian army.[27] In the Ukraine the situation was even worse. Once again the invading German army was composed almost entirely of *Landwehr*,[28] but here the Soviets did not even have a sem-

24 *Ibid.*, 112
25 *Protokoly TsK*, 194-5
26 DVP, vol. I, 105
27 Fraiman, *Revoliutsionnaia Zashchita Petrograda*, 63
28 N.I. Suprunenko, *Ocherki Istorii Grazhdanskoi Voiny i Inostrannoi Voennoi Interventsii na Ukraine* (Moscow, 1966) 22-3

blance of a front. All that stood between Hoffmann and Kiev was the Red Guard of Antonov-Ovseenko. These troops were invincible when pitted against those of the Rada, but entirely outclassed when faced with the lame, the blind, the incapacitated, but organized reservists of the German *Landwehr*. 'It is the most comical war I have ever known,' wrote Hoffmann, 'it is almost entirely carried on by rail and motorcar. We put a handful of infantrymen with machine guns and one gun on a train and push them off to the next station; they take it, make prisoners of the Bolsheviks, pick up a few more troops and go on. This proceeding has, at any rate, the charm of novelty.'[29]

Soviet sources confirm Hoffmann's account. Propaganda was the first and only defence the Bolsheviks had against a German attack, and when it failed to destroy the discipline of Hoffmann's army they had no recourse but to order their remaining troops to abandon the northern front. Krylenko ordered a general retreat. All military supplies were to be evacuated and all bridges along the way were to be destroyed, but resistance was to be offered 'only where this seems possible.'[30] Even these orders were not obeyed, and the retreat promptly turned into a rout. Panic swept through the Russian army, and on 18 February, fewer than sixty German soldiers captured Dvinsk without firing a shot. Worse still, bridges over the Dvina fell into German hands undamaged. The victorious *Landwehr* simply drove across the river and pursued the retreating Russians for another fifteen kilometers before night brought a short end to their advance.[31] In despair, Stavka telegraphed Smolny: 'The front is melting away by the hour. Our one and only care is to save equipment. Demobilization is occurring spontaneously. Peace of any kind is needed at once. All units and establishments must be withdrawn.'[32]

News of the military debacle did not reach Petrograd until late in the afternoon. Until then the Central Committee had received only sketchy reports about the German preparations to launch an offensive. Planes had flown over Dvinsk, an attack was expected on Reval, and four new German divisions were reported to have arrived from the western front. On the previous day Lenin had again sought to convince his colleagues that they should resume negotiations with Germany. He had failed but had

29 Hoffmann, *War Diaries*, vol. 1, 207
30 Fraiman, *Revoliutsionnaia Zashchita Petrograda*, 69
31 *Ibid.*, 70
32 Chubar'ian, *Brestskii Mir*, 166

scored an important tactical victory when a plurality of the Committee agreed that if the Germans resumed their offensive the Soviet government would have to sue for peace. Six, including Trotsky, had voted with Lenin. Bukharin, Lomov, Uritskii, and Krestinskii abstained, while only Ioffe voted against the proposition. When word of the German preparations reached Petrograd Lenin summoned his colleagues to a morning meeting where he attempted to persuade them to decide in favour of peace. He argued that the conditions foreseen in the previous day's voting had already materialized, and that as a consequence negotiations should be resumed at once. Both Trotsky and Bukharin spoke against his motion. Trotsky argued that it was still too early to determine what the German masses would do and that the German army had not yet been called upon to advance into Russia. Bukharin agreed and was sufficiently bold to point out that Lenin was indulging in euphemisms, that he was not talking about negotiations, but capitulation. When the Committee voted it divided seven to six against Lenin. Trotsky had returned to the side of the left Bolsheviks again giving them a majority in the Central Committee.[33]

The question remained in suspense throughout the day. In the late afternoon Lenin found time for a short walk with Krupskaia, and they strolled along the Neva Embankment discussing the day's events. This brief interval captured by Krupskaia's pen offers us a quick glimpse into Lenin's mind on that fateful day. It shows that despite his steadfast demand for peace, Lenin was still not absolutely convinced that Trotsky might not be right after all. Let Krupskaia tell it. As they walked, Lenin 'kept repeating over and over again the reasons why the standpoint of "no war, no peace" was fundamentally wrong. On our way back Ilych suddenly stops, and his tired face lights up and he lets fall: "You never know!" – meaning a revolution may have started in Germany for all we know. In Smolny he reads the latest telegrams reporting that the Germans are advancing. His face becomes clouded and drawn, and he goes into his office to ring up.'[34]

The Central Committee was called to meet for the second time that day, this time under the dark cloud of the disastrous news from the front. Lenin was no longer prepared to tolerate procrastination, and undoubtedly the first person he informed of this fact was the foreign commissar. Trotsky, it will be recalled, had made a bargain with Lenin in January agreeing to oppose the advocates of revolutionary war in exchange for a

33 *Protokoly TsK*, 194-5, 196-200
34 Krupskaia, *Reminiscences*, 449

trial of his 'no war, no peace' strategy. Lenin, as Trotsky recalls, now reminded him of his political debt. The first instalment of this debt had come due the day before when Trotsky had voted in principle for Lenin's motion to sue for peace if the German offensive actually materialized. The time had now come for his second payment. When the Committee assembled Lenin demanded that the German peace terms be accepted. The evidence was now at hand; the German offensive was a reality; no military defence was possible. 'War is no joke ... The Germans will now take everything. This thing has gone so far that continued sitting on the fence will inevitably ruin the revolution ... We cannot afford to wait. This would simply mean consigning the Russian revolution to the scrap heap ... The issue now is that while playing with war we have been surrendering the revolution to the Germans.' Trotsky and Bukharin took immediate umbrage at the phrase 'playing with war' and struck back. The whole policy, said Trotsky, had been based on 'imponderable quantities' but that was no reason to make accusations such as this. 'No one is playing with war,' he said, repeating this phrase several times as if to convince himself, if not Lenin, that this was true. Nevertheless, he still contended that it was necessary for the Soviet government to act 'morally' by which he presumably meant that it was necessary to keep the faith of proletarian internationalism and give the German proletariat an opportunity to act against their imperialists. Bukharin expressed his astonishment at Lenin's accusation; 'nothing,' he said, 'could be further from the truth.' With an equanimity which Lenin in his turn must have found astonishing, Bukharin went on to say that rather than being surprised at what was happening he believed that 'events are happening just as they had to happen ... All that is taking place we foresaw. We said that either the revolution would spread beyond Russia or we would perish under the pressure of imperialism.' No one was playing with war according to Bukharin, because no one had it in his power to do so; instead, everything was developing according to the 'iron logic' of history. Imperialism, because of its very nature, was seeking to destroy the socialist revolution, and it was necessary to mobilize the workers and peasants to fight it. 'All we have,' he said, 'is our tactic of world revolution.' Lenin immediately pounced on Bukharin's last statement, and, no doubt with a meaningful glance toward Trotsky, declared that Bukharin had not even noticed 'how he went over to the position of a revolutionary war ... But if that is what we want we should not have demobilized the army.' 'A revolutionary war,' he said, 'must not be a mere phrase,' and, as he could not see anything with which the Soviet government could wage a revolutionary war, he would not support such a policy. Contrary to the views of Bukharin, Lenin said that the Germans were not necessarily seeking to destroy the revolution; instead, they might only want to loot the Russian empire. If they wanted the Baltic provinces they could have them in exchange for peace. Lomov contended that there was still insufficient evidence on which to base a decision, but Lenin demanded an immediate vote on the proposal to capitulate.

The moment of truth had arrived. If Trotsky honoured his obligation to Lenin, the motion to capitulate would pass; if he did not, it would fail. Painfully writhing in the tentacles of the dilemma of whether he should betray Lenin or his own conscience, Trotsky equivocated to the last. He proposed a substitute motion which sought to delay the decision, but the other members of the Committee decided to vote on Lenin's motion. Trotsky finally had to decide, and he chose to vote against his conscience. His one ballot gave Lenin a majority of seven to six in favour of capitulation. This decision was immediately made binding on the Bolshevik members of the Sovnarkom and Lenin was instructed to prepare a telegram to the German government expressing Soviet willingness to sign the terms presented at Brest-Litovsk.[35]

Lenin lost no time in exercising his mandate. Within hours the message had been drafted, presented to the Sovnarkom for endorsement,[36] and sent by radio to Berlin.[37] It was received in Brest-Litovsk on the morning of 19 February and forwarded to the German capital. Hoffmann, however, was not yet ready to make peace. His offensive had barely gotten under way, and he had no intention of ending it until he had conquered every mile he intended to demand at the peace table. If his over-age warriors were making good headway against negligible resistance they were still a long way from Narva, Pskov, and Kiev. Although the Russian army was disintegrating so also were the Russian roads, and his Quartermaster Corps was already complaining of insufficient horsepower to supply the needs of the army. More to the point, Berlin had not yet formulated the 'precise peace terms' now requested by the Bolsheviks. Hoffmann had his own ideas on this subject and had just informed Ludendorff of the terms he felt should be demanded, but they had not yet been approved by Kreuznach much less the Wilhelmstrasse.[38] Suspecting that it might be some time before he had terms which he could dictate to the commissars

35 *Protokoly TsK*, 201-5
36 Oznobishin, *Ot Bresta do Iur'eva*, 86
37 DVP, vol. I, 106
38 DSB, vol. I, 418-19

he chose to delay matters for a while by informing Petrograd that he could not consider their radio message as an official communication 'because it lacks authentic signatures.' Before considering the request to resume peace talks he demanded written confirmation of their message which was to be delivered to the German commandant at Dvinsk.[39] When Petrograd radio responded almost at once that a courier was on his way with the requested document Hoffmann noted rather irritably in his diary: '[Trotsky] seems to be in a devil of a hurry – we are not!'[40]

Unaware of Hoffmann's problems, but acutely conscious of their own, the Soviet government placed the worst possible construction on the German refusal to negotiate – the Germans intended to crush the revolution. Leaflets being distributed by the German army seemed to substantiate this conclusion as they proclaimed that Germany had launched its offensive to 'cleanse Russia which was sick and suffering from Bolshevism and Red Terror.'[41] Other leaflets spread by low-flying aircraft described the invasion as a 'police action' and attempted to portray the German army as a riot squad racing into Russia to save the local population from the 'blood-stained hands' of Bolshevik 'criminals.' Germany, it was said, was marching 'not against the Russian people, but against the fraudulent Bolshevik government and their myrmidons – the Red Guard.' Most ominously, the German proclamations declared 'it is our purpose to be just, as soon as the representatives of the Russian people establish themselves and turn to us to conclude peace.'[42]

Nor did news from the front improve. In the south the Germans captured Lutsk, Rovno, and Sarny, and virtually nothing stood between them and Kiev.[43] Reports from the northern front made even worse reading. Whole divisions had ceased to exist; entire corps were in flight; and all units were losing contact with those on their flank. On 20 February, the twelfth army reported that its men were 'retreating before the Germans, scattering in every direction without even returning their fire.' The first army informed Smolny that it had lost all contact with its troops and had no idea at all where the front might be located or what was happening there.[44] The Bolsheviks were faced with military disaster.

39 *Ibid.*, 417
40 Hoffmann, *War Diaries*, vol. I, 206
41 M. Philips Price, *My Reminiscences of the Russian Revolution* (London, 1921) 240
42 DSB, vol. I, 221; Bunyan and Fischer, *The Bolshevik Revolution*, 512
43 Suprunenko, *Ocherki Istorii*, 22-3
44 Fraiman, *Revoliutsionnaia Zashchita Petrograda*, 74-5

The only good news was of a purely negative character. The absence of reports identifying Austrian military units among those advancing into Russia and the Ukraine gave rise to hope that Austria had been unable to resume the war. Trotsky subscribed to this view, and, in general, all those who still hoped to avoid signing an annexationist peace grasped this slender Austrian straw in the maelstrom then engulfing the Russian revolution. A telegram was hastily sent to Vienna inquiring 'whether Austria-Hungary also considers itself to be in a state of war with Russia' and suggesting in the event that it did not, that the two governments 'proceed to the practical accomplishment of working out an agreement in Petrograd.'[45] No reply was received, but various rumours began to circulate in Petrograd and Moscow asserting that Austria had fallen out with Germany and would not resume the war. The left Bolsheviks immediately seized on these stories and argued that it was only necessary to wait a little longer for the paralysis supposedly gripping Austria to spread to Germany. Lenin poured cold water on these wildly exaggerated hopes, informing his Moscow comrades that 'I personally, in distinction to Trotsky, do not consider this communication confirmed; they say it was sent by radio and was then telegraphed here from Stockholm, but I have not seen such a document.'[46] Nor would he ever see it, for it did not exist. The rumour soon proved to be without foundation. Although Austria did hesitate to resume the war, and the German offensive badly strained Austro-German relations, the alliance between Vienna and Berlin did not break.[47] In late February, Austrian troops joined those of Germany in the Ukraine, and when the Soviet peace delegation returned to Brest-Litovsk the Bolsheviks found the Austrians in their accustomed position, lodged firmly under the German thumb. The war continued without the intervention of the central European proletariat in defence of the Russian revolution.

The extreme gravity of the situation required the Soviet government to take prompt and decisive action. If Germany would not make peace the Bolsheviks would have to fight. But with what? On 20 February, Krylenko reported to the Sovnarkom that the old army would not fight, and there was nothing to prevent Hoffmann from reaching Petrograd. Nor could the government rely on the garrison of the capital. Although it theoretically numbered one hundred thousand men, its actual strength had dwindled to

45 DVP, vol. I, 107
46 Lenin, PSS, vol. XXXV, 365
47 Oleh S. Fedyshyn, *Germany's Drive to the East and the Ukrainian Revolution, 1917-1918* (New Brunswick, New Jersey, 1971) 97-100

less than fifty thousand and, like the rest of the army, it lacked all will to fight. During December and January the capital had been stripped of its most dependable fighting forces in order to reinforce the Red Guards on the Don and in the Ukraine. Less than six thousand reliable troops remained in the city.[48] Having listened to this depressing report the Sovnarkom decided to accelerate the formation of the Red army, issue a special appeal to the population and form a Council of Workers and Peasants Defence to organize and coordinate those measures which could be taken to defend the revolution against the German offensive.[49]

The Council of Defence began its work by issuing a proclamation on the morning of 21 February explaining the attempt to reach a peaceful settlement with Germany, denouncing the resumption of hostilities and warning that the Germans might be seeking to 'smash Soviet power.' Although continually stressing the Soviet desire for peace the proclamation called for 'all conscious and courageous fighters of the revolution' to enlist in the Red army, for the existing army to purge itself of all 'corrupt elements, hooligans, marauders and cowards' and for the bourgeoisie to be forced 'in the most decisive and unmerciful manner' to 'do their duty' to the revolution. 'We are prepared,' said the Soviet government, 'to defend the conquests of the revolution to the last drop of blood.'[50] The same day Krylenko placed the capital under martial law, and the Petrograd Soviet independently joined the act by forming a Committee for the Revolutionary Defence of Petrograd designed to mobilize the civilian sector of society. Agitators were sent into the factories, recruiting centres were established for the Red army, luckless members of the bourgeoisie were conscripted to dig trenches and all materials needed to wage war were confiscated. Independent from these committees the recently formed Extraordinary Commission (the Cheka) began to arrest anyone even vaguely suspected of sympathizing with the Germans. On the following day, 22 February, an administrative amalgamation took place in which all agencies working to defend Petrograd were combined into one large Committee for Revolutionary Defence chaired by Iakov Sverdlov. M.D. Bonch-Bruevich, the last chief of the Russian general staff, was entrusted with the operational command of the Red army. In three days a very promising start had been made in organizing and deploying a genuine armed force to meet the German attack.[51]

48 Fraiman, *Revoliutsionnaia Zashchita Petrograda*, 63-7
49 Chubar'ian *Brestskii Mir*, 167; Fraiman, *Revolutsionnaia Zashchita Petrograda*, 78
50 DVP, vol. I, 107-9
51 Fraiman, *Revoliutsionnaia Zashchita Petrograda*, 78-84; Chubar'ian, *Brestskii Mir*, 167

Promise was one thing, fulfillment another, and the military situation remained grim. When Lenin placed the defence of Petrograd in the hands of Bonch-Bruevich he had told him: 'You and your friends shall have to start figuring out immediate measures to defend Petrograd. We haven't any troops. *None at all.*'[52] The best Bonch-Bruevich could do was send the first units of the Red army to locate the Germans. Having established that elementary bit of military intelligence the scouting parties were then to act as a 'screen' remaining in contact with the enemy but falling back on the capital as the Germans advanced. As new units were formed they would be sent to reinforce the 'screen' and hopefully make a stand before the Germans reached the Nevsky Prospekt.[53] Meanwhile all Petrograd awaited the reply of the German government to the Soviet peace proposal, but, as time passed, fear spread that Berlin would not reply and intended to throttle the Soviet government in its crib on the Neva.

So critical had the situation become by 22 February, that yet another proclamation entitled 'The Socialist Fatherland in Danger' was issued by the Soviet government. Written by Lenin, it brilliantly exemplified the fear rampant in Petrograd that the Germans intended to restore their version of 'order' to the city. Lenin, who since January had insisted that it was possible to purchase peace from Germany, now took up the refrain of the left Bolsheviks that Germany was 'fulfilling the task with which it has been charged by the capitalists of all countries ... to strangle the Russian and Ukrainian workers and peasants, to return the land to the landowners, the mills and factories to the bankers and power to the monarchy.' On the basis of this assumption the Sovnarkom placed 'the country's entire manpower and resources entirely at the service of revolutionary defence,' ordered 'all Soviets and revolutionary organizations to defend every position to the last drop of blood,' directed 'all able-bodied members of the bourgeois class, men and women, to dig trenches under the supervision of Red Guards' and specified that 'those who resist are to be shot.'[54]

Three observations are in order. First, it should be noted that both this proclamation and the one of the previous day called specifically for *revolutionary defence* against German aggression, not *revolutionary war* against world imperialism. Lenin carefully skirted the political demands of the left Bolsheviks and staked out his own ground on which he would stand or fall

52 Mikhail D. Bonch-Bruevich, *From Tsarist General to Red Army Commander* (Moscow, 1966) 245. Emphasis in original
53 *Ibid.*, 246ff
54 Lenin, PSS, vol. XXXV, 357-8

in the challenging days to come. This is made all the clearer by a second observation, that both proclamations emphasized the emphatic desire of the Soviet government for peace. While the two proclamations of 21 and 22 February raised a great cry for the defence of the revolution, they expressed not just the willingness, but the eagerness, of the Soviet government to make peace with the German 'bandits.' Contrary to the wishes of many of his colleagues Lenin kept his proclamations centred on the quest for peace and did not yield to the temptation of issuing an emotionally satisfying but hollowly dangerous declaration of war against imperialism. The sudden call to arms, Lenin made clear, was solely the responsibility of German militarists who refused to make peace with Soviet Russia. If the Germans should decide to make peace then the Soviet government would be willing to resume negotiations. In short, the fundamental policy of the Soviet government had not changed, only the circumstances in which it was conducted had been altered.

Finally, it should be observed that these proclamations made no call for a *levée en masse* based on the principle of *union sacrée*. They were exactly the opposite – a call for class warfare of the proletariat against the bourgeoisie, foreign and domestic. Here was Lenin's concept of a ruthless war against the bourgeoisie translated into the new circumstances created by the seeming unwillingness of the Germans to make peace. Contrary to the wishes expressed by the bourgeois and moderate socialist parties for an end to class enmity and the dictatorship of the proletariat, Lenin actually ordered the intensification of these policies. No appeal was made to the national pride of the Russian bourgeoisie, no invitation was extended to them to join the fight against the invader; instead, they were to be rounded up, organized into work gangs and, like beasts of burden, driven to the front where, at gun point, they were to be forced to dig the trenches from which the proletariat would attempt to defend the revolution. Lenin equated the Russian bourgeoisie with the German invaders, lumping members of the former ruling classes with German spies and saboteurs, and called upon the proletariat to strike down both with the same ruthless efficiency.

These measures astonished and puzzled foreign observers who could not understand how, in the hour of national disaster, Lenin could continue to stoke the fires of civil war. French observers in particular found it incomprehensible, both Noulens and Niessel, the head of the French military mission in Russia, telegraphing Paris that the Bolsheviks were simply 'unable to understand *union sacrée*.'[55] In this they were profoundly mis-

55 MAE, Guerre, Russie, 23/213 and 221

taken. Lenin understood the principles of *union sacrée* perfectly and, in those circumstances most likely to give birth to that hated doctrine, did all in his power to prevent its spontaneous appearance. His policy had the manifold advantage for him of deepening class hatreds, disposing of the bourgeoisie, intensifying proletarian pride, making any future reversal of the revolution more difficult and, most importantly, shifting the entire political spectrum of Russia to the left, leaving the moderate socialist parties dangling dangerously on the far right wing of the political world. It was a political masterstroke.

The political genius of Lenin is clearly evident in these events. The hallmark of that genius was his ability to maneuver untiringly in the shifting and dangerous sands of political change, finding some political profit in *every* situation which he could add to the power which he already exercised. In February 1918 the last thing Lenin wanted to do was wage war against Germany, but finding himself apparently backed into a corner where he had no other alternative, he did not hesitate to seize the initiative, make the policy of revolutionary defence *his* policy, shape it to fit *his* requirements and, in the process, secure immense political advantage for the future. Throughout the crisis Lenin never lost sight of his twin goals of personally retaining power and imbedding forever the principles of *his* revolution in Russia. Everything else was secondary, and he treated it accordingly.

His political genius is also evident in the question, which arose at this time, of whether Soviet Russia should accept allied aid in fighting Germany. With the resumption of hostilities it was a natural question to ask and quickly became a controversial issue in Petrograd. The allies had grown increasingly disillusioned with the various anti-Bolshevik groups which they had supported, and, as a consequence, when the peace conference at Brest-Litovsk broke up on 10 February, they were more than eager to fish in troubled waters.[56] For the first and only time in the dismal history of allied involvement in the Russian revolution there was nearly gen-

---

56 One of the officials of the British foreign office wrote at this time: 'We have backed every anti-Bolshevik movement; every one has collapsed. Every man on the spot ... considers that we are backing the wrong horse. In practice all our horses have now been scratched, and I venture to think that we have much to gain and nothing to lose by frankly acknowledging the fact.' Continuing the same metaphor which seems to have sprung naturally to the sporting minds of the foreign office another official wrote: 'The Ukrainian Rada was certainly a bad horse to back, Cossack is almost a non-starter, but Bolshevik would be the worst horse of the lot on which to lay our money, although we may run him as a pacemaker.' PRO FO 371/3299/31250

eral agreement among western leaders and their representatives in Russia on the proper policy to pursue in that country. With the exception of the American government, which disregarded the advice of its missions in Russia,[57] all agreed that everything possible should be done to support the Bolsheviks once they had resumed hostilities with Germany. Thus, on 17 February, the French foreign minister instructed Noulens to inform the Bolsheviks that if they were 'to resist the German menace and defend their country against our enemies, who are also their own, we will extend to them our cooperation in money and in material,'[58] and, on 21 February, Balfour informed Bruce Lockhart, his newly arrived representative in Russia, that he could assure the Bolsheviks of British cooperation if they chose to resist German aggression. Given Bolshevik objectives, he said, such cooperation would be based on 'calculation, not love,' but 'in so far as the Bolsheviks are opposing or embarrassing our enemies, their cause is our cause.'[59]

Lenin would have been sickened by the thought of being loved by the high priests of British imperialism, but an illicit liaison based on pure political expediency was completely within the range of his understanding. The proposals contained in the directives of the French and British foreign ministers, therefore, might well have served as the basis for allied-Soviet cooperation against the Germans, but London and Paris, it turned out, had much more in mind than simple cooperation against a common enemy. The allied governments placed no trust in the ability of the Bolsheviks by themselves to resist a German attack and wanted to stiffen their resistance by including other forces in the front to be formed against the central powers in eastern Europe. The French, in fact, were seeking to have a Japanese army form the nucleus of the anti-German front in Russia,[60] and the British wanted to continue and even expand assistance to Russian political movements other than the Bolsheviks. 'The very principles which induce us to co-operate with the Bolsheviks,' wrote Balfour, 'urge us to support any forces in Russia which seem likely to offer resistance to our enemies or aid to our friends ... We cannot pledge ourselves to abstain from such action in other parts of Russia as may in our opinion

57 Kennan, *Russia Leaves the War*, 432-3
58 MAE, Guerre, Russie, 29/91. For the development of French policy regarding the Bolsheviks see M.J. Carley, 'The origins of the French intervention in the Russian civil war, January-May 1918: a reappraisal,' *Journal of Modern History*, XLVIII, no. 3 (Sept. 1976) 413-39.
59 PRO FO 371/3299/32015
60 MAE, Guerre, Russie, 29/99-104

help to win the war.'[61] As if such intentions were not sufficient to destroy the basis for any cooperation with the Bolsheviks, the British and French had other motives in offering assistance to the Soviet government. The French hoped to secure political and economic concessions from the Bolsheviks,[62] and the British, despite their insistence on flagrantly meddling in Russian internal affairs, demanded that the Bolsheviks promise to abstain from spreading their propaganda in Britain. It is very difficult not to agree with Trotsky who bluntly told Lockhart that the allied leaders were like 'roulette players ... scattering chips on every number.'[63]

The Bolsheviks were well aware that the allies were supporting numerous counter-revolutionary movements in Russia and shrewdly suspected that London and Paris were attempting to draw Japan into the cauldron of eastern Europe. Any attempt to negotiate with the allies, therefore, was fraught with danger, but failure to do so was even more perilous. Trotsky admitted candidly to Lockhart that 'although he hated British capitalism almost as much as German militarism he could not fight against the whole world at once.'[64] There was also the nagging fear that the entente and Germany would reach a bargain at Russia's expense, and no meeting between Trotsky and allied representatives took place without the foreign commissar anxiously quizzing his visitors about that possibility. Nothing Lockhart, Sadoul or Robins could say set Trotsky's fears to rest, and this phobia, which sprung so naturally from the Marxist assumptions of the Soviet leaders, was to form a constant backdrop against which the problem of allied assistance would be played. At one and the same time it constituted the most serious obstacle erected by the Bolsheviks in the path of cooperation and most compelling reason driving them to seek allied assistance. A perfect dialectic emerged between the Bolshevik dread of being entangled in a monstrous imperialist conspiracy and the hope of smashing that conspiracy by reaching an agreement with the allies.

With the resumption of the German offensive the problem assumed great importance. The first two days passed without panic, but on the third day, when it became clear that Hoffmann was deliberately stalling, Trotsky began to sound the allied representatives about the possibility of receiving military assistance. Sadoul, as he described it, decided 'to strike a grand coup' and offered Trotsky the aid of the French military mission in

61 PRO FO 371/3299/32015
62 MAE, Guerre, Russie, 29/91
63 Lockhart, *British Agent*, 231
64 PRO FO 371/3299/31645

Petrograd to halt the German advance. Trotsky showed immediate interest, but knowing the ambiguous status of Sadoul insisted on receiving 'the word of the ambassador in the same sense.' Sadoul promised to arrange this, but noted in his diary that 'the only problem is that I have made this proposal on my own authority.'[65] Such a minor detail did not concern the audacious captain, and he promptly concocted a story to dispose of it. Not wishing to anger his volatile superior by informing him that he had usurped the ambassadorial prerogative, Sadoul told Noulens that it was Trotsky who had first solicited the aid of France. As Noulens had already been instructed to promise assistance if requested by the Soviet government, he fell in with the plan to put the French military mission at the disposal of Trotsky. Then Noulens began to talk about the conditions which would be attached to this aid, and it was only with the greatest difficulty that Sadoul was able to convince him that other matters could wait on the successful defence of Petrograd. 'Better late than never,' thought Sadoul, as Noulens picked up the telephone and informed Trotsky that 'in your resistance against Germany you may count upon the military and financial assistance of France.'[66]

Would the Soviet government accept this assistance? The question was discussed in the Sovnarkom on the evening of 21 February, but the left SRs objected so violently that no decision was reached, and the problem was referred to the Central Committees of the two governing parties.[67] When the Bolshevik Central Committee convened the next day, the issue appeared to be in considerable doubt. Despite the precarious position of Soviet Russia no one was eager to associate himself with Anglo-French imperialism. Moreover, all factions in the Central Committee now shared the suspicion that the imperialist powers had temporarily put aside their differences to preside over the funeral of the Russian revolution. Might not the allied offer be a trick designed, as the left Bolsheviks would have it, to discredit proletarian internationalism, or, as others suggested, to provoke the Bolsheviks into waging a self-destructive war against Germany? Trotsky laboured under the same phobic burden as the others, yet at this meeting came forward without apology to propose that the allied offer be accepted. In doing so he earned the fearful charge that he had become an ententeophile.[68]

65 Sadoul, *Notes*, 241-2
66 *Ibid.*, 243. Also see Henri A. Niessel, *Le triomphe des bolcheviks et la paix de Brest-Litovsk: Souvenirs, 1917-1918* (Paris, 1940) 277-8, and MAE, Guerre, Russie, 23/212
67 Oznobishin, *Ot Bresta do Iur'eva*, 91
68 Concerning this charge see Lockhart, *British Agent*, 229-32

Curiously, Lenin and several of his lieutenants were absent from the meeting, and Trotsky had to present his proposals to a Committee almost evenly divided between left Bolsheviks and lesser Leninists. The minutes of the meeting are available, but like the sanitized records of any executive committee they conceal more than they disclose. It is evident, however, that when Trotsky presented his proposal he was attacked from every side. Both left Bolsheviks and Leninists denounced the idea, Bukharin describing it as a plan to convert Russia into a colony while Sverdlov said that the allies were simply trying to use Soviet Russia as a tool against Germany. Everyone, except for Trotsky, agreed there was no advantage for Soviet Russia in becoming associated with the allies. Not a single member of the Committee spoke in support of Trotsky's motion, and near the end of the meeting he was reduced to tendering his resignation as foreign commissar. Bukharin, who had led the attack against accepting allied aid, sought to make his victory complete by submitting a resolution which amounted to a vote of non-confidence in Trotsky. Bukharin proposed that the Soviet government 'should not enter into any agreements concerning the purchase of weapons or the utilization of the services of officers and engineers from the French, English and American missions.'[69]

Given the nature of the preceding debate, this motion should have passed easily, but such was not the case. For reasons which the compiler of the minutes was careful to conceal the exact opposite occurred. Thus, immediately following Bukharin's motion Trotsky is recorded as making a vigorous defence of his own proposal which then passed by a vote of six to five! What happened? The only additional document available to explain this extraordinary occurrence is the famous note of Lenin laconically declaring that 'I ask that my vote be recorded in favour of taking potatoes and weapons from the brigands of Anglo-French imperialism.'[70] In abstract studies of Leninist theory this document is frequently and quite rightly cited as evidence of the Soviet leader's pragmatism, but its significance in the concrete circumstances of 22 February has been overlooked. Isaac Deutscher, for example, simply states that at the meeting Trotsky 'eventually ... converted the Central Committee to his view, and Lenin firmly supported him.'[71] But which came first, the conversion of the Central Committee or Lenin's support? Trotsky's memoirs make it clear

69 *Protokoly TsK*, 206-7
70 Lenin, PSS, vol. L, 45
71 Deutscher, *The Prophet Armed*, 386

140 Revolution and survival

that Lenin's support was responsible for the conversion of the Committee. Thus, he wrote: '*Lenin came vigorously to my aid, and* the Central Committee adopted my resolution by six votes against five. As far as I can remember now, *Lenin dictated the resolution* in these words: "That Comrade Trotsky be authorized to accept the assistance of the brigands of French imperialism against the German brigands." He always preferred formulas that left no room for doubt.'[72] Ten years after the actual event Trotsky could not be expected to remember the actual wording of Lenin's note, but the sequence of events remained imprinted on his memory.

What did happen that day in the Central Committee? With the aid of Trotsky's memoirs and the minutes of the meeting the following account can be reconstructed: Trotsky came to the meeting to argue for his policy of accepting aid from the British and French. Having presented his case, he found everyone against him. The left Bolsheviks, objecting for reasons of principle, feared that the revolutionary war for which they yearned and which seemed on the verge of realization, would be sullied by the touch of Anglo-French imperialism; the Leninists dissented presumably because they felt the proposal was a step backwards from the decision to sue for peace. Trotsky found himself isolated, and having submitted his resignation was about to be humiliated by the passage of Bukharin's motion. At this point Lenin's message arrived and fell with devastating impact on the united front arrayed against Trotsky. The Leninists switched sides, Bukharin's motion was forgotten and, with Lenin's ballot cast in his favour, Trotsky carried the day by one vote. Bukharin was so outraged by what had happened that he broke down and cried, saying that the party was being turned into a 'dungheap.'[73] Not wishing to dwell in filth he resigned from the Central Committee and the editorship of *Pravda*.

All of this raises some very interesting questions. Why, for instance, was Lenin absent from the meeting? More important, why were Stalin and Zinoviev, Lenin's lieutenants who could have given a lead to his lesser followers, also absent from the meeting? Was it merely fortuitous that Lenin's note arrived when it did? Or did someone, perhaps Sverdlov, slip from the meeting and bring back the note which signaled the switch to Trotsky's side? Unfortunately there is no evidence to answer any of these questions. 22 February was a very busy day for Lenin, and the need to organize the defences of Petrograd might well have kept him away from the Central Committee. The same could be said for Stalin and Zinoviev,

72 Trotsky, *My Life*, 389. Emphasis added
73 *Ibid.*

but it seems highly fortuitous that key members of the Leninist faction should be absent while the left Bolsheviks were present in sufficient force to stage a devastating attack on Trotsky. The consequences of the meeting also seem too spectacular to have occurred by chance. Lenin, who on that day believed it might be necessary to fight the Germans and who was already talking about the possibility of having to retreat to the Urals, had good reason for casting his ballot in favour of accepting 'potatoes and weapons from the brigands of Anglo-French imperialism,' but in doing so, and especially in the manner in which he did it, he also provided a much needed lesson for all members of the Central Committee, especially Trotsky and Bukharin, as to where real power in the party lay. The foreign commissar had assumed full responsibility for defending his policy of accepting aid from the entente, yet within minutes of his presentation he found himself attacked on every side and compelled to offer his resignation from the government. Bukharin, who had championed the cause of revolutionary war and who on 22 February had good reason to believe that his day of glory was about to dawn, assumed the responsibility for attacking the foreign commissar and was on the verge of uniting the entire Central Committee behind his leadership. Then as quickly as disaster had befallen Trotsky and fortune had smiled on Bukharin the situation was reversed by Lenin, who, not even bothering to appear himself, sent only a note which his followers accepted as sufficient warrant to abandon their previous position. The lesson was lost on no one, least of all Trotsky. Whether by deliberate preparation or chance occurrence, the confrontation in the Central Committee of 22 February was to have lasting consequences.

Ironically, the decision to accept allied aid was reversed almost at once. Although Trotsky moved quickly, arranging with General Niessel for French officers to direct the demolition of roads, bridges, and railways in the vicinity of Petrograd, cooperation with the allies never progressed beyond this point. When Trotsky spoke with the French general on the afternoon of 23 February, in fact, the German answer to the Soviet note had just arrived, and Bolshevik attention had already shifted from accepting 'allied potatoes' to satisfying the rapacious appetite of Germany. Trotsky knew this but said nothing to Niessel. Instead he worked out the basic guidelines of cooperation with the French military mission and listened to Niessel's plans for defending Petrograd. When the French general asked for authorization to begin the destruction of bridges south of the city, however, Trotsky had to backtrack. There were two possibilities, he said, the continuation of the war, in which case Niessel's plans would be implemented, or the conclusion of peace. If Russia made peace with Germany, he asked, 'would France agree to leave a military mission to organize a new army?' Niessel was not quite ready for this question and equivocated, saying that such a decision would depend upon actual events, but it was his personal opinion that as long as Russia remained a factor in the war against Germany cooperation of some kind could be arranged. The question of French assistance was left in limbo for the next few days with Niessel's detachments awaiting orders which never arrived. When it became clear that Russia would capitulate Niessel gave up hope and, in late February, ordered his mission to leave for France.[74] Cooperation with Great Britain proved even more ephemeral. Britain had no large military mission in Russia, and, consequently, given the rapid pace of events, cooperation never proceeded beyond Lockhart's verbal assurances that the British government would assist Soviet Russia in its war against Germany.[75] The entire question of allied aid was effectively aborted by the German message of 21 February agreeing to resume peace negotiations.

The German message was received on the morning of 23 February. Prepared at Kreuznach and reluctantly approved by Kühlmann it had been transmitted to Dvinsk, where, on the morning of 22 February, it was delivered to a Soviet courier waiting to receive it. In addition to the previous terms presented to the Bolsheviks at Brest-Litovsk the Germans now demanded that Russia surrender Livonia and Estonia, evacuate Finland and the Ukraine, recognize the independence of these two countries, demobilize the Russian army including the Red Guards, disarm all Russian warships, restore the trade treaty of 1904, and pay a substantial indemnity.[76] The Bolsheviks were given forty-eight hours to accept these conditions. The courier took more than twenty-four hours to reach Petrograd, and, consequently, when the Central Committee met to hear the German demands, more than half the time given to consider the document had elapsed. Once again 'the beast' had sprung quickly.

A decision was needed at once. When the meeting came to order Lenin declared that 'the policy of revolutionary phrases is at an end,' and if it should continue he would resign from the government and Central Committee. He absolutely refused to hear any further arguments in favour of a revolutionary war, declaring that 'for a revolutionary war, an army is needed. There is no army. This means we must accept the [German] con-

74 Niessel, *Le triomphe des bolcheviks*, 281ff
75 Lockhart, *British Agent*, 231-2; PRO FO 371/3284/34849
76 DSB, vol. I, 425-6

ditions.' A majority of those present attempted to escape this logic, confessing again their faith in the international revolution, insisting that the situation was not as bad as it appeared, arguing that the Germans would soon present new demands and asserting that men and material were available to wage war against Germany. Over the meeting, however, hovered Lenin's threat of resignation, and with the exception of Lomov, who passionately asserted that the obvious majority in favour of war should not be coerced by a single man, no one else chose to tempt the wrath of their leader. Lomov continued to argue that the majority should 'take power without Vladimir Il'ich,' but with the memory of the previous day fresh in everyone's mind, no one chose to give this advice serious consideration. Trotsky in particular declared that 'we cannot conduct a revolutionary war with a split in the party.' If Lenin chose to lead his faction into opposition the war would be lost before it even started. Krestinskii, Ioffe, and Dzerzhinskii shared this view and, like Trotsky, said they would not assume responsibility for splitting the party. Bukharin and his followers were left in a minority, and when Lenin called a vote on his proposal to accept the new German conditions, the motion passed seven to four with Trotsky, Ioffe, Dzerzhinskii, and Krestinskii abstaining. As the latter four had passionately wished to reject the German conditions, the result meant that a minority had prevailed over the majority, and in reality one man had bent all the others to his will.

A further word needs to be added about Trotsky's abstention. Given the perspective of time it is clear that the decision reached at this meeting was crucial in determining the fate of the revolution in Russia, but this is obvious only with the benefit of historical hindsight. Viewed from the rough and tumble circumstances of that feverish day in Petrograd the significance of the decision was not at all obvious. Trotsky, in particular, was not convinced that the decision would have lasting consequences, for he doubted that the Germans were willing to make peace. This belief arose from the manner in which he accounted for the failure of his 'no war, no peace' policy. Either the military extremists had gained power in Berlin, he calculated, or Germany and the entente had struck a bargain. In either case the Germans would continue their advance, and the Soviet government would have no option but to fight. In abstaining, therefore, Trotsky was keeping open what, in his mind, was the real possibility of launching a revolutionary war against Germany in a short period of time. With his vote he avoided a disastrous split in the party, paid the last instalment on his political debt to Lenin, and left himself a free hand to deal with the future. Just as Lenin had neutralized Trotsky's opposition to his policy by agreeing to give the foreign commissar an opportunity to test his 'no war, no peace' gambit, so now Trotsky was preparing to neutralize Lenin's opposition to a policy of revolutionary war. If Lenin failed in his bid for peace, then the road would be clear for a united Bolshevik party to wage all-out war against German imperialism.[77]

Understandably the members of the Central Committee whom Lenin had just bludgeoned were in a rather foul mood, and after the vote had been taken there was a great flurry of note writing as those who felt they had been roughly handled hastened to record their frustrations for posterity. Krestinskii, Ioffe, and Dzerzhinskii submitted a joint note justifying their abstentions by saying, in effect, that they had chosen the lesser of two evils. If a decision to wage revolutionary war had produced a split in the party, they said, 'then the position of the Russian Revolution would be much more dangerous than in the event of simply having signed peace.' The left Bolsheviks, who truly felt aggrieved by the circumstances of their defeat, prepared a much sharper note and resigned from all responsible party and state posts. Ominously, they also declared that they were 'preserving for themselves full freedom of agitation, both inside and outside of the party, in support of their position.'[78] This was a clear threat to split the party, and Stalin, who even at this time showed many of the characteristics which would later terrify two continents, was ready to read them out of the party. Not so Lenin. If necessary, he would accept the full consequences of his victory, rip the party in two and wage unrelenting political warfare against the left Bolsheviks, but not if such a struggle could be avoided. A firm believer in psycho-prophylaxis, Lenin had already begun to anoint Bukharin's traumatized ego with political patent medicine. As soon as his motion had passed, Lenin promptly sponsored another resolution calling for the party to begin immediate *preparation* for a revolutionary war. He brushed aside Stalin's crude response to the left Bolsheviks and pointing to his second resolution soothingly told Bukharin, Lomov, Uritskii, and Bubnov that there was no reason for them to assume a hostile attitude toward the party. The Central Committee had merely decided to *sign* a peace treaty, this did not mean that the treaty would be ratified or actually put into force. Only the Party Congress could decide that issue, and if it decided against peace, then preparations necessary to wage the revolutionary struggle desired by the left would already

77 Trotsky, *Sochineniia*, vol. xvii, part I, 135ff
78 Kommunisticheskaia Partiia Sovetskogo Souiuza, *VII Kongress, Stenograficheskii Otchet* (Moscow, 1928) 209

have been started. Was it not possible, he asked, for Bukharin and his associates to wait until the Congress had resolved the issue before deciding to submit their resignations? Did this mean, the left Bolsheviks replied somewhat suspiciously, that if they elected to retain their posts that they could still agitate against the decision of the Central Committee? 'Certainly,' answered Lenin, who for the moment radiated sweet reason in every direction. Moreover, he told them, he intended to circularize the Moscow and Petrograd Soviets seeking their views on the question, and until the results of this survey were known the dissidents should avoid any rash action.[79]

Making use of a complete repertoire of such arguments Lenin sought to dull the senses of his opponents and induce them to reconsider their decision to bolt the Central Committee and launch an immediate struggle against peace with Germany. He had several reasons for doing this. First, he was not certain himself that the Germans would agree to peace; if they did not, he would need the loyal support of everyone – especially Bukharin. If the Germans did agree to peace it would be immeasurably better to face his critics with a *fait accompli* than to do political battle over an issue which was not yet decided. Most important, however, Lenin knew that he did not have time to mount a full scale defence against the left Bolsheviks. In less than eighteen hours the German ultimatum would expire, and the decision to capitulate had yet to be ratified by the Central Executive Committee. Seemingly not understanding that they were once again being led down the garden path the left Bolsheviks agreed to reconsider their resignations while Lenin hastened off to present the Central Executive Committee with the decision to accept the new and more onerous terms demanded by Germany.

The Central Executive Committee proved to be just as difficult to convince as his colleagues. Energized by a large block of left SRs who were even more set against peace than Bukharin the meeting dragged on for hours, first as a closed session embracing only representatives of the two governing parties and then as a plenum including all members of the Committee. Speaker after speaker rose to accuse the Bolsheviks of everything from opportunism to treachery while such ardent opponents of peace as Karl Radek and Alexandra Kollontai prowled the hall in search of support for a policy of revolutionary war. Lenin spoke twice in favour of his motion to accept the German ultimatum,[80] but despite the fact that no

79 *Protokoly TsK*, 216-18
80 Lenin, PSS, vol. XXXV, 372, 376-80

one could argue with his logic, few would associate themselves with the conclusion that peace was an absolute necessity. Only the recitation of the terrible facts about the total collapse of the front made an impact on the deputies. Even then the debate dragged on while the deadline of the German ultimatum drew near. Finally, at five o'clock in the morning of 24 February, the question was called, and by a show of hands the German conditions were accepted, 112 against 84 with 24 abstentions.[81] The Sovnarkom promptly convened to act officially on the decision of the Central Executive Committee and with only minutes to spare Radio Tsarskoe Selo transmitted the Soviet decision to Berlin.[82]

Lenin had won, but there was still much to be done. While a courier was sent to Brest-Litovsk bearing an authentic copy of the message just sent over the wireless, Lenin prepared to defend his policy in the public forums of the capital. The left Bolsheviks, he knew, were planning to put their case before the workers, and if they were not to win the day by default he had to prepare his arguments against them. For several days, in fact, he had already been publishing major articles in *Pravda* under the pen name of Karpov. These articles were masterpieces of the polemicist's art and through reason and ridicule he had demolished every argument in favour of war.[83] Now, having come completely into the open in support of a capitulationist policy, Lenin threw off the guise of Karpov, acknowledged the earlier articles as his own[84] and splashed his Twenty-One Theses of January across the front pages of *Pravda* and *Izvestiia*. Consequently, when Bukharin, Kollontai, Radek, and the other left Bolsheviks reached the great industrial plants of the city, party activists had already been exposed to Lenin's point of view and were not easily swayed by emotional arguments. The British journalist M. Philips Price records that the war hawks 'came back to the Smolny in the afternoon, convinced that resistance was impossible.'[85]

Lenin also took another important step to strengthen his position. On the previous day he had promised Bukharin that he would solicit the views of the Moscow and Petrograd Soviets on war against Germany. This promise undoubtedly played a significant role in convincing Bukharin and his associates that they should reconsider their decision to resign from the Central Committee, for the Moscow and Petrograd Soviets were both

81 Price, *Reminiscences*, 246ff; Oznobishin, *Ot Bresta do Iur'eva*, 105ff
82 DVP, vol. I, 112
83 Lenin, PSS, vol. XXXV, 343-53; 361-4
84 *Ibid.*, 366-8
85 Price, *Reminiscences*, 249

hotbeds of revolutionary militancy, and the left Bolsheviks could reasonably assume that they would favour a continuation of the war. True to his word Lenin did address inquiries to the Moscow and Petrograd Soviets, but he also sent identical messages to *every* Soviet and revolutionary organization throughout Russia. The telegrams which poured out of Petrograd that day described the German peace proposals, explained the decision to capitulate, presented the two conflicting points of view on the question of peace and asked the local revolutionary authorities throughout the country to submit their opinion on whether peace, once signed, should be ratified.[86] Lenin had again outmaneuvered the left Bolsheviks, for instead of merely soliciting the views of the two most volatile cities of Russia he had gone to the country at large. He was convinced that Russia wanted peace and that the response from the country as a whole would support his policy.

Having reversed Bolshevik policy in an attempt to save the Soviet government from destruction Lenin also sought to salvage the revolution in the Ukraine. At his command, Stalin dispatched a telegram on 24 February to the People's Secretariat in Kiev explaining the action of the Soviet government in Russia and saying that the Kievan regime: 'should send its own delegation to Brest and there declare that if Vinnichenko's adventure is not supported by the Austrians and Germans, the People's Secretariat will not object to the basic provisions of the treaty concluded by the former Kievan Rada.' Stalin described the German terms as 'ferocious' but stressed the importance of the two Soviet governments working together.[87] Kiev reluctantly agreed, and on 27 February, as German troops were nearing the Ukrainian capital, announced that it was sending a delegation to Brest-Litovsk.[88]

But who among the Bolsheviks would take the road to Canossa? Who would be saddled with the onerous duty of signing the hateful treaty? Trotsky had resigned as foreign commissar and would have nothing further to do with the negotiations. No one else volunteered to take his place. When the Central Committee met on the afternoon of 24 February, Lenin suggested that Ioffe make the journey, but he emphatically declined the honour. He continued to refuse even when Lenin explained that, despite their ultimatum, the Germans might still allow actual negotiations once

86 Lenin, PSS, vol. XXXV, 491-2
87 Joseph Stalin, *Works.* 13 vols. (Moscow, 1952-4) vol. IV, 42-5
88 Theophil Hornykiewicz (ed.), *Ereignisse in der Ukraine, 1914-1922.* Four vols. (Philadelphia, 1968) vol. II, 47

the Soviet delegation reached Brest-Litovsk, and, in that case, it would be desirable to have a representative who had participated in the previous meetings of the peace conference. When Sokol'nikov spoke up urging Ioffe to make the journey, all eyes turned in his direction, and before he knew what had happened Sverdlov had suggested that he should join Ioffe on the trip to Brest-Litovsk. Now it was the turn of Sokol'nikov to object, and an incredible scene ensued with Sokol'nikov hastily nominating Zinoviev and Zinoviev assuring the Committee that his unwanted sponsor was truly better qualified. Sokol'nikov was trapped, and he could not escape. In effect, the Committee ganged up on Ioffe and Sokol'nikov, two of their most junior members, and forced them to accept the assignment. Ioffe was granted the privilege of accompanying the delegation only as far as Dvinsk where he could remain unless the Germans should actually appear ready to open genuine negotiations, but Sokol'nikov was stuck with serving as head of the delegation.[89]

Lenin filled out the delegation with three members from the government: G.I. Petrovskii, an old and trusted comrade then serving as commissar of internal affairs; Lev Karakhan, the secretary to all the previous peace delegations, and Chicherin. For the sake of appearances it was, of course, necessary to send someone from the Narkomindel, but in view of the lack of enthusiasm displayed by Ioffe and Sokol'nikov, it is not unlikely that Lenin had other motives in attaching Chicherin to the delegation. With good reason Lenin feared a further attempt to prevent the signing of peace, and, as will be shown in relation to the actual journey of the delegation, he was particularly concerned that Ioffe and Sokol'nikov might yet back out of their unwanted assignments. Lenin may therefore have sent Chicherin as insurance that the treaty would actually be signed. This was the view of DeWitt Clinton Poole, the American consul-general in Moscow and one of the most discerning foreign diplomats in Russia. It was his opinion that Lenin: 'turned to Chicherin who was his pèrsonal Man Friday. He knew he could count upon Chicherin – Chicherin was completely devoted to Lenin ... Knowing that he could be sure that Chicherin would do as he was told and do it promptly and exactly, Lenin picked him out and made him Commissar of Foreign Affairs and Chicherin signed the Treaty of Brest-Litovsk for Russia.'[90] With the possible exception of Petrovskii, whose views at this time are completely unknown, Chicherin was

89 *Protokoly TsK*, 219-25
90 Memoir of DeWitt Clinton Poole, Columbia University Oral History Project; Columbia University, New York City, New York, vol. II, 191

the only member of the delegation who wholeheartedly subscribed to Lenin's position. Ioffe was an ardent opponent of the treaty, Sokol'nikov was lukewarm at best, and Karakhan was soon to impress the Germans as an outspoken enemy of peace.[91] Lenin on the other hand had already won Chicherin's allegiance. Thus, Chicherin wrote: 'For all of us the break from our previous views of an underground revolutionary party to the political reality of holding state power was extraordinarily difficult, and at the time of my first conversation with Vladimir Il'ich I still had not succeeded in resigning myself to the necessity of signing the "obscene" peace. However, I completed the break and went to Brest-Litovsk.'[92]

The trip of the peace delegation to Brest-Litovsk was fraught with danger and uncertainty. The delegation left Petrograd late on the evening of 24 February, but, due to the disruption caused by the German offensive, made very slow progress, arriving at the small station of Novosel'e, forty-six kilometers from Pskov, at eight the next morning. Here they came to a stop, because the track was jammed with abandoned railway cars, and it was decided to split up the delegation, Sokol'nikov and Petrovskii proceeding toward Pskov while the rest of the party remained behind to inform Petrograd of their predicament. Both groups were to spend an eventful twenty-four hours. After many adventures Sokol'nikov and Petrovskii eventually reached Pskov where they found a small German garrison which had just occupied the city. Sokol'nikov promptly reported to the commandant, asking that Hoffmann be informed of their arrival, but was told by the embarrassed officer that the advance of the German army had been so rapid that he had lost contact with Brest-Litovsk. Having been promised that Hoffmann would be informed as quickly as possible, the Soviet delegation was taken to a hotel where they were given rooms for the night.

Back at Novosel'e, Karakhan, after some difficulties, finally succeeded in contacting Petrograd, but his message was so inexact that Lenin replied at once: 'We do not fully understand your telegram. If you are wavering this is inadmissible. Send out truce envoys and attempt to reach the Germans quickly.'[93] Another telegram was sent explaining the situation in

91 Germany. Auswärtiges Amt. Politisches Archiv. Russland 82. Band 2, folio 45. Rosenberg to Auswärtiges Amt, 1 March 1918. Saint Antony's College Microfilm Collection, reel no. 141

92 Georgii Chicherin, 'Lenin i Vneshniaia Politika.' In *Mirovaia Politika v 1924 godu. (Sbornik statei pod redaktseii F. Rotshteina)* (Moscow, 1925) 4. This article is reprinted in *Voprosi Istorii*, no. 3 (1957) but with significant omissions from the original.

93 *Leninskii Sbornik*, vol. XI, 29

more detail, but there was no way to comply with Lenin's instructions. A message had arrived from Sokol'nikov indicating that it was impossible to reach Pskov by rail, and, worse yet, 'idlers and some suspicious looking types of individuals began to poke about the train, staring in the frost covered windows and crowding about the doors.' The delegation decided to wait until the next day to continue their journey and ordered the train removed several miles down the track to escape the unwanted attention of the crowd. The next morning, having succeeded in moving the abandoned railway cars off the track, the train proceeded to Toroshino where a demolished bridge made further progress impossible. The Red Guard had to scour the countryside to find sufficient sleighs to carry the delegation to Pskov. At mid-day on 26 February, Chicherin and the rest of the delegation rejoined the advance party at their hotel.

The agony of the journey was not yet over. Pskov had just fallen to the Germans, and while Soviet authority had collapsed the German army did not yet have complete control of the city. Local counter-revolutionaries now came into the open and thronged the streets to taunt the Soviet delegation. The arrival of Chicherin's party in a long string of sleighs gave birth to the rumour that the Soviet government had fallen, and word spread quickly that 'Lenin and Trotsky had arrived in Pskov on their way to safety in Berlin.' An ugly crowd gathered in front of the hotel demanding that 'Trotsky' be turned over to them. When the Soviet delegation called on the German commandant the mob gathered around their auto and began to shout 'Death to the damned Bolsheviks!' The Germans dispersed the crowd, but the frightened Soviet delegation could draw little comfort from a situation in which their safety depended on German protection. Nor was the situation improved by a bemused German officer who remarked that if it was not for his troops 'the crowd would make short work of the Bolsheviks.' 'Yes,' Sokol'nikov shot back, 'they take us for your friends.' Later the delegation was escorted out of town to a deserted lodge where they passed the night under German guard. In the morning they left for Brest-Litovsk where they arrived on the afternoon of 28 February, having spent nearly four terrifying days in reaching their destination.[94]

No time was wasted in beginning negotiations. Three hours after the Soviet arrival the first organizational meeting convened. Rosenberg, who in the absence of Kühlmann now headed the German delegation,

94 Gorokhov, *Chicherin*, 34-8; S. Zarnitskii and A. Sergeev, *Chicherin* (Moscow, 1968) 70-5; G. Sokolnikov, *Brestskii Mir* (Moscow, 1920)

sketched his idea of how the conference should proceed. He suggested that political, economic, and legal commissions be formed to expedite the work of the delegates and that a draft treaty prepared by the German foreign office serve as the basis of negotiation. Sokol'nikov, not knowing exactly what Rosenberg had in mind, equivocated, hoping that the German diplomat would make his purpose clear. He reserved the Soviet position on the first suggestion, promising to deliver it on the following day, but rejected the proposal that a document which he had not yet seen should form the basis of negotiation. Instead, he suggested that the German ultimatum be used. Rosenberg agreed but, fearing that the Soviets might be seeking to evade the full rigour of Germany's demands, emphasized that 'there could be no discussion of the already accepted ultimatum.' Only the manner in which the ultimatum would be translated into a final treaty was open to negotiation. Rosenberg then laid down the law to Sokol'nikov, saying that the Soviets had only three days to conclude peace and that if the negotiations broke down the conference would be ended at once. In view of this time limit, he said, the Russians should 'avoid all theoretical discussions, retrospective recriminations and propaganda declarations.' Sokol'nikov was left with no illusions about the manner in which the conference would be conducted. He icily indicated that he understood the importance of bringing the negotiations to a swift and successful conclusion but, deciding to make one last effort to determine if any negotiations of substance were possible, asked that hostilities be suspended for the duration of the conference. As long as fighting continued, he asserted, 'there could be no genuine consideration of the conditions of peace.' This was the acid test which would determine the future course of the conference. In his memoirs Sokol'nikov noted that the Soviet delegation presented this proposal 'without any hope of success' but to determine if the Germans, as Lenin hoped, might still agree to meaningful negotiations.[95] They would not. Rosenberg simply pointed to the previous statements of the German government and reiterated that hostilities would continue until peace had actually been signed. On that note the meeting adjourned until next morning when the full conference would convene. The Germans, who had not yet completed the occupation of all territory which they wished to seize, magnanimously informed Sokol'nikov that the three days in which peace had to be concluded would be counted from 1 March.[96]

95 Sokol'nikov, *Brestskii Mir*, 15
96 DSB, vol. I, 446-8

Rosenberg had sought to convey a hard and uncompromising image in this first meeting, and he succeeded only too well. 'We were dealing with an imperialist Shylock who had firmly resolved to receive the pound of flesh due him,' Sokol'nikov wrote. How then should he play the role of Portia? Except for the admonition that the Soviet delegation should not leave Brest-Litovsk without signing a peace treaty the Central Committee had not provided it with any instructions, so the actual handling of the negotiations was left completely to the discretion of the delegation. It was clear, they decided, that the Germans would not alter the terms contained in their ultimatum, and while Rosenberg might agree to minor changes such concessions would be meaningless and would be designed simply to conceal the 'indecency of imperialist violence.' As they desired 'clarity' as much as General Ludendorff they decided unanimously to deny Rosenberg the luxury of clothing the nakedness of his treaty with artificial fig leaves. Instead, they would conduct negotiations in such a way that the final treaty would clearly bear the cloven imprint of 'imperialist violence' and 'forced revolutionary capitulation.' Reinforced by their belief that any agreement which they signed would only be an 'intermission without lasting historical consequences,' the members of the Soviet delegation decided to approach the negotiations from 'an agitational point of view,' continuing the same basic strategy of the earlier negotiations. In the altered circumstances of March 1918 this meant that instead of haggling over every detail of the treaty as Trotsky had done, they would accept every demand presented by Rosenberg, ostentatiously ignoring the peace terms to which they would place their signatures.

When the full conference assembled the next day Sokol'nikov rejected the German proposal to establish separate commissions and proposed instead that the treaty be dealt with in plenary session. As soon as Rosenberg had satisfied himself that the Soviet delegation was not attempting to delay proceedings he agreed to the unorthodox procedure and much to his surprise promptly found himself locked into a pattern dictated by Sokol'nikov. What ensued rapidly became embarrassing as, without discussion, the Soviet delegation accepted each part of the German treaty as it was read to them including a new demand that Russia surrender Kars, Ardahan, and Batum to the Turks. Rosenberg had wanted speedy negotiations, but the talks now were proceeding *too* rapidly. Not only would it be glaringly obvious that no real negotiations had taken place, but if matters continued in this way the talks would end before the German army had time to complete its conquest of the Baltic. Germany could demand and receive anything which it wanted from Soviet Russia, but as a matter of 'honour' the German army insisted that it conquer by the sword every-thing which Russia would surrender in the peace treaty. When the treaty was finished, therefore, and Sokol'nikov proposed that it be signed the following morning Rosenberg refused. 'Technical difficulties' in preparing the final document, he explained, would prevent its signing before the afternoon of 3 March. Unable to protest, the Soviet delegation retired to inform Petrograd of what had happened.[97]

Mere communication, however, was a serious problem for the Soviet delegation. Once at Brest-Litovsk they were held almost incommunicado by the Germans. Despite the evident desire of the Bolsheviks to conclude peace as quickly as possible, the Germans still feared they would attempt to use the resuscitated peace conference as a forum from which to spread propaganda, and they established a tight surveillance over the commu-nication of the Soviet delegation with Petrograd. Rosenberg confidently informed Berlin that it need not fear any leakage of information from Brest-Litovsk. The Bolsheviks, he wrote, can:

send couriers, but it will take them three or four days to reach Petrograd. We can, moreover, control how quickly they travel. The Hughes apparatus which was earl-ier available to them has been disassembled ... We will place our radio station at their disposal for very limited and important communication with their govern-ment. Thus, all that they wish to send, they must give over to us, and we can censor and exclude from transmission all that which we do not want them to send.[98]

Ironically, these measures were to lead directly to the initiation of armed intervention by the allied powers in Russia. Thus, shortly after the meeting of 1 March, Karakhan prepared two radio messages for transmis-sion to Petrograd. One was in code, explaining how matters stood at the conference; the other was in clear and asked that a train 'with an ample guard detachment' be sent to Toroshino for the return of the peace dele-gation to Petrograd. Both were handed to the Germans at the same time, for it was obvious that peace would soon be signed, and the delegation, not wishing to sample the hospitality of Pskov for a second time, wanted to assure themselves a speedy and uninterrupted journey home. Taken

97 Sokol'nikov, *Brestskii Mir*, 15-17. Also see Hahlweg, *Der Friede von Brest-Litowsk*, 634-43, 644-9, 651-3. The decision to approach the negotiations from 'an agitational point of view' was sanctioned retroactively by the Soviet government. See *Vladimir Ilich Lenin: Biograficheskaia Khronika*, vol. v, 297

98 DSB, vol. I, 447-8

together, the meaning of the two messages was clear, but if separated, the second became ambiguous and the most alarming implications could be read into it. The Germans, too clever by half, sent the second message at once while holding back the first for decoding. This was to have spectacular consequences, for when the second telegram arrived in Petrograd without the first, it created panic. Lenin interpreted the message to mean that the peace negotiations had broken down and that imminent disaster confronted the Soviet government. He immediately prepared a telegram addressed 'to all Soviets, to all, to all' which was sent to all parts of Russia reporting Karakhan's message and declaring that: 'this telegram, in all probability, signifies that the peace negotiations have been ruptured by the Germans. It is necessary to be prepared for a prompt attack by the Germans on Petersburg and in general on all fronts. It is obligatory to mobilize everyone and intensify measures of guard and defence.'[99]

Sent at eight o'clock on the evening of 1 March, this telegram created consternation throughout all Russia, but nowhere so much as in Murmansk. For weeks rumours had circulated in the north about an imminent German attack on the Murmansk railway, and when Lenin's telegram was received the Murmansk Soviet immediately wired back asking if, in the circumstances, it should enlist the assistance of allied military missions to defend the city and railway against German attack.[100] The inquiry reached Petrograd late the same night and was delivered to Trotsky. He ordered the Murmansk Soviet 'to accept any and all assistance from the allied missions and use every means to obstruct the advance of the plunderers.'[101] This was interpreted as a peremptory command, and on the following day, the Murmansk Soviet signed an agreement with the local allied forces placing regional military authority in the hands of a council dominated by allied officers.[102] While these events were in progress, Rosenberg, having discovered that Karakhan was not attempting to bootleg propaganda over the German radio, allowed his first message to proceed, and Petrograd, with great relief, discovered that its fear had been unwarranted. Lenin sent another circular telegram informing the local So-

99 Lenin, PSS, vol. L, 48
100 Partiinyi Arkhiv Murmanskogo Obkoma KPSS, Arkhivnyi Otdel UVD Murmanskogo Oblispolkoma i Gosudarstvennyi Arkhiv Murmanskoi Oblast, *Bor'ba za ustanovlenie i uprochenie sovetskoi vlasti na murmane. Sbornik dokumentov i materialov* (Murmansk, 1960) 145-6. Hereafter cited as BZU
101 BZU, 146-7
102 Mikhael Sergeevich Kedrov, *Bez Bolshevistskogo Rukovodstva (iz istorii interventsii na murmane)* (Leningrad, 1930)

viets that peace would apparently be signed after all, but warning them of possible German treachery. He issued an 'unconditional order' for local soviets to stiffen their defences against enemy attack.[103] For the moment no one noticed what had happened at Murmansk where even prior to Lenin's second telegram military authority had passed into allied hands. Four days later Royal Marines from HMS *Glory*, then at anchor in Murmansk harbour, went ashore, and a military build-up began which would soon lead to open hostilities between Soviet Russia and the allied powers. As one war was coming to an end another was in the process of starting.

At Brest-Litovsk the negotiations were at an end. The Soviet delegation suggested that the treaty be signed on 2 March, but the Germans politely refused. The Germans 'must be given their due,' wrote Sokol'nikov. 'Not once did they treat the Soviet delegation "incorrectly."' This led him to observe that 'the division of labour in capitalist society was brilliantly expressed in this contrast of unceremonious plunder at the front and mannerly gentlemanliness behind the green table.' Finally Rosenberg could not delay matters any longer, and, on the afternoon of 3 March, the fully inscribed copies of the Treaty of Brest-Litovsk were laid out on the green tables ready for signatures. Keeping in mind the 'agitational character' he wished to attach to the treaty, Sokol'nikov bitterly attacked the document before affixing his signature. Russia, he said, was being forced to sign 'a strictly imperialist and annexationist peace.' He characterized it as a peace dictated at 'the point of a gun,' a peace which Russia was compelled to accept 'with its teeth clenched,' but a peace which would be of short duration. 'We are signing the peace treaty presented to us as an ultimatum immediately,' he declared, 'refusing to discuss it ... waiving all discussions as completely useless in the given circumstances.' Only Hoffmann interrupted this Soviet curse pronounced over the yet unsigned treaty. 'The same old gibberish' he remarked when Sokol'nikov dared declare that 'the triumph of German imperialism is only temporary.' The other delegates saved their comments until Sokol'nikov had finished, the Austrian representative then expressing his regret that the last day of the negotiations should be marred by the Soviet statement and Rosenberg cynically asserting that 'Russia has not been forced to sign peace. It depends on the free will of the Russian people whether to accept the German conditions or continue the war.' The prize for hypocrisy went to the Turkish delegate who praised the treaty as the crowning realization of the principles of the Russian revolution, particularly in that it assured the self-determination

103 Lenin, PSS, vol. XXXV, 410

of the peoples of such areas of Kars, Ardahan, and Batum.[104] Choking on these statements, but refusing to be provoked, the Soviet delegates signed the treaty and left for Petrograd. The terribly disillusioning attempt by Soviet Russia to force a revolutionary peace upon the world was at an end.

7
Brest-Litovsk: an evaluation

Germany ... and Russia ... are resolved to live henceforth in peace and amity with one another. Article I, Treaty of Brest-Litovsk. 3 March 1918

The previous negotiations at Brest-Litovsk ... made it sufficiently evident that the so-called 'peace by agreement' is in fact an imperialistic and annexationist peace ... a peace dictated at the point of the gun ... and which revolutionary Russia is compelled to accept with its teeth clenched. Sokol'nikov, 3 March 1918

The Peace of Brest-Litovsk has not fared well in the annals of history. It has called forth nearly universal condemnation, and almost as if echoing the frightful curse of Sokol'nikov, historians have reserved their harshest words to describe its contents. British, French, and American historians have painted the document in the darkest colours and held it up as an example of what would have befallen the western powers if they had been so unfortunate as to have been defeated by Germany. Soviet historians have been even more severe than their western colleagues. From first to last they have seen the treaty as nothing less than a monstrous imperialist land grab, an interpretation which since the nineteen-thirties, when they began to dress themselves in the garb of Russian nationalism, has grown increasingly shrill. Nor has the treaty been popular in Germany. Many Germans found the treaty unpalatable from the start, and its subsequent use to justify the much less onerous, yet painful, conditions imposed on them at Versailles did nothing to increase its popularity. Present day historians in both Germanies accord the treaty much the same treatment as historians elsewhere.[1] Most historians agree on the fundamental interpre-

---

1 A notable exception is Winfried Baumgart, 'Brest-Litovsk und Versailles: Ein Vergleich zwier Friedensschlüsse,' *Historische Zeitschrift* CCX, no. 3 (June 1970) 583-619. In this

tation of the treaty, arguing primarily over which pejoratives to use in describing it. The simple fact that the treaty had an effective life of only eight months has also contributed to the near universal scorn in which it is held. More frequently than not the Treaty of Brest-Litovsk is remembered as the 'dictated peace' or, thanks to J.W. Wheeler-Bennett, the 'forgotten peace.'

What exactly were its terms? Contained in fourteen crisp articles, one map, and several voluminous appendices they solemnly, but prematurely, celebrated the triumph of German militarism over the revolutionary masters of the old Russian empire. With one blow, article three separated Poland, Lithuania, and Courland from Russia. Articles four and six effectively severed even greater areas from the Russian state, requiring that Ardahan, Kars, and Batum in the Caucasus; Estonia, Livonia, Finland, and the Aaland Islands in the Baltic; and the whole of the Ukraine 'will, without delay, be cleared of Russian troops and the Russian Red Guards.' Furthermore, Russia was obligated to 'conclude peace at once with the Ukrainian People's Republic,' 'recognize the treaty of peace between that State and the Powers of the Quadruple Alliance,' acknowledge that the fate of Ardahan, Kars, and Batum would be settled by the people of those districts in agreement with Turkey, and agree that 'Estonia and Livonia will be occupied by a German police force until security is ensured by proper national institutions and until public order has been established.' In concrete terms Germany sheared 780,000 square kilometres of territory from the former Russian empire, reduced its population by fifty-six million people, and deprived it of one-third of its rail network, seventy-three per-cent of its iron ore production, and eighty-nine per-cent of its coal supply. For Russia the hands of time were set back to the mid-sixteenth century when Muscovy barely extended west of Smolensk or south of Kursk.

Nor was that all, for during the two weeks after the resumption of hostilities the German army advanced even beyond its own ambitious line of conquest. To avoid the creation of large and militarily unmanageable salients in the Baltic and the Ukraine Hoffmann had been forced to undertake

article Baumgart attempts to abstract the Treaty of Brest-Litovsk from its immediate historical setting and compare it with other peace settlements, particularly Versailles. He finds many parallels between the two and, provided both are viewed as preliminary, rather than definitive settlements, believes that they are comparable with earlier peace treaties. Although it may be argued that some of his conclusions are rather strained, it is difficult to dissent from his call for historians to use a broader frame of reference when evaluating Brest-Litovsk and Versailles.

an offensive in central Russia as well. By 3 March, his legions had advanced to Polotsk, Orsha, and Bobruisk, and he had no intention of evacuating this region. Instead, article four of the treaty provided that only when 'general peace is concluded and Russian demobilization is carried out' would Germany be obligated to surrender this large bloc of territory. Until then Hoffmann would sit on the doorstep of Smolensk, the gateway to Moscow, and offer a constant reminder to the Soviet government of its numerous obligations to Germany. Moreover, in case the Soviet government should harbour any thoughts of resuming the war, the treaty provided that Russia was to be disarmed. She was required to 'carry out the full demobilization of her army inclusive of those units recently organized by the present Government,' and 'bring her warships into Russian ports and there detain them until the day of the conclusion of a general peace or disarm them forthwith.' Germany also demanded the political disarmament of Soviet Russia, requiring that 'the contracting parties will refrain from any agitation or propaganda against the Government or the public and military institutions of the other party.' This clause also extended to the territories occupied by the central powers and those areas stripped from the Russian empire. Gagged, as well as bound, the Soviet state was to await the pleasure of the conqueror.

Economically, the treaty spelled out the manner in which Germany would begin to exploit its new found dominion in Russia. With seeming idealism article nine declared that 'the contracting parties mutually renounce compensation for their war expenses ... as well as compensation for war losses ... inclusive of all requisitions effected in enemy country.' But behind the idealism lurked German rapacity, for the war had been fought primarily on Russian soil and the Germans had liberally helped themselves to Russian property. This article, therefore, legalized the requisition of Russian resources and foreclosed any attempt by Russia to claim compensation. But there was more, for in a supplement to the treaty the two states agreed 'to reimburse the expenses incurred by the other party for its nationals who had been made prisoners of war.' As the number of Russian prisoners in Germany far exceeded that of German prisoners in Russia this meant that Russia, in disguised form, would be forced to pay a very substantial war indemnity. To add insult to injury, it was known that Russian prisoners of war had been efficiently employed in German agriculture and industry and had played a large role in assuring the success of Germany's *Kriegswirtschaft*. In effect, therefore, although Russia was exempt from paying the expenses of those prisoners actually employed in industry or agriculture, the stipulation forced Russia to subsidize the German economy, not only providing the labour needed to keep it in operation, but also much of the capital needed to pay the living expenses of this several million man pool of forced labourers. Russia would pay the bills while Germany collected the profits. Nor was there any guarantee that this inequitable arrangement would end with the signing of peace. On the contrary, the conditions governing the exchange of prisoners were extraordinarily vague, and there was nothing to stop Germany from returning only those prisoners who were a drag on the German economy while retaining those whose labour could be profitably exploited. In fact, repatriation of Russian prisoners of war proved to be a very slow process, and in 1920, a large number of Russian prisoners of war remained in Germany.

Germany did not stop here. At the last minute Berlin changed its mind about reinstating the German-Russian trade treaty of 1904 and insisted instead that the Russian tariff of 1903 be resurrected until a new trade treaty could be negotiated. By itself the tariff of 1903 was highly favourable to Germany, but it was made even more advantageous by the specification contained in the treaty that until the negotiation of a new trade agreement Germany would enjoy most favoured nation status in all commercial and economic relations. This would reduce duties on German imports to a very low level, and in the chaotic state of the Russian economy leave Russian manufacturers almost unprotected. Nor could Russia seek to protect her natural resources, for another clause in the treaty specified that Russia was to place no ban or tax upon exports of timber and ores to the Reich. Furthermore, German investments in Russia, sequestered during the war, were to revert to their previous owners, and Russia undertook to pay full compensation for the expropriation of any property acquired by German subjects either before or after the conclusion of the treaty. The Germans had a strangle hold on Russia and intended to tighten their grip. Presumably for comic relief the treaty specified that the two states 'are resolved to live henceforth in peace and amity with one another.'

This was black humour at its worst. With a treaty of this type 'peace and amity' between Russia and Germany were impossible. Given its conditions, relations could only grow worse, for the treaty fostered the illusion in Germany that anything could be demanded of Russia and the conviction in Russia that any violation of the treaty was justified. Much in the way that unlimited printing of paper money destroys its value the unilateral imposition of onerous terms destroys the value of international agreements. From beginning to end this treaty was recognized in both lands as a fraud and a swindle, devoid of all moral force, and dependent entirely upon armed might for its enforcement. If the mailed fist should disappear the treaty would collapse. Well aware of this, both sides chose to ignore the terms of the agreement, which were by themselves meaningless, and concentrate on the utilization of raw power, the one and only reality of their relationship. Peace had been signed, but a *de facto* war continued. In the circumstances of March 1918 peace was impossible. Too much was at stake for the men in Berlin and Petrograd to allow anything to stand in the way of their single-minded, but separate, pursuit of power. As long as the German high command remained confident of victory over the entente, and the Bolshevik Central Committee continued to believe that the world war would inevitably give birth to world revolution, nothing would stop them from waging war on each other and anyone else who crossed the path of their ambitions. In these conditions a peace treaty was a mockery of the millions who had died and would die on the farflung battlefields of Europe.

The treaty concluded at Brest-Litovsk, however, was a valid reflection of existing power relationships in eastern Europe. At the time of its signature Germany was at the zenith of her power and Russia reduced to impotence. Why then should Germany not force its brand of peace upon a prostrate Russia? Kühlmann knew, but the army would not listen to him. Russia, he tried to tell Ludendorff, would not remain forever prostrate at the feet of Germany. Ludendorff, on the other hand, assumed that he could eliminate Russia as a great power. The ease with which his armies overran the country, and the speed with which the Soviet government capitulated simply confirmed his judgment. The only reason that he did not make even more extortionate demands was that, for the moment, he had nothing further which he wanted from Russia. He assumed that anything he wanted in the future would be his for the asking and that Russia had become a region reserved for German exploitation.

In its turn this belief was based in part on the assumption, generally accepted throughout Europe at this time, that Russia was not, and never had been, quite 'European' in nature. Those elements of European civilization which Russia did enjoy, it was felt, were the result of borrowing from the west and were nothing but a thin veneer over Russia's 'Asiatic' core. Russia owed her status as a great power to the tireless efforts of the 'better elements' of her population, mainly of foreign origin and principally German extraction, who had imposed civilization on an 'Asiatic' society. If the revolution had done anything, it was believed to have stripped this veneer from Russia and destroyed those 'better elements' who had been responsible for Russian greatness. Deprived of them, Russia would wallow indefinitely in chaos and disorder. The German attitude toward Russia was shaped in no small part by these racist assumptions. Combined with the previous history of increasing European exploitation of the non-European parts of the globe these assumptions inclined German leaders to look upon Russia as a potential India or China, a region to be dealt with first on the basis of unequal treaties and then as a colony. It might be necessary to deal with other imperial powers attempting to poach on this German preserve, but it certainly was not necessary to come to terms with the Russians. They would be forced to do the bidding of Berlin.

These were comforting thoughts but not valid assumptions. If the treaty reflected *existing* power relationships it disregarded the manner in which those relationships might evolve in the future. More an act of wish-fulfillment than a serious political venture, the treaty ignored almost everything which had shaped the destinies of eastern Europe. It overlooked the manner in which Russia had shaken off past conquerors, the immense social upheaval which had just occurred, the difficulties of administering such a vast and unstable territory and the ruthless dynamism of the Bolsheviks. Most of all it ignored the social and political forces unleashed by the Great War and the manner in which they were already undermining the foundations of European society. It was a treaty built on sand. By attempting to freeze a moment of history into permanency the German militarists miscalculated very badly. Not only did they disregard the potential strength of Russia and the Bolsheviks, they also chose to treat eastern Europe as a vacuum which only they could fill. If Russia did not revive and seek to redeem itself other ambitious states were bound to rush into the vacuum. The treaty, therefore, was not merely sterile, doomed to die in a short period of time, it was dangerously counter-productive of anything which could even remotely be called German 'national interest.' By demanding its pound of flesh, as Sokol'nikov called it, Germany was foreclosing her entire future in Russia.

It was no accident that the leading German diplomats and politicians opposed this treaty. They were the ones who would have to pick up the pieces once the war was over, and they instinctively knew the damage which would be done by this monstrous caricature of their art. Kühlmann had pleaded in vain for the Kaiser to recognize that the seizure of Estonia would alienate not only the Bolsheviks, but *any* Russian government. The Bolsheviks might not matter, but at some time in the future Germany would want Russian cooperation and, having stolen the gateway to Petrograd, was not likely to be received cordially. Payer had

pleaded for an understanding of the internal damage which an annexationist policy would create, but he too was ignored. It was the generals and, to
a lesser extent, the bureaucrats who demanded that an annexationist
peace be forced upon Russia. The generals with their single-minded pursuit of military 'necessity' and the bureaucrats who believed that everything could be handled 'administratively' failed to understand the far-
reaching political significance of what they were doing. For them it was
just another military maneuver or administrative procedure requiring
'clarity' for best results. They did not realize that in politics 'clarity' is a
fleeting phantom present at one moment and gone the next. Kühlmann
understood this, but neither the Kaiser nor the army would listen to him.

Kühlmann was an imperialist and one of the foremost advocates of a
German dominated *Mitteleuropa*, but unlike his opponents, he had a clear
and consistent view of what he hoped to accomplish. Of equal importance,
he realized the limits of German power. Rather than staking the entire
future of Germany on the success of military operations he wanted to
consolidate the German position in central Europe, prepare for negotiations and bargain with the entente from a position of strength. His Russian
policy was an integral part of this larger political framework and subordinate to it. With rip tides of incalculable political energy racing across the
continent it is questionable if *any* foreign policy could, at that late date,
have saved Germany from the forces unleashed by the Great War, but, in
contrast to the adventurist policies actually adopted, Kühlmann's proposals did offer some hope of security for German society as it was then
structured. In many ways Kühlmann was trying to save German society
from itself, for that society entrusted vast and irresponsible power to a
military elite primarily concerned with its own narrow interests and aspirations. Only the emperor could call the military 'demi-gods' to account, and
Wilhelm II was not the man to do this. Sharing the ethos and attitudes of
his generals, Wilhelm reinforced rather than limited the power of the
high command to commit Germany to policies based on military considerations alone. Governed in this manner the Reich was almost certainly
doomed to destruction, for Germany's military leaders only poorly understood the relationship between means and ends. Germany simply did not
have the resources to impose its will on the continent, and any attempt to
do so was indulging in fantasy and courting disaster. Time and again German military leaders had failed to comprehend the essentially political
nature of the struggle in which they were involved, and by attempting to
solve their problems by brute force had only made them worse. With the
irony which so frequently accompanies great events the German militar-

ists completely disregarded Clausewitz, their greatest theorist, while the diplomats and politicians clamoured in vain to remind them of his words.

Ignored in his native land Clausewitz found an avid disciple on the Neva. Lenin never forgot that 'war is the continuation of politics by other means.'[2] While the left Bolsheviks pronounced in favour of a revolution-ary war as an article of faith in proletarian internationalism Lenin insisted on posing the question in Clausewitzian terms. A revolutionary war he said could be justified only if it would assist the outbreak of revolution in central and western Europe. But where were the revolutionary move-ments in those parts of Europe? Certainly they existed and were maturing rapidly, but how long would it be before they ripened sufficiently to benefit from a revolutionary *jihad* in the east? And what resources were available for that war? 'For a revolutionary war, an army is needed,' he lectured his colleagues, 'There is no army,' and thus there could be no revolutionary war. His logic was irrefutable. To avoid this logic his oppo-nents had to transcend rationality and enter the realm of emotion, but when they did Lenin ridiculed their flight from reason. For men who prided themselves on their 'scientific' socialism such criticism was deva-stating.

But Lenin did not stop here. He also posed the question in terms of Marxist analysis. Which social classes, he asked, would war benefit? If it did ignite revolution in central and western Europe then undoubtedly it would benefit the proletariat, but what if it failed? Without adequate pre-paration a revolutionary war would fail, and failure would mean the end of the revolution in Russia. Was it worth staking the entire revolution on the slim possibility that a revolutionary war would bring the quiescent central European proletariat to life? Not for Lenin. If there had been any sign of revolutionary quickening in Germany (as there was in Hungary in 1919 when Soviet Russia did seek to aid a foreign revolution) Lenin would have been the first to preach a crusade, but in the circumstances of early 1918 he could not justify such a policy. When the left Bolsheviks threw his own words in his face and asked why he was now hesitant when in October he had been bold, he had two cogent replies. In October, he said, Russia had already enjoyed seven months of unfettered revolutionary freedom, that at that moment the revolutionary movement in Russia had been at flood tide and that the fortunes of the Kerensky government had been at low ebb. Where in central Europe had a revolution even started? Where had

2 For example see Lenin's praise of Clausewitz as 'one of the greatest authorities on military matters.' Lenin, PSS, vol. XXVI, 292

March, let alone November, arrived? His second response was equally to the point. A conspiratorial party, he said, could afford to take chances; if it failed it could always regroup and try again. A party which formed the government of a revolutionary state could not do this, for it held the fate of the revolution in its hands. It could not gamble with the revolution, for the masses who had fought and suffered to make it a reality would not understand this. If it failed it would be hopelessly discredited.

Lenin was adamant. He argued that a revolutionary war proclaimed in the absence of a strong revolutionary movement in central Europe would be nothing less than counter-revolutionary in nature. It would benefit only the allied imperialists and the Russian bourgeoisie, the former because it would distract Germany from the western front, and the latter because it would allow them to escape the full rigour of the revolution. If Soviet Russia embarked on a revolutionary war without first having set its own house in order the conflict might well turn into a *national* war against Germany in which, for the sake of mere survival, it would be necessary to compromise with the bourgeoisie. Above all else Lenin feared the dread spectre of *union sacrée*, and, even in mid-February when it appeared as if he had no choice but to fight Germany, he formulated a policy of proletarian defence based on intensified class conflict rather than declare a revolutionary war which might eventually force a compromise with the bourgeoisie. So fearful was Lenin of the compromises which a revolutionary war might force on the Soviet government that he was prepared to resign and wage war on his own party rather than join his colleagues in a venture which he was certain would fail.

All this serves to call attention to Lenin's pragmatism, but it also highlights the burning emotions which lay behind it and which were obscured by the icy logic and cold rationalism of his argument. Lenin, in fact, was quite emotional and approached politics with a passion unsurpassed by any of his colleagues. It was his entire life and consumed all the other emotions which might have dissipated its burning fury. No wonder then that at every stage of his political career he fought so fiercely for his policies. In this instance he desired a world workers' revolution as passionately as the left Bolsheviks, but where they would allow their emotions, of which he hardily approved, to lead them into disaster he chose to find an outlet elsewhere for his own. The difference between Lenin and his opponents was not that of emotion, but the manner in which they chose to channel those emotions. Instead of focusing his hatred on the German bourgeoisie which was effectively beyond his grasp he turned it against the former Russian ruling classes who were at his mercy. If he allowed himself the luxury of attempting to fight both at once, he reasoned, the latter would escape him while the former would probably destroy the revolution.

For Lenin, therefore, war was a serious proposition and nothing to be played with. For him, it was, as Clausewitz would have it, one more tool of the politician's trade, and like any other master craftsman Lenin did not misuse his tools. In his skilful hands war became a very effective instrument of policy. Lenin understood that it is always better to deal in threats than actual war. Once begun, a war is difficult to end, and its results can not be foreseen. Threats and promises, on the other hand, were merely words and committed him to nothing; if he actually launched a revolutionary war not only would he lose the use of those valuable instruments, he would also have to make good his promises. Lenin, therefore, refused to be provoked. Just as he had held back from launching the revolution in July 1917, so also he refused to declare a revolutionary war in February 1918. On neither occasion was he ready for a fight to the finish, and rather than accept combat at the time and place chosen by his enemy he preferred to suffer temporary set backs while awaiting a better opportunity to strike.

The left Bolsheviks, on the other hand, were willing to be provoked. Their faith in proletarian internationalism was so strong, their fear of betraying their creed so great that they would prefer closing their eyes to brutal reality and attacking the German war machine at the peak of its power. Bukharin, in particular, seems to have been gripped by a strange eschatological fatalism driving him to believe in the certainty of either total success or total failure. As such he was easy prey for Lenin's dynamic tactics which steadily eroded his political position and left him and his chief supporters isolated.

Lenin's task in securing the acceptance of peace with Germany, however, was far from easy. Before anyone else he realized the necessity of such a step, but before he could act he had several obstacles to surmount. First, there was the deep conviction, which he had dinned into the masses during the previous year, that if the Russian revolution was carried to its logical extreme it would lead to the world workers' revolution. 'Permanent revolution' had provided a panacea for all of Russia's ills and an answer to all objections about deepening the revolution in wartime, but, by early 1918, it was no longer a viable hypothesis on which to base Soviet foreign policy. It had become potentially lethal to cling to this doctrine, yet it still retained its popularity. This popularity and the optimism which it engendered had to be overcome before peace could be signed. Trotsky was a second and more formidable barrier. As the author of 'permanent revolution' and, with Lenin, a co-founder of the Soviet state, he occupied a position of great influence and authority. Trotsky did not subscribe to the 'all-or-nothing' philosophy of Bukharin yet he too hankered after a revolutionary war and unlike the left Bolsheviks would have made a credible leader of such a crusade. But Trotsky was too hard-headed to embark on war with Germany in a heedless manner. When he gauged the deep desire for peace racing through the army he knew it was not simply a matter of issuing a few revolutionary commands and watching the imperialist enemy flee before hordes of revolutionary warriors. Moreover, he respected Lenin's judgment and, even more, his political authority. What developed was a muted struggle for power, Lenin vetoing revolutionary war while Trotsky rejected capitulation. 'No war, no peace' was a temporary and highly unstable compromise developed by Trotsky to bridge the gap created by the conflict between Lenin and the advocates of revolutionary war on the one hand and the revolutionary aspirations of the Soviet state and its meager resources on the other. It might be described as trying to foment revolution 'on the cheap,' but it did have the virtues of avoiding a split in the Bolshevik party, postponing an openly annexationist peace and preserving the moral integrity of the revolution. Unfortunately the compromise depended entirely on German cooperation, and when they refused, it collapsed.

At this point two observations are in order. First, it should not be assumed that Trotsky's scheme was doomed from the start. If Hertling, Payer, and Kühlmann had had their way it would have been accepted, but in Germany at this time the voice of the civil authorities was weak and drowned out by the stentorian tones of Ludendorff. In somewhat different circumstances Germany might well have accepted Trotsky's declaration as an easy way out of an embarrassing situation. Second, if this had happened the Soviet government might well have found itself in an even worse position than it did after signing the onerous peace of Brest-Litovsk. Kühlmann had calculated the consequences of such a makeshift arrangement rather well, and it is hard to argue with his logic. 'No war, no peace' was clearly conceived more as a way of overcoming political difficulties in the Bolshevik Central Committee than as the basis for a realistic foreign policy, and if the Germans had proven acquiescent, the results might not have proved as satisfactory as Trotsky assumed. As Soviet Russia was to find following the end of hostilities in Europe, the role of an outlaw state in international politics is not an easy one, and such would have been her fate in 1918, as well as 1919, if Germany had followed Kühlmann's advice. In the absence of both a peace treaty and firm Bolshevik control over

the old Russian empire Germany could have sown havoc through the borderlands and supported anti-Bolshevik movements inside Russia itself. As
it was, Germany acquired almost a proprietary interest in the Bolshevik
regime and while the Soviets were free to undermine the German government, Berlin, paradoxically, found it necessary to shore up the Bolsheviks.
A state of 'no war, no peace' would have avoided this ironic situation.

Germany, however, did not accept Trotsky's declaration and the resumption of hostilities had the effect of sweeping aside the last resistance
to Lenin's policy. The disastrous reports from the northern front were
sufficient to destroy the credibility of the left Bolsheviks and shift Trotsky,
remorsefully but decisively, behind Lenin. The Germans were the last
barrier to the realization of Lenin's policy, and they agreed to accept the
Soviet capitulation. If they had not Lenin would have had to admit the
bankruptcy of his policy and try to make the best of attempting to defend
the revolution without an army. Lenin's much talked about 'Ural-Kuznetsk Republic' would probably have become reality with the Soviet government transferring its seat to one of the industrial towns of the Ural
industrial region for a last ditch stand against its enemies.

Such measures did not prove necessary. The Germans did agree to accept the Soviet capitulation, and if Lenin paid an exorbitant price for peace
it was worth the cost. Although forced to surrender the entire western and
southern borderlands of the Russian state the Bolsheviks were granted
invaluable time to consolidate their hold over the remainder of the old
empire. Political circumstances were so unstable in early 1918 that the
losses could hardly be considered permanent, and, in the event German
imperialism should go bankrupt, Soviet Russia, because of the strength of
the revolutionary movement in the borderlands, could be said to hold a
first mortgage on the territories just lost. Yet, at any time prior to 10
February 1918, the Bolsheviks could have purchased peace at a much
lower price than they eventually paid. It is a truism that the 'poor always
pay more,' and in international relations power is the coin in which diplomats and generals trade. As the revolution deepened in Russia, the Soviet
state grew weaker, and hence, in terms of international relations, more
poverty stricken. As the Germans realized this their appetite for Soviet
territory increased, and they began to demand more for the peace which
Russia desired. The problem was that the Soviet government did not want
simply a separate peace for Russia but a general peace for the entire world,
and not simply peace defined as an end to hostilities and a return to an
altered *status quo ante bellum* but the radically new peace which they
believed would be brought about by the international workers' revolution.

Thus the first month of the peace conference passed with the opposing delegations working at cross purposes to one another, talking not so much with each other as to the constituencies which they represented. Both sides hoped to benefit from this discourse so the meaningless conference continued. All the while the German appetite grew, and when they finally called a halt to these proceedings the bill they presented the Bolsheviks was truly staggering. Even then, as the last minute bargaining indicated, the Soviets could probably have escaped without losing the Ukraine. To do so, however, Trotsky would have had to junk his policy of 'permanent revolution' and bargain seriously to obtain the best terms available. If he had done this and offered to give up Poland, Lithuania, and Courland while agreeing to endorse the treaty negotiated by the Rada, he might still have saved the Ukraine. Trotsky chose to disregard this possibility and decided to stake the Ukraine and, indeed, all of Russia on proletarian internationalism. His gamble failed, and when the next Soviet delegation journeyed to Brest-Litovsk the price of peace had increased still further. All Sokol'nikov could salvage from the wreckage of Trotsky's policy was the 'agitational character' which he was able to attach to the peace treaty. Given the manner in which it was obtained this privilege cost the Soviet state dearly. But at Brest-Litovsk no one won. The Germans secured a peace built on sand, while the Soviets saw the authority of their state shaken to its foundations. Neither would recoup their losses for years to come. In a sense, Germany never recovered from the errors made at Brest-Litovsk, while in Russia the entire course of the revolution was irrevocably altered.

25 *Ibid.*, 98-9
26 Lenin, PSS, vol. XXXVI, 34

8
The new foreign policy

Marxists have never forgotten that violence must inevitably accompany the collapse of capitalism in its entirety and the birth of socialist society. That violence will constitute a period of world history, a whole era of various kinds of war ... This epoch, an epoch of gigantic cataclysms, of mass decisions forcibly imposed by war, of crises, has begun – that we can see clearly – and it is only the beginning. Lenin, March 1918

To gain time, I want to surrender space to the actual victor. That and that alone is the whole point at issue. Lenin, March 1918

If you are unable to adapt yourself, if you are not inclined to crawl on your belly in the mud, you are not a revolutionary but a chatterbox; and I propose this not because I like it, but because we have no other road. Lenin, March 1918

In late February, Lenin had won an enormous political victory, defeating the left Bolsheviks, neutralizing Trotsky, and rallying about himself the majority of the Bolshevik party. After nearly two months of procrastination and fruitless argument the onrushing tide of German infantry had forced his colleagues to face reality and admit the bankruptcy of the regime's first foreign policies. 'Permanent revolution' had failed and 'no war, no peace' had proved to be made of tissue paper. The Central Committee faced with the choice of revolutionary war or capitulation had opted for the latter, tacitly abandoning the ideological baggage which threatened the survival of the revolution. Lenin had received a mandate to salvage what he could from the wreckage of Trotsky's policies. Not much was left, but from the debris he saved the Soviet state, the badly damaged myth of proletarian internationalism, and a slim chance for future revolutionary aggrandizement. The rest he allowed to sink from sight never again to be honoured in its land of origin.

The decision of 23 February marked a major divide in the history of the Russian revolution. On one side lies the political naiveté, buoyant optimism and idealism inherited from the European and Russian revolutionary movements, unfettered by state power and innocent of the responsibilities which such power brings; on the other is the hard-headed, seemingly unemotional realism of Lenin, singlemindedly intent on maintaining and expanding the base of Soviet power. As the one receded into the past the other came dramatically to the fore, rapidly bringing about a profound transformation in the nature and substance of the revolution. Those qualities which previously had marked Lenin's personal style of politics now became dominant in the Soviet state, shouldering aside the more flamboyant approach of Trotsky and the doctrinal intensity of the left Bolsheviks. Never again would the advocates of ideological purity divorced from *raison d'état* receive a serious hearing in Bolshevik councils. In the days following his victory, Lenin moved swiftly to overhaul both party and state, forging policies which reflected his uncompromising views on the future course of the revolution.

His first task was to have his victory ratified by the Party Congress which had been summoned to render a definitive answer to the question of war or peace. Originally scheduled to meet in late February the congress had been postponed due to the 'eleven days war' with Germany and did not assemble in Petrograd until 6 March, a scant three days after the conclusion of the Peace of Brest-Litovsk. This was a very poor time to debate the merits of revolutionary war, but an excellent opportunity for Lenin to exploit his victory. In January, his demand for a party congress had been a tactical measure designed to forestall Bukharin's effort to summon a party conference, but after the events of late February the congress quickly assumed strategic importance. Known in the annals of Soviet historiography as the Seventh 'Extraordinary' Congress this gathering unquestionably deserves its description. Never before or afterward was there a party congress quite like this one. Rather overlooked in most studies of the Russian Communist party, the Seventh Congress deserves much more attention than it has received.

The most striking feature of the Congress was its diminutive size. In comparison with the Sixth Congress which had met in June 1917 and was attended by 267 delegates (157 possessing the right to vote and 110 with a 'consultative' mandate) representing 176,750 party members, the Seventh Congress was composed of only 70 delegates (46 possessing the right to vote and 24 with a 'consultative' mandate) representing less than 150,000 Bolsheviks. In the interval between the Sixth and Seventh Congresses the party had grown from less than 200,000 to more than 300,000 members,[1] meaning that in March 1918, less than half of the party was represented at the Congress. Of the 46 delegates with the right to vote, 27 represented party organizations in Moscow and Petrograd while at least five of the remaining nineteen delegates supposedly drawn from the provinces actually worked in the capital and had little if any contact with their nominal constituencies. Iakov Sverdlov and N.N. Krestinskii, for example, attended the Congress as delegates from the Urals while P.I. Stuchka was said to represent the Latvian members of the party. In short, the Congress was composed primarily of delegates drawn from the central organs of party government with only a few representatives from the provinces. This can be explained by the sudden decision to summon the Congress and the chaotic conditions existing in Russia at the time. In early March, with railway transportation totally disrupted, the larger number of delegates simply could not reach Petrograd. This did not prevent Lenin from proceeding with the Congress as he was able to argue with considerable justification that the military emergency required a final answer to the question of war or peace.

Lenin had no problem with the delegates. They were few in number, drawn mainly from the two capitals and easily influenced by the strong current of public opinion favouring peace. This current was quite genuine, fed by the steady flow of demoralized soldiers fleeing the front, but in late February, it was given new direction and force as Lenin began consciously to pump it into politically useful channels. In the two weeks separating the meeting of 23 February and the opening of the Congress the Bolshevik Central Committee brought enormous pressure to bear on the regional and district organizations in Moscow and Petrograd, and by the time the Congress opened most of these organs had fallen into line and announced their support for ratification of the peace treaty.[2] In addition, the replies to Lenin's telegram soliciting the views of local Soviets and land committees on whether the government should wage revolutionary war or ratify the peace treaty with Germany had begun to pour into the capital. Although the first batch of these replies showed sixty-one in favour of war against sixty opposed to continuing the conflict later returns revealed a steady

1 Kommunisticheskaia Partiia Sovetskogo Soiuza, *VII Kongress, Stenograficheskii Otchet*, 1-7. Hereafter cited as *VII Kongress*
2 Oznobishin, *Ot Bresta do Iur'eva*, 169-79

trend in favour of peace. When all results were tabulated it was found that 262 local soviets and land committees had voted for ratification of the peace treaty while 233 opposed it.[3] Lenin, therefore, could claim that this poll supported his position. His opponents had been outmaneuvered every step along the way with Lenin having seized control of the Central Committee, undermined their previous predominance in Moscow and Petrograd and secured a mandate from the country at large. Possessing neither the prestige, information nor resources of the Central Committee the left Bolsheviks were unable to generate any enthusiasm for their program. They had to stand to one side, powerless to prevent the sudden and massive erosion of their political position, unable even to prevent the defection of delegates who arrived in Petrograd bearing instructions from their local party organizations requiring them to vote for war.[4] Before the Congress met the issue had already been decided in favour of peace.

With full control of the Congress Lenin had only to decide how he would exploit the unprecedented opportunity which the meeting offered him. As he had no desire to drive his opponents from the party he decided to make their defeat as painless as possible. When the Congress convened, therefore, Bukharin even received a seat on the presidium and Sverdlov, despite his open support for Lenin, conducted the meetings in a reasonably impartial manner. Bukharin was allowed to argue his case, those who supported revolutionary war were given every opportunity to be heard and, despite considerable invective, particularly from Karl Radek, no attempt was made to muzzle the left Bolsheviks. Lenin made a great show of allowing free discussion. He could do this because the left Bolsheviks were isolated, Bukharin was incapable of inspired leadership and Trotsky would not join the opposition. Only an alliance of Bukharin and Trotsky could have defeated Lenin, but Trotsky was not interested in such a bloc.[5] The circumstances which had led him to abstain from voting in the Central Committee on 23 February still prevented him from making common cause with the left Bolsheviks.[6] Unwilling either to assume leadership of the left or play second fiddle to Lenin, the lion was reduced to a pathetic role justifying his conduct at Brest-Litovsk and seeking a vote of confidence from the delegates. Trotsky, in fact, was irrelevant to the proceedings of the Congress, a completely neutral factor in the uneven con-

3 *Leninskii Sbornik*, vol. XXXVI, 30
4 *VII Kongress*, 102-3
5 Trotsky, *My Life*, 387
6 See above, 142-4

test. This neutrality was the key to Lenin's success at the Congress, just as it had been two weeks earlier in the Central Committee. If Trotsky had passed into opposition the entire balance of power within the party would have shifted dramatically, probably resulting, as Trotsky feared, in an open and, most likely, armed conflict between the two Bolshevik factions. Unprepared to assume the responsibility for such a conflict Trotsky remained neutral and, without effective opposition, Lenin was able to run in slippered feet over his other opponents. On the afternoon of 8 March, the delegates voted thirty to twelve with four abstentions in favour of Lenin's resolution recognizing 'the necessity to confirm the extremely harsh, humiliating peace with Germany.'[7]

With this resolution the Congress placed its seal of approval on Lenin's policy. Henceforth the party was bound by this decision, and, as a consequence, ratification of the Treaty of Brest-Litovsk by the Bolshevik-dominated All-Russian Congress of Soviets became a foregone conclusion. When that body met a week later it voted 784 to 261 in favour of peace. The defeat of the left Bolsheviks and Trotsky had thus been confirmed, a sufficiently momentous event in itself, but only the thin end of the wedge as far as Lenin was concerned. He had prevailed over his opponents, but he had laboured not merely to defeat them on this one issue but also to free himself of their obstruction in the future. Having won a major victory he now proceeded to exploit it, turning the defeat of his opponents into an absolute rout.

Even before the final ballot on his motion to accept the Treaty of Brest-Litovsk he had moved decisively in this direction. When, near the end of the debate, Trotsky had roused himself to complain about the sweeping nature of Lenin's motion, the Bolshevik leader was ready to offer one of those 'rotten compromises' for which he was so justly famous. The international situation, Trotsky had argued, could change very quickly, and within a few days the Bolsheviks might not wish to ratify the peace treaty. Yet under the terms of Lenin's motion the party would be bound to support ratification in any circumstances. Instead of recognizing 'the necessity' of confirming the treaty Trotsky suggested that the Congress acknowledge 'that it is permissible' to do so. He also objected to Lenin's apparent readiness to make peace with the German-dominated governments in Finland and the Ukraine and proposed amendments to the resolution forbidding the Soviet government to follow such a policy.[8] Lenin,

7 *VII Kongress*, 132
8 *Ibid.*, 127

who saw in these proposals yet another attempt to escape reality, rejected the amendments saying that 'we must in no way bind our hands in any strategic maneuver. Everything depends on the relationship of forces and the time of the attack against us by these or those imperialist countries.' But Lenin was not about to leave the matter stand as it was, for Trotsky's attempt to limit his freedom of action offered him an opportunity to expand that freedom infinitely. Trotsky's contention that circumstances might suddenly change accorded perfectly with his own view of the situation, a view which he hastened to share with the Congress, adding that the Soviet government because of unexpected circumstances might soon be in a position 'not merely to refrain from concluding peace, but to declare war.' Therefore, supposedly to meet Trotsky's objections, he proposed that the Congress 'empower the Central Committee of the Party both to break all the peace treaties and to declare war on any imperialist power or the whole world when the Central Committee of the Party considers that the appropriate moment for this has come.'[9] The Congress accepted this extraordinary amendment *unanimously*, thus vesting the Central Committee with unlimited power in the field of foreign affairs. By once again playing on the bellicose passions of the left Bolsheviks, holding out to them the hope of imminent revolutionary war, Lenin had scored another major victory over his politically naive opponents, painlessly and with their full approbation, extracting from them plenary power to conduct Soviet foreign policy in any manner which he saw fit.

But there was more, much more. In the same 'resolution on war and peace' Lenin also included an important section on domestic policy. 'The Congress,' read the resolution:

declares that it recognizes the primary and fundamental task of our Party ... to be the adoption of the most energetic, ruthlessly determined and Draconian measures to improve the self-discipline and discipline of the workers and peasants of Russia ... to create everywhere soundly co-ordinated mass organizations held together by a single iron will, organizations that are capable of concerted, valorous action in their day-to-day efforts and especially at critical moments in the life of the people and lastly, to train systematically and comprehensively in military matters and military operations the entire adult population of both sexes.[10]

This too was passed, and one week later, was translated into law for all revolutionary Russia by the Fourth All-Russian Congress of Soviets. In

9 *Ibid.*, 128
10 Lenin, PSS, vol. XXXVI, 35-6

view of its all-encompassing nature, virtually charging the Central Committee to establish an unfettered military dictatorship, it is surprising to
observe that hardly any of the delegates took notice of it. Only D.B. Riazanov, a former Menshevik and trade union leader, called attention to the
sweeping powers granted the Central Committee and called for their
modification through substitution of 'persuasion' for the 'Draconian measures' which Lenin wanted.[11] His objection, however, was so incoherent
that no one paid any attention to him. Riazanov, in fact, was an object of
ridicule throughout the entire Congress and a lone voice of moderation
crying in the wilderness. Everyone else was so hypnotized by the debate on
foreign policy that they failed to realize the immense significance of
Lenin's resolution concerning internal affairs. Even if they had, it is unlikely that any of the left Bolsheviks would have objected strongly to
Lenin's proposals, for in principle, if not in actual practice, Bukharin and
his associates agreed with the Bolshevik chief that the most extreme measures were needed if the revolution was to survive. Where they differed
was in defining the purpose of those dictatorial powers. Lenin saw them as
a form of retrenchment, a *long*-term commitment to prolonged struggle,
while the left viewed them as a *short*-term commitment to the preparation
of an imminent revolutionary war. Once again the left Bolsheviks proved
more than willing, even eager, to sacrifice everything in pursuit of their
illusory goal. Lenin allowed his opponents to delude themselves, playing
all the while on their blinding passion to gather ever greater power in his
own hands. The left had no idea what Lenin meant by such a vague expression as 'ruthlessly determined and Draconian measures' nor how
single-minded the 'iron will' of which he spoke would actually be; nor did
they realize just how much of the spontaneous and libertarian quality of
the revolution which they valued would be lost through their agreement
to impose Lenin's sanctions upon Russian society. In the months to come
they would have ample opportunity to learn.

Up to this point the Congress had dealt only with affairs of state, laying
down those policies, foreign and domestic, which the Central Committee
through its control of the Soviet government was to translate into law for
the revolutionary republic. The debate on these measures had stretched
over three days, and so, on the evening of 8 March, when the delegates
assembled for their fifth and final meeting, they had no reason to believe
that, except for the election of a new Central Committee, any further
business of substance would be transacted. Lenin, however, had a surprise

11 *VII Kongress, 126*

for them, because he chose this moment to present recommendations for changing the name of the party and completely transforming its program. The first proposal was not controversial as no one objected to exchanging the discredited title of Russian Social Democratic Labour Party, which seemed to associate them with the 'social-chauvinists' of Germany and France, for the more illustrious and untainted designation of Russian Communist Party of Bolsheviks. The proposed change in party program was a different matter. Discussion of program revision had been under way since the previous year, and at the beginning of the Congress this question had been placed on the agenda, but owing to the limited time available no one had really expected the issue to be discussed. Nevertheless, when the final session opened that evening Lenin presented a resolution calling for the fundamental reform of the party program. The theoretical portion of the old program, he said, should be retained, as 'there is nothing incorrect in it' but to this section which analysed the development of capitalism he wanted to add a 'definition of imperialism and the era of the international socialist revolution that has begun.' Equally important, he felt, was a change in the political section of the document, replacing the outmoded portions dealing with the struggle for power with 'the most accurate and comprehensive definition possible of the new type of state, the Soviet Republic, as a form of the dictatorship of the proletariat.' Other sections of the program were to be 'recast in the same spirit and direction. The centre of gravity must be a precise definition of the economic and other reforms begun by our Soviet power, with a definite statement of the definite tasks which Soviet power has set itself, and which proceed from the practical steps we have taken towards expropriating the expropriators.'[12]

Lenin's proposals for the new party program fit perfectly with his view of the manner in which the revolution would develop in the future, relying fundamentally on the instrumentalities of an all-powerful state, liquidating the old order and proceeding to the transformation of Russia into a socialist society. With such a program, it was clear, there could be no question of conducting an adventurous foreign policy or of launching the revolution on a ruinous crusade against imperialism. There would certainly be war, but it would not be the 'all or nothing' type of romantic conflict which the left Bolsheviks advocated. Instead, in his address introducing the changes he wished to make in the party program, Lenin gazed deeply into the future and explained to the delegates how he envisaged the way in which the revolution would spread to the rest of the world. It sum-

12 Lenin, PSS, vol XXXVI, 58-9. Also see p. 46

marizes his basic assumptions and expectations so well that it is worth presenting in its entirety.

Marxists [he said] have never forgotten that violence must inevitably accompany the collapse of capitalism in its entirety and the birth of socialist society. That violence will constitute a period of world history, a whole era of various kinds of wars, imperialist wars, civil wars inside countries, the intermingling of the two, national wars liberating the nationalities oppressed by the imperialists and by various combinations of imperialist powers that will inevitably enter into various alliances in the epoch of tremendous state-capitalist and military trusts and syndicates. This epoch, an epoch of gigantic cataclysms, of mass decisions forcibly imposed by war, of crises, has begun – that we can see clearly – and it is only the beginning.[13]

Here, brilliantly illuminated, is the fundamental difference between Lenin and his opponents at the Seventh Congress. For him, the great era of violence was just beginning, and he foresaw it continuing unabated for an indefinite period of time. It would, in his view, be an era of untold danger, a Darwinian jungle of international proportions in which the weakest and least adaptable of the 'species' would most surely perish. Resolved that his fledgling state would survive the terrible years to come, he saw his task as one of preparing Soviet Russia for the contest. The left Bolsheviks would not agree that the era of violence had only begun. Steeped in the wisdom of nineteenth-century Europe, which had not imagined that anything so terrible as the Great War could drag on for as long as it did, they believed that the years of destruction were drawing to a close and would be terminated by the world workers' revolution. Rather than entrenching the revolution in the inhospitable soil of Russia, therefore, they proclaimed that it was necessary to make only one last supreme effort to achieve the revolutionary breakthrough which would bring both the war and imperialism to their well-deserved end. Believing this, Bukharin quite naturally opposed Lenin's proposed revision of the party program and submitted his own design for the consideration of the delegates. Like that of Lenin, Bukharin's proposed program mirrored his expectations for the future. As he believed that the days of capitalism were numbered, his first wish was to exclude the section in the old program which dealt with its development. In its place he wished to include an extensive description of socialism and communism as they would soon function,

13 *VII Kongress*, 148-9

placing special emphasis on the way in which all states, including the dicta-torship of the proletariat, would wither away to nothing. Rather than cele-brating the virtues of the Soviet state as Lenin wished, Bukharin called for a party program which would map out its destruction.[14]

Lenin would have none of this. He immediately attacked Bukharin's proposals, reaffirming the usefulness of the state, declaring that the day of ultimate revolutionary victory was 'still a long way off' and asserting that there was virtually nothing which could be said at that moment about the future functioning of socialist society in its developed form.[15] With totally different visions of the future Lenin and the left Bolsheviks had no com-mon basis for agreement, and in essence, were locked in the eternal debate between the Janus-like concepts of voluntarism and determinism found at the heart of Marxist doctrine. Agreement, however, was not necessary as Lenin commanded the votes needed to pass his resolution. At the end of this peculiar debate, in which the opposing sides appeared to be describing events occurring on two separate planets, the Congress ac-cepted Lenin's guidelines for the revision of the party program. As time did not permit the immediate elaboration of these guidelines into an ac-tual program the Congress struck a seven-man commission to prepare a final draft for submission to the next party congress. Although Bukharin was elected to this commission, his presence was merely nominal as he was isolated in the midst of a Leninist majority which was obviously not prepared to be influenced by the left Bolsheviks. Lenin, in fact, did not want anyone to influence his commission, for he even rejected a proposal that it should canvas the party to obtain a wide range of views on the new program. Far from agreeing to this proposal he insisted that the commis-sion publish its program even before the meeting of the next congress.[16] The pliable delegates agreed, and thus, Lenin received a blank cheque to prepare and publish a new party program which would reflect his own revolutionary philosophy. Just as he had locked the Soviet state into a political program of his own design he now succeeded in locking the party into the same framework.

In the long run none of this would have been of value had Lenin not also secured control of the Central Committee. The vast powers just voted by the Congress had been vested in that body, and its decrees guided the policies of all agencies of the Soviet government. The last and ultimately

14 *Ibid.*, 154-9
15 *Ibid.*, 159-60
16 *Ibid.*, 167-8

most important victory won by Lenin at the Seventh Congress, therefore, was the election of a Central Committee subordinate to his will. So absolute was Lenin's hold on the delegates, however, that the election appeared almost anti-climactic. Some of the left Bolsheviks, discouraged by their earlier defeats, did not even wait for the election, but left the Congress beforehand. The others might just as well have done so, because the obedient delegates promptly provided Lenin with the Central Committee which he wanted. To begin with, following Sverdlov's motion from the chair, the Congress agreed to reduce the number of members on the Central Committee from twenty-one to fifteen. Theoretically this was done to improve the efficiency of the Committee, but it takes little imagination to see that it also facilitated the removal of left Bolsheviks whose presence Lenin found embarrassing. This purpose became clear when one of Lenin's followers submitted what amounted to an official slate of candidates which excluded all left Bolsheviks except Bukharin and included only four other men who might, from time to time, hold views contrary to the Bolshevik leader. Of these, Trotsky, Zinoviev, and Dzerzhinskii had already shown that in a major crisis they would collapse under pressure, while the fourth, Krestinskii, could reliably be expected to follow the lead of Trotsky. The other nine members were either old and reliable associates such as Sverdlov, Stalin, and Sergeev or completely new men who could be counted upon to follow Lenin's leadership. With their election the Central Committee had been restructured to prevent any serious challenge to his rule.[17] Not only were the left Bolsheviks cast into the political wilderness, but Trotsky had been deprived of his pivotal position as holder of the balance between Lenin and the left. Rather than having to count on Trotsky's good will in any future conflict, Lenin could be assured of a two-thirds majority in the Central Committee. His hands were now free to manage the affairs of the Soviet state in any way he saw fit, unchecked by doctrinal fetters or vexatious colleagues. Lenin, in fact, left the Seventh Congress clothed in virtually absolute power. No longer was he merely *primus inter pares* in the revolutionary leadership of Russia, he had very nearly become *princeps.*

Despite his vastly expanded powers and now undisputed authority within the party, Lenin had no desire to turn the quarrel with his opponents into a vendetta. Vendettas were foreign to Lenin, for he knew from long experience that an enemy in one dispute might become an ally in the next, and it was wise to leave as many options as possible for future man-

17 *Ibid.,* 172-7

euver. Throughout the Congress and afterward, despite bitter words exchanged with his opponents, he never failed to stress the essential identity of their views with his own. 'The fact that we are together,' he said at the Congress, 'shows that we are ninety per-cent in agreement.'[18] Their differences, he disingenuously claimed, were concerned with tactics, and he tried to paper over the many areas where he and the left Bolsheviks were in fundamental disagreement. He did this, because, above all else, he wanted to draw his opponents back into the mainstream of the Bolshevik movement and utilize their talents for his own advantage. Trotsky, in particular, was too valuable to be left in the political dustbin, and if Lenin no longer trusted him to conduct Soviet foreign policy his energy and intelligence could be used elsewhere. Shortly after the Seventh Congress, therefore, Lenin accepted Trotsky's resignation as foreign commissar but immediately appointed him commissar of war. The left Bolsheviks were another matter. Far more irreconcilable than Trotsky they left the Congress in a foul and uncompromising mood. Bukharin swore he would not accept his election to the Central Committee and his followers, some of whom had been elected candidate members of the Central Committee, said the same. They continued to publish their journal *Kommunist* and, pointing to the party members represented and delegates actually present at the recent congress, began to question its authority to reach decisions binding on the party as a whole.[19] This attitude seriously worried Lenin, and he described the left Bolsheviks as 'slipping further and further towards a completely disloyal and impermissible violation of Party discipline.' Their refusal to accept the posts to which they had been elected, he said, represented 'absolutely disloyal, uncomradely actions that violate Party discipline, and such behaviour was and remains a *step towards a split*.'[20] Nevertheless, in the circumstances of 1918, even if Lenin had been inclined to take disciplinary action against them he could not afford to do so, for, as in the case of Trotsky, he needed the special talents which they possessed. They might be terrible politicians (hardly a serious failing in Lenin's eyes), but, to a man, they were also outstanding propagandists, polemicists, and party organizers. Such men were valuable, and while Lenin methodically ridiculed their ideas, leaving them no scope to expand their following, he also was careful to keep the way open for them to return to the fold.

18 *Ibid.*, 113
19 *Ibid.*, xlii
20 Lenin, PSS, vol. XXXVI, 77. Emphasis in original

While continuing to fence with the left Bolsheviks, Lenin's main concern was to elaborate his new foreign and domestic policies. The new foreign policy followed logically from the decision of 23 February and was based on the same fundamental circumstances which had governed that decision. 'To gain time, I want to surrender space to the actual victor. That and that alone is the whole point at issue,' he had said.[21] But much more was involved than military necessity, for, as in every move made by Lenin, there was an overriding political consideration involved. 'Strategy *and politics*,' he told the Party Congress, 'prescribed the most disgusting peace treaty imaginable.'[22] By this he meant that in addition to the patent impossibility of resisting German aggression any attempt to do so would play into the hands of the Russian bourgeoisie, alienate the peasantry, and undercut the foundations of Soviet power. 'I know quite well that it is the bourgeoisie who are bawling for a revolutionary war,' he said, 'Their class interests demand it, their anxiety to see Soviet power make a false move demands it.'[23] Only by inciting the revolutionary government to wage a war it could not win, he felt, did the bourgeoisie stand a chance to regain power. Nor was he alone in believing this, for at the Party Congress delegates from the provinces reported that the bourgeoisie had been the first to respond to the call for national defence while the proletariat and particularly the peasantry showed little interest in continuing the war.[24] The war-weariness of the peasantry was, in fact, the key to Lenin's political calculations. The peasantry wanted peace, and to declare war would undercut the alliance of the peasantry and proletariat which had originally allowed the Bolsheviks to seize power in November. Thus Lenin had no patience with the left Bolsheviks who charged that the party was allowing the peasantry to dictate its foreign policy. He expressed 'amazement' at such views, remonstrated with those who made 'contemptuous references to the exhausted state of the peasantry' and repeatedly reaffirmed the Bolshevik alliance with the countryside. 'Without this alliance,' he said, 'it would be senseless to make any attempt to establish power.'[25] In essence, Lenin submitted that the continuation of the war with Germany would be 'the surest way of getting rid of us today.'[26]

21 *Ibid.*, 27
22 *Ibid.*, 34. Emphasis added
23 *Ibid.*, 100
24 *VII Kongress*, 100-2
25 *Ibid.*, 98-9
26 Lenin, PSS, vol. XXXVI, 34

The policy which emerged from these calculations was one of sheer desperation designed to secure the survival of Soviet Russia and little else. Lenin explicitly abandoned the great hopes of late 1917, repudiated the prospect of a great 'field revolution,' denied that victory could be attained through a 'triumphant march with flying banners' and described the imminent coming of the world workers' revolution as 'a very beautiful fairy tale.' 'I quite understand children liking beautiful fairy tales,' he cruelly declared, 'but I ask, is it proper for a serious revolutionary to believe in fairy tales?'[27] Having thereby junked the foreign policy on which his government had come to power he now called for a retreat into the depths of Russia, to any part of that vast country, where Soviet power might be retained and strengthened.

If Lenin had smashed the idol of *imminent* world revolution he, of course, had to retain the myth of proletarian internationalism and the prospect of *eventual* world revolution. These he had carefully salvaged from the wreckage of Trotsky's foreign policy, and he immediately gave them positions of honour in his own political pantheon. This was necessary not only to camouflage the sharp reversal of policy but also to provide a shield against the Bukharinist left who charged him with betraying the revolution. Moreover, not even Lenin, realist that he was, could afford to admit that the revolution might remain isolated in Russia. Such an admission would have made nonsense of *all* his former policies and, in a Marxist framework, would have destroyed the theoretical and practical justification of the revolution, smashing all hope for its survival. Thus he readily acknowledged the ultimate dependence of the Russian revolution on the broader revolutionary movement in Europe as a whole. 'In all events, under all conceivable circumstances,' he told his comrades, 'if the German revolution does not come we are doomed.' He was also careful to assure his listeners that revolution would eventually come to Germany. Time and again, as if to convince himself as well as others, he repeated the assertion that 'the world socialist revolution would come – because it is coming; would mature because it is maturing and will reach full maturity.'[28] In the days after Brest-Litovsk, however, Lenin shoved the probable date for this revolution further back into the voluminous folds of the indefinite future, allowing it to assume a rather shadowy existence somewhat akin to the second coming of Christ. Where before he had said

27 *Ibid.*, 19
28 *Ibid.*, 11

that there were 'ninety-nine chances in a hundred' that the revolution would spread from Russia to the rest of Europe he now abandoned percentages entirely and virtually took his text from the ancient proverb 'all good things come to him who waits.' Thus he consoled his followers: 'One may dream of the field revolution on a worldwide scale, for it will come. Everything will come in due time.' In addition, he began to stress ever more forcefully the difficulties which the revolution would encounter in central and western Europe. 'The revolution will not come as quickly as we expected,' he said, 'History has proved this, and we must be able to take this as a fact, to reckon with the fact that the world socialist revolution cannot begin so easily in the advanced countries as the revolution began in Russia – in the land of Nicholas and Rasputin.'[29] Until the revolution spread beyond Russia, therefore, the Soviet government would have to hold fast and rely on its own resources for survival. He ridiculed those who, in the short run, would 'bank on the international socialist movement' and say 'I can commit any piece of folly I please; Liebknecht will help us out, because he is going to win, anyhow.'[30] Liebknecht, the leader of German revolutionary socialism, would win, Lenin believed, but not before Soviet Russia had passed through hell in its attempt to withstand German imperialism.

Lenin made no attempt to conceal how difficult it would be for the revolution to survive. 'We need no self deception,' he declared, 'We must courageously look the bitter, unadorned truth straight in the face. We must measure fully to the very bottom that abyss of defeat, dismemberment, enslavement and humiliation into which we have now been pushed.'[31] Having measured the depth of this abyss he did not hesitate to report the alarming results to his comrades. 'We have no army,' he told them, 'but we have to go on living side by side with a predator who is armed to the teeth, a predator who still remains and will continue to remain a plunderer and is not, of course, affected by agitation in favour of peace without annexations and indemnities.'[32] For political reasons, in fact, Lenin took great pains to paint the situation in the darkest possible colours, justifying in this way the peace of Brest-Litovsk and the enormous burdens which he intended to impose on Russia. In this manner he

29 *Ibid.*, 15-16
30 *Ibid.*, 12
31 *Ibid.*, 79
32 *Ibid.*, 11

also prepared everyone for even worse days to come, stating bluntly that 'at Brest the relation of forces corresponded to a peace imposed upon the one who had been defeated ... at the next stage, a peace four times more humiliating will be dictated to us.'[33] 'The Soviet Republic,' he said, 'may be reduced to slavery.'[34] So gloomy were his predictions that he even demanded that the party reaffirm its willingness to work within the despised framework of parliamentary government should events force it from power. 'An epoch of most grievous defeats is ahead of us, it is with us now, we must be able to reckon with it, we must be prepared for persistent work in conditions of illegality, in conditions of downright slavery to the Germans.'[35] Much like Churchill in 1940 he promised his followers nothing but blood, sweat, and tears. 'We must be prepared for extraordinary difficulties, for extraordinary severe defeats which are inevitable,' he proclaimed.[36]

To minimize these defeats and retain a basis of power Lenin decreed that the tactics of the Soviet Republic in conducting its international relations must be 'those of manoeuvering, retreat and waiting for the moment when the international proletarian revolution ... fully matures.'[37] By man-euver he meant the difficult and dangerous expedient of exploiting the highly unstable political situation in Europe, seeking whatever advantage could be derived from the continuing war among the great powers. The Soviet regime, he believed, had survived since November only because of 'a special combination of international circumstances that temporarily shielded us from imperialism. Imperialism had other things to bother about besides us; ... the engine that was supposed to bear down on us with the force of a railway train bearing down on a wheelbarrow and smashing it to splinters was temporarily stalled – and the engine was stalled because the two groups of predators had clashed.'[38] Due to the mistaken policy of 'no war, no peace' this protective shield had been lost. Rather than staying the hand of German imperialism Trotsky had provoked it, calling attention to Russia's debilitated state and virtually asking for the crushing military defeat which Hoffmann had administered. But even after Brest-Litovsk, Lenin believed, not all was lost. Although Russia lived in the shadow of the German war machine she still remained a factor in interna-

33 *Ibid.*, 23
34 *Ibid.*
35 *Ibid.*, 26
36 *Ibid.*, 16
37 *Ibid.*, 277
38 *Ibid.*, 8-9

tional politics. Weak as Russia was, Lenin realized that the favour of the Soviet government was something with which to conjure, and, by threatening to magnify or promising to diminish the problems of one or the other great coalitions, the revolutionary regime could still bargain for its freedom. In the delicately balanced state of the war a Soviet threat to tip the scales in one direction or the other would have to be taken seriously. Nor was the international framework in which Soviet Russia could maneuver limited merely to two dimensions, for a third, and very important, dimension was provided by the existence of rivalries within the two coalitions. Thus, not only could Soviet Russia extend or withhold its cooperation from one or the other coalition, it could also take advantage of the conflicting ambitions of the separate states which composed those coalitions. Each state had aspirations which differed significantly from those of its partners, and, in the case of Germany and Turkey in the Caucasus and the United States and Japan in the far east, these differences were sufficiently great to offer the tempting possibility of exploitation for Soviet benefit. In Russia's weakened condition, without the means to fend off armed attack, this was a very dangerous policy, but in early 1918, Russia really had no other path to follow. 'We shall be protected ... by the continuing struggle between the two giants of imperialism in the West,' wrote Lenin, 'We have just one chance until the outbreak of the European revolution ... the continuation of the struggle of the international imperialist giants.'[39]

Retreat and patient waiting for future opportunities were integral parts of Lenin's new foreign policy. He unhesitatingly sounded the call for retreat everywhere from the Baltic to the Black Sea exhibiting absolutely no shame in ordering the most far-reaching strategic withdrawals. He did this, he said, 'to prevent things from getting worse,' and firmly rebuffed any attempt to confuse reality with appeals to honour, duty or other aristocratic-bourgeois concepts which he loathed. 'Suppose,' he said:

we have two armies of a hundred thousand each and there are five armies against them; one army is surrounded by two hundred thousand, and the other must go to its aid; knowing that the other three hundred thousand of the enemy are ambushed to trap it, should the second army go to the aid of the first. It should not. That is not treachery, that is not cowardice ... it is no longer a personal concept. By

39 *Ibid.*, 254

acting in this way I preserve my army, let the other army be captured. I shall be able to renew mine ... That is the only way to argue; when military arguments are mixed up with others, you get nothing but empty phrases.[40]

Against those who attempted to introduce such 'empty phrases' into the debate Lenin turned a withering fire of sarcasm and ridicule. The left Bolsheviks, who never tired of lecturing him on revolutionary honour, particularly drew his fire. 'Their newspaper,' he said, 'bears the title *Kommunist*, but it should bear the title *Szlachcic* because it looks at things from the point of view of the szlachcic, who dying in a beautiful pose, sword in hand, says "Peace is disgraceful, war is honourable." They argue from the point of view of the szlachcic; I argue from the point of view of the peasant.'[41] Whereas his opponents spoke loftily of the millions of peasants who would flock to the banners of a Soviet army engaged in revolutionary warfare Lenin bluntly declared that 'any Russian who contemplated the task of overthrowing international imperialism on the basis of Russian forces would be a lunatic.'[42] Instead of contemplating victories yet unwon Lenin counted the days he had actually secured for the evacuation of Petrograd. He treasured each day, literally gloating over every twenty-four hours he snatched from the Germans. Each day was valuable, for it meant that proletarian warriors, skilled craftsmen, and party organizers could be withdrawn to the relative safety of Moscow where they would form the cadre of a new Soviet striking force. Thus, with evident relish and satisfaction Lenin counted these days and denounced Trotsky's policies which had led to the loss of valuable time. 'We must not brag, but must be able to take advantage of even a single day of respite ... I say again that I am ready to sign, and that I consider it my duty to sign a treaty twenty-times, a hundred-times more humiliating in order to gain at least a few days in which to evacuate Petrograd.'[43] If the Germans demanded a new pound of flesh from the bleeding body of Russia, then Lenin was prepared to give it to them, withdrawing further and further into the depths of the continent. Nor did he attempt to make out that these withdrawals were anything short of a headlong retreat, a near rout. 'We cannot hide the incredibly bitter, deplorable reality from ourselves with empty phrases,' he told his

40 *Ibid.*, 31-2
41 *Ibid.*, 22
42 *Ibid.*, 253
43 *Ibid.*, 24

comrades, 'we must say: God grant that we retreat in what is half-way good order. We cannot retreat in good order, but God grant that our retreat is half-way good order ... you cannot stop an army in flight.'[44]

The primary purpose behind this policy of maneuver, retreat and waiting was, in Lenin's words, 'to hold out in the positions we have won.'[45] By this, of course, he did not mean holding onto any specific geographic areas, even the chief industrial regions of Russia, for he was willing to exchange almost any amount of territory for time to regroup his forces. Instead he meant that he was seeking, in any circumstances, to hold onto state power and the ability to influence events both inside and out of Russia. 'Our task, since we are alone, is to maintain the revolution, to preserve for it at least a certain bastion of socialism ... until the revolution matures in other countries, until other contingents come up to us.'[46] This was not merely a question of self-preservation, but of broader revolutionary strategy. Through the Bolshevik seizure of power, he believed, Russia had become the vanguard of the world revolutionary movement. If the Soviet regime perished, therefore, it would do nothing to strengthen revolutionary movements elsewhere. To the contrary, the destruction of Soviet Russia would hinder other revolutionary movements, play into the hands of reactionary governments and frighten the masses 'who would be scared by the defeat of Soviet Russia just as the British workers were scared by the defeat of the Paris Commune in 1871.'[47] In his eyes, success in Russia involved the fate of the revolution everywhere. If the Bolsheviks held onto power long enough, their struggle might kindle the fires of revolution in the rest of the continent; if they did not, their failure would serve as a deterrent to revolutionary socialists everywhere.

But how was the revolutionary government to survive, let alone gather strength to renew the struggle with its enemies? The Treaty of Brest-Litovsk seemed to erect insuperable barriers against significant recovery, and the left Bolsheviks declared that it would be the death of the revolution. Lenin, however, viewed the Treaty of Brest-Litovsk and any other concessions which he might have to make to the Germans as essential steps in the direction of recovery. When his critics claimed that he had taken leave of his senses he replied: 'It is ridiculous not to know the

44 *Ibid.*, 18
45 *Ibid.*, 252
46 *Ibid.*, 250
47 *Ibid.*, vol. xxxv, 403

history of war, not to know that a treaty is a means of gathering strength ... There are some people who are just like children, they think that if we have signed a treaty we have sold ourselves to Satan and have gone to hell.'[48] For him, the treaty was meaningless, and he consistently compared its obligations to those the Bolsheviks had assumed a decade earlier when 'signing scraps of monarchist paper' saying 'that they would faithfully and truly serve the Emperor Nicholas II.' Just as the Bolsheviks had once signed these 'scraps of paper' to secure the right to sit in the State Duma and thereby improve their political position in Russia, so now the Bolshevik government was signing the German 'scrap of paper' to secure the opportunity to improve its political position in the future. Lenin also compared the Peace of Brest-Litovsk with that of Tilsit which Napoleon had forced Prussia to sign in 1807. He never tired of pointing out that the Peace of Tilsit imposed much more onerous terms on Prussia than the Treaty of Brest-Litovsk did on Russia, yet Prussia had been able to regain its strength and resume the struggle against Napoleon. He intended to follow the same pattern and found it incredible that anyone should ask him if he actually intended to fulfill the obligations contained in Russia's treaty with Germany. 'If it were a three-year-old child who asked me,' he exclaimed, 'it would be both pleasant and naive,' but for an adult revolutionary to do so 'is indeed worthy of children.'[49] When asked this question only a few days after the actual conclusion of 'peace' he shot back: 'Yes, of course, we are violating the treaty; we have already violated it thirty or forty times.'[50]

How did Lenin intend to translate these general principles of his foreign policy into concrete reality? It was one thing to say that the peace treaty was 'a means of gathering strength' and quite another to draw energy from its hostile pages. Yet Russia's armed forces, the most tangible measure of Soviet strength, provide a ready example of Lenin's plan in action. As everyone realized, these forces had deteriorated badly in the previous year, and by early 1918, they no longer represented a military organization of any significance. As long as the war continued, however, the Soviet government had no choice but to perpetuate the fiction that the Russian army was a viable fighting force and maintain its decimated divisions along the entire front from the Baltic to Galicia. No matter how weak and use-

48 *Ibid.*, vol. XXXVI, 31
49 *Ibid.*, 119-20
50 *Ibid.*, 22

less the army had become it was impossible to disband it while negotiations were still in process or actual combat was under way. The 'eleven days war,' however, had revealed the true state of the old Russian army and left no illusions that it could still be maintained as an effective fighting force. Demoralized and disorganized it had simply vanished in the face of the enemy. The peace treaty with Germany finally made it possible to dispose of this phantom army. Lenin described it as the 'sick part of the organism' and said 'the best thing we can do is to demobilize it as quickly as possible.'[51] By March, spontaneous demobilization had largely solved this problem, and the Soviet government could turn its attention to the formation of the new Red army.

Strictly speaking, of course, the formation of a new army was prohibited by the Treaty of Brest-Litovsk, but the Soviet government had a ready answer for this problem. 'We are obligated to proceed to the full demobilization of our army,' Chicherin told the Fourth All-Russian Congress of Soviets, 'including our newly organized armed forces, i.e. the Red army. But here it is a question of demobilization not disbandment, the transfer of the army to a peacetime basis not the total elimination of the army.'[52] This loophole left ample scope to build a large and efficient army, for on the basis of the strength of Russia's pre-war military forces it would be a long time before Germany could claim that the Soviet government was exceeding a peace-time military establishment. Moreover, given the unsettled condition of eastern Europe the Germans were unlikely to be in a position to compel the Soviet government to limit the size of its armed forces. Simply on the basis of maintaining internal order the Soviet government could justify a very large army, and the Germans, knowing that almost any group other than the Bolsheviks would denounce the Treaty of Brest-Litovsk, would have to look benignly upon Soviet efforts to crush counter-revolutionary movements. Finally, given the immensity of Russia, the Germans would find it difficult to determine even roughly the size of the emerging Red army; the Soviet government would certainly do nothing to assist them in such investigations. Under cover of the onerous Treaty of Brest-Litovsk, therefore, the Red army began to come into existence, protected and encouraged by the very document that it was designed to destroy.

But if the Red army was to expand and the Soviet state was to survive all of Russian society had to be restructured. By capitulating at Brest-

51 *Ibid.*, 14
52 Georgii Chicherin, *Stati i Rechi po voprosam mezhdunarodnoi politiki* (Moscow, 1961) 28-9

Litovsk Lenin was buying time to make far-reaching changes in Russia. At the Seventh Party Congress he had secured dictatorial powers to carry out this task, and he lost no time in using them to strengthen the Soviet state in the manner he felt necessary. He said his task was 'to exert every effort to ensure the country's speediest economic recovery, to increase its defence capacity, to build up a powerful socialist army.'[53] Here, as in Soviet Russia's foreign policy, Lenin's realism came rapidly to the fore, puncturing cherished illusions and overturning wasteful practices which had emerged during the first year of the revolution. 'We must learn to work in a new way,' he lectured his comrades, ' ...we must produce order and we must produce all the energy and all the strength that will produce the best that is in the revolution.'[54] If the new army was to have any chance for success, he said, 'we need a strong and organized rear.'[55] It was necessary to transform 'the state economic mechanism into a single huge machine, into an economic organism that will work in such a way as to enable hundreds of millions of people to be guided by a single plan.' To do this he contemptuously rejected the old 'hurrah' methods, saying that 'anyone who attempted to apply these methods ... would only prove his bankruptcy as a politician, as a socialist, and as an active worker in the socialist revolution,' and insisted that 'only by the hard and long path of self-discipline would it be possible to overcome the disintegration that war had caused.' This, he said, would be a 'hundred times more difficult' than anything yet attempted by the Soviet government and would be a 'fight which promises no spectacular opportunities' but was a battle which had to be won if the revolution was to survive.[56]

To win this struggle he prepared a whole series of innovations which he began to enforce upon Soviet society, summing them up under the rubrics of 'accounting and control,' 'labour discipline,' and 'increased productivity of labour.'[57] They added up to nothing less than a complete reversal of those attitudes and practices which the revolution had engendered in Russia and a reversion to norms and methods existing prior to the overthrow of the tsarist regime. Arguing that the destruction of capitalism and the creation of the dictatorship of the proletariat had completely altered social and economic relationships in Russia he asserted that the wasteful practices which had emerged with the collapse of capitalism would no

53 Lenin, PSS, vol. XXXVI, 277
54 *Ibid.*, 25-6
55 *Ibid.*, vol. XXXV, 408
56 *Ibid.*, vol. XXXVI, 6-8
57 *Ibid.*, 278-9

longer be tolerated. Instead, each factory, plant, and work shop was to be held accountable by the state for the allocation and efficient utilization of its resources. Workers, who for the past year had devoted more time to political meetings than actual labour, were to return to their work benches. Politics was to be de-emphasized, and the press in particular was to 'give priority to labour questions in their immediate practical setting.' The press, in fact, was to be converted entirely 'from an organ purveying sensations, from a mere apparatus for communicating political news ... into an instrument ... for telling the masses how to organize work in a new way.' Lenin defined this new way of work as 'democratic centralism in the economic sphere' and clearly intended to apply the same criteria of discipline in the factories of Russia as he applied within the Bolshevik party. The authority of managerial personnel to regulate the tempo and conditions of labour was to be restored and even buttressed. Lenin now spoke almost lyrically of 'one man responsibility' and the 'absolute necessity that the instructions of individual leaders be carried out.'[58] Lenin proposed to reintroduce piece work, restore the Taylor system and make 'the payment of wages commensurate with the general results of the work of a factory.'[59] Trade unions also had to fall in line. Where formerly their primary task had been to defend the class interests of the proletariat they were now to become 'state organizations' having prime responsibility 'for the reorganization of all economic life on a socialist basis.' Anything less, said Lenin, would be 'counter-revolutionary' and amount to 'renouncing the socialist tasks of the working class.'[60]

Lenin was aware that these measures would be just as unpopular as the decision to sign peace with Germany. 'The slogan of practical ability and businesslike methods has enjoyed little popularity among revolutionaries,' he wrote, 'One can even say that no slogan has been less popular.'[61] He knew, however, that they would have to live with these slogans and all the measures he had in mind to strengthen the Soviet state. By slamming the door on an immediate revolutionary crusade Lenin had left his followers no other recourse than to follow the difficult path which he marked out for them. Using both the carrot and stick he urged them relentlessly forward, ascribing Russia's unparalleled danger to the devastated and anarchic state of her social-economic organization and promising salvation

58 *Ibid.*, 156-8
59 *Ibid.*, 279
60 *Ibid.*, 160
61 *Ibid.*, 158

only through the elimination of these obstacles. Counting upon the humiliation and impotent rage of his followers to work in his favour he did not hesitate to remind them constantly of their fate, literally wiping their noses in the foul-smelling situation in which they found themselves. 'Organize self-discipline, strict discipline,' he dinned into everyone's head, 'otherwise you will have to remain lying under the German jackboot as you are lying now, as you will inevitably have to lie until the people learn to fight and to create an army capable not of running away but of bearing untold suffering.'[62] The world workers' revolution remained the shrine at which the Russian revolution worshipped and its golden hope for ultimate deliverance from the hands of the capitalist world, but in the meanwhile, Lenin made clear, and others grudgingly had to admit, that the revolution in Russia would survive only through its own efforts.

This meant hard work, drudgery, and sacrifice. For professional revolutionaries still bemused by chiliastic dreams of imminent utopia and unaccustomed to the type of labour necessary simply to keep a society together, let alone rebuild it from top to bottom, this was an almost impossible challenge. Yet this was the substance of Lenin's words. In summarizing the problems which had to be solved if the revolution was to survive Lenin put this challenge very clearly. 'If the European revolution is late in coming,' he said, 'gravest defeats await us because we have no army, because we lack organization, because at the moment, these are two problems we cannot solve. If you are unable to adapt yourself, if you are not inclined to crawl on your belly in the mud, you are not a revolutionary but a chatterbox; and I propose this, not because I like it, but because we have no other road.'[63] The previous November, when initially embarking on the revolution, Lenin had urged his followers to scale the heights of political power, boldly smashing the patterns of previous generations and, in so doing, bringing revolution to the rest of the world; now he had hurled an even greater challenge to them, many times more difficult to fulfill because it called upon them to smash the illusions, not of other men, but of themselves, while assuming a posture which appeared both unheroic and unrewarding. If any of Lenin's listeners believed that their leader was exaggerating or that they would not do just as he foretold, they were sadly mistaken. 'Grit your teeth, don't bluster and muster your forces,' he told them, and for the next eight months that was exactly what

62 *Ibid.*, 21
63 *Ibid.*, 18

they had to do. The proud revolutionaries who had so light-heartedly seized power the previous November dreaming of the unopposed sweep of their movement across the face of the earth found themselves face down in the mud clawing the slime simply to survive.

9

War and peace: Soviet-German relations after the peace of Brest-Litovsk

If we entice the German financiers ... then we might be able to hang heavy weights on the feet of these soldiers. Ioffe to Lenin, early May 1918.

As long as there remains even a slight chance of preserving peace or of concluding peace with Finland, the Ukraine and Turkey, at the cost of certain new annexations or losses we must not take a single step that might aid the extreme elements in the war parties of the imperialist powers. Lenin to Central Committee, 10 May 1918

The Treaty of Brest-Litovsk brought an official end to the state of war between Soviet Russia and Imperial Germany. The two governments ordered their armies to cease hostilities, and on 4 March, after the Germans had seized their last strategic objectives near Narva, fighting came to an end along the battlefront extending from the Baltic to White Russia. It was, however, an uneasy peace. The treaty had yet to be ratified, powerful groups in both countries opposed it and the two governments suspected each other of treacherous intent. In his telegram announcing the end of fighting Lenin warned that the Germans might resume their offensive at any time and directed local Soviets to redouble their preparations to meet such an attack.[1] On the German side, General Hoffmann, doubting that the Bolsheviks would actually ratify the treaty, made plans for his army to occupy Petrograd.[2] To the surprise of nearly everyone these precautions proved unnecessary. Germany was too deeply involved elsewhere and Russia too exhausted for either to resume hostilities. The war along Russia's *western* frontier was at an end.

1 Lenin, PSS, vol. xxxv, 410
2 Hoffmann, *War Diaries*, vol. I, 208

To the north and south, in Finland and the Ukraine the situation was different. In these areas nationalist regimes had sprung into existence and fought desperately against determined Bolshevik resistance. There the war not only continued but intensified. The conclusion of peace in central Russia only transferred the theatre of war to the borderlands, for if the Soviet government had been forced to renounce Russian sovereignty in the Ukraine and Finland, the Bolshevik party had not abandoned its ambition to rule in Kiev and Helsinki.[3] This clashed with Germany's desire to purge these areas of Russian influence, and Berlin's decision to assist the Rada in the Ukraine and the anti-Bolsheviks in Finland led once again to the clash of German and Soviet armed forces. The renewed struggle posed an immediate threat to the Peace of Brest-Litovsk, because the uneven contest soon resulted in the Germans outflanking Soviet Russia in both the north and south. At Brest-Litovsk a western frontier had been established for Russia and fighting had ceased along a line from Narva to Orsha, but with the intervention of German troops in Finland and the Ukraine this line was left hanging in mid-air, rendered absolutely meaningless by the German drive to the east. Central Russia in effect became a massive salient in the German line of advance, vulnerable to attack at any point. The absence of internationally recognized frontiers separating Russia from her former provinces magnified this problem, for the Rada and Finland proclaimed their sovereignty over as wide an area as possible while Soviet Russia sought to reduce their claims to a minimum. The ensuing conflicts, with German troops enforcing the claims of Kiev and Helsinki, soon threatened to draw Russia and Germany again into full-scale war.

The situation was especially critical in the Ukraine. Here the German advance had begun with the resumption of hostilities on 18 February and continued unchecked after the conclusion of peace. Despite the collapse of the Rada the Germans continued to recognize it as the legitimate government of the Ukraine. Acting on advice from Lenin and Stalin the Soviet government of the Ukraine had made repeated offers to sign the treaty which the Rada had concluded with the central powers on 9 February, but each attempt had ended in failure, the German civil and military authorities being unwilling to enter into relations with the People's Secretariat.[4] As a consequence the German army swept rapidly through the

---

3 *VII Kongress*, 178-9; Lenin, PSS, vol. XXXVI, 32
4 Stalin, *Works*, vol. IV, 42-5; Arkhivnoe Upravlenie pri sovete ministerov UkSSR, Tsentral'nyi Gosudarstvennyi Arkhiv Oktiabr'skoi Revoliutsii i Sotsialisticheskogo Stroitel'stva UkSSR, Institut Istorii AN UkSSR, *Grazhdanskaia Voina na Ukraine.* Three vols. in four. (Kiev, 1967) vol. I, part 1, 20-2. Hereafter cited as GVU

western Ukraine restoring the Rada in Kiev on 1 March. The Soviet Ukrainian government withdrew first to Poltava and then Taganrog, unable to halt the avalanche which had suddenly descended upon it.[5]

Worse was to come, for the Ukrainian Bolsheviks were badly divided among themselves. Regional loyalties, doctrinal differences, and personality problems split them into feuding factions with the Kharkov Bolsheviks fearing subordination to Kiev and the Kievans denouncing the independent ways of their Kharkov comrades. Under the stress of the German invasion the party in the Ukraine began to disintegrate.[6] Alarmed by this dissension Lenin wrote his military commander Antonov-Ovseenko, who had sided with the Kievan faction: 'For heaven's sake, apply every effort to *remove all and every friction* with the Central Executive Committee (Kharkov). *This is super important for the sake of the state.* For heaven's sake, make up with them and grant them *any* sovereignty.'[7] His words fell on deaf ears. By February, the Kharkov Bolsheviks, fed up with both Antonov-Ovseenko and the Kievan faction, broke away from the Ukrainian Soviet Republic and formed their own Donets-Krivoi Rog Soviet Republic. In the following month, as Soviet power crumbled west of the Dnepr, the left bank Bolsheviks did nothing to assist their comrades in Kiev, even congratulating themselves on their timely secession from the Ukrainian Soviet Republic, believing that this gesture would save the eastern Ukraine from the Germans. As late as 6 March, when German columns had already crossed the Dnepr and were marching on Kharkov, the leaders of the new republic declared their intention of uniting with Russia and proclaimed that 'the proletariat of the Donets Republic must focus all its efforts in the direction of asserting its autonomy and independence from the Ukraine.'[8]

This attempt to disassociate the left bank of the Dnepr from the moribund Ukrainian Soviet Republic was doomed to failure. Regardless of Bolshevik sentiments the Rada had proclaimed the provinces of Taurida, Poltava, Kharkov, and Ekaterinoslav to be integral parts of the Ukrainian Republic and had no difficulty in convincing the Germans to extend their military operations into those areas.[9] Lenin realized that if he was to organize any defence against the German invasion he would first have to

---

5 Suprunenko, *Ocherki Istorii*, 26
6 Arthur E. Adams, *Bolsheviks in the Ukraine* (New Haven, 1963), 13-20; Pipes, *Formation of the Soviet Union*, 126ff
7 Lenin, PSS, vol. L, 34-5. Emphasis in original
8 Pipes, *Formation of the Soviet Union*, 131
9 Baumgart, *Deutsche Ostpolitik*, 120-1

overcome the demoralization and divisiveness which was crippling the party in the south. On 15 March, the Central Committee met to ponder the chaotic situation in the Ukraine, handing down a series of decrees ending the scandalous *raskol* between Kiev and Kharkov. To start, it pronounced a death sentence on the Donets-Krivoi Rog Soviet Republic. It was to be liquidated and reunited with the rest of the Ukraine, a new Soviet government composed of representatives from all parts of the Ukraine replacing the separate regimes existing since February. Nor would the Committee tolerate the refusal of Kharkov to assist in the defence of the right bank. 'All party members,' read the resolution of the Central Committee, 'are charged with the obligation to work jointly for the formation of a single defence front.'[10] A week before Antonov-Ovseenko had taken charge of the Kievan armed forces and now he was named commander of the army available in the Donets Basin. Grigori Ordzhonikidze, the representative of the Central Committee in the Ukraine, was given full powers to enforce these resolutions. The day before, in confident expectation of the Committee's action, Lenin had written Ordzhonikidze instructing him to take the most vigorous action to remove all political obstacles to the formation of a 'united battle front from the Crimea to Great Russia.' Dismissing as 'absurd,' 'capricious,' and 'ruinous' all objections to the creation of this front he told Ordzhonikidze to remind the southern comrades that their territory 'could be gobbled up in passing by the Germans.' Lenin also instructed his envoy to 'Ukrainianize' all Soviet military units in the south and have such quasi-Ukrainians as Antonov-Ovseenko assume a totally Ukrainian identity. Thus the Soviet military commander was to drop the Russian 'Antonov' of his hyphenated name and style himself simply as 'Ovseenko.' Anyone who did not cooperate, said Lenin, 'is to be referred to me.'[11]

Ordzhonikidze obtained quick results. The day following the decision of the Central Committee the Sovnarkom of the Donets-Krivoi Rog Republic published a proclamation announcing the formation of a single military command with the Ukrainian Soviet government and recognized Antonov-Ovseenko as the supreme commander of its armed forces.[12] Equally important, Kharkov dispatched representatives to the Second All-Ukrainian Congress of Soviets where they combined with the Kievan Bolsheviks to dominate the meeting and form a new all-Ukrainian govern-

10 GVU, vol. I, part I, 44-5
11 Lenin, PSS, vol. L, 49-50
12 Suprunenko, *Ocherki Istorii*, 28

ment dedicated to national defence.[13] Finally, a month later, the separate party organizations were dissolved at the founding congress of the Ukrainian Communist party.[14] The newly united party was to remain a constant embarrassment and source of trouble for its Russian parent, but at least the amazing spectacle of one faction of the party refusing to assist the other against a foreign invader was not to be repeated.

The damage had already been done. While the various Bolshevik factions had quarreled the Germans had advanced and, by late March, had already begun to approach the eastern industrial region of the Ukraine. After the evacuation of Kiev, Antonov-Ovseenko had concentrated his forces west of Kharkov, but his army was too small to shield the eastern Ukraine from the Germans. Even after it had been reinforced by detachments from the Donets, Ovseenko's army did not exceed twenty-five thousand men, and he had no chance of establishing a continuous front from the Crimea to Great Russia. When the Germans resumed their drive eastward, Ovseenko decided to pass over to partisan warfare, breaking his army into small detachments and leaving them behind the lines of the German army. Within a short time these partisan detachments, reinforced from the local population, began to take a heavy toll of the invader, but the immediate effect was to open the entire eastern Ukraine to occupation. On 8 April, Kharkov fell, followed quickly by the rest of the industrialized left bank; in early May German troops reached the Don and stood at Rostov, the gateway to the Caucasus.[15]

The disaster in the Ukraine had the most serious consequences for Soviet Russia. The Germans had uncovered the entire southern flank of Great Russia, exposing the provinces of Orël, Kursk, and Voronezh to invasion and posing a serious threat to Moscow itself. With the arrival of German troops near Kursk in early April, the Soviet government was forced to make a painful decision regarding the Ukraine. Until then Moscow had provided substantial support for the Ukrainian Bolsheviks, supplying them with financial aid, arms, and military reinforcements, but if the Soviet government continued this policy it would provide the Germans with a ready-made excuse to extend their military operations into the heart of Russia. Even without this excuse there was no guarantee that the German juggernaut would stop at Kharkov, but if Soviet Russia con-

---

13 Pipes, *Formation of the Soviet Union*, 131; Suprunenko, *Ocherki Istorii*, 32-4
14 Suprunenko, *Ocherki Istorii*, 41; Pipes, *Formation of the Soviet Union*, 132; Adams, *Bolsheviks in the Ukraine*, 19
15 GVU, vol. I, part 1, 18ff; Suprunenko, *Ocherki Istorii*, 30ff

tinued to aid the Bolsheviks in the Ukraine it was virtually certain that Russia would again be drawn into direct conflict with Germany. This would spread disaster from the Ukraine to Russia, for the Red army was no more prepared to face the Germans in April than it had been in March. But if armed resistance was out of the question any other policy meant the recognition of the hated Rada as the government of the Ukraine. The terrible dilemma which Trotsky had forecast at the Seventh Party Congress had materialized. Soviet Russia had to choose between abandoning its friends in the Ukraine or jeopardizing its own respite from German attack.

Lenin did not hesitate to make a decision. Although bitterly attacked by the left Bolsheviks for once again surrendering to German imperialism he replied that the disaster in the Ukraine had confirmed and fully justified his earlier policies. 'Our "Lefts,"' he said, 'merely brandish a cardboard sword when they ignore the universally known fact, of which the war in the Ukraine has served as an additional proof, that peoples utterly exhausted by three years of butchery cannot go on fighting without a respite.'[16] He was unwilling to sacrifice Russia's breathing space to wage a heroic, but senseless war in the name of Ukrainian self-determination, and, just as he had abandoned the Baltic provinces in March, he abandoned the Ukraine a month later. It was necessary, as he had predicted, to sacrifice yet more space to gain additional time to rebuild Russia. The inescapable corollary of this policy was the initiation of peace negotiations with the Rada to establish an acknowledged frontier, trading off Soviet recognition of the Rada as the legal government of the Ukraine in exchange for safeguarding Russia from German invasion.

The moment of decision came on 2 April. On that day Moscow received a radio message from the Rada accusing Soviet Russia of active participation in the Ukrainian civil war, demanding an end to this interference and proposing that the Russian-Ukrainian peace negotiations called for in the Treaty of Brest-Litovsk begin as soon as possible.[17] In the circumstances, with German and Ukrainian troops rapidly approaching the Russian frontier, a Soviet response could not long be delayed. A meeting was held with the Ukrainian Bolsheviks who agreed that it was necessary for Soviet Russia to bow to reality and negotiate with the Rada. In return they received Moscow's sympathy in their struggle against the German invader.[18] As

16 Lenin, PSS, vol. XXXVI, 288-9
17 DVP, vol. I, 232
18 GVU, vol. I, part 1, 101-2

circumstances would soon show, they must also have received more substantial, if unofficial, promises of material assistance, for even after the final collapse of Soviet power in the south, Ukrainian Bolsheviks were allowed to continue their struggle from bases in Russia.[19] For the moment, however, this political legerdemain allowed Chicherin to respond affirmatively to the Rada's proposal to open peace negotiations, the foreign commissar suggesting that the talks begin in Smolensk on 6 April.[20]

The decision came none too soon, for on the same day that it was made, German and Ukrainian troops crossed into Russia, occupying districts in the southern part of Kursk province. This created alarm in the Soviet capital, for it was not known if this was the spearhead of an attack on Moscow or merely a military operation of limited local significance. Seeking information Chicherin sent the German government a radio message protesting the incursion, describing the occupied region as being 'indisputably Russian territory' and asserting that even in its 'one-sided declarations' the Rada had made no claim to Kursk.[21] When Berlin replied two days later that 'all contentious questions concerning the extent of Ukrainian territory' would have to be settled by Russian-Ukrainian negotiations and reminded Chicherin that these negotiations were called for by the Treaty of Brest-Litovsk, Moscow had good reason to hope that the way was open to bring the dangerous situation on its southern frontier under control. Although the German answer could hardly be described as friendly it betrayed no overt hostility and seemed to rule out an attack on Moscow. This led Chicherin to reply that Soviet Russia had already proposed peace talks with the Ukraine but had received no answer. He asked the German government to bring his message to the attention of the Rada, reaffirming Russia's willingness to meet Kiev's representatives in Smolensk at the earliest possible moment.[22] The problem created by the German advance towards Kursk appeared on the way to solution.

Appearances were deceiving. A week passed before Berlin replied, and as days fled by without a response the foreign commissar twice more brought the question of Russian-Ukrainian negotiations to the attention of the Wilhelmstrasse.[23] When the Germans finally replied on 14 April, their response was hardly comforting, for it completely ignored Soviet willingness to negotiate and saddled Moscow with the entire responsibility

19 Adams, *Bolsheviks in the Ukraine*, 19-21
20 DVP, vol. I, 232
21 *Ibid.*, 234
22 *Ibid.*, 232-3
23 *Ibid.*, 238-9

for the explosive situation near Kursk. Germany had been forced to occupy the south-western part of Kursk province, the *Auswärtiges Amt* contended, because in suppressing the 'disorders' in the Ukraine its troops had continuously been attacked by armed bands which sought safety by escaping into Russian territory. 'As long as the Russian government does nothing to disarm these bands,' warned the Germans, 'there is not the slightest possibility of ending military operations at the border.'[24] Not one word about Moscow's repeated attempts to initiate peace talks with the Ukraine! Chicherin promptly communicated Moscow's 'surprise' at this omission,[25] and six days later, on 22 April, when the Soviet government still had not received any further response from Berlin, followed it with an exasperated inquiry 'if the absence of an answer must be taken to mean that the German government wishes to remove the [question of Russo-Ukrainian peace negotiations] from the German-Russian treaty.'[26]

The German silence meant no such thing. As usual Berlin had tied itself in knots trying to define Germany's policy in eastern Europe, and the long delay in responding to the Soviet peace initiative simply indicated that the German civil and military authorities had been unable to agree on their future course of action in the Ukraine.[27] As Ludendorff continued to dominate the German political world nothing could be done without his approval, and the foreign office, therefore, had found it necessary to procrastinate and respond evasively to Moscow's messages. Only after the German army had successfully completed the occupation of the northeastern Ukraine and had taken up positions along the entire Ukrainian-Russian frontier was Ludendorff willing to permit the negotiations to proceed. Kiev was then given the green light, and the Rada responded to the Soviet proposal of 3 April with its own suggestion that peace talks begin at Kursk. The Soviet government promptly accepted the proposal, and in late April, a Soviet delegation composed of Joseph Stalin, Christian Rakovskii, and Dmitri Z. Manuilskii left for Kursk to begin talks with the Rada.[28]

Before negotiations could begin, events in the Ukraine left them in shambles. Conservative elements in Kiev, seeing their chance to regain power, had secured the blessing of the German military authorities and seized control of the city. The Rada was overthrown, and a more conser-

24 *Ibid.*, 246
25 *Ibid.*, 245-6
26 *Ibid.*, 257
27 Baumgart, *Deutsche Ostpolitik*, 60ff
28 DVP, vol. I, 281

vative government headed by Hetman Pavel Skoropadskii took its place. Unaware of the *coup d'état* the Soviet delegation arrived at Kursk only to discover that their Ukrainian counterparts had failed to appear. Puzzled and unsure of themselves, they informed Moscow of their predicament and asked the Narkomindel to make inquiries at Kiev. This was not nearly good enough for Lenin, who always suspected his peace delegations of shirking responsibility, and he replied with a sharp message instructing the delegation to search everywhere for the missing Ukrainians.[29] Eventually the Bolsheviks located the Rada delegation, but by then they were already on their way back to Kiev and made it clear that they would not be returning to Kursk.[30]

This left the Soviet government back where it had started a month before, and Chicherin rather caustically turned to Berlin for clarification of the situation. The conservative restoration in the Ukraine was grist for the Soviet mill, and the foreign commissar lost no time in making political capital of the German role in the *coup*. Did the German government, he asked, still want peace negotiations at Kursk? If so, with whom did Berlin expect that the Soviet government should negotiate? 'In the event that supreme authority in the Ukraine has been transferred by the German military authorities to any kind of Ukrainian institution,' he concluded, 'the Russian Soviet government asks the German government to transmit to this new Ukrainian authority its invitation to consider whether or not the previous proposal of the Rada to conduct negotiations at Kursk is still in effect.'[31] It was not necessary, however, for the Bolsheviks to await the formation of a new Ukrainian government in order to secure an end to hostilities south of Moscow. The German military authorities proved willing to negotiate with the Soviet peace delegation, and on 4 May, an armistice was signed.[32] This was only a local agreement, but it reduced tension along that part of the border which most concerned the Soviet government. Moreover, it set a precedent for similar agreements, and Lenin lost no time instructing Soviet military authorities to open negotiations everywhere along the border to secure the same type of armistice.[33] The southern frontier was still far from safe, and any incident was capable of touching off a disastrous confrontation with the German army, but in early May the focus of Soviet concern shifted from Kursk to the northern shore of the Black Sea.

29 Lenin, PSS, vol. L, 66, 421
30 DVP, vol. I, 281
31 *Ibid.*
32 GVU, vol. I, part 1, 136-7
33 *Ibid.*, 137

The crisis which developed along the Black Sea coast stemmed from many of the same causes which had led to the resumption of the hostilities further north. Just as at Kursk, the absence of recognized frontiers provided the basis for conflict. In neither area had the territorial limits of the new Ukrainian state been established, and in the south particularly, the Rada and Soviet Russia put forward sharply conflicting claims. Kiev had proclaimed its sovereignty over the entire Black Sea coast from Odessa to Azov, excluding only the Crimea, while Moscow, pointing to the substantial Russian population of this region, especially in such cities as Odessa, Nikolaev, and Kherson, disputed the Rada's claim. With a total absence of natural barriers to stop them, military forces bent on enforcing the will of their respective governments were able to move freely from one district to another. Both north and south the contested regions were sucked into the vortex of the great conflict then under way in the Ukraine with neither the Germans, Ukrainians, nor Bolsheviks paying any attention to potential or actual frontiers. With their greater mobility and striking power the Germans, in particular, simply roamed at will over both Russian and Ukrainian territory.

Although similar in origin, the crises soon differed from each other in two significant ways. From the start the Soviet government found it difficult to control events in the south. While it was easier for Moscow to communicate with Kursk than Odessa, more was involved than mere technical difficulties. Bolshevik discipline in the south was weaker than in the north, and Bolsheviks there frequently found it necessary to share power with the more volatile left SRs. This made it more difficult to prevent accidental clashes from developing into full-scale hostilities and allowed hotheaded commanders to give full rein to their inclination to fight against impossible odds. Rather than giving ground to superior force the Bolsheviks along the Black Sea coast contested the advance of the German army, provoking even further assaults as a consequence. The higher stakes involved in the Black Sea conflict provided a second distinctive feature. Ultimately it made little difference if Russia won or lost a few additional square miles of farmland in the regions around Orël, Kursk, and Voronezh; it made a great deal of difference if Russia was cut off from the Black Sea. Furthermore, a large part of Russia's fleet was concentrated in the Black Sea ports and this prize made the southern contest especially acute, coming eventually to dominate the entire conflict.

The struggle in the south originated in much the same manner as that further north. German troops swept into the region around Odessa, encountered resistance from the Red Guard and demanded its immediate surrender. The Odessa Soviet, influenced by sailors from the Black Sea Fleet, decided that the city would not be surrendered without a struggle.[34] The Germans were easily able to overcome this resistance, occupy the city and continue their advance along the coast to Kherson. Near that city Antonov-Ovseenko made a brief stand against the Germans, calling upon the Black Sea Fleet to aid him in this effort. The Soviet military commander apparently envisaged a great naval display including the battleships based at Sevastopol, but he received the assistance of only a few light ships which shelled German positions near Nikolaev and later at Kherson.[35] By this time, the Black Sea Fleet, which was described by its commander Admiral Sablin as 'being in a shattered condition,'[36] could no longer fight as a unit and was held together more by inertia than anything else. Armed resistance proved impossible.

Diplomatic protest was equally futile. When word reached Moscow that the Germans had occupied Odessa Chicherin sent a radio message to Berlin, reaffirming Russian sovereignty in that city and demanding its immediate evacuation.[37] On 24 March the *Auswärtiges Amt* rejected this protest saying that the Rada claimed not only Odessa but all of Kherson province, and that, consequently, Germany, acting at the specific request of the Ukrainian government, had not violated either Russian territory or the Treaty of Brest-Litovsk.[38] This declaration, with its implication that Germany had assumed the burden of enforcing the Rada's claim to disputed territories, prompted a double-barreled inquiry from Chicherin, the foreign commissar, asking the German government on 26 March how it defined the borders of the Ukrainian Republic and on 'what document bearing an international character' this definition was based.[39] These were astute questions, for not only were they designed to secure information concerning the extent of Germany's intended military operations along the Black Sea coast, but, as no 'document bearing an international character' existed on which the Ukraine could base its claim, they were also well calculated to embarrass the Wilhelmstrasse. In its answer the German foreign office simply referred the Soviet government to 'proclamations of the Ukrainian Central Rada' for a definition of Ukrainian frontiers and

34 *Ibid.*, 41
35 *Ibid.*, 48, 69-70, 77, 118
36 'Dokumenty po istorii chernomorskogo flota v marte-iune 1918 g.' *Archiv Russkoi Revoliutsii*, XIV (1924) 155. Hereafter cited as 'Dokumenty po istorii chernomorskogo flota'
37 DVP, vol. I, 214
38 *Ibid.*
39 *Ibid.*

asserted that a final solution of this question would have to await a Russian-Ukrainian peace treaty. Until that time, the Germans said, the Reich would recognize the Rada's claim to nine provinces of the former Russian empire including Kherson, Taurida (without the Crimea), Ekaterinoslav, and Kharkov.[40] This left no doubt that the Germans intended to seize the entire Black Sea coast west of the Dnepr and press on to the east, perhaps as far as the Don. In fact, both Kherson and Nikolaev fell to the Germans before the end of March, and the Black Sea ports were lost to the Soviet Republic.

Much worse was to follow, for as their note implied, the Germans had no intention of ending their military operations at the Dnepr. The Ukraine claimed the northern half of Tauride province and, on this basis alone, the German army could have continued its march eastward along the Black Sea, but Ludendorff's aspirations extended even further than this. The nearly effortless advance of the German army had whetted his appetite for further conquests, and from early March he had begun to cast covetous glances south of Perekop. The intervention of the Black Sea Fleet in the fighting at Nikolaev and Kherson, ineffective as it had been, provided him with the excuse he needed to realize his new aspirations. Claiming that this intervention had been a violation of the Treaty of Brest-Litovsk, Ludendorff loudly demanded the liquidation of the 'pirate's nest' at Sevastopol.[41]

Time and again Lenin had cautioned his colleagues against heedlessly provoking the German generals, and in April, the Soviet government was to receive yet another lesson in the wisdom of his warning. Nothing could have been more obvious than the absurdity of sending a handful of warships to strike a few passing blows at the enemy. Nothing had been gained and much had been lost by this futile gesture, for not only did it violate every law of military and political science, it also provided Ludendorff with the pretext he needed to invade the Crimea and detach it from Soviet Russia. He had begun to think of the peninsula as a 'German Riviera,' and following the use of Russian warships at Nikolaev and Kherson he began to prepare for the seizure of the Crimea. Although the German foreign office objected, pointing to the damage which the seizure of the Crimea would do to Germany's relations with Soviet Russia, the army went ahead with its plans and, by mid-April, was ready to launch its attack.[42]

40 *Ibid.*, 217
41 Baumgart, *Deutsche Ostpolitik*, 152-3
42 *Ibid.*, 153-4

Long before this Moscow had grown concerned about the safety of the Crimea and the fleet at Sevastopol. There were virtually no Soviet troops in the peninsula, and once the Isthmus of Perekop was lost the Germans could reach Sevastopol in a matter of days. As the Soviet government knew that Antonov-Ovseenko would have to abandon Perekop it began to give serious consideration to the evacuation of the Black Sea Fleet to Novorossiisk. [43] After studying the problem, however, the Supreme Military Soviet was reluctant to order this move as they feared that the Germans might consider it a violation of the Treaty of Brest-Litovsk.[44] But what then was to be done? Not only was the council aware that German troops were massing opposite Perekop, they also noted that Berlin in its message of 29 March, while excluding the Crimea from the territorial limits of the Ukrainian Republic, had not specifically recognized the peninsula as an integral part of Russia. From this they concluded that while the Treaty of Brest-Litovsk guaranteed the 'inviolability' of the Black Sea Fleet, 'experience has shown how lightly the Germans violate the norms of international law as well as their own obligations.' They resolved, therefore, to accept *in principle* the proposal to transfer the fleet to Novorossiisk but to delay the move until Trotsky had consulted with the Narkomindel to 'clarify the political side of this complicated question.'[45]

The delicate state of Russo-German relations justified the caution of the Supreme Military Soviet. No evidence is available to indicate the result of Trotsky's consultations with the Narkomindel, but as no further action was taken by the council prior to the German invasion of the Crimea, it is safe to assume that the foreign commissariat advised against any move which might antagonize Berlin. But it was not good enough simply to avoid offending Berlin; the Narkomindel had to determine Germany's probable reaction to a movement of the fleet to Novorossiisk without actually informing Berlin that this was what the Soviet government intended. Chicherin did this by raising questions tangential to the central problem of the Black Sea Fleet, seeking first to initiate negotiations for the return of Russian ships seized by the Germans at Nikolaev[46] and then, two days later, filing a rather vague protest against hostile acts of German warships in the Black Sea. In the latter he went far out of his way to stress

43 'Dokumenty po istorii chernomorskogo flota,' 155-7
44 GVU, vol. I, part 1, 93-4
45 *Ibid.*, 98-9
46 DVP, vol. I, 240

the 'definitive and strict' neutrality observed by the Russian Black Sea Fleet, even asserting that since the signing of peace with Germany the ships had never left port.[47] If he did this hoping to coax some response from the German foreign office revealing its attitude toward the fleet at Sevastopol he was not disappointed, for the German reply left no doubt of how Berlin felt on this question. With Ludendorff's invasion of the Crimea only days away Berlin took this opportunity to justify the forthcoming attack, charging that Russia had violated the peace treaty by employing its fleet against German and Turkish forces. The Germans demanded an end to these activities, said they would no longer tolerate further violations of the peace treaty, and informed Moscow that after 20 April any Russian warship contravening article five of the Treaty of Brest-Litovsk would be considered as 'outside the law' and be dealt with accordingly.[48]

The German message, amounting to an ultimatum, left the Soviet government in a considerable dilemma. If it ordered the Black Sea Fleet to Novorossiisk the Germans could describe it as a violation of the peace treaty and thereafter treat the Russian ships as 'outside the law;' if, on the other hand, the Soviet government left the fleet at Sevastopol and the Germans did invade the Crimea, the ships would be captured at their moorings. Despite the ominous ring of the German message, with its perplexing reference to 20 April as having some special significance, the Soviet government decided against provoking a crisis by ordering the fleet to Novorossiisk. Instead, on 17 April, Chicherin responded to Berlin's charges by disputing the German interpretation of the naval clauses of the peace treaty and proposing the formation of a special commission to regulate the issue. He denied any misconduct by the Black Sea Fleet and blamed the hostile acts against Turkish forces on 'Caucasian counter-revolutionaries' who he said had appropriated some of the smaller vessels of the Russian fleet at Batum and were using them contrary to the wishes of the Soviet government. He was careful, however, not to mention the incident at Kherson. Instead, with an eye to the possibility that events might force the Black Sea Fleet to seek safety in Novorossiisk, he placed heavy emphasis on the Soviet interpretation of the naval clauses of the peace treaty, asserting that they did not compel Russian warships to remain in port but gave them the right to navigate Russian coastal waters from one Russian port to another. Pending resolution of this issue, said

47 *Ibid.*, 242-3
48 *Ibid.*, 248

Chicherin, he was 'certain' that Germany would abstain from any hostile acts against Russian warships exercising the rights which Moscow claimed for them.[49]

Chicherin, of course, was certain of no such thing. Powerless to influence Berlin, he could only wait in suspense while the German government made up its mind. As usual Berlin found this impossible, and instead of one German response there were two. The foreign office found the Soviet proposal acceptable and suggested that Moscow send representatives of the Russian fleet to Berlin to meet with the naval representatives of Germany and her allies to settle questions arising from the disputed articles of the peace treaty.[50] It did so in the hope of restraining the German army from further expansion into Russia,[51] but Ludendorff was not to be denied. He had his heart set on conquering the Crimea, and he would not allow the last minute Soviet proposal to stop him from carrying out his plans. On 18 April, a German army commanded by Field Marshal Mackensen seized Perekop and marched into the Crimea. Ludendorff had again triumphed over the foreign office, revealing once more the schizophrenia rampant at the centre of the German power structure.

In the Crimea, German troops soon reached Simferopol less than fifty miles from the anchorage of the Black Sea Fleet.[52] No armed force barred their way, nor were they stopped by protests from the Soviet government. Neither that of Centroflot (the highest organ of Soviet authority in the Black Sea Fleet) filed with Mackensen,[53] nor that of the Narkomindel sent to Berlin,[54] had any effect. In his protest Chicherin had warned that 'interests of self-preservation' would force the Black Sea Fleet to resist the invasion, and when Mackensen did not respond to its protest Centroflot dispatched armed sailors to Simferopol to block the road to the naval base. The sailors managed to stem the German advance for about a week, but they were too disorganized to establish a permanent perimeter around Sevastopol. Worse yet, under the pressure of the German attack, the frail unity of the fleet began to collapse. As Mackensen approached Sevastopol Ukrainian sympathizers convinced many war-weary sailors that the only way to save themselves from German internment was to swear allegiance

49 *Ibid.*, 246-8
50 *Ibid.*, 247
51 Baumgart, *Deutsche Ostpolitik*, 157-8
52 Suprunenko, *Ocherki Istorii*, 38
53 GVU, vol. I, part 1, 128
54 DVP, vol. I, 253-4

to the Rada. One ship after another raised the Ukrainian flag, and by the time orders finally arrived from Moscow to evacuate Sevastopol only part of the fleet was willing to leave. When Sablin weighed anchor on 27 April most of the mine-sweepers, the old battleships, and all of the submarines remained behind. The rest of the fleet including the two modern dreadnoughts followed Sablin to Novorossiisk.[55]

The escape of a large part of the Black Sea Fleet soon plunged Russian-German relations into even deeper crisis. The first hint of further trouble came on 3 May when Berlin responded to the Soviet protest against the occupation of the Crimea. The note denied that Germany was seeking to detach the Crimea from the Russian federation explaining that the occupation had been motivated by reasons of 'purely military significance.' Germany, it said, recognized the right of the Crimea to self-determination and was content that its fate be decided in a future Russian-Ukrainian peace treaty. Given the German definition of self-determination and support of the Ukraine this alone was enough to alarm the Kremlin, but it was the remainder of the note which was truly frightening. Here, Berlin justified the invasion of the Crimea on the basis of 'the attack by the Sevastopol fleet against Kherson and Nikolaev.'[56] If Germany could justify her action in the Crimea on the basis of the threat posed to Mackensen's army by the Black Sea Fleet, she could also use the presence of that fleet at Novorossiisk as a pretext for an invasion of the Kuban.

This was exactly what Ludendorff had in mind. No sooner was the occupation of the Crimea complete than he began to demand new measures to force the surrender of those ships which had escaped Mackensen at Sevastopol. Pointing to the fighting at Simferopol as fresh evidence of Soviet unwillingness to honour the peace treaty he proposed that a new ultimatum be sent Moscow demanding the surrender of the warships at Novorossiisk. If the Russians did not surrender the ships Mackensen would march into the Kuban after them and, if necessary, chase them all the way around the Black Sea until they had no further harbor in which to find refuge.[57] Still master of the political situation in Berlin, the general had little difficulty in overcoming the resistance of the *Auswärtiges Amt*, and, on 10 May, the new German demands were sent to Moscow.[58] Russian-German relations entered a new and critical phase precipitated by

55 Suprunenko, *Ocherki Istorii*, 38-40
56 DSB, vol. I, 614-15
57 Baumgart, *Deutsche Ostpolitik*, 159-62
58 DVP, vol. I, 284

Ludendorff's insatiable appetite for new conquests and Moscow's inability to cope with the military power of Imperial Germany.

The situation was just as bad on Russia's northern flank. While German armies marched through the Ukraine, occupied the Crimea and stood ready to invade the Kuban, other German troops landed in Finland. This had been foreshadowed in early March when German troops went ashore in the Aaland Islands but had been delayed by unfavourable weather and the inability of the German government to decide if it wanted to intervene in the Finnish civil war.[59] When Ludendorff succeeded in forcing this decision on the government the German foreign office reluctantly began to prepare for intervention by warning Soviet Russia about its activities in Finland. The Treaty of Brest-Litovsk strictly prohibited the Soviet government from interfering in the internal affairs of Finland, but, as in the Ukraine, Moscow provided its friends with as much assistance as it could spare from its meager resources. Lenin, in fact, boasted of this assistance at the Seventh Congress and hoped with the aid of Russian arms and money to maintain Soviet power in Finland.[60] Berlin, therefore, had a good case and, on 23 March, issued its first warning demanding that Soviet Russia put an immediate end to the delivery of arms and ammunition to Helsinki.[61] Lenin took this warning very seriously and ordered that a detailed reply be made answering the charges of the German government.[62] This was sent on 27 March, but, of necessity, was a rather lame response to the German protest.[63] It made absolutely no impression in the German capital where final preparations for intervention in Finland were already under way. On 1 April the *Auswärtiges Amt* fired back a second protest complaining of the movement of Red Guards from Petrograd to Finland. With German troops already aboard the transports which would carry them to Hanko, Berlin warned that if Soviet Russia did not abide by its treaty obligations Germany would 'be forced to take steps of its own for the restoring of the situation prescribed by the treaty.'[64] This triggered alarm bells in Moscow where Lenin, sensing that Berlin meant what it had said, desperately sought to forestall German intervention. Upon receipt of the German protest he telephoned Petrograd ordering the withdrawal of

59 Baumgart, *Deutsche Ostpolitik*, 93-7
60 Lenin, PSS, vol. XXXVI, 32
61 DVP, vol. I, 218
62 Meijer, *The Trotsky Papers*, 31
63 DVP, vol. I, 217-18
64 *Ibid.*, 222

all Red Guards from Finland, repeating his order a second time when Soviet officials in the former capital proved reluctant to comply.[65] Chicherin sent an urgent message to Berlin assuring the Germans that neither 'the central Soviet government nor local organs of power are sending Red Guards to Finland.'[66]

The last minute effort to avert German intervention in Finland proved too little and too late. The German 'beast' was poised to spring again, and on 3 April, the Baltic Division went ashore at Hanko. In conjunction with Finnish troops under General Carl Mannerheim it made short work of the Red Guards, entering Helsinki on 13 April and clearing all Finland of Soviet troops within a month.[67] Just as in the Ukraine, Soviet power collapsed under the hammer blows of the German army. With its demise a bourgeois government hostile to Soviet Russia took power in Helsinki. Headed by P.E. Svinhufvud, the new government considered itself to be in a state of war with Moscow and acted vigorously to defend its new-won independence. Unlike the Rada it was soon able to stand on its own feet and dispense with German military assistance, but as it remained closely tied to Berlin it represented a serious threat to Soviet security. Mannerheim's army moved up to the Soviet frontier in early May, and as no international agreement identified the precise line separating Russia from Finland numerous incidents occurred which threatened to lead to full-scale hostilities. The fears and aspirations of Finnish nationalists greatly enhanced this threat, for in the interest of self-defence they claimed the right to occupy Russian territory and in the name of a yet greater Finland they demanded the annexation of East Karelia. Mannerheim's troops seized strategically important regions in the vicinity of Petrograd and Finnish irregulars invaded East Karelia. As tension began to mount Svinhufvud even sought to convince Germany that it should detach Petrograd from Russia in order to eliminate the danger which that city posed to Finland.[68] In short, the victory of the anti-Bolsheviks in Finland threatened to unhinge Russia in the north in the same way as the victory of the Rada had done in the south.

The crisis in the north soon came to focus on Fort Ino, a key bastion defending the sea approaches to Petrograd. Situated on the north shore of the Gulf of Finland, approximately sixty miles from the Neva, it was claimed by both Moscow and Helsinki. The Finns demanded its surrender

65 Lenin, PSS, vol. L, 54-5
66 DVP, vol. I, 221
67 C. Jay Smith, Jr, *Finland and the Russian Revolution, 1917-1922* (Athens, Georgia, 1958) 73-85
68 Mauno Jääskeläinen, *Die Ostkarelische Frage* (Helsinki, 1965) 84-5

because the fort was situated well within their borders; the Bolsheviks wished to keep it, as they feared that the surrender of one of the key elements in the defence of Petrograd would encourage the Germans to launch a seaborne assault on the city. Well protected and provided with the latest in coast defence artillery, Fort Ino was not easily captured. Although by early May the Finns had placed the fort under siege, its garrison could still be supplied by sea, and Helsinki soon conceded that it could not be captured without the assistance of large warships. Turning to Berlin, they found the German navy reluctant to risk its treasured battleships against the fixed fortifications at Ino. Such a contest was contrary to accepted naval practice, and although Ludendorff urged the admirals to accommodate the Finns, the foreign office encouraged them to refuse. While debate continued in Berlin, the Soviet government settled the question by suddenly evacuating the fort. On 15 May, the Russians removed their garrison, destroying the guns and fortifications before they left.[69]

Why did the Soviet government do this? In part, Moscow misjudged the extent to which Germany was prepared to support Finland. Left reeling by the speed with which Germany had overrun the Ukraine, Finland, and the Crimea, the Soviet government could not have guessed that the German navy would prove reluctant to risk its capital ships against fixed fortifications. Since February, Germany had backed every claim of its eastern clients against Soviet Russia, and Moscow had no reason to believe that Berlin would default in this instance. The Bolshevik leadership was so psychologically prepared to expect extortionate demands from Germany that in the case of Fort Ino Berlin did not even have to present a formal demand for its surrender. Instead, a German note warning that the continued presence of Russian troops on Finnish territory would 'undermine trust in the sincerity of the peace policy of the Soviet authorities'[70] proved sufficient to convince Lenin that the fortress would have to be surrendered. Not wanting to provoke Germany into mounting an attack on Ino which could easily be expanded to include Petrograd, Lenin on 6 May asked for and received authorization from the Central Committee 'to yield to the German ultimatum' and surrender the fortress to Finland.[71] Subsequent inquiries in Berlin revealed that the German foreign office did not object to the destruction of the fortress, and, consequently, Lenin ordered that it be reduced to rubble before abandoning it.[72]

69 Baumgart, *Deutsche Ostpolitik*, 99-101; Jääskeläinen, *Die Ostkarelische Frage*, 116-17; Smith, *Finland and the Russian Revolution*, 84-5
70 DVP, vol. I, 278
71 Lenin, PSS, vol. XXXVI, 315, 607
72 *Ibid.*, 344-5

But more was involved in the surrender of Fort Ino than psychological conditioning and unwillingness to provoke Germany. Coming as it did with the concurrent crisis in the Ukraine, the threat to Russia's northern frontier formed only part of the larger problem of how to deal with Germany's insatiable appetite for Soviet territory. Lenin had tried to purchase peace at Brest-Litovsk by conceding everything which Germany demanded, but the Reich had merely increased its demands, adding to them those of the Rada and White Finland. The experience of March and April had shown that it did the Soviet government absolutely no good to deal with individual crises as they arose, for no sooner would one problem be settled to Russia's disadvantage than Germany would create a new and more serious one to take its place. If Soviet Russia was to survive, Lenin had to find some way to stop the Germans from amputating one province of the former Russian empire after another. As the Red army could not possibly assist in this task the Soviet government had no other recourse than to attempt to engage Berlin in new negotiations designed to reach a general settlement of all problems existing between the two states. In reaching this conclusion Lenin did not delude himself with the hope of regaining lost territory. His one aim was to prevent the loss of further territory or, at least, to keep such losses to a minimum. In this larger framework, the loss of Fort Ino, as serious as it was, meant relatively little and was easily justified as a tactical retreat necessary for the attainment of broader objectives.[73]

The first step in this direction came on 13 May when Chicherin, in a radio message to Berlin, proposed the initiation of wide-ranging talks aimed at the settlement of major differences existing between Soviet Russia and Germany. Strictly speaking this was a response to the German message of 11 May demanding the return of the Black Sea Fleet to Sevastopol, but on the basis of guidelines prepared by Lenin,[74] the foreign commissar tied the satisfaction of Germany's demand to the larger issues which interested Moscow. Taking as his theme 'the goal of establishing a durable peace in all parts of Russia' Chicherin coyly informed Berlin that the Soviet government was prepared to return the Black Sea Fleet to Sevastopol. This would be done, he added, 'only if agreement on this question is part of a general agreement ... establishing final limits to German, Austro-Hungarian, and Turkish occupation in all parts of Russia as well as

73 *Ibid.*
74 *Ibid.*

the borders of Finland and the Ukraine, which in its turn presupposes the unconditional termination of military action in all parts of Russia.' Nor was that all. Chicherin carefully differentiated between the internment of the Black Sea Fleet and its surrender, ruling out the latter as unacceptable and specifying that if the ships were returned to Sevastopol, Germany would first have to evacuate the city and return it to Soviet control. Nor would the Soviet government agree to the internment of its fleet simply in return for an end to military operations in Russia. Chicherin also linked the satisfaction of the German demand to a settlement of problems in the Caucasus where, since March, Turkish forces had pressed steadily forward into Georgia and Armenia. This advance threatened both the southwestern shore of the Black Sea and the oil-rich city of Baku on the Caspian. Any settlement with Germany, Chicherin made clear, would be incomplete without Berlin agreeing to use its influence to end Turkish military operations in the Caucasus.[75] In substance, then, the foreign commissar told Berlin that Moscow would give up the Black Sea Fleet only if Germany was ready to end the three-month-old war against Soviet Russia.

On the whole this was hardly an attractive package, for all it promised in return for the many concessions demanded from Germany was the return of the Black Sea Fleet, a fugitive easily within the grasp of Mackensen. If this had been all which Moscow could throw into the balance it is unlikely that Berlin would have shown much interest, but in addition to the Black Sea Fleet the Bolsheviks also had Russia's continued neutrality in the Great War with which to bargain. As will be shown in the next chapter, the deterioration of Soviet-German relations had led to a resurgence of allied interest in drawing Russia back into the war, and as Lenin had predicted, Soviet Russia was able to play on Germany's fear that Moscow might once again join the entente against the central powers. Rumours that the Soviet government was contemplating such a move had begun to circulate in Moscow, and the Bolsheviks did nothing to discourage their spread. Quite to the contrary, Chicherin did his best to encourage them. Thus, at the height of the crisis he provided Morgan Philips Price, Moscow correspondent of the *Manchester Guardian*, with an interview in which he said: 'At the present moment the policy of the Soviet Government is to keep Russia neutral. But if either of the great world groups shows to it more hostility than the other, it may be compelled to act with the less hostile one. Thus, if Germany attempts to occupy part of Great Russia, she may meet

with the resistance of British bayonets side by side with Russian bayonets.'[76] To be sure, in order to balance his political equation and not give
undue encouragement to the allies, he added that 'if Japan attempts to
occupy Siberia, she may meet with German bayonets on the Urals,' but at
the time the interview was given Chicherin's formula was specifically designed to alert Germany to the danger involved in pressing Soviet Russia
too far. It was not necessary, however, for the foreign commissar to rely
entirely on the unsure medium of the press to convey his message to
Berlin. By this time Soviet Russia and Germany had exchanged ambassadors and it was possible for Chicherin to bring this matter directly to the
attention of the Wilhelmstrasse. He instructed the Soviet ambassador in
Berlin to: 'call the attention of the German Government to the fact that
the present state of affairs creates among the masses that fear which
yesterday poured out into the press in a whole series of rumours and false
news reports about the supposedly impending rupture of relations between Germany and Russia. We have denied these rumours, but no assurance of ours can pacify the masses of Russia when the actions of German
policy flow in the opposite direction.'[77] In addition, Count Wilhelm von
Mirbach, the German ambassador in Moscow, took these rumours seriously. As early as 10 May, he informed Berlin that he had received a
report from a 'good but not yet fully proven source' that the entente had
offered military assistance to Russia as a means of inducing her to re-enter
the war. The Soviet government, he said, was not likely to accept the
offer, but as Bolshevik leaders were 'incensed about the advance in the
South' it was 'not impossible that there may be surprises.'[78]

The Narkomindel worked overtime to impress Mirbach with the seriousness of the situation. In addition to Chicherin, who for the record had
to soft-pedal the rumours of an impending rupture, the German ambassador was encouraged to speak with some of the more bellicose Bolsheviks,
Karl Radek in particular, who favoured more resolute action to stem Berlin's *drang nach osten*. Returning from one such conversation Mirbach
reported the 'deep-seated excitement' then prevalent in Moscow governing circles and warned Berlin that the Bolsheviks were having no easy time
in restraining the 'Hotspurs' in their camp 'who were doing everything
possible to promote a breach' with Germany. Despite their 'international

76 Price, *My Reminiscences of the Russian Revolution*, 276
77 DVP, vol. I, 284
78 Z.A.B. Zeman (ed.), *Germany and the Revolution in Russia: Documents of the German Foreign Ministry* (Oxford, 1958), 123-4

socialist exaggerations,' he explained, they deeply resented the humiliating spectacle of their country being torn to shreds by the German Army. 'I have the distinct impression,' he concluded, 'that [the Bolsheviks] would prefer once and for all to be informed about our final aims, no matter how exaggerated they might be, than to have to bear patiently, this constant partial amputation.'[79] Two days later, on 13 May, Mirbach went even further, warning Berlin that 'any further advance on our part might drive the Bolsheviks into the arms of the Entente or, in the event of their fall, bring successors favourable to the Entente into power.' As this would undermine Germany's entire position in eastern Europe, he advised Kühlmann that 'our interests still demand the continuation in power of the Bolshevik Government.'[80]

These were exactly the views which Lenin wanted Mirbach to convey to Berlin. Only if the German government could be persuaded that it was in its own interest to assist the Bolsheviks to stay in power was there any hope of ending the march of the German army into Russia, and Mirbach's reports represented a long step in that direction. Together with Chicherin's proposal to open new negotiations with Berlin they marked the opening phase of the successful Soviet effort to bring the war with Germany to a genuine conclusion. They were, however, only two elements in a larger plan to achieve this goal, for Moscow knew that it was insufficient merely to convince the German foreign office of the wisdom of reaching a final settlement with Soviet Russia. If the Soviet government was to succeed in ending German military operations in Russia, Lenin understood that he first had to find some way of reducing the army's influence in the formation of German foreign policy.

Soviet leaders had been aware of the pre-eminence of the army high command in German politics since December 1917 when peace talks had begun at Brest-Litovsk. The split between the German civil and military authorities had been apparent at the peace conference, but because of Trotsky's commitment to a revolutionary strategy the Soviet government had been unable to capitalize on it. Nor had Lenin been able to cope with the independent role of the army high command in shaping German policy. Although there was seldom any doubt in his mind as to who actually made decisions in Berlin, he had no knowledge of the other landmarks of the German political world. He had in effect been steering blindly without benefit of a political roadmap identifying the paths of power in Berlin. By

---

79 Cited in Baumgart, *Deutsche Ostpolitik*, 163
80 Zeman, *Germany and the Revolution in Russia*, 124-5

itself this absence of reliable information had badly crippled Soviet policy, and it was not until the third week of April, following the exchange of ambassadors, that Moscow began to receive the information which it needed to evaluate the situation in Berlin.

The delay in exchanging ambassadors arose primarily from the continuation of hostilities. The route between Moscow and Berlin was controlled by the German army, and with operations in the Ukraine and Finland under way they had little interest in assisting the passage of diplomatic missions. Finally, after repeated delays, the problem of dispatching two substantial delegations through war-torn western Russia was solved, and on 20 April, A.A. Ioffe arrived in Berlin to take up his duties as Soviet ambassador in the German capital.[81] Ioffe proved to be a good choice for the post. Energetic but soft-spoken, willing to listen as well as to argue, he was sufficiently flexible in his approach to men of other persuasions to gather the information needed in Moscow. From his first day in the German capital he saw a steady stream of visitors from the German political and business world, and from them he learned a great deal. He quickly confirmed that a wide split existed between the German civil and military authorities and reported that German big business opposed the army's policies in the east. The interest which representatives of major German banks and industries showed in the establishment of commercial relations with Moscow convinced him that they were opposed to a resumption of the war. 'In any event,' he reported, 'if they were considering the possibility of a rapid renewal of the war against us, they would not be coaxing us as they are now.' Their eagerness to share in the Russian market also suggested a way of hobbling the German army. Summarizing his proposal, he wrote: 'If we entice the German financiers, who even apart from this do not approve the policy of the extreme militarists, then we might be able to hang heavy weights on the feet of these soldiers.[82]

This was the type of information for which Lenin had been waiting. He used Ioffe's reports to formulate a new set of theses accounting for the failure of his peace policy and laying the basis for a new effort to make it work. He presented his ideas to the Central Committee on 10 May, arguing that 'since Brest the war party has gained the upper hand in German politics in general, and this party could now, at any moment, gain the

81 Baumgart, *Deutsche Ostpolitik,* 208-9
82 I.K. Kobliakov, 'Bor'ba sovetskogo gosudarstva za sokhranenie mira s germaniei v period deistviia brestskogo dogovora (Mart – Noiabr' 1918),' *Istoriia* SSSR, no. 4 (1958) 12

upper hand on the question of an immediate general offensive against Russia.' Despite that danger, he contended there was still hope for peace. 'It is an undoubted fact,' he said, 'that the majority of the imperialist bourgeoisie in Germany are against [the policy of the war party] and at the present moment prefer the annexationist peace with Russia to a continuation of the war for the simple reason that war would divert forces from the West and increase the instability of the internal situation in Germany ... it would also make it difficult to obtain raw materials.' From these postulates he drew the conclusion that 'the foreign policy of Soviet power must not be changed in any way.' Instead, he asserted that 'as long as there remains even a slight chance of preserving peace or of concluding peace with Finland, the Ukraine and Turkey, at the cost of certain new annexations or losses, we must not take a single step that might aid the extreme elements in the war parties of the imperialist powers.'[83] The Central Committee accepted Lenin's theses, and four days later, the All-Russian Central Executive Committee approved a much abbreviated version of this policy statement.[84]

With his foreign policy approved by the central organs of the party and state Lenin was left with the responsibility of making it work. But where, to use Ioffe's idiom, was he to find the weights to hang on the feet of Ludendorff? Obviously they would have to be heavy objects indeed, and since Lenin wanted to interest German capitalists in a political alliance against their own army these objects would have to be made of pure gold. Keeping this in mind, as well as the near certainty that he would not have another chance to stop Ludendorff short of the Ural-Kuznetsk redoubt, Lenin prepared a massive bribe to tempt German big business into partnership with Soviet Russia. In a set of new theses outlining a policy of economic cooperation with Germany he called for the resumption of economic relations with the Reich, a large loan from German banks to the Soviet government, the payment of interest on this loan with Russian raw materials, large Soviet purchases in Germany, concessions to German companies for the exploitation of Russian natural resources and German assistance in construction of railways and modernizing agriculture. First, however, Germany would have to agree not to interfere in Russia's internal economic policies, abstain equally from interfering in Soviet economic relations with countries which previously formed a part of Russia, recog-

83 Lenin, PSS, vol. XXXVI, 322-6
84 Ibid., 327-45, 608

nize Soviet legislation nationalizing banks and trade, guarantee delivery of at least half of the total iron ore production from Krivoi Rog and assist in the establishment of a Soviet frontier with the Ukraine which would assure Russia possession of the Donets coal basin.[85] Lenin lost no time in communicating these proposals to the German government. Drafted on 14 May, they were presented to a rather surprised German ambassador the next day. In a short speech elaborating on Lenin's economic program, M.G. Bronskii, Soviet commissar of trade, explained to Mirbach that the Soviet government wished to act on the proposals quickly and suggested that formal negotiations begin as soon as possible. So that there would be no misunderstanding the purpose of these proposals, Chicherin pointedly informed the German ambassador that 'these economic suggestions presupposed a settlement of political questions such as would not completely throttle Russia.'[86] Within hours both Lenin's program and Chicherin's statement were on the wires to Berlin where they proved decisive in bringing about the shift in German policy desired in Moscow.

Lenin had carefully timed the presentation of his proposals so that they would arrive in Berlin shortly after Chicherin's message calling for the negotiated settlement of Russia's border problems. Only forty-eight hours separated the two, and their sequential arrival in the German capital had the effect, as Lenin wished, of strengthening Kühlmann in his struggle with Ludendorff for control of Germany's *Ostpolitik*. Using the two proposals Kühlmann was able to prepare an irrefutable argument against the continuation of German military operations in the east, proposing instead a negotiated settlement with Moscow. As a start, they permitted him to destroy Ludendorff's contention that the Bolsheviks would not fulfill their obligations except at the point of a gun. The Soviet proposals indicated that the Bolsheviks were not only prepared to abide by the Treaty of Brest-Litovsk, but, if allowed to do so, were even willing to provide Germany with the economic reinforcement it needed in the last phase of the Great War. Lenin's economic proposals virtually marked Kühlmann as a prophet, for no less than a fortnight before, in an effort to appeal to the anti-semitic prejudices endemic in German ruling circles, he had predicted that the Soviet leaders as 'Jewish businessmen' would 'soon give up their theories in favour of a profitable practice in trade and commerce.'[87]

85 DSB, vol. I, 622-7
86 Zeman, *Germany and the Revolution in Russia*, 126
87 Baumgart, *Deutsche Ostpolitik*, 386

Most importantly, Lenin's economic proposals allowed Kühlmann to outmaneuver Ludendorff, using the General's own words to box him in. This opportunity arose from a letter of 3 May which Ludendorff had sent to the Reichschancellor stressing the importance of promoting close economic ties with Russia. When the war in Europe ended, said Ludendorff, a bitter economic struggle with the entente would continue, and only 'through the intense economic utilization of Russia' could Germany remain strong. Russia, rich in raw materials and hungry for manufactured goods, would have to replace Germany's traditional markets and be brought under German tutelage. Ludendorff, however, had little idea of how to do this and could only suggest 'propaganda and the dependence upon us into which Russia has fallen for the duration of the war' as the means available to achieve his goal.[88]

Nor was Ludendorff the only German leader who worried about the post-war world. On 16 May, the day following the delivery of Lenin's economic proposals to Mirbach, the barons of the German steel industry presented a memorandum to the Imperial Treasury containing views similar to those just expressed by Ludendorff. The names of the men and firms signing this memorandum read like a who's who of the German economic world, including Thyssen, Stinnes, Vogler, and Krupp. They too believed that an economic struggle with the western powers would follow the end of the war and feared that Germany would be unable to win back its former markets. A substitute was needed, and, in their eyes, Russia would be an ideal replacement for the markets lost to the entente. They were willing to invest heavily in this enterprise, proposing the creation of a huge consortium capitalized at two billion marks to control German trade with Russia, but insisted that such an enormous venture would require substantial government support. First and most important, they said, the German government would have to take the political initiative to guarantee Russia as an area of German economic exploitation.[89]

With men such as Thyssen, Stinnes, Vogler, and Bruhn demanding close economic relations with Russia, and Lenin offering to open Russia to German economic exploitation, the balance of power on the question of Germany's eastern policy swung dramatically in favour of Kühlmann. He now had the means to fight Ludendorff, and he lost no time in using his new weapons. Marshalling all the evidence which Lenin had so carefully placed at his disposal he argued that the Soviet regime was the only

---

88 DSB, vol. I, 613-14
89 *Ibid.*, 629-33

imaginable Russian government willing to abide by the Treaty of Brest-Litovsk, let alone agree to close economic ties with Germany, and consequently, the Reich in its own interests, could not afford to jeopardize Bolshevik rule in Russia. Ludendorff's policy, especially the 'constant partial amputations' which Mirbach said were creating political instability in Moscow, had to be changed. Otherwise, said the foreign secretary, Germany would soon be faced with an openly hostile Russian government and lose its chance to develop the economic ties demanded both by German industry and Ludendorff himself. Hoist with his own petard, Ludendorff was unable to reply to Kühlmann's argument, and on 19 May, at the request of the foreign secretary, the Kaiser ordered a halt to further German military operations in Russia.[90] The next day Kühlmann told Ioffe of this order, informing him that the German government was prepared to begin the negotiations suggested by Moscow.[91] Lenin had succeeded in hanging his weights of gold on the feet of the German army.

How long would they restrain the dynamic Ludendorff? Lenin moved quickly to get the negotiations started, having Chicherin propose a six-point agenda (comprising the situation in the Caucasus, the Crimea, the demarcation line established by the Treaty of Brest-Litovsk, prisoners of war, and economic questions) on 22 May,[92] but this was not fast enough to stop Ludendorff from regaining the initiative. The general had been temporarily outmaneuvered but not defeated. He remained as intransigent as before, hating the Bolsheviks and not wishing to do anything to support them. Due to his inadequate reserves of men and material, as well as the absence of a realistic alternative to put in their place, he was forced to tolerate the Bolsheviks, but toleration did not include the negotiation of any further agreements with them. If the Bolsheviks could not be eliminated they could at least be kept off balance. This would prevent them from organizing any effective resistance to future German demands and leave them vulnerable once the war in France was over. Lenin's offer to open economic negotiations, therefore, seriously disrupted Ludendorff's calculations, and the interest which this offer had excited in the German business and political world made it politically inexpedient to challenge directly the Kaiser's decision to accept the offer. Instead he was forced to adopt obstructionist tactics in an effort to prevent the civil authorities from reaching a new agreement with Moscow.

90 Baumgart, *Deutsche Ostpolitik*, 163-4, 269
91 DVP, vol. I, 311, 315
92 *Ibid.*, 315-16

Least successful of these tactics was his attack on Lenin's economic proposals. Dismissing the Soviet program as 'inadequate' he said Germany should be satisfied with nothing less than total domination of Russia's foreign trade. Any possibility that Moscow might trade with the west had to be eliminated, and Russia, which he said 'will never be our friend' had to be weakened still further and *'tied to us by force.'*[93] Despite Ludendorff's violent words his response was weak, for it was backed by nothing but his own hot air. No-one in the upper echelons of the German government believed that his demands were realizable, and Kühlmann had only to ask 'how can this be done?' in order to reveal the void lurking behind the general's bombastic phrases. If Ludendorff was to obstruct negotiations with Moscow he would have to find some pretext other than the Soviet economic proposals.

He found his most effective means in that area where he still held the initiative and exercised effective control over the contested ground. That was in Russia itself and concerned the still unresolved question of the Black Sea Fleet. Lenin, by voluntarily agreeing to negotiate the return of the fleet to Sevastopol and tying those negotiations to many other questions, had temporarily reduced the tension on this issue, but Ludendorff, recognizing the leverage which it offered him, lost little time in reviving the dispute. As early as 21 May, two days after the Kaiser had ruled an end to further German military operations in Russia, Ludendorff insisted that it was necessary 'to clear the table ... in order to obtain security on the Black Sea.' Let negotiations proceed, he said, but first let the Black Sea Fleet return to Sevastopol where it could not harm German interests in the Ukraine. The Kaiser proved sympathetic to this argument but not to the general's demand that the Bolsheviks be given six days to surrender their fleet. Kühlmann argued that purely technical reasons might make it impossible for the Bolsheviks to comply and that in any case an ultimatum would not contribute to the pacification of eastern Europe. The Kaiser agreed,[94] and the message sent to Moscow on 23 May was drafted by Kühlmann rather than Ludendorff. In it Kühlmann said that the return of the Black Sea Fleet could not await settlement of the other issues raised by the Soviet government but was careful to assure Moscow that the ships would remain Russian property and would be returned to the Soviet government at the conclusion of a general peace. He set no specific date by which time the ships would have to reach their former anchorage but

93 Cited in Baumgart, *Deutsche Ostpolitik*, 269. Emphasis in original
94 *Ibid.*, 164-5

warned that any delay could be justified only on the grounds of technical difficulty and in no case could extend beyond a period of from six to ten days. If the ships were returned within the specified time the German army would not advance beyond the line which it had already reached.[95] While still containing a substantial element of menace, therefore, the message tended to emphasize agreement rather than controversy and was certainly not the ultimatum which Ludendorff had wanted. Moreover, following its dispatch, both Kühlmann and Hertling reiterated their opposition to any action which might endanger Germany's relations with Russia. Kühlmann insisted that the army abandon its plans to advance on Novorossiisk telling Ludendorff that to do so 'would shake the Russian trust in our *bona fides*, something which could have serious consequences,' while Hertling told the general that the possession of a few ships was not worth the 'extraordinary political consequences' which would result from an invasion of the Kuban. Rightly fearing the explosive potential of this issue, Kühlmann hastened to instruct Mirbach to urge the Bolsheviks to agree to the prompt return of the ships 'as a sign of their good will.'[96]

Kühlmann's plea fell on deaf ears. Good will toward Germany was understandably at a discount in the Soviet capital, and the Bolshevik leaders were in no hurry to give up the remnants of the Black Sea Fleet. With the exception of the economic bait which they were then dangling in front of the Germans and the intangible value of their continued neutrality in the Great War the fleet was all that they had to bargain with, and Lenin was determined to get as high a price as possible for its return to Sevastopol. At this point, however, the Soviet leaders got their signals very badly tangled, and whereas Moscow's first reaction was to scoff at the German message of 23 May, Ioffe acted otherwise. The Soviet ambassador had agreed to the foreign secretary's terms, reporting his action in a radio message which reached Moscow at approximately the same time as the German note.[97] This brought an almost instant response from Chicherin, the foreign commissar, who wired back: 'Your radio message not understood, repeat imprecise statement about Black Sea Fleet.' To remove any doubt from the mind of the ambassador, he again spelled out Russia's precise terms for the return of the fleet to its former base, stressing that Moscow would agree to this only if Sevastopol was returned to Soviet control. 'This,' he concluded, 'is an unalterable condition.' Lenin

95 DVP, vol. I, 351-2
96 Baumgart, *Deutsche Ostpolitik*, 165
97 *Ibid.*

turned livid when he discovered what his ambassador had done. 'How can Ioffe make such a mistake?' he wrote. 'How can he have "sold" so cheaply? How was it possible that on such an important question that he could send a note *on his own authority* without asking for advice; I do not understand this.'[98] But the damage was done, and the Soviet government had to retreat. The German government, fearing Ludendorff's wrath, would not negotiate further and dug in its heels. Chicherin attempted to save something from the débacle by offering to accept the important railway junction of Bataisk in southern Russia instead of Sevastopol, but this too was rejected.[99]

As time passed and the Russian ships did not return to Sevastopol, Berlin began to grow restive. Ludendorff, of course, inquired why Russia had not complied with Germany's demand,[100] and Kühlmann reluctantly had to instruct Mirbach to turn the screws on Chicherin. On 6 June, the Soviet government was informed that Berlin 'attached significance' to receiving an answer to its note of 23 May within six days' time.[101] Mirbach did not say what consequences would follow from a Soviet failure to reply, but Moscow reasonably drew the conclusion that continued silence would lead to further military action. Consequently, the Bolsheviks capitulated and assured the Germans that the Soviet ships would return to Sevastopol within the next ten days. On 8 June Moscow radio broadcast a special order from Trotsky instructing the Black Sea Fleet to return to Sevastopol.[102]

This did not settle the controversy, nor was the crisis to pass so easily. Instead, events in the south were moving in the opposite direction. Near Rostov, at the far north-eastern corner of the Sea of Azov, the quasi-autonomous Black Sea-Kuban Soviet Republic, struggling for its life against a variety of enemies including the Germans, inopportunely decided to launch a sudden sea-borne assault behind the lines of Field Marshal Mackensen's army. Unaware of the crisis in Russian-German relations,[103] Soviet leaders in the south unleashed their attack on the morning of 8 June with armed merchant ships shelling German positions near Ta-

98 *Leninskii Sbornik*, vol. XXXVI, 43-4. Emphasis in original
99 DVP, vol. I, 330-1; DSB, vol. I, 655
100 Baumgart, *Deutsche Ostpolitik*, 166
101 DSB, vol. I, 655
102 'Dokumenty po istorii chernomorskogo flota,' 216
103 A report from Rakovskii to Trotsky dated 7 June 1918, gives a graphic account of the lack of communication and coordination which then existed between Moscow and Soviet authorities in southern Russia. See Meijer, *The Trotsky Papers*, 45-7

ganrog and landing troops to link up with other Soviet units striking west from the Don. Although there was no proof to show that these ships came from Novorossiisk,[104] Ludendorff immediately seized on the attack as new evidence of Soviet treachery and demanded authorization to eliminate the 'pirates' nest' at Novorossiisk.[105] Kühlmann was able to prevail upon the Kaiser to give him one more chance to secure the surrender of the Black Sea Fleet without a German advance to Novorossiisk, but it was his last chance, and he drafted his note to the Soviet government with Ludendorff breathing down his neck. The foreign secretary, therefore, couched his demands in peremptory language, demanding an end to the Soviet military operations near Taganrog and the return of the Black Sea Fleet to Sevastopol. The German army, he concluded, would be forced 'to take further measures, solely determined by military considerations' if within three days the Soviet government did not comply with his demands.[106]

Ioffe, who had to bear the brunt of German anger, did his best to quiet the storm. He blamed the incident on the unsettled military situation in southern Russia and promised to work for the acceptance of the German demands. He placed a special direct wire call to Moscow in order to urge compliance with the German demands and warn Lenin that 'any inadvertent act of provocation on our side, even if it be a trivial one, will be immediately turned to account from a military point of view.'[107] Lenin fully shared this view and assured his ambassador that everything possible was being done to cope with the crisis. 'We are taking all measures,' he said, 'to secure both the transfer of the ships to Sevastopol and also a cessation of hostilities or anything resembling hostilities on our side. I repeat: everything possible is being done.'[108]

This was true only in so far as it involved ending hostilities. Lenin and Chicherin succeeded in contacting the Soviet forces operating against Taganrog and ordered an immediate cease fire, threatening anyone who violated the order with 'strict accountability before a revolutionary tribu-

---

104 Sablin, in fact, had repeatedly refused to send his ships to aid the Black Sea-Kuban
   Soviet Republic. See 'Dokumenty po istorii chernomorskogo flota,' 194. The troops and
   ships attacking Taganrog sailed from Eisk on the Sea of Azov and received absolutely no
   support from the Black Sea Fleet. V.T. Sukhorukov, *XI Armiia v Boiakh na Severnom
   Kavkaze i Nizhnei Volge, (1918-1920 gg)* (Moscow, 1961) 34
105 Baumgart, *Deutsche Ostpolitik*, 166-7
106 DSB, vol. I, 657
107 Meijer, *The Trotsky Papers*, 49-55
108 *Ibid.*

nal.'[109] Trotsky also issued a general order to the Red army forbidding offensive action of any kind against the Germans.[110] The text of this order was promptly communicated to the Germans, and Chicherin informed Mirbach that the Soviet government accepted the German ultimatum without reservation. He promised to do everything possible to meet the German deadline but stressed that difficulties in communicating with Novorossiisk might make it impossible for the ships to reach Sevastopol by the fifteenth. Mirbach accepted this explanation and passed it on to Berlin where it was generally credited as having been made in good faith.[111]

The German government was profoundly in error, for Lenin had no intention of surrendering the fleet without receiving substantial compensation. As early as 24 May, one day after receiving the second German demand for its surrender, he had decided to destroy the fleet rather than relinquish it on the terms which Berlin offered,[112] and, on 28 May, he secretly ordered that the ships at Novorossiisk be scuttled.[113] The plan nearly failed, because the sailors of the Black Sea Fleet were totally confused by the conflicting orders which they received. Radio Moscow repeatedly urged them to return to Sevastopol[114] while ciphered instructions sent secretly to the naval base insisted that they scuttle their ships at Novorossiisk. The sailors found it difficult to believe that the order broadcast *en clair* from Moscow was designed only to confuse the Germans and were reluctant to act until they received unambiguous instructions. Lenin entrusted these instructions to F. Raskol'nikov who was ordered to proceed at once to Novorossiisk and sink the Black Sea Fleet. The day before his arrival, however, six destroyers and one dreadnought sailed for Sevastopol. On 18 June Raskol'nikov succeeded in sinking the remaining ships. The Black Sea Fleet had ceased to exist.[115]

The sinking of the Black Sea Fleet removed the last obstacle to new negotiations with Germany. Soviet treachery in destroying, rather than surrendering, the fleet could have led to a new crisis in relations between

109 Sukhorukov, *XI Armiia*, 36
110 SGO, vol. I, 558
111 Baumgart, *Deutsche Ostpolitik*, 167
112 Lenin, PSS, vol. L, 81
113 GVU, vol. I, part 1, 168
114 'Dokumenty po istorii chernomorskogo flota,' 216-17
115 V.K. Zhukov, *Chernomorskii Flot v Revoliutsii 1917-1918 gg.* (Moscow, 1931) 277ff
    Also see F. Raskolnikov, *Rasskazy Michmana Il'ina* (Moscow, 1936) 19-46

Moscow and Berlin, but the German government chose to accept Chicherin's rather lame explanation[116] and close its eyes to what actually had happened. Ludendorff, to be sure, roared angrily about Soviet duplicity and demanded sanctions against the Bolsheviks, but no one else in the German government cared if the Black Sea Fleet was in Sevastopol or at the bottom of the sea.[117] Ludendorff had based his entire case for the surrender of the fleet on the threat it posed to German interests in the Ukraine, and with that threat removed government and industrial circles were unwilling to allow a few unwanted ships to stand in the way of the projected economic and political negotiations.

Lenin had gambled that Berlin would react in this way and probably reasoned as well that the sinking of the fleet, together with the earlier destruction of Fort Ino, would serve as a good lesson for the Germans. Having consciously excited German avarice it was of the utmost importance that he now convince them that they could not satisfy their greed except through cooperation with the Soviet government. Since May he and his representatives had been dinning this message into German heads, regaling Berlin with stories of the abundant wealth of Russia but always pointing to the Ukraine as an example of what would happen if Germany attempted to use force to take what it wanted from Russia. In the Ukraine, they reminded Berlin, the German army had occupied the entire country and established a regime subservient to its wishes, but, nevertheless, had been unable to extract the food and raw materials needed to supply the German economy.[118] 'The German merchants,' said Lenin in a letter to Ioffe, had to be made to understand 'that by war with us they will get *nothing*, but through agreement with us, *everything*.'[119]

Lenin's message was clearly understood in Berlin. Although minor skirmishes continued to occur along Russia's exposed frontier, these were small local conflicts and did not threaten a resumption of full-scale war. Instead, under prodding from Berlin, the governments in Kiev and Helsinki agreed to end hostilities with Russia. Although the unresolved question of East Karelia prevented more than a *de facto* cease-fire with Finland,[120] the Hetmanate signed an actual armistice with Soviet Russia.[121]

116 DVP, vol. I, 372-3
117 Baumgart, *Deutsche Ostpolitik*, 169-70
118 *Ibid.*, 275-6
119 *Leninskii Sbornik*, vol. XXXVI, 46-7. Emphasis in original
120 Jääskeläinen, *Die Ostkarelische Frage*, 122-3
121 John S. Reshetar Jr, *The Ukrainian Revolution, 1917-1920* (Princeton, New Jersey, 1952) 190

The same uneasy calm which had earlier settled over western Russia now descended in the north and south.

Lenin had succeeded in plumbing the depths of German greed, and if he had been forced to promise Berlin a substantial share of the actual and potential wealth of all Russia he had finally succeeded in obtaining the long-sought, but ever-elusive, respite which he wanted. This was no mean accomplishment, for it neutralized the greatest threat to Bolshevik rule in Russia. Until June, Lenin and his colleagues had lived in the shadow of the German juggernaut, Ludendorff's war machine drawing ever nearer their seat of power and threatening to topple them at any moment. Even if the Germans had simply continued their 'partial amputation' of the Russian provinces the political instability generated by their action might have been sufficient to overturn the Bolsheviks. This threat had now been reduced, if not eliminated, and with the coming of summer the Soviet government could turn its meager military resources against internal enemies gathering in Siberia and the southeast. Nearly eliminated in March, these forces had sprung to life again during the three months in which Soviet power appeared to disintegrate under the hammer blows of the German army and, in mid-year, once more constituted a major threat to the Bolsheviks. Worse yet, this problem was magnified by the mounting hostility of the allied powers and the increased assistance which they began to provide anti-Bolshevik forces in Russia. The Bolsheviks, having successfully ransomed themselves from the Germans, were now faced with a new threat from the allies as a result of their success.

10

Soviet Russia and the allies after Brest-Litovsk: the failure of cooperation

Our ways are not your ways. We can afford to compromise temporarily with capital. It is even necessary, for if capital were to unite we should be crushed at this stage of our development ... So long, therefore, as the German danger exists, I am prepared to risk a co-operation with the allies, which should be temporarily advantageous to both of us. Lenin to Lockhart, 1 March 1918

Two groups of powers wish to interfere in Russia; if we remain passive, the history of the first partition of Poland will repeat itself to our detriment. Cooperation on our part has fewer inconveniences, but you have refused to propose it to us with precision. Chicherin to Lavergne, 4 May 1918

War against Germany threatens greater losses and calamities than against Japan. Decision of Bolshevik Central Committee, 5 May 1918

Throughout 1918 the barometer of Soviet-allied relations rose and fell in direct proportion to the actual or anticipated role of Russia in the world war. The allies, deeply engrossed in the struggle with the central powers, framed policies on the basis of their calculated contribution to the defence of western interests and the eventual defeat of Germany, while the Bolsheviks, in an attempt first to spread revolution and then simply to survive, trimmed their political sails with every storm generated by the continuing conflict. The Bolshevik decision to sign the Peace of Brest-Litovsk shattered the fragile basis of Soviet relations with the allied powers, and within days the western representatives began to leave Petrograd. Convinced that they were in danger of being taken prisoner by the Germans, the allied missions scattered in all directions, the British and French embassies seeking safety in Scandinavia, the French Military Mission leaving for Murmansk and the Americans departing for Vladivostok. Allied-Soviet relations sank to their lowest level since the Bolshevik seizure of power.

Viewed through western eyes the Bolshevik capitulation was nothing short of disaster, for London and Paris believed that the coming year would determine the outcome of the war. Bled white by four years of slaughter the western allies feared that they would be unable to survive if Germany was allowed to draw on the abundant natural resources of Russia and concentrate all its forces on the western front. For this reason they had not hesitated to intervene in the Russian revolution aiding those groups which promised to continue the war and even throw their support behind the Bolsheviks when circumstances made it appear that they would be forced to fight Germany. The Soviet surrender put paid to that chapter of the allied search for collaborators in Russia and, more importantly, exhausted all the Russian groups available for use against Germany. By late February the revolution had done its work so thoroughly that, except for the Bolsheviks, no political force remained in Russia around which the allies could build a bulwark against the central powers. Not one of the many movements upon which the allies had pinned their hopes commanded any significant support.

So desperate was their position that even prior to the collapse of their last effort to recruit allies in Russia, western leaders had begun to cast about in search of a foreign force capable of re-establishing allied influence in eastern Europe. Given the exhaustion of their own armies and the assignment of the American Expeditionary Force to France only Japan could provide the necessary troops. As early as January, Japan had said it was prepared to send its army into Siberia, but fearing the American reaction to that thrust, Tokyo insisted that it would first have to receive the explicit approval of the United States. This the American government steadfastly refused, but as Tokyo was reluctant to promise that it would extend its military operations from Siberia into eastern Europe, the western allies did not make a major issue of Washington's refusal to sanction Japanese intervention in Russia.[1] The Bolshevik

1 Kennan, *Russia Leaves the War,* 275-329, 470-85; Ullman, *Intervention and the War,* 82-103; James William Morley, *The Japanese Thrust into Siberia, 1918* (New York, 1957) 122-30; W. B. Fowler, *British-American Relations, 1917-1918: The Role of Sir William Wiseman* (Princeton, New Jersey, 1969) 164-9; David R. Woodward, 'The British government and Japanese intervention in Russia during world war I: *Journal of Modern History,* XLVI, no. 4 (Dec. 1974) 663-85

capitulation swiftly altered the situation, and, in late February, the western allies again turned to the Japanese gambit, pressing it upon the reluctant Americans with clamorous insistence.[2]

Reports concerning allied intervention soon reached Soviet ears. Rumours of possible Japanese action in Siberia had been circulating for
months, but with the collapse of Bolshevik resistance to Germany vague
accounts of the actual discussions among allied leaders began to leak into
the western press.[3] These stories were monitored in Petrograd where gov-
ernmental circles received them with concern. Since the stories tended to
reinforce suspicions deeply rooted in the Bolshevik consciousness Soviet
leaders took them seriously and initiated measures to delay and, if possible, frustrate western efforts to reach agreement on intervention. This
was made difficult, not only by the critical state of Soviet negotiations with
Germany but also by the withdrawal of the allied ambassadors from Petrograd. By the end of February only Bruce Lockhart and Jacques Sadoul
remained in the Soviet capital, and neither had much influence with his
government.

The Soviet leaders turned first to Lockhart who, unlike Sadoul, was at
least an official agent of his government. He was called to Smolny on 1
March for an interview with Lenin. The significance of Lenin meeting
with Lockhart and later Robins should not be overlooked. Since November Trotsky alone had dealt with the allied representatives, but now, in the
absence of Chicherin, who was still at Brest-Litovsk, Lenin assumed the
responsibility. Trotsky attended the meeting, but, Lockhart observed, 'the
Lion' remained in the background and Lenin did all the talking. This was
Lockhart's first meeting with the Bolshevik chieftain, and at first he was
not impressed, thinking that Lenin looked 'more like a provincial grocer
than a leader of men.' This impression soon faded, and he found himself
captivated by Lenin's 'tremendous will-power, relentless determination
and lack of emotion.' Lockhart admired Trotsky, but now he concluded
that Lenin was the greater of the two. 'Morally,' he wrote, '[Trotsky] was
as incapable of standing against Lenin as a flea would against an elephant.'
Together with this impression Lenin conveyed his intention to continue
the struggle with Germany. Russia was making peace, he said, but it
would not be a durable peace; instead the war against German imperialism
would continue on terms which would not threaten the existence of the
Soviet state. Consequently, cooperation with the western powers was

2 Ullman, *Intervention and the War*, 104; Kennan, *Russia Leaves the War*, 474
3 Kennan, *Russia Leaves the War*, 492

still possible, but he insisted that Paris and London would have to understand that the Soviet government would 'not be made the cat's paw for the Allies' and would not sacrifice itself in their interest. He was, however, skeptical about the possibility of cooperation and said Britain was more likely to support the 'Russian reactionaries.' Lockhart naturally attempted to convince Lenin that cooperation was possible, but he also challenged the contention that it could be effective if Russia made peace with Germany. What, he asked, would become of the Bolsheviks if Germany should defeat the western allies? Lenin laughed at this shop-worn question and accused Lockhart of thinking 'only in concrete military terms.' The war, he said, would be decided 'in the rear and not in the trenches;' but even from a purely military perspective, he contended, the conclusion of peace would not injure the western powers. Instead the 'robber's peace' would force Germany to commit more, rather than fewer, troops to eastern Europe.[4]

Lenin made no attempt to deal specifically with the question of intervention, seeking only to breathe new life into possible allied-Soviet cooperation and convince Lockhart that Russian withdrawal from the war would not be fatal for the allied cause. He left the problem of Siberia to Trotsky, who after Lockhart's talk with Lenin informed the British agent of Soviet fears of Japanese action in the far east. Such a step, said Trotsky, 'would throw all Russia into the hands of the Germans' making Russian socialists believe that this action was a 'direct result of a secret understanding between the Allies and Germany.' That evening Lockhart cabled London reporting that there were 'still considerable possibilities of organizing resistance to Germany,' and saying he would remain in Russia 'as long as there is the slightest hope.'[5] If that hope was to be realized, he added, the allies could not act precipitously and intervene militarily without Bolshevik assent. In particular, he said, it was necessary to restrain Japan and 'delay action until it is proved that the Bolsheviks are unable to organize any opposition to the Germans.'[6]

For the moment at least Lenin and Trotsky had enlisted Lockhart against intervention, but by himself the young British agent was unlikely to carry much weight in allied councils. Moreover, the logic of power politics in the Pacific, where the United States was the chief rival of Japan, called for a Soviet strategy based on convincing Washington, rather than

4 Lockhart, *British Agent*, 236-40
5 Cited in Ullman, *Intervention and the War*, 121
6 PRO FO 371/3285/40028

London, of the need to restrain Japanese intervention. But with the departure of the American ambassador from Petrograd how was this to be done? Not only had Francis left, but Raymond Robins, the ubiquitous Red Cross officer who had served as liaison with Smolny for the Americans, had gone with him. Only when it was learned that the Americans had interrupted their journey at Vologda did it become possible for the Soviet government to re-establish contact with them. For tactical reasons, the Bolsheviks decided to ask the help of Sadoul, as they believed that the Americans, angered by the decision to make peace, were more likely to listen to a French officer than a Soviet envoy. Sadoul, who was very sympathetic to the Soviet cause, had no influence with his own government, but was a friend of Robins and might be able to convince him to oppose intervention. Both Lenin and Trotsky spoke to the French captain on 2 March asking him to undertake this mission on their behalf. As with Lockhart they stressed the tenuous nature of the peace negotiated at Brest-Litovsk and the manner in which a Japanese descent on Vladivostok would throw Russia into the arms of Germany. Sadoul, who looked upon the Japanese as 'the Germans of the far east' and feared a potential alliance between Tokyo and Berlin, agreed, and left the next day to bring Francis and Robins up-to-date on events in Petrograd. Specifically, he was instructed to enlist American aid for opposing Japanese intervention in Siberia.[7]

Sadoul arrived in Vologda in the evening of 4 March. Robins had already departed, having returned to Petrograd on receiving news that peace had been signed at Brest-Litovsk, but the French captain had little difficulty in convincing Francis that if the Bolsheviks could obtain allied assistance they were prepared to continue the war against Germany. Sadoul, who had a rather low opinion of the ambassador, describing him as a 'respectable old man of a trifle slow intelligence,'[8] was careful to present his case in terms understandable by Francis. Playing on American idealism and fear of Japan the captain stressed the importance for the allies of avoiding any action of an 'anti-Russian character.' The United States, he said, must reassure the Russian people of allied good intentions and 'protect the general interests of the entente' against Japanese encroachment.[9] Francis responded favourably and sent Colonel Ruggles, his military attaché, back to Petrograd with Sadoul to consult Trotsky on the

7 Sadoul, *Notes*, 251
8 *Ibid.*, 254
9 *Ibid.*, 255

assistance which Russia would need if the Soviet government did not ratify its peace treaty with Germany. More importantly, he adopted a negative attitude to intervention. At the time he left Petrograd he had called
upon the allies to occupy Russian ports in the far north and Pacific, but
now he reversed himself. In light of the seeming Bolshevik readiness to
resist Germany, he told Washington, the seizure of these cities would be
'unwise.'[10]

Independent of these events, the American government was painfully
and erratically attempting to formulate its policy on the chaotic and disastrous situation in Russia. Assaulted by both the British and French governments, which vehemently demanded American cooperation in fore-
stalling a German seizure of all Russia, Wilson's objections to Japanese
intervention had begun to crumble. Still unwilling to sponsor such a move
the president, nevertheless, decided on Friday, 1 March, that he could no
longer object to his allies asking Japan to act in Siberia. Although Britain
and France were informed of this decision, sentiment in Washington
quickly forced Wilson to reverse it. 'We can not wash our hands of this
matter,' argued William Bullitt, who one year later would lead an American mission to Soviet Russia and later still become Washington's first ambassador in Moscow. 'Unless we oppose, we assent. Pontius Pilate washed
his hands. The world has never forgiven him.'[11] Bullitt convinced Colonel
House, Wilson's chief confidant, that the president's decision would undermine the 'moral position' of the United States, and House agreed to
review the policy with the president. On Monday, while Sadoul was still on
his way to meet Francis at Vologda, the president drafted another statement on intervention, assuming a position diametrically opposed to that
of the previous Friday. Instead of giving Tokyo a green light to proceed
with intervention Wilson once more reiterated American opposition to
the landing of Japanese troops in Siberia.[12] Delivered the next day, Wilson's note was sufficient to give pause to the Japanese. Two days after
receiving it the Japanese foreign minister informed the British that pending American approval his government would be unable to take further
action.[13] For the moment, the threat of a Japanese invasion of the Soviet
far east subsided.

10 FRUS, *1918, Russia* vol. 1 392; cf. 384
11 Kennan, *Russia Leaves the War*, 475-80
12 *Ibid.*, 481-2
13 Morley, *The Japanese Thrust into Siberia*, 133

Unaware of this, Lenin and Trotsky continued to woo the Americans. When Robins reached Petrograd early on the morning of 5 March, Trotsky lost no time involving him in the Soviet effort to avert Japanese intervention. Using the lure of Russia possibly continuing the war against Germany, Trotsky captivated Robins by energetically reopening the question of allied assistance in the event the Bolsheviks failed to ratify the Treaty of Brest-Litovsk. Although the ink on that treaty was barely dry Trotsky declared that if Lenin could get 'economic co-operation and military support from the Allies he [would] refuse the Brest peace, retire, if necessary from both Petrograd and Moscow to Ekaterinberg, re-establish the front in the Urals, and fight with Allied support against the Germans.' This was exactly what Robins wanted to hear, but knowing, as he said, that Lenin was 'running this show,' he demanded to speak with the Bolshevik leader.[14] Trotsky agreed, and a meeting was arranged with Lenin prior to which Robins received a vague and curious document purporting to be a statement of Soviet inquiries concerning American intentions should a number of hypothetical circumstances occur.

This document provided the basis of discussion in Robins' meeting with Lenin and is worth close examination. It can not be described as a 'state paper,' for it came to Robins unsigned and without benefit of any formal assurance that it was an official act of the Soviet government. Much to the contrary, when Robins first asked Trotsky to commit his proposals to paper, providing in this manner an official statement of Soviet intent, the commissar had replied with shock: 'You want me to give you my life, don't you?'[15] Robins had then suggested that if it was too dangerous for Trotsky to provide a written statement of Soviet proposals for cooperation with the allies it might be possible to convey their substance in a less explicit manner. The result was the convoluted, unorthodox document which Trotsky presented Robins before their meeting with Lenin. Although Robins considered it a document of extraordinary importance it is difficult to share his opinion or see it as anything more than a contingency paper of no official standing. On its face, in fact, the document could have originated anywhere and have been designed for almost any purpose. It was, of course, prepared by Trotsky, probably in collaboration with Lenin, and was meant specifically to convince Robins that Russia was truly ready

14 United States of America, *Bolshevik Propaganda Hearings before a Subcommittee of the Committee on the Judiciary, United States Senate, Sixty-Fifth Congress* (Washington, 1919) 800-1.
15 *Ibid.*

to resume the war with Germany. In reality it did not commit the Soviet government to anything at all. It merely cited three contingencies – Soviet refusal to ratify the peace treaty with Germany, a continued German offensive, and Soviet renunciation of the peace treaty – in which, as it said, it would be 'very important for the military and political plans of the Soviet power for replies to be given' to a number of questions. These questions fell into two categories, the first concerned entirely with the extent to which Soviet Russia could rely on allied, and particularly American, assistance in the event of renewed hostilities with Germany, and the second bearing on the problem of possible allied intervention in Russia. 'What step would be taken ... especially by the United States,' it asked, 'to prevent a Japanese landing on our Far East.'[16] Here was the key to the document, for whereas Robins sought to draw out the Bolsheviks on their plans to resist Germany, Lenin and Trotsky preferred to talk about the threat of intervention. Lenin, as he would explain a few days later at the Seventh Congress,[17] was seeking to play off one belligerent coalition against the other and use allied interest in Russia's resumption of the war to stave off Japanese invasion in the far east.

Of course, much more than this was involved, for when Lenin spoke with Robins on the afternoon of 5 March he had no way of knowing if the peace with Germany would endure. He did not even know if he could convince his supporters to ratify the peace treaty. If his policy failed he had to have some line of retreat prepared beforehand. Just as important, given the strength of the war party in Petrograd, he had to reinforce his credibility as a leader ready to carry on the war if his policy should fail. Much still depended on Trotsky's willingness to live up to his bargain, and until Lenin could restructure the Central Committee at the forthcoming congress he had to humour his more bellicose colleagues and convince them he was acting in their interest as well as his own. In part Robins understood this, realizing that Lenin was not a fervent partisan of renewed belligerency, but that which he did not understand was the length to which Lenin would go to avoid the resumption of war with Germany. Swept up in the wartime psychosis of national hatreds and totally enveloped in a shroud of assumptions meaningless in the context of Leninist politics, he was certain that German rapacity would force Soviet Russia back into the war. But Lenin was directing a totally different policy than that pursued by

16 C.K. Cumming and Walter W. Petit (eds.), *Russian-American Relations: March 1917–March 1920. Documents and Papers* (New York, 1920) 81-82; DVP, vol. I, 208-9
17 See above, 185-6

any of the belligerents and had no intention of being dragged into the war unless faced with a mortal threat to the regime or presented with an opportunity to improve his position substantially. In a veiled form, probably written by Lenin, this was mentioned in the document Robins received from Trotsky. Here it said that all the questions raised in the first part of the document were: 'conditioned with the self-understood assumption that the internal and foreign policies of the Soviet Government will continue to be directed in accord with the principles of international socialism and that the Soviet Government retains its complete independence of all non-socialist governments.'[18] Robins did not understand the meaning of these words, and Lenin did not enlighten him. Instead he allowed the eager American to leave the meeting convinced that Russia would soon rejoin the allies in the struggle against Germany.

Robins returned to Vologda where he reported to Francis. The ambassador promptly informed Washington of Robins' conversation with the Bolshevik leaders and reaffirmed his earlier warning against a Japanese move into Siberia. Fear of such a move was driving Russia to ratify the Treaty of Brest-Litovsk, he said, and an actual invasion 'would result in non-resistance [to Germany] and eventually make Russia a German province.'[19] Within hours of sending this message Francis received a telegram from Colonel Ruggles who had reached Petrograd and spoken with Trotsky. Ruggles told much the same story as Robins and stressed Trotsky's insistence that the United States 'take the necessary steps to prevent action by Japan or other Allies at this critical time.'[20] This led Francis to reinforce his first warning against intervention with a second telegram, describing possible Japanese action in Siberia as 'folly' and virtually invoking the 'yellow peril' as an argument against it. Tying renewed Russian participation in the war to American restraint of Japan he endorsed the proposition which Lenin and Trotsky had drilled into Robins and Ruggles.[21] These warnings, of course, played no part in Wilson's decision to continue his opposition to Japanese intervention, but together with others which followed, they did serve to reinforce and justify this decision.[22] Although Lenin did not fully understand the basis on which American policy was made he did succeed in feeding information into

18 Cumming and Petit, *Russian-American Relations*, 80-1
19 *Ibid.*, 84-5. Also see Kennan, *Russia Leaves the War*, 499-500
20 Kennan, *The Decision to Intervene*, 112
21 Cumming and Petit, *Russian-American Relations*, 85-6
22 Kennan, *Russia Leaves the War*, 509

official American channels which played an important role in delaying armed intervention in the far east.

From the avid interest shown by Sadoul, Lockhart, and Robins in re-opening talks aimed at Soviet military collaboration with the allies the Bolshevik leaders knew that they had succeeded in again opening channels of communication with the western capitals. Not wishing to reduce the zeal of the allied agents, the Bolsheviks carefully massaged their egos, flattering them with the notion that they had come to occupy positions of prime importance in the great political events then unfolding in Europe. This was a very heady brew for men as young and inexperienced as the trio of allied agents,[23] and it discernibly influenced their judgment, subtly pre-judicing them to accept the arguments of the Soviet government. Sadoul, who despite his lack of influence with the French government served to buoy up the hopes of the other allied agents, received constant praise from the Soviet authorities and was led to believe, as he records in his journal, that the Bolsheviks were 'enchanted' with the success of his mission to Vologda.[24] Lockhart became the recipient of many favours, being given free access to Trotsky and Chicherin while being fed a steady diet of belli-cose assurances that peace with Germany would be of short duration. Typical was Chicherin's statement made immediately after his return from Brest-Litovsk. 'The German terms,' he assured Lockhart, 'had raised a feeling of resentment in Russia similar to that in France after 1870 ... The peace was a dictated peace which Russia would break as soon as she was strong enough.'[25] It was Trotsky, however, who provided the greatest encouragement. Lockhart accompanied him everywhere and was able to observe with his own eyes how energetically Trotsky took charge of the Red army. 'Almost in a night,' he later recalled, Trotsky 'had be-come a soldier.'[26] Trotsky's military spirit excited Lockhart, and he lis-tened uncritically as the 'Lion' described his plans for opposing Germany. Robins received much the same treatment and, as seen from his meeting with Lenin and Trotsky, was no more able to resist their flattery than his colleagues. Even the crusty old Francis, isolated in Vologda, began to mel-low under the constant wash of favourable reports from Petrograd and

23 Robins at 43 was the oldest of the three but had absolutely no previous diplomatic expe-rience; Lockhart at 31 was the youngest but had served in the British consular service since 1912.
24 Sadoul, *Notes*, 255
25 Lockhart, *British Agent*, 240
26 *Ibid.*, 243-6

modified somewhat his previously hostile attitude toward the Soviet government.

The way in which the Bolsheviks exploited their good relations with the allied agents is illustrated by an incident which occurred just prior to the departure of the Soviet government for Moscow. In the midst of packing, the Narkomindel received word from Vladivostok that the Consular Corps in that city had published a strong public protest against the reorganization of municipal government along the lines of Soviet administration.[27] Taken in the context of the Japanese threat to the Russian far east and the presence of foreign warships in the harbour the local authorities viewed the protest as evidence of impending intervention and asked Petrograd for assistance. Upon receiving the request Chicherin turned at once to Robins and Lockhart. The British agent was summoned to the Narkomindel where he found Chicherin and Karakhan 'in a state of excitement' over what they termed the 'ultimatum handed to the local Soviet authorities at Vladivostok by the Consular Corps.' The message, he said, had 'produced the most painful impression' and was regarded 'as having a direct connection with Japanese intervention in Siberia.' Lockhart found this news particularly embarrassing as only hours before he had assured Karakhan that the allied powers would not interfere in Russian internal affairs. Saying that both Chicherin and Karakhan were 'in favour of a policy of agreement with the Allies as long as our interests lie along the same lines,' he declared that he could 'only predict the most gloomy results' if the allies should embark on either intervention or interference in the internal affairs of Soviet Russia. Either course, he warned, 'must be fatal to any pro-Ally feeling in Russia and may even lead eventually to a Russo-German Alliance.'[28]

Having impressed Lockhart with the seriousness of the situation, Chicherin conveyed the same message to Robins. As the American 'colonel' had already left to confer with Francis, the foreign commissar telegraphed Vologda with the news from Vladivostok, expressing his certainty that the American embassy would 'use all means to solve at its earliest convenience this new complication.'[29] Robins and Francis reacted in the same way as Lockhart, hastening to inform Washington of the Soviet protest and asking for an explanation of the consular action at Vladivostok. Within a few days answers arrived from Washington and London indicat-

27 Kennan, *The Decision to Intervene*, 61
28 PRO FO 371/3290/45119
29 FRUS, *1918, Russia*, vol. II, 74

ing that the consuls had issued the protest on their own authority in response to the deterioration of public order in the city.[30] This information, which both Lockhart and Robins passed along to Chicherin, did nothing to relieve Soviet fears of Japanese intervention, but did confirm that two-way communication with the west had been restored. For the foreseeable future Moscow could rely on Robins and Lockhart to bring the Soviet view to the attention of the allied governments.

These governments, however, were distinctly cool to the advice which they were receiving from their agents in Russia. Lockhart, in particular, became a prime target for all those in Whitehall who opposed cooperation with the Bolsheviks, and during March confidence in his judgment fell precipitously. 'Don't you think the time has come,' wrote Lord Robert Cecil to Balfour on 7 March, 'when we should hint to Lockhart that it is his business to persuade Trotsky that we are right, not to persuade us that Trotsky is right?'[31] Balfour agreed and sent Lockhart a sarcastic telegram criticizing his entire perspective of the Russian problem.[32] General Knox, who prior to the sudden Bolshevik capitulation had supported Lockhart, was even more critical. In a venomous memorandum he declared that 'Lockhart's advice has been in a political sense unsound and in a military sense criminally misleading.' 'Why,' he asked, 'is he retained in Russia?'[33] Why indeed? None of the permanent officials at the foreign office were prepared to defend Lockhart, and Lord Hardinge, the under-secretary of state, agreed fully with the general, saying of Lockhart that 'all his forecasts have proved wrong, and we do not even know whether he presses our views. He is hysterical and has achieved nothing.' Balfour, nevertheless, stood by his envoy and despite the withering sarcasm of his telegram shielded Lockhart from dismissal. In no way did this indicate that the foreign secretary was prepared to listen to his agent in Russia, only that for the moment, while the American government had not yet agreed to intervention and Whitehall had no effective way of significantly influencing events in Russia, Lockhart, who seemed at least to possess the confidence of the Bolsheviks, might just as well remain at his post. Perhaps Balfour also derived malicious satisfaction from leaving Lockhart in Moscow, for he had not been consulted when it was decided to send the young envoy to Russia. That decision had been made by Lloyd George on

30 *Ibid.*, 79; PRO FO 371/3290/45119
31 PRO FO 800/205/248
32 Ullman, *Intervention and the War*, 125
33 PRO FO 371/3290/51340

the advice of Lord Milner, Balfour's rival at the war office.[34] The foreign secretary, therefore, could not be held responsible for Lockhart, and it was distinctly to his advantage to retain Milner's discredited protegé in Russia where he promised to embarrass the secretary for war even further. Lockhart, then, was free to speak his mind without the slightest possibility of anyone listening to what he said. 'Although Mr. Lockhart's advice may be bad,' wrote one senior official at the foreign office, 'we can not be accused of having followed it.'[35]

Nor was the American government following the advice of Robins. Much of what he had to say, in fact, was not even getting through to Washington, being held back by Francis who only transmitted what he felt was politically expedient. As a result, Washington remained ignorant of much which Lenin and Trotsky had told Robins on 5 March, although, as noted above, the concern of the Soviet leaders about Japanese intervention had reached Washington where it served to reinforce the policy of the United States in the far east. The odd manner in which Washington and Robins were working at cross purposes, while ironically serving Lenin's interest, can be seen in the message which Wilson decided to send the All-Russian Congress of Soviets in the middle of March. The American government wished to influence the congress against ratification of the Treaty of Brest-Litovsk, and it occurred to Colonel House that 'a reassuring message to Russia' would play a part in this. But more was involved than simply influencing the Congress of Soviets, for as he wrote Wilson on 10 March, 'my thought is not so much about Russia as it is to seize this opportunity to clear up the Far Eastern situation but without mentioning it or Japan in any way. What you would say about Russia and against Germany could be made to apply to Japan or any other power seeking to do what we know Germany is attempting.'[36] The result was a brief message which Wilson prepared 'for the people of Russia through the Soviet Congress.' Sent to Moscow on 11 March it was in Lenin's hands the following day. While serving House's purpose of warning the Japanese against action in Siberia it had the immediate effect of undermining Robins' effort to influence the Soviet government to reject the Treaty of Brest-Litovsk, for although it conveyed the 'sincere sympathy' of the American government 'for the Russian people,' decried the German effort 'to turn back the whole struggle for freedom,' and promised that the American govern-

34 Lockhart, *British Agent*, 198-9
35 PRO FO 371/3290/51340
36 Cited in Kennan, *Russia Leaves the War*, 510

ment would 'avail itself of every opportunity to secure for Russia once more complete sovereignty and independence,' it said absolutely nothing about cooperation with the Soviet government. Indeed, Wilson's message openly admitted that the United States 'is unhappily not now in a position to render the direct and effective aid it would wish to render.'[37]

This admission had the effect of vastly strengthening Lenin's hand at the Congress, for it made clear that Soviet Russia could expect no material support from the western world if war with Germany was resumed. If the United States was not in a position to render aid to Russia then none of the other allies, hard pressed on the western front, would be able to do so. Wilson's message, therefore, provided the last bit of evidence that Lenin needed to prove that Soviet Russia had no option other than ratification of the peacy treaty and completed the disarmament of those, such as Trotsky, who still wanted to continue the conflict. It also absolved Lenin from any obligation which Robins might have felt the Bolsheviks had incurred as a consequence of the meeting of 5 March and placed the onus of failure to develop allied-Soviet cooperation squarely on American shoulders; in the future, therefore, Robins could be used as a channel of communication without Lenin fearing that this service would necessarily commit the Soviet government to any binding obligations. Finally, Wilson's message provided Lenin with an opportunity to reaffirm his faith in the revolution at one of the darkest moments in Soviet history. Speaking through the Congress of Soviets he responded to Wilson in the same manner as the president had addressed him. Just as Wilson had ignored the Soviet government, Lenin now ignored the American government, addressing his reply instead to 'the American people, and in the first instance to the toiling and exploited classes of the United States of North America.' Into this brief message Lenin packed the substance of his revolutionary creed, expressing confidence that 'the happy time is not far distant when the toiling masses of all bourgeois countries will throw off the yoke of capitalism and will establish a socialist order of society, which alone is capable of assuring a firm and just peace as well as the cultural and material well being of all the toilers.'[38] Here was a fit response to Wilson, for just as the president had aimed his message at the great powers and, to a lesser extent, the Russian people, Lenin keyed his reply to fellow revolutionaries and secondarily to the peoples of Europe and America. The two messages, so different and yet so similar, are a telling commentary on

37 FRUS, *1918, Russia*, vol. I, 395
38 DVP, vol. I, 211

Soviet-allied relations at that time. Given the vast gulf which divided them, a gulf of truly gargantuan dimensions created by violently conflicting social, political and intellectual assumptions, there was little possibility that even a limited form of cooperation could develop between Soviet Russia and the west. The distance between the two may be judged by the reply of the American government to Francis when, in mid-March, the ambassador belatedly sent Washington a summary of the Bolshevik document handed Robins on 5 March. The state department, replied Washington, 'considers President's message to the Russian people ... adequate answer.'[39]

Yet the charade of negotiations continued, for the allied agents and Trotsky had too much political capital invested simply to abandon the effort to reach agreement. Robins and Lockhart had both staked their reputations on the success of these talks and Trotsky, if he was to have any chance of resisting Germany, had to have western assistance. By the end of March the negotiations had made some headway with both sides agreeing that western officers and railway specialists should assist in the organization and supply of the Red army.[40] This much even Lenin would have accepted, as an agreement on this basis would have strengthened the Red army without committing Soviet Russia to a resumption of war against Germany. But for that very reason the allied agents could not be satisfied with an agreement limited solely to material and technical assistance. Instead they wanted a broader understanding, linking technical assistance to a resumption of the war. Lockhart, in particular, could not ignore London's strident demand for Soviet action against Germany and, consequently, had to press Trotsky to accept the use of Japanese troops in Russia. Here agreement broke down, for only in the most disastrous conditions would Lenin think of inviting another imperialist power on to Soviet territory. Nevertheless, given the circumstances of late March, with the Germans advancing through the Ukraine and approaching the southern provinces of Russia itself, the Bolsheviks had to allow for this possibility and at least make it appear as if they were seriously considering the allied proposals. This became imperative when the allied military representatives in Russia joined the negotiations with Trotsky. These men, reinforced by the French consul-general Grenard, proved more difficult to persuade than the impressionable Robins and Lockhart. Grenard, in particular, took a dim view of the Soviet position, believing that 'whatever

39 Kennan, *Russia Leaves the War*, 514-6
40 Kennan, *The Decision to Intervene*, 112-7

sincerity and vigour [Trotsky] may have, it is improbable that he has the time or the means to attain any very effective results.'[41] Grenard held an even lower opinion of Bolshevik promises to resume the war against Germany. 'All these sterile and hypocritical rodomontades,' he reported to the Quai d'Orsay, 'must not be taken seriously.'[42] By late March it must have been apparent to the Bolsheviks that if they wished to retain allied interest in the possibility of military collaboration it would be necessary to accommodate, in part, the demand for foreign reinforcement of the Red army. If they could not invite Japan into Russia to oppose Germany, the time had come when they had to *appear* ready to do so.

The Bolsheviks did this by deftly shifting the basis of discussion from that which they were prepared to accept at the moment to that which they promised to accept in the future. On 25 March, Chicherin told Lockhart 'that as soon as war breaks out [with Germany] Russia will be glad to accept not only material help from the Allies, but also help in men including the Japanese Corps.' The allies, he added, would be expected to guarantee both the inviolability of Soviet territory and non-intervention in the internal affairs of Russia.[43] When Trotsky repeated these assurances the following day[44] Lockhart accepted them at face value and informed London that only patience was necessary to secure everything which the allies wanted from the Bolsheviks. 'The whole situation is turning rapidly in our favour,' he reported, 'and I earnestly trust that Japanese intervention will be postponed until we can reach a proper agreement with the Russian Government.'[45] Here was the major reason for the sudden Soviet willingness to accept intervention, for by promising to invite the allies into Russia at some unspecified time in the future they were seeking to stave off their unwanted presence a bit longer. Lockhart did not understand this and thus painted a rose-coloured picture of imminent Bolshevik action against Germany.[46]

Lockhart's optimism was completely without foundation. Even if Lenin was not purposely misleading him and was prepared, in certain circumstances, to act against Germany, events were already under way which would undercut the basis for any agreement with the Bolsheviks. Foremost among these was the sudden arrival of Joseph Noulens at the diplo-

41 MAE, Guerre, Russie, Dossier general, 24/126
42 *Ibid.*, 24/111
43 PRO FO 371/3290/55299
44 *Ibid.*, 371/3285/56926
45 *Ibid.*, 371/3290/55299
46 *Ibid.*, 371/3285/56926

matic encampment at Vologda. The French ambassador had travelled a circuitous route and arrived only after a month-long odyssey which had carried him far into Finland in his effort to reach France. Balked by the civil war then raging in Finland, Noulens and his staff had become separated from the British diplomatic party with whom they had been travelling. In mid-March they found themselves dangerously isolated at Tammersfors deep in the interior of Finland and, fearing capture by the Germans, decided to return to Russia.[47] Noulens returned with the conviction that the Soviet government had to be overthrown and a new Russian regime established under the protection of allied bayonets. On 9 March he cabled the Quai d'Orsay from Tammersfors: 'We must create one or more centres around which all the elements favourable to our influence and to the reconstitution of a powerful Russia can gather. Even inconsequential inter-allied forces which we can establish at designated places will constitute a point of departure for a military organization which will check German expansion and oblige our enemies to commit forces of occupation which would otherwise be engaged on our front. These centres of resistance seem to me to be Vladivostok for the Americans and Japanese and Archangel and Murmansk for the other allies.'[48] He had hoped to return to Russia aboard an allied warship, but when this proved impossible he made a virtue of necessity and asked Paris for permission to join Francis at Vologda. There he hoped to contact 'Russian elements favourable to the allies and await the hour when we will be ready to install ourselves at Archangel under the protection of warships and pursue a new policy with the cooperation of a Russian government constituted under our auspices.'[49] Thus, when Noulens reached Vologda on 29 March, he came with the express purpose of pursuing a policy directed against the Bolsheviks and aimed at their overthrow.

Although Paris did not officially endorse this policy the Quai d'Orsay allowed Noulens to proceed with his plans. On 21 March, Pichon approved the journey to Vologda and, nine days later, sent the ambassador a long telegram outlining French policy in Russia. This policy was based on non-recognition of the Soviet government which, said Pichon, 'to the stain of its illegitimate origin has now added the shame of the German peace.'

47 Noulens, *Mon Ambassade*, vol. II, 20-2; MAE, Guerre, Russie, Action des Allies, 34/95. Also see Carley, 'The origins of the French intervention in the Russian Civil War.' Carley illuminates the complex nature of French policy at this time and emphasizes the long-term political and economic motives of leading figures at the Quai d'Orsay.
48 MAE, Guerre, Russie, Action des Allies, 34/96-8
49 *Ibid.*, 34/166-8

Noulens was instructed to adhere 'rigorously' to this principle and 'vigorously defend' the interests of France and her citizens. France, said the foreign minister, looked forward 'to the day when the revolutionary upheaval is over and Russia will again be a friend and an ally.' Pichon assured Noulens that his scheme for intervention was being given the most serious consideration, and that allied action was only being delayed by 'the grave events on the western front.' While awaiting this action Noulens was directed to 'assist the grouping of indigenous elements favourable to the reconstruction of a Russian government sympathetic to the interests of France.'[50] One week later the Quai d'Orsay instructed its consul-general in Moscow to act in a similar manner. Grenard was told to encourage any political demonstration favourable to the allies and 'extend thanks in the name of the French government, in terms appropriate to each circumstance, to all personalities and groups which previously have acted in this manner and those which do so in the future.' They were to be informed that 'despite the maximalists and their disastrous peace ... our sentiments for the Russian people have not changed.'[51]

But the French government was desperate. On 21 March the German offensive had begun on the western front and even while Pichon was writing to his representatives in Russia Ludendorff was advancing on Paris. Therefore, while encouraging Noulens to pursue a policy directed at overthrowing the Soviet government, the foreign minister also instructed him not to interfere with the unofficial negotiations then under way with the Bolsheviks. The situation on the western front was so critical that France could not afford to spurn a Bolshevik offer of cooperation against Germany. 'It is a question of struggle against our enemies,' Pichon explained somewhat apologetically. Yet if such an offer was made it would have to be examined 'with care, prudence and intelligence,' and Pichon warned Noulens not to accept any proposal until he had first established that the Bolsheviks possessed the 'will to fight effectively against the central powers.'[52]

In short, France, like her ally Britain, was scattering its chips all over the roulette table of Russian politics; no opportunity, however slight, was to be overlooked in the effort to restore a fighting front in eastern Europe. The essence of Pichon's message, however, was clear: the French government would prefer to rely on the anti-Bolsheviks rather than the Soviet government. Only if some strange turn of events occurred were the Bol-

50 *Ibid.*, 29/225-7; see also 34/181
51 MAE, Guerre, Russie, Dossier general, 24/247
52 MAE, Guerre, Russie, Action des Allies, 29/225-7

sheviks to be supported in preference to their enemies. Noulens needed no more encouragement than this to proceed forcefully along the path which he had chosen for himself. Paris might choose to scatter French chips on the Soviet numbers, but the ambassador intended to stack them all on the side of the counter-revolution.

Noulens had very little difficulty doing this, for when he reached Vologda he found the allied representatives demoralized and virtually without leadership. As dean of the diplomatic corps Francis should have dominated the situation, but he had largely abdicated his authority in favour of the more dynamic Robins, Sadoul, and Lockhart. Although the American ambassador supported the effort to convince Lenin and Trotsky to resume the war against Germany he did so hesitantly and without much enthusiasm. This gave Noulens the opening he needed to assume leadership of the allied political representatives in Russia, for not only did Francis doubt the wisdom of courting the Bolsheviks, he also resented the manner in which the initiative had passed into the hands of the junior agents in Moscow. Noulens played on these sentiments and easily convinced Francis that a thorough re-examination of allied policy in Russia was necessary.[53] Early in April word was sent to Moscow for the military attachés then negotiating with Trotsky to come to Vologda for a meeting with the allied diplomats. Significantly, Robins, Sadoul, and Lockhart were not invited to attend.

And no wonder, for under the skilful guidance of Noulens the conference which met on 3 April reached conclusions which made further collaboration with the Bolsheviks impossible. Although the allied representatives reaffirmed the desirability of obtaining Bolshevik consent prior to intervention, their other decisions reduced this declaration to an empty gesture. Noulens succeeded in convincing the other allied representatives that before reaching an accord with Lenin and Trotsky they should first require 'guarantees concerning the true purpose of the Bolshevik Government with regard to the Allies.' The guarantees which they specified were Bolshevik 'acceptance of Japanese intervention' and 'concessions to Allied nationals of at least the same advantages, privileges and compensations accorded by Russia to German subjects by the peace treaty of Brest-Litovsk.' The conference also decided that allied aid in organizing the Red army would be withheld until western military authorities were satisfied that adequate discipline would be enforced in the new army.[54]

53 Noulens, *Mon Ambassade*, vol. II, 50-60
54 FRUS, *1918, Russia*, vol. II, 111

These were exactly the conditions which the Bolsheviks were least likely to accept, because they threatened to undermine the authority of the Soviet regime. In obtaining the support of the other allied representatives Noulens advanced a long way toward frustrating the effort of Lockhart, Sadoul, and Robins to negotiate a military agreement with the Bolsheviks and clearing the ground for his own policy of uninvited intervention. The extent of his success can be measured in a telegram which Lockhart sent London the day allied representatives met at Vologda. In it he reported further progress toward conclusion of a military pact with the Bolsheviks, but pointing to the crucial role which Trotsky was playing in the negotiations cautioned against asking too much from the commissar of war. In particular he specified that Trotsky would be unable to agree to allied military assistance which was 'predominantly Japanese' or 'under Japanese control.' 'Trotsky has a biggish load to carry with his own people,' he warned, 'so ... care should be taken not to overburden him from our side.'[55] Given the results of the meeting at Vologda, Lockhart was speaking into the past; Noulens had already put together a load which Trotsky would find impossible to bear.

Events in the far east soon rendered Soviet collaboration with the allies even more unlikely. In Vladivostok tension between the local revolutionary authorities and the foreign colony had been mounting since the consular protest of early March, and on 4 April, when two clerks of a Japanese business house were murdered while resisting an armed robbery, the situation exploded. The commander of the Japanese naval squadron at Vladivostok proclaimed that public order in the city had collapsed and, acting on his own authority, landed two companies of marines to protect Japanese lives and property. The British naval commander took the same action, and by 6 April, when the Japanese landed four more companies of marines to reinforce their first detachment, foreign troops had established effective control of the city.[56]

The Russian reaction was predictably hostile. A wave of revulsion swept across the country, uniting, for a moment, both Bolshevik and anti-Bolshevik against what was seen as a Japanese grab for Russian territory. The racist overtones of this protest were particularly evident as even those elements of Russian society which were clamouring for the allies to overthrow the Bolsheviks did not wish to be liberated by the Japanese and

55 PRO FO 371/3285/59400
56 Morley, *The Japanese Thrust into Siberia*, 146-7

pleaded with the allies to hold back the 'yellow tide' from Siberia.[57] Throughout the episode the presence of the Royal Marines alongside the Japanese was largely ignored even by the Bolsheviks who might have been expected to be less discriminating in their attitude toward the invading forces. Racial prejudice was particularly evident in Vladivostok where all segments of society demanded the withdrawal of the Japanese marines from the city.[58] The Bolsheviks, fearing that they were losing control of the situation, acted at once to reassert their authority. This included measures to restrain 'the criminal element and sinister forces' blamed for the violence which triggered the landing, but was concerned primarily with mobilizing the far east against a full-scale Japanese invasion. The Siberian Central Executive Committee sounded the alarm throughout all Russia, placing the whole of Siberia in a state of military emergency and establishing a Siberian military-revolutionary staff to coordinate the work of local military councils.[59] Moscow issued a proclamation saying: 'The course of events leaves no doubt whatsoever that all this was prearranged and that the murder of the two Japanese was only a pretext for the imperialist attack from the east which has been contemplated for some time. The imperialists of Japan wish to strangle the Soviet revolution, to cut off Russia from the Pacific Ocean, to grab the rich territories of Siberia and to enslave the Siberian workers and peasants. The bourgeoisie of Japan advance as the deadly enemy of the Soviet Republic.'[60] Lenin applauded the initiative of his Siberian comrades and advised them to take even further steps 'to put defence preparations on a sound footing.' Although he promised to 'begin negotiations with the ambassadors' concerning events in the far east he warned that little could be expected from these talks. 'It is clear,' he said, 'that no faith can now be put in any assurances and that solid military preparations on our part constitute the sole reliable guarantees.'[61] In a later telegram he instructed the Siberian Bolsheviks to use armed force to oppose any Japanese attempt to advance beyond Vladivostok.[62] The Japanese landing at Vladivostok, therefore, only served to heighten Bolshevik suspicion of allied motives and made further progress toward any kind of agreement with the western powers infinitely more difficult.

57 See reports of the French consul-general in Moscow on this subject during March 1918. MAE, Guerre, Russie, Dossier general, 24/passim
58 Morley, *The Japanese Thrust into Siberia*, 148-9
59 Meijer, *The Trotsky Papers*, 33-5
60 DVP, vol. I, 225
61 Meijer, *The Trotsky Papers*, 35
62 *Ibid.*, 41

The new tension in allied-Soviet relations was felt at once. Allied representatives were summoned to the Narkomindel where late on the evening of 5 April, Chicherin demanded an explanation of the landing at Vladivostok. 'It is hard to believe,' he exclaimed, 'that the allies could be guilty of supporting such an act just when the Bolsheviks were preparing to conclude an alliance with them.' Lockhart and Robins, who knew even less about the incident than Chicherin, tried to pass it off as a 'purely local affair' but quickly informed their governments of the Soviet protest.[63] Lockhart, who feared that London might approve the Japanese action, pleaded with Balfour to oppose it and offer the Soviets 'as satisfactory an explanation as possible.' The incident, he said, 'is deplorable in every way and must seriously affect our chances of coming to terms with the Bolsheviks.'[64] Robins was even more emphatic, warning Francis that if the incident was not settled quickly the Soviets would 'declare war on Japan.' In that event, he continued: 'the latent hostility of all Russian people to Mongolian domination will transform present resentment against Germany into far more bitter resentment against Allies ... We are at most dangerous crisis in Russian situation, and if collossal blunder of hostile Japanese intervention takes place all American advantages are confiscated.'[65]

The following day Trotsky met with the allied representatives. Abrasive at the best of times, his temper had been rubbed raw by the events in the far east, and he unleashed his anger on the unfortunate trio. In what Lockhart described as a 'long and violent discussion' Trotsky informed them of exactly what he thought of their explanation of the landing at Vladivostok. 'It is what the wolf says to the unfortunate hare which it has just grabbed by one paw. Don't be disturbed. It is a purely local incident.'[66] Trotsky believed that the landing was the beginning of a full-scale Japanese invasion and demanded to know what the other allied powers intended to do about it. Only if they would guarantee not to interfere in the internal affairs of Russia, promise to collaborate with the Soviet government, and restrain the Japanese could there be any further talk of a military alliance. Trotsky, however, made it clear that he still was interested in negotiating an alliance, even going so far as to say that if the Japanese insisted on payment for their cooperation then the price had to be fixed beforehand

63 DVP, vol. I, 230-1
64 Alfred Milner Papers, Bodleian Library, Oxford. Box B, document 173
65 Cumming and Petit, *Russian-American Relations*, 134-5
66 Sadoul, *Notes*, 294

252 Revolution and survival

and would have to be borne in part by the western allies. 'As intervention will serve equally the interests of Russia and the Allies,' he was reported as saying, 'it would be just that the latter should also participate in payment of Japan and should examine the possibility of territorial or economic concessions from their own territories in the Far East.'[67]

It is difficult to know exactly what to make of this statement. Was Trotsky sincere or was he simply trying to determine the extent of allied demands in the far east? Had he been authorized to make such a proposal or did he act on his own initiative? For the moment these questions can not be answered, for Soviet sources do not mention this offer or the circumstances leading up to it. It could be argued that if the Soviet government had decided to enlist allied support against the Germans they would not have hesitated to pay for this assistance with Siberian real estate, but there is no evidence that the Soviet government had made any such decision. Nevertheless, the landing at Vladivostok coincided exactly with the arrival of German troops in the vicinity of Kursk, and when Trotsky spoke with the allied representatives on 6 April, neither he nor the Soviet government had any idea if the Germans would stop at the Russian frontier or drive north to Moscow. In this critical situation Trotsky may well have been authorized to offer the allies Soviet territory in the far east or at least to lay the basis for such a bargain. Some credence might be lent this interpretation by a telegram which Lenin sent Soviet authorities in Irkutsk and Vladivostok on the day following Trotsky's meeting with the western representatives. In it he categorically stated: 'the Japanese will certainly attack. This is inevitable. Probably all the allies without exception will help them.' From this he drew the conclusion that his Siberian comrades should not set themselves 'unrealistic aims' but instead prepare to withdraw in the direction of Irkutsk. 'Above all,' he said, 'attention must be devoted to correct withdrawal, retreat and removal of stores and railway materials.'[68] In light of Trotsky's statement to the western representatives it does not take much imagination to see this order as part of a larger plan to surrender the distant Soviet far east, perhaps as far as Irkutsk, in exchange for allied assistance against the rapidly advancing Germans. On the the other hand, the absence of corroborating evidence might indicate that nothing but simple realism led Lenin to issue this order. Trotsky might well have been acting on his own initiative, thinking that with the advance of the German army such a bargain was well within the realm of possibility

67 PRO FO 371/3285/62282
68 Lenin, PSS, vol. XXXVI, 216

or that in any case it would be useful to gauge allied intentions in the far east. As it stands, however, these intriguing questions must remain unanswered as even the circumstantial evidence is insufficient to warrant a tentative resolution of the problem.

No such mystery enshrouds the allied response to Trotsky's proposals. Washington, London, and Paris had already grown suspicious of the negotiations under way in Moscow and were not prepared to commit themselves to supporting the Bolsheviks without a searching examination of Soviet intentions. Even prior to Trotsky's meeting with the allied agents of 6 April, the American government had ruled out any commitment until it was satisfied that the Bolsheviks were negotiating in good faith,[69] and London had expressed deep concern over Trotsky's insistence that Japanese participation in intervention be kept to a minimum. Balfour had told Lockhart: 'The only Power which has forces available for a Far Eastern campaign is Japan, and yet in the face of this obvious fact Trotsky wants the Japanese, if admitted into Siberia at all, to be admitted only in a subordinate position. On this point you tell me he is "absolutely adamant." No wonder there are skeptics who doubt his sincerity.'[70] The French were most skeptical of all, seeing the Soviet offer as nothing more than a clever Bolshevik scheme to prepare the Red army to fight indigenous enemies rather than Germany. Noulens denounced the Soviet protest against the Japanese landing at Vladivostok as 'arrogant' and ridiculed the very idea of 'loyal collaboration' with the Bolsheviks.[71] The French government was somewhat more interested in Trotsky's proposals than Noulens, but Pichon ruled out any pact involving actual recognition of the Soviet regime.[72] Essentially Paris left the question to be decided by Noulens, and the ambassador ruled against further talks with the Bolsheviks. So pervasive had Noulens' influence become that shortly thereafter the American and French military representatives in Moscow even ceased to play an active role in the talks with Trotsky. Although all three western governments quickly and honestly denied that the Japanese landing at Vladivostok was the prelude to an invasion of Siberia, Sadoul, and Robins were unable to report any readiness to negotiate a military pact with Moscow. By mid-April, therefore, the possibility of an allied agreement with Soviet Russia had virtually evaporated. Not only had the allies failed to bargain

69 FRUS, *1918, Russia*, vol. I, 495
70 PRO FO 371/3285/61467
71 MAE, Guerre, Russie, Action des Allies, 30/66-7
72 *Ibid.*, 30/88-9

seriously, but the military emergency of early April, which might have induced the Bolsheviks to accept allied aid, had also passed. By mid-month Lenin had begun to think in terms of reaching a new agreement with Germany rather than with the allies.

Only Lockhart was able to continue meaningful talks with the Soviet government. Robins and Sadoul were obstructed by their respective ambassadors; he was responsible only to London and did not have to contend with any British authority in Russia higher than himself. Consequently, even after Francis and Noulens had hobbled their agents in Moscow, Lockhart was able to persist in his effort to reach an agreement with Trotsky. This led on 13 April to another long conversation with the war commissar who again put forward his proposals of the previous week as a basis for agreement. In addition he asked for British help in reorganizing the Black Sea Fleet, in running the Russian railways and in managing the port of Archangel. A few days later he also asked Lockhart for British assistance against the Turks in the Caucasus. Equally important, Lockhart reported that Trotsky appeared ready to grant Japan a major role in intervention and only demanded suitable guarantees of Russian territorial integrity.[73] London found these proposals more interesting than any which it had received previously from Moscow, and on 22 April, Balfour wired Lockhart that they might be suitable as 'a basis for discussion.' The foreign secretary was prepared to guarantee Russian territorial integrity and to agree not to interfere in Russian internal affairs, but he believed other parts of Trotsky's proposals required modification. These modifications are most revealing as they illuminate clearly how far the British and Bolsheviks were from agreement. Thus, Trotsky had asked the allies to pledge 'loyal co-operation with the Soviet Government,' but Balfour, claiming that this might conflict with the pledge not to interfere in the internal affairs of Russia wished to change this to 'loyal co-operation with Russian authorities against the common enemy.' Similarly, the war commissar had called for an allied declaration that their forces would 'cross Siberia solely in order to reach the war zone,' while the foreign secretary wished to substitute a statement saying that allied forces would 'cross Siberia solely for the purpose of carrying out military operations against the enemy.'[74] These seemingly minor changes were of major importance, for they had the effect of completely altering the nature of the proposed

73 PRO FO 371/3285/68677. See also FO 371/3285/69968
74 PRO FO 371/3285/69968

agreement. In making its proposals the Soviet government had in mind an agreement among sovereign states which would have placed it on a par with the western governments and recognized its authority to act in the name of Russia. Balfour's proposals provided no such recognition and in fact were designed to avoid that recognition. Instead they would have provided the allies with a 'passport' to enter Russia, justified their cooperation with any Russian authority with whom they chose to deal, and authorized military operations anywhere in Russia they claimed to see 'the enemy.' Given French objections to the recognition of the Soviet government, Balfour's counter-proposals can be seen as essential to the maintenance of allied unity, but given the highly developed Bolshevik instinct for survival they can only be seen as lethal to any agreement with Soviet Russia. Their implementation would have been diastrous for the Bolsheviks, and it is inconceivable that they could ever have been accepted in Moscow. How the Bolsheviks might have reacted to Balfour's counter-proposals will never be known, for before the foreign secretary's telegram could reach Moscow a new political storm burst over Russia which rendered the question of cooperation entirely academic.

The storm burst on 23 April following the publication of a statement given by the French ambassador to the Russian press. Appearing in all non-Bolshevik newspapers the statement was a thinly veiled attack on the Soviet government and an attempt to justify uninvited allied intervention in Russian affairs. In it, Noulens attributed the Japanese landing at Vladivostok to the 'prolonged state of trouble and uneasiness in that city' which 'inevitably' had been bound to 'necessitate armed intervention aimed at guarding the security of foreigners.' In landing troops the Japanese had only acted to defend their citizens against the 'excesses of the streets.' Nor was that all. 'The Japanese issue,' he continued, could be localized in Vladivostok provided that Japan was 'given the satisfaction which it rightly demands,' but the allied powers could not be satisfied with the simple restoration of order in a single sea port. 'The allies,' he asserted, could not 'with equanimity accept the success of the Austro-Germans' in the heart of Russia itself. As Germany was seeking to subordinate to itself 'all of Russia economically' and 'to organize in Siberia a centre of colonization,' the allies, he said, 'may be compelled to intervene in order to meet this menace which is directed against them, and, to a much greater extent, against the Russian people.' In such an event, he concluded: 'they will act solely in the capacity of friends, which, while not interfering in the internal affairs of Russia, without any kind of ulterior motives of any kind of conquests, and with the single care of defending common interests and in full agreement with Russian public opinion, will be a force resisting the German seizure of eastern Europe.'[75]

As Sadoul recorded, the Bolsheviks were 'furious' over Noulens' statement. They saw it as an effort to disrupt their negotiations with Lockhart and, beyond that, a peremptory challenge to their authority in Russia.[76] They had long been aware of the contacts between French representatives and counter-revolutionary organizations, but as long as there had been hope of reaching agreement with the allies they had chosen to ignore them. With Noulens' open appeal to Russian public opinion for support of an allied policy of uninvited intervention they could no longer feign disinterest in the activities of allied agents, and they decided to force a confrontation with the western powers over the question of their relation to the Soviet government. Noulens, however, had taken them by surprise, and they required several days to work out their full response. While preparing it Chicherin issued an interim reply. His statement, published the following day, was moderate and dignified, characterized more by restraint than absence of emotion. Expressing his 'deep regret' that the issue had arisen he challenged the premises on which the ambassador had based his argument. Referring to Noulens' assertion that the collapse of order in Vladivostok had compelled the Japanese to act, the foreign commissar declared: 'In reality it is Soviet power, the dictatorship of the toiling masses, and not anarchy, which has ruled and continues to rule in Vladivostok. This, of course, is not at all to the liking of the exploiters, be they native Russians or foreigners. The same Soviet power governs all the Russian Republic, and if in Noulens' opinion the existence of that system of government had to lead to foreign invasion at Vladivostok then, in principle, this means that he is calling for the foreign seizure of all Russia for the purpose of restoring the authority of the exploiters.' Turning to the question of Russia's difficulties with Germany, Chicherin admitted the serious nature of the problem, but having catalogued the areas of conflict existing between Soviet Russia and Germany went on to state: 'All this can have nothing in common with any situation in which each power would be free to tear hunks of territory from our mutilated country. Russia is far removed from such a state of affairs, and it will fight with all its strength against such an attitude on the part of other nations.' In summary, Chicherin described the ambassador's position as being 'completely inadmis-

75 DVP, vol. I, 271-3
76 Sadoul, *Notes*, 320

sible' and expressed the hope that Paris would understand 'what unfavourable consequences it, without doubt, will have for relations between Russia and France if the French government either openly or silently supports the position taken by Mr. Noulens.'[77]

Here was the substance of the Soviet response as it emerged in the next few days: either France, and with it the other western powers, disowned Noulens and the policies for which he stood or the possibility of Soviet cooperation with the allies was at an end. The Bolsheviks were determined to drive Noulens from a position where he could obstruct the further development of allied-Soviet relations; failing that, they would have no choice but to draw the necessary conclusions and act accordingly. Thus, on 25 April, notes were delivered to Sadoul, Robins, and Lockhart informing them of the discovery of an anti-Soviet conspiracy involving allied consular representatives in Siberia. Documents purporting to establish the facts of the conspiracy were appended to the note and the western governments were invited to recall their consular agents from Vladivostok, investigate the activities of their other agents in Russia and declare 'in specific and unequivocal form' their relation to the Soviet Russian government.[78] The next day, the Narkomindel sent another note to the allied powers asking them to clarify their relation to 'the bands of counter-revolutionary conspirators' operating in Siberia. Chicherin said: 'the Narkomindel expresses the hope that the answer given by the governments of the entente powers will be such as to exclude in the future the participation of their agents in activities and efforts directed against existing Soviet authorities as the provision of this support by the agents of these powers is reflected so very seriously in relations between them and the Russian Soviet Republic.'[79] The conclusion of this fast-moving campaign came two days later when the Soviet government formally asked Paris for the recall of its ambassador. Citing Noulens' statement of 23 April, Chicherin declared that the ambassador had 'contributed to the worsening of relations between France and Russia' and 'could no longer be tolerated within the borders of the Russian Republic.'[80] With the delivery of these notes the fate of future relations between Soviet Russia and the west passed into the hands of allied leaders. If they did not provide suitable answers to the questions asked by the Soviet government, and France did not recall Noulens, the

77 Chicherin, *Stati*, 33-6
78 DVP, vol. I, 265-8
79 *Ibid.*, 268-9
80 *Ibid.*, 271-3

symbol and protagonist of militant anti-Bolshevism, the negotiations for a military agreement would collapse.

The western reaction to the Soviet campaign was entirely negative. Unprepared to extend any form of official recognition to the Bolsheviks, Washington, London, and Paris chose to ignore Chicherin's demand for a clarification of their relations with the Soviet government. Similarly, Paris chose not to recall Noulens. At Vologda, the French ambassador gloried in the success of his efforts to disrupt allied-Soviet relations and struck an heroic pose in expectation of his forcible expulsion from Russia. 'If they expel me by force [he cabled Paris] there can be no doubt that they will act under orders from Germany, and in that case I would like to believe that our British and American allies will understand that they can not have any dealings with the maximalist government. I will congratulate myself on the violent measure taken against me if it has the effect of unleashing allied military action in the far east.'[81] Noulens miscalculated, for the Bolsheviks denied him martyrdom. Lenin personally ordered that the French ambassador be undisturbed, and during the next three months he was simply ignored.[82] Whatever their personal animosity against Noulens the Bolsheviks were aware that their difficulties with the allies originated in the western capitals and not in Vologda. By demanding his recall and the explicit clarification of allied policy on Russia they had sought to determine if it was worthwhile to continue their negotiations with the western powers. The loud silence which met their demands provided an unequivocal answer to the question. By early May it was clear that the allies had no intention of negotiating seriously and would not recognize the Soviet government as a legitimate bargaining agent for Russia.

On this basis the Bolsheviks had to reach a final decision on the future course of their foreign policy. This was made all the more urgent by the exchange of ambassadors with Germany and the development of proposals to seek a new, if even more costly, settlement with the Reich. Yet up to the last minute the Bolsheviks attempted to determine if there had been a change of heart in the west. As late as 4 May, Chicherin called the French General Lavergne to the Narkomindel to learn if Paris had assumed a less hostile attitude to the Soviet government. Lavergne, however, had just received strict instructions from Noulens forbidding him to do anything further to promote 'any form of intervention which offered

81 MAE, Guerre, Russie, Action des Allies, 30/178
82 Chicherin, 'Lenin i Vneshniaia Politika,' 9

the Bolsheviks even a chance of accepting,'[83] and he could only repeat the stale formulae which allied representatives had been chanting for months. In an effort to pry something new from the general, Chicherin told him bluntly: 'Two groups of powers wish to intervene in Russia; if we remain passive, the history of the first partition of Poland will repeat itself to our detriment. Cooperation on our part has less inconveniences, but you have refused to propose it to us with precision.'[84] The meaning of Chicherin's words was clear: if the Bolsheviks could not obtain suitable terms from the allies, they would have to seek agreement with Berlin. 'The clear impression which emerges from this conversation,' reported Lavergne, 'is that the Soviet government wishes to know if it is a question of struggle with or against it. It assumes that we intend to fight it. It will be our adversary.'[85]

And indeed that was the way in which the situation developed. The day following Chicherin's conversation with Lavergne the Bolshevik Central Committee accepted Lenin's thesis that it was too dangerous to reject the new demands which Germany had so rudely presented to Soviet Russia. This, it was recognized, would almost certainly lead to a clash with the allied powers, but, as the brief decision of the Committee states, it was their opinion that 'war against Germany threatens greater losses and calamities than against Japan.' Lenin, accordingly, was empowered to proceed with a new effort to purchase peace from Germany, and the door to collaboration with the allies was closed.[86]

Admittedly that door had never been more than slightly ajar, and, given Bolshevik prejudice and suspicion, it was unlikely to have opened much further, but western prejudice, suspicion, and indecision also played an important role in foreclosing the possibility of cooperation. Although in the spring of 1918 both Soviet Russia and the allies were mortally threatened by German military power, and in the abstract logic of power politics nothing made more sense than mutual assistance against their common foe, it proved impossible for them to scale the barriers of mistrust and suspicion which they had built around themselves to forge an alliance beneficial to both. In part this was due to the personalities involved, but more importantly, both Soviet Russia and the allies perceived

83 PRO FO 371/3285/88696
84 MAE, Guerre, Russie, Action des Allies, 31/22
85 *Ibid.*, 31/19-20
86 Lenin, PSS, vol. XXXVI, 315

that the exclusive aims each was pursuing would drain any agreement of real benefit. While the western powers wanted military victory over Germany, the Bolsheviks, if more cautiously than in November, continued to aim at nothing less than the world workers' revolution. Consequently the two could find common ground only in their fear of Germany and sought elsewhere for means of attaining their ultimate objectives. Momentary circumstances encouraged this search, for neither the Bolsheviks nor the allies saw each other as permanent fixtures in the political geography of Europe. Western leaders saw the Bolsheviks as nothing more than a passing phenomenon and even the most enthusiastic advocates of cooperation did not believe Soviet Russia would survive the war; similarly, Bolshevik leaders, Lenin in particular, never tired of sounding the death knell of *all* bourgeois regimes, those of the allies included. Why then, men on both sides asked, should they join hands with a corpse? The allies looked for the future rulers of Russia in the ranks of Lenin's enemies, men who exercised no power in the spring of 1918, but who, in the rose-coloured dreams of allied leaders, would certainly do so in the near future. The Bolsheviks sought their future partners among the revolutionary proletariat of the western states, and if they were not so fortunate as the allies in being able to send agents in search of potential comrades, they nevertheless indulged in the same type of dreams, *mutatis mutandis*, as clouded the calculations of allied governments. In the meanwhile, they had the option of seeking a new pact with Germany which, if politically and personally humiliating, at least posed fewer risks than an accord with the allies. Not only was it less dangerous in a military sense to renew the effort to purchase peace from Germany, it was also less damaging ideologically to the image which the Bolsheviks had of themselves. A new agreement with Germany could quite truthfully be portrayed as one more installment of the 'robbers' peace' of Brest-Litovsk and justified on the basis of simple survival. An agreement with the allies would not have this justification and would imply a Bolshevik willingness to link themselves voluntarily with one alliance of imperialists against the other. Moreover, as Lenin never failed to point out, alliance with the western powers was the policy of the Mensheviks and right Socialist Revolutionaries. In Lenin's mind these groups served the interests of the Russian bourgeoisie and their policies therefore were counter-revolutionary in nature. To ally himself with the western powers, he feared, was to play the game of the Russian bougeoisie and shamelessly betray the revolution.

Yet there were those among the Bolsheviks, Trotsky in particular, who were eager to obtain military assistance from the allies, and in the black days of late March and early April, when the Germans appeared ready to march on Moscow, even Lenin may have been prepared to gamble recklessly on western assistance. Allied failure to capitalize on this momentary willingness to accept assistance critically injured the possibility of ever reaching an accord. The movement of the allies toward uninvited intervention, particularly after the Japanese landing at Vladivostok, further damaged the prospects of cooperation, while the calculated efforts of Noulens to destroy any basis for agreement put paid to the entire project. By early May the Bolsheviks could be certain that in the future they would encounter only mounting allied hostility, and that to seek any longer to balance the west against Germany would be to invite a second tiger into Russia. They thus had little choice but to turn to Germany and seek, at almost any cost, to purchase peace from their most immediate enemy. This policy, of course, meant that the western powers would almost certainly turn from veiled hostility to open violence in an effort to achieve their goals in Russia, but faced as they were with the immediate threat from Germany, the allied menace could count for little in Bolshevik calculations. If they could obtain peace from Germany they would stand a reasonable chance of surviving the allied challenge. Following the decision of 6 May, therefore, Soviet policy turned away from the option of possible cooperation with the western powers and toward the task of reducing, as far as possible, the danger which the allies posed to Bolshevik rule.

11
The road to war:
last efforts to avert allied intervention

We are witnessing a situation in which the stormy waves of imperialist reaction, of the imperialist slaughter of nations, are hurling themselves at the small island of the socialist Soviet Republic, and seem about to sink it any minute, while actually these waves are only breaking against each other. Lenin, early May 1918

... we are presented with demands almost in the nature of an ultimatum; if you cannot protect your neutrality, we shall wage war on your territory. Lenin, 14 May 1918

We have been plunged into war, we are in a state of war ... now we are faced with British and French imperialism. Lenin, 26 July 1918

The Bolshevik decision to make a new attempt to purchase peace from Germany had been made with the full realization that it would almost inevitably precipitate a violent response from the allied powers. The anticipated allied action, however, did not particularly frighten Lenin. It paled in comparison with the threat posed by Germany and receded even further into the background when measured against the possibility of all belligerents uniting in a common anti-Soviet alliance. The spectre of a united imperialism, ferocious and vengeful, had long haunted his worst nightmares, but the one glimmer of hope on the dark political horizon of May 1918 was the failure of that terrible apparition to materialize. Looking out on western Europe, Lenin, almost in disbelief, noted the intensification, rather than slackening of the contradictions dividing the capitalist powers. This seemed incredible, for according to his analysis, 'the main economic trend of the capitalist system' unequivocally demanded a 'general alliance of the imperialists of all countries.' Yet the facts were clear. 'This enmity, this struggle, this death grapple,' he wrote, as if defining a new theorem of his political geometry, 'proves that in certain circumstances the alliance of world imperialism is impossible.' For Soviet Russia this was vitally important. Almost in awe he concluded: 'We are witnessing a situation in which the stormy waves of imperialist reaction, of the imperialist slaughter of nations, are hurling themselves at the small island of the socialist Soviet Republic, and seem about to sink it any minute, while actually these waves are only breaking against each other.'[1]

Such a situation could not last. Lenin believed, in fact, that it could disappear in a few days, and then the Bolsheviks would be left to face a pan-imperialist alliance dedicated to the destruction of the revolution in Russia.[2] The task of Soviet foreign policy, therefore, was to encourage the contradictions within the capitalist system and feed the fires of hatred which divided the imperialist powers. To do so Lenin intended to tantalize Germany with the economic riches of Russia and terrify the allies with the prospect of German aggrandizement in the east. Soviet weakness made this a very dangerous policy. Unable yet to command a sizeable army Lenin had to rely on political legerdemain as his first and virtually only defence. One miscalculation, one serious error, and the entire flimsy structure of his foreign policy would collapse. Therefore, 'the greatest caution, discretion and restraint' were his watchwords, while 'maneuver, withdraw, wait and prepare' remained the principles guiding his policy.[3] Although it was a dangerous policy, it was not adventurous. Instead, it reflected the political realities of the moment and scrupulously accorded each adversary the respect its power demanded.

'Caution, discretion, and restraint' especially characterized Soviet policy toward the western powers in the summer of 1918. The decision to negotiate a new settlement with Germany virtually guaranteed a future conflict with Britain and France, but it was necessary to postpone that clash for as long as possible. The new German orientation in Soviet policy, therefore, brought with it no immediate change in Moscow's outward relations with the allies. Instead, Trotsky continued to express a warm interest in military collaboration, and Chicherin carefully left the door of the Narkomindel open to allied agents. The foreign commissar even announced the readiness of the Soviet government to agree to the mobilization of an allied army on the far eastern frontier of Russia in expectation

1 Lenin, PSS, vol. XXXVI, 328-9
2 *Ibid.*, 329
3 *Ibid.*, 323-4

of a request from Moscow that the allies intervene militarily against Germany.[4] Beneath the surface, however, a fundamental change had occurred. From potential allies in the struggle against Germany, Britain, and France became potential enemies, posing a serious threat to the Soviet state. The impact of this change was almost immediately reflected in Soviet policy, appearing first in Moscow's attitude to the allied position in northern Russia.

The allies had first established themselves at Murmansk in the midst of the chaotic circumstances surrounding the conclusion of peace with Germany. At first this presence caused no particular concern in Moscow where the problem of German aggression monopolized Soviet attention. Stalin chided the Murmansk Soviet for concluding a military agreement with the allied forces but merely advised them to seek 'written confirmation' that the British and French would not interfere in local affairs.[5] Chicherin assumed a similar off-hand attitude, assuring Lockhart on 10 March, that the Soviet government was not concerned about the situation in the north and would not seek, as required by the Treaty of Brest-Litovsk, to expel the allies from Murmansk.[6]

Circumstances in the north soon caused Moscow to reconsider this attitude. Within days of the first allied landing additional warships arrived, and before the end of March a substantial allied squadron was anchored at Murmansk.[7] More importantly, the Council established by the agreement with the allies had begun to function, and under its urging the Murmansk Soviet had assumed control of the region as far south as Kandalaksha.[8] Although Admiral Kemp, senior allied officer at Murmansk, attempted to mask his activities behind the authority of the Murmansk Soviet, local revolutionary groups, especially militant sailors and railwaymen, began to inform Moscow of their fear of the mounting allied presence in the north.[9] By the end of March, Chicherin felt compelled to warn Lockhart about the 'high-handed behaviour of British and French authorities at Murmansk'

4 France. Archives du Ministère de la Guerre, Vincennes. Campagne contre Allemagne. Record group 6N. Vol. 221. General Lavergne à Clemenceau, télégrammes 255-6, Moscou, le 6 mai 1918. Hereafter cited as MG, followed by record group and volume numbers.
5 BZU, 148-9
6 PRO FO 371/3290/45119
7 BZU,151; Kennan, *The Decision to Intervene*, 50
8 Mikhael Sergeevich Kedrov, *Bez Bolshevistskogo Rukovodstva (iz istorii interventsii na Murmane)* (Leningrad, 1930) 35
9 BZU, 152-4

and ask that the allied officers 'use proper tact in dealing with a difficult situation.' For his part, Chicherin reaffirmed that the Soviet government wished to avoid a clash with the western powers and had issued 'strict instructions to co-operate with the Allies as far as possible.' Moscow's new concern could be seen, however, in Chicherin's statement that a 'special commissioner' would be sent to Murmansk 'to promote good relations' with the allied military authorities.[10]

The Soviet government had very good reason to view the situation with concern, for London was preparing the most far-reaching plans for utilizing the Russian north in the war against Germany. In early April when Chicherin pressed Lockhart for a statement denying rumours that Great Britain was planning to occupy Archangel as well as Murmansk,[11] the foreign office ruled against such a declaration. A firm denial, wrote Lord Robert Cecil, 'would tie our hands; on the other hand any qualified answer would arouse suspicion.'[12] Lord Robert had no wish for the British government to tie its hands, for as one of the foremost advocates of intervention he believed action in the north would precipitate a Japanese movement into Siberia. 'It seems very important,' he wrote, 'that the western Allies show their flags at Archangel ... [because] if we begin to move the Japs will be stirred to activity.'[13] When the question was discussed in cabinet on 12 April, Cecil and Milner, strongly seconded by Sir Henry Wilson, chief of the imperial general staff, argued forcefully in favour of seizing both Murmansk and Archangel. 'This place,' said Wilson, 'will belong to us or the Boche.' Lloyd George was highly critical of this view. 'I fear that we are treating the Bolshevik Government as though it were no Government,' he told his colleagues. 'Under the old regime you would not have gone to Murmansk and Vladivostok without the tsar's permission. You are out for the same policy as during the French Revolution – seizing Toulon, and one place after another.' More than a rehearsal of past history Lloyd George feared the American reaction to uninvited intervention in Russia. If the allies proceeded without the president's sanction might they not undermine American willingness to send a large army to France? 'America is sending divisions to the Western Front. I shall be surprised if we don't get 300,000 infantry. Better a certain American support than a doubtful Japanese support.' For the moment, all

10 PRO FO 371/3307/56759
11 DVP, vol. I, 222
12 PRO FO 371/3305/59948
13 Balfour Papers, British Museum, Add. Mss. 49738

Lloyd George would accept was a commitment to proceed with preparations for the reinforcement of Murmansk and the possible seizure of Archangel at some unspecified time in the future.[14]

Germany soon added to the problem. The allied presence in the north had aroused German concern, and when rumours reached Berlin that six thousand British troops had landed at Murmansk, the *Auswärtiges Amt* demanded an explanation.[15] The German protest was especially embarrassing, for at this time the Soviet government had still not decided if it wished to conclude a military agreement with the allies. As long as the future orientation of Soviet foreign policy remained in doubt Chicherin could not alienate the western powers by demanding their withdrawal from Murmansk. Accordingly he asked Lockhart to suggest a satisfactory reply. Pointing to the exaggerated nature of the report contained in the protest, Lockhart suggested that the entire story be denied and no attempt be made to explain the smaller allied force at Murmansk.[16] Chicherin adopted this proposal, and although he subsequently presented Lockhart with several protests 'against the prolonged stay of the British at Murmansk' he raised no genuine objection to the allied presence in the north. When Lockhart asked him what he was to do with the Soviet protests Chicherin cynically declared, 'you can put them in your wastepaper basket.'[17]

All this changed with the Bolshevik decision to initiate new negotiations with Germany. As late as 2 May Lockhart had been able to reassure the foreign office that 'relations at Murmansk are the best,'[18] but five days later he reported that Chicherin had informed him that the situation there had become 'extremely critical.' Ostensibly this had occurred as a result of stories appearing in the bourgeois press reporting bellicose remarks made by allied officers at Murmansk, but the solution which Chicherin proposed for this 'crisis' betrays a very different reason for his warning. 'It seemed to him,' Lockhart reported Chicherin as saying, 'that we should either withdraw from Murmansk or greatly increase our forces there.'[19] The ever sanguine Lockhart interpreted this to mean that the Bolsheviks were again urging military collaboration, but in early May, with the Germans drawing

---

14 Thomas Jones, *Whitehall Diary.* Two vols. (Oxford, 1969) vol. I, 59-61. See also FO 371/3307/66525
15 Baumgart, *Deutsche Ostpolitik,* 101
16 PRO FO 371/3307/74559
17 Lockhart, *British Agent,* 253
18 PRO FO 371/3307/84551
19 *Ibid.,* 371/3285/82257

ever closer to Paris, Chicherin knew very well that the allies could not 'greatly increase' their forces in northern Russia. Instead, he seems to have been hinting that the allies should withdraw. Two days later, as if to underline his meaning, Chicherin told Lockhart that certain Russian trawlers which Trotsky had promised would assist British operations at Murmansk would not be made available.[20]

On 14 May, addressing the All-Russian Central Executive Committee, Lenin sounded the keynote of the new Soviet attitude toward the allied presence at Murmansk.

It is natural [he said] that the question of Murmansk, to which the Anglo-French have laid claim, should give rise to even greater aggravation, because they have spent tens of millions on the port's construction in order to safeguard their military rear in their imperialist war against Germany. Their respect for neutrality is so wonderful that they make use of everything that is left unguarded. Furthermore, sufficient excuse for their grabbing is their possession of a battleship, while we have nothing with which to chase it away ... The British landed their military forces at Murmansk, and we were unable to prevent this by armed force. Consequently we are presented with demands almost in the nature of an ultimatum; if you can not protect your neutrality, we shall wage war on your territory.[21]

Even Lockhart could understand these words, and he hastened to determine if Trotsky shared the opinion of his chief. It was clear that Trotsky did not, but it was equally obvious that he was powerless to alter Lenin's policy. This embarrassed Trotsky, and he reacted very defensively. 'I asked what he thought of Lenin's speech on foreign policy,' Lockhart reported, 'he replied that he had not had time to read it and that his whole time was now given to the army!' It was over a month since he had asked the western powers for specific proposals on military collaboration, he exclaimed, and now 'he had given up all hope of getting anything definite from the Allies.' He suggested that Lockhart discuss Lenin's speech with Chicherin, for, in his words, 'he had no longer anything to do with foreign affairs.' When Lockhart continued to press him, asking for an hour to discuss the question, Trotsky cut him short, saying that 'if the Allies would put forward definite proposals, it was not an hour he would give me, but a whole day!'[22] London drew the logical conclusion from this and

20 *Ibid.*, 371/3307/84418
21 Lenin, PSS, vol. XXXVI, 344
22 PRO FO 371/3286/92955

subsequent reports about the situation at Murmansk. 'The only moral,' wrote one foreign office observer, 'is that our forces in the North should be made as strong as possible'.[23]

A contest now developed between the Bolsheviks and the British for control of Murmansk. As both had already committed most of their military resources to other theatres of war neither could send a significant force, and the two had to dig deeply into their last reserves to muster the men required on the shores of the Arctic Ocean. The British could spare only six hundred men unfit for duty elsewhere to reinforce the small allied garrison at Murmansk, but they also sent a small training mission that they hoped would be able to recruit a local Russian force and re-organize several Czechoslovakian regiments then on their way to Archangel from central Russia.[24] If the British plan had been fully realized they would eventually have commanded an army of nearly one hundred thousand men, but until that plan could be translated into reality they were actually limited to a diverse force of less than three thousand troops most of whom were of questionable military value. The Bolsheviks could not match even this trifling force. They were reduced to organizing their railway guards for possible use against the British.[25] Their number was so small that they could not even hope to face the Royal Marines already ashore at Murmansk.

In the first instance, therefore, the Bolsheviks had to rely on political rather than military suasion and moral rather than armed force. To begin, this took the form of minatory telegrams admonishing the Murmansk authorities to mend their ways. On 12 May, Chicherin warned the Murmansk Soviet that its 'reckless' policy of cooperation with the British was leading the northern region into 'ruin,'[26] and five days later, Sverdlov sent a similar message. The chairman of the All-Russian Central Executive Committee demanded an end to collaboration with the British, because 'to aid one imperialist power against another' was contrary to the policy of the central government.[27] When these warnings were ignored Chicherin resorted to open threats, telling the Murmansk Soviet on 22 May, that if they continued to defy his authority 'very decisive measures' would be taken against them.[28]

23 *Ibid.*, 371/3307/93608
24 Major-General Sir C. Maynard, *The Murmansk Venture* (London, 1928) 12. For the involvement of the Czechs, see below, 271-80.
25 Kennan, *Decision to Intervene*, 260
26 DVP, vol. I, 286
27 BZU, 174-5
28 DVP, vol. I, 313

These messages had no effect. The prestige of the central government had steadily declined in the north, and the sudden flood of orders from Moscow did nothing to restore its authority. Instead, it washed away the last foundations of that authority leaving the Murmansk Soviet more dependent on the allies than before. The Russians at Murmansk simply could not understand the logic behind the orders issued by Chicherin and Sverdlov. Haunted by the twin spectres of starvation and German attack they had turned to the allies for help. Not only did the allies shield the region from Germany they also supplied much of the food consumed in the area. Supplies from the south no longer reached Murmansk, and only Britain kept the region alive by delivering food from abroad. Additional sustenance was drawn from the sea, but this too had come to depend on the allies, for in early 1918 a German submarine had begun to operate in the Arctic Ocean and fishing boats could not put to sea without the protection of allied warships. All this served to tie the north to the allies and to prejudice the region against instructions issued by Moscow.[29]

Until early June the Soviet government did not realize how seriously its authority had deteriorated. Due to the absence of a strong Bolshevik movement in Murmansk and the desperate state of affairs elsewhere Moscow had paid little attention to that distant region and had little reliable information on which to base its judgment of the problems there. To remedy this Lenin dispatched a special commissar, S. P. Natsarenus, to take charge of the situation. Natsarenus arrived on 25 May, charged with the difficult task of reorganizing the Murmansk Soviet and altering its relations with the allies. To make his task more intricate, he had been given strict instructions 'not to give the allies any formal grounds for breaking relations and for aggressive measures against Russia.'[30] This reflected Moscow's cautious approach to the allies, but it gave Natsarenus little room for maneuver and almost no leverage to use against the Murmansk Soviet. Although he tried to explain the subtleties of Soviet policy to the local authorities he made little headway. Thus, his demand that the Murmansk fishing fleet cease sailing under the protection of allied warships was flatly rejected. Moscow opposed this practice not only because it exacerbated relations with Germany but also because it reinforced existing local ties with the allies. In the north, however, allied protection of the fishing fleet was universally popular, and even the most revolutionary sail-

29 Kennan, Decision to Intervene, 245-76; Leonid I. Strakhovsky, *The Origins of American Intervention in North Russia* (Princeton, New Jersey, 1937)
30 Kedrov, *Bez Bolshevistskogo Rukovodstva*, 86

ors refused to sail without it. As a result Natsarenus had to agree that the practice could continue although in a somewhat less obvious manner than before.[31]

Natsarenus found his talks with allied officers equally disturbing. They were complete masters of the situation and thoroughly uninterested in Moscow's point of view. Worse yet, a day before his own arrival an American cruiser had reached Murmansk bearing a British general, F.C. Poole, to command the allied forces in northern Russia. The presence of another western warship was bad enough, but the appointment of a general to command the miniscule garrison at Murmansk was fraught with the most sinister implications. Natsarenus had no way of knowing how many additional allied troops were on their way to the Russian north, but from the simple fact of Poole's appointment he had no difficulty in guessing that the garrison would soon be reinforced. Adhering to his instructions, however, he did not seek to challenge the authority of the new allied commander and sought only to sound out the general concerning his mission. What he learned was not reassuring, for Poole continually stressed the importance of the Soviets joining the allies against Germany and discounted the possibility of cooperation outside this context. Although his relations with the general were very cordial (Poole later described the Soviet commissar as 'quite a good old bird!')[32] Natsarenus soon decided that he could not alter the situation at Murmansk, and on 2 June he left for Moscow.[33] With his return the Soviet government was left no further illusions about their status in the north. If they wished to restore their authority it would require more than a single commissar and a handful of railway guards.

If the crisis in the north had remained an isolated phenomenon it is conceivable that the Bolsheviks might have chosen not to challenge the allied presence at Murmansk. No matter how injurious that presence became, even if Murmansk broke away from Soviet Russia, it could not compare with the threat to the regime elsewhere and could have safely been tolerated for some time to come. The crisis in the north, however, was not to remain an isolated phenomenon, and precisely at the time Natsarenus returned to Moscow it merged spectacularly with the much larger emergency created by the insurrection of the Czech legion in Siberia.

31 Kennan, *Decision to Intervene*, 273-4
32 Maynard, *The Murmansk Venture*, 26
33 Kennan, *Decision to Intervene*, 274-5

The complicated story of the Czechoslovakian legion has been re-counted in detail elsewhere[34] and does not require re-examination here. It is sufficient to recall briefly how the Czechs became involved in the chaos of revolutionary Russia and came to play such a significant role in the tumultuous events of 1918. Originally, the legion had been formed from Czechoslovakian soldiers captured by the Russians in the first year of the war. These soldiers, feeling no loyalty to the Habsburg monarchy and wishing to fight for the liberation of their homeland, willingly volunteered to take up arms against the central powers. In 1917 they were organized into several regiments and sent to the front. There, in the midst of the disintegrating Russian army, they not only retained their discipline but grew in number to form a full army corps of two divisions. The Bolshevik revolution found them in the Ukraine, and although the legion promptly declared its neutrality in the civil war which erupted, the German invasion forced it to fight on the side of the Bolsheviks in an effort to retreat from the region. Even before this, the Czechoslovakian National Council, under whose auspices the legion had first been formed, had begun nego-tiations with the Bolsheviks to permit the evacuation of their army to France by way of Vladivostok. In mid-March the Soviet government agreed, and shortly thereafter, the first echelons of the legion began to move eastward from Kursk toward Siberia.

Problems arose at once, and the Czechs were able to proceed only slowly, their progress blocked everywhere by impediments thrown up by the Soviet authorities. Part of these difficulties were caused, no doubt, by the manifold problems of moving such a large number of men across a vast territory in troubled times, but there is also evidence to suggest that the Soviet government had many second thoughts about permitting the Czechs to enter Siberia at a time when the far east was threatened by Japanese attack. More importantly, Soviet authorities in Siberia were terrified by the prospect of the Czech legion passing through their terri-tory. Thus, on 22 March, the Omsk Soviet wired Kazan: 'Sixty trains of Czechoslovaks armed to the teeth are proceeding from Kursk to Eastern Siberia. You are hereby ordered to stop these trains at any cost.' Although Moscow countermanded this order and directed local Soviets to allow the

---

34 See J.F.N. Bradley, *La Légion Tchécoslovaque en Russie, 1914-1920* (Paris, 1965); *idem Allied Intervention in Russia* (London, 1968); Kennan, *The Decision to Intervene.* Also see the editorial postscript of Peter Sedgwick in his translation of Victor Serge, *Year One of the Russian Revolution* (London, 1972) 415-24

Czechs to pass, the legion still found its way blocked at every turn.[35] Trotsky, who was instrumental in retarding the Czechs, may have had ulterior motives in promoting this delay. At the time he still hoped for collaboration with the allies, and, as a consequence, he may have been reluctant to see the legion leave Russia. This at least is what he confided to the French military mission in mid-March, saying that if the war against Germany resumed he wanted to use the Czech contingents 'as the nucleus of a new Russian army.'[36] In any case, by late March the advance elements of the Czech legion had only succeeded in reaching the Volga while the larger part of the force remained far to the west, some units not even having left Kursk.

The allied powers were rather slow in recognizing the political and military potential of the Czech legion. As late as 19 March the British foreign office knew virtually nothing about it, and Lord Hardinge, when shown a telegram from Moscow reporting that 'the Tchech corps of seventy thousand men will soon be leaving Kursk district for Vladivostok on the way to the French front' expressed utter amazement. 'Surely the number must be wrong,' he exclaimed, 'seventy thousand Czechs would require an enormous amount of transport!'[37] The figure did prove wrong, the Czech corps comprising only forty-two thousand men, but even that number excited the imagination of British officials casting about for some force to use against the Germans in Russia. By the end of March, the war office had come to believe that the Czechs should be left in Russia where they might be used more effectively than in France. Significantly, Archangel was among the places suggested where the Czechs could be used, the director of military intelligence saying that at that port they could 'keep open the road to Siberia.'[38] This suggestion soon won general acceptance, and in early April utilization of the Czechs in Russia became the policy of the British government.

French policy was different. Clemenceau desperately needed fresh troops to stem the German advance on Paris, and his insistence that the Czechs be brought to France as quickly as possible led to a protracted debate with the British. In this debate the British had the advantage, for only they had sufficient tonnage to move the Czechs. While not flatly refusing to do this they expanded on the difficulties involved in moving so

35 James Bunyan, *Intervention, Civil War and Communism in Russia. April-December 1918. Documents and Materials* (Baltimore, 1936) 81
36 PRO FO 371/3323/59310
37 *Ibid.*, 371/3323/50420
38 *Ibid.*, 371/3323/57789

many men half-way around the world and continually argued for their own plan of using the Czechs in Russia. In early May, a compromise was reached by which the British agreed to evacuate part of the Czech legion by way of Archangel rather than the far east. The French agreed that the Czechs west of Omsk were to be sent north to Archangel, and the British promised 'to do their best' to transport the entire legion to France.[39] The British obviously got the better of this bargain, for while not committing themselves to anything substantial they obtained French agreement to a plan compatible with their own intention of building northern Russia into a centre of resistance against Germany. British intentions can best be gauged by their failure to make any provision for the transport of the legion to France. Instead, they elected to send a training mission to Archangel to reorganize the Czechs for use in northern Russia.[40] They also advised their consul in Vladivostok that those Czechs who had already reached Omsk would be left in Siberia. There they 'might be used ... in connection with allied intervention should this materialize.'[41] Needless to say, Clemenceau reacted angrily when he discovered that the British had misled him,[42] but he might just as well have saved his breath. Commanding the world seaways, Whitehall had decided, whether France liked it or not, to regroup the Czechs at Archangel and Vladivostok for the purpose of waging war against Germany in Russia.

Success in either the French or British venture depended on a certain amount of cooperation from the Soviet government. Whether the Czechs were evacuated from Russia or clandestinely organized as the nucleus of a new allied army the western powers needed Bolshevik assistance in the early phase of the project. Moscow had agreed to allow the Czechs to go to Vladivostok, not Archangel, and the Anglo-French agreement of 2 May recognized that the allies would have to negotiate a change in route with the Soviet authorities. This was left to the British who, unknown to their French ally, had anticipated the decision by instructing Lockhart on 20 April to secure Soviet permission for some of the Czech units to change their destination from the Pacific to the Arctic Ocean.[43] As Trotsky had earlier suggested such an arrangement[44] Lockhart had no difficulty in obtaining authorization for the change in plans, and the Soviet government

39 *Ibid.*, 371/3323/79525
40 See above, 268
41 PRO FO 371/3323/84358
42 Cited in Ullman, *Intervention and the War*, 171
43 PRO FO 371/3323/68874
44 *Ibid.*, 371/3323/73544

issued immediate orders to stop the Czech trains and re-route them to Archangel.[45] With the British, French and Soviet governments in agreement, the Czech problem appeared on the way to a momentary solution.

But not quite. The Czechs themselves had not been consulted, and the speed with which the Soviet authorities acted to stop their progress toward Vladivostok left no time even to inform them of the decision. On orders from Moscow, the long line of trains was simply halted, and everywhere from Penza to Vladivostok, along five thousand miles of the trans-Siberian railway, the surprised Czechs learned that the corps was to be divided into two parts with those echelons west of Omsk to proceed northward to the Arctic Ocean.

They immediately suspected treachery, and imaginations fertilized by a year's exposure to the wonderland of revolutionary Russia conjured up the terrible spectre of a divided corps dispersed to remote regions and led off to captivity. Months of uncertainty, rumour, and frustration had taken their toll, and the terrified Czechs refused to obey the new order. The widely scattered regiments quickly established telegraphic contact with each other, and it was unanimously agreed that the corps would not move until it could be positively established that the legion was not being led into a trap. Even a belated telegram from the Czech National Council informing them that their new orders had been issued at the express request of the allied governments did nothing to restore their confidence, and they decided to send delegates to Moscow to investigate the situation there. They also decided that a congress of the 'Czechoslovakian Revolutionary Army' previously summoned to meet in Cheliabinsk to discuss the internal organization of the corps should also determine its future course of action.[46]

These events set the stage for a direct conflict of the Czech legion with the Soviet government. Although neither wished such a conflict the mistrust generated by the episode served effectively to prejudice the two against each other. Both, however, made an effort to resolve their differences, the Czechs by sending representatives to Moscow, and the Bolsheviks by receiving these delegates and, together with allied agents, explaining the reasons for dividing the corps. Within a few days the Czech representatives were satisfied with the explanation given them and were ready to return to their units and report that the corps could safely resume

45 Bradley, *Allied Intervention in Russia,* 89
46 Kennan, *Decision to Intervene,* 149-51; Bradley, *Allied Intervention in Russia,* 89-90

its journey in the manner desired by the allied and Soviet governments.[47]
If this could have been done quickly, confrontation might have been
avoided, but in the volatile circumstances of May 1918, delay was dangerous as anything could happen to complicate even the most complex of
problems. So it was with the Czechs, for while their representatives in
Moscow were amicably settling the misunderstanding, an incident occurred at Cheliabinsk which translated insubordination into mutiny. The
incident erupted on 14 May when a train bearing Hungarian prisoners-of-
war came to a stop next to one containing elements of the Czech legion.
Insulting words were exchanged, a fight broke out and before it was over
one Hungarian was dead. When the local Russian authorities arrested several Czechs engaged in the brawl their comrades objected, marched into
town, liberated the prisoners and seized the city arsenal. Once tempers
had cooled the Cheliabinsk Soviet was able to restore good relations with
the Czechs, but when the Soviet government learned of the incident it
reacted violently. Not only did it arrest the two Czech representatives in
Moscow, forcing them to send telegrams to Cheliabinsk calling on their
comrades to surrender their weapons to local authorities, but Trotsky also
ordered all Soviets along the trans-Siberian railway to remove the Czechs
from their trains and disarm them.[48] This only served to inflame the situation as the Siberian soviets were in no position to impose their will on the
Czechs, and the latter, especially after the incident at Cheliabinsk, were
unwilling to surrender their weapons to anyone. When the congress of the
'Czechoslovakian Revolutionary Army' met on 23 May and learned of
Trotsky's orders the delegates voted unanimously against allowing the
corps to be divided into two parts. Over the heated objection of French
officers sent to Cheliabinsk to restore the obedience of the corps to allied
orders, the delegates passed a resolution defiantly proclaiming 'to Vladivostok, armed and even against the will of the Soviets.'[49] Both the allies
and the Bolsheviks had lost control of the situation.

Moscow reacted quickly, but ineffectively, to the challenge flung in its
face by the Cheliabinsk resolution. Trotsky reinforced his previous order
by instructing soviets along the railway that: 'Every armed Czechoslovak
found on the railway is to be shot on the spot; every troop train in which

47 Bunyan, *Intervention*, 85-6. These events are confirmed in Lavergne, 'Le conflit
  Tchéco-Slovaque' (Moscou, le 21 juin 1918). MG, Campagne contre Allemagne 6N, 220
48 *Ibid.*, 88
49 Bradley, *Allied Intervention in Russia*, 91

even one armed man is found shall be unloaded, and its soldiers shall be interned in a war prisoners' camp. Local war commissars must proceed at once to carry out this order; every delay will be considered treason and will bring the offender severe punishment.' But Trotsky was speaking into a military vacuum. The local soviets were not strong enough to execute his order, and the attempt to do so simply led to one-sided clashes with the well-armed Czechs who in a few days time proceeded to seize most of the trans-Siberian railway from Samara to Irkutsk. An entirely new front had been opened in the Russian civil war, and the Bolsheviks were completely unprepared to defend it. Only by draining the Urals and Lower Volga of their remaining Red Guards was it possible to recapture Penza and establish a thin defence against a possible Czech thrust into the heart of central Russia.[50] The Soviets had suffered a grave defeat. Not only were they faced with a new and determined enemy, but they had also lost the trans-Siberian railway, the most populous region of Siberia, and contact with the far east. Much worse, the Czech success gave heart to Bolshevik enemies everywhere, stimulating a rash of new anti-Soviet insurrections and firing the imagination of all those who opposed the revolutionary regime.

The allied representatives in Russia had no hand in the actual revolt, but they were not slow in appreciating its significance. Noulens, in particular, believed the mutiny would hasten the fall of the Bolsheviks and immediately proposed that the allies should support the Czechs in their refusal to submit to Soviet authority.[51] Although the allied military representatives still favoured cooperation with the Bolsheviks in moving the Czechs to Archangel and Vladivostok, Noulens had his way and couriers were sent to Siberia to inform the Czechs of this decision. This message, however, did not reach Cheliabinsk before the Czechs on their own authority had decided to resist disarmament and, as an ironic consequence, French officers at the congress actually pleaded with the legion to lay down their arms and submit to the Soviets. Even as this was happening, however, the allied representatives at Vologda had already decided to go beyond mere moral support of the Czechs and plunge even deeper into

50 Glavnoe arkhivnoe upravlenie pri Sovete Ministrov SSSR, Tsentral'nyi gosudarst-venny arkhiv sovetskoi armii, Institut voennoi istorri ministerstva oborony SSSR, *Direktivy Glavnogo Kommandovaniia Krasnoi Armii (1917-1920). Sbornik Dokumentov* (Moscow, 1969) 91-5. Hereafter cited as DGKKA. Also see Bunyan, *Intervention*, 91

51 Noulens, *Mon Ambassade*, vol. II, 85-6. Lavergne confirms the role of Noulens and the subsequent action of French officers in attempting to influence the Czech Corps. See MG, Campagne contre Allemagne, 6N, 220

the Siberian imbroglio by seeking to interpose their authority between the Bolsheviks and the mutinous legion.

They did this in response to a Soviet request for allied assistance in ending the Czech insurrection. On 28 May, Chicherin had officially informed Lockhart and Grenard of the mutiny and called upon them to use their 'moral influence' in having the Czechs surrender their weapons. While hinting darkly of suspected allied complicity Chicherin did not address the western representatives in a hostile manner. 'We agree,' Chicherin assured Lockhart, 'that [the Czechs] must be permitted to leave our country, but they must be promptly disarmed. This affair is extraordinarily serious, and we are certain that you will assist us in subduing the armed resistance which has arisen.'[52] Even before receiving this note Lockhart had spoken with Trotsky, and the commissar of war had expressed the same views stressing, however, that disarmament of the Czechs was a prerequisite for Soviet cooperation. 'Trotsky absolutely insists on this last measure,' Lockhart informed the foreign office,[53] and Chicherin reemphasized this demand in his message. But the allied representatives had already decided against disarmament, and when the demand was received in the form of an official communication the ambassadors at Vologda instructed their agents in Moscow to reject it emphatically.[54]

The allied response to Chicherin was made on 4 June, when the allied agents appeared at the Narkomindel and informed him that 'any attempt to disarm the Czechs or to interfere with them in any way would be regarded as an act inspired by Germany and hostile to the Allies.' Lockhart, who had only recently been converted to the interventionist position,[55] made his statement especially strong, falsely accusing the Bolsheviks of acting under German pressure and having 'wantonly attacked those who had always been their friends.'[56] Chicherin was shocked and, together with Karakhan, listened in stunned silence to the allied declarations. Lockhart later wrote that throughout the meeting the two Bolsheviks 'were scrupulously polite. Although they had a case, they made no attempt to argue it. Chicherin, looking more like a drowned rat than ever, stared at us with mournful eyes. Karakhan seemed stupidly bewildered. There was a painful silence. Everyone was a little nervous and none more than myself,

52 DVP, vol. I, 326-7
53 PRO FO 371/3323/93425
54 Kennan, *Decision to Intervene*, 307
55 See R. K. Debo, 'Lockhart plot or Dzerzhinski plot?' *Journal of Modern History* XLIII, no. 3 (Sept. 1971) 413-39 for the circumstances of this conversion
56 Lockhart, *British Agent*, 283-4

whose conscience was not quite clear. Then Chicherin coughed. "Gentlemen," he said, "I have taken note of what you said." We shook hands awkwardly and then filed out of the room.'[57] This version of the meeting may capture the tension which gripped the room that June afternoon, but it does not adequately reflect what was actually said. From Lockhart's report to the foreign office, prepared shortly after speaking with Chicherin, it is clear that the foreign commissar did not content himself with simply taking note of the allied statement. Instead, he declared that 'the demand that the Czechs should be left with their arms was equivalent to an ultimatum' and asked 'if this demand was the prelude to a declaration of war on the Soviet Government.' Lockhart denied the allegation, saying that the 'question concerned only the Czechs and was not to be considered otherwise,' but this did not calm Chicherin, whom the British agent described as being 'very seriously frightened.' Although Chicherin still said it 'was impossible to allow the Czechs to retain arms after all that had happened' he did not allow his visitors to leave without assuring them that 'he was most anxious to negotiate and give every guarantee that the Czechs would be sent anywhere we liked with the utmost rapidity possible.'[58] This attempt to end the meeting on a positive note failed completely, for according to the American consul-general, the French representative took advantage of Chicherin's statement to sharpen the allied position even further, curtly informing the foreign commissar that 'the retention of their arms by the Czecho-Slovaks must always be a condition precedent to any further discussion.'[59] A total impasse had been reached.

This was exactly the result which Noulens wanted. Anticipating the initiation of armed allied intervention at any time, the French ambassador had again succeeded in exacerbating relations with the Soviet government. In this he had the active cooperation of Lockhart, who despite his earlier opposition to uninvited intervention, now joined whole-heartedly in the effort to overthrow the Soviet regime. 'French and Italians are striving their hardest to use this incident so as to force intervention as soon as possible,' he reported on 6 June, 'and I fully sympathize with their endeavours.' 'We could never have a more favourable opportunity [he continued]. Moment is ripe, almost over-ripe. Counter-revolution is raising its head on all sides. Famine is sowing discontent among workmen and

57 *Ibid.*, 284
58 PRO FO 371/3323/10785
59 Poole to Francis, 5 June 1918, David Francis Papers, Missouri Historical Society, St Louis, Missouri

peasantry, and Bolshevism as a force is rapidly losing ground. Delay and indecision of Allies are losing us supporters every day, and if we do not act within the next few days, Germans may engineer a counter-revolution which would leave us in an almost hopeless position.'[60] Of equal importance, Noulens had the unwitting cooperation of the American ambassador. Francis, who was too inexperienced to realize how he was being used by Noulens, had joined eagerly in what he thought was a simple effort to rescue the hard-pressed Czechs. 'I have no instructions or authority from Washington to encourage these men to disobey the orders of the Soviet Government,' he wrote to his son, '[but] I have taken chances before ... and another little chance will do me no harm.'[61] Consciously or otherwise, by early June, all the major representatives of the western powers were working together to set the stage for allied intervention in Russia.

It did not take the Bolsheviks long to appreciate this fact. Following further fruitless efforts by Radek, Chicherin, and Karakhan to influence Lockhart, [62] the Soviet government reaffirmed its decision that settlement of the problem would have to be based on Czech disarmament and allied guarantees that the corps would be promptly evacuated from Russia. Chicherin notified Litvinov on 6 June[63] and six days later, sensing no change in the allied attitude, delivered official notes to the western agents in Moscow rejecting the allegations made at their meeting with him. Russia, he reminded them, had withdrawn from the war, and to permit the movement of armed detachments of foreign troops through its territory would be a violation of Soviet neutrality. The commissar also pointed out that it was the Czechs who had taken up arms against the Soviet government, and, by itself, this left Moscow no other choice but to take 'decisive steps' to restore its authority in Siberia.[64] In a private conversation with Lockhart, Chicherin went further, bluntly informing the British agent that the Soviet government viewed the mutiny as an 'Allied plot and a prelude to intervention.' In such circumstances, he said, the Bolsheviks had no other course but 'to fight to the end.' Still claiming that Moscow wished to avoid an open break with the western powers, he nevertheless added that 'relations could not be the same any longer' and that the Bolsheviks

60 PRO FO 371/3224/107587
61 Cited in Kennan, *Decision to Intervene*, 306
62 PRO FO 371/3224/107587
63 DVP, vol. I, 347
64 *Ibid.*, 354-6

'would also be forced to alter their attitude toward [the Allied position] at Murmansk.'[65]

The Soviets then had accepted the challenge flung at them by the allied representatives. All possibility of cooperation was now forgotten, and the Soviet advocates of such a policy, Trotsky in particular, were discredited. The commissar of war, who in previous weeks had grown increasingly cool to Lockhart, now refused to see him at all,[66] and henceforth the British agent had to conduct his remaining business with the Soviet government through the unsympathetic foreign commissariat. Although the Czech revolt had led to the near collapse of allied-Soviet relations, the struggle in Siberia soon ceased to play a central role in the residual contacts between the two. Both the western representatives and the Soviet government were locked into their respective positions, and when the allied governments ratified the stand taken by their agents in Russia[67] no further negotiation was possible. Shortly thereafter the Czechs seized control of Vladivostok, and armed forces from all the major allied powers landed in Siberia.[68] This effectively brought an end to the Czechoslovakian controversy, engulfing it in the larger problem of Siberian intervention and leaving only northern Russia as a question of political, rather than military, dispute between the allies and the Bolsheviks.

The Czech revolt had completely altered the situation in the Russian north. Like a flash of lightning the disaster in Siberia had illuminated the danger inherent in Soviet toleration of the allied presence at Murmansk, and, thereafter, the Bolsheviks could no longer pursue the limited objective of seeking to reduce the extent of collaboration between the Murmansk Soviet and the allies. It became imperative for the Bolsheviks to expel the allies from Murmansk or at least establish an adequate defence against their presence in the north. The seriousness with which the Soviet government viewed the situation can be seen in the role which Lenin played in directing the new policy. Whereas earlier his name had not even appeared on the messages exchanged with Murmansk, he now became fully involved in the struggle to prevent the north from falling into the

---

65 PRO FO 371/3286/111410
66 *Ibid.*
67 *Ibid.*, 371/3324/113393. Also see Bradley, *Allied Intervention in Russia*, 98
68 See Kennan, *Decision to Intervene*, 381-404; Bradley, *Allied Intervention in Russia*; John Silverlight, *The Victors' Dilemma* (New York, 1970); Betty Miller Unterberger, *America's Siberian Expedition, 1918-1920* (Durham, North Carolina, 1956); Ullman, *Intervention and War*

hands of the western powers. This involvement began on 6 June, when he joined the foreign commissar in warning the Murmansk Soviet of a possible 'English expedition' to seize the Soviet north. Lenin and Chicherin demanded nothing less than the expulsion of all foreign military forces from Russian territory. 'In the most categorical manner,' they wrote, 'we insist on the observance by the Murmansk Soviet of those obligations required by the neutrality of Russia. Cooperation and goodwill toward foreigners who violate that neutrality would be a crime and a breach of the Treaty of Brest-Litovsk.'[69]

The same day, Chicherin informed Lockhart of the new policy. In the past when he had objected to the presence of allied forces at Murmansk he had accompanied his protest with a sly wink indicating that it could safely be ignored; those days were past, for Chicherin now went so far as to include a veiled threat of Soviet counter-measures should the British fail to heed his warning.[70] Lockhart took this warning seriously and, in asking London for instructions, added: 'I would recommend you most earnestly to make every effort to induce the Murmansk Soviet to declare itself independent from Russia.'[71]

Although the Murmansk Soviet was not yet ready to declare its independence, events in the north were rapidly moving in that direction. British influence was growing with every passing day, and General Poole had no reason to fear that the local authorities would slip from his grasp. He had established very cordial relations with the leaders of the Murmansk Soviet and familiarly referred to two of them, Zvegintsev and Vesselago, as 'Swiggens and Vessels.' One British source records that the general treated them 'as a house-master might treat a couple of his prefects; giving them to understand that they must realize their responsibilities, and act for the good of the house, yet determined none the less that no action taken by them should run contrary to his own preconcerted plans.'[72] Poole's 'prefects' behaved in exactly this way, for in mid-June when Chicherin again demanded that the Murmansk Soviet force foreign warships to leave Russian waters,[73] they replied defiantly that the people of northern Russia looked upon the western powers as their protectors. Until such time as the Soviet government could protect northern Russia the

69 DVP, vol. I, 348
70 *Ibid.*, vol. I, 347-8
71 Milner Papers, Box D4, document 220
72 Maynard, *Murmansk Venture*, 38-9
73 DVP, vol. I, 367-8

Murmansk Soviet refused to implement directives from Moscow.[74] The prestige and authority of the Soviet government had collapsed at Murmansk. In these circumstances the British could safely ignore Chicherin, and, on 15 June, when Lockhart received a categorical demand from the foreign commissar for the withdrawal of all British forces from Murmansk[75] the British agent simply dismissed it as 'insolent' and advised London to disregard it completely.[76] The views of the Soviet government had ceased to interest the allied representatives in Russia.

This was bad enough, but to make matters even worse the Germans again began to take an interest in the Russian north. For a short while they had been reasonably satisfied with Bolshevik efforts to dislodge the allies from Murmansk, but with the Czech mutiny and the diversion of Soviet military strength to the Volga they grew concerned that the Russians would be unable to dispose of both the allied force at Murmansk and the Czechs in Siberia. This led the German general staff to prepare a plan by which the Bolsheviks could concentrate their meager armed forces against the Czechs while Finland would be assigned the task of driving the allies out of Murmansk. Germany would guarantee that Finland would not take advantage of this agreement to seize Petrograd or to prejudice the Soviet claim to the far north. The German foreign office was not particularly impressed with the plan, but, on 9 June, when Ioffe unexpectedly proposed a variation of this scheme, suggesting that Germany guarantee the safety of Petrograd to free Russian troops for use at Murmansk, the proposal took on new life. Thinking Moscow had instructed Ioffe to take the initiative, Kühlmann directed Mirbach to discuss it further with Chicherin, but on 19 June, when the German ambassador sought to do so, the foreign commissar disclaimed all knowledge of the subject. From the available evidence it is not possible to determine if Ioffe's proposal was just another *faux pas* of the inexperienced ambassador or a trial balloon launched by Moscow to determine the direction in which German policy was moving. In any case the alacrity with which Berlin reacted to the proposal gave the Soviet government fair warning of Germany's intentions. For the moment Chicherin was able to pour cold water on the suggestion, saying that Soviet Russia would require a political settlement with Helsinki before concluding a military agreement for cooperataion against the British, but it took little foresight for the Bolsheviks to realize that if they

74 BZU, 199
75 DVP, vol. I, 366-7
76 PRO FO 371/3286/116258

could not handle the situation at Murmansk the Germans would feel compelled to shoulder the burden themselves.[77]

This realization stimulated the Bolsheviks to organize a military force for use in the far north. On the day following his conversation with Mirbach, Chicherin warned Soviet authorities in Petrograd of the impending crisis at Murmansk. 'We must send military forces against the landings of the British,' he wrote, 'it is necessary to restrain the local soviet and take the defence of Murmansk into our own hands.'[78] The next day this policy was adopted by the Sovnarkom and the commissariat of war was directed to provide two thousand men for the defence of Murmansk. Trotsky, however, was not entrusted with this task. Instead, the Sovnarkom delegated this responsibility to S.P. Natsarenus whose powers as extraordinary commissar of the Murmansk region were widened to encompass the entire White Sea district, including Archangel, and expanded to include 'without exception, all organizations and institutions' in the far north.[79] Apparently Trotsky objected to this decision, for on 24 June, Chicherin found it necessary to write the commissar of war imploring him to cooperate with Natsarenus. As Chicherin's letter provides a clear statement of the underlying assumptions of Soviet policy, it is well worth reproducing. He wrote:

In view of the fact that an English invasion at Murmansk, *if not resisted by our armed forces, will inevitably lead to an invasion of German-Finnish troops and serve as the opening skirmish of the two imperialisms on Russian territory*, the Narkomindel most urgently insists that the dispatch of armed forces to Murmansk is incomparably more important than the presence of significant armed forces on the western front in the provinces of Pskov or Vitebsk. In as much as recent information indicates the approaching realization of the threat of English invasion, not a single minute can be wasted in providing Comrade Natsarenus with armed forces for the discharge of his duties.[80]

Unfortunately, Trotsky's side of the argument is not available. Presumably he objected to the plan because he would have to provide the men for an expedition over which he would have no control, but his reluctance to cooperate may have been based more on political than administrative

---

77 Jääskeläinen, *Die Ostkarelische Frage*, 122-3; Baumgart, *Deutsche Ostpolitik*, 101-5
78 DVP, vol. I, 370
79 BZU, 201-2
80 DVP, vol. I, 375. Emphasis added

considerations. Until June, Trotsky had stood for cooperation with the allies against Germany, and, consequently, after the Czech mutiny he had been accused by other Bolsheviks of having put too much trust in western promises. Stung by this criticism Trotsky had severed his relations with the western agents, and on 12 June, Lockhart had reported that the commissar of war was 'angry with himself and with the Allies.' 'I should not be surprised,' Lockhart added, 'if he now makes a violent change in the opposite direction.'[81] By the time the Murmansk crisis reached full boil, Trotsky seems to have made this change, for when Lockhart visited Chicherin, the foreign commissar commented how strange it was that 'this military idea had gone to Trotsky's head.' In March, Chicherin said, 'Lenin had to use his influence to prevent Trotsky from declaring war on Germany. Now it was Lenin's cool brain which is holding Trotsky back from declaring war on the Allies.'[82] From this it is possible to infer that Trotsky wanted to pursue a much more aggressive policy than Lenin, and if he had been given a free hand would have launched a direct attack on Murmansk seeking to drive the British and French from northern Russia. This is nothing more than hypothesis, for there is insufficient evidence to substantiate it, but if true, it would explain why Trotsky was denied authority over Bolshevik forces in the north. Even in late June, Lenin wished to avoid an armed clash with the allies and still hoped to secure his objectives at Murmansk through the threat, not the actual use, of force. If Trotsky had argued forcefully for a more aggressive policy, Lenin, remembering the debacle at Brest-Litovsk, might well have chosen this means of keeping the commissar of war out of mischief. In his turn, Trotsky, who could no longer challenge Lenin on a political level, may have responded by throwing up an administrative road block against the policy adopted by the Sovnarkom. Whatever the case, Lenin was not prepared to tolerate delay, and on 25 June, orders were issued for units of the Red army to proceed north to Murmansk.[83] The stage for a final showdown with both the allies and the Murmansk Soviet had been set.

Lenin himself arranged the props for this confrontation. In a stinging telegram of 25 June, he told the Murmansk Soviet that 'any collaboration, direct or indirect, with the invading hirelings must be considered a state crime and punished according to martial law'[84] and, the next day,

81 PRO FO 371/3286/111410
82 Lockhart, *British Agent*, 289
83 BZU, 205
84 *Ibid.*

warned: 'If you still refuse to understand Soviet policy – a policy equally hostile to the English and to the Germans – you have only yourself to blame.'[85] His warnings, however, went unheeded, and four days later the Murmansk Soviet concluded a new agreement with the western powers placing their relationship on even firmer foundations.[86] When this was learned in Moscow a final bitter exchange took place between Chicherin and Iur'ev, the chairman of the Murmansk Soviet, in which the commissar accused the northern authorities of being allied puppets and Iur'ev accused Chicherin of being controlled by the Germans. It ended abruptly with Chicherin reading a prepared statement saying that 'in the name of the Soviets and Comrade Lenin, I proclaim you and all who share your point of view to be outlaws.'[87] With this statement the telegraph was shut down, and the two-month debate between Moscow and Murmansk came to an end. The effort to regain control of Murmansk by moral and political suasion had failed.

The use of armed force proved equally disastrous. Rather than waiting to organize the heterogeneous forces assigned him by Trotsky, Natsarenus committed his troops piecemeal, rushing each unit north separately as it arrived in his district. Given the urgency of the situation it is easy to understand his reason for doing this, but it had the effect of dividing Soviet strength and leaving the isolated detachments vulnerable to surprise attack. When the first encounter with British troops occurred Soviet units were strung out along the entire length of the Murmansk railway from Kandalaksha to Petrograd. Worse yet, the commanders of these isolated detachments had little idea of what they were to do when they came in contact with the British. No preparations were made against surprise attack, and, in general, it would seem that the advance elements of the Red army did not even expect to meet resistance.

The British were better prepared to cope with the situation. Not only had General Maynard arrived with reinforcements on 23 June, but two days later Lenin's telegram to the Murmansk Soviet warned them that the Red army was on its way north. Although still substantially outnumbered Maynard decided that: 'holding Murmansk meant holding the railway; and within limits, the further south we could hold it, the better for us ... if [the Bolsheviks] succeeded in collecting ... a force at Kem it would be bad enough; if at Kandalaksha it would be doubly serious; and if at

85 DVP, vol. I, 376
86 Kennan, *Decision to Intervene*, 374
87 Strakhovsky, *Origins*, 68

Murmansk itself it might well prove the death blow to all our hopes.'[88] Consequently, on 27 June, he set off down the railway with a small force to intercept the Bolshevik troops before they could reach Murmansk. He was just in time, for he was able to surprise and disarm Soviet detachments which he found at Kandalaksha and Kem. No actual fighting took place as the Soviet units, both substantially larger than his own, surrendered without resistance.[89] The result of Maynard's *bahnkrieg* was to establish the British more than three hundred miles south of Murmansk at the railway centre of Kem. Without firing a shot Natsarenus had lost the initiative, part of his command and a vast territory to the British. Rather than commanding the situation at Murmansk with a numerically superior force he had been forced back on his primary base at Petrozavodsk, five hundred miles south of his objective.

The political consequences of this military disaster were even worse. The Murmansk Soviet, which prior to the defeat of Natsarenus had still hesitated to sign a political agreement with the western powers, now put aside their last remaining doubts and concluded a virtual treaty with General Poole specifying the terms on which they would cooperate with the allies. These terms were very favourable to the western powers and had the effect of establishing an allied protectorate over northern Russia.[90] On 6 July 1918 (the same day allied forces assumed control of Vladivostok and President Wilson decided to send seven thousand American troops to Siberia) the allied agreement with Murmansk was signed; for the next year, London rather than Moscow would rule in the Russian north.

The Bolsheviks had suffered a severe defeat, but viewed in perspective it can be seen that their predicament could have been many times worse. Maynard captured Kandalaksha and Kem with fewer than two hundred men – all that could be spared from the tiny garrison at Murmansk. If he had commanded a larger force there is no doubt that he could have continued south along the Murmansk railway and overrun the Bolshevik headquarters at Petrozavodsk. This would have completely disrupted Soviet military operations in the north and opened the gateway to Petrograd. In the chaotic days of early July almost anything could have happened. As it was, six days passed before Natsarenus even learned of the disaster

88 Maynard, *Murmansk Venture*, 30
89 *Ibid.*, 39-53
90 *Ibid.*, 53

which had befallen his troops in the north, and his first reaction to this news was panic. While hastily preparing to evacuate Petrozavodsk he wired Moscow that 'Anglo-French troops *numbering approximately twelve to fifteen thousand* have occupied all of the northern part of the Murmansk Railway, including Kem ... In the near future they will possibly move south of Kem ... The situation is serious.'[91]

With good reason Moscow responded rather slowly to this startling news. No matter how serious the situation in the north had become it could not compare with the crisis which suddenly exploded during the first days of July when the left SRs attempted to seize control of the Soviet capital. The tumultuous events of 6 July, including the assassination of Count Mirbach and the consequent threat of war with Germany,[92] effectively paralysed the Soviet government. Not until Moscow was once again safely in Bolshevik hands could Lenin spare the time for consideration of the debacle at Murmansk. Even then his directives proved insubstantial to the point of being superficial. The best he could do was to advise Natsarenus to rip up the railway line south of Kem and arrest anyone suspected of aiding the allied cause. He put two million rubles at the disposal of his special commissar, but at a time when it appeared as if Natsarenus needed men, not money, all Lenin could promise was a 'special communication' on this subject at some unspecified time in the future.[93] The war commissariat did attempt to reinforce Natsarenus,[94] but there is no evidence to indicate that such forces reached Petrozavodsk until much later.

In truth, of course, Natsarenus did not require reinforcement, for instead of the twelve to fifteen thousand allied troops which he believed to be at Murmansk, Poole, and Maynard commanded no more than two thousand five hundred men. Of these, approximately half were British, but many 'had been certified as belonging to a physical category so low as to render them unfit for duty in France.' The remainder consisted of French, Serbian, Polish, and Finnish detachments riddled with scurvy and other debilitating diseases.[95] Natsarenus could handle this force with the troops already assigned him, especially after he had destroyed the railway track south of Kem. This made it impossible for the allies to repeat May-

---

91 DVP, vol. I, 379. Emphasis added. Also see BZU, 210
92 See below, 311ff
93 BZU, 211
94 DGKKA, 59-60
95 Maynard, *Murmansk Venture*, 14, 28

nard's daring dash down the Murmansk railway,[96] and had the effect of bringing military operations to a virtual standstill. Except for routine patrols neither side ventured far from their advanced outposts, and the two settled down to watching each other through the pine forests of northern Russia. With their many troubles elsewhere the Bolsheviks were not going to challenge Maynard, and the British, having carved out a spacious enclave, shifted their attention across the White Sea to the strategically important port of Archangel.

The allies had become interested in Archangel largely as a result of the rapid development of their plans for the use of the Czechoslovak legion. Only then was it seen that Archangel with its railway linking the White Sea to Siberia could serve as a point of entry or egress for armed forces operating in the heart of the Eurasian continent. The French came to see Archangel as a port from which the Czechs could be evacuated from Russia, but the British saw it as a ready-made means of linking an allied force in northern Russia with a Japanese army in Siberia.[97] As luck would have it this plan was compromised first by the refusal of the Czechs to proceed to Archangel and then by adverse climatic conditions in the Arctic. A late summer delayed the break-up of ice in the White Sea and made it impossible for the military mission sent out from Britain to proceed directly to Archangel. It had to land at Murmansk and wait until the Arctic summer finally melted the ice in the White Sea. Despite these setbacks the British intended to proceed with their plans, substituting other allied forces for the absent Czechs and waiting only for the ice to melt before launching their expedition. They still anticipated that a significant indigenous force could be raised in the Russian north to form the mass of an allied army to fight against the Germans. In the summer of 1918 anything seemed possible, and, in a desperate effort to improve their position against Germany, first Britain and then the other western powers proved willing to gamble on such an ill-considered policy. By mid-June each of the major western allies had agreed to send a small expeditionary force to Archangel.[98]

The Bolsheviks had little difficulty in determining allied strategy. In one of his last telegrams to Murmansk, Lenin had said of the allied plan: 'Its immediate aim is to link up with the Czechoslovaks and, if successful,

96 Maynard, of course, had no plan to repeat his earlier performance and was quite content with the situation as it stood. 'The destruction of the railway bridges,' he wrote, '... had played our game; ... for the moment, it suited me well to know that there was small likelihood of interference from the south.' Maynard, *Murmansk Venture*, 53
97 PRO FO 371/3305/109403. Also see above, 272-3
98 Kennan, *Decision to Intervene*, 363-80; Ullman, *Intervention and War*, 194-6

with the Japanese, in order to crush the worker-peasant government and establish the dictatorship of the bourgeoisie.'[99] This served to highlight the importance of Archangel and, given the Bolshevik experience at Murmansk, to put them on guard against a repetition of their previous mistakes in the far north. Fortunately for them, Archangel was under better control than Murmansk. It had no allied garrison, the only foreign warship in the harbour was a British ice-breaker, and the local Soviet was loyal to the Bolsheviks. The approach of summer threatened to change the situation, for once the White Sea was free of ice the allies would have no difficulty in putting an expeditionary force ashore at Archangel. Then everything would depend on the strength in which the allies arrived. If they came in substantial numbers there was little the Bolsheviks could do to stop them, because Moscow simply could not spare any troops to reinforce the Red Guards at Archangel. In the event of a large allied landing the city would have to be abandoned, but, in the meanwhile, the Bolsheviks took precautions to improve their position, tightening local security and ordering the British icebreaker to leave the harbor. Although the British captain at first refused to comply, a display of force, including the movement of artillery within range of the vessel, had the desired effect and the icebreaker withdrew to Murmansk.[100] None of these measures could save Archangel from a determined allied attack, but the Bolsheviks hoped they might prove effective against a lesser assault.

The Bolsheviks also had to deal with the problem of the allied diplomatic community at Vologda. Heretofore it had made little difference to the Soviet government if the allied diplomats chose to remain there, but with the threat of an allied landing at Archangel their presence assumed sinister implications. Vologda was the key to the entire northern rail network, for through it passed the Archangel line leading south to Moscow and the Petrograd track extending east to the Urals. In allied hands Vologda would provide access to the Czechs in Siberia and to Moscow itself. When in early July, a right SR insurrection occurred at Iaroslav, just a short distance south of Vologda, the Soviet government feared that the ambassadors might try to organize a force to seize the rail junction and hold it until allied reinforcements could arrive from Archangel. Such a situation was too dangerous to tolerate, and in mid-July the Soviet government felt compelled to dislodge the allied diplomats from their distant retreat.

99 BZU, 204
100 Ullman, *Intervention and War*, 182

Moscow had good reason to fear the diplomatic community at Vologda. Heartened by the insurrections at Moscow and Iaroslav the allied ambassadors had sent a joint telegram to Admiral Kemp on 7 July urging an immediate allied landing at Archangel to support the anti-Bolshevik rebellions. On the next day the insurgents at Iaroslav appealed to them for assistance, and they again wired Murmansk stressing the need for resolute action.[101] But the White Sea was still clogged with ice, and no action was possible. Without western assistance the rebels were crushed, and the Bolsheviks were able to restore their authority in the Moscow region. The significance of the allied inability to act can be seen in the memoirs of Boris Savinkov, the right SR leader of the Iaroslav insurrection. Savinkov wrote: 'Our aim was to cut off Moscow from Archangel, where the allies proposed to land a force. According to that plan, the allies having landed at Archangel could very easily take Vologda and menace Moscow if Iaroslav were in our hands ... Iaroslav ... was held for seventeen days, a period more than would have been necessary for the allies to arrive from Archangel. But the allies did not come.'[102] The allied ambassadors agreed. Francis Lindley, the British *chargé d'affaires* who had just joined the other diplomats at Vologda reported to his government: 'There can be little doubt that had a force of 3000 Allied troops been able to land during the first week of July, the whole course of subsequent events would have been different.'[103]

Despite the threat posed by the ambassadors at Vologda the Soviet government did not feel that it could simply remove them by force. Lenin still hoped to avoid an open break with the western powers and, therefore, proceeded very cautiously. The problem was left with Chicherin who in a telegram to Francis endeavoured to convince the dean of the diplomatic corps that the allied representatives should come to Moscow. Given the events of early July, the foreign commissar chose an unfortunate argument to justify his proposal, saying that the security of the allied representatives could best be assured in the Soviet capital. Equally unfortunate was the Soviet decision to send Karl Radek to Vologda 'in order to execute

101 Kennan, *Decision to Intervene*, 443. Uldis Germanis, 'Some observations on the Yaroslav Revolt in July 1918,' *Journal of Baltic Studies* IV, no. 3 (1973) 236-43. For allied, and especially French, involvement in the anti-Bolshevik insurrections of July 1918 see MAE, Europe 1918-29, Russie, vols. 205, 206, and 207. On the same subject also see MG, Campagne contre Allemagne 6N, 221. Lavergne à Clemenceau, télégrammes 531-3 (Moscou, le 29 juin 1918)
102 B.V. Savinkov, *Bor'ba s Bol'shevikami* (Warsaw, 1920) 32
103 PRO FO 371/4018/174096

this measure and remove any difficulties.'[104] In view of the murder of Mirbach and Radek's abrasive personality it is difficult to imagine an argument or individual less likely to convince the allied representatives to comply with the Soviet request. The acerbic French ambassador described Chicherin's telegram as 'this burlesque document which ... invited us to entrust our security to the place where circumstances had just demonstrated it would be the least assured,'[105] while Lindley said that 'the telegram from M. Chicherin opened what may properly be described as telegraphic hostilities.'[106]

David Francis may have left much to be desired as an ambassador, but as an old Missouri politician he excelled at verbal fencing. In the 'telegraphic hostilities' which followed he succeeded in thoroughly obfuscating the issue and wrapping it in an opaque tissue of his own choosing. Even the British *chargé d'affaires* commented that the ambassador's 'natural verbosity and diffuseness of mind were inadequately restrained by the advice of his colleagues.'[107] At the time, however, Francis' evasiveness served the purpose of the allied ambassadors who were not eager to debate the Soviet proposal on its own merits. Instead, on 11 July, Francis replied to Chicherin: 'We have no fear of the Russian people, whom we have always befriended, and we have full confidence in the population of Vologda. Our only anxiety is concerning the forces of the Central Empires with whom we are at war and, in our judgement, they are much more likely to capture Moscow than Vologda.'[108]

The arrival of Radek on 12 July did not improve the situation. Instead, it led to a test of will between the determined Bolshevik agent and the resolute allied diplomatic corps. The ambassadors were neither impressed by Radek's concern for their safety nor by the picture he painted of the security offered them in Moscow. They were even less impressed by his arrogance and rudeness, finding special fault with the manner in which he prominently displayed a large revolver which he carried in his belt. Given the insurrection in the Moscow region Radek had good reason for carrying a revolver, but the excitable Francis was so incensed by this ostentatious exhibition that his colleagues could barely restrain him from strapping on his own six-gun in imitation of the Bolshevik envoy. The talks proceeded in an unfriendly atmosphere thick with suspicion and mistrust. The senti-

104 DVP, vol. I, 385
105 Noulens, *Mon Ambassade*, vol. II, 144
106 PRO FO 371/4018/174096
107 *Ibid.*
108 Francis, *Russia from the American Embassy*, 246

ments expressed in the earlier exchange of telegrams were again rehearsed resulting in almost immediate deadlock. Radek sought to break this deadlock by warning the ambassadors that the Soviet government could no longer guarantee their safety in Vologda. When that made no impression he demanded a public statement absolving the Soviet government of all responsibility for what might happen to them in the future. The ambassadors courteously declined to make such a statement leaving Radek in a dilemma as how to deal with his adversaries. Although the British journalist Arthur Ransome, who had accompanied Radek to Vologda, informed Lindley that the Soviet emissary was empowered to remove the diplomats by force,[109] it would seem that Radek never seriously contemplated such a step. His entire game was bluff and intimidation, the use of all measures short of physical violence, and having failed to intimidate them in one way he chose another to secure their cooperation. Posting guards around their quarters he informed them that no one would be allowed to enter their 'chanceries' without his express permission. They could see whomever they wished, but their visitors would first have to be screened by his agents. This, he claimed, was designed to avoid a repetition of the Mirbach tragedy. Incidentally, of course, it also prevented anti-Bolshevik agents from meeting with the allied representatives, and thus reduced the danger inherent in their presence at Vologda. This brought a cry of outrage from the ambassadors, but did not make them any more receptive to the idea of moving to Moscow. Instead it confirmed their deeply-held conviction that if they went to Moscow they would simply place themselves at the mercy of the Soviet government. Nothing Radek could say would shake this conviction, and five days after his arrival he had to leave Vologda having failed to convince the diplomatic corps to accompany him.[110]

Even while Radek remained at Vologda the 'telegraphic hostilities' between Francis and Chicherin continued, each seeking to maneuver the other into a politically disadvantageous position. In this logomachy the commissar and ambassador expanded the themes of their original exchange, each emphasizing his own good will while casting aspersions upon the sincerity of the other. In an effort to give the impression that he was prepared to respect the views of the allied ambassadors Chicherin made a

109 PRO FO 371/4018/174096
110 Francis, *Russia from the American Embassy*, 247ff; Noulens, *Mon Ambassade*, vol. II, 145ff. Also see protocols of Radek's meeting with Francis on 12 July 1918 in *Ofitsal'naia Perepiska Diplomaticheskago Korpusa v" Vologde c" Narodnym" Kommissariatom" po Inostrannym" Delam" po Voprosu o Pereezde Pervago iz Vologdy v" Moskvu* (Vologda, 1918) 5-7

'new' proposal. 'If you don't like living in Moscow,' he said on 14 July, 'we can offer you a beautiful dacha in its vicinity.' This, of course, did nothing to meet the ambassador's real objection to leaving Vologda, but Francis could not say so. Instead, he thanked the foreign commissar for his 'kind invitation' but, pointing to the interruption of telegraphic contact with the outside world, declared that the diplomatic corps could not accept the offer until they had consulted their governments.[111] At this inconclusive stage of the telegraphic exchange Radek gave up and returned to Moscow.

His departure was not a victory for the allied ambassadors. Even with Radek gone all the restraints on their liberty remained. They were cut off from the outside world, surrounded by hostile guards and subject to the whims of a government which at any moment might use physical force to abduct them. Their ability to influence events had obviously come to an end, and when a courier arrived to inform them that General Poole believed they should join him at Murmansk the allied representatives began preparations to leave Vologda.[112] When these were only half complete they were startled to receive an extraordinary telegram from Chicherin imploring them to leave Vologda at once. 'In the most serious manner [he said] I ask you to leave Vologda and come here; danger is approaching, tomorrow may be too late; when a battle rages it is impossible to distinguish among houses. If, during the clash of hostile forces everything is smashed in your houses, the responsibility is yours because you have remained deaf to all entreaties. Why cause a catastrophe which you can avoid?'[113] As the message confirmed their belief that an allied landing at Archangel was imminent the diplomats accelerated their preparations for departure and informed Chicherin that they were ready to leave Vologda.[114] What they did not tell him was that they intended to go to Archangel, not Moscow; only when the Soviet authorities at Vologda refused to provide them with locomotives for the trip did they inform Chicherin of their plans. This brought a final plea to reconsider their decision, but when the ambassadors remained adamant he ordered the locomotives released for their use.[115] Early on the morning of 25 July the diplomatic trains left Vologda, arriving at Archangel the next day. From there they took ship for Kandalaksha, landing at the British-held port on 29 July, just one day

111 *Ofitsal'naia Perepiska,* 8-17
112 Kennan, *Decision to Intervene,* 450
113 DVP, vol. I, 402-3
114 *Ibid.,* 403
115 *Ibid.,* 403-6

before General Poole launched his long-delayed expedition to seize Archangel.

The departure of the western ambassadors clearly signalled the final and concluding stage in the long crisis in allied-Soviet relations. With Poole at Murmansk, the Czechs in Siberia and a landing expected at Archangel, a definitive rupture could not long be delayed. But given the basic outline of Soviet foreign policy, emphasizing non-alignment with either belligerent coalition, Moscow still wished to postpone the break for as long as possible. Not bound by the traditional canons of international relations the Soviet government was more than willing to maintain political contact with the western governments while fighting off their armies in various parts of Russia. Before the allied ambassadors had even left Vologda, Chicherin made this clear. In a public statement of 24 July, he expressed his 'deep regret' that the allied embassies had elected to leave Russia, emphasizing that their action was 'wholly undesired' by the Soviet government. Fearful that this step might be interpreted to mean that Soviet Russia had decided to align itself more closely with Germany he took care to underline the basic principles of Soviet foreign policy and reiterate that they had nothing in common with the goals of either belligerent coalition. The Soviet government, he said, remained dedicated to peace, and if it should be necessary to use armed force to oppose allied military operations on Soviet territory this did not mean that the Soviet government wished to break off diplomatic relations. 'Even after the departure of the Vologda diplomats,' he said in conclusion, 'the Soviet government sees no cause which would impede the maintenance of diplomatic relations with the entente powers through their representatives located in Moscow.'[116]

This was a forlorn hope. As Chicherin must have known, the remaining British and French agents in Moscow – Bruce Lockhart in particular – had already ceased to play the role of diplomatic representatives and had assumed the function of conspirators clandestinely seeking to overthrow the Bolsheviks. Since May Lockhart had progressed steadily along this path, gradually shedding his original sympathy for the Bolsheviks to listen attentively to the plans of their enemies. By July, he and Grenard had established contact with 'the Centre,' a broadly based counter-revolutionary coalition embracing such unlikely bedfellows as the Socialist Revolutionary Boris Savinkov, the constitutional democrat Peter Struve, and the tsarist General Alekseev, which promised to establish a military dictatorship in Russia and resume the war against Germany in exchange for suitable as-

116 *Ibid.*, 407-8

sistance from the allies. As a first instalment they demanded ten million rubles. Lockhart and Grenard paid this sum and soon plunged even deeper into anti-Bolshevik conspiracies.[117] With the exception of the American consul-general and his staff, the remaining western agents in Moscow all had a hand in these operations.

When the allied ambassadors decided to leave Russia these plans had not yet reached fruition. Believing that success was close at hand, the western agents wished to remain in Moscow, and when Lindley advised Lockhart to depart with the embassy, he received a reply saying the British agent 'felt unable to leave some important work on which he was engaged.'[118] Lockhart and the other agents in Moscow did take the precaution of visiting Chicherin 'to feel out his position.' They found, rather to their surprise, that the commissar was 'studiously polite' and urged them to remain in Moscow, assuring them that whatever happened they would be allowed to leave whenever they wished.[119] 'This is a little difficult to understand,' Lockhart told London, but ascribing it to little more than a continuation of their earlier policies, he confirmed his intention to remain in Moscow. 'Anything is possible,' he added cryptically.[120] This, of course, referred to his clandestine operations, but he would have been less optimistic had he known that the Bolsheviks were already aware of the conspiracy in which he was involved. The Cheka had picked up the scent of this conspiracy and was actively investigating the relations of the allied agents with known counter-revolutionaries. Rather than simply arresting Lockhart and his associates, the Cheka chose to bide their time and await further developments, expecting that the allied agents would lead them to the heart of the conspiracy. In late July and early August, therefore, an additional element of unreality was added to the hyper-tense atmosphere of Moscow, the allied agents feverishly going about their business of seeking to unseat the Soviet government while the Cheka carefully played out long strands of rope in the belief that the conspirators would soon hang themselves.[121]

Reality, however, continued to break through this shroud of make-believe. On 29 July, with the allied landing at Archangel only hours away, Lenin addressed a meeting of the All-Russian Central Executive Commit-

---

117 PRO FO 371/3287/131278 and 129986. For further details see Debo, 'Lockhart plot or Dzerzhinskii plot?'
118 PRO FO 371/4018/174096
119 Lockhart, *British Agent*, 304
120 PRO FO 371/3300/135024
121 Debo, 'Lockhart plot or Dzerzhinskii plot?'

tee and launched a blistering attack on the 'vultures of Anglo-French imperialism.' In contrast to Chicherin, who always avoided the word 'war' when describing the conflict between Soviet Russia and the allied powers, Lenin stated bluntly: 'We have again been plunged into war, we are in a state of war, and it is not only civil war, war against the kulaks, the landowners and the capitalists who have united against us – now we are faced with British and French imperialism.' To the worried western agents who received a second-hand account of the speech it seemed as if Lenin had declared war on the allies,[122] but a careful reading of the entire address suggests that Lenin only wanted to shock his audience and impress them with the perilous situation which faced the Soviet republic. Seen as a whole it is clear that Lenin's speech was intended to breathe new life into the faltering Soviet military effort and to attack the war-weariness which had begun to sap the strength of the revolutionary cadre. Most of his speech, in fact, was devoted to exposing the mistakes and inadequacies of the Soviet response to the allied challenge and, in substance, was an emotionally laced appeal for a redoubled effort to save the revolution from the new attack which had been launched against it.[123]

The allied agents had no way of knowing this. The exact text of Lenin's speech was not published until a year later, and, consequently, when they met on the morning of 30 July, the western representatives could only consider the garbled account at their disposal. After some debate they decided to call on Chicherin to clarify the situation. Did the Soviet government, they asked, consider itself in a state of war with the allied powers? 'No,' replied Chicherin, not a state of war, but a 'state of defence.' As this left the situation more confused than ever, the allied agents continued to press him for a further explanation, but they received nothing more specific than the commissar's assurance that existing circumstances did not require a rupture of relations. An extraordinary incident which punctuated the meeting, however, served to convey Chicherin's actual feelings. It òccurred when a secretary interrupted the meeting to deliver a report that Field Marshal von Eichhorn, the German military commander in the Ukraine, had been assassinated. The news had an electrifying effect on the foreign commissar who jumped from his seat and danced a jig around the desk. 'You see what happens when foreigners intervene against the wishes of the people!' he exclaimed. The allied representatives left the meeting profoundly depressed and concerned about their personal safety.[124]

122 Poole, 'Reminiscences,' Columbia University
123 Lenin, PSS, vol. xxxvii, 1-19
124 Lockhart, *British Agent*, 305; Poole, 'Reminiscences,' Columbia University

For the moment they had no need to fear for their lives or freedom. As key figures in the anti-Bolshevik conspiracy Lockhart and Grenard were much too valuable to harm or even imprison. Poole was immune from arrest, because the Bolsheviks still treasured the hope that Washington would exercise some restraint on Japan. Their immunity, however, did not extend to other members of the allied community, and on 4 August, when word of the British landing at Archangel reached Moscow, the Soviet authorities arrested British and French citizens who still remained in Russia. For a short while the police even detained the staffs of the British and French consulates, but they were soon released. For the rest of the month the remaining allied representatives in Russia were allowed a precarious and closely circumscribed existence. They were free to get themselves in as much trouble as the Cheka could arrange.

By August 1918, Soviet relations with the allied powers had virtually come to an end. All that remained was a desperate and increasingly dangerous game of espionage and counter-espionage played between the allied agents and the Cheka. With allied armies fighting Soviet forces in the Russian north and Siberia the entire future of allied-Soviet relations had been committed to the military for solution. On a political level, nothing of substance remained to be discussed, a fact recognized by Moscow on 1 August when, for the first time since early 1918, the Sovnarkom issued a direct appeal to the 'toiling masses' of the western states. This appeal, the first of many to follow in the coming two years, outlined the Soviet position on intervention and called for the workers of the western countries to rally to the defence of the revolution in Russia.[125] As long as there had been any hope of avoiding a rupture with the western powers the Soviet government abstained from this type of propaganda, but in circumstances devoid of any other means of influencing political decisions in allied countries the Soviet government reverted to this earlier and less effective method of having its voice heard in the west. Just as surely as the withdrawal of the allied embassies and the landing of allied troops in Russia this appeal marked the breakdown of the Soviet effort to avoid open hostilities with the western powers.

It is difficult to conceive a manner in which this could have been avoided. Given the allied aim of restoring a second front against Germany and the impossibility of the Bolsheviks cooperating in that venture the Soviet effort to avoid war with the allies almost certainly had to fail. Lenin had no way of enticing the allies, as he did Germany, to cooperate with his government. Whereas the Germans needed Russian raw materials, the

125 Degras, *Soviet Documents*, vol. 1, 88-92

allies did not. The western powers could be satisfied with military collaboration and nothing else. As this was out of the question the Bolsheviks could seek only to postpone actual hostilities for as long as possible. In doing so they showed both ingenuity and restraint, resisting what must have been, given the wild outburst of Chicherin on 30 July, an overwhelming urge to strike back at the aggressive measures of the allies. Given the level of their military preparedness they had good reason for restraint; military impotence rather than doctrine dictated a policy of appeasement. Those instances when emotion got the better of reason illustrate the wisdom of Lenin's policy. Trotsky, for example, would seem to have destroyed the Soviet position in Siberia when he ordered the disarming of the Czechs. The Bolsheviks themselves recognized this, Karakhan telling Lockhart in September 1918 that 'in attacking the Czechs Trotsky had made a political mistake.'[126] On the other hand, in its later stages Soviet policy may be criticized as having been excessively moderate. In early June, for example, the Bolsheviks could certainly have eliminated the small British garrison at Murmansk and thereby made it more difficult, if not impossible, for the allies to seize northern Russia. In making such a criticism, however, it is essential to keep in mind the broader outline of Soviet policy. Given the danger of German aggression, particularly in early June, Lenin could ill afford to attack allied forces at Murmansk. Lenin, in fact, did not appear to object to a token British presence in the north as long as it served the useful purpose of reminding Germany that theoretically the Bolsheviks could still re-enter the war on the side of the allies. But anything more than a token force was unacceptable. Not only would a large allied force endanger Soviet security, it could also easily lead to a clash of 'the two imperialisms on Russian territory.'

Lenin sought to avoid this nightmare by striking a balance between the two rival coalitions. The British at Murmansk were to be balanced against the Germans in Finland with a thin line of Red Guards between them. He meant to neutralize the north and prevent it from becoming a major theatre of war. This was a very precarious balance and could be realized only with the cooperation of everyone concerned. In fact, no one would cooperate. The allies were intent on using the north as a staging area for a strike into central Russia; the Germans wanted to smash the allied base before it could threaten them; worst of all the Murmansk Soviet threw in its lot with the allies. By early June, Lenin's original plan was a shambles and a new strategy was needed. Yet Lenin hesitated, and only when it became

126 PRO FO 371/3344/186867

clear that Germany was ready to act unilaterally did Lenin take decisive action. Even then it would not have been too late for the Bolsheviks to master the military situation in northern Russia, but the brief delay caused by Trotsky gave the British just time enough to consolidate their position at Murmansk. Indecision, hesitation, and internal dissension combined with military weakness to bring about the debacle in the Russian north.

The Bolshevik failure to avoid war with the allies had substantial consequences. As will be seen in the next chapter, it had the immediate effect of thrusting the Bolsheviks further into the arms of Germany. Of equal importance, it assured counter-revolutionary groups of new and substantial support – a development which guaranteed the intensification of the civil war. In general, the Bolshevik failure to appease the allies led to a great reduction in their freedom of maneuver in international affairs. Much against their will the Bolsheviks became more dependent than ever on German benevolence during the remaining months of world war I.

12

The road to peace: negotiation of the supplementary treaties with Germany

It is clearer than ever to us that our tactics were right. Lenin, 5 July 1918

Our entire policy must be based on proving to the Germans that if they bend the stick too far, we will be forced to fight and then they will get nothing, for we will create a waste land from Russia, but give them none of it. Ioffe to Lenin, mid-July 1918

Whether we like working with [the Bolsheviks] or not is irrelevant so long as it is useful ... to refuse to benefit from working with the Bolsheviks out of reluctance to incur the odium of having to do with the Bolsheviks – that is dangerous. Hintze, 6 August 1918

In March 1918, Soviet Russia had adopted a new foreign policy. Based on the realism of Lenin this policy had frankly repudiated Trotsky's concept of permanent revolution and recognized the stern necessity of coming to terms with Imperial Germany. This had meant surrender, humiliation, and the steady loss of territory. Finland, the Baltic provinces, the Ukraine, and the Crimea all disappeared down the insatiable maw of the German war machine, and in June, Ludendorff held the heartland of Russia in an iron vise, one jaw securely anchored in Estonia, the other embedded in the west bank of the Don. Even then the German army continued to stir restlessly, and the crisis precipitated by the controversy over the Black Sea Fleet brilliantly illuminated the narrow margin of Soviet security. A 'breathing space' had been won, but would it be of long duration? Territory had been exchanged for time, but was time truly working in favour of Soviet Russia? Pride and conscience had been sacrificed, but would the sacrifice save the revolution?

Lenin answered all these questions affirmatively. In late June and early July his every word exuded buoyant optimism. While admitting the slender margin of Soviet security he took great comfort in the contradictions which riddled the German position in Europe. Ludendorff was victorious everywhere, but what advantage had his victories brought Germany? The food campaign in the Ukraine had failed, and the German offensive in France had proved similarly dysfunctional. Ludendorff had forced the allied armies to retreat, but he had not broken their will to resist. From these circumstances Lenin drew the conclusion that 'the more Germany is victorious the clearer it becomes to all, even to many representatives of the big bourgeoisie in Germany, that the war is hopeless.'[1] But his dialectic did not end there, for Lenin proclaimed that while the war was hopeless, peace was equally impossible. Britain and America would 'not reconcile themselves to Germany retaining the huge booty she had seized.' Drawing on their superiority in men and material they would organize new armies to recoup the losses suffered in France. As their strength increased that of Germany would decline, but the war would continue, for Germany would never voluntarily give up the immense territory she had conquered. Thus 'the victory of German arms was making peace between the imperialist countries impossible.' They remained 'locked in a life and death struggle.'[2] For Lenin these circumstances amply justified his foreign policy. '*It is clearer than ever to us,*' he told the Fifth All-Russian Congress of Soviets, '*that our tactics were right.*' The breathing space was a reality; every day brought the revolution closer; imperialism was tearing itself apart.[3] Yet imperialism remained dangerous and caution was still necessary. To declare revolutionary war would be suicidal, and Lenin heaped scorn on the idea. Those who opposed his foreign policy, he said, were either 'hysterical' or 'acting in the interests of restoring the power of the landowners and capitalists.'[4]

Chicherin evaluated the international situation in the same way. In a lengthy report to the Fifth All-Russian Congress of Soviets he elaborated on many of the views expressed by Lenin and stressed the 'radically new form' of Soviet foreign policy. Originally, he said, the Soviet government had launched 'a revolutionary offensive aiming at the expected world revolution,' but 'when the failure of the proletariat of other countries to lend its immediate support brought about the defeat of revolutionary Rus-

1 Lenin, PSS, vol. XXXVI, 438-9
2 *Ibid.*, 487
3 *Ibid.*, 491ff. Emphasis in original
4 *Ibid.*, 514-5

sia,' the Soviet government had been compelled 'to adopt a waiting policy, to avoid the dangers which menaced us from all sides.' This policy was based on the conviction that 'the social changes called forth by the war will lead to new relations among nations' and that in time the growing proletarian movement in other countries would mature and come to the assistance of the Soviet Republic. Until then, the Soviet government had no choice but to pursue a policy of maneuver and retreat in order to buy time for the revolution to take root in Russia. Soviet Russia, he emphasized, was not anxious for 'military revenge.' It sought to strengthen those elements in capitalist countries which were working for peace with Soviet Russia. 'Some imperialists in both coalitions,' he said, 'think of the future after the war, of economic relations with Russia, this world market most capable of expansion. Instead of a policy of robbery, these elements would prefer a policy of trade, of concessions and economic conquests.' He expressed special interest in German capitalists who wished to establish close economic relations with Soviet Russia. Provided that they would recognize the socialist nature of the Soviet economy and 'understand that the best way to exploit the national wealth of Russia is through cooperation with the Soviet government,' Chicherin said, it was possible to reach an agreement with them. 'We are prepared to give Germany that which we can without damage to our vital interests and that which does not compromise our country as a neutral.'[5]

In Germany the Soviet offer to negotiate agreements to supplement the Treaty of Brest-Litovsk had received a mixed reception. In general, business and government circles found the offer attractive while the army high command had dismissed it as 'inadequate.' Despite Ludendorff's objection the German government had accepted the offer, and on 20 May Kühlmann informed Ioffe that Germany was prepared to negotiate a settlement of problems left unresolved by the peace treaty. Before these talks could begin the simmering crisis over control of the Black Sea Fleet came to a boil, and serious negotiations were postponed until the problem was settled.[6] The crisis, however, did not prevent the two governments from making preliminary arrangements, and on 2 June, they decided that the talks would be held in Berlin. Shortly thereafter, discussion of minor issues began, but nothing of importance was dealt with until the remnants of the Black Sea Fleet returned to Sevastopol.[7]

5 Chicherin, *Stati*, 37-61
6 See above, 223-7
7 Baumgart, *Deutsche Ostpolitik*, 271

Lenin appointed seven men to represent Soviet Russia in the negotiations. Of these only A.A. Ioffe and Leonid B. Krasin played an active role. Ioffe, who had been instrumental in initiating the talks, served as head of the delegation while Krasin, an old Bolshevik and former director of the Siemens and Schuckert office in Russia, acted as spokesman on economic questions. Both were highly regarded in Berlin where the *Auswärtiges Amt* saw them as serious negotiators sincerely interested in reaching an agreement with Germany.[8] The other members of the Soviet delegation played little part in the negotiations. V.R. Menzhinskii, Soviet consul-general in Berlin, and V.V. Vorovskii, Soviet diplomatic representative in Stockholm, do not appear to have even participated in the talks while N.I. Bukharin, G.Ia. Sokol'nikov, and Iu. Larin played only minor roles. It is difficult to understand why the last three were even included in the delegation. All had opposed the peace of Brest-Litovsk and remained hostile to any agreement with Germany.[9] Lenin even thought it necessary to give Ioffe 'a little warning' about the three before they left Moscow. Bukharin, he said, was 'loyal, but has overdone "left-stupidity" till he is sick;' Sokol'nikov had 'gone astray again;' and Larin was a 'first-rate bungler.' 'Be archly careful of all these prize and very beautiful delegates,' he said scornfully, 'Be on your guard!'[10] Ioffe was so suspicious of Larin that he demanded the right to send him back to Russia at any time he felt this was necessary.[11] All three were kept well in the background. The German police, who watched their movements closely, reported that Bukharin spent most of his time with members of the Independent Socialist party while the other two devoted their energies to the production of Bolshevik propaganda.[12] The three may have been sent to Germany primarily for these purposes or simply to allow them to take the temperature of German society for themselves. In any case Ioffe and Krasin dominated the negotiations.

A somewhat similar situation prevailed within the German delegation. Although the army, industry, and chancellor were all represented, the *Auswärtiges Amt* retained control of the negotiations and was able to reduce the number of actual participants to a minimum. Apart from members of the *Auswärtiges Amt* only Paul Litwin and Gustav Stresemann, who represented German industry, played a significant role in the negotiations.

8 *Ibid.*, 272
9 *Ibid.*, 271
10 *Leninskii Sbornik*, vol. XXXVI, 46-7
11 Lenin, PSS, vol. L, 90
12 Baumgart, *Deutsche Ostpolitik*, 271

Richard von Kühlmann and his successor Paul von Hintze formulated the policies of the German delegation but left the detailed bargaining to their subordinates. Of these, Johannes Kriege, director of the legal department, and Rudolf Nadolny, the office's specialist in Russian affairs, were of special importance. With good reason the army looked upon Kriege as the 'evil genius' of the negotiations, for his skill and patience contributed substantially to their success. Success was possible, however, only because Kühlmann and Hintze refused to be intimidated by Ludendorff. In opposing the treaties Ludendorff found his hands tied both by the deteriorating military situation in France and the wholehearted support given the negotiations by German industry. Stresemann in particular used all his influence to pacify the army and secure its tacit consent to a new treaty with Russia.[13]

In these circumstances the negotiations began. Political questions were first discussed on 29 June when Kühlmann and Ioffe outlined their basic positions. For Ioffe this meant an elaboration of the Soviet program of 15 May,[14] while Kühlmann stressed the importance of Russia giving Germany a free hand to settle the fate of Estonia and Livonia. He also informed Ioffe that Georgia, which earlier had declared its independence of Russia, had appealed for German assistance against Turkey. Germany was prepared to give this assistance but first wanted the Soviet government to recognize Georgian independence so Germany could not be accused of interfering in the internal affairs of Russia. He also hinted at possible German-Soviet cooperation in the Caucasus and reminded Ioffe of the Turkish threat to Baku. In the past Ioffe had complained bitterly of Turkish violation of the Treaty of Brest-Litovsk,[15] and Kühlmann now suggested that it was in the interest of both Soviet Russia and Germany to stop the Turks before they reached the Caspian. There was, of course, a price. If Germany could induce Turkey to end its military operations in the Caucasus, Berlin expected to receive a share of the petroleum produced at Baku. Other issues, such as the British presence at Murmansk, would also have to be settled, but preliminary agreement on problems in the Baltic and the Caucasus was necessary before proceeding further. Soviet renunciation of sovereignty over Livonia and Estonia, Kühlmann emphasized, was essential to any agreement.[16]

---

13 *Ibid.*, 274-5
14 See above, 219-20
15 Baumgart, *Deutsche Ostpolitik*, 183-5
16 *Ibid.*, 281; Lenin, PSS, vol. L, 109

Two days later, the German foreign minister and Soviet ambassador met again. In the interval Ioffe had informed Moscow of the first meeting and received permission to accept the new German demands. Lenin, who had fearfully been watching the steady Turkish advance toward the Caspian, was especially pleased with the German proposal for cooperation in the Caucasus and telegraphed Stalin at Tsaritsyn to relay this report to Baku. It was a question of accepting the 'principle of giving in order to receive' and Lenin embraced it eagerly, telling Stalin that 'now there is a serious chance of holding on to Baku.'[17] In relaying the message Stalin described the situation more bluntly. 'The Germans, who wish to leave Baku to us,' he said, 'demand a certain amount of oil as a tip. We can naturally agree to this "demand".'[18] When Ioffe met Kühlmann on 1 July, therefore, he told him that if Berlin could restrain the Turks, Moscow would provide Germany with oil from Baku. Furthermore, Lenin was prepared to accept a German protectorate in Georgia. In exchange, he wanted Germany to end its support of the Don Cossacks. German troops would have to be withdrawn from the Don and the region acknowledged as an integral part of Soviet Russia. Extending the principle of 'giving in order to receive,' Ioffe said that the Soviet government was ready to give up Livonia and Estonia if Germany would provide compensation elsewhere. Parts of White Russia he suggested would be suitable for this purpose. In addition, of course, Berlin would have to agree to the original Soviet demand for German evacuation of the Donets coal basin and cooperation in the negotiation of a favourable frontier with the Ukraine.[19]

Kühlmann found the Soviet counter-proposals quite acceptable. In his view Germany had no interest in either White Russia or the Don and could profitably exchange them for Soviet concessions in the Baltic and Caucasus. He was also prepared to accept the other Soviet proposals, for he believed they would heighten Russian-Ukrainian tension and increase the dependence of both Moscow and Kiev on Germany. Most of all, he favoured the Soviet proposals, because he believed they would help the Bolsheviks remain in power. Kühlmann valued the Bolsheviks, for he was convinced that no other Russian party would accept Germany's political and economic demands. Therefore, if Germany was to exploit her dominant position in eastern Europe she had to do everything possible to shore up the Bolsheviks. In addition, he believed that a Bolshevik Russia

17 Lenin, pss, vol. L, 109

18 *Dokumenty po istorii grazhdanskoi voiny v SSSR* (Moscow, 1940) 289-90

19 Baumgart, *Deutsche Ostpolitik,* 281

meant a weak Russia, and with Germany fighting for its life on the western front a weak Russia was essential to German security. White Russia, the Don, and the Donets basin, therefore, were a trifling price to pay for the continued services of such a useful band as the Bolsheviks, and Kühlmann did not hesitate to recommend that it be paid.[20]

As usual the army had other ideas. Ludendorff had never reconciled himself to the subtleties of Kühlmann's policy and had not abandoned hope that circumstances might make it possible for him to impose his will on the *Auswärtiges Amt*. Temporarily frustrated by the Soviet surrender of the Black Sea Fleet, Ludendorff quickly found another weapon to use against Kühlmann's *Ostpolitik*. This was presented to him by Major Wilhelm Schubert, the German military attaché in Moscow, who throughout June had filed a steady stream of reports describing the waning power of the Bolsheviks and the growing strength of the Russian monarchists. Schubert believed that the time had come for Germany to switch its support from the Bolsheviks to the monarchists and take decisive action against the Soviet government. In his opinion the Bolsheviks were so weak that two German battalions would be sufficient 'to restore order' in Moscow and establish a monarchist government.[21]

Nor was Schubert alone in advocating the overthrow of the Bolsheviks. By late June, hatred of Bolshevism permeated the German embassy in Moscow and, inflamed by violent anti-Semitism, seriously warped the political perspective of its members. Baron von Bothmer, one of the German officials in Moscow, confided to his diary that when the Bolsheviks fell he looked forward with 'pleasure' to seeing 'a few hundred of the Jewish louts hanging next to one another on the Kremlin wall. In order to heighten the effect the hangings should be carried out in such a way so that death comes slowly.'[22] Count Mirbach did not give vent to such grisly sentiments, but he too joined the chorus of embassy officials calling for the overthrow of the Soviet government. Bolshevism, he told Kühlmann in a letter of 25 June, was 'dangerously ill' and would soon fall victim 'to the process of internal disintegration which is devouring it.' He therefore called for a change in German policy. When the Bolsheviks fell, he argued, their successors would be backed by either Germany or the entente. If Germany did not act quickly the entente would win by default. Unlike Schubert he did not favour the monarchists whom he dismissed as

20 *Ibid.*
21 *Ibid.*, 216-20; Hoffmann, *War Diaries*, vol. II, 228-9
22 Cited in Baumgart, *Deutsche Ostpolitik*, 221

'too confused and too lazy' to govern effectively. Instead, he touted the Octobrists and Kadets as the nucleus of a new Russian government. His plan was to reach an agreement with these parties and topple the Bolsheviks. This could be done, he believed, simply by resuming military operations. Then, 'the new organ of government, which we would be holding in readiness and which would be entirely at our service would step into the ensuing gap.'[23] Kühlmann was not impressed. He rejected any change in policy and insisted that Mirbach continue to support the Bolsheviks.[24] Kühlmann, however, had no control over Schubert, and the major's reports were read avidly by Ludendorff who saw them as a vindication of his own views. If the Soviet government was about to fall there was no reason to continue Kühlmann's policy, and the prospect of joining hands with the Russian monarchists appealed to him.

When the Kaiser summoned a crown council to meet in Spa on 2 July, the general pressed vigorously for a new orientation of German policy in Russia. Repeating Schubert's words he emphasized the declining strength of the Bolsheviks and the desirability of coming to terms with the Russian monarchists.[25] Kühlmann was absent, having fallen into disfavour because of a speech in which he had suggested that a purely military victory was no longer possible,[26] but his policy was defended by the chancellor who reminded the Council of the vaulting ambitions of the Russian monarchists. They dreamed of restoring a Great Russia, united and indivisible, and this dream was hardly compatible with German policy in eastern Europe. No one was prepared to argue with this statement, but several Council members suggested that the Russian monarchists might be prepared to settle for something less than their avowed goal. There could be no question of returning Poland or the Baltic provinces, but Germany might agree to a reunification of Russia and the Ukraine. The Kaiser endorsed this suggestion, but Ludendorff, who was not prepared to make concessions even to the monarchists, insisted that they would first have to accept the Treat of Brest-Litovsk. As it was obvious that it might take some time to convince the Russian monarchists to accept a bargain of this nature the Council agreed that Germany could not yet dispense with the Bolsheviks. The result was a rather equivocal decision that '*for the present* the fall of the Bolshevik government should not be induced, but close

23 Zeman, *Germany and the Revolution in Russia*, 137-9. See also Baumgart, *Deutsche Ostpolitik*, 221
24 Baumgart, *Deutsche Ostpolitik*, 220, 222
25 DSB, vol. I, 674-6
26 Baumgart, *Deutsche Ostpolitik*, 88

ties should be established with the monarchists for later use. This must be done on the basis of the Brest Peace Treaty. They can be left the hope of a later restoration of Great Russia.'[27]

Other questions concerning Russia were also discussed at Spa. Without much debate it was decided to continue the negotiations which had just begun in Berlin. Other decisions, however, revealed the absolute inability of the German government to formulate a coherent policy. Thus, on some issues the Crown Council proceeded as if working on the assumption that the negotiations would lead to a firm agreement with the Bolsheviks while on others it appeared to assume the opposite. In line with the first assumption the Crown Council resolved to seek Russian recognition of Georgian independence and to conclude an agreement guaranteeing Russia possession of Baku and Germany a share of its oil production. If necessary German troops would even be sent to the Caspian to stop the Turks from seizing Baku. Similarly, the Council decided that the British presence in north Russia was intolerable and resolved to assist the Bolsheviks in driving the allies from Murmansk. On other issues the Council made decisions which seemed to be based on the assumption that the Bolsheviks would soon fall and that it was only necessary to string them along for a while longer. Ludendorff, for example, was no longer satisfied with Soviet renunciation of sovereignty in Livonia and Estonia. He now demanded the surrender of Dvinsk whose rail link with Riga he said was indispensable for future military operations. The Council accepted this demand and agreed that it would be presented to Moscow. The question of the Don Cossacks was dealt with in a less straightforward manner. Ludendorff, who was supplying the Cossacks with arms and money,[28] objected strenuously to the proposal that Germany recognize the Don as an integral part of Soviet Russia. It would be a mistake, he said, to sacrifice the Cossacks to reach an agreement with Moscow, for only the Cossacks stood between the German army in the Ukraine and the Czechs on the Volga. If the Cossacks threw in their lot with the Czechs, Germany would again be faced with an allied army on the eastern front. The council equivocated, deciding to withhold official German support for the Cossacks but allowing Ludendorff 'as an unconditional military necessity' to provide them secretly with arms and money. If necessary the civil authorities could deny any knowledge of the army's activities. In no case would an agreement

27 DSB, vol. I, 685. Emphasis in original
28 Baumgart, *Deutsche Ostpolitik*, 140-6

with Moscow be reached at the expense of the Cossacks.[29] This revealed
with particular clarity the schizophrenia afflicting German *Ostpolitik.*
Unable to resolve their differences German policy-makers projected them
on to the broad screen of eastern Europe where they distorted and complicated the already compromised German position.

The Soviet government also found it difficult to maintain a unified policy in relation to Germany. Whereas the German problem arose from
discord within the ruling oligarchy, the Soviet problem was generated by a
clash of personalities made worse by poorly defined lines of communication and authority. The importance of the supplementary treaties and the
difficulty of coordinating their negotiation with the day-to-day work of the
Narkomindel also played important roles in the clash. On one side was the
foreign commissar, responsible for the harmonious conduct of government policy and intent on preserving the prerogatives of his office; on the
other was the Soviet ambassador in Germany, irritated by his subordination to Chicherin and wanting greater freedom of action. In the middle
was Lenin to whom both appealed for assistance.

Chicherin and Ioffe had both rendered distinguished service to the Soviet state. Chicherin had become Lenin's 'Man Friday' in foreign affairs[30]
and, due to his conscientious administration of the fledgling foreign commissariat had been promoted to full *Narkom* from the position of acting
commissar which he had occupied since the resignation of Trotsky. Ioffe
had been active in Soviet foreign affairs since the first days of the revolution. Although opposing the Treaty of Brest-Litovsk he had agreed to accept the difficult post of ambassador in Germany. There he had originated
the plan of 'hanging heavy weights' on the feet of German soldiers,[31] and
when it proved successful, Lenin enthusiastically promised his support in
carrying out the policy. Not only did he allow Ioffe to conduct the negotiation of the supplementary treaties he also promised to assist him in resolving practical problems which might arise in Moscow during the course of
the negotiations.[32]

This had the effect of involving Lenin in the ambassador's quarrel with
Chicherin, for Ioffe used his direct access to the Soviet leader to attack the
foreign commissar. Although Ioffe's side of the correspondence has not

29 DSB, vol. I, 685-6
30 See above, 148-9
31 See above, 218-19
32 Lenin, PSS, vol. L, 90; *Leninskii Sbornik*, vol. XXXVI, 43-4

been published it is clear from that of Lenin that the ambassador accused Chicherin of incompetence and sought independence of his control. There is good reason to believe that Ioffe's objective was the Narkomindel itself and that he was seeking to advance his own claim to the office. As long as he did not make this too obvious Lenin proved sympathetic to his plea for greater freedom of action, but even then warned him against exaggerating his differences with Chicherin. 'Don't be in an irritable mood,' he cautioned, '... don't act hastily.'[33]

But Ioffe's irritation increased and with it, apparently, the stridency of his accusations. In early June, Lenin felt it necessary to lecture the ambassador on his relationship with Chicherin. Lenin wrote that he had heard it said that 'Comrade Ioffe is removing the Commissariat of Foreign Affairs to Berlin.' Gently hinting that the friction between the embassy in Berlin and the Narkomindel was damaging the ambassador's standing in Moscow he attempted to remove the friction by applying a thick coat of reassurance and flattery to Ioffe's ego. 'I have received the impression from your letters and am firmly convinced that the frictions are unimportant (chaos is everywhere, inaccuracies are everywhere – they are present in all commissariats and the cure for this evil is slow). Patience and perseverance and the frictions will be removed. Chicherin is an excellent worker; your line of policy loyally carries out the Brest Treaty; you are *already* successful in my opinion – and hence the friction will easily be removed.'[34]

This did not satisfy Ioffe, for he still coveted the office of foreign commissar. Thus in a letter of 27 June, Leonid Krasin wrote his wife that '[Ioffe] would like me to devote myself seriously to foreign policy, and perhaps stay on here permanently as the Soviet Ambassador, while he went back to Russia to take charge of the Ministry of Foreign Affairs.'[35] Fortunately, Krasin had no interest in this suggestion, because Ioffe had no chance of replacing Chicherin. Outraged by Ioffe's back-biting Lenin responded on 1 July: 'I am growing angry with you, to tell the truth extremely angry.' He then condemned the '*personal* sallies, attacks and taunts' to which Ioffe had subjected Chicherin and blunty informed the ambassador that he would not be used as a tool against the foreign commissar.

33 *Leninskii Sbornik*, vol. XXXVI, 44
34 *Ibid.*, 46-7. Emphasis in original
35 Liubov Krasin, *Leonid Krassin: His Life and His Work* (London, 1929) 92

Chicherin is a magnificent worker, most conscientious, intelligent and skilful. Such people must be valued. That his weakness is insufficient executive experience is not a misfortune. Few people are without fault upon close examination!

It is possible to work with Chicherin; he is easy to work with, but it is also possible to make work impossible, even with Chicherin.

You have picked a quarrel with him, but the commissar of foreign affairs justly has complaint of you, for you do not take him into consideration, and *without* administration and decisions of the foreign commissar, of course, ambassadors are unable to take rational steps.[36]

In order to put an end to Ioffe's insubordination, Lenin personally went to the Narkomindel on 29 June and together with Chicherin drafted a set of statutes regulating the administration of the commissariat. First and most important was an ordinance explicitly subordinating Soviet Russia's foreign representatives to the commissar of foreign affairs. Only in the most exceptional circumstances could an ambassador act without the approval of the Narkomindel, and, in such circumstances, the government would hold the individual personally responsible for his decision.[37] The next day Lenin submitted these statutes to the Sovnarkom which approved them, adding a special admonition personally warning Ioffe not to reach any agreement with Germany without first consulting the Narkomindel.[38] Nor did Lenin stop here, for he also sent a secret message to Krasin revealing his displeasure with Ioffe and demanding that the ambassador change his ways. Krasin was instructed to make this clear to his associate and inform Lenin of the result.[39] Unfortunately this response has not been published, but presumably Ioffe got the message. Following the hurricane of letters, directives, and warnings he could have had little doubt about his personal standing in the Soviet capital.

Not all threats to the unity of Soviet policy could be dealt with so easily. The rejection of Lenin's entire foreign policy by the left Socialist Revolutionary party was much more serious. The left SRs had objected to Lenin's policy since March when, following the ratification of the Treaty of Brest-Litovsk, they had resigned from the government and begun a violent propaganda campaign against the peace with Germany. As they only sur-

36 *Leninskii Sbornik*, vol. XXXVI, 54-5. Emphasis in original
37 Trush, *Vneshnepoliticheskaia Deiatel'nost' V.I. Lenina*, 144-5; Vygodskii, *U Istokov Sovetskoi Diplomatii*, 40-1
38 Vygodskii, *U Istokov Sovetskoi Diplomatii*, 41
39 *Leninskii Sbornik*, vol. XXXVI, 55

rendered their posts in the Council of People's Commissars while keeping their seats in other Soviet institutions the Bolsheviks had found it difficult to muzzle them. Throughout the spring their call for war grew increasingly loud and with the Bolshevik decision to send foraging parties into the countryside to gather food for the starving cities the split between the two parties widened into a vast gulf. The left SRs accused the Bolsheviks of betraying the revolution and stealing grain from the peasantry. They called for a great national uprising to wage partisan warfare against the Germans and drive them from the country. The Bolsheviks responded with equally venomous charges. By demanding the resumption of war and opposing the seizure of grain, they said, the left SRs had revealed themselves as the party of the petite bourgeoisie. The Bolsheviks said grain was not taken from the poor peasants, who by definition had none to give, but only from the rich peasants who were hoarding it in expectation of higher prices. Without grain the cities would starve and without peace the revolution would be crushed. Despite all objections from the left SRs, therefore, the Bolsheviks insisted that they would maintain the Peace of Brest-Litovsk and extend the policy of class warfare into the countryside, seizing grain from the rich peasants to feed the cities and mobilizing the poor peasantry in support of this program. The policies of the two parties were irreconcilable and an open clash could not long be delayed.

The left SRs took the initiative in provoking this clash. On 24 June, in preparation for the Fifth All-Russian Congress of Soviets, their Central Committee resolved that 'in the interests of the Russian as well as of the international Revolution, an immediate end must be put to the so-called "breathing space" created by the Treaty of Brest-Litovsk.' They decided 'to organize a series of terrorist acts against the leading representatives of German imperialism' in the hope that these acts would incite Germany to resume the war and inspire the Russian masses to resist the invaders. Although the left SRs Central Committee regarded their action 'as an attack on the present policy of the Soviet government, not as an attack on the Bolsheviks themselves' they recognized that it might 'involve a collision with the Bolsheviks' and resolved to defend themselves 'with force of arms' should the Bolsheviks take 'aggressive counteraction.' The preparation of these measures was left to a small sub-committee headed by the famous terrorist Maria Spiridonova.[40]

Spiridonova was greatly assisted by the role which left SRs played in the All-Russian Extraordinary Commission. Although the Cheka was directed

40 Isaac N. Steinberg, *Spiridonova, Revolutionary Terrorist* (Freeport, New York, 1971) 208-9

by Felix Dzerzhinskii and staffed primarily with Bolsheviks, the left SRs, even after their party had left the Soviet government, held positions of great trust within the Commission. Of special importance were Dzerzhinskii's deputy, P.A. Aleksandrovich, and D.I. Popov, commander of the special detachment of Cheka security troops stationed in the capital. Spiridonova built her plans around these men. Alexandrovich was able to provide her with men, money, and documents to carry out her plan, while Popov, with his detachment of six hundred men personally loyal to himself, was to protect the left SRs during the first dangerous hours of their operation. Popov was also able to requisition supplies for left SR battle squadrons which Spiridonova ordered to Moscow from the provinces. By early July she had a force of more than one thousand men at her disposal and was ready to execute the mandate of the left SR Central Committee.[41]

What was her plan? Based on the terrorist tradition of the Socialist Revolutionary party and the belief that Germany could be goaded into resuming the war against Russia, Spiridonova assumed that the spectacular assassination of 'leading representatives of German imperialism' would so enrage German militarists that they would rupture relations with the Soviet government and march on Moscow. She chose the German ambassador in Moscow as the central figure in her political drama. Since his arrival in Moscow the left SRs had conducted an unrelenting campaign of vilification against Count Mirbach, and Spiridonova could assume that his assassination would have the symbolic quality required for the success of her plan. Once Mirbach had been killed, she seems to have believed that war with Germany would follow almost automatically.

Although in the aftermath of the left SR action the Bolsheviks were to claim that Spiridonova intended nothing less than the overthrow of the Soviet government this charge, in its strictest sense, can not be substantiated. The left SRs spoke of nothing more than forcing a change of foreign policy on the Bolsheviks, and Spiridonova testified that her party 'never mentioned the overthrow of the "Bolshevik" government. What happened was merely a result of the excitement with which the Russian government rushed to the defence of the assassinated agents of German imperialism.'[42] Furthermore, in the actual uprising it is difficult to discern any attempt to seize power. Instead, with the exception of the initial provoca-

---

41 D.L. Golinkov, *Krakh Vrazheskogo Podpol'ia* (Moscow, 1971) 93-4; K. Gusev, *Krakh Partii Levykh Eserov* (Moscow, 1963) 195; Bunyan, *Intervention*, 219. Also see L.M. Spirin, *Krakh Odnoi Avantiury: Miatezh Levykh Eserov v Moskve 6-7 Iiulia 1918 g.* (Moscow, 1971)
42 Bunyan, *Intervention*, 219-20

tive incident designed to elicit the desired change in Soviet policy, all other actions of the left SRs appear to have been forced by Bolshevik countermeasures. Rather than actively seeking power the left SRs were content to await developments. Nevertheless, had Spiridonova's plan succeeded it almost certainly would have led to the fall of the Soviet government. Once the German army had begun to move the Bolsheviks would have had little choice but to adopt her policy of partisan warfare, and once they had done that they would have had to abandon class warfare in the countryside. Even then, Moscow and Petrograd could not have been defended, and with their fall the entire apparatus of the Soviet state could have collapsed. Resistance would have continued, in fact probably increased, but the struggle against the invader would have been conducted on the terms of the left SRs rather than the Bolsheviks. In this sense left SR policy *was* aimed at the overthrow of the Soviet government and was an *oblique*, rather than direct, attack on the Bolsheviks.

To insure the success of her plan Spiridonova required a national forum in which to present her policy, and this was provided by the Fifth All-Russian Congress of Soviets. When it opened at the Bolshoi theatre on 4 July, one left SR after another rose to denounce the Bolsheviks and demand a resumption of war against Germany. The keynote was given by a Ukrainian delegate who delivered an address characterized by Jacques Sadoul as 'one long cry of bitterness, heat and despair against the German oppressors.' His words led to an ugly demonstration directed against German representatives who were observing the Congress from the diplomatic box. 'Down with Brest! Down with Mirbach! Down with the flunkies of Germany!' screamed the left SRs.[43]

The left SRs did not stop with mere gestures. Following the demonstration they immediately moved that the representatives of the Ukraine be officially seated and given the right to vote. If the motion had passed it would have increased the number of delegates prepared to vote for war and symbolically have torn up the Treaty of Brest-Litovsk, announcing to the world that the supreme legislative body of Soviet Russia no longer recognized the separation of Russia and the Ukraine. Given the excitement of the moment the motion might well have passed, but the discipline of the Bolshevik delegates held firm, and the wave of sympathy for the Ukraine broke on the rocks of political realism. This did not stop the left SRs, for as soon as Trotsky rose to deliver his report they resumed their attack, bitterly assailing him for his attempt to control the situation

43 Sadoul, *Notes,* 392-3

on Russia's southern frontier. Near Kursk, Trotsky reported, units of the Red army had attempted to attack German forces in the Ukraine. Not only had one detachment already crossed the border, others had mutinied, lynching their commissars and firing on a government commission sent to investigate. Trotsky denounced the attempt of individual army units to decide the question of war and peace themselves and demanded that the Congress call for an end to this insubordination. Boris Kamkov, speaking for the left SRs, opposed the resolution and extolled the revolutionary virtue of those soldiers who wanted to drive the Germans from the Ukraine. Saying that the left SRs supported 'this healthy revolutionary movement' he proposed that the Congress 'send greetings to those workers and solders who recognize their duty.'

Kamkov's motion precipitated an open confrontation. The Bolsheviks could not ignore this challenge, and when Zinoviev rose to speak he declared that the two parties had 'come to a parting of the ways.' The government, he said, could never accept such an irresponsible proposal and pointed out that Bolshevik commissars had been killed by those individuals to whom the left wanted to send greetings. 'If this is a challenge to battle, we accept it. I raise the question whether you will pick up the gauntlet thrown down by Comrade Trotsky.' Spiridonova did so. 'Comrades Bolsheviks,' she proclaimed, 'we pick up the gauntlet!' Convulsed by the charges which Spiridonova then levelled against the Bolsheviks the meeting collapsed into a bog of accusations and counter-accusations with neither side yielding to the other in the invective which they used. The Bolshevik motion proclaiming that the 'power of decision in matters of war and peace belongs only to the All-Russian Congress of Soviets' eventually passed, but before it was put to the vote the left SRs demonstrably left the hall in order to disassociate themselves from the decision.[44] With good reason Jacques Sadoul, who had witnessed the entire spectacle, wrote that as a result of the first day of the Congress 'an abyss so deep' had been opened between the two parties 'that rupture appears henceforth inevitable. ... The bridges are burned.'[45]

On the following day the acrimonious debate continued. Spiridonova again spoke for the left SRs while Lenin took the podium for the Bolsheviks. Both were intent on buttressing their position and neither was willing to admit the possibility of compromise. In effect they were not talking to

---

44 *Piatyi Vserossiiskii S"ezd Sovetov Rabochikh, Krest'ianskikh Soldatskikh Kazach'ikh Deputavov. Stenograficheskii Otchet* (Moscow, 1918) 20-36
45 Sadoul, *Notes,* 394

one another, or even to the Congress, but to the people of Russia in search of support for their respective programs. Even as they spoke their minds were elsewhere, Spiridonova planning for the next day and Lenin vainly attempting to fathom her intentions. Lenin in particular was preoccupied, and observers noted that his mind seemed constantly to drift away from the Congress. Precautions, of course, had been taken, but the Bolsheviks had concentrated their forces in the wrong place. They had reinforced the Latvian guard at the Bolshoi theatre and warned the commandant of the Kremlin, who was in charge of security at the Congress, 'to be on the alert ... that we could expect all kinds of mean tricks from the Left Socialist-Revolutionaries.'[46] Much like generals thinking in terms of the previous war they thought in terms of the last revolution and failed to realize that the left SRs would not strike at the Congress of Soviets, the symbol of revolutionary legitimacy, but at the hated figure of Mirbach. Even while the verbal battle at the Congress was under way Spiridonova made her final preparations, summoning a young member of her party to the hall and instructing him to murder the German ambassador.

Iakov Bliumkin, the assassin-elect, was twenty years old, a member of the Cheka and an experienced killer. Due to the unseemly exuberance with which he publicly prepared lists of his victims he had incurred the wrath of Dzerzhinskii, and a few days before his meeting with Spiridonova he had been suspended from the Cheka pending an investigation of the charges brought against him. Before his suspension, however, he had been engaged in counter-espionage activities and, in the course of his work, had acquired a fair knowledge of the layout and organization of the German embassy. With the help of Aleksandrovich he was able to obtain a pass allowing him to enter the embassy, and in the company of Nikolai Andreev, another left SR member of the Cheka, he called on Count Mirbach on the afternoon of 6 July.[47]

The assassination took place according to plan. Bliumkin and Andreev arrived at about three o'clock and were received by Dr Riezler the councillor of the embassy. Although he was suspicious of the two, their credentials, bearing the authentic seal of the Cheka and a well-forged signature of Dzerzhinskii, appeared in order, and after some hesitation he allowed them to speak with the ambassador. Shortly after the conversation had begun Bliumkin took a pistol from his briefcase and opened fire. Mirbach

46 Pavel D. Malkov, *Reminiscences of a Kremlin Commandant* (Moscow, n.d.) 245-6
47 *Iz Istorii Vserossiiskoi Chrezvychainoi Komissii. 1917-1921 gg.* (Moscow, 1958) 154;
   V. Vladimirova, 'Levye Esery v 1917-1918 gg,' *Proletarskaia Revoliutsiia*, no. 4 (63)
   (1927) 117; Golinkov, *Krakh*, 93-4

attempted to run from the room, but a short distance from safety he was shot through the head and fell to the ground mortally wounded. The assassins hurried from the room, throwing a bomb behind them to cover their retreat.[48]

Bliumkin's bomb exploded at three-thirty on the afternoon of 6 July, and within minutes the crisis which was to test the stability of Soviet Russia's tenuous peace with Germany had begun. After the smoke had cleared Riezler lost no time in telephoning Chicherin who immediately relayed the councillor's report to Dzerzhinskii and Lenin. Dzerzhinskii went to investigate, and Lenin sent V.D. Bonch-Bruevich, secretary of the Sovnarkom, to the German embassy with a company of Latvian riflemen to take charge of the situation. The pieces of the puzzle came together only slowly, and when Bonch-Bruevich phoned his first report to Lenin there was still no evidence to warn the Bolsheviks that the assassination was part of a larger conspiracy. Dzerzhinskii, of course, had been shown the document with which the assassins had gained entry to the embassy, but on seeing Bliumkin's name he only remembered the irresponsibility which had led him to suspend the young Chekist and did not connect the left SRs with the murder.[49] Then disturbing facts began to emerge. Dzerzhinskii noticed that the seal on Bliumkin's document was genuine, and when he tried to phone Aleksandrovich to determine how Bliumkin had gained access to the seal his deputy did not answer. Other members of his staff were also unavailable. The tense situation in the city and the fact that the men whom he could not contact were all left SRs began to worry him. Nevertheless, when Lenin arrived at the embassy the Soviet leaders still did not suspect the magnitude of the problem which faced them. Their first communique, issued approximately an hour after the assassination, spoke only of 'monarchists or similar provocateurs' as being responsible for the attack on the German ambassador.[50]

Lenin had decided to visit the German embassy just as soon as Bonch-Bruevich informed him that Mirbach was dead. The political situation in Germany was so delicate that the murder of the ambassador could easily tip the scales against those who favoured peace with Russia, and Lenin was determined to do everything possible to prevent the assassination

48 Bunyan, *Intervention*, 217-19; Karl Bothmer, *Mit Graf Mirbach in Moskau* (Tübingen, 1922) 70ff; G. Hilger and A.G. Meyer, *The Incompatible Allies* (New York, 1953) 11ff; Alfons Paquet, *Im kommunistischen Russland* (Jena, 1919) 24ff
49 *Iz Istorii Vserossiikoi Chrezvychainoi Komissii*, 154-5
50 Lenin, PSS, vol. L, 112-13; Vladimir D. Bonch-Bruevich, *Izbrannye Sochineniia*. Three vols. (Moscow, 1963) vol. III, 231ff

from injuring, or even possibly destroying, Soviet relations with Germany. 'At any price we must exercise our influence on the manner in which the Germans will inform Berlin about what has happened,' he told Trotsky.[51] Although he went through the motions, expressing his deepest regret to the officers of the German embassy and promising to apprehend and punish the criminals responsible for the death of their chief, Lenin's exercise in diplomatic hyprocrisy was not entirely successful. His underlying ambivalence showed through his official facade, and his coldness repelled the Germans. 'He did it in such a repulsive manner,' one German told a representative of the foreign commissariat, 'that his condolence was as cold as a dog's muzzle.'[52] Obviously neither side drew any satisfaction from this ritual, and by mutual consent it was kept as brief as possible.

Before leaving the German embassy Lenin conferred with other Soviet leaders about what to do next. While they talked word arrived that the Cheka detachment commanded by Popov had refused to accept further orders from the Soviet government. This report assumed even more importance when it was learned that Bliumkin had been seen entering Popov's headquarters in the mansion of the former Russian sugar king Morozov. To make matters even worse a phone call informed Dzerzhinskii that a short while before Alexandrovich and other left SRs whom he had been trying to contact had all suddenly left the offices of the Cheka taking the Commission's treasury with them. Dzerzhinskii grew more alarmed with each report and wanted to go in person to the Morozov mansion to investigate. Bonch-Bruevich warned that this might be dangerous, but Lenin raised no objection. On the other hand, Lenin was growing more worried about the situation and agreed with Bonch-Bruevich that prudence demanded the mobilization of an armed force to use against Popov should Dzerzhinskii fail in his mission. On returning to the Kremlin the Bolshevik leaders sent for Nikolai Podvoiskii, their most trusted military specialist, and directed him to prepare for an armed confrontation with the left SRs. As an added precaution they ordered the Kremlin itself prepared to withstand a siege, and, within minutes, the seat of the revolutionary regime was transformed into its traditional role of the ultimate bastion of the Russian government.[53]

---

51 Trotsky, *Lenin*, 135
52 Cited in Baumgart, *Deutsche Ostpolitik*, 228
53 V.D. Bonch-Bruevich, *Izbrannye Sochineniia*, vol. III, 235-6; N. Zubov, *F.E. Dzerzhinskii* (Moscow, 1965) 177; Malkov, *Reminiscences*, 249-50

While Lenin took these precautions Dzerzhinskii arrived at Popov's headquarters on the Trekhsviatitelskii Lane. With three members of his staff he stormed into the Morozov mansion and demanded the surrender of Bliumkin and an explanation of why the detachment had refused to carry out the orders of the Soviet government. He quickly discovered, however, that he was in no position to demand anything, for in short order he was disarmed and placed under arrest. Confronted by Spiridonova and the rest of the left SR Central Committee he had to listen while they explained the motives of their action. Resistance was useless, they said, because Mirbach's murder was a *fait accompli* and with it the Bolsheviks could no longer continue their policy of peace with Germany. 'The Brest Treaty is ruptured, and war with Germany is inevitable,' they crowed. 'We don't want power, let it be the same here as in the Ukraine. We are going underground. You may remain in power, but you will have to quit playing the lackey for Mirbach.' Germany could occupy the country 'all the way to the Volga;' the left SRs would make Russia the graveyard of German imperialism. Dzerzhinskii argued with them, denouncing their scheme as a betrayal of the revolution and of benefit only to the 'Anglo-French imperialists' but, of course, convinced no one. He was put under lock and key while the left SRs retired to an adjacent room to discuss the next step of their desperate policy.[54]

Judging from Dzerzhinskii's reaction to their plan the left SR Central Committee could no longer hope that the Bolsheviks would tamely accept the *fait accompli.* If they were to succeed, therefore, they would have to take additional steps to defend themselves and win public support. Thus, they decided to fortify the Morozov mansion, send patrols into other parts of the city to seize hostages and despatch units to occupy the telephone exchange, telegraph office, and Cheka headquarters. At the telephone exchange the left SRs encountered a patrol of Latvian riflemen sent from the Kremlin and were unable to dislodge them from the premises, but both the telegraph office and Cheka headquarters fell without a fight. Once in control of the telegraph office they sent messages to all corners of Russia proclaiming proudly that they had assassinated 'the torturer of the Russian toilers' and appealing for a national uprising against the Germans. At Cheka headquarters they managed to bag the remainder of Dzerzhinskii's staff and cart them off to Trekhsviatitelskii Lane. By a simple ruse M.Ia. Latsis, the second-ranking Bolshevik on the Cheka, was able to get a tele-

54 Gusev, *Krakh*, 203-4; Zubov, *Dzerzhinskii*, 177-8

phone call through to the Kremlin informing the government what had happened, but by then the damage had been done and the Cheka building, a veritable fortress itself, was securely in the hands of the left SRs. Long before the sun set on the evening of 6 July, twenty-six Bolshevik commissars including Latsis and the chairman of the Moscow Soviet, had joined Dzerzhinskii in the Morozov mansion.[55]

These moves took the Bolsheviks by surprise. After receiving the phone call from Latsis and reports of the appearance of left SR patrols in the centre of the city the Soviet leaders could glimpse the outline of what appeared to be an attempted *coup d'état*, but they were unable to respond effectively. For the moment the forces available to the left SRs outnumbered their own, and all Podvoiskii could do with the few companies of Latvian riflemen at his disposal was to hold the Kremlin and a few key points such as the telephone exchange and the railway stations. By itself this was important, because control of the telephone exchange insured the integrity of government communications and command of the railway stations prevented the insurgents from being reinforced from outside the city. Early that evening, in fact, the Bolsheviks disarmed and arrested a detachment of left SRs from Petrograd who suddenly arrived at Moscow's Nikolaevsk station. For the most part, however, the evening of 6 July was one of nerve-racking apprehension, and it is clear that the Bolshevik leaders feared that they were on the verge of losing power. Half jokingly, Sverdlov suggested that the Council of People's Commissars would again have to become a military revolutionary committee, and Lenin described the whole episode as a 'monstrous convulsion of the petite bourgeoisie.' Lenin considered the situation so serious that at one point he even considered the advisability of the government evacuating Moscow, but Podvoiskii assured him that he could hold the city until morning. By then reinforcements would arrive, and it would be possible to take the offensive. Despite this reassurance the Bolsheviks spent a night of torment feverishly seeking to strengthen their forces against the insurgents. 'What an affair!' sighed Trotsky, 'We can not complain that life is dull.'[56]

The Bolsheviks were very fortunate that Spiridonova's plans did not call for the arrest of the Soviet government. Consequently the insurgents did not press the advantage which they enjoyed on the evening of 6 July

55 Zubov, *Dzerzhinskii*, 180; Gusev, *Krakh*, 205; Steinberg, *Spiridonova*, 213-14; Vladimirova, 'Levy Esery,' 120-2; Bunyan, *Intervention*, 215-16
56 Gusev, *Krakh*, 206-7; Steinberg, *Spiridonova*, 214-16; Zubov, *Dzerzhinskii*, 180-1; Trotsky, *Lenin*, 135-6; V.D. Bonch-Bruevich, *Izbrannye Sochineniia*, vol. III, 239-42

and only proceeded with their plan of mobilizing the masses in support of war with Germany. The telegrams dispatched to the provinces were part of this plan, but Spiridonova reserved the centre of the stage for herself and intended to launch her primary appeal for support from the floor of the Congress of Soviets. While her comrades entrenched themselves in the Morozov mansion, therefore, she left Trekhsviatitelskii Lane to go to the Bolshoi theatre. There she hoped to sway a majority of the delegates to support the policy of all-out war against Germany.[57] No one, least of all the Bolsheviks, genuinely liked Lenin's policy, and with the sharp sword of German retribution hanging over the Congress, her oratory might be sufficient to kindle the flame of revolutionary fanaticism which smouldered among the delegates.

The Bolsheviks had no intention of giving Spiridonova an opportunity to bewitch their delegates. They controlled the presidium of the Congress, and following the murder of Mirbach they postponed the opening of the day's session, continuing to delay it as the crisis deepened. When it became clear that the government was faced with an insurrection they quietly called the Bolshevik delegates from the hall, locked the doors and placed the left SRs under armed guard. When Spiridonova arrived she was admitted, but her bodyguard was arrested and she found no one to harangue but her own followers. Her demand to address the Congress was rudely rejected, and the left SRs were told that they were being held as hostages to guarantee the safety of Bolsheviks detained by the insurgents. Spiridonova and her band spent the rest of the night cooped up in the theatre. For all the good they did their cause the remainder of the left SR Central Committee might just as well have joined them, because all they did that night was to retire into the fortified headquarters of the Popov detachment and wait for events to take their course. The next morning they were still entrenched in the sugar king's mansion on Trekhsviatitelskii Lane.[58]

The Bolsheviks wasted no time. During the night they marshalled their forces, and in the early morning hours of 7 July, Podvoiskii launched his attack. As he had been ordered to crush the insurgents quickly he made prompt use of his artillery, opening a deadly fire against the Morozov mansion. At about seven in the morning the left SRs began a disorderly

57 Steinberg, *Spiridonova*, 215; Zubov, *Dzerzhinskii*, 178-80
58 Steinberg, *Spiridonova*, 215-16; P.G. Sofinov, *Ocherki Istorii Vserossiiskoi Chrezvychainoi Komisii, (1917-1922 gg)* (Moscow, 1960) 73; Gusev, *Krakh*, 206-7; Malkov, *Reminiscences*, 247-8

retreat, breaking out of their fortifications and scattering in all directions. Most sought to flee the city but were overtaken by the Kremlin guard which was sent after them in hot pursuit. By mid-afternoon the insurgents had been crushed, several hundred taken prisoner and the rest dispersed in harmless groups subject to later apprehension. Twenty-four hours after it had begun the insurrection was at an end.[59]

The political consequences of the insurrection were not without benefit for the Bolsheviks. In the previous months the left SRs had become a very troublesome thorn in the side of the Soviet government and had used their status of legal, but not overly loyal, opposition to incite resistance to Bolshevik policies. Now they could be silenced. In quick succession decrees spilled out of the Kremlin ordering the imprisonment of Spiridonova and other rebel leaders, the expulsion of the left SRs from the Congress of Soviets, and the suppression of all their newspapers. But if the Bolsheviks had been content with mere repression they would only have driven their enemies underground and made efforts to cope with them more difficult. Instead, the Bolsheviks drew the line of guilt very finely, readily accepting Spiridonova's claim that she and the Central Commitee had acted without the knowledge of most members of their party. Thus, when Trotsky reported to the Congress of Soviets on the suppression of the insurrection he said: 'The entire party is not guilty of this. Instead ... the Central Committee of the Left SRs, behind the back of probably 90% and perhaps even 98% of their party, conducted this stupid adventure, and many representatives of the party have indignantly disassociated themselves from this scandalous act.'[60]

The Bolsheviks, in fact, did everything possible to encourage individual left SRs to disassociate themselves from Spiridonova and swear loyalty to the Soviet government. If they did, they were left in peace, allowed to continue in the posts which they occupied and even form new parties, socialist revolutionary in orientation but distinct from the existing party of Spiridonova. This allowed the Bolsheviks to picture themselves as defenders of the revolution against fanatical extremists. Already in the early

59 Malkov, *Reminiscences*, 250-2; Gusev, *Krakh*, 208; Leon Trotsky, *Kak Vooruzhalas' Revoliutsiia*. Three vols. (Moscow, 1923-5) vol. I, 280-3; Steinberg, *Spiridonova*, 216; Lenin, PSS, vol. L, 114-115; V.D. Bonch-Bruevich, *Izbrannye Sochineniia*, vol. III, 244-50. Also see 'Likvidatsiia levoeserovskogo miatezha v Moskve v 1918 g.' *Krasnyi Arkhiv*, 1940, no. 4, and Ia. Vatsetis, 'Vystuplenie levykh eserov v Moskve,' *Etapy bol'shogo puti* (Moscow, 1963)

60 Trotsky, *Kak Vooruzhalas'*, vol. I, 276, 290

morning of 7 July, Lenin described the insurgents as 'hysterical adventurers' and predicted in a telegram to Stalin that 'All who are against war will
be for us.' Within hours this policy had crystalized, and Lenin defined his
response to the left SR insurrection in a telegram to K.A. Mekhonoshin, member of the Revolutionary Military Council of the Eastern Front.
'I do not doubt,' he said, 'that the stupidly hysterical and provocative
adventure ... will drive from [the left SR Central Committee] not only the
majority of workers and peasants, but also many members of the intelligent-
sia.'[61] To exploit this political opportunity the Bolsheviks had to be merciful to the bulk of the left SRs, but this cost them nothing. Not only was the
majority of the rival party genuinely innocent, but clemency for the rank
and file did not rule out punishment for the guilty. The Bolsheviks, however, dealt lightly even with the leaders of the insurrection, and only the
Chekists who had joined the conspiracy were actually shot. Spiridonova
was too popular to be dealt with in this manner, but she was put safely
behind bars. Although the majority of the left SR Central Committee escaped arrest the defection of their followers made them virtually impotent. If
in early July they could not mount more than a one-day uprising they were
not likely to threaten the Bolsheviks later. In political terms, therefore, it is
difficult to disagree with Trotsky who later wrote that the left SR insurrection
'did not weaken [the Bolsheviks] but strengthened [them].'[62]

61 Lenin, PSS, vol. L, 116
62 Trotsky, *Lenin*, 158; Golinkov, *Krakh*, 93-4, 173ff; Gusev, *Krakh*, 217-28. This interpretation rejects the sensational thesis of George Katkov that Lenin, rather than Spiridonova, was the instigator of Mirbach's assassination. Except for vague innuendo, Katkov
can produce no evidence to support his thesis, and when stripped of its supporting network of supposition, it rests on the unquestionable, but irrelevant, fact that the left SRs
responsible for the assassination were treated very leniently by the Bolsheviks. In particular, Katkov points to the escape of Iakov Bliumkin, who was not captured until 1919 and
was then almost immediately granted amnesty and allowed to rejoin the Cheka. In effect,
Katkov asks if Lenin would have been so lenient with the left SRs if he had not ordered
the murder of Mirbach himself. The answer is *yes*, for Lenin was not interested in vengeance, a goal which he rarely sought, but in political profit. Lenin's great gift was the
ability to extract political gain from almost any situation, and following the insurrection
he quickly realized that there was immense political profit to be won by treating the left
SRs in the manner which he did. Essentially his policy was that of the 'united front from
below' seeking to attract as many left SRs to his banner as possible. He would not accomplish this by venting his anger on the left SRs nor would he accomplish it by making
martyrs of Spiridonova and her associates. Only if he thoroughly discredited the leadership of the rival party while projecting an image of benign moderation could he hope to
obtain his objective.

The same could not be said of the impact of the insurrection on the Bolshevik military position. In early July the Red army was barely holding its own against the Czech legion, and the uprising shook the Soviet eastern front to its very foundations. M.A. Muraviev, a left SR and commander-in-chief of the eastern front, was the cause of this disaster. Although unaware of Spiridonova's plans he was dissatisfied with the policies of the Soviet government and was psychologically prepared to take part in a rebellion against the Bolsheviks. He did not act precipitously, however, and when informed of the uprising in the capital, he even denounced its instigators and swore an oath of loyalty to the Soviet government. Lenin himself agreed to accept the oath, and on 7 July ordered Mekhonoshin to let Muraviev retain his command.[63] But Muraviev had lied, and three days later he disappeared from his headquarters, gathered a

Bliumkin's case is also explained easily. If the assassin had been apprehended in July he undoubtedly would have been executed; Germany would have demanded the life of Mirbach's murderer, and Lenin would not have hesitated to send him to the gallows. By 1919, however, the Imperial German government had fallen, and Lenin no longer had to fear its wrath. Why then should he punish Bliumkin who had only killed the treacherous representative of a hostile regime which could no longer harm Soviet Russia? To act against Bliumkin in 1919 would only have revived bitter memories, and Lenin remained just as eager as before to possess the good will and voluntary cooperation of former left SRs. As long as Bliumkin caused no further trouble, he was *politically* more valuable alive than dead. For Lenin this was the prime consideration.

The most telling argument against Katkov's thesis, however, is the entire development of Lenin's foreign policy during the summer of 1918. This policy was firmly based on reaching a negotiated settlement with Germany, and, at the time of Mirbach's assassination, negotiations had already begun in Berlin and were proceeding smoothly. To be sure, Mirbach had argued against further cooperation with the Bolsheviks, and it is more than likely, as Katkov suggests, that Lenin knew of the ambassador's proposal to overthrow the Soviet government. It does not follow from this possibility, however, that Lenin chose assassination as a way of opposing German intervention in Russia. Mirbach was simply one of many German leaders who wanted to overthrow the Bolsheviks, and to lop off his head would not slay the hydra of intervention but only enrage its other, vastly more influential, advocates. Lenin's response to those Germans who advocated resumption of war with Russia was to encourage their political enemies in Germany to oppose them by holding out the prospect of profitable economic relations with Soviet Russia. It is inconceivable that Lenin, who constantly cautioned his followers against provoking Germany and repeatedly warned that 'this beast springs quickly,' would place his entire foreign policy, and with it the existence of his regime, in jeopardy by ordering the murder of the German ambassador. The assassination of Mirbach was the desperate act of a party which wished war with Germany, not of a government which wanted to maintain the peace. See George Katkov, 'The assassination of Count Mirbach,' *St. Antony's Papers 12* (Soviet series 3) (1962) 53-93. Cf. Baumgart, *Deutsche Ostpolitik*, 224

63 Lenin, PSS, vol. L, 116

thousand men and went to Simbirsk where he proclaimed an end to the struggle against the Czechs and a declaration of war on Germany. A new government would be formed, he promised, and the true invader of Russia driven from the country. Within a day the Bolsheviks were able to deal with Muraviev personally, gunning him down at a meeting on 11 July, but the damage which he had done was enormous. As a result of his treachery the entire eastern front was opened to the Czechs, the Red army was demoralized and organized resistance virtually came to an end. Lenin sent I.I. Vatsetis to retrieve the situation, but in the circumstances all he could do was plead for reinforcements.[64] By the middle of the month Lenin was draining troops from every part of Russia to reinforce the Volga, and on 20 July he wrote Zinoviev: 'It is essential to move the *maximum* number of workers from Petrograd. Otherwise *we shall fall*, for the situation with the Czechoslovaks is *as bad as could be* ... we shall certainly *perish* owing to the Czechoslovaks unless we make *desperate* efforts to add hundreds and thousands of *leading* workers in order to convert the jelly into something solid.'[65] The situation, however, remained out of control, and during late July the Czechs advanced westward against virtually no opposition. Although the left SR insurrection had failed politically, its military consequences threatened, *ex post facto*, to bring down the Soviet government.[66]

The international consequences of the left SR insurrection were potentially even more serious than Muraviev's treachery. Even while the Volga crisis was at its worst the Bolsheviks could still hope to shore up the eastern front; if the Germans chose to use the murder of Mirbach as a pretext to resume their offensive there was absolutely no way they could be stopped. Petrograd, Moscow, and all other parts of European Russia were within their grasp. In February, Lenin could heroically claim that, if necessary, the Soviet government would retreat into a Ural-Kuznetsk redoubt in order to keep the flame of revolution alight in Russia, but with the Czechs on the Volga this option was no longer available. In case of a resumption of war with Germany the Bolsheviks had no other choice but to fight and fall in central Russia. If they wished they could then elect to continue the struggle in the form of partisan warfare, but they would no longer possess state power, the instrument which Lenin believed essential for the fight against counter-revolution in Russia and imperialism throughout the world.

64 DGKKA, 102
65 Lenin, PSS, vol. L, 124-5. Emphasis in original
66 See David Footman, *Civil War in Russia* (London, 1961) 141-5; A.P. Nenarokov, *Vostochnyi Front 1918 g.* (Moscow, 1969) 97-148

The spectre of war haunted Lenin, and he did everything possible to avert that catastrophe. He realized that while official expressions of condolence might help, the Germans would be interested primarily in the stability of the Soviet government. Resumption of the war, he believed, would result not from German anger over the murder of their ambassador, who was expendable, but from a conviction that the murder signalled the imminent fall of the Soviet regime. 'There is more than enough reason for military intervention,' he told Trotsky, 'especially if one takes into account the fact that Mirbach, no doubt, must have been reporting all the time that we are weak and that the slightest shock would hurt us.'[67] It had been essential, therefore, that the Bolsheviks crush the left SR insurrection quickly, for otherwise the Germans, believing that the Bolsheviks were falling, might have decided to act on their own initiative. As long as the issue was in doubt Lenin remained fearful of German intervention. 'We are a hair's breadth from war,' he telegraphed Stalin at one o'clock on the morning of 7 July.[68]

In reality the situation was not as critical as Lenin imagined. The fundamental cleavage within the German oligarchy remained unchanged by the murder of Mirbach, and first Kühlmann and then Hintze were able to convince the Kaiser not to authorize the army to retaliate against Soviet Russia. Kühlmann placed responsibility for the murder on agents of the entente, and Wilhelm accepted this interpretation.[69] Although Ludendorff attempted to use the murder to advance his pet project of hoisting the monarchists to power in Russia he could not shake the Kaiser's commitment to the policy of the foreign office.[70] When Hintze, whom Wilhelm described as his only advisor who 'really knew Russia,'[71] took charge of the *Auswärtiges Amt* this commitment deepened, and much to the consternation of Ludendorff the Kaiser even listened to a foreign office proposal that if the Bolsheviks were unseated Germany should help Lenin regain power.[72] Convinced that western agents had engineered Mirbach's murder the Kaiser believed that any measure designed to weaken the Bolsheviks would play into the hands of the entente. 'Right now,' he wrote

67 Trotsky, *Lenin*, 135
68 Lenin, PSS, vol. L, 114
69 Wilhelm Joost, *Botschafter bei den Roten Zaren* (Vienna, 1967) 18; also see Baumgart, *Deutsche Ostpolitik*, 224
70 A.A. Akhtamazian, *Ot Bresta do Kila* (Moscow, 1963) 145-6
71 Baumgart, *Deutsche Ostpolitik*, 222
72 *Ibid.*, 225

on 11 July, 'we have to support the Bolsheviks under any circumstances.'[73]

As usual when the Kaiser rejected the army's advice Lüdendorff sought to have the decision reversed. The response to Mirbach's assassination was no exception, and, as in June, the general had the assistance of the embassy in Moscow. The events of 6 July had only confirmed the views which they had held earlier, and following the murder of Mirbach they filed a steady stream of reports intended to influence the German government against providing further support to the Bolsheviks. Riezler openly suggested that the murder should be used as a pretext to break with the Bolsheviks,[74] and even after the *Auswärtiges Amt* rejected his suggestion he continued to bombard Berlin with proposals designed to weaken the Bolsheviks.[75] Major Schubert, however, provided the proposal on which Ludendorff chose to act. Given the unstable situation in the Soviet capital, said the military attaché, a battalion of German troops armed with machine guns, mortars and flamethrowers should be sent to Moscow to protect the embassy. The army high command promptly endorsed this proposal and submitted it to the chancellor.[76] For tactical reasons, the *Auswärtiges Amt* accepted the proposal and, on 14 July, ordered Riezler to present it to the Soviet government. The proposal which left the Wilhelmstrasse, however, was quite different from that made by the army, for whereas the high command had suggested something akin to an ultimatum the foreign office presented the measure as a 'request' adding solemnly that it did not indicate that Germany wished to occupy Moscow. Moreover, the foreign office instructed Riezler to stress the positive side of the proposal and point to the value of a German battalion in the event of future trouble in Moscow.[77] The *Auswärtiges Amt* had again managed to turn a suggestion directed against the Soviet government into one designed to strengthen it.

The Bolsheviks were able to discern only an occasional shadow of this struggle within the German oligarchy. That which they saw, however,

73 Gerald Freund, *Unholy Alliance* (London,.1957) 22
74 Karl Helfferich, *Der Weltkrieg* (Berlin, 1919) 648-9
75 Baumgart, *Deutsche Ostpolitik*, 224-5, 230. For an evaluation of Riezler's role in these events see Konrad H. Jarausch, 'Co-operation or intervention? Kurt Riezler and the failure of German Ostpolitik, 1918,' *Slavic Review*, XXXI, no. 2 (June 1972) 381-98. Also see Akhtamazian, *Ot Bresta do Kila*, 145-6, and Helfferich, *Der Weltkrieg*, 648
76 Akhtamazian, *Ot Bresta do Kila*, 146
77 Baumgart, *Deutsche Ostpolitik*, 231

made them somewhat less apprehensive of German intervention. The first indication that the situation was not as serious as it originally seemed came late on the night of 6 July when an uncoded teletype message from Berlin revealed that Kühlmann believed the murder of Mirbach was a provocation by the entente. The Bolsheviks quickly picked up this theme, and thereafter took great pains to implicate the entente in the murder.[78] Even while Chicherin was industriously seeking to convince the allied ambassadors to leave Vologda and come to Moscow[79] the Soviet press rang with stories alleging that these same diplomats were responsible for the murder of Mirbach. As long as the Germans believed that the allied powers were responsible for the murder the Bolsheviks could be reasonably certain that Berlin would not resume the war against Soviet Russia.

The first reports from Ioffe concerning German reaction to the assassination were equally encouraging. No demonstrations had taken place, and German leaders continued to express their wish to improve relations with Soviet Russia.[80] Most important, Ioffe reported that the German government apparently had no intention of breaking off negotiation of the supplementary treaties. Kühlmann, in fact, had referred to the assassination as a weighty reason for accelerating the talks,[81] and on the day following the murder Ioffe and Krasin had a very important meeting with Stresemann in which the three men discussed the basis of Soviet-German cooperation at great length.[82] These reports were received with great relief in Moscow[83] and allowed the Soviet government to relax somewhat.

The German request to station a battalion of troops in Moscow brought an end to this relaxation of tension. From the moment Riezler appeared at the Narkomindel on the evening of 14 July a new crisis developed. Chicherin branded the proposal as 'blackmail' and, after consulting with Lenin, told Riezler it was unacceptable.[84] The Soviet government was prepared to provide the embassy with a guard of one thousand of its 'most loyal soldiers,' but it could not permit a German battalion to be stationed in Moscow.[85] 'No foreign mission in Russia has, nor can have, detachments of

78 *Ibid.*, 229
79 See above, 289-94
80 Kobliakov, 'Bor'ba sovetskogo gosudarstva,' 18
81 Baumgart, *Deutsche Ostpolitik*, 230
82 See below, 333-4
83 Zarnitskii and Sergeev, *Chicherin*, 89
84 *Ibid.*, 90-1
85 DVP, vol. I, 400

their own army for protection,' said Chicherin, 'because Russia has no desire to be lowered to the level of a colonial country such as Morocco and fall into dependence on foreigners.'[86] Rather than negotiate with Riezler, whose hostility was well known to the Bolsheviks, Chicherin chose to deal directly with Berlin. Ioffe met with under-secretary of state von dem Bussche that afternoon and informed him that the Bolsheviks would not accept the proposal. The ambassador made it clear that Bolshevik prestige was at stake and added that if the Soviet government accepted the proposal it would be relegated to 'the ranks of small oriental states and be deprived of all authority.' At the same time, however, Ioffe revealed that Moscow was ready to discuss a compromise. In addition to Chicherin's offer of a Soviet guard for the embassy, Ioffe said that the Bolsheviks were prepared to allow Germany to reinforce the *internal* security of its mission by sending a force of three hundred men to Moscow provided that they came without uniforms and were armed only with pistols. They were to be used only inside the embassy while Soviet troops were to be stationed outside.[87]

That evening Lenin spoke to the All-Russian Central Executive Committee, attacking the German proposal to send a battalion of troops to Moscow. He compared this proposal with the wishes of 'leading commercial and industrial circles' in Germany and warned that the 'considerable progress' which had been made in the negotiations under way in Berlin could be lost if the German government insisted on stationing troops in Moscow. This was a direct appeal to the groups in Germany which he hoped would oppose the disruption of political and economic relations with Russia. 'There are limits,' he said, 'beyond which even the most peace-loving masses of the working people will be compelled to rise, and will rise, as one man to defend their country with arms in hand.' The German request to send a battalion of troops to Moscow was such a case, and he underlined that 'on no account and under no circumstances' could the Soviet government satisfy this request. If Germany should formulate its request as a categorical demand the Soviet government would be 'obliged to respond as we have responded to the Czechoslovak mutiny and to the military operations of the British in the north ... War would then be for us a fateful but absolute and unconditional necessity, and this would be a revolutionary war waged by the workers and peasants of Russia shoulder to shoulder with the Soviet government till the last breath.'[88]

86 *Ibid.*, 400-1
87 Baumgart, *Deutsche Ostpolitik*, 232
88 Lenin, PSS, vol. XXXVI, 523-6

In making this statement Lenin was taking a calculated risk that he could forestall a German ultimatum with one of his own. By presenting the Soviet position in such a clear-cut fashion, he was, in effect, presenting the Germans with a *fait accompli*, gambling that they would prefer to accept the compromise secretly conveyed to them that afternoon than lose the prospect of a negotiated settlement with the Soviet government. Due to the progress of negotiations in Berlin[89] he could do this with a certain amount of confidence, but Lenin was far from certain that he would succeed. Only hours before he spoke to the All-Russian Central Executive Committee the war commissariat issued a warning to all military units along the demarcation line to prepare for a German attack. 'The German war party is rattling its weapons,' M.D. Bonch-Bruevich told the commander of the Soviet western front, 'the situation remains tense.' The commander's response illustrates the seriousness of the situation. He promised to do his best to defend the front, but added 'God grant that we can do it, for there is no bread, no one will provide it and, moreover, there is no flour anywhere.'[90] If the Germans attacked the front would crumble.

The Germans did not attack. Although the embassy in Moscow argued that the Soviet refusal to comply with the request provided Germany with a 'good way out' of its entangling relations with the Bolsheviks[91] the *Auswärtiges Amt* had no intention of allowing the problem to hinder the negotiations under way in Berlin. Instead it pressed Ludendorff to accept the Soviet compromise, arguing that 'for the moment we doubtless have an interest in maintaining the Bolsheviks, at least until the conclusion of the present negotiations.'[92] A week later the general agreed, but, in the interval, Riezler continued to stir up trouble. Still hoping to excite an emotional response to the death of Mirbach he focused attention on the Soviet failure to offer sufficient atonement for the assassination. He demanded to know how many left SRs would be executed for their part in the murder and insisted that 'exemplary punishment' should be meted out to the 'intellectual originators' of the conspiracy.[93] Although Chicherin assured him that several hundred left SRs would be executed Riezler did not

89 See below, 331-5
90 Glavnoe arkhivnoe upravlenie pri Sovete Ministrov SSSR, Institut voennoi istorii minis-terstva oborony SSSR, Tsentral'nyi Gosudarstvennyi Arkhiv Sovetskoi Armii, *Direktivy Kommandovaniia Frontov Krasnoi Armii (1917-1922 gg). Sbornik Dokumentov.* Four vols. (Moscow, 1971–), vol. I, 221-2. Hereafter cited as DKFKA
91 Akhtamazian, *Ot Bresta do Kila*, 148
92 Baumgart, *Deutsche Ostpolitik*, 232
93 Zarnitskii and Sergeev, *Chicherin*, 91-2; Baumgart, *Deutsche Ostpolitik*, 229-30

believe him. The Soviets had covered their repression of the left SRs with 'a thick veil of untruthfulness,' he reported and said, 'that for the most part' the trial of the rebel leaders would 'be played only as theatre.'[94] By this time the Bolsheviks were not really concerned with Riezler, for they continued to receive encouraging news from Ioffe who reported on 21 July that 'Germany does not want war with us.' 'Our entire policy,' he advised, 'must be based on proving to the Germans that if they bend the stick too far, we will be forced to fight and then they will get nothing, for we will create a waste land from Russia, but give them none of it.'[95] Finally, on 23 July, the *Auswärtiges Amt*, having received Ludendorff's approval, accepted the Soviet compromise. The Germans insisted, however, that the three hundred men be allowed to travel to Moscow in uniform. Chicherin submitted this proposal to Lenin who accepted it.[96] A final compromise settled the issue. Although the Germans could come in uniform, they would wear no distinguishing insignia; on 30 July, Major Schubert filed his official request that two companies of one-hundred-fifty men each be sent to reinforce the internal security of the embassy in Moscow.[97] The crisis provoked by the left SR insurrection was at an end.

While these events disturbed relations between Germany and Soviet Russia the negotiation of the supplementary treaties had continued without interruption. The rapid progress of these talks, in fact, accounts for the relative ease with which the crisis caused by the murder of Mirbach was overcome; their substance, moreover, helps explain why the *Auswärtiges Amt*, German industry and even the Kaiser were unwilling to break with the Bolsheviks. The negotiation of the supplementary treaties, therefore, can be described as the sheet anchor of German-Soviet relations providing stability at a time of great unrest.

In the negotiations conducted during July, Ioffe and Krasin went far beyond the original Soviet proposals presented in mid-May. Not only did they show a great readiness to accommodate Germany's economic and territorial demands, they also submitted proposals which foresaw far-reaching political cooperation between Germany and Soviet Russia. Thus, in a meeting with Paul Litwin on 5 July, the two Soviet representatives outlined specific economic plans which they said 'would serve as the basis for construction of further economic and political relations between Germany and Russia.' Both countries possessed an interest in exploit-

94 Baumgart, *Deutsche Ostpolitik*, 230
95 Kobliakov, 'Bor'ba sovetskogo gosudarstva,' 13-14
96 Trush, *Vneshnepoliticheskaia Deiatel'nost' V.I. Lenina*, 154
97 Baumgart, *Deutsche Ostpolitik*, 233

ing the agricultural resources of the Ukraine, they said, but Germany had failed to obtain any sizeable quantity of food from that region and, by itself, would probably be unable to collect sufficient grain to meet its requirements. They proposed, therefore, that Germany authorize Russia to collect grain from certain unspecified parts of the Ukraine with the two countries dividing the spoils equally and Russia paying for her share by delivering rubber, textiles, and copper to Germany. Such an agreement, said Ioffe, would allow the Soviet government to relieve the famine rampant in Russia's great cities and 'provide an opportunity to cultivate and influence Russian public opinion in a manner favourable for Germany.' The Soviet representatives stressed that a change in Russian public opinion was the 'fundamental pre-requisite for a more intimate association' of the two countries. As a start, Moscow was willing to recognize the Treaty of Brest-Litovsk, suitably modified to meet Germany's wishes in the Baltic, as the basis of future cooperation and was prepared to enter into a new agreement 'which would pave the way for a German-Russian alliance.' As long as the Russian people remained hostile to Germany 'a publicly acknowledged alliance ... would not be possible,' but with German cooperation Russian public opinion could be reversed 'in a relatively short period of time (in a few months) so that a publicly acknowledged German-Russian alliance could be proclaimed.' Ioffe and Krasin virtually bubbled with enthusiasm saying there was no question which could not be settled to the mutual advantage of the two countries. Ioffe assured Litwin that Germany had no need to worry about the presence of allied troops in Russia, for if Berlin would agree not to attack Russia the Soviet government would be able to expel the Czechs and British, thus eliminating the danger of a new war in eastern Europe. Moreover, Ioffe promised that Russia could deliver all the raw materials which Germany needed, adding slyly that Germany would obtain these commodities 'more quickly and surely' through an agreement with the Soviet government than by the methods she was then using. In general, Ioffe and Krasin left Litwin with the impression that the Bolsheviks 'were prepared to give up their utopian goals and carry through a practical socialist policy.' Germany could deal profitably with such a government, and Litwin was impressed with the proposals made by the Soviet negotiators. At the very beginning of the negotiations, therefore, Ioffe and Krasin succeeded in dazzling the Germans, putting such an attractive package before them that in the weeks to come Berlin would find it difficult not to cooperate with the Soviet government.[98]

98 Hans W. Gatzke, 'Dokumentation zu den deutsch-russischen Beziehungen im Sommer 1918.' *Vierteljahrhefte für Zeitgeschichte*, no. 3 (1955) 77-9

This difficulty was compounded by the programs of other political groups in Russia. The moderate socialists remained firmly committed to the allies while the monarchists refused to renounce their goal of restoring 'Russia, one and united.' The rapid movement of the Kadets away from their British and French orientation had excited interest in Berlin, but talks with Pavel Miliukov convinced the Germans that nothing was to be gained by supporting the Russian moderates. Miliukov had made virtually the same demands as the monarchists, calling for the abrogation of the Treaty of Brest-Litovsk as his price for cooperation.[99] Such demands were wholly unacceptable to German leaders, and Gustav Stresemann, who had journeyed to Kiev in order to survey the Russian situation, returned from the Ukraine disillusioned with the possibility of doing business with the Kadets.[100] This left only the Bolsheviks, and although Stresemann would later write that 'one does not like to be seen on Unter den Linden with a tramp,'[101] it was clear that with harlots as well endowed and free with their favours as the Bolsheviks he did not really object to linking arms.

Stresemann spoke with Ioffe and Krasin for the first time on 7 July. Aware of their conversation with Litwin he was particularly interested in obtaining a further elaboration of their views on German-Soviet cooperation. As the two Soviet representatives knew that Stresemann was closely linked with German industry and the army high command they were more than pleased to satisfy his curiosity and, for five-and-a-half hours, regaled him with the potential delights of doing business with Soviet Russia. Just as they had impressed Litwin by making concrete proposals for German-Soviet cooperation they used the same strategy to interest Stresemann in their prospectus. They said that the Soviet government was very eager to resume commercial relations with Germany but complained that negotiations had made very little headway. So eager was Russia to begin trade, said Krasin, that the Soviet government did not even want to wait until negotiations were completed and suggested that trade begin at once with the sale of a small amount of coal which could serve as a pilot project for further exchanges. This, in fact, became the start of the first post-war commercial exchange between Russia and Germany, German ships unloading coal on the wharves of Petrograd within

99 George A. Brinkley, *The Volunteer Army and Allied Intervention in South Russia, 1917-1921* (Notre Dame, Indiana, 1966) 44-5
100 Gatzke, 'Dokumentation,' 81
101 Cited in Freund, *Unholy Alliance,* 27

seven weeks of this meeting,[102] but Ioffe and Krasin were interested in much more than simply acting as brokers for the Soviet coal trust. The conversation slid easily from economic to political questions, and the two Soviet representatives carefully stressed the relationship between Germany ending her intervention in Russia and the ability of the Soviet government to cooperate economically with Germany. The Bolsheviks were prepared to live with the Peace of Brest-Litovsk, they said, but as long as Germany continued to seize additional territory from Russia it would be impossible to restore the Russian economy and achieve a level of productivity essential to supply Germany with the goods she wanted. This amputation of territory not only inflamed Russian public opinion, making it impossible to acknowledge publicly any policy of cooperation with Germany, it also undermined the essential unity of the Russian economy. Without coal, oil, and grain from the regions which Germany had torn from Russia, the Russian economy simply could not function and there could be no trade with Germany. Only if Germany and Russia agreed to exploit the economic resources of Russia jointly would either country benefit. All this made a considerable impression on Stresemann, and he recognized the necessity of Germany returning such areas as the Donets basin and the rail lines linking central Russia with the Kuban and the Caucasus. On the same day as the left SR insurrection was being liquidated, therefore, Ioffe and Krasin had made a very important breakthrough in the negotiation of the supplementary treaties. Although for obvious reasons Stresemann inquired if the Soviet government was actually in control of Russia he was satisfied with the answer that no other group had any power behind them. Subsequent events would confirm this evaluation, but as the Germans were prepared to provide all the power any group needed to establish itself as the government of Russia a much more important consideration was the readiness of these groups to accept the heavy burdens which the Germans insisted Russia carry. Ioffe and Krasin left no doubt in the minds of the German negotiators that the Bolsheviks were prepared to accept those burdens.[103]

After the meetings with Litwin and Stresemann the negotiations proceeded rapidly. By mid-month, when the issue of the guard battalion was disturbing the surface of German-Soviet relations, the representatives of

102 M.E. Sonkin, *Okno vo vneshnii mir* (Moscow, 1964) 82-8; Baumgart, *Deutsche Ostpolitik*, 283-4
103 Gatzke, 'Dokumentation,' 79-83

the two governments had already reached a basic understanding concerning the treaties which would regulate their future association. They had agreed that the treaties would satisfy the primary demands of both sides, Germany receiving Estonia and Livonia, recognition of Georgian independence and compensation for the nationalization of German property in Russia, while Russia would receive additional territory in White Russia, a pledge of non-interference in its internal affairs and a favourable adjustment of its frontier with the Ukraine. The further advance of the German army in Russia was to be stopped and German troops withdrawn from railways connecting central Russia with the Kuban and Caucasus. When the rail connection with the south was restored Russia and Germany would share the grain and raw materials of the Kuban and Caucasus, the division being overseen by a mixed commission appointed by the two governments. For the duration of the war Russia would bar its territory to any undertaking directed against Germany. Still unsettled in mid-month was the amount of indemnity due Germany for losses suffered from the nationalization of German property in Russia, the exact share of raw materials each country would receive and the manner in which Russia would guarantee that her territory would not be used for an allied attack on Germany. Berlin wanted the Soviet government to agree that if it was unable to clear Russia of allied troops within a short period of time that it would ask for German military assistance, but neither this nor the demand that Russia first offer Germany the sale of any surplus raw materials before selling to other countries had been accepted by Ioffe and Krasin.[104]

Negotiations proceeded so smoothly that if the *Auswärtiges Amt* had fully controlled the German side of the bargaining a final agreement could probably have been reached in late July or early August. The foreign office, however, had to consult the army on the question of the evacuation of Russian territory, and this delayed, and even threatened to prevent, the signing of the treaties. Ludendorff continued to object to any agreement which would sacrifice the Cossacks to the Bolsheviks, and when Ioffe demanded the evacuation of Rostov and Taganrog, together with the Rostov-Voronezh and Taganrog-Kursk railways, the general saw this as a measure directed against Ataman Krasnov. Troops, as well as grain, he said, could be carried by these railways, and surrender of Rostov and Taganrog to the Soviets would make Krasnov ready prey to the Bolsheviks. Hintze attempted to reason with Ludendorff, arguing that a treaty binding the Soviet and all future Russian governments to the concessions

104 *Ibid.*, 85-6

which the Bolsheviks were willing to make was well worth a few Cossacks, but for the moment the general would not be budged. With the Czechs victorious on the Volga he was more fearful than ever of driving Krasnov into the arms of the allies, and although he knew that the Don Cossacks were shielding and even providing arms to the volunteer army of General Alekseev south of the Don he was not alarmed by this arrangement.[105] Alekseev had openly proclaimed his loyalty to the allies, but due to the small size of his army did not constitute a threat to Germany. Moreover, as Chicherin observed on 28 July in a telegram to Ioffe: 'In reality there is no such opposition between the German and English orientation among the Cossacks as there is between Germany and England on the field of battle, because in the final analysis the entire counter-revolution benefits both. And even, perhaps, England is being duped, because if Alekseev, Dutov and all the anglophile whiteguardists are victorious, then the victorious reaction will have to lean more on Germany than on England.' Ioffe was instructed not to sign the supplementary treaties without obtaining German evacuation of Rostov, Taganrog, and their railways.[106] Without such an agreement there was no way the Soviets could reach the Kuban and thus fulfill their obligations to Germany and provide themselves with grain and raw materials. The negotiations, therefore, had reached an impasse, and Ludendorff had again found a way to disrupt the policy of the foreign office.

Equally disruptive was the appointment of a new German minister in Moscow. The post had remained vacant throughout most of July, but at the end of the month Karl Helfferich, a former finance minister and leading political figure, was named as minister. For reasons which remain obscure even to his biographer Helfferich had eagerly sought this dangerous assignment.[107] Whatever his reasons may have been for wanting the position, however, they do not seem to have included any of the objectives which would later be associated with his mission. According to his own testimony he wished to have a hand in shaping the development of German-Russian economic relations,[108] but there is no evidence that he went to Russia with the aim of overthrowing the Bolsheviks or seeking to upset the policy of the German government. Nevertheless, within ninety-six

105 Baumgart, *Deutsche Ostpolitik*, 285-8; Zarnitskii and Sergeev, *Chicherin*, 95-6; Kobliakov, 'Bor'ba sovetskogo gosudarstva,' 19
106 Zarnitskii and Sergeev, *Chicherin*, 95
107 John G. Williamson, *Karl Helfferich, 1872-1924* (Princeton, New Jersey, 1971) 272-3
108 Helfferich, *Der Weltkrieg*, 642-3

hours of his arrival in the Soviet capital these were exactly the goals which he set himself.

To be sure, the circumstances of Helfferich's first four days in Moscow were unlikely to have impressed him favourably or inspired confidence in the Soviet government. On the contrary, almost everything he saw and heard could only have contributed to a belief that the days of the Bolsheviks were numbered. His arrival was handled by the Soviet government with all the melodrama of a cheap novel. He was met at the Russian frontier by a representative of the Narkomindel, taken aboard a heavily armed train and whisked through the Russian countryside to a point approximately forty kilometers from Moscow. There he was met by Riezler and Karl Radek who informed him that it would be safer to make the rest of the trip by automobile. In the dead of night the trio set out in Radek's automobile, eventually reaching the German embassy by a roundabout route which carried them through the back streets of the Soviet capital.[109] On the next day, 29 July, Helfferich had his first meeting with the foreign commissar. Chicherin, whom he described as resembling a 'woebegone and frightened scholar,' attempted to assure him of the stability of the Soviet government but seems to have succeeded only in convincing him of the opposite. 'The fate of the revolution hinges on the villages,' Chicherin explained, 'and the Soviet government, therefore, was trying to mobilize the "village poor" against the "village rich" ... In this manner the Soviet government would succeed in holding power.' For Helfferich, who knew virtually nothing of Russia, this policy made no sense and appeared to augur ill for the Bolsheviks.[110]

But he was primarily concerned about his own safety and that of the embassy. The left SRs had again become active in the Soviet capital, and when their Moscow committee learned of Helfferich's arrival they announced their intention to kill him. The following day word arrived from Kiev that Field Marshal Eichhorn had been assassinated, a murder for which the left SRs promptly took credit. Alarmed by these developments Helfferich called on Chicherin to complain about the apparent freedom with which the left SRs were going about their deadly business,[111] but received little satisfaction. Although Chicherin promised to reinforce the guard at the German embassy he could not resist ridiculing the German

109 *Ibid.*, 649-50
110 *Ibid.*, 650-1
111 Compare Chicherin's earlier reaction in the presence of the allied agents, 296

proposal to send a guard battalion to Moscow. If all the German troops in Kiev could not save Eichhorn, he said maliciously, then a single battalion would certainly be unable to protect Helfferich![112] As if this was not bad enough, the German minister soon discovered that he could not move freely in the Soviet capital, for the Russians informed him that if he left his embassy they would be unable to guarantee his safety.[113] In effect, he found himself a virtual prisoner and increasingly fearful that the Bolsheviks could not really control the situation in Moscow.

Riezler and the other members of the embassy staff played on these fears. From the first night of his arrival they had indoctrinated him with their violently anti-Bolshevik views,[114] and by the morning of 1 August, Helfferich was quite ready to agree with them. He sent a long telegram to Hintze in which he predicted the imminent fall of the Soviet government and urged that Germany seek new partners in Russia. He proposed to forge a broad alliance of parties, including the 'Right-Centre,' the Latvian regiments, the Provisional Government of Siberia, and the Don Cossacks, which under German tutelage would overthrow the Bolsheviks and restore 'order' in Russia. As a first step he suggested the withdrawal of the embassy from Moscow, preferably to Petrograd, where it would be possible to establish closer contacts with anti-Bolshevik groups. This should be done immediately, for in his opinion the Bolsheviks were failing so quickly that if Germany did not get rid of them promptly they would be overthrown by groups favourable to the entente.[115] Helfferich, in short, had swallowed the entire policy advocated by Riezler and his associates, returning essentially to the proposals made by Mirbach prior to his assassination.

While the German minister drafted this telegram an important meeting was taking place in the Kremlin. Word had just reached Moscow of the British landing at Onega and shelling of Archangel,[116] and Soviet leaders had been hurriedly summoned to consider the situation. Unfortunately, the minutes of the meeting have not yet been published so it is impossible to establish what was said, but even without them it is reasonable to assume that the mood of the commissars must have been gloomy indeed. The Soviet position was desperate. The Bolsheviks were over-extended everywhere, and they simply had no troops to oppose the Brit-

112 Helfferich, *Der Weltkrieg*, 661-2
113 *Ibid.*, 662
114 *Ibid.*, 650
115 Baumgart, *Deutsche Ostpolitik*, 238-40
116 DKFKA, vol. I, 224-5

ish. They still had not succeeded in stabilizing the eastern front, and every available man was needed to stem the Czechoslovak tide. Yet the British had to be contained, and at the emergency meeting Lenin made a bold and desperate decision; he decided to turn to Germany for help. Three weeks later, recalling his earlier decision to seek aid from Britain and France at the time of the German offensive in February, Lenin would write: 'However much the Anglo-French and American imperialist sharks fume with rage, however much they slander us, no matter how many millions they spend on bribing the right Socialist-Revolutionary, Menshevik and other social-patriotic newspapers, *I shall not hesitate one second* to enter into a *similar* "agreement" with the German imperialist vultures if an attack upon Russia by Anglo-French troops calls for it.'[117] Although in this 'Letter to American Workers' he used the future tense he was actually referring to an event which had already happened, for on the evening of 1 August, immediately following the meeting in the Kremlin, Chicherin went straight to the German embassy and asked Helfferich for German military assistance against the British.[118]

Chicherin chose his words very carefully. He stressed that the Soviet government was not seeking an alliance with Germany but only 'de facto parallel action.' For the moment, he said, the two countries were confronted by the same enemy, and although Russian public opinion made an open alliance impossible it was in their common interest to prevent the allies from overruning further Russian territory. Presumably the British would follow their landing on the White Sea with a thrust at the heart of Russia, and to counter this attack the Soviet government intended to withdraw its forces from in front of Murmansk and concentrate them around Vologda to defend Moscow. The Soviet government wanted Germany to assume responsibility for the Murmansk front, sending troops to pin down the British in Karelia. Chicherin attached three conditions to this proposal, saying that the Soviet government wanted guarantees that Germany would not occupy Petrograd, would avoid Petrozavodsk, if possible, and agree that the military operation would not prejudice the future political status of the Russian north. In addition Chicherin asked for German support in the south, again calling for 'de facto parallel action.' Here the object was to free the Kuban of forces hostile to the two countries. Russia was prepared to give up its demand that Germany evacuate Rostov and Taganrog if Germany would agree to give the Soviet government free use

117 Lenin, PSS, vol. XXXVII, 26. Emphasis in original
118 Chicherin, 'Lenin i Vneshniaia Politika,' 7

of the railways running through these cities and launch an offensive against Alekseev. Chicherin did not insist that Germany attack Krasnov, but as the Ataman was supporting Alekseev he asked Berlin to cease aiding the Don Cossacks.[119]

In requesting German assistance the Soviet government had its eye on Berlin as well as Archangel. As usual Lenin had displayed his uncanny ability to perceive a method of obtaining political profit from even the most disastrous circumstances, and he was seeking not only to stop the British in the north but also to accelerate the negotiation of the supplementary treaties. These talks were stalled by Ludendorff's refusal to evacuate Rostov and Taganrog, so what better way to get around this problem than by making a virtue of necessity and yielding the cities in order to obtain the benefit which their possession was expected to bring. Plus, of course, German assistance against the British. Plus the rapid conclusion of the treaties. For over a month Berlin had been pressing the Bolsheviks to accept German help in driving the British from the north. Why not accept this offer, especially at a time when help was genuinely needed and its acceptance might reasonably be expected to hasten the conclusion of the negotiations in Berlin?[120] The risk was great, as the Soviet reservations concerning Petrograd, Petrozavodsk, and Murmansk show, but in a situation where the Bolsheviks really had little to lose Lenin's proposal was a political master stroke designed to obtain a maximum of benefit for a minimum of cost.

The chief danger of this policy was that the Germans might interpret it as a sign that the Soviet government was on the verge of collapse. Helfferich placed exactly this interpretation on Lenin's proposal and submitted it to Berlin in support of his own plan of action against the Bolsheviks. The request for assistance, he said, provided 'striking proof' of Bolshevik weakness and argued that Germany should feign acceptance of the Soviet proposal while actually implementing the plan which he had submitted earlier. At the last moment, when the German army had begun to

---

119 Helfferich, *Der Weltkrieg*, 652-3; Baumgart, *Deutsche Ostpolitik*, 106ff
120 The German reaction to an earlier Soviet suggestion of this possibility had been very positive. On 2 July, when an article entitled 'Last warning' had been published in *Izvestiia* merely suggesting the possibility of Soviet-German military cooperation against the entente, the *Auswärtiges Amt* had promptly informed the Russian embassy 'that the trust in us of the Russian government made known in the article could only favourably affect the present negotiations' (Baumgart, *Deutsche Ostpolitik*, 107). If the suggestion of possible cooperation could favourably affect the treaty negotiations then it is reasonable to assume that Lenin anticipated an even more favourable result from his actual proposal of joint military action against the allies.

advance into Russia, it could turn on the Soviet government and in collaboration with Krasnov drive the Bolsheviks from power.[121]

Helfferich's ingenious scheme received no support from the *Auswärtiges Amt*. Hintze rejected the plan of his minister, endorsing instead the Soviet request for military assistance and asking Ludendorff to send German troops to northern Russia. The general responded enthusiastically saying that he was prepared to begin military operations against the British in Russia if his army could first occupy Petrograd and use it as a base for the campaign. This was in direct contradiction to the Bolshevik plan, but Hintze did not immediately inform the Soviet government. Instead, he told Moscow that if 'necessary prerequisites for carrying out the operation' were met the German army was ready to assist Russia in Karelia. The disparity between the two plans, however, could not long be concealed and once exposed proved to be a permanent barrier to 'de facto parallel action.' As long as the British did not launch an actual offensive from their base at Murmansk the Soviet government would not agree to the German occupation of Petrograd, and without this agreement the German army would not mount an operation against the British. Moreover, when Ludendorff and Helfferich both associated German occupation of Petrograd with plans for the overthrow of the Soviet government the foreign secretary began to reconsider the whole proposal. Realizing that the problem would not be settled quickly and that the Bolsheviks required immediately military relief Hintze accepted a plan suggested by Ioffe which would permit the Soviet government to concentrate its armed forces in areas where they were needed most. On 7 August, he and the Soviet ambassador reached a tacit agreement whereby Germany pledged not to attack Russia if the Bolsheviks withdrew their armed forces from the demarcation line separating Soviet territory from that occupied by the German army.[122] Even before this agreement the Soviet government had begun to withdraw some of its forces from the demarcation line, but on 10 August, Lenin ordered that 'all military units capable of doing battle' were to be sent from the western frontier to the Volga.[123] The Bolsheviks also withdrew some of their troops from Karelia, transferring them to Vologda and stations south of Archangel.[124] By redistributing its available manpower the Soviet government was able to cling to power,

121 Helfferich, *Der Weltkrieg*, 653-4; Baumgart, *Deutsche Ostpolitik*, 109
122 Baumgart, *Deutsche Ostpolitik*, 110-11
123 DGKKA, 108-9
124 DKFKA, vol. I, 224-5

stabilizing the front south of Archangel and building a small reserve to strike against the Czechs. Instead of overthrowing the Bolsheviks at the moment of their greatest weakness the Germans contributed substantially to saving the Soviet government.

Helfferich looked on in agony as Berlin acted to reinforce the Bolsheviks. During the first five days of August he sent one telegram after another to Berlin explaining that if Germany would only withdraw its support from the Bolsheviks the Soviet government would fall.[125] His problem, however, was not in convincing Hintze that the Bolsheviks would fall without German support, but that their fall was desirable. Hintze believed as strongly as Helfferich that without German support the Bolsheviks would fall, but the foreign secretary's policy rested on the belief that it was not in the German interest to topple the Bolsheviks. This was the obstacle which Helfferich, like Mirbach and Riezler, could not overcome. Finally, on 5 August, Helfferich demanded that Hintze present their rival views to the chancellor for a final decision on the controversy.[126]

The clash between Hintze and Helfferich was virtually no contest. Secure in the confidence of both the Kaiser and chancellor, the foreign secretary had only Ludendorff to fear, and although the general immediately informed the *Auswärtiges Amt* that he had more than enough divisions to install a new government in Moscow,[127] Hintze had no difficulty in defending his policy. In a telegram to Ludendorff of 6 August, Hintze heaped scorn on Helfferich, saying that except for the Bolsheviks every other party in Russia was prepared to take up arms against Germany to overthrow the Peace of Brest-Litovsk. The Siberian regime which Helfferich touted as a potential ally was in fact closely linked with the western powers and had even declared war on Germany! Although Hintze characterized the Bolsheviks as being 'very evil and antipathetic people' he reminded Ludendorff that they had proved to be very useful. 'We have got out of them what we could,' he said, 'and our drive for victory demands that we should go on doing so, so long as they are in power.' Hintze then read Ludendorff a lecture in *Realpolitik* worthy of Bismarck or Machiavelli:

Whether we like working with [the Bolsheviks] or not is irrelevant, so long as it is useful. History proves that to introduce feelings into politics is an expensive lux-

125 Baumgart, *Deutsche Ostpolitik*, 237-9
126 *Ibid.*, 245
127 *Ibid.*, 110

ury. In our position it would be irresponsible to allow ourselves such a luxury. A man who works with the Bolsheviks as the men *de facto* in power and then sighs over the nastiness of the company is harmless; but to refuse to benefit from working with the Bolsheviks out of reluctance to incur the odium of having to do with the Bolsheviks – that is dangerous. Politics have always been utilitarian, and will be so for a long time to come.[128]

Here was a language which Ludendorff could understand, and he made no further effort to support Helfferich. When Helfferich demanded that Hintze submit their dispute to the chancellor, therefore, the foreign secretary could safely order the minister to return at once to Berlin.[129]

Before leaving Moscow Helfferich made one last effort to influence the development of German policy in Russia. He had come to Russia with the authority to remove the embassy from Moscow if he thought German lives were in danger, and, as his last official act, he exercised this power to transfer the embassy to Petrograd. At his final meeting with Chicherin he explained that the embassy would be more secure in Petrograd than Moscow.[130] Although his fear was undoubtedly authentic it is difficult to accept this explanation. Given his plan to overthrow the Soviet government Helfferich probably hoped to facilitate German contact with the anti-Bolsheviks active in the former capital. This was the interpretation of Hintze, who on learning of Helfferich's order immediately directed the German embassy to leave Russia entirely.[131] This was the safest course to follow, for at one stroke it eliminated the possibility of relations with Russia being complicated either by assassination or the mischief of individuals such as Riezler and Schubert. Moreover, by withdrawing the entire mission Hintze could postpone the appointment of a new minister and keep control of relations with the Soviet government in his own hands. The foreign secretary remained in close contact with Ioffe while leaving a consul-general in Moscow to handle routine affairs. In this way relations with Russia were not ruptured but strengthened. Within a few days Riezler and the remainder of the German embassy were safely out of Russia and relocated behind the demarcation line at Pskov. A major source of difficulty in Soviet-German relations had been removed.

Purely by chance Helfferich became involved in an incident which could have proved fatal to him and disastrous for Soviet-German rela-

---

128 *Ibid.*, 392-4
129 *Ibid.*, 246
130 Helfferich, *Der Weltkrieg*, 663-4
131 Baumgart, *Deutsche Ostpolitik*, 247

tions. The day he left Moscow the left SRs staged an uprising in the provinces west of the capital, and the route along which he travelled took him directly into the centre of the insurrection. The left SRs continued to demand war with Germany, and the insurgents called for the use of force against any Germans they could find. At Orsha, where the minister was scheduled to cross into German occupied territory, the Soviet garrison mutinied and delivered a declaration of war to the German commandant on the other side of the demarcation line.[132] It is easy to imagine the consternation which these reports must have caused in Moscow. The life of the German minister was obviously in danger and, with it, peace with Germany. The Bolsheviks clearly realized that the German government would find it difficult to overlook the murder of a second plenipotentiary within a single month and took urgent measures to avert a new catastrophe. While a message went down the line ordering Helfferich's train to return to Viazma orders were issued to quell the mutiny at Orsha. Karl Radek was sent to explain the situation to Helfferich who was detained at Viazma until the situation was brought under control. Only then was Helfferich allowed to resume his journey, accompanied to the demarcation line by Radek and a reinforced guard. When his train reached Orsha fighting was still under way in the hills above the city, but the minister was able to cross safely into German controlled territory. Without further mishap Helfferich proceeded to Berlin where he received a very cold and formal reception from Hintze. His short but tempestuous mission to Russia was at an end.[133]

While Hintze quarreled with Helfferich, Lenin was again having trouble with Ioffe. The ambassador had obviously not been informed of the reasons for his government's dramatic turn against the entente, and in late July, he protested strongly against this change in policy. His letter is not available, but from other evidence it would seem that the ambassador took particular exception to Lenin's speech of 29 July,[134] and said that Chicherin had not tried hard enough to prevent the departure of the allied ambassadors from Vologda. Ioffe appealed for a continuation of the policy of 'maneuver' and may have suggested further steps to appease the allies. There is no way of knowing what arguments he used to support his views, but he appears to have threatened to resign and take his case to the Central Committee if Lenin did not reaffirm the former Soviet policy. He also

132 Gusev, *Krakh,* 230; Vladimirova, 'Levy Esery,' 136; Helfferich, *Der Weltkrieg,* 664
133 Helferrich, *Der Weltkrieg,* 664-5
134 See above, 295-6

asked Lenin to let him come to Moscow to present his case in person. His letter brought a savage response from Lenin who was not prepared to listen to further criticism from Ioffe or look kindly upon the possibility that the ambassador might abandon his post at the most crucial moment in the negotiation of the supplementary treaties. 'All that you write in your last letter is absurd to the point of the supernatural,' Lenin told him, 'To conduct the "former" policy of non-rupture with the entente after Onega – is ridiculous. It is impossible for a woman with children to be innocent again.' Ridiculing Ioffe's proposals Lenin asserted that contrary to the ambassador's assumption, fundamental Soviet policy had not been changed. The Soviet request for German assistance was just one more 'maneuver,' Moscow simply 'proposing to the Germans to take that which is *already taken* by the entente and by doing that impeding and delaying the Anglo-American, Japanese smothering of Russia.' If Ioffe wished to pursue the matter further, Lenin said he could 'hand in a declaration to the Central Committee,' but added viciously, 'before your declaration to the Central Committee, before the acceptance of your resignation by the Central Committee, before sending you a deputy, before his arrival, you, of course, as a member of the Party (that you write yourself) do your duty!'[135]

Ioffe's duty was to bring the negotiation of the supplementary treaties to a successful conclusion. Given the kaleidoscopic manner in which the political situation in both Germany and Russia could change Lenin waited impatiently for the completion of the treaties. He wanted results and thought nothing of intimidating Ioffe, even ordering Radek to remain at Orsha ready to proceed to Berlin should the ambassador fail in his task. Ioffe, however, was soon able to complete the negotiations himself, blaming the delay on Larin and Sokol'nikov whom he claimed had consistently 'put a stone' in his path.[136] On 10 August, while Helfferich vainly sought an interview with Hintze, the supplementary treaties were initialled, and shortly thereafter Ioffe left for Moscow to present them to the Soviet government.[137]

The treaties were well received in Moscow where the German consul-general reported leading figures of the Soviet government had expressed their satisfaction with the results of the negotiations.[138] Although Chicherin submitted a long and detailed criticism of the vague language used

135 Lenin, PSS, vol. L, 134. Emphasis in original. See also Zarnitskii and Sergeev, *Chicherin*, 94
136 Baumgart, *Deutsche Ostpolitik*, 288-9
137 Helfferich, *Der Weltkrieg*, 665
138 Baumgart, *Deutsche Ostpolitik*, 256

to describe the demarcation line separating Soviet from German occupied territory[139] Ioffe was authorized to sign the treaties. No record of the debate which preceded this approval has yet been published, but presumably Lenin justified the additional sacrifices which the treaties imposed on Soviet Russia by arguing that the new regime still required peace and that the only way to prolong the breathing space was to purchase time from the military masters of eastern Europe. Undoubtedly, he also referred to the purely temporary nature of the agreements promising as usual that when the revolution spread to Germany the treaties would be scrapped. Although by August this promise was becoming trite Lenin's colleagues had little choice but to accept it. When Ioffe returned to Berlin on 17 August, he confidently told his staff that he had 'full powers to sign any treaty, for due to the impending revolution in Germany none of these agreements will ever be carried out.'[140]

Despite this boast, the treaties were not signed immediately. Two issues arose which delayed the signing, and they show that if the Bolsheviks were not concerned about long-term obligations which they assumed, they were vitally interested in the immediate effect of the treaties. Both issues concerned German interference in what the Bolsheviks considered the internal affairs of Russia and highlight the fundamental importance which Moscow attached to this question. Before his trip to Moscow, Ioffe had told the Germans that their pledge not to interfere in the internal affairs of Russia was the only acceptable part of the agreement,[141] and the Soviet government did not intend to allow Germany to subvert this clause before the treaty was even signed.

The first issue concerned German support of Krasnov. Since spring the Germans had been supplying him with arms, and the Bolsheviks were determined to bring this practice to an end. Although Ludendorff prevented Hintze from including a specific prohibition of German support of the Cossacks in the treaty the clause prohibiting interference in the internal affairs of Russia proved broad enough to satisfy the Soviet government that the agreement would block further aid to Krasnov. Or at least it satisfied the Soviet government until Ioffe returned to Berlin and learned that Skoropadskii was allowing Krasnov to recruit openly in the Ukraine and was on the verge of recognizing the Don Republic as an independent state. Ioffe protested at once, saying that 'what the Ukrainians do is done

139 GSO, vol. I, 593-4
140 Baumgart, *Deutsche Ostpolitik*, 290
141 *Ibid.*, 289

with the approval of Germany,' and refused to sign the treaty until this problem was dealt with.[142] But worse was to come, for Ioffe soon learned that the Duke of Leuchtenberg, travelling as an ambassador from Krasnov, had arrived in Berlin seeking German recognition of the Don Republic and had been personally received by Ludendorff and Hindenburg. This brought a stiff protest from Chicherin who described Krasnov as a rebel and said that the reception of 'Nicholas Leuchtenberg' in Germany was a violation of the treaty just concluded with Soviet Russia.[143] As the treaty had not yet been signed this was not quite true, but it served to define the major issue involved in the controversy. If Germany recognized Krasnov's regime before signing the supplementary treaties she would not violate any specific agreement with the Soviet government; on the other hand, recognition of the Don Republic would certainly violate the spirit of the new agreement and, as a consequence, the Soviet government might refuse to sign the treaties. Ludendorff, of course, supported recognition, but Hintze refused even to consider this possibility. 'To support the Cossacks and take the field ... against the Bolsheviks is to cut off the branch on which we sit,' he said.[144] Germany did not recognize the Don Cossacks and to calm Bolshevik fears concerning the Ukraine, Hintze agreed to include a special section in the letters exchanged at the time the supplementary treaties were signed. 'Germany undertakes ...,' it said, 'to see that the formation of independent state units within the Russian State should not obtain military support from the Ukraine.' The Cossack problem which had plagued the negotiations was settled.

The second issue involved Baku and arose as a result of German inability to stop the Turkish advance toward the Caspian Sea. Despite their best efforts neither the German government nor army high command was able to get the Turks to stop. The Ottoman government countered every German threat with one of its own, even warning that it would terminate the alliance with Germany if Berlin did not cease meddling in the Caucasus.[145] As Turkish troops approached Baku the problem grew even more complicated, because the large Armenian segment of the city's population, swollen by refugees and fearing for its safety, rebelled against Bolshevik rule, overthrew the government of S.G. Shaumian, and invited the British to come to its rescue. The fall of the Soviet regime in Baku and

142 *Ibid.*, 291
143 DVP, vol. I, 434-5
144 Baumgart, *Deutsche Ostpolitik*, 291
145 Ulrich Trumpener, *Germany and the Ottoman Empire, 1914-1918* (Princeton, New Jersey, 1968) 167-99

the arrival of British troops completely altered the situation for Germany, because it transformed the problem from one of mediation among allies to open confrontation with the British. When Ioffe returned to Berlin in mid-August, therefore, he was faced with a German demand that the principle of armed assistance accepted by the Bolsheviks in the case of Murmansk be extended to cover Baku. Moscow, which really had very little idea of what was happening in the Caspian city,[146] was very reluctant to agree. As long as Lenin had any hope that Shaumian might be able to regain power he insisted that the Germans limit themselves to keeping the Turks out of Baku. The Germans, however, had already begun preparations for an assault on Baku, and they insisted that the Bolsheviks give their sanction to this operation. When Lenin finally learned that Shaumian had been imprisoned he gave in to the German demands. Applying his own principle enunciated in the case of Murmansk, he agreed that the Germans should be allowed to take that which the British had already taken from the Soviet government. This decision would appear to have been made easier by the willingness of Hintze to delay the signing of the treaties until Germany could prove that it would fulfil its promises to the Soviet government. If the Soviets wished, said the foreign secretary, the signing of the treaties could be delayed until Germany had driven the British from Baku and confined the Turks behind a specified demarcation line.[147] In the circumstances Moscow decided that this was neither necessary nor wise, and on 27 August, the supplementary treaties were signed by the representatives of the two governments. The long process of negotiating peace with Germany was finally complete.

The agreements signed at Berlin included two treaties and an exchange of confidential notes. In the political treaty Russia renounced sovereignty over Estonia and Livonia while acknowledging that Germany was free to decide the fate of these provinces 'in agreement with their inhabitants.' Northern Russia was dealt with very briefly, details of the actual agreement being reserved for the confidential exchange of notes. In the treaty Russia merely promised to 'employ all the means at her disposal to expel the entente forces from North Russian territory' while Germany pledged for the duration of this operation not to permit a 'Finnish attack of any kind on Russian territory, particularly on Petrograd.' The Treaty was also

146 As late as 9 August, Lenin wrote to N.A. Anisimov in Astrakhan: 'The situation in Baku is entirely unclear to me. Who is in power? Where is Shaumian?' Lenin, PSS, vol. L, 141-2. For an examination of events in Baku itself, see Ronald G. Suny, *The Baku Commune, 1917-1918* (Princeton, New Jersey, 1972)
147 Baumgart, *Deutsche Ostpolitik*, 292

intentionally vague about the Caucasus. Publicly Russia only agreed to provide Germany with a quarter of the oil produced at Baku and to sanction Germany's recognition of Georgia as an independent state, while Germany pledged not to give assistance 'to any third power in any military operation in the Caucasus.' Georgia, where Germany already maintained a military force, was specifically excluded from this agreement, but Germany promised in addition 'to take measures to prevent the military force of any third power in the Caucasus' from overstepping a line drawn from the mouth of the Kuban River to Baku. Germany made a number of other concessions to the Soviet government. From the Bolshevik viewpoint the most important was contained in article four where Germany promised that: 'in so far as it is not otherwise prescribed in the peace treaty or in this Supplementary Treaty, Germany will in no way interfere in the relations between the Russian state and parts of its territory and will thus in particular neither cause nor support the formation of independent states in those territories.' In addition, Germany agreed to favour Russia in the drawing of its frontier with the Ukraine and to begin the evacuation of White Russia at the same time the Soviet government began to make the payments stipulated in its financial agreement. In a last minute change designed to thrust the burden of fighting Alekseev on to the Bolsheviks Germany agreed to evacuate the Rostov-Voronezh railway and the city of Rostov. Germany also met the Russian demand for economic concessions within the territory she occupied adjacent to the Black Sea, agreeing that both the Taganrog-Rostov and Taganrog-Kursk railways would be made available for the shipment of grain and other goods to Soviet Russia and promising to provide coal for Russia from the Donets basin.[148]

The most controversial aspects of the political agreement were all contained in an exchange of confidential notes. In part this secrecy was dictated by the need to conceal future military operations from the entente, but it also served to shield the two governments from political embarrassment. In view of their repeated statements in defence of national self-determination, for example, both governments would have found it difficult to explain why they had agreed to draw the Russian frontier in such a way as to leave Narva and Dvinsk under German control. This was done at the insistence of the German high command, but in the ideologically charged atmosphere of 1918 neither government wished to admit that the whim of the German army had dictated their decision. Even more embarrassing for Germany would have been the public exposure of concessions made Russia at the expense of the Ukraine and Georgia. Thus, in addition to promising the Soviet government that it would prevent the Ukraine from fostering separatism within the Russian state, Germany also pledged that a third of Ukrainian iron production would be made available to Russia and that Berlin would use its influence in the negotiation of the future Russian-Ukrainian peace treaty to insure that Russia would obtain most of the Donets basin. Similarly, Germany promised Russia one-quarter of the manganese ore produced in Georgia. For Germany, however, the most compromising portion of the confidential exchange concerned Turkey. Here Germany declared that in the 'unfortunate' case of an armed conflict between Russia and Turkey in the Caucasus that 'as long as Russian troops do not cross the frontier of Turkey or the borders of Georgia' it would lend no assistance to its Ottoman ally. In short, if the Russians could drive the Turks out of Azerbaijan and Armenia Germany would let them do it.

The secret exchange of notes also contained the political foundations for the military cooperation of the two governments. Here Germany made clear that it expected the Soviet government to devote most of its military resources to Central Russia and to 'take all possible measures in order to crush immediately the insurrection of General Alekseev and the Czecho-slovaks.' The Soviet government was also to be given an opportunity to drive the British from northern Russia and Baku, but if it failed Germany said that she 'would find herself obliged to undertake this action.' In that event Berlin expected 'that the Russian Government would not consider such action as an unfriendly act' and would 'not oppose it in any way whatsoever.' Northern Russia and Baku were dealt with in two separate notes, but in both Germany made the the same promise. If Russia cooperated with German military operations the Soviet claim to the two regions would not be challenged. In the case of Murmansk, Germany pledged not to send troops into the region south of Lake Lagoda (i.e., Petrograd) without Soviet permission and to evacuate the region north of it after the conclusion of a general peace. Similar pledges were given concerning Baku.[149]

149 The Soviets have not published this exchange of notes. A German copy of the note dealing with all subjects except Baku was published in *Europaische Gesprache* (March 1926), and is translated in Wheeler-Bennett, *The Forgotten Peace*, 435-8. The note concerning Baku has been published by Winfried Baumgart as an appendix to 'Die "Geschäftliche Behandlung" des Berliner Ergänzungsvertrags vom 27 August 1918,' *Historisches Jahrbuch*, vol. LXXXIX (1969) 146-8. The significant portion of the note has also been published in translation by Trumpener, *Germany and the Ottoman Empire*, 192

The financial treaty was an extension of the political agreement. Its central feature was contained in the Russian pledge to pay six billion marks to compensate Germany for losses suffered by its citizens as a result of the war and Soviet legislation nationalizing German property in Russia. This removed the threat of a German challenge to the Soviet decree of 28 June nationalizing virtually all private property in Russia, including that of German citizens, but it left Russia saddled with an enormous debt which it had to pay Germany. The treaty specified that Russia was to pay Germany one-and-a-half billion marks in gold and bank notes while another billion was due in the form of commodities. The gold and bank notes were to be delivered to Germany in five instalments, the first payable on 10 September and the last on 31 December 1918. The commodities were to be delivered to Germany at specified dates from November 1918 to March 1920. In addition, one billion marks was earmarked for possible payment by the Ukraine and Finland, but in so far as these countries did not discharge this debt Russia was to be held responsible for its payment. Finally, Russia was to pay two-and-a-half billion marks by issuing bonds in Germany bearing six per cent interest and secured by specific national revenues, 'in particular the rental dues for certain economic concessions to be granted to Germans.' Here was the engine for Germany's economic domination of Russia. Russia, which was to be drained of its gold reserve and sucked dry of commodities, would be bound hand and foot to the German economy, German financiers securing a first mortgage on every profitable enterprise in Russia. With an eye to the uncertainties of the future, however, the Germans were careful to add clauses to the treaty which provided that if in the future a Russian government should denationalize any of the German property seized by the Soviet government this property, upon return of the compensation granted under the agreement and with adjustments made for improvements and damages, would revert to its original German owners. Thus, regardless of whether the Soviet government adhered to its existing policies or reverted to a capitalist form of economic organization Germany was certain to dominate the Russian economy. It would have been difficult to devise a more efficient instrument of exploitation than the financial treaty supplementing the Treaty of Brest-Litovsk.[150]

At the Seventh Congress Lenin had warned the Bolsheviks to be prepared for 'downright slavery to the Germans.' The supplementary treaties amply fulfilled this prediction. No other term than slavery adequately

150 DVP, vol. I, 445-53

describes the level to which the Bolsheviks were reduced by these agreements. At Brest-Litovsk they had been stripped of Russia's western borderlands and had their illusions of imminent world revolution shattered. Viewed at the time as an unparalleled disaster the losses suffered at Brest-Litovsk paled in comparison with the sacrifices made at Berlin. Lenin had predicted this too, telling the Seventh Congress that at the next stage in Russia's relations with Germany 'a peace four times more humiliating will be dictated to us.' And so it was, for although some of the worst aspects of the supplementary treaties were shrouded in secrecy or partially concealed by the fig leaves of diplomacy the Soviet leaders knew the truth. They had succeeded in out-bidding every other group in Russia for the favour of Germany, but in doing so they had committed themselves to an association which bore an unfortunate resemblance to that which Berlin had established with Finland, the Ukraine, and Georgia. Like the other states of eastern Europe, Soviet Russia had become a client of Germany, pleading its case in Berlin and accepting alms from the table of its master. The Bolsheviks had acknowledged that Germany would decide the fate of Russia, distributing Russian provinces and cities to its miscellaneous vassals as required by the German interest. Already Germany had assumed partial responsibility for the defence of its Russian satellite, marking out the areas from which it would drive the entente while designating those which the Bolsheviks were to handle. If the Soviet government proved incapable of shouldering its share of the burden there was little doubt that the Germans would expand their activities, moving further into the heart of Russia. Militarily, therefore, the only hope which the Bolsheviks had to avoid further German occupation of Russian territory was to succeed in the task set them by their masters. The same was true economically. At Berlin the Bolsheviks had made far-reaching commitments to supply German industry with raw materials. To be sure, Germany had agreed to supply Russia with raw materials from those areas of the former Russian empire under its control, but only to permit the Russian economy to serve German interests more efficiently. When these deliveries were made the Germans would expect a great outpouring of Russian wealth to fuel their industry and compensate them for the great losses suffered during the war. If the Bolsheviks did not fulfill these expectations they could anticipate the same consequences as would follow from failure to complete the military tasks which the Germans had set them. To avoid complete German control of the Russian economy the Bolsheviks would have to deliver faithfully everything which they had promised Germany. Like slaves they existed at the sufferance of their master and were condemned to do his bidding upon command.

Despite the thraldom to which they were condemned the Bolsheviks viewed the signing of the supplementary treaties as a great victory. The negotiations in Berlin had extended the 'breathing space' through the summer and promised a further extension of indeterminate length. For at least six months the Soviet government could look forward to a respite from the problems which had haunted it since February. Ioffe had succeeded in hanging heavy weights on the feet of Germany's soldiers, and they were now shackled by perhaps the most effective chain of all, the golden dream of great expectations. As long as dreams of Russian natural resources obediently delivered by willing Bolsheviks danced through the heads of German statesmen, industrialists, and financiers Soviet Russia was reasonably safe from those in Germany who wanted to crush the revolution. To be sure, the treaty had nothing in common with the agreement which Chicherin in early July had said the Soviet government wanted to negotiate with Germany.[151] The treaties gravely injured Russia's vital interests and wholly compromised its neutrality, but they did shield the Bolsheviks from German attack. Consequently Bolshevik leaders hailed the treaties as a triumph of Soviet diplomacy.

In late July, when the outline of the treaties was already visible, Lenin publicly celebrated their imminent conclusion saying: 'we have won freedom to carry on socialist construction at home, and have taken steps in this direction which are now becoming known in western Europe and constitute elements of propaganda that are incomparably more effective than any before.'[152] Due to the attempt on his life which left him incapacitated in early September; Lenin did not comment further on the treaties, but on 2 September when Chicherin presented the documents to the All-Russian Central Executive Committee for ratification he declared that they represented a 'significant improvement' of the Soviet position in international relations.[153] Radek, who in the absence of Lenin assumed the burden of popularizing the treaties, took much the same line, declaring emphatically that the agreements worked in favour of Soviet Russia.[154] While Chicherin based his argument on the advantage of regulating Rus-

151 See above, 301-2
152 Lenin, PSS, vol. XXXVII, 13
153 Chicherin, Stati, 66
154 Karl Radek, *Die internationale Lage und die äussere Politik der Räteregierung* (Berlin, 1919) 3-5

sia's relations with Germany and stressed the common interests which the two countries temporarily shared, Radek took his text from Lenin and emphasized the added time for encouraging world revolution which had been obtained by negotiating the new treaties. Chicherin's real feelings can be gauged from a comment made in private to one of his associates. 'The seventh circle of hell is reserved for tyrants who thirst for blood and gold,' he said, 'If Dante was writing the Divine Comedy today he would certainly place the Prussian Junkers with their upturned moustaches in the seventh circle.'[155] But neither he nor Radek said anything publicly about the negative aspects of the treaties, and in the changed political environment of September 1918, so different from that of earlier in the year, they did not have to fear a challenge from hostile critics. In March the Treaty of Brest-Litovsk had been bitterly attacked both within the Bolshevik party and throughout Russia as a whole. In September a treaty many times worse was greeted silently by the disciplined members of the All-Russian Central Executive Committee. Lenin had seen to this, for the suppression of dissent within Russia guaranteed the silent consent needed by the Bolshevik leaders to conduct their dangerous policy of seeking security in the shadow of Germany.

The success of this policy, however, depended in large part on Soviet Russia never having to fulfill its commitments to Germany. At Berlin the Bolsheviks had exchanged their freedom of action for the privilege of continuing as the government of Russia, a bargain which every passing day and every additional German demand would make more difficult to keep. Ioffe had said that 'time and peace' were the 'profit' which Soviet Russia obtained from the supplementary treaties,[156] but both these commodities were highly abstract and could easily be lost. To obtain them Lenin had thrown the last of his political capital into the balance, and once it was lost his cause was bankrupt. What the Germans had given they could just as easily take away, and Hintze's words[157] make it clear that even the so-called 'peace party' in Germany was not prepared to tolerate the Bolsheviks one day longer than their usefulness demanded. How long would that be? Certainly no longer than it took the Bolsheviks to default on one of the major pledges made at Berlin. And given the truly desperate state of the Soviet economy could it possibly fulfill the expectations of Germany? Lenin himself had said that 'chaos is everywhere ... and the

155 Zarnitskii and Sergeev, *Chicherin*, 87
156 Baumgart, *Deutsche Ostpolitik*, 301
157 See above, 342-3

cure for this evil is slow.'[158] The 'cure' in fact had hardly begun, and in the late summer of 1918 the direction of the Soviet economy was down, not up. The Soviet government could barely feed its own people, and industrial indices were sinking lower with every month. All of Russia that remained to the Bolsheviks was being mobilized for war with transport monopolized by the Red army. The supplementary treaties may have obtained peace with Germany, but they also pledged the Bolsheviks to intensify their struggle against Alekseev and the Czechs. In such circumstances it was impossible to squeeze any significant surplus from the Russian economy for delivery to Germany. The Soviet government had knowingly misled the Germans, convincing them that the Russian economy could quickly regain its vitality and serve as a useful auxilliary to that of the Reich. This had been necessary to win German favour, but having signed the supplementary treaties Soviet Russia was faced with the hopeless task of making good its promises.

Or at least it faced this dismal prospect if the long-expected revolution or some similar cataclysm did not soon overtake Germany. In one of his last speeches before the attempt on his life Lenin again predicted the imminence of the German revolution,[159] but he had been making such predictions for more than a year, and the German war machine still held Russia in its grip. Yet by August there were hopeful signs which began to lend substance to Soviet expectations. On 8 August, the 'Black-Day' of the German army, Marshal Foch had taken the offensive in France. The news from Flanders made just as cheerful reading in Moscow as in Paris, for Soviet leaders realized that the steady retreat of the German army in the west would influence events in eastern and central Europe.[160] But in what way? Would the German crisis ripen before it was too late to save the revolution in Russia or would the collapse of German militarism also find Bolshevism in ruins? The answer to these questions would determine whether Lenin's policy had simply prolonged the agony of the revolution or had indeed saved Soviet Russia from extinction at the hands of Germany.

158 See above, 310
159 Lenin, PSS, vol. XXXVII, 74-8
160 See, for example, *ibid.*, 65-70, 74-8

13
Survival

The external foe of the Russian Soviet Socialist Republic at present is British, French, American and Japanese imperialism. Lenin, early August 1918

Our present situation, for all its contradictions, might be expressed by saying, firstly, that never before have we been so near the world workers' revolution, and secondly, that never have we been in such a perilous position. Lenin, 22 October 1918

World capital itself is now coming for us. Lenin, early November 1918

In August, while the Bolsheviks extricated themselves from the grip of the German army, the western powers had intensified their efforts to overthrow the Soviet government. From the north, south, and east, allied forces struggled to penetrate the heart of Russia while in Moscow and Petrograd western agents sought to install a new Russian government willing to link itself with the entente. Step by step, the Bolsheviks were forced to retreat from the Urals, the White Sea and Baku. Barely clinging to a foothold on the Middle Volga they were faced with the prospect of losing their last granary as well as the vital link with the Caspian Sea. In central Russia, the class conflict which the Bolsheviks had fostered in the villages spiralled into open civil war and threatened to engulf the land in turmoil. Day by day the last stocks of grain were consumed, and if the Bolsheviks were unable to drive their enemies from the Volga and overcome peasant resistance Soviet Russia would succumb to its enemies.

Lenin, who had previously concentrated on placating Germany now became absorbed with the threat posed by the western powers and redefined the tasks of Soviet foreign policy. Sometime in the first part of

August, he penned another of his emotion-filled essays which summarized his views and served to guide Soviet policy. Here he declared that 'the external foe of the Russian Soviet Socialist Republic at present is British, French, American and Japanese imperialism.' This enemy was: 'attacking peaceful Russia with the ferocity and voracity of the Germans in February, the only difference being that the British and Japanese are not only out to seize and plunder Russian territory, but to overthrow the Soviet government so as to "restore the front," i.e., to draw Russia again into the imperialist (or more simply, the predatory) war between Britain and Germany.' The western powers, he said, were 'counting on alliance with the internal enemy of the Soviet government,' not only the capitalists ists and landowners, but also the kulaks. As usual in this type of memorandum prepared for his own use, Lenin gave vent to a veritable hurricane of hatred, defining the kulaks as 'the rabid foes of the Soviet government' who 'everywhere' were 'joining with the *foreign capitalists* against the workers of their own country.' 'These bloodsuckers ... spiders ... leeches ... vampires ...' had to be destroyed. 'Either the kulaks massacre vast numbers of workers, or the workers ruthlessly suppress the revolts of the predatory kulak minority ... There can be no middle course.' He demanded: 'Ruthless war on the kulaks! Death to them! Hatred and contempt for the parties which defend them – the right Socialist Revolutionaries, the Mensheviks, and today's left Socialist Revolutionaries! The workers must crush the revolts of the kulaks with an iron hand, the kulaks who are forming an alliance with the foreign capitalists against the working people of their own country.'[1]

This became the leitmotif of Soviet policy during August and served to complement the bitter struggle against the allies. Anyone who sympathized with the western powers or might benefit from their intervention became the enemy of the Soviet government, and the Bolsheviks did not hesitate to adopt the most brutal methods to deal with them. As the internal and external position of the Soviet government deteriorated, Bolshevik frustration found an outlet in the repression of their political enemies. Jails began to fill with suspected counter-revolutionaries, and when it became known that the British and Czechs had executed Bolshevik prisoners the Soviet government ordered hostages taken from among the former property-owning classes. Every new blow, every pressure added to the shrinking boundaries of Soviet Russia increased internal tensions and brought the spectre of a great bloodbath closer to realization.

1 Lenin, PSS, vol. XXXVII, 38-42. Emphasis in original

The breaking point came on 30 August, when two terrorists acting independently of each other, struck at the heart of the Soviet government. In the morning, Moses Uritskii, the chairman of the Petrograd Cheka, was shot and killed, and the same evening Lenin was gunned down as he left a workers' meeting in Moscow. Gravely wounded, he was not at first expected to live. This double-barrelled assault caused a convulsive spasm to pass through the Soviet government, and, recoiling like a badly wounded animal, it struck out wildly at its enemies. Sverdlov issued a decree calling for 'merciless mass terror against all the enemies of the revolution,'[2] and within hours the execution of hostages began. Before the bloody assize had run its course, thousands were dead, and the civil war in Russia had assumed a new and more ferocious dimension.

The terror evoked a strong protest from the last remnants of the diplomatic corps. Reduced to the ministers of the neutral powers and the consuls-general of Germany, Austria-Hungary, and the United States, they were, for the most part, concentrated in Petrograd where they were closely associated with the anti-Bolshevik movement in the city. Some, such as Breiter, the German consul-general, and Scavenius, the Danish minister, made no effort to conceal their hatred of the Soviet government, while others only sought to alleviate the desperate circumstances into which old friends and associates had fallen. All, however, recoiled in horror from the massacre which followed the attempt on Lenin's life. On 3 September, they visited Zinoviev to protest 'in the name of humanity' against what they termed 'these indiscriminate executions *en masse* of people who were in no way whatever connected with the attacks on Uritsky and Lenin.' The Swiss minister Odier spoke for the corps, asking Zinoviev 'to put a stop to these barbaric executions.' Breiter, who together with his Austro-Hungarian colleague had spontaneously asked to participate, said much the same thing. Although Chicherin was later to describe this protest as 'the first concentrated diplomatic step of both imperialist coalitions against the proletarian revolution,'[3] the Soviet government took no formal notice at the time. Zinoviev only listened and said that 'he did not wish to interfere' with the work of the Cheka.[4]

The Soviet government was soon forced to abandon its silence. Not only did the American consul-general in Moscow add his voice to the

2 Sverdlov, *Izbrannye Proizvedeniia*, vol. III, 5

3 *Izvestiia*, 6 Nov. 1919

4 W.J. Oudendijk, *Ways and By-Ways in Diplomacy* (London, 1939) 286. See also Baumgart, *Deutsche Ostpolitik*, 313

remonstrance,[5] but, on 5 September, the diplomatic corps addressed a written protest to the Narkomindel. The representatives of the neutral powers, now acting without Breiter who had been ordered by Berlin to disassociate himself from the action,[6] used even stronger language than before. Again claiming to speak in the name of 'humanity' they denounced the 'red terror,' saying that the 'murder' of 'hundreds of unfortunate individuals ... whose only guilt was to belong to the bourgeois class' had 'provoked the indignation of the entire civilized world.' Denying that they wished to interfere in the internal affairs of Russia they nevertheless 'reserved for their governments the right to exact necessary satisfaction and personal juridical responsibility of those who are guilty and will be guilty of these arbitrary acts.'[7] Although the Bolsheviks were unimpressed by this threat they could no longer remain silent. By invoking 'the entire civilized world' and assuring wide publicity for their protest the diplomatic corps virtually forced the Bolsheviks to challenge the interpretation of the 'red terror' which they had given.

The Soviet reply was delivered on 12 September. In it Chicherin skilfully combined ridicule with sarcasm, impeaching the right of the neutral ministers and their governments to speak in the name of 'humanity.' Claiming the right of the Soviet government to represent 'not only the Russian working class but the whole of exploited humanity,' he proudly displayed the triumphs of the Russian revolution, pointing in particular to the destruction of tsarism whose 'bloody regime' he observed had 'provoked no protests from the neutral powers.' Although admitting that 'abuses' had occurred he shrugged them off, saying that 'abuses on the part of individuals occur in every war, and we are engaged in a civil war.' Chicherin devoted the major part of his response to illustrating the hypocrisy of the neutral ministers and their governments. Did they know, he asked:

that it is now the fifth year of the world war into which small groups of bankers, generals and bureaucrats have flung the masses of the people of the entire world ... that in this war not only have millions died at the front, but both belligerents have dropped bombs on open cities and killed defenceless women and children ... that one of the belligerent parties in this war has condemned tens of

5 FRUS, *1918, Russia*, vol. 1, 683
6 Baumgart, *Deutsche Ostpolitik*, 318
7 'Un échange de notes diplomatiques sur la terreur blanche et la terreur rouge' (Zurich, 1918). Also see FRUS, *1918, Russia*, vol. 1, 697

millions to death by starvation by cutting them off from their food supply ... that the other party takes prisoner hundreds of thousands of defenceless peaceful 'enemy' citizens and sends them to forced labour?

Had they not heard about the 'massacres of the Sinn Feiners in Dublin ... about the White Terror in Finland ... about the mass execution of workers and peasants in the Ukraine, about the mass execution of workers by the gallant Czechoslovaks, the hired bandits of French-English capital'? The governments of 'the so-called neutral powers' had heard about all this, he said, 'but it has never occurred to them to protest against these abuses by the bourgeoisie' because they were so enmeshed in the imperialist system, so involved in growing rich from the war, so fearful of their own working masses 'that they did not even want to protest;' consequently they could hold no brief for 'the civilized world' or speak in the name of 'elemental humanity.' Concluding with a stern warning, Chicherin rejected 'the interference of the neutral capitalist powers in favour of the Russian bourgeoisie' and declared that the Soviet government would 'regard every attempt on the part of the representatives of these powers to exceed the limits of the lawful protection of the interests of their nations as an attempt to support the Russian counter-revolution.'[8] Given the circumstances this was no idle threat, and Chicherin's response put an end to protests from the neutral ministers. More importantly, it constituted a forceful reply to the foreign critics of the Soviet regime. It would, of course, carry no weight with those who for political reasons already hated Soviet Russia, but in the ranks of European socialists, among actual and potential revolutionaries, it put the best face possible on the blood-smeared countenance of the Bolsheviks.

No matter how Chicherin might justify the 'red terror,' it still did untold damage to the international position of Soviet Russia. Not only did it strain the tenuous ties with the neutral powers and damage the Bolshevik image in western and central Europe, it also complicated the negotiations with the western powers for the exchange of prisoners, hostages and official agents detained since the outbreak of hostilities. These negotiations had proceeded slowly. Although the Bolsheviks quickly released most of the allied citizens arrested after the British landing at Archangel the western consuls no longer had any confidence in their ability to influence the Soviet government, and on 9 August hauled down their flags and committed the safety of allied citizens in Russia to the representatives

8 DVP, vol. I, 472-4

of the neutral powers.[9] As a consequence, negotiations for the exchange of prisoners had proceeded through the medium of the Dutch minister, the Danish minister, and the Swedish consul-general in Petrograd. The technical difficulties involved in this cumbersome process had caused delay which was further compounded when the Bolsheviks repeatedly altered the conditions on which they would agree to an exchange.[10] Primarily, however, the negotiations were impeded by the Cheka which knew the allied agents were involved in a wide-ranging conspiracy against the Soviet government and wanted them to remain in Russia, free to become involved in as much mischief as possible. During August, therefore, the Soviet government found one reason or another to delay the departure of the allied agents, all the while giving them free rein to organize their conspiracy and thus assist the Cheka in its investigation. The attempt on Lenin's life put an end to this game.[11] The hysteria of the moment demanded prompt action, and although its investigation was not complete the Extraordinary Commission had to arrest most of the remaining western citizens in Soviet Russia including Lockhart and the other allied agents. This was bad enough, but in Petrograd the result of the 'red terror' was even worse. There, an angry mob, believing that the assassin of Uritskii had taken refuge in the British embassy, stormed into the building and was met by the naval attaché, Captain Cromie. Cromie, on being told to stand aside or 'be shot like a dog,' opened fire himself and was killed in the ensuing gunfight.[12] The death of Cromie and the imprisonment of the remaining allied personnel in Russia evoked a sharp response from the British government which, in addition to arresting Litvinov, informed Moscow that: 'Should the Russian government fail to give complete satisfaction or should any further acts of violence be committed against a British subject His Majesty's Government will hold the members of the Soviet Government individually responsible and will make every endeavor to secure that they shall be treated as outlaws by the governments of all civilized nations and that no place of refuge shall be left to them.'[13] Paris had already issued a similar declaration, and in succeeding days the allied governments generated an immense international storm designed to blacken the name of Bolshevism throughout the world. Even in Berlin,

9 Ullman, *Intervention and the War*, 286-7
10 Oudendijk, *Ways and By-Ways*, 287-8; Ullman, *Intervention and the War*, 287-8; PRO FO 371/3335/138594, 141743. Also see PRO FO 371/3330/150249.
11 Debo, 'Lockhart plot or Dzerzhinskii plot?' 437
12 London *Times*, 24 Oct. 1918
13 *Ibid.*, 5 Sept. 1918

chancellor Hertling suggested that the German government file a protest against the 'red terror' and was only dissuaded from enlisting Germany in what was essentially an allied cause by Hintze who refused to mix sentiment and politics.[14] Thus, on two accounts the Bolsheviks suffered as a consequence of the 'red terror.' The premature arrest of the allied agents and the opportunity given the allies to launch a political offensive against Moscow did nothing to enhance the security of the Soviet state.

It was no easy task to sort out the wreckage left by the 'red terror.' So serious was the lack of trust that foreign representatives calling at the Narkomindel even found themselves staring down the barrel of a revolver when they talked with the deputy commissar.[15] The Dutch minister William Oudendijk, who was carrying the burden of negotiations for the release of allied citizens in Russia, was particularly distrustful of Chicherin whom he characterized as a 'reptile' and 'beneath contempt.'[16] It is doubtful if Chicherin had any higher regard for the Dutch minister, but the foreign commissar also had to contend with the Cheka which, after Lockhart and the other allied agents had ceased to be of further use, was not inclined to be merciful. Oudendijk feared for their safety and insistently demanded that the Narkomindel restrain the Cheka.[17] That the lives of the allied agents were spared was due not to mercy but cold political calculation. Several years later Chicherin would recall that the departure of the allied ambassadors from Vologda 'in a fully correct fashion' had 'facilitated future relations with their governments,'[18] and undoubtedly this consideration influenced the Bolshevik decision to free the allied conspirators. Given the bloodbath of early September no further lives were needed to prove that the Soviet government would deal ruthlessly with its enemies, and in the rapidly changing conditions of war-torn Europe it took little imagination to conceive of circumstances in which the Soviet government might wish to resume direct relations with the allied powers. If the Bolsheviks executed Lockhart and the other allied agents it was unlikely that the western states would agree to a restoration of diplomatic relations. Reason demanded a clean break with the western governments,

14 Baumgart, *Deutsche Ostpolitik*, 317
15 Oudendijk, *Ways and By-Ways*, 293
16 FRUS, *1918, Russia*, vol. I, 678. Also see Richard K. Debo, 'Dutch-Soviet relations, 1917-1924: the role of finance and commerce in the foreign policy of Soviet Russia and the Netherlands,' *Canadian Slavic Studies* IV, no. 2 (summer 1970) 199-204
17 Oudendijk, *Ways and By-Ways*, 294
18 Chicherin, 'Lenin i Vneshniaia Politika,' 7

and on 6 September, Chicherin resumed negotiations for an exchange of prisoners.

This took the form of an official statement released by the Narkomindel explaining the position of the Soviet government. Chicherin repeated the charges against the allied agents and defended the necessity of depriving them 'of those conditions under which they could continue to pursue their criminal activities,' but reaffirmed the willingness of the Soviet government to allow them to leave Russia. Once Litvinov was free to leave England, he said, the allied agents could leave Russia. He shrugged off the British and French declaration holding members of the Soviet government personally responsible for the safety of allied citizens in Russia, saying that 'there is nothing new in this, for the entente powers have already used this form of reprisal, including the execution of Soviet workers, in regions of Russia which they occupy.' He added, however, that the Soviet government would abstain from reprisals if the entente would do so as well.[19] The same day he communicated the substance of this declaration to the Swedish consul-general who was asked to convey it to the allied powers.[20]

The Soviet declaration took the allied governments by surprise. When the first reports of the 'red terror' reached western Europe it was assumed that the entire allied community in Russia had been murdered, and the warning contained in the British and French messages of 5 September, notifying Soviet leaders that they would be treated as outlaws, had been no idle threat. Almost at once the allies had begun to canvas the neutrals seeking their agreement to measures outlawing the Soviet regime. Now everything had changed, and it appeared that allied citizens in Russia were safe and that the Soviet government was prepared to allow them to leave. Moreover, the neutral governments had not reacted favourably to the allied proposal and, in the altered circumstances, would be even less inclined to agree to the measures proposed by London and Paris. The allied governments, therefore, had to change gears, and on 11 September they empowered the neutral representatives in Russia to resume negotiations with Chicherin. The neutrals were asked 'to do everything that is possible to get [allied citizens] away at once.' Litvinov would be allowed to leave England together with any other Russians who wished to accompany him. In return the allies demanded 'full reciprocity' and the release of all their

19 DVP, vol. I, 469-70
20 *Ibid.*, 468

citizens, 'officials or otherwise,' including military personnel. Nothing further was said about reprisals.[21]

Full reciprocity was unacceptable to the Bolsheviks. They could agree to exchange the allied agents for Litvinov and repatriate some British and French citizens, but they were not prepared to release all western prisoners. If they did they would be unable to influence the manner in which allied forces occupying parts of Russia treated captured Bolsheviks and would also lose a valuable means of inducing the western powers to negotiate with the Soviet government. The allied citizens held in Russian jails, therefore, were to be used not merely as hostages to insure good treatment for Bolsheviks who might fall into allied hands, but as potential diplomatic pawns. Thus, Chicherin rejected the allied proposal of 11 September and submitted his own plan for an exchange of prisoners. In his note of 16 September, he offered to exchange allied official agents, consular personnel, and members of the military missions for Litvinov and his associates. In addition, 'working class' civilians, together with women, children and older 'bourgeois' males would be repatriated. 'Bourgeois males from fifteen to forty-eight years of age' plus all French officers and enlisted men not included as official members of military missions were to be detained until further conditions were met, the French military personnel until France agreed to return Russian soldiers in France, and bourgeois males of military age until all Russian citizens in allied countries, including those forced into service in the British army, were returned to Russia. No reprisals would be taken against allied citizens as long as the western powers did not mistreat Russians in Britain, France, or Russian territories occupied by allied armies.[22] This was a very neat package well designed to meet the requirements of international law, Bolshevik propaganda and *Realpolitik*. If accepted by the allies, the Bolsheviks would get back Litvinov, dispose of the weakest and most troublesome of their prisoners and retain a select group of British and French citizens whose fate could be expected to have a moderating influence on allied policy. If it was rejected the question of prisoners would simply remain open, and Moscow would retain all of its existing leverage.

The British government realized the weakness of its position. Winter was fast approaching, the fall of the Bolsheviks did not appear imminent and reports from Moscow cast doubt on the ability of many of the prisoners to survive the Russian winter. Moreover, it was impossible to pre-

21 PRO FO 371/3336/154406
22 DVP, vol. I, 482-3

dict if the 'red terror' would again flare up, and if it did what the consequences might be for the hostages still in Bolshevik hands. A decision had to be made quickly, and against the wishes of the French government Whitehall decided to accept Chicherin's terms. On 19 September this decision was reinforced when Chicherin suddenly demanded that Bolshevik commissars arrested at Baku be included with Litvinov in the exchange for Lockhart and other allied agents.[23] This demand made it imperative that allied prisoners be repatriated as quickly as possible, because the commissars whom Chicherin wanted returned had already been murdered by the Transcaspian government of Ashkhabad into whose hands they had fallen after escaping from Baku.[24] Aware of this, but anxious to keep it secret from the Bolsheviks,[25] the foreign office pressed forward with the exchange, informing Moscow that while the British government could not 'engage at once to comply with further demands' it was prepared to accept all the conditions set forth in Chicherin's note of 16 September.[26] This response went by radio directly to Moscow where it made a good impression on the Soviet government. Chicherin replied on 30 September, telling Balfour that his 'kind wireless message ... had facilitated the solution of pending difficulties' by disjoining 'the question of the immediate repatriation of the official representatives ... from the more complicated question of the repatriation of the other citizens.' Lockhart, said Chicherin, would be allowed to leave Russia just as soon as the Narkomindel was informed by the Norwegian consul that Litvinov had left Aberdeen for Bergen.[27]

Within a few days the exchange had taken place. Litvinov quickly reached Norway, and on 7 October Lockhart with a party of fifty-four crossed into Finland.[28] By mid-month more than one-hundred-fifty allied citizens had left Russia. Those left behind were destined to remain there for more than a year, because the Bolsheviks showed little interest in discussing their repatriation until the allied powers began to retreat from Russia. Then, as Chicherin had undoubtedly anticipated, they became the pawns which the Soviet government advanced to initiate more extensive negotiations with the western powers. Such negotiations could take place,

23 *Ibid.*, 489
24 G.H. Ellis, *The British 'Intervention' in Transcaspia, 1918-1919* (Berkeley, California, 1963) 57-65; Ullman, *Intervention and the War*, 321-3; Suny, *The Baku Commune*, 337-43
25 PRO FO 371/3336/164159
26 *Ibid.*, 371/3336/161133
27 *Ibid.*, 371/3336/164855
28 *Ibid.*, 371/3337/169656

however, only after the Soviet government had become so strong that the western powers could no longer reasonably hope to destroy it.

In early September 1918, Soviet Russia did not give the appearance of strength. With Lenin gravely wounded and the Red army in retreat the Bolshevik position appeared critical. When Trotsky addressed the All-Russian Central Executive Committee on 2 September, he tried to put the best possible interpretation on the Soviet military position but could only report that Soviet forces were growing stronger and that discipline within the army, stiffened by drafts of workers from Moscow and Petrograd, had begun to improve. He had no victories to report, and he slid over the concrete details of the military situation very quickly, choosing instead to stress the need for greater sacrifices and harder work. He looked forward to winter when the harsh climate of Russia would paralyze the enemy, but emphasized that until winter came the Republic was in deadly peril. 'We must mobilize people, we must mobilize soldiers, and,' he said, 'we must mobilize the spiritual and ideal strength of the country, so that everyone, everywhere, particularly on the British stock market where they are now quoting the blood of the Russian people, will know that we will spare no one, and that we will fight to the last drop of our blood.'[29]

Already, however, the Soviet military and political position had begun to improve. Although badly wounded Lenin recovered quickly, and by mid-September was again at work, gradually resuming all his former responsibilities. In the north, the allies proved unable to advance, and in the south, the Bolsheviks successfully defended Tsaritsyn against the forces of Ataman Krasnov. Most important, the eastern front finally solidified, and the Czechs were first stopped and then rolled back. On 10 September, Soviet forces captured Kazan and two days later overran Simbirsk. Behind the Czech lines, which now began to crumble, the heterogeneous Russian political elements trying to form a national government to direct the struggle against the Bolsheviks started to quarrel among themselves and soon gave way to an unpopular and incompetent military dictatorship. The Red army rolled eastward, conquering a vast territory which was to provide the Soviet regime with food in the bitter months to come. By the end of September, the Bolsheviks occupied a stronger position than anyone thought possible at the beginning of the month.

This improvement was due in no small measure to the *détente* with Germany. Not only did the supplementary treaties free Soviet Russia from the threat of German attack, permitting the Red army to concentrate

29 Trotsky, *Kak Vooruzhulas'*, vol. I, 320-4

its forces on the eastern front, they also allowed the Bolsheviks to call on Berlin for assistance in the regulation of difficulties with their other neighbors. In this sense, Soviet enlistment as a client of Germany proved to be a great boon to Moscow, and the Bolsheviks exploited their new status to the utmost.

The most important aspect of the new Soviet relationship with Germany was the vastly altered manner in which the two countries dealt with problems confronting them. Before the conclusion of the supplementary treaties, Soviet Russia had been faced with one German ultimatum after another with retribution certain if Moscow did not promptly comply with German wishes. In September this changed, and the Soviet government no longer had to knuckle under to German demands. Germany now had a very real stake in the continued existence of the Soviet regime, and as long as Berlin remained confident of political and economic profit from a satisfactory relationship with its Russian client it could not afford to treat the Bolsheviks in the same high-handed manner of the past. This allowed the Soviet government to adopt a dilatory approach to its problems with Germany, directing disputes into relatively harmless channels, thereby defusing them before they became critical. This was the manner in which Moscow dealt with both 'Operation Schlussstein' and the problem of the maritime defence of Petrograd.

Operation Schlussstein was the code name given by the German army to its proposed campaign against allied forces in northern Russia. Even prior to the Soviet request for German assistance[30] General Hoffmann had prepared plans for this operation, and in early August, when Chicherin petitioned Berlin to assume responsibility for the defence of the Murmansk railway both Hintze and Ludendorff gave their permission for the campaign to begin.[31] Ludendorff, however, had assumed that his forces would be free to occupy Petrograd, and when the Soviet government refused to permit this occupation the general called a halt to the operation. Ludendorff and Hoffmann, however, still wished to proceed and pressured the *Auswärtiges Amt* to secure Soviet approval for the German occupation of Petrograd. Fearful of the anti-Bolshevik implications which both generals attached to the operation Hintze did little to convince the Soviet government that it should accede to the demand and even included a clause in the secret notes attached to the supplementary treaties prohibiting Germany from occupying Petrograd without the sanction of the Bol-

30 See above, 338-40
31 Baumgart, *Deutsche Ostpolitik*, 110

368 Revolution and survival

sheviks. Moreover, by late August the Soviet government was no longer as worried about Murmansk as it had been at the beginning of the month. Even with the skeleton force left in Karelia, Natsarenus was able to hold the front. Consequently, Soviet interest in German assistance declined while suspicion of Ludendorff's motives increased. To gain time Hintze and Ioffe decided that the question of Soviet-German military cooperation required further study, and the German government officially asked Moscow to send a high-ranking military officer to Berlin 'with the purpose of discussing the military requirements of the projected operations against Murmansk.' Instead of one officer the Bolsheviks sent an entire commission which, together with their German counterparts, concluded that a team of German officers should conduct an 'on the spot' investigation of the communication lines leading from Petrograd to Petrozavodsk. While these officers were tramping the roads and railways of Russia time was passing quickly, and when they filed their report at the end of September the entire military situation in Europe had undergone a profound change. Instead of clamouring for permission to occupy Petrograd the German high command began to cast about for ways of withdrawing from the secondary theatres of war to concentrate their divisions in areas vital for the defence of the Reich. 'Operation Schlussstein' was forgotten and with it the Soviet problem of resisting a German occupation of Petrograd.[32]

German objections to Bolshevik measures to strengthen the maritime defences of Petrograd were dealt with in a very similar manner. The problem arose from the failure of the Soviet government to comply with the requirement contained in the Treaty of Brest-Litovsk that it sweep Russian mine fields from the waters adjacent to Petrograd and abstain from laying any new mines. The Bolsheviks had been very reluctant to remove the mines protecting Petrograd and had devised numerous excuses to explain their failure to fulfil the obligation. As long as the Germans did not seriously plan to occupy Petrograd they were not unduly concerned with the problem, but when General Hoffmann began to prepare 'Operation Schlussstein' the question of naval support became important, and, at the insistence of the German navy, Berlin began to press Moscow for removal of the mines.[33] The question became critical in mid-August when the Germans discovered that not only had the Bolsheviks failed to remove the old mines, they were secretly laying new ones. This brought a sharp protest from Berlin which warned that if any further attempt was made to lay new

32 *Ibid.*, 107-11
33 *Ibid.*, 112-13

mine fields 'it would be stopped by armed force' and in that event 'the resumption of military activities would be the responsibility of the Russian government.'[34]

The Bolsheviks, who had resumed mining at the direct order of Lenin,[35] responded cautiously, Chicherin denying the charge and giving the standard Soviet excuses for their failure to remove the old mines. He also called attention to a forthcoming naval conference to be held in Libau and declared that the question of minefields could best be discussed at that meeting.[36] The Germans, however, had grown weary of Bolshevik procrastination and initiated their own measures to dispose of the minefields. Berlin informed the Soviet government that the German navy would sweep navigation channels up to a distance of three miles from Soviet territory.[37] Alarmed by this news Chicherin instructed Ioffe to enter a strong protest with the *Auswärtiges Amt.* 'This is extremely serious,' he said, 'for if they reach Kronstadt there will be a clash.'[38] One day after this message was sent the supplementary treaties were signed, and the foreign commissar increased his pressure on Berlin. Chicherin warned the German government that any attempt to sweep the mines from the eastern end of the Gulf of Finland could 'only be regarded by the Russian government as incompatible with friendly relations between Russia and Germany.'[39] The situation, he told Ioffe, was 'extraordinarily serious,' for if the Germans were allowed to approach the three-mile limit 'either we literally open Kronstadt or there will be a battle which we absolutely do not want but which in spite of our wishes might spontaneously erupt as a result of the sailors' excited frame of mind.'[40]

The same circumstances which caused the German government to postpone 'Operation Schlussstein' also caused it to delay minesweeping operations in the Gulf of Finland. The strong Soviet protest led to a reconsideration of the action, and Berlin decided to await the results of the Libau conference. For obvious reasons the Soviet government was in no hurry for this conference to begin, and when it finally convened in early October the Russian delegates refused to discuss minesweeping until the

34 DVP, vol. I, 424
35 R.N. Mordvinov, *Kursom 'Avrory.' Formirovanie sovetskogo voenno-morskogo flota i nachal ego boevoi deiatel'nosti (noiabr' 1917 – mart 1919 gg.)* (Moscow, 1962) 287
36 DVP, vol. I, 423-4
37 *Ibid.*, 455
38 *Ibid.*, 437
39 *Ibid.*, 454-5
40 *Ibid.*, 455-6

question of a demarcation line in the Gulf of Finland was settled first.[41] Due to the steadily declining fortunes of Germany the Soviet government was able to drag out the negotiations, and when Germany finally collapsed in November the question of minesweeping had still not been settled. Kronstadt and Petrograd remained secure from an unexpected attack by foreign warships.

Following the conclusion of the supplementary treaties the Bolsheviks were also able to strengthen their position in relation to the Ukraine and the Don Cossacks. The Cossacks might still receive weapons from the German army, but Ludendorff had to recall his liaison officer from Krasnov's headquarters,[42] and Moscow could reasonably assume that if it could crush the Ataman militarily the Germans would not intervene. More importantly, the Bolsheviks could take a hard line in their negotiations with the Ukraine. The Germans had agreed to confine the Ukraine to the territory claimed in the Third Universal and to force Kiev to surrender the most important parts of the Donets basin to Russia. Consequently, the Bolsheviks were able to stiffen their position and insist upon the Hetman recognizing the territorial integrity of the Russian state as defined by the Soviet government. The Ukrainians refused to comply with this demand, and in early September the negotiations reached an impasse. Less than two weeks after signing the supplementary treaties, therefore, Moscow was able to invoke the secret clauses of the political agreement and petition Berlin for assistance in its negotiations with the Ukraine. Describing the situation as 'intolerable' Ioffe asked the German government to intervene on the side of Soviet Russia.[43] Although the Germans failed to respond, and the negotiations eventually collapsed without result,[44] this made no difference to the Soviet government, for in the rapidly changing political circumstances of late 1918 the opportunity of acquiring the entire Ukraine became a distinct possibility.[45] In September, however, before the kaleidoscope of European politics had again begun to spin, the Bolsheviks were able to take advantage of their new relationship with Germany by launching a political offensive against their enemies in the south.

In the Caucasus the Bolsheviks were even more aggressive. Germany had promised them Baku, and they were determined to enforce their claim to the city. Even while the fate of the eastern front remained in doubt they

41 *Ibid.*, 507-8; Baumgart, *Deutsche Ostpolitik*, 112
42 Baumgart, *Deutsche Ostpolitik*, 146
43 DVP, vol. I, 470-1
44 Reshetar, *The Ukrainian Revolution*, 191
45 See below, 376

began to prepare a military operation to recapture Baku from the British. On 6 September, in what must have been one of his first orders issued after the attempt on his life, Lenin feverishly sought to move his forces into position. Hinting broadly at the bargain which had just been struck with Germany he informed the Soviet authorities in Petrograd: 'The struggle for the south and the Caspian is in progress. In order to retain the entire region for ourselves (and it can be retained!) we need several light torpedo boats and a couple of submarines. I implore you to break down all barriers and expedite the ... delivery of that which is required. Baku, Turkestan and the Northern Caucasus will (unconditionally!) be ours, if you will promptly fulfil this demand.'[46] Before the Bolsheviks could move against the British, however, the situation changed radically. On 14 September, the Turks drove the British from Baku and occupied the city. Turkey, rather than Britain, became the prime antagonist of the Bolsheviks for control of the Caspian.

Soviet reaction to the Turkish victory was predictably hostile. Ioffe remonstrated with Hintze, even threatening to denounce the supplementary treaties,[47] while Chicherin handed Hauschild a very stiff protest, describing the Turkish action as a 'violation' of the German-Soviet agreements of 27 August. Germany, said the foreign commissar, would have to assume responsibility for evicting Turkey from Baku.[48] While the Germans sought to mediate the dispute the Soviet government issued a virtual declaration of war, officially proclaiming on 20 September that Turkish actions had 'destroyed the peaceful relations between Russia and Turkey' and that the peace treaty between the two countries was 'no longer in force.'[49] Although *Izvestiia* had already published the Soviet declaration Hintze persuaded Ioffe to delay its delivery to the Turkish ambassador in Berlin until a further effort had been made to resolve the issue peacefully. Making liberal use of both carrot and stick Hintze convinced the Turks that they should allow Germany to settle the fate of the Caucasus. In a secret protocol signed on 23 September, Turkey agreed to evacuate the Caucasus and surrender Baku to Germany in exchange for a German pledge to provide Turkey with petroleum and the promise that Berlin would seek to obtain Soviet recognition of the independence of Armenia

46 DGKKA, 80-1. Emphasis in original
47 Baumgart, *Deutsche Ostpolitik*, 205
48 DVP, vol. I, 492-3
49 *Ibid.*, 490-2. English translation in Degras, *Soviet Documents on Foreign Policy*, vol. I, 109-10

and Azerbaijan.[50] It is doubtful if Moscow would have accepted this compromise, but the Soviet government did not have to give it serious consideration. In late September, both the Mesopotamian and Balkan fronts of the central powers collapsed, and Turkey, caught in a giant nutcracker, was opened to invasion from both south and west. The Turkish government had to recall all its forces from the Caucasus and could not wait for them to be replaced by German troops whose arrival, in any case, was now questionable.

In an effort to save Azerbaijan from Soviet attack Turkey entered into direct negotiations with the Bolsheviks. Talaat Pasha, the Grand Vizier of the Ottoman empire, informed Ioffe that Turkey intended to withdraw its troops from the Caucasus and wished to settle its differences with Russia peacefully. Ioffe agreed to negotiate but insisted that the Turks would have to surrender the Caucasus to Soviet Russia as they withdrew from the region. When Talat proved reluctant to accept this demand Ioffe responded by delivering the Soviet declaration of war.[51] Hintze made one last effort to mediate, and although Ioffe urged his government to accept a compromise proposed by the Germans,[52] Moscow would not hear of it. In a teletype message of 7 October, Lenin ordered his ambassador not to sign any agreement which did not provide for the prompt transfer of Baku directly to the Soviet government. 'Without this point,' he said, 'there is every reason to suspect a secret agreement with the entente about the transfer of Baku into its hands.'[53]

This was Moscow's last word on the subject and reflected the immense change which had occurred in one week. During September, the Bolsheviks had aggressively asserted their right to Baku, relying on the German guarantee contained in the supplementary treaties to give substance to their demands. By the first week in October, the guarantee of Germany meant nothing, and Moscow was already peering fretfully over Berlin's shoulder at the advancing armies of the western powers. While German power had lasted, however, Soviet Russia had made good use of Berlin in strengthening its hold upon Russia and speaking with greater authority in eastern Europe. To be sure, the Bolsheviks paid a price for this, millions of marks in gold delivered to Germany under the terms of the financial agreement of 27 August, not to mention the intangible cost of consistently going hat-in-hand to plead their case in Berlin, but by paying this

50 Baumgart, *Deutsche Ostpolitik*, 205-6; Trumpener, *Germany and the Ottoman Empire*, 196
51 DVP, vol. I, 509-10
52 Baumgart, *Deutsche Ostpolitik*, 206
53 Lenin, PSS, vol. L, 372

price they had contributed substantially to the survival of the Soviet government in the period of its greatest peril. The late summer of 1918 marked the nadir of Bolshevik fortunes; the coming of fall witnessed a great transformation in the affairs of the Soviet state and, indeed, the entire world.

This transformation was caused by the military defeat of the central powers. Suddenly and unexpectedly the stalemate in the Great War was broken, and the sanguinary conflict began to rush toward a rapid conclusion. First Bulgaria, then Turkey and Austria-Hungary collapsed and, with them, the quadruple alliance. The train of events set in motion on 26 September, when Bulgaria sued for peace, led directly to the end of hostilities. With the collapse of Bulgaria the entire Balkan peninsula was thrown open to allied invasion, outflanking both Turkey and Austria-Hungary. Turkey, which simultaneously suffered the collapse of its Mesopotamian front, and Austria-Hungary, whose dissident nationalities had already begun to secede from the empire, could not continue the war and were forced to plead for peace. This left only Germany and, open to attack on all sides, the Reich could no longer hope to continue the conflict. When word of Bulgaria's defection reached Ludendorff at the same time the allies launched an offensive in Flanders he panicked and, on 29 September, informed a startled German government that the war was lost and an immediate armistice was necessary. Within days Europe shook with the political consequences of Germany's defeat. Where before the word of Berlin had been law, the German writ meant nothing, and throughout the continent all eyes turned toward the western powers as the new arbiters of Europe.

Lenin again revised his foreign policy, but until the fate of Germany was sealed he remained cautious. When Kamenev wrote him in late September suggesting that Germany could be forced to renegotiate the Treaty of Brest-Litovsk, Lenin told him that it was still necessary '*to bide our time.*' He added, however, that recent events made it advisable for the Bolsheviks to 'begin to shift' their policy and implied that it might no longer be possible for Soviet Russia to maneuver between the rival coalitions. 'If Germany is defeated,' he said, 'then it becomes impossible to maneuver because there will not be two belligerents *between whom we can maneuver*!!' From this he concluded that it was vitally important to strengthen the Soviet armed forces. 'Without the Red army,' he said, 'England will gobble us up.'[54]

54 *Ibid.*, 184-5. Emphasis in original

The German political situation quickly forced Lenin to abandon his initial caution. When he learned of the plan to form a German government 'possessing the confidence of the people' he grew excited and concluded that Germany was on the brink of revolution. Reports that the new government would include Ebert, Scheidemann, and other German Social Democrats, whom he considered 'social-chauvinists' akin to Russian Mensheviks, whetted his appetite for action. On 1 October, he sent notes to Sverdlov and Trotsky saying 'affairs in Germany have so "accelerated" that we must not lag behind. And today we have already fallen behind ... the international revolution has approached *in a week* to within such a distance that it is to be reckoned with as an event of the *immediate future.*' He told them to summon a joint meeting of the governing bodies of all major Soviet institutions to discuss the revolutionary situation in Germany and define Soviet policy. In his note Lenin sketched the outlines of this policy. There would be, he said, 'no alliances either with the government of Wilhelm or the government of Wilhelm plus Ebert and other scoundrels.' The Soviet government would pursue a policy of 'fraternal alliance' with the 'German working class masses,' supplying grain to break the allied blockade and military assistance to defend the German revolution. To prepare for the German revolution he said it was necessary for the Bolsheviks to generate 'ten times more effort in procuring grain' and 'ten times more *enrollment* in the army.' 'Sweep up *all* stocks [of food] both for ourselves and *for the German* workers,' he ordered and demanded that by spring an army of three million men be ready 'to help the international workers' revolution.'[55]

Lenin, who was at Gorky recovering from the wounds suffered in the attempt on his life, wanted to return to Moscow at once, but his doctors insisted that he continue his convalescence. On 3 October, therefore, when the All-Russian Central Executive Committee assembled in joint session with numerous other Soviet bodies, Sverdlov presided and read a letter from Lenin to the meeting. This letter is interesting, for while it faithfully echoed the themes contained in his earlier notes to Sverdlov and Trotsky it also qualified his initial views on the situation in Germany. Written after further information had reached Russia it may have reflected the wary advice of Ioffe. At any rate, it displayed a greater understanding of the complexities inherent in the embryonic German revolution and took a more sober view of what might happen as it developed. Although Lenin still painted a picture of Germany tottering on the brink

55 *Ibid.*, 185-6. Emphasis in original

of revolution, he now tended very subtly to downgrade the crisis, saying that it meant '*either* that the revolution has begun *or* at any rate that the people have realized it is inevitable and imminent.' He said that 'the most kaleidoscopic changes' were still possible and warned that 'there may be attempts to form an alliance between German and Anglo-French imperialism against the Soviet government.' This obviously worried Lenin, for although he said that 'circumstances *may* require us to come to the aid of the German people' he was careful to specify that for the present 'the Soviet government will certainly not help the German imperialists by attempting to violate the Brest-Litovsk Peace Treaty.' Even when the German workers were victorious he predicted that they 'would have the gravest trials ahead of them, because the defeat of German imperialism will for a while have the effect of increasing the insolence, brutality, reaction and annexatory attempts of British and French imperialism.'[56] Here was the key to Lenin's caution, for no matter how welcome a revolution in Germany might be, it would have the immediate consequence of vastly strengthening the entente and perhaps give the western powers an opportunity to strangle the revolution in Russia. These thoughts weighed heavily on Lenin and influenced the emphasis which he placed on building an ever-stronger Red army. In the weeks to come they would take more definite form.

When Trotsky rose to speak he struck a much more optimistic note. Amidst prolonged applause he publicly acknowledged the wisdom of Lenin's foreign policy which had permitted Soviet Russia to survive and witness the beginning of the revolution in Germany, but while not taking issue with his chief, he again assumed a stance at variance with him. Trotsky's entire address exuded confidence, celebrating in triumphant rhetoric the collapse of German imperialism. Whereas Lenin peered anxiously at the advancing wave of 'western imperialism' Trotsky proclaimed that revolutionary Germany would unite with Soviet Russia to form a bloc of two hundred million people 'about which all the waves of imperialism will shatter.' The distance which Trotsky had travelled in the few days since the beginning of the German crisis can be seen by comparing his address of 3 October with remarks he made on 30 September. In the latter, he had warned of the danger from the western powers and spoken of the necessity of convincing them that the Bolsheviks only wanted to 'live and let live.'[57] On 3 October, this was all forgotten, and he proclaimed that

56 *Ibid.*, vol. XXXVII, 97-100. Emphasis added
57 Trotsky, *Kak Vooruzhulas'*, vol. I, 365

given the success of the German revolution the 'fundamental task' for Soviet Russia would be 'not to know national borders in the revolutionary struggle.' His fertile imagination, in fact, had already skipped over the Rhine and settled comfortably in the streets of Paris. The victory of the revolution in Germany, he assured his listeners, would radically alter the entire world situation and be of especial importance for France. Heretofore the French workers had been deterred by the fear of German imperialism, but 'on the day after the working class seizes power in Germany,' he predicted, 'the barricades will go up in Paris.'

Trotsky also pointed to the 'special significance' which the collapse of Germany had for the Ukraine. With the demise of German imperialism it would be possible to make good the losses suffered at Brest-Litovsk. Revolutionary enthusiasm, he said, was already mounting sharply in the Ukraine, and it would soon be possible to restore Soviet rule in the south. Bowing to Lenin he admitted that Soviet Russia could not indulge in 'any reckless adventurous steps,' but it was clear that he impatiently awaited the day when he could order the Red army to march on Kiev, Berlin, and perhaps even Paris.[58]

In early October, therefore, many of the differences which had distinguished Lenin and Trotsky earlier in the year could still be observed in their reaction to the emerging revolution in Germany. Despite Trotsky's tardy endorsement of Lenin's foreign policy the two men remained as far apart as ever, divided more by temperament and thought processes than by doctrine. Both subscribed to the same faith, worshipped at the same shrines and had their eyes fixed on the same goal, but whereas the brilliant mind of Trotsky, in reaching out to encompass the entire world, tended repeatedly to confuse wish with reality, the more penetrating intellect of Lenin did not suffer from this affliction. Lenin, who daily revised his estimate of the political situation, delighted in shaping theories to explain the phenomena which he observed but thought nothing of scrapping even his most treasured theories once new data showed that they distorted rather than clarified reality. In the excitement generated by the news from Germany, Trotsky virtually reverted to the views which he had held earlier in the year and dreamed of the triumphal march of the revolution to Paris and beyond. Lenin, after a few brief hours of revolutionary exaltation, saw clearly the dangers which lurked in the shadows of the new political configuration in Europe and, while hoping for the best, began to prepare for less attractive contingencies.

58 *Ibid.*, 366-74

The foreign commissariat shared Lenin's concern. Although *Pravda* and *Izvestiia* churned out a steady stream of glowing reports about the revolutionary situation in central Europe, and Karl Radek distinguished himself in journalistically kicking the yet unburied 'corpse' of world imperialism,[59] the Narkomindel viewed events in Germany and the rest of Europe with apprehension and even trepidation. Radek might jest with Ioffe, telling him that the Germans were taking too long to reorganize their government and suggesting that the ambassador show them 'how according to our experience it is done,' but Ioffe was not amused. He was appalled by the sudden burst of revolutionary propaganda and warned Moscow that the unexpected turn in Soviet policy 'would spoil everything.'[60] Chicherin had also been disturbed by Lenin's first pronouncement on the German revolution,[61] and although his mind had been set at ease by the letter read to the meeting of 3 October, he still viewed the changing international scene with anxiety. On 4 October, he wrote Ian Berzin, the Soviet representative in Switzerland, that 'the position grows more complicated with each day. We feel that the situation has never been so dangerous as now.'[62]

During October, the Soviet sense of insecurity continued to mount. Each day brought the defeat of Germany closer and, with it, the destruction of the shield which the supplementary treaties had momentarily erected over Russia's exposed western and southern frontiers. In essence, Germany's disintegration was proceeding *too rapidly* for the good of Soviet Russia. On the one hand, the Bolsheviks needed more time to rebuild Russia's armed forces, while on the other, radical groups in Germany needed more time to organize a revolutionary party-capable of seizing power when the old regime finally fell. On 9 October, Lenin lamented: 'Europe's greatest misfortune and danger [read: *my* greatest misfortune and danger] is that it has *no* revolutionary party. It has parties of traitors like the Scheidemanns, Renaudels, Hendersons, Webb and Co., and of servile souls like Kautsky. But it has no revolutionary party.' It was possible, he believed, that 'a mighty, popular revolutionary movement may rectify this deficiency, but it is nevertheless a serious misfortune and a

59 See Radek's articles in *Izvestiia* written under the pseudonym 'Viator,' 4, 5, 18, and 20 Oct. 1918
60 Baumgart, *Deutsche Ostpolitik*, 329
61 Zarnitskii and Sergeev, *Chicherin*, 105
62 Gorokhov, Zamiatin, and Zemskov, *G.V. Chicherin*, 47

grave danger.'[63] To M. Philips Price he confided: 'I fear that the social revolution in Central Europe is developing too slowly to provide us with any assistance from that quarter.'[64]

Every day brought entente forces closer to Soviet Russia. Lenin viewed the disintegration of Ottoman Turkey with special alarm. Collapsing at an even faster rate than Germany it was only a matter of days before it would capitulate to the allies. And what then? The Black Sea and the Caucasus would be open to the western powers, and they would no longer have to wage war against Soviet Russia in the inhospitable wastes of the Arctic and Siberia. For this reason Lenin had pressed the Turks to surrender Baku, and the refusal of the sultan's government to hand over the city augured ill for the future. Lenin's eyes were riveted on the Dardanelles, and on 18 October, he wrote Ioffe that 'everything is centered on whether the entente can disembark a large force on the Black Sea.' If they could, Soviet Russia would be in deadly peril, for the Red army remained woefully unprepared to oppose a large and well-equipped western force. 'The fundamental difference between February 1918 and now, is that at that time we *had* the possibility of playing for time and surrendering land,' he told Ioffe, adding ominously, 'now *there is no* such possibility.'[65]

The Soviet leaders began to crank up their distress signals. Believing that public opinion had to be prepared for the struggle against the entente they began to pour cold water on the expectation of immediate success for the world revolutionary movement. On 20 October, Sverdlov led off by telling the delegates to a Bolshevik conference that: 'We have perhaps never been so close to catastrophe as now. We must count on an attack of English-French troops.'[66] Lenin followed two days later with an address to a special session of the All-Russian Central Executive Committee meeting jointly with the Moscow Soviet and trade union leaders. Sounding the key note of the campaign Lenin began his presentation by stating that 'our present situation, for all its contradictions, might be expressed by saying, firstly, that never before have we been so near the world workers' revolution, and secondly, that never have we been in such a perilous position.' In words almost reminiscent of the bleak days of February, he declared that 'the people at large scarcely realize the full danger bearing down on us' and said that 'the chief task of the representatives of the Soviet gov-

63 Lenin, PSS, vol. XXXVII, 110. Emphasis in original
64 Price, *Reminiscences*, 345
65 Lenin, PSS, vol. L, 195. Emphasis in original
66 I.I. Mints and E.N. Gorodetskii (eds.), *Dokumenty o razgrome germanskikh okkupantov na Ukraine v 1918 g.* (Moscow, 1942), 191

ernment is to bring home to the people the full truth of the present situation, however difficult this may sometimes be.' He skipped over his first proposition quickly, saying that 'it has been spoken about time and again' and concentrated on dispelling the false optimism rampant in Russia. Due to the success of the Russian revolution and the example which it set for the working class of all other lands, he said, Soviet Russia had become a serious threat to the world bourgeoisie. Realizing that there was 'no force, no counter-revolution' in Russia which could overthrow the Soviet government, the western powers were now compelled to take matters in their own hands. Those in Russia who believed that the defeat of the Cossacks and Czechs had settled everything were mistaken, for they did not realize 'that there is a new enemy, a far more formidable one: British and French imperialism.' It was necessary 'to open the people's eyes,' for soon the new enemy would descend on Russia 'either through the Dardanelles and Black Sea or else overland through Bulgaria and Rumania.' It was no good, he declared, to expect the German revolution to save Soviet Russia, because it was impossible to determine how the revolution in Germany would develop. That revolution might fall short of Bolshevik expectations. 'A popular revolution and *perhaps* a proletarian revolution' was 'inevitable' in Germany, but in the meanwhile, he warned, 'a tacit bargain has most definitely been struck between the German bourgeoisie and that of the entente powers,' in which the former would allow the latter to occupy the Ukraine in exchange for leaving 'a portion of the spoils' to Germany. The southern front, he said, had become a 'front against British and French imperialism' and, consequently, it was essential to give 'prime attention to the army.' Stressing the importance of expanding the Red army he concluded with a declaration which again emphasized how little he counted on the German revolution. '*Our forces*,' he declared, 'must grow daily, and *this constant growth is, as it was, our chief and complete guarantee* that world socialism will triumph!'[67]

Long before this address, Lenin had already initiated measures to cope with the threatening international situation. They may be grouped under five general headings and described as measures to enhance Soviet military potential, to utilize the borderlands for the defence of Russia, to influence the developing revolutionary situation in central Europe, to initiate negotiations with the western powers, and to take advantage of German weakness to escape the obligations assumed at Brest-Litovsk and Berlin.

67 Lenin, PSS, vol. XXXVII, 111-25. Emphasis added

Militarily, there was no way to fulfil Lenin's rhetorical demand for a ten-fold increase in the size of the Red army, but in October new measures were introduced to enlarge it as quickly as possible. This, of course, would take time, and as it was decided on 23 October to pour the new recruits into a reserve army subordinate directly to the supreme command,[68] the immediate threat of western attack had to be met in the same way as the Czechs had been overcome in August and September. The Bolsheviks had to drain troops from fronts which were secure to reinforce areas threatened by the entente. Essentially this meant postponing a further development of offensive operations in the east and the transfer of all available military formations to the southern front. As early as 7 October, the Red army supreme command had pointed to the need for this redistribution of forces. In a lengthy memorandum I.I. Vatsetis, the newly appointed commander-in-chief, argued that economic as well as strategic considerations demanded this change. 'In the east,' he said, 'we are separated mainly from bread and fat, but in the south, we are separated from almost everything that the country needs to live – bread, livestock, fat, and especially fuel and raw materials for industry.' By launching an offensive in the south, he concluded, 'we will sooner attain the necessary means for life without which the centre of the country can not exist.'[69] The collapse of Turkey and the anticipated appearance of the British fleet in the Black Sea reinforced his arguments. If the Red army did not launch a major offensive against Krasnov before the arrival of western forces, said the commander of the southern front, the entente would be able to form a powerful anti-Soviet alliance composed of the Cossacks, the volunteer army, and the Ukraine. It was necessary, he believed, to strike at the centre of this alliance before it could come into existence and eliminate Krasnov as a threat to Soviet Russia.[70] Lenin agreed, but before transferring troops from the east it was first necessary to secure the Volga from enemy attack. The important Izhevsk and Votkinsk region, with its vital munitions factories, was not overrun until early November,[71] and only in the middle of the month was it possible to order the movement of a sizeable number of troops to the south.[72] By then the rapid development of the international situation had shifted the focus of Soviet interest from the

68 DGKKA, 194-5
69 *Ibid.*, 117-27
70 *Ibid.*, 240-7
71 Lenin, PSS, vol. L, 197; 202; 451, n.201
72 DGKKA, 284-5; DKFKA, vol. I, 708

Don to the Ukraine where a decisive confrontation with the western powers had begun to take shape.

In preparing their defence against the expected allied attack, the Bolsheviks faced a special problem in the borderlands and particularly in the Ukraine. On the one hand, they would have liked to expel the Germans from these regions as quickly as possible, but, on the other, they did not wish to provoke Germany prematurely and give the advocates of a German 'conspiracy' with the allies a pretext to launch an anti-Bolshevik crusade. The issue was further complicated by Bolsheviks from the borderlands who clamoured for assistance in expelling the German army and those who argued against such assistance in the belief that the occupying forces, if left unmolested, would fall ready prey to Bolshevik propaganda and, like the Russian army a year before, throw in their lot with the revolution. Prudence dictated a policy of watchful waiting, and it is no doubt significant that Lenin, unlike Trotsky, made no reference to the borderlands in his messages of early October. The absence of any substantial force with which to drive the Germans from the borderlands probably proved decisive in resolving the issue.

On 22 October, in his speech to the All-Russian Central Executive Committee, Lenin made a special point of addressing himself to this problem. Using the Ukraine as an example he expressed his understanding of those who wished 'to give vent to their pent-up hatred and resentment by attacking the German imperialists at once, regardless of everything,' but insisted that such emotions had to be suppressed and that the question be viewed solely from the 'internationalist' point of view. From this perspective, he said, it could be seen that any premature effort to liberate the borderlands would only play into the hands of German imperialism and interfere with the demoralization and disintegration of the German army. 'Our chief task,' he said, 'is to carry on propaganda for a revolt in the Ukraine' while abstaining for the moment from any provocative act against the Germans.[73] This ruling was immediately enforced upon the Ukrainian Communist party and the Bolshevik organizations active in the other regions of the former Russian empire occupied by Germany. Both groups were meeting in Moscow at this time, and resolutions were passed at the Second Congress of the Ukrainian Communist party and at a conference of Bolsheviks from White Russia, Lithuania, Latvia, Poland, Estotonia, and Finland denouncing any unauthorized initiation of partisan war-

73 Lenin, PSS, vol. XXXVII, 120-1

fare or efforts to provoke insurrections against the German army. Instead, the Bolsheviks of these regions were called upon to expand their party organizations, *prepare* for armed insurrection, conduct vigorous propaganda among the German occupation forces and coordinate their activities with the Communist party of Russia.[74] For its part, the Soviet government began to prepare for the moment when it would be possible to re-occupy the borderlands. To provide troops for this enterprise the supreme command decided to organize a new army to be stationed along the Ukrainian frontier; based at Orel, its divisions were to be operational no later than 1 December.[75] Furthermore, recruits from the Ukraine were encouraged to join this army,[76] and in early November two Ukrainian divisions were added to its structure.[77] Recruits from the other occupied territories were also formed into units for later use in the liberation of their homelands.[78]

These measures proved inadequate. Based on the assumption that imperial Germany had a life expectancy somewhat longer than proved to be the case Soviet military preparations were overtaken and passed by the sudden eruption of revolution in the Reich. The equally sudden capitulation at Compiègne and the stipulation included in the armistice that the German army should maintain order in eastern Europe until replaced by allied troops rendered the preparations useless. The entire policy had to be junked and a new one improvised to cope with the vastly altered situation. On 12 November, the Soviet government decided to invade the Ukraine, appointing Vladimir Antonov-Ovseenko to command this operation and giving him ten days to prepare his attack.[79] Shortly thereafter Moscow also ordered the Red army into the Baltic provinces and the occupied portion of White Russia. Ready or not, the Bolsheviks had to move quickly if they were to recapture the borderlands before the arrival of western armies.

Bolshevik measures to influence the developing revolutionary situation in central Europe were also tardy and inadequate. Due to insufficient documentation it is not yet possible to examine this question fully, but the

74 Institut Istorii Akedemii Nauk Lit. SSR, Institut Istorii Partii pri TsK KP Litvy – filial Instituta Marksizma-Leninizma pri TsK KPSS, Arkhivnoe Upravlenie pri SM Litovskoi SSSR, Tsentralynyi Gosudarstvennyi Arkhiv Lit SSR, *Bor'ba za Sovetskuiu Vlast' v Litve v 1918-1920 gg. Sbornik Dokumentov* (Vil'nius, 1967) 32-3. Hereafter cited as BzSVvL. Also see GVU, vol. I, part 1, 377-9
75 DGKKA, 194-5
76 GVU, vol. I, part 1, 384
77 DGKKA, 195-6
78 BzSVvL, 33
79 Vladimir A. Antonov-Ovseenko, *Zapiski o grazhdanskoi voine.* Four vols. (Moscow, 1924-33) Vol. III, 11-15

available evidence suggests that, contrary to views expressed at the time and in subsequent years, the Bolsheviks actually did little to hasten the pace of revolution outside the frontiers of the former Russian empire. In the provinces of the old empire occupied by German troops they still could command an illegal party apparatus and were able to conduct an extensive propaganda, especially in the last months of 1918,[80] but elsewhere in Europe they were severely hampered by the absence of clandestine organizations capable of outwitting the police. Ioffe found ways of publishing some illegal literature in Germany and disseminated it through his contacts among German radicals,[81] but only in Switzerland were the Bolsheviks able to publish freely. This left them with the problem of transporting their publications to other parts of Europe where they might prove useful in the struggle against their enemies. Little evidence is available to indicate how successful they were in this venture, but leaving this question aside there remains that of how much revolutionary literature Bolshevik agents actually produced at this time. From Lenin's correspondence it would seem that prior to mid-October very little literature had been prepared by the Soviet representatives in Switzerland and Germany. Thus, on 15 October, Lenin wrote Ian Berzin in Switzerland: 'I have just received from Sverdlov a complete set of your publications (there would have been nothing wrong in sending me this complete set). Little!!! *Hire* a group of translators and publish ten times more ... (It is necessary to hire translators in order to publish in *four* languages: *French*, *German*, *English*, and *Italian*.) You have *nothing* in the last two. Scandal! Scandal!'[82] Three days later, Lenin wrote in a similar manner to Ioffe, telling him: 'We ought to play the role of a bureau for ideological work of an international character, and we have not done anything!! It is necessary to publish one hundred times more. There is money. Hire translators. And we are not doing anything! Scandal ...'[83] But time was passing swiftly, and the Bolshevik propaganda machine was never able to go into high gear. Lenin's order for the accelerated publication of Bolshevik literature was not issued until mid-October, and by early November it was already out of date. On 5 November, Ioffe together with the entire staff of the Soviet embassy in Berlin was expelled from Germany, and, a week later, Berzin was forced

---

80 Selesnjow, 'Die Propaganda,' 158-9
81 See below, 391-2
82 Lenin, pss, vol. l, 192-3. Emphasis in original
83 *Ibid.*, 194-5

to leave Switzerland. The entire apparatus for the distribution of Soviet propaganda in central Europe was smashed and played little role in the tumultuous events which rocked the continent in November 1918.

Soviet efforts to negotiate with the allied powers were begun somewhat earlier than other measures to cope with the changing international situation but enjoyed no greater success. As early as mid-September, the Narkomindel had begun to extend peace feelers to the western powers. While Lockhart was still imprisoned in the Kremlin, Karakhan visited him on several occasions, 'nominally,' in the words of the British agent, 'to discover how I was being treated, [but] in reality to talk about the political situation.'[84] Karakhan said the Bolsheviks 'were prepared to go a long way in order to induce the allies to abandon intervention' and quite bluntly asked Lockhart 'what England and Japan would "take" to withdraw.' In return for an end to hostilities, he said, the Soviet government was prepared to reconsider the repudiation of loans contracted by previous Russian governments and 'to offer commercial and even territorial privileges to the Allies.' Lockhart, who rather relished the 'absurdity' of this situation in which he, an accused 'murderer and assassin' was being asked to convey peace overtures to his government, held out little hope that the Bolshevik proposals would be accepted. Nevertheless, given the delicacy of his position, he was careful to keep the Bolsheviks interested in continuing the talks until his departure and informed the foreign office of them when he reached London.[85]

French representatives returning from Russia brought similar proposals. General Lavergne, who was allowed to leave Moscow at the same time as Lockhart, reported that the Bolsheviks were eager to initiate negotiations with France, while Paul Dufour, arriving two weeks later, carried a detailed plan for the settlement of Franco-Soviet differences. Dufour, a businessman who had served as French consular agent at Nizhni Novgorod, was also an acquaintance of Leonid Krasin. Krasin and Chicherin had told him that the Soviet government was ready to recognize Russia's prewar debts, compensate French businessmen for the loss of property nationalized by the Soviet state and grant concessions to those entrepreneurs interested in developing Russian natural resources. The same economic privileges accorded to Germany by the supplementary treaties of 27

84 Chicherin was rather vague on this particular question, simply saying, without providing any details, that 'from the first difficulties with the entente, Vladimir Il'ich insisted on our turning to their governments with peace proposals.' Chicherin, 'Lenin i vneshniaia politika,' 7
85 PRO FO 371/3344/186867

August 1918 would be extended to France. Chicherin had put these proposals in writing and asked Dufour to submit them to the French government.[86]

Nothing came of these Bolshevik initiatives, but even before the British and French agents had left Russia the Soviet government began to seek other ways of involving the allies in peace negotiations. On 30 September, in response to a British radio message concerning the exchange of prisoners,[87] Chicherin ostentatiously thanked the British foreign secretary for his 'kind message' and emphasized the 'particular pleasure' of the Soviet government in receiving a communication directly from London. Such communication, he said, would facilitate the exchange of prisoners and permit the two governments to settle their differences without the meddlesome interference of the Dutch envoy in Petrograd. Oudendijk, said Chicherin, had blundered consistently, and his rude behaviour made it difficult to negotiate even the simplest agreements; his conduct, in fact, made 'it impossible ... to continue the transactions through his medium.'[88] This was an obvious hint that the Bolsheviks wanted to initiate direct negotiations with London, but the British turned a deaf ear to Chicherin. His message was ignored at the foreign office.

By mid-October, the Bolsheviks had grown more desperate. By then they had fully evaluated the threat posed by the victorious western alliance and were more eager than ever to initiate negotiations. On 11 October, Chicherin wrote Ioffe:

At any time, we ... are prepared to do that which is necessary to secure peace for us, if only the conditions will be acceptable. This task is one of the most important for all our representatives who have the possibility of meeting with representatives of the entente or politicians connected with them. While not appearing too eager and not conveying the impression that it seems we are crying for mercy, it is necessary, if the opportunity offers itself, to make it understood that we desire nothing but to live in peace with everyone. They must tell us their conditions. Of course, we are unable to sanction an occupation by the entente replacing that of the Germans. If they will tell us precisely what they want, however, we will consider it.[89]

86 MG, Campagne contre Allemagne 6N, 237, l'attaché militaire à Clemenceau (Stockholm, le 10 octobre 1918). MAE, Europe 1918-29, Russie, vol. 6, 37-40
87 See above, 364-5
88 PRO FO 371/3336/164855
89 Cited in Gorokhov, Zamiatin, and Zemskov, G.V. Chicherin, 47-8

Presumably this message was also sent to the Soviet representative in Stockholm, for a week later Vorovskii made overtures in this vein to Sir Mansfeldt Findlay the British minister in Norway. Acting through Ludwig Meyer, a Norwegian socialist, Vorovskii informed Findlay that he was ready to travel to Kristiania if this would promote negotiations between the Soviet and British governments. Meyer urged Findlay to accept this proposal, saying that he believed that it was possible to arrive 'at an arrangement with the Bolshevik government through which Russia might enter into a more peaceful phase of development.' Findlay, however, refused to meet Vorovskii without the permission of his government, and, in London, the foreign office rejected the proposal. 'I can not believe,' wrote Sir Ronald Graham, 'that any arrangement is possible with the Bolsheviks, now or in the future ... They are fanatics who are not bound by any ordinary codes.'[90] The foreign office similarly ignored statements made by Litvinov in Stockholm that the Soviet government wished to renew negotiations with Britain.[91]

The failure to interest London in direct negotiations forced Moscow to look elsewhere for a way of involving the western powers in peace talks. Like so many other governments at this time the Soviet government turned to Woodrow Wilson, but unlike the others which went hat in hand to the American president the Soviet government assumed a very different posture. The enormous prestige which Wilson had acquired through the growth of American power represented both an opportunity and a threat to Soviet Russia; an opportunity because Wilson might be prepared to negotiate a settlement with Moscow, a threat because his immense prestige might be put at the service of the pan-capitalist alliance which the Bolsheviks feared. At the very least Wilson championed a political creed totally alien to the Bolsheviks and was a formidable rival for the hearts and minds of the European masses. The Bolsheviks hoped to negotiate a settlement with Wilson, but before doing so they had to show the world that they were not intimidated by the American president or ready to accept his ideals as anything but the crassest hypocrisy. In October 1918, Soviet leaders obviously looked upon Wilson as a serious threat and decided to 'soften him up' before making a direct approach in search of peace.

Lenin personally directed this task. On 10 October, he ordered the Narkomindel to compose an 'arch-detailed, polite but poisonous' letter to the American president. 'We shall say to Wilson,' wrote Lenin, 'that we con-

90 PRO FO 371/3344/175192
91 *Ibid.*, 371/3321/179604

sider it our duty to propose peace – even to governments of capitalists and billionaires – in order to seek to end the bloodshed and *to open the eyes of the people.*' He suggested that Chicherin address Wilson in the following terms: 'Don't the capitalists want part of the forests of the North [and] part of Siberia? Don't they want the interest on the seventeen billion [rubles of the tsarist debt]? If this is so, then they shouldn't hide this. We welcome you: state directly, *how much*? Concerning the Brest peace Germany has agreed to remove her troops. What's the matter? Wouldn't you like *your troops* to take the place of the Germans?'[92] Chicherin, Karl Radek and other sharp-penned members of the Soviet government spent nearly two weeks in preparing their slashing attack on Wilson.[93] The resulting screed, broadcast to the world on 24 October, represents one of the finest products of the propagandist's art. Sarcastically addressing Wilson as 'Mr President' and subjecting his fourteen points to a devastating analysis, the authors first indicted him as a treacherous villain dealing in hypocrisy, plunder, and murder. After they had contemptuously dismissed him as a tool of Wall Street, however, they proceeded to declare the willingness of the Soviet government to negotiate with him. They said:

... since we have no desire to wage war against the United States, even though your government has not yet been replaced by a Council of People's Commissars and your post is not yet taken by Eugene Debs ... we finally propose to you, Mr. President, that you take up with your allies the following questions and give us precise and businesslike replies: will the governments of the United States, England and France cease demanding the blood of the Russian people ... if the Russian people agree to pay them a ransom, such as a man who has been suddenly set upon pays to the one who attacked him? If so, precisely what tribute do the governments ... demand of the Russian people? Do they demand concessions, do they demand territorial concessions, some part of Siberia, or the Caucasus or perhaps the Murmansk coast?

Anticipating that Wilson would not reply to this message they concluded by saying that if they did not receive an answer 'the Russian people will then understand that the demands of your government and of the Governments of your allies are so severe and extensive that you are unwilling to communicate them to the Russian government.'[94]

92 Lenin, PSS, vol. L, 188-91. Emphasis in original
93 Price, *Reminiscences*, 344
94 DVP, vol. I, 531-9

Unfortunately for the Soviet government, the fast-moving events of late October and early November robbed their note of most of its propaganda value. Amid the rumble of crashing thrones and collapsing empires it was barely noticed. Worse yet, the magnitude of allied victory grew with every passing day, and the Soviet government had to accelerate its peace offensive, shifting from propaganda to a straightforward campaign to initiate negotiations with the western powers. It was no longer possible to seek peace secretly or anticipate that the allies, aroused by propaganda broadsides or discrete hints dropped in high places, might initiate negotiations themselves. The allies had to be approached directly, and on 3 November, Chicherin addressed a note to the Norwegian and Swedish ministers in Petrograd asking them to transmit peace proposals to the western capitals. These were unambiguous and totally devoid of propaganda, simply stating that the Soviet government wished to end hostilities between its armed forces and those of the allies and proposing the prompt beginning of negotiations to liquidate the conflict. Chicherin asked the allied governments to set the time and place of the negotiations.[95] In confidence, the foreign commissar also asked the Norwegian minister to inform the western capitals that the Soviet government was 'prepared to go very far with regard to concessions to the entente powers with a view of arriving at an understanding.'[96]

The official Soviet peace proposal received a very cold reception in the western capitals. At the lowest level of the foreign office, E.H. Carr was bold enough to suggest that 'an understanding with the Bolsheviks could ... be reached on the basis of the present position,' but further up the official ladder there was no sympathy for an agreement of any kind with Soviet Russia. 'Now that our enemies are defeated,' wrote Lord Robert Cecil, 'the chief danger to this country is Bolshevism.'[97] This sentiment was shared by the French government. Pichon, the French foreign minister, wrote on the telegram bearing the Soviet peace proposal: 'We do not have the least desire to enter into talks with the Bolsheviks.'[98] The allied and associated powers quickly agreed with the British decision that it was 'premature to enter into any relationship with the Bolshevik Government in Russia or, for the present, to send any reply to the advances which they have made through the Norwegian Government.'[99] On 13 Novem-

95 *Ibid.*, 549
96 PRO FO 371/3344/184126
97 *Ibid.*
98 MAE, Europe, 1918-29, Russie, vol. 154, 10
99 PRO FO 371/3344/188836

ber, the war cabinet studied the Russian situation in depth, but did not even consider the Bolshevik proposal. Instead they endorsed a plan to enlarge, rather than reduce, British involvement in the Russian civil war.[100] Although France and Italy would soon take issue with various aspects of this plan they agreed in principle that the allies should aid those in Russia who were fighting the Bolsheviks. Nor were the Americans inclined to promote peace in Russia. In mid-October, Wilson had told Sir William Wiseman: 'My policy regarding Russia is very similar to my Mexican policy. I believe in letting them work out their own salvation, even though they wallow in anarchy for a while. I visualize it like this: A lot of impossible folk, fighting among themselves. You can not do business with them, so you shut them all up in a room and tell them that when they have settled matters among themselves you will unlock the door and do business.'[101] By early November nothing had happened to change his mind.[102] While the war in western Europe was ending, therefore, the conflict in Russia was destined to intensify. The entente, eager to consolidate its victory, was preparing to increase its support for the anti-Bolsheviks, and Wilson, for the moment, had decided to stand aside. Although the Bolsheviks hurriedly publicized their desire for peace, issuing declarations on 6 and 8 November that they wished nothing more than 'an end to the bloodshed,'[103] it was no use; their peace offensive had failed. The war in Russia would continue.

The changed international situation did provide Soviet Russia with one advantage: it no longer had to fear an attack from Germany. As early as 30 September, Trotsky had told the All-Russian Central Executive Committee that 'Germany no longer counts as a danger for us,'[104] and in succeeding weeks the Soviet government was able to treat the Imperial regime with an increasing firmness which sometimes bordered on insolence. Thus, Soviet leaders made no effort to conceal their satisfaction with the mounting internal turmoil within Germany, and on 22 October, Lenin even sent his greetings to Karl Liebknecht when the leader of the Spartacist movement was released from prison.[105] In general, however, the new Soviet attitude was expressed in the number and tone of official notes

100 *Ibid.*, 371/3344/188740
101 *Ibid.*, 800/214/32
102 For the later shift in Wilson's view see A.J. Mayer, *Politics and Diplomacy of Peace Making* (New York, 1967) 21-3
103 DVP, vol. I, 556, 557-8
104 Trotsky, *Kak Vooruzhulas'*, 364
105 Lenin, PSS, vol. L, 198-9

addressed by the Narkomindel to the Imperial government protesting German violation of the Treaty of Brest-Litovsk and its supplements. These protests were concerned primarily with the seizure of Russian property by German troops withdrawing from White Russia and the assistance given anti-Bolshevik organizations in the regions still occupied by Germany. The Narkomindel demanded full compensation for the loss of Russian property[106] and warned Berlin that in the very near future the anti-Bolshevik military organizations which it was sheltering might well 'be converted into an English army to be used against Germany.'[107]

These complaints provided the Soviet government with a convenient pretext for denouncing the financial obligations which Russia had assumed in signing the supplementary treaties. In accepting these onerous obligations the Bolsheviks had believed they would receive something of value in return, and, at first, they had, but by late October, it was obvious to everyone that imperial Germany had become a derelict in international waters, hopelessly awash and wholly unable to fulfill its commitments. There was no further reason for the Bolsheviks to honour their promises, and, on 29 October, after peppering the Wilhelmstrasse with one last barrage of protests,[108] Chicherin announced that Soviet Russia would refuse to pay the third installment of the indemnity due Germany under the terms of their financial agreement. The Soviet government, he said, would make this payment only when Germany ceased violating the political agreement, returned the property which the German army had stolen in White Russia and discontinued aid for the anti-Bolsheviks which it protected.[109] In a confidential message to Ioffe, however, Chicherin revealed that the inability of Germany to meet its broader commitments to the Soviet government had caused Moscow to suspend the financial agreement. Pointing to Turkey's withdrawal from the war and Germany's failure to take any action to bar the Dardanelles, Chicherin asked: 'Why should we give them money, if, for their part, they cease observing the treaty and have openly passed to the side of those who, in fact, are conducting an offensive against us?' The foreign commissar instructed Ioffe to inform the German foreign ministry that the financial agreement would not be reinstated until Germany was able to fulfil all of its commitments to Russia.[110]

106 See for example DVP, vol. I, 510-11, 530-1
107 *Ibid.*, vol. I, 530. See also 529, 539-40, 540-1
108 *Ibid.*, 541-3
109 *Ibid.*, 543-4
110 Zarnitskii and Sergeev, *Chicherin,* 106

But the time for diplomatic bargaining had passed. The revolutionary tide was mounting in Germany, and the old Reich, quaking with each blow delivered by the allies, was ready to fall. Frustrations built up by years of authoritarian rule began to burst forth, and every group in Germany possessing a grievance against the old order came forward to present it. 'Only on my arrival here did I realize how completely the old Prussian system had broken down,' wrote the chancellor, Prince Max of Baden on 15 October, '... We are already in the middle of a revolution.'[111] In these circumstances the Bolsheviks were no longer primarily interested in their formal relations with the German government. On 18 October, Lenin wrote Ioffe that while he was not opposed to a continuation of Soviet diplomatic activity in Berlin, he believed that 'its significance has decreased,'[112] and Chicherin was later to write that during October, 'the rising revolutionary wave in Germany gradually forced the technical diplomatic work into the background.'[113] To the fore came assistance for the emerging revolutionary forces in Germany. Ioffe himself testified that the Soviet embassy in Berlin served 'as staff headquarters for a German revolution.' Almost every night, he said, 'left-wing Independent Socialist leaders slipped into the embassy building on Unter den Linden to consult on questions of tactics.'[114]

What assistance did the revolutionary forces in Germany receive from the Soviet embassy? According to Ioffe, who is the only Soviet source on the subject, he subsidized newspapers, collected information, paid for the printing of revolutionary literature and provided several hundred thousand marks for the purchase of arms. Most of this money, he said, was given to the Independent Social Democratic Party and the Revolutionary Shop Stewards who received it through various intermediaries.[115] It should be noted, however, that Ioffe gave his testimony *after* the German revolution had failed to develop in a manner satisfactory to the Bolsheviks and that his disclosures took the form of a polemic against the Independent Social Democrats and the Revolutionary Shop Stewards, both of which the Bolsheviks accused of betraying the revolution. Furthermore, Ioffe's statements are notable for the absence of any reference to the Spartacists,

111 Maximilian, Prince of Baden, *The Memoirs of Prince Max of Baden.* Two vols. (New York, 1928) vol. II, 85-7
112 Lenin, PSS, vol. L, 195
113 *Izvestiia*, 6 Nov. 1919
114 Louis Fischer, *Men and Politics: An Autobiography* (New York, 1941) 26
115 *Izvestiia*, 6 and 17 Dec. 1918; reprinted in Degras, *Soviet Documents on Foreign Policy*, vol. I, 127-8

the revolutionary group in Germany most closely akin to the Bolsheviks. It is inconceivable that the Bolsheviks did not subsidize Karl Liebknecht whom Lenin had publicly hailed as 'the representative of the revolutionary workers of Germany.'[116] Thus, in addition to providing assistance to the Independent Social Democrats and the Revolutionary Shop Stewards it is likely that he also provided substantial aid to the Spartacists as well. In all, he probably spent something in excess of a million marks attempting to promote a Bolshevik style revolution in Germany.

The German government had repeatedly been warned that the Bolsheviks might use the extra-territorial immunity of the embassy on Unter den Linden to spread revolutionary propaganda in Germany. From the time when diplomatic relations were established with Soviet Russia the Army high command had objected to the presence of 'offe in Berlin, and throughout the summer and fall, reports from German missions in Russia never failed to emphasize the danger of allowing the Soviet embassy to remain in Germany.[117] The *Auswärtiges Amt*, however, had shrugged off all these warnings, saying that it could not justify jeopardizing Germany's entire policy in Russia without substantial evidence to prove that the Bolsheviks were interfering in the internal affairs of Germany. The German police, in fact, were never able to obtain any evidence that Ioffe was violating his diplomatic immunity, and the foreign office, which placed a high value on the maintenance of German relations with Russia, would not allow any action to be taken against the Soviet embassy.

Military defeat, the decision to sue for peace and the rise of social unrest changed all this. Writing to Hintze on 22 October, Wilhelm Solf, the new foreign secretary, declared that the time had come to alter Germany's relations with Soviet Russia. Citing the Bolshevik dream 'of revolutionizing Germany' and the 'ever greater dimensions' of Soviet propaganda he said that while 'all possible measures' were being taken to end Soviet interference in the internal affairs of Germany 'it appears that only a complete breach of relations could snip off the threads leading from Russia to our country.' But this was not his primary concern. Foreseeing an end to the war he calculated that the Bolsheviks 'would then have everyone against them, and their rule will come to an end, probably in rivers of blood.' 'In these circumstances,' he concluded, 'I incline to the view that it would be better not to wait, but at a time of our choosing, act against them so that the expected bloodbath will not be put against our account as

116 Lenin, PSS, vol. L, 198-9
117 Baumgart, *Deutsche Ostpolitik*, 304-5

a result of our friendship with them.'[118] Solf, however, had little time to devote to Germany's relations with Russia. In the hectic days of October, with Germany desperately trying to negotiate an armistice with the western powers, he was transfixed by the conundrum of how to salvage the German empire from the wreckage of a lost war. Although in the middle of the month the government approved measures designed to save Germany's position in the Ukraine,[119] October passed without the cabinet having promulgated a new policy on Russia. In this vacuum the permanent officials of the foreign office simply continued to follow the policy in force under Kühlmann and Hintze. As late as 30 October, Kriege, acting under the stimulus of Chicherin's suspension of Soviet indemnity payments, pleaded with the army to cease requisitions in White Russia in order to avert a total renunciation of the supplementary treaties by the Bolsheviks.[120]

With the *Auswärtiges Amt* distracted by armistice negotiations the departments of the German government charged with protecting the internal security of the Reich took the lead in forcing a review of the policy which permitted Ioffe to remain in Berlin. As a result of their action the war cabinet of Prince Max von Baden discussed the problem on 28 October. At this meeting, the Prussian interior minister argued strongly that the Bolshevik embassy should be expelled from Berlin, but Rudolf Nadolny of the foreign office said that the proposed action would do more harm than good. Not only would it endanger the lives of Germans in Russia, it would also have an adverse impact on Germany's foreign policy. Again he pointed out that the police had no evidence to link the Soviet ambassador with German revolutionaries and reminded the meeting that Ioffe had dealt satisfactorily with every complaint filed against him. In conclusion, he remarked that although he personally suspected that the Bolsheviks were, in fact, spreading revolutionary propaganda in Germany it would do no good to expel their embassy because they would only find 'more refined' ways of bringing propaganda into the country.[121]

Nadolny's concluding remarks revealed a rather ambiguous side to his presentation. The memorandum which he read to the meeting undoubtedly reflected the prevailing views at the *Auswärtiges Amt*, but since late

118 *Ibid.*, 406-7
119 Max of Baden, *Memoirs*, vol. II, 102-42; also see Borowsky, *Deutsche Ukrainepolitik 1918*, 272-7
120 Baumgart, *Deutsche Ostpolitik*, 328
121 DSB, vol. I, 785-6; Erich Matthias and Rudolf Morsey (eds.), *Die Regierung des Prinzen Max von Baden* (Düsseldorf, 1962) 397-8, 412-15

September, Nadolny himself appears to have soured on continued relations with the Bolsheviks.[122] Moreover, in the discussion following the presentation Nadolny seems to have provided the meeting with a suggestion of how the police might obtain evidence which would warrant a rupture of relations with Soviet Russia. A month before, he explained, Soviet porters carrying a chest destined for the German consul-general in Petrograd had dropped it on the steps of the railway station causing it to break open and reveal a consignment of pistols being sent Breiter and his staff for their protection. 'Of course,' he said, 'that would never happen here.'[123] Due to the opaque quality of the minutes, obviously designed to conceal, rather than illuminate, the discussion, and the somewhat contradictory testimony contained in the memoirs of the men present at the meeting, it is unclear who first suggested this possibility. The minutes say nothing about Nadolny's comment but record that Philipp Scheidemann, the representative of the Social Democrats, suggested that evidence could be obtained by having one of the Soviet trunks 'accidentally' broken open to see if it contained propaganda. In his memoirs Scheidemann relates that he said there were two possibilities: 'a higher official might be found willing to "get the sack" for breaking into the Russian legation on his own ... [or] that somebody should instruct a few railway porters in the way of dropping a box ... in such a manner that it was bound to break.'[124] Regardless of who first thought of the idea it became the basis of the plan used to dispose of Ioffe and his embassy. Although the minutes simply record a decision to increase surveillance of the Soviet embassy in an effort to obtain evidence that the Bolsheviks were distributing propaganda in Germany it is evident that more than one individual left the meeting intent on ransacking the trunks being brought by diplomatic courier to the Soviet embassy. It is worth noting that at the end of the meeting Nadolny emphasized that if the Soviet embassy was to be expelled from Berlin it should be done in a 'refined manner' to minimize the consequences for Germans still inside Russia.[125]

In the next few days, events moved swiftly. In the north, sailors of the German fleet mutinied, and in the south, the revolution which had broken out in Austria threatened to sweep across the frontier into Bavaria. Almost hourly the crisis deepened, fed by reports from those parts of the

122 Baumgart, *Deutsche Ostpolitik*, 324-6
123 Rudolf Nadolny, *Mein Beitrag* (Wiesbaden, 1955) 62
124 Philipp Scheidemann, *The Making of a New Germany, The Memoirs of Philipp Scheidemann.* Two vols. (New York, 1929) vol. II, 534-5
125 Matthias and Morsey, *Die Regierung,* 414-15

Reich where the revolution had already begun. On 4 November, troops sent to restore order at Kiel and Wilhelmshaven went over to the side of the sailors, and the triumphant insurgents, following the example set in Russia, began to elect councils of deputies to represent them. With revolution imminent, leading figures of the German government decided to expel the Russian embassy from Berlin. It is still impossible to determine where, when, and by whom this decision was made. Perhaps the exact details will never be known, but it can be established that after the cabinet meeting of 28 October, officials at the *Auswärtiges Amt* reconsidered their policy regarding Russia and, by 31 October, Nadolny had prepared a memorandum in which he agreed that it was desirable for Germany to sever relations with the Bolsheviks. In contrast to his earlier view that it would do no good to drive the Soviet embassy from Berlin he now contended that 'the expulsion of the embassy, as the demonstrative central organ of Bolshevism in Germany, would bring with it a certain easing of the situation.' Primarily, however, he adopted Solf's argument that the end of the war would lead to the fall of the Bolsheviks, and, consequently, there was no reason for Germany to maintain its relations with a government which would soon perish anyway. He still insisted that Ioffe be expelled 'without any roughness' but outlined the 'official reasons' which could be given to explain the action of the German government. Bolshevik propaganda, refusal to pay the indemnity called for in the supplementary treaties and failure to provide adequate atonement for the murder of Mirbach would provide sufficient justification for the break. He advised, however, that before any steps were taken the army should be consulted to ascertain if there was any danger that the action might provoke a Russian attack.[126]

Hoffmann's assurance that the Bolsheviks were too weak to attack Germany reached Berlin at approximately the same time as a group of Bolshevik couriers bringing over one hundred trunks consigned to the Soviet embassy.[127] The police had kept a careful watch on the train bearing the couriers from the time it had crossed the demarcation line and were convinced that the trunks contained revolutionary literature. Due to the vigilance of the couriers, however, the police had been unable to break into the trunks and obtain the incriminating evidence they desired.[128] The police did not let this discourage them, and, undoubtedly with government

---

126 Baumgart, *Deutsche Ostpolitik*, 357
127 *Ibid.*
128 Matthias and Morsey, *Die Regierung*, 414, n.6

support, they developed a plan to cope with the situation. Someone, in fact, did 'instruct a few railway porters in the way of dropping a box,' and, in the words of the German chancellor, 'on the evening of 4 November, the Russian courier's packing case went to pieces ... *according to plan.*'[129] Leaving nothing to chance, the zealous police raced to the scene of the 'accident' with a bundle of revolutionary leaflets which they mixed with the other contents of the trunk.[130] Promptly 'discovering' the leaflets the police impounded the entire Soviet shipment and informed the *Auswärtiges Amt* that the Bolshevik couriers had been caught in the act of trying to smuggle revolutionary literature into Germany.

The machinery of the German government was promptly set in motion to rid Berlin of the Bolshevik menace. When Ioffe arrived at the Wilhelmstrasse on the morning of 5 November to protest against the action of the police he was met by a stony-faced official who gravely informed him of the leaflets 'discovered' in the broken trunk and the decision to expel the Soviet mission from Germany. A special train was already waiting, and the Bolsheviks would leave the next day. In the meanwhile the teleprinter link to Moscow had been severed, and the embassy surrounded by police. Anyone who wished could enter the building but no one would be permitted to leave.[131] Early on the morning of 6 November, a small caravan of police cars conveyed the 186 members of the Soviet embassy to the railway station where they were put aboard a train which would return them to Russia. The Bolsheviks had lost their outpost in Germany at exactly the moment when civil unrest was about to blossom into open revolution.

The action of the German government came as a complete surprise to the Bolsheviks. One member of Ioffe's mission described it as coming 'like a stroke of lightning out of a bright sky,'[132] and the speed with which the police acted left Ioffe little time to put his affairs in order. Before being escorted to the railway station the Soviet ambassador managed to transfer his remaining funds to Oskar Cohn, a member of the Reichstag and legal advisor to the embassy, whom he charged with disposing of them 'in the interests of the German revolution.'[133] Cohn evidently was unable to

---

129 Max of Baden, *Memoirs*, vol. II, 289. Emphasis added
130 This aspect of the 'accident' was not revealed until much later when *Klassenkampf*, the official organ of the Austrian Social Democratic party disclosed on 1 December 1927 that the revolutionary leaflets 'discovered' in the Soviet trunk were actually prepared and printed in Germany by the Spartacists.
131 Matthias and Morsey, *Die Regierung*, 541-2
132 M.J. Larsons, *Als Expert im Sowjetdienst* (Berlin, 1929) 31
133 *Izvestiia*, 17 Dec. 1918

make much use of this money. In December, he testified that most of it remained unspent and two months thereafter indicated that only a trifling amount had been used in the manner which Ioffe had wanted.[134] The expulsion of the Soviet embassy, therefore, would seem to have disrupted whatever financial support the Bolsheviks were providing German revolutionaries. The rupture evoked equal surprise in Moscow. After receiving an initial report from Ioffe concerning the action of the German government the teleprinter link with Berlin went dead, and the Narkomindel was left without further information until Hauschild called on Chicherin bearing the official German announcement of the rupture of relations.[135] On the following day Chicherin succeeded in contacting Nadolny, who had transferred the teleprinter terminal of the Soviet embassy to his own office, but the German diplomat simply repeated the official reasons which he had concocted to explain the break in relations. Nadolny probably enjoyed a good laugh when Chicherin, with obvious perplexity, spoke of the 'mysterious circumstances' surrounding the discovery of propaganda leaflets in the Soviet trunk and asserted that the leaflets 'as had been mentioned in yesterday's official statement, truly had not been sent by us.'[136] By this time Ioffe was already many miles from Berlin, and the rupture was an accomplished fact. Wholly unprepared for this unforeseen event the Bolsheviks were unable to do anything to redeem the losses suffered as a consequence of the expulsion of their embassy from Berlin.

Soviet reaction to the rupture of relations with Germany took two forms. On the surface, the Bolsheviks attempted to shrug off the event as being of little consequence. In the developing revolutionary situation in central Europe, with 'Germany ... on fire and Austria ... all ablaze,' the breach of relations was said to pose no danger to Soviet Russia. The German decision, said Lenin, was 'ridiculous' and 'shows not so much that they want to fight us as that they have completely lost their heads.' The German government, he continued: 'is now making this move not because the situation has in any way changed, but because it formerly felt stronger, and was not afraid that one "burning" house on the streets of Berlin would set all Germany alight. The German government has lost its head, and now that the whole of Germany is ablaze it thinks it can put out the fire by turning its police hose on a single house.'[137]

134 *Das Werk des Untersuchungsausschusses der Deutschen Verfassunggebenden Nationalversammlung und des Deutschen Reichstag 1919-1928. Vierte Reihe: Die Ursachen des Deutschen Zusammenbruchs im Jahre 1918* (Berlin, 1927-9) vol. v, 69, 204-5
135 DVP, vol. I, 559
136 Baumgart, *Deutsche Ostpolitik*, 358, n.95
137 Lenin, PSS, vol. XXXVII, 150

On another level, however, the Bolsheviks took the rupture of relations very seriously. On learning of the German action Soviet leaders warned the Red army to prepare for a possible German attack or, what they considered more likely, 'an attack by the White Guard forces' which had been organized and protected by the German army.[138] To defend against either contingency the Soviet government ordered its armed forces to station armoured trains at strategic locations, to make preparations for destroying major railway centres and to launch 'extensive intelligence operations' to uncover whatever plans the Germans might have.[139] But the Soviet government was not primarily worried about an imminent attack either by the Germans or the bands of white-guardists camped on the German side of the demarcation line. Moscow was much more concerned that the rupture of relations signalled the first step in the forging of an anti-Bolshevik alliance against Soviet Russia.[140] If this alliance materialized it would threaten the very existence of Soviet Russia, and the Bolsheviks carefully scanned the political horizon for any sign of its appearance. On 8 November, in his major address to the Sixth All-Russian Congress of Soviets, Lenin again warned of this possibility and even suggested that the Soviet Republic might be 'suddenly wiped out' as a consequence of the new political configuration created by the end of the Great War in Europe.[141]

The sudden eruption of the German revolution provided a brief moment of optimism in the midst of these gloomy predictions. The situation appeared all the more promising, because, in addition to the genuine news concerning the fall of the Hohenzollerns, the first bulletins reported that the peace delegation sent by the imperial government to negotiate an armistice with the allied powers had been arrested when it reached the front and that German troops had taken the negotiations in their own hands, initiating peace talks directly with the French soldiers in the trenches opposite them.[142] Russian events of the year before seemed to be repeating themselves in Germany, and amidst the jubilant celebrations in Moscow[143] even Lenin gave vent to renewed optimism. Instead of completing his polemic, 'The Proletarian Revolution and the Renegade Kautsky,' he wrote: 'the conclusion which still remained to be written to my pamphlet on Kautsky and on the proletarian revolution is now super-

---

138 DVP, vol. I, 555-6. Also see Meijer, *The Trotsky Papers*, 171-2
139 DGKKA, 172-3
140 Lenin, PSS, vol. XXXVII, 148, 150
141 *Ibid.*, 156
142 *Ibid.*, vol. L, 202-3
143 See Price, *Reminiscences*, 348-9

fluous.'[144] The glorious events in Germany, it seemed, would deal more effectively with Kautsky than any amount of barbed rhetoric which might be hurled in his direction.

The Soviet government immediately gave its full attention to Germany. On the morning of 10 November telegrams and radio messages began to flow from Moscow in a steady stream seeking to link the Bolsheviks with the German revolution and exploit its impact on the international scene. While the Soviet radio relayed reports from Germany throughout Russia, stressing the importance of bringing them to the attention of German soldiers at all border points,[145] Lenin sent secret orders to Orel and Kursk instructing Soviet officials in the two provinces to contact the German troops in the Ukraine and advise them of what was happening in their homeland. 'It is necessary... ,' said Lenin, 'to advise them to attack the troops of Krasnov, because together we will then capture tens of millions of poods of grain for the German workers and repel the invasion of the English who now have a squadron approaching Novorossissk.'[146] At the same time the Narkomindel sought desperately to contact Ioffe. The German army was holding the Soviet ambassador and his party a short distance from the demarcation line, waiting to exchange the Bolsheviks for German diplomats still in Russia, but Chicherin could not locate them. When the ambassador could not be reached the foreign commissar telegraphed the headquarters of the German army hoping that revolutionary soldiers had displaced Hoffmann and would be able to assist Ioffe in returning to the German capital.[147] As the day wore on, however, the reports from Germany began to diminish, and by the end of the day, the British and French radio was providing more information about events in Germany than German transmitters. Worst of all, it had proved impossible to establish two-way contact with Berlin or German military formations in the occupied territories.

The next day the Soviet government tried again to contact Germany. In special session the All-Russian Central Executive Committee acted on Lenin's proposal to rush food to Germany and resolved to dispatch two trains bearing more than fifty thousand poods of grain to Berlin where it was 'to be put at the disposal of the struggle for the dictatorship of the proletariat and the power of the Soviet of Workers and Soldiers in Ger-

144 Lenin, PSS, vol. XXXVII, 331
145 *Ibid.*, 183-4
146 *Ibid.*, vol. L, 202-3
147 Zarnitskii and Sergeev, *Chicherin,* 108

many.'[148] Radio Moscow immediately broadcast this resolution together with a renewed appeal for the revolutionary authorities in the German capital to arrange a full restoration of diplomatic relations with Russia. While this message was being transmitted, German prisoners-of-war took charge of the German consulate-general in Moscow. The Narkomindel gladly recognized this change in management, and Chicherin hurried to the consulate-general to congratulate the new proprietors and ask for their assistance in contacting Berlin. The self-proclaimed German representatives succeeded in putting Chicherin in contact with Oskar Cohn but were unable to make any further connection with parties in Germany with whom Chicherin wished to speak.[149] Late that evening, in a desperate effort to bring the views of the Soviet government to the attention of German revolutionary leaders, Chicherin prepared a radio message for transmission to Berlin. Taking the form of a response to one of the first messages from Germany announcing the outbreak of revolution Chicherin's reply expressed 'the great joy' of the Soviet government over 'recent events in Berlin' but proceeded immediately to warn of the dangers which Moscow saw in the new situation. He expressed particular concern about the chaos which seemed prevalent in Germany, saying that it was an 'impediment to the liberation of the masses.' Essentially, however, Chicherin was eager to provide guidance for German revolutionaries sympathetic to Soviet Russia, and in his message he formulated both a creed and a practical program for their consideration:

We see salvation for the masses in the consistent revolutionary struggle against all enemies; we see the bearers of this struggle in the revolutionary movement directed by Liebknecht and connect with it our hopes in which we are certain of future victory. We are seeking to attain full unity with the revolutionary movement headed by Liebknecht. We put forward as practical tasks which must be accomplished the evacuation of the occupied region, the conclusion of an offensive and defensive alliance of the revolutionary socialist republics of soviets to which we add as necessary an active participation on the part of German troops against Krasnov's counter-revolutionary bands.[150]

148 DVP, vol. I, 564-5
149 Germany. Auswärtiges Amt. Politisches Archiv. Deutschland 131, Band 54, folio 129. St Antony's College Microfilm Collection, reel no. 102. Also see Winfried Baumgart (ed.), *Von Brest-Litowsk zur Deutschen Novemberrevolution. Aus den Tagebüchern, Briefen und Aufzeichnungen von Alfons Paquet, Wilhelm Groener und Albert Hopman. März bis November 1918* (Göttingen, 1971) 236
150 SGO, vol. I, 677

Neither this nor any of the other Soviet messages sent during the first days of the German revolution reached their intended recipients. Nadolny studiously avoided answering any of the messages which arrived on the direct wire from Moscow and also managed to intercept incoming radio traffic from Soviet Russia. 'I made use of the radio messages which were suitable for my purpose,' he later wrote, 'and threw the others in the wastepaper basket.' His purpose, of course, was to quarantine Germany from Bolshevik influence, and during the first critical days of the revolution he succeeded. The new government of Majority and Independent Socialists which had taken power on 9 November wanted nothing to do with the Soviet government and had readily agreed when Nadolny suggested that the entire question of Germany's relations with the Bolsheviks be dealt with in a 'dilatory manner.' When representatives of the Berlin Soviet, which was eager to have Ioffe return to the German capital, called on Nadolny seeking information concerning the whereabouts of the Soviet ambassador, he suffered a convenient lapse of memory. In response to their question of where the Russian embassy was located, he writes, 'I naturally answered that I did not know. I had to assume that the Russian embassy had already been in Moscow for some time. In reality it was still at Borisovo.'[151]

Although the Narkomindel finally located Ioffe, efforts to convince the German soldiers' council at Kovno to arrange his return to the German capital or accept delivery of the two train loads of grain for 'Red Berlin' proved unsuccessful.[152] The soldiers' councils in the Baltic and White Russia, in fact, were unwilling to cooperate with the Soviet government in any way. Unlike those which sprang up in Germany during the first days of the revolution the soldiers' councils formed in the field armies were called into existence from above, by the German general staff, which hoped by creating councils of trusted men to forestall the appearance of genuine soviets in the German army. The conclusion of an armistice with the western powers and the obligation to return Germany's far-flung armies to the Reich provided the German general staff with precisely the circumstances it needed to insure the maintenance of discipline within the ranks. Appealing to the army to retain its discipline in order to insure the prompt return of all soldiers to Germany the officer corps and their councils of trusted men succeeded in stemming the revolutionary tide.[153] Conse-

151 Nadolny, *Mein Beitrag*, 64
152 *Izvestiia*, 12 Nov. 1918
153 F.L. Carsten, *The Reichswehr and Politics, 1918-1933* (Oxford, 1966) 7-12

quently, the soldiers' council at Kovno would do nothing to assist the Bolsheviks and the great masses of soldiers, hypnotized by the prospect of rapid demobilization, were not prepared to take any action which might jeopardize their return home. The situation was similar in the Ukraine where Lenin had hoped that the German soldiers might become the allies of the Bolsheviks. Rather than taking up arms against Krasnov the German soldiers in the Ukraine grasped eagerly at the prospect of early demobilization. Although the soldiers of one small garrison fraternized with the Red army and sent their greetings to Lenin,[154] the German army in the Ukraine retained its discipline and remained subordinate to the officer corps. The Soviet appeal for a Russian-style revolution went unheeded. Already on 12 November, the pace and quality of the German revolution had diverged so greatly from the Russian model that the Soviet government felt compelled to issue a statement warning that extreme caution had to be exercised in evaluating the situation in Germany. The German revolution, said the Sovnarkom, might only have reached the stage of 'February' and not that of 'October.'[155]

Events of the following days fully justified this warning. The government of Ebert and Scheidemann steadily strengthened its hold on Germany and showed no inclination to restore diplomatic relations with Soviet Russia. On 14 November, in fact, Berlin announced that it did not recognize the authority of the German prisoners of war who had seized control of the German consulates-general in Russia, and demanded the immediate release of its official representatives. Ioffe and his staff, said the German government, would be brought to Orsha where they would be allowed to cross the demarcation line when the German diplomats from Moscow and Petrograd were permitted to leave Russia. This message with its obvious implication that the German government did not intend to restore diplomatic relations evoked an angry response from Moscow. The same day Chicherin directed two telegrams to the new German government, one asking sarcastically if it intended to pursue the old policies of the Hohenzollern regime and the other accusing it of deliberately flouting the will of the Berlin Soviet which had called for the return of the Soviet ambassador to the German capital.[156] More importantly Chicherin also broadcast a radio message to the various soviets in Germany, appealing to them for the first time over the heads of the newly constituted

154 Lenin, pss, vol. L, 205-6; GVU, vol. I, part 1, 426
155 *Izvestiia*, 12 Nov. 1918
156 DVP, vol. I, 568-9

government of Majority and Independent Socialists. Outlining the proposals of the Soviet government relating to Russian-German cooperation he declared: 'We turn to you comrades, in order with your aid, to communicate with comrades in Berlin and *finally* to receive from them answers to some extraordinarily important questions. For some unexplained reason we have not received any answers to these questions. We are beginning to suspect that our questions have not yet even been received by those to whom they were addressed.'[157] The foreign commissar might just as well have saved his breath. Nadolny still controlled the channels through which the soviet government communicated with Germany, and he did not allow any of these messages to be made public. The German cabinet read all the messages from Moscow but continued to pursue the 'dilatory' policy recommended by the *Auswärtiges Amt*.[158] On 18 November, when they finally debated Germany's future relations with Soviet Russia they decided to spin out the question even further by asking Moscow 'to explain the radio messages in which it expressed doubts about the present government and to investigate the circumstances under which the arrest of the consuls-general in Moscow and Petrograd took place.' They assumed that long before these questions could be answered satisfactorily the Bolsheviks would fall, and Germany would be able to start with a clean slate in Russia. 'The Soviet government,' said Kautsky, 'is not likely to stay in power for long; in a few weeks it would be all over.'[159]

Even before the German government reached this decision the Bolsheviks had cast aside their last illusions concerning possible cooperation with the new authorities in Germany. On 16 November, the Narkomindel was finally able to establish direct contact with Berlin and found Hugo Haase, the leading member of the Independent Social Democrats in the Ebert cabinet and the people's commissar responsible for foreign affairs, at the communication centre of the *Auswärtiges Amt*. In a two-hour conversation conducted by direct wire linking Moscow with the teleprinter in the foreign office, Chicherin and Radek had their worst fears confirmed concerning the situation in Germany. Without actually saying it Haase revealed that the new German government intended to ignore Soviet Russia and build its foreign policy on cooperation with the western powers. Step by step, it emerged from the conversation that Ger-

157 *Ibid.*, 567-8. Emphasis added
158 Charles B. Burdick and Ralph H. Lutz (eds.), *The Political Institutions of the German Revolution, 1918-1919* (New York, 1966) 66-8
159 *Ibid.*, 70-4

many would not allow Ioffe to return to Berlin, that the German government did not need to accept the grain offered by the Bolsheviks because it expected to receive food from the United States, and that the armistice with the western powers was not just a political ploy designed to gain a 'breathing space' for the reorganization of Germany but a genuine effort to negotiate peace with the allies. When the two Bolsheviks attempted to present the Soviet program for Russian-German cooperation, including an offensive and defensive alliance, joint military operations against Krasnov, Alekseev and the allies in the region of the Black Sea and the admission of Soviet agitators to Germany for the purpose of conducting propaganda among allied troops on the Rhine, Haase refused to discuss the proposals without first consulting his colleagues. Radek lost all patience and told Haase that the German government had twelve hours in which to respond to the Soviet proposals. 'If the German government does not do everything possible in order promptly to reach agreement with us over the regulation of these questions,' he warned, 'it will be necessary for us, on our own initiative and on our own responsibility to do what the situation demands.'[160] The exchange ended with this ultimatum and was never resumed. From this one conversation it was clear that the Russian Bolsheviks and the German Social Democrats had nothing to discuss. Dedicated to halting the leftward drift of the revolution and bringing an end to the war with the allies the German Social Democrats could not even consider the Bolshevik proposals; desperately seeking some way to save themselves from the expected western onslaught the Bolsheviks could not tolerate the collaboration of the German Social Democrats with the allies. In Moscow the importance of the conversation was understood at once. If Haase was unwilling to endorse German cooperation with Soviet Russia neither would the other members of the Ebert government. Chicherin has recorded: 'as soon as I read the ribbon of my conversation with Haase to Vladimir Il'ich, he said, "nothing will come of it; this must be stopped."'[161]

A few days later, in fact, the teleprinter link with Germany was permanently severed, and, thereafter, the relations between the two revolutionary governments grew steadily worse. Representing two different schools

---

160 Germany. Auswärtiges Amt. Politisches Archiv. Deutschland 131, Band 55, folios 50-7. Partly printed in Gerhard A. Ritter and Susanne Miller (eds.), *Die Deutsche Revolution 1918-1919. Dokumente* (Frankfurt am Main, 1968) 271-9. Also see Baumgart, *Deutsche Ostpolitik*, 362-3; Nadolny, *Mein Beitrag*, 65-6; Karl Radek, 'Noiabr'. Stranichka iz vospominanii,' *Krasnaia Nov'*, no. 10 (1926) 142-3
161 Chicherin, 'Lenin i Vneshniaia Politika,' 7

of socialism, each government challenged the Marxist credentials of the other and accused its antagonist of bad faith. Relying on the arguments formulated in the last months of the war the Bolsheviks branded the German Social Democrats as 'social traitors' while the German Social Democrats responded by describing Bolshevism as an 'oppressive tyranny' having nothing in common with Marxist socialism. The conflict between the two, however, was not long confined to the exchange of angry words. Insurgent Bolsheviks and Soviet troops hastening to seize the borderlands before the arrival of the allies soon clashed with the rearguard of the German army as it withdrew from eastern Europe. These clashes added to the bitterness of the argument between Moscow and Berlin putting a final seal of violence on the long-standing dispute between the Bolsheviks and German Social Democrats.

In the midst of this mounting violence the long-delayed exchange of German and Soviet official representatives took place at Orsha. In the vain hope that new circumstances might still permit Ioffe to return to Berlin the Soviet government had delayed this event for as long as possible, but on 23 November, when the last detail had been settled, Moscow was forced to proceed with the exchange. As the train bearing the Soviet ambassador slowly crossed the demarcation line that of the German diplomats leaving Russia passed in the opposite direction.[162] This exchange, conducted according to the ritual of international law, was highly symbolic, for it marked the end of the Bolshevik dream of revolutionary cooperation with a socialist Germany. Ioffe, who had been sent to Berlin to assist the German revolution, was returning in failure. The German revolution, the shining hope of Bolshevik dreams, was revealed as a leaden grail.

Rather than salvation the German revolution brought immense peril for the Bolsheviks. Soviet Russia was caught in a giant international vortex created by the liquidation of German dominance in Europe. Everywhere around them the other clients of Berlin were being smashed to bits. By mid-November only Finland and Soviet Russia stood amidst the rubble of Germany's former empire in the east, each in its own way exhibiting those elements of strength which had originally called it into existence. To be sure, the liquidation of the German empire had its advantages for Soviet Russia. With perfect safety the Bolsheviks could denounce the Treaty of Brest-Litovsk, proclaim Soviet sovereignty over the borderlands and seek to establish their form of order in the chaos which prevailed in eastern Europe. Everything was up for grabs, and no claim unbacked by sub-

162 Baumgart, *Deutsche Ostpolitik*, 360; Hilger and Meyer, *Incompatible Allies*, 21-3

stantial force had any hope of recognition. Moreover, with the withdrawal of Germany from eastern Europe, the Bolsheviks momentarily possessed greater military and economic resources than any of their neighbors. Given time they could consolidate their hold on Russia and extend it to the borderlands, but it was inconceivable that the victorious allies would give the Bolsheviks the opportunity to entrench themselves in power. The political riptides which were sweeping Germany out of eastern Europe were sweeping the western powers into the heart of this maelstrom. When they arrived a violent clash was certain.

Could Soviet Russia survive this clash? Due to the flexibility of Lenin's foreign policy the Bolsheviks had survived the terrible threat posed by Germany earlier in the year, but would they be able to confront the challenge posed by the victorious allies? It did not seem likely. Even the Bolsheviks doubted their ability to survive. Chicherin would later recall that at the time Germany signed its armistice with the western powers, Lenin had fearfully confided to him that 'world capital itself is now coming for us.'[163] Other remarks made by Lenin at this time leave no doubt that he anticipated a combined assault by the great capitalist powers and did not rule out the possibility that Soviet Russia might be 'suddenly wiped out' by this attack.

This was not a cry of despair, but a sober appraisal of the threatening international situation. Given the circumstances Soviet Russia might well be 'wiped out,' but Lenin did not consider disaster to be a certainty. Mixed with his pessimism was a certain confidence that Soviet Russia could survive the impending onslaught. The liquidation of German hegemony had come much too suddenly for the Bolsheviks to draw much advantage from it, but with winter already settling comfortably over Russia there was still time to shape a new policy to cope with the vastly altered situation. Although Soviet Russia could no longer maneuver between Germany and the western powers it might be possible to neutralize Germany and find some way to exacerbate tensions among the allies. It might also be possible to frame a policy designed to heighten class conflicts within the war-weary societies of western Europe and reduce their potential to wage war in Russia. Most important, the Red army would be able to play a larger role in the defence of Soviet Russia than it had in the previous year. During 1918, Lenin had been forced to shape his foreign policy in the sure knowledge that he had little if any armed force with which to pursue his objectives. In the spring of 1919, he would have a genuine

163 *Izvestiia*, 7 Nov. 1923

army on which to base the security of the Soviet state. By itself this army would not constitute a certain guarantee of victory, but it would serve as a shield behind which a determined political struggle could be waged to preserve and consolidate Soviet Russia. In November 1918, therefore, the Soviet government began to prepare itself for a new struggle of survival. The contest with imperial Germany was over, that with the allies was just beginning.

14
Conclusion

From the very beginning of the October Revolution foreign policy and international relations have been the main questions facing us. Lenin to Sixth All-Russian Congress of Soviets, November 1918

Soviet foreign policy in the first year of the Bolshevik revolution was essentially that of Vladimir Il'ich Lenin. Even when Leon Trotsky served as foreign commissar and pursued a policy of 'permanent revolution' the conduct of Soviet international relations was largely determined by the Bolshevik leader. 'Permanent revolution' was not merely Trotsky's policy, but that of the Bolshevik party as a whole, and through the Central Committee Lenin kept a close rein on the foreign commissar. In the euphoria of late 1917, however, there was little disagreement over foreign policy. Lenin, Trotsky, and the other Bolshevik leaders shared the belief that the fate of the revolution in Russia depended on its spread to the remainder of Europe. The war of nation against nation would have to be converted into an international struggle of class against class if the revolution was to survive. The Decree on Peace, the publication of the secret treaties, and the initiation of peace negotiations with Germany were all dictated by this assumption.

When 'permanent revolution' failed it demoralized the Bolsheviks. Badly divided, the Central Committee split into feuding factions which bitterly debated the propriety of holding power in Russia if the revolution did not spread to the rest of Europe. In this debate Trotsky held the balance of power, and both Lenin and the left Bolsheviks had to court his favour. This allowed the foreign commissar to formulate his own policy and, against the better judgment of his colleagues, secure approval for its implementation.

The failure of 'no war, no peace' put an end to Trotsky's short-lived independence. In the crisis which followed Lenin was able to regain control of Soviet foreign policy and establish his unquestioned primacy within the party. With the very existence of Soviet Russia in jeopardy the frightened delegates of the Seventh Party Congress voted him virtually unlimited powers to refashion the party and state. Utilizing these powers he moved swiftly to implement a wholly new foreign policy, seeking desperately to buy peace from Germany, outmaneuver the allies, and consolidate power in Russia. Assisted by Chicherin, but guided only by his own instincts, he steadfastly adhered to a course which, despite the most humiliating subservience to Berlin, eventually freed Soviet Russia from the threat of German aggression and preserved the revolutionary regime in Russia until the collapse of the Wilhelmine Reich.

It is difficult to overestimate the importance of Lenin's foreign policy in determining the development of the revolution in Russia. During 1917 four successive Russian governments had fallen largely because of their inability to cope with the problems created by the war.[1] Not only the tsar, but Miliukov, Tsereteli, and Kerensky had been unable to frame policies which could mobilize popular support and secure Russia from attack. After the fall of the tsar, the problem grew more acute, and it was generally accepted that the revolution would 'kill the war' or the war would 'kill the revolution.' In effect, the failure of Miliukov, Tsereteli, and Kerensky 'killed' their particular editions of the revolution, foreclosing first the democratic and then the moderate socialist approaches to the problems of Russia. The failure of the moderate socialists prepared the way for the Bolsheviks. From the time Lenin returned to Petrograd the Bolsheviks hammered away at their contention that nothing but a radical break with the past and the adoption of a foreign policy based on spreading the revolution to western and central Europe could bring an end to the war. The Bolshevik panacea grew increasingly popular, winning widespread support especially in the army and large cities of Russia. The credibility of the Provisional Government crumbled, and with the Bolshevik seizure of power Lenin and Trotsky were given an opportunity to put their theory into practice.

They had to act quickly, for if their revolution failed to 'kill' the war, they were clearly marked for destruction. 'From the very beginning of the October Revolution,' Lenin told the Sixth All-Russian Congress of Sovi-

1 See Rex A. Wade, 'Why October? The search for peace in 1917,' *Soviet Studies* xx, no. 1 (July 1968) 36-45

ets, 'foreign policy and international relations have been the main questions facing us.'[2] The Bolshevik promise to end the war had been instrumental in bringing them to power, but once there it became an albatross around their necks. Their difficulties multiplied with every passing day, and Trotsky quickly discovered that a revolutionary foreign policy involved more than simply 'issuing a few revolutionary decrees and then shutting up shop.' When it became apparent that the revolution would not spread quickly to the rest of Europe the Bolshevik position became critical. Either they had to shape new policies or suffer the fate of their predecessors.

Amidst the scandalized protest of his colleagues, Lenin chose to discard the party's original foreign policy. Retreating from the utopian heights of November he entrenched himself in the realities of early 1918 and demanded that Soviet foreign policy be based on the unpleasant facts of the international situation. These facts – the isolation of the revolution in Russia, the military unpreparedness of the Bolsheviks, the war-weariness of the Russian peasantry, and the undisputed preponderance of Germany – dictated a 'disgusting' policy of surrender, retreat, and compromise. This led not only to the Treaty of Brest-Litovsk but to the virtual conversion of Soviet Russia into a client of Imperial Germany. Moscow was bound tightly to the German chariot, but Soviet control over the heart of the old tsarist empire was preserved. Within this territory – roughly equivalent to sixteenth century Muscovy – the Bolsheviks gathered their strength and prepared for the day when they could again move into the borderlands.

Lenin compared the Treaty of Brest-Litovsk to that of Tilsit and proclaimed that agreement with Germany was the only way by which Soviet Russia could regain its strength. 'Time and peace' were the only 'profit' obtained from collaboration with Germany, but Lenin used his 'breathing space' effectively. In the interval between March and November 1918 his government created the Red army and deployed it for maximum effect. During the same period the Bolsheviks eliminated their political rivals within Russia and began to exercise a tight control over the few economic resources at their disposal. Meanwhile the Great War continued, exhausting both coalitions and providing a measure of added security for the Soviet state. The Bolsheviks emerged at the end of the war immeasurably stronger than in early 1918. Although still tormented by appalling military, economic, and administrative deficiencies they could seriously plan

2 Lenin, PSS, vol. XXXVII, 153

to defend themselves against the victorious western allies. The difference may be seen by comparing the Bolshevik position in early 1918 with that of November. In February, when the German army was marching on Petrograd, Lenin had only the Red Guard to defend the capital. In November, not only did Lenin have the Red army, but he had begun to organize a strategic reserve and could send the Soviet armed forces into the borderlands to meet the allies before they could penetrate the heart of Russia. 'World capital itself' might be 'coming' for the Bolsheviks, but in November 1918, Lenin had an army with which to fight and a year's experience on which to base his policies. Lenin's original foreign policies had largely accomplished their objectives. The first had played a key role in hoisting the Bolsheviks into power, the second had succeeded in keeping them there in the last tumultuous months of the war.

Soviet foreign policy clearly reflected the personality of its author. Victor Chernov who had no reason to admire the Bolshevik leader has described Lenin as possessing 'an imposing wholeness. He seems to be made of one chunk of granite. And he is all round and polished like a billiard ball. There is nothing you can get hold of him by. He rolls with irrepressible speed.'[3] And so it was with Lenin's foreign policy. No other statesman of the era had so little to work with or accomplished as much.

His 'imposing wholeness' was largely a consequence of the manner in which he formulated his policies. Little escaped him, and he consistently revised even his most cherished theories. It is difficult to escape the conclusion that he re-examined his position every day, weeding out anything which had ceased to be of value while carefully nurturing everything which was of use. As a Marxist who would have to justify his proposals to other Marxists he developed his policies within a theoretical framework of dialectical materialism, class conflict, and the heritage of the European and Russian revolutionary movements. Unlike some of his colleagues, however, his Marxism was not a thin excrescence covering a philosophic void or a dogmatism which mindlessly tied him to every word of his mentor. He used the work of Marx and Engels as a guide rather than a detailed road map and made special use of their method of social-political analysis to construct his own policies. As such, Marxism served him well, for through it he identified his adversaries, analyzed their concrete interests and plotted the political direction in which they were moving. Combining this analysis with the most rigorous and objective calculation of the power

3 Robert Paul Browder and Alexander F. Kerensky, *The Russian Provisional Government, 1917.* Three vols. (Stanford, California, 1961) vol. III, 1209

available to each adversary he was then able to determine which groups might assist him in reaching his own objectives. Within Russia this dictated the temporary alliance with the peasantry, and in foreign affairs it pointed to the equally temporary arrangement with German big business. The first provided him with the broad base of support which he needed to assume power while the second permitted him to cling to power in the closing months of the World War.

The speed with which Lenin identified and sought agreement with temporary allies has frequently led to the charge that the Bolshevik leader was an 'opportunist' or worse. If by 'opportunism' his critics mean that Lenin grasped every 'opportunity' to strengthen his position then the description is certainly accurate; if, however, his critics mean that he was bereft of principles then the charge can not be substantiated. As a Marxist Lenin believed that all history was developing in a specific manner and, despite the 'zig-zags' which characterized its development, would inexorably bring mankind to the age of proletarian socialism. In his view history had reached the decisive moment when bourgeois capitalism, having attained its highest and ultimate expression in the imperialist competition which characterized the early twentieth century, was ready to give way to proletarian socialism. Although Marx had stressed the inevitability of this transition Lenin was not prepared to wait for history to take its course. The Great War had literally torn Europe apart, and he believed that if the conflict was not brought to a speedy and revolutionary conclusion the devastation which it wrought would enormously complicate the task of building the new socialist order. Proletarian internationalists, his own Bolshevik party in the vanguard, had to act decisively to convert the war of nation against nation into an international conflict of class against class. In addition to the seizure of power and the dynamic pursuit of revolutionary objectives, decisive action included the forging of temporary alliances with many diverse groups. Much like Canning a century before, Lenin could say that the Bolsheviks had no permanent allies, only permanent interests. When Bolshevik interests paralleled those of other groups it was necessary to march in the company of even the most unlikely allies. Thus, one day Lenin could solicit 'potatoes and weapons from the brigands of Anglo-French imperialism' while on the next he would try to interest the German financial world in a first mortgage on the entire Russian economy. When Bolshevik objectives diverged from those of their erstwhile allies, however, it was necessary to part company. Given the rapidity with which the political map of Europe was changing these alliances were made and broken with the most devastating swiftness. The ally of one day became the enemy of the next. As these rapid changes bewildered even Lenin's closest associates, causing Bukharin to weep, Trotsky to rage and even Chicherin to blink, it is not surprising that Lenin has been charged with opportunism. Far from opportunism, however, they were simply his realism displayed at its very best. The results, judged by his own standards and objectives, largely justified his decisions.

On a tactical level, Lenin's political genius is even more apparent. With good reason Chernov wrote that Lenin 'rolls with irresistible speed,' for once the Bolshevik leader had formulated his strategy he would seize the initiative and move forward on a broad political front. Combining reasoned argument with emotional propaganda, mass politics with the most subtle pressure, sarcastic rhetoric with administrative manipulation, Lenin would literally devastate his opponents. He always sought to divide his enemies, winning over the less steadfast and isolating the remainder. Once he had secured his objective he became sweet reason itself, offering meaningless 'concessions' to the vanquished. At all times he was the master of 'rotten compromise,' proposing bargains which unobtrusively, but unfailingly, worked to his own advantage. As long as any group or individual remained potentially useful Lenin was careful not to alienate them entirely. Today's adversaries, he knew, might be tomorrow's allies, and as a consequence, he sought to disarm rather than destroy those who opposed him. Thus, Zinoviev, who had fought bitterly against the seizure of power, became Lenin's ally in the struggle to conclude peace with Germany, and almost all those who opposed peace with Germany eventually came to play important roles in preserving it. Trotsky, Bukharin, and Radek all enlisted in the effort to maintain the breathing space won at Brest-Litovsk, and after Spiridonova's insurrection Lenin succeeded in marshalling the rank and file of the left SRs behind his own banner. Lenin used the same tactics internationally, always seeking to seize the initiative, launch a many-sided attack, and sow confusion in the enemy camp. On this immense stage his talent for political maneuver was displayed with particular clarity as he balanced the warring coalitions, pitting one against the other, and, as a consequence of what must have been the most 'rotten' and spectacular 'compromise' of his entire political career, eventually securing German assistance in holding the Bolshevik regime in power.

Given the subtlety of Lenin's politics there was virtually no circumstance from which he could not profit. In situations which seemed devoid of any conceivable political gain he could always find some way to benefit. Thus, in February, when Germany resumed the war against Russia, Lenin used the crisis to isolate Trotsky, intimidate a majority of his colleagues, and force his policy through the Central Committee. During the same disastrous days Lenin carefully formulated a policy of 'revolutionary defence' rather than 'revolutionary war,' thus exorcising the spectre of *union sacrée* while plunging Russia ever deeper into the ruthless class warfare which he desired. On a different plane, but of equal significance, is Lenin's masterstroke of early August when Soviet Russia was threatened simultaneously by the possible breakdown of negotiations with Germany and the landing of allied troops at Archangel. To overcome both problems at once he invited Germany to assist in the defence of Soviet Russia. This served to remove the last obstacle to the completion of the supplementary treaties and allowed the Bolsheviks to concentrate their armed forces in areas where they were needed most. When circumstances were favourable the results were even more spectacular. Thus, at the Seventh Party Congress Lenin did not seek ratification of the Treaty of Brest-Litovsk merely as an end in itself, but as a means to a greater end. He encouraged the delegates to spend their time debating foreign policy, and when that issue was finally resolved in his favour, he presented the Congress with a series of far-reaching resolutions which, when adopted, gave him virtual plenipotentiary powers in the affairs of party and state. In the waning hours of the Congress Lenin succeeded in convincing the delegates to equip him with a Central Committee of his choice and power to revise the party program, make and break treaties, declare war, and reorganize the entire economy of Russia according to his own wishes. Regardless of how one feels about *what* was accomplished it is necessary to recognize this as the work of political genius.

This is not meant to imply that Lenin was omniscient or somehow merits the quasi-deification to which he has been subject in the Soviet Union. Far from omniscience, Lenin frequently erred, and erred badly. Most significant in this regard was his belief that the revolution in Russia would lead to similar revolutions throughout Europe. Time and again he proclaimed that there were ninety-nine chances in one hundred that a Bolshevik revolution in Russia would spread proletarian internationalism to Germany, and in this, of course, he was profoundly mistaken. Permanent revolution proved to be of inestimable value in hoisting the Bolsheviks to power but was a leaden grail throughout the rest of the continent. The problem of Lenin's utopianism in November 1917 will be dealt with below, but at this point it is necessary to note that after late 1917, Lenin erred more frequently on the side of caution than rashness. In early October and mid-November 1918, it is true, his enthusiasm of the previous fall returned, and for brief instants he again trumpeted the imminent arrival of the world workers' revolution, but these were mere episodes in an otherwise unbroken record of prudence and restraint. Following the failure of 'permanent revolution,' Lenin grew immensely cautious and his errors of judgment reflected that caution. Thus, in March 1918 the situation in which Soviet Russia found itself was bad, but not nearly as bad as Lenin imagined. Throughout the month, he literally counted the days snatched from Germany allowing him to evacuate men and resources from Petrograd, and he thought even Moscow would fall to General Hoffmann. Similarly, in April, when the Japanese landed at Vladivostok, he anticipated an immediate loss of the far east and wrote off all Siberia east of Baikal. Nor can his judgment of the allied threat to north Russia be considered particularly sound. Too permissive in March and April he only tardily awoke to the danger of the western presence at Murmansk and, even then, did not act as decisively as he might, failing to strike energetically when he could still have denied the far north to the allies. In his defence, however, it must be noted that at the time – late June – he could not be certain that he would succeed in buying off the Germans, and he had to keep some path to the allies open in the event Germany should attempt to unseat his government. Lenin had to prepare for the worst, and this had the effect of causing him to err on the side of caution.

The genius of Lenin was not in his infallibility but in being able to adjust rapidly to kaleidoscopic change. On the occasions noted above and in other instances he was essentially misled by insufficient information and was forced to make decisions on the basis of appearance and the terrible nightmares which prowled his conscious and subconscious mind. Here Marxism did not serve him well, for in the absence of concrete data, he frequently fell back on the Marxist stereotypes and dogmatism which he decried in his colleagues. On such occasions he would tend to pursue chains of deductive logic to their final frightening conclusion, mistaking the *reductio ad absurdum* for reality. As hard data became available, however, and he could glimpse even the broad outline of his adversary's intentions he never failed to junk his original distorted evaluation and forge new policies in accord with the information at his disposal. This is strikingly evident in his decision to renew the effort to purchase peace from Germany. Backed against the wall by Germany's continued aggression after Brest-Litovsk, Lenin appears to have been on the verge of seeking an accommodation with the allies. The arrival of Ioffe's first reports from Berlin with solid data concerning the split in the German oligarchy changed all that. Lenin could conclude that at the cost of the most extortionate of bribes he could 'hang heavy weights' on the feet of German generals and avoid the incalculable risk of resuming the war with the questionable assistance of the allied powers.

Just as Lenin could move from pessimism to optimism, formulating realistic policies to cope with a changing situation, he could also move in the opposite direction, formulating equally realistic policies in the process. Thus, his original enthusiasm over the October constitutional crisis in Germany quickly gave way to a realization of the dangers inherent in the new situation, and his joy over the fall of the Hohenzollerns faded quickly with the awareness that Ebert rather than Liebknecht would rule in Berlin. In both instances he overcame both his initial error in judgment and subsequent disillusionment to formulate policies to cope with the new and ever more threatening situation. In no instance did he waste any time lamenting the sad circumstances in which he found himself; no matter how execrable the situation he always found some way to benefit from it.

Having placed such a heavy emphasis on Lenin's realism and undogmatic approach to Marxism it is difficult to explain his utopianism on the occasion of the Bolshevik seizure of power. At the time Lenin proclaimed his certainty of the imminence of the world workers' revolution – the 'great field revolution' which he would so caustically deride a few months later. The very seizure of power, in fact, was premised on the assumption that the new proletarian internationalist regimes which were expected to arise in the more highly-developed parts of the continent would come to the aid of Russia and assist her in the transformation of what was essentially a peasant society into a functioning part of the new socialist order. Without that assumption the fate of the revolution in Russia – from a Marxist point of view – appeared hopeless. How then was Lenin able to jettison this assumption when it proved wrong? Was it mere rhetoric designed to provide a plausible excuse for his seizure of power in a peasant-dominated society or did Lenin actually believe in 'permanent revolution'? The speed with which he disassociated himself from this theory and adopted a foreign policy based on the principles of *Realpolitik* would seem to point to the conclusion that his original foreign policy was based on little more than internal criteria and was never taken seriously by the Bolshevik leader. It strains credibility to assume that Lenin was equally sincere in his evaluation of the international situation both before and after the revolution, and to believe that Lenin did not cynically concoct one policy to raise himself to power and another to keep himself there.

Yet it strains credibility even further to believe the opposite. Given the circumstances of late 1917, with Russia's overwhelming peasant population, shattered army and collapsing economy, would Lenin have launched the revolution if he had not believed that his seizure of power had a very good chance – ninety-nine in one hundred to use his odds – of touching off the world workers' revolution and bringing prompt aid from the more highly-developed parts of the continent? Would Lenin really have chosen to face Germany barehanded and without hope of external assistance? Such an interpretation assumes either an insouciant adventurism or a malevolent irresponsibility which is simply inconsistent with everything else that is known about Lenin. Whatever Lenin may have been he was neither an adventurer nor irresponsible; he may have been profoundly in error, but he always tried to calculate the political odds carefully and act accordingly. Similarly, such an interpretation would have to assume that either Lenin was willing to seize power for the sake of seizing power or possessed a perspicacity surpassing even that claimed for him by the present day high priests of the Leninist cult. Since we know the depths of Lenin's dedication to the success of his movement we can dismiss the first assumption; he would be the last to assume an attitude of *aprés moi le deluge* and seize power for the sake of exercising it for a few brief days, only to be forcibly and perhaps fatally removed from the stage of history forever. The second assumption can also be dismissed. The 'zig-zags' of history took Lenin as much by surprise as anyone else, and in November 1917 he had no premonition of the terrible journey through hell that he and his party would make in the year 1918.

We are left, therefore, with the conclusion that in November 1917 Lenin did implicitly believe that his uprising would mark the beginning of the triumphal world workers' revolution. There is no evidence to the contrary, and alternative interpretations strain the imagination even more than this enormity. How then can we explain Lenin's naive trust in such a fanciful doctrine as 'permanent revolution'? The first prerequisite of such an explanation requires that we strip ourselves, in so far as possible, of our knowledge of what was to follow the Bolshevik seizure of power. The events of 1918 were a closed book to the Bolsheviks of 1917, and they did not have the slightest way of even imagining what was in store for them. Instead, we must concentrate on the experience of these men *prior* to their revolution. In all cases, Lenin in particular, this included their profound alienation from existing society, the subscription to an all-encompassing interpretation of history which stressed the imminent arrival of the socialist millenium, years of grinding toil in the service of their creed, the horrendous impact of what was, to then, mankind's most sanguinary and vicious war, and the rapid movement of Russia through all the stages of revolutionary development within an eight month span of time. Given their assumptions and experience, especially in the years from 1914 to 1917, it is very easy to understand their utopian optimism in November 1917. Within Russia everything was moving in the direction which they had predicted, and this experience reinforced the chiliastic inclinations of the creed to which they subscribed. Cut off from the outside world by a continent at war, they could catch only brief and distorted glimpses of events and developments elsewhere. Everything they saw was viewed through ideological spectacles which filtered out disturbing facts not conforming with their assumptions and magnified those which did. Thus, wherever they looked they found evidence to support their assumptions and plowed resolutely forward. In late 1917 the revolution appeared to be at flood tide, and the Bolsheviks could see no reason why it should not inundate the entire continent. Lenin, to whom burning emotion[4] and utopian expectation[5] were no strangers, believed the time was ripe, even over-ripe, to force the revolutionary pace and breach the dikes of conservatism everywhere. Within Russia this gave the Bolsheviks a dynamism and self-assurance which other groups lacked and provided an emotionally satisfying answer to the vexing question of how to end the war. In the struggle for power the doctrine of 'permanent revolution' was a weapon of inestimable value made all the more efficient by the sincerity of those who wielded it.

Once in power this weapon became a paper sword more dangerous to the Bolsheviks than their adversaries. Inspiring false confidence and unwarranted optimism it threatened to destroy the revolution itself. Step by step its flimsiness was revealed. Contrary to Bolshevik expectations the seizure of power and Decree on Peace elicited little in the way of positive response from the outside world. Nor did the publication of the much vaunted secret treaties fall with the devastating impact which they had anticipated. Only Germany responded to their appeal for an armistice, and when negotiations began at Brest-Litovsk the Bolsheviks had to face the German generals alone. In the following weeks the Bolsheviks could not stir the European proletariat; the one glimmer of hope – the January demonstrations in Central Europe – seemed to mock their expectations. These hard and bitter facts made an obvious impact on Lenin. Long before any other Bolshevik he began to take them into account, and, by early December, he had already ceased to mention the imminent spread of

4 See above, 63-4
5 See Rodney Berfield, 'Lenin's utopianism: state and revolution,' *Slavic Review* XXX, no. 1 (March 1971) 45-56

revolution beyond Russia. He fell silent, and it does not stretch the imagination to picture him desperately trying to determine how to deal with this unexpected development. Every passing day provided additional evidence that 'permanent revolution' was a failure. What was to be done? Despite the assumptions on which he had taken power it was obvious that he could not admit his error and resign. That would destroy the party and perhaps the revolution itself, demoralizing and discrediting proletarian internationalism everywhere. The hands of time could not be set back. The only thing he could do was to move forward, trying to shape a new policy which had some chance of success. Such a policy had to be based on the harsh realities of the moment and, given his bitter experience with 'permanent revolution,' exclude all elements over which he had no control.

Seeking simple survival Lenin pushed theory into the background and made it distinctly subordinate to the preservation of the Soviet state. In the words of Chicherin, a transition had taken place from 'an underground revolutionary party to the political reality of holding state power.' Preservation of the Soviet state became the keystone of Lenin's new policy and dictated all the 'disgusting' compromises which he would make in the months to come. Although Lenin did not abandon hope in the world workers' revolution he pushed it ever further into the future, allowing it to assume a shadowy existence somewhat akin to the second coming of Christ. This served to legitimize all the new policies, for in theory they were meant to preserve the revolution in Russia 'until other contingents came up to it.' The effect, however, was to shift the focus of Bolshevik policy from promoting world revolution to guaranteeing the survival of the Soviet state. As with early Christianity when it attained the status of a state religion, original doctrine was subordinated to the welfare of a secular institution. Almost at once, the original content of the faith which had called the institution into existence began to wither as the institution itself loomed ever larger in the minds of those who had created it. 'Permanent revolution' had proved unattainable, but given the substantial resources at their disposal as masters of Russia the Bolsheviks could realistically hope to save the Soviet state. Each success in defending their creation made it more dear and reinforced their concentration on preserving it rather than original doctrine. As with early Christianity the institutionalized manifestation of doctrine survived, grew strong, and flourished; the doctrine itself underwent one subtle change after another, eventually losing its original meaning and coming to serve the masters of the institution in any way they felt necessary. In a sense, therefore, the Soviet state survived and the revolution perished, certainly one of the choicest ironies in all history.

Soviet foreign policy in the first years of the Bolshevik revolution, then, was an amalgam of ideology and expediency, utopian expectation and realistic calculation, daring innovation and classical diplomacy. Ideology, expectation, and innovation particularly characterized Bolshevik policy in the first months of the revolution, finding concrete expression in the Decree on Peace, the original Bolshevik peace proposals, and Trotsky's brilliant presentation of the Soviet program. The limits of this policy were reached by January 1918, and in February it failed completely. Trotsky's great peroration of 10 February unwittingly proclaimed the failure of Soviet Russia's first foreign policy; his declaration of 'no war, no peace' marked its utter bankruptcy. Even after the failure of 'permanent revolution,' however, ideology was not abandoned, expectation of eventual world revolution remained high and the conduct of Soviet foreign policy continued to be innovative. But no further attempt was made to transcend the entire existing framework of international relations. The dominant characteristics of Soviet foreign policy after February 1918 were definitely those of expediency, realistic calculation, and classical diplomacy. Lenin very carefully calculated the limits of Soviet power, and Chicherin conducted a diplomacy worthy of the most traditional foreign office. Within this context an entirely new policy was formulated which subtly, but decisively, shifted the entire purpose of Bolshevik policy from advancing the case of world revolution to that of preserving the embattled Soviet state. This was to have the most far-reaching consequences, leading eventually to the uneasy incorporation of Soviet Russia into the world order which emerged from the Great War. In no small measure this was due to the conduct of Soviet foreign policy, the policy of Lenin, a policy of revolution and survival.

Selected bibliography

UNPUBLISHED DOCUMENTS AND PAPERS

The most important unpublished materials used in the preparation of this work were:

FRANCE. Archives du Ministère des Affaires Etrangères, Paris
- Archives du Ministère de la Guerre, Vincennes

GREAT BRITAIN. Public Record Office, London. Minutes of the War Cabinet
- Foreign Office

Other unpublished materials used were:

GERMANY. Auswärtiges Amt. (St Antony's College Microfilm Collection)

UNITED STATES. National Archives, Washington, DC. Records of the Department of State
- Arthur Balfour Papers (British Museum, London)
- David Francis Papers (Missouri Historical Society, St Louis, Missouri)
- Alfred Milner Papers (Bodleian Library [formerly at New College Library], Oxford)
- Reminiscences of DeWitt Clinton Poole (Columbia University oral history project, New York City)

PUBLISHED DOCUMENTS AND PAPERS

Akademiia Nauk SSSR, Institut Slavianovadeniia i Pol'skaia Akademiia Nauk, Sektor Istorii Pol'sko-Sovetskikh Otnoshenii. *Dokumenty i Materialy po Istorii Sovetskogo-Pol'skikh Otnoshenii.* Six vols. (Moscow, 1963-9)

Arkhivnoe Upravlenie pri Sovete Ministerov UkSSR, Tsentral'nyi Gosudarstvennyi Arkhiv Oktiabr'skoi Revoliutsii i Sotsialisticheskogo Stroitel'stva UkSSR, Institut Istorii AN UkSSR. *Grazhdanskaia Voina na Ukraine.* Three vols. in four (Kiev, 1967)

WINFRIED BAUMGART (ed.) 'Die militärpolitischen Berichte des Freiherrn von Keyserlingk aus Petersburg, Januar-Februar 1918.' *Vierteljahrhefte für Zeitgeschichte,* no. 1 (1967) 87-104

– *Von Brest-Litovsk zur Deutschen Novemberrevolution. Aus den Tagebüchern, Briefen und Aufzeichnungen von Alfons Paquet, Wilhelm Groener und Albert Hopman* (Göttingen, 1971)

ROBERT PAUL BROWDER and ALEXANDER KERENSKY (eds.), *The Russian Provisional Government of 1917: Documents.* Three vols. (Stanford, California, 1961)

JAMES BUNYAN, *Intervention, Civil War and Communism in Russia. April-December 1918. Documents and Materials* (Baltimore, 1936)

– and H.H. FISHER, *The Bolshevik Revolution, 1917-1918: Documents and Materials* (Stanford, California, 1934)

CHARLES B. BURDICK and RALPH H. LUTZ (eds.), *The Political Institutions of the German Revolution, 1918-1919* (New York, 1966)

GEORGII CHICHERIN, *Two Years of Soviet Foreign Policy* (New York, 1920)

– *Stati i Rechi po Voprosam Mezhdunarodnoi Politiki* (Moscow, 1961)

C.K. CUMMING and WALTER W. PETIT (eds.), *Russian-American Relations: March 1917-March 1920. Documents and Papers* (New York, 1920)

JANE DEGRAS (ed.), *Soviet Documents on Foreign Policy.* Three vols. (Oxford, 1951)

'Dokumenty po Istorii Chernomorskogo Flota v Marte-Iune 1918 g.' *Archiv Russkoi Revoliutsii* XIV (1924) 151ff

Dokumenty po Istorii Grazhdanskoi Voiny v SSSR (Moscow, 1940)

OLGA GANKIN and H.H. FISHER (eds.), *The Bolsheviks and the World War. The Origin of the Third International* (Stanford, California, 1940)

HANS W. GATZKE 'Dokumentation zu den deutsch-russischen Beziehungen im Sommer 1918,' *Vierteljahrhefte für Zeitgeschichte,* no. 3 (1955) 67ff

Glavnoe Arkhivnoe Upravlenie pri Sovete Ministrov SSSR, Institut Voennoi Istorii Ministerstva Oborony SSSR, Tsentral'nyi Gosudarstvennyi Arkhiv Sovetskoi Armii, *Direktivy Kommandovaniia Frontov Krasnoi Armii (1917-1922 gg). Sbornik Dokumentov.* Four vols. (Moscow, 1971–)

– Tsentral'nyi Gosudarstvenny Arkhiv Sovetskoi Armii, Institut Voennoi Istorii Ministerstva Oborny SSSR, *Direktivy Glavnogo Komandovaniia Krasnoi Armii (1917-1920). Sbornik Dokumentov* (Moscow, 1969)

WERNER HAHLWEG (ed.), *Der Friede von Brest-Litovsk* (Düsseldorf, 1971)

THEOPHIL HORNYKIEWICZ (ed.), *Ereignisse in der Ukraine 1914-1922.* Four vols. (Philadelphia, Pennsylvania, 1968)

Institut Istorii Akademii Nauk Lit. SSR, Institut Istorii Partii pri TsK KP Litvy – filial Instituta Marksizma-Leninizma pri TsK KPSS, Arkhivnoe Upravlenie pri SM Litovskoi SSR, Tsentral'nyi Gosudarstvennyi Arkhiv Lit. SSR, *Bor'ba za Sovetskuiu Vlast' v Litve v 1918-1920 gg. Sbornik Dokumentov* (Vil'nius, 1967)

Institut Istorii Partii TsK KP Ukrainy – filial Instituta Marksizma-Leninizma pri TsK KPSS, Arkhivnoe Uprvalenie UkSSR. *Bol'shevistskie organizatsii Ukrainy v Period Ustanovleniia i Ukrepleniia Sovetskoi Vlasti (Noiabr' 1917– Aprel' 1918 gg).* (Kiev, 1962)

Institut Leninizma pri TsK VKP (b), *Protokoly Tsentral'nogo Komiteta RSDRP (b): Avgust 1917 g. – Fevral' 1918 g.* (Moscow, 1929)

Institut Marksizma-Leninizma pri TsK KPSS, *Vladimir Il'ich Lenin: Biograficheskaia Khronika.* Seven vols. (Moscow, 1970-6)

A.A. IOFFE (ed.), *Mirnye Peregovory v Brest-Litovske* (Moscow, 1920)

Kommunisticheskaia Partiia Sovetskogo Soiuza, *VII Kongress: Stenograficheskii Otchet* (Moscow, 1928)

V.V. KUTUZOV, 'Dokumenty o Bratanii,' *Sovetskoe Arkhivy*, no. 4 (1968) 98-101

V.I. LENIN, *Leninskii Sbornik.* 36 vols. (Moscow, 1924-59)

– *Polnoe Sobranie Sochinenii.* Fifth ed. 55 vols. (Moscow. 1958-64)

ERICH MATTHIAS and RUDOLF MORSEY (eds.), *Die Regierung des Prinzen Max von Baden* (Düsseldorf, 1962)

JAN M. MEIJER (ed.), *The Trotsky Papers* (The Hague, 1964)

Ministerium für Auswärtige Angelegenheiten der DDR, Ministerium für Auswärtige Angelegenheiten der UdSSR, *Deutsch-Sowjetische Beziehungen von den Verhandlungen in Brest-Litowsk bis zum Abschluss des Rapallovertrages.* Two vols. (Berlin, 1967-71). Russian edition: *Sovetsko-Germanskie Otnosheniia ot Peregovorov v Brest-Litovske do Podpisaniia Rapall'skogo Dogovora.* Two vols. (Moscow, 1968-71)

Ministerstvo Inostrannykh Del SSSR, *Dokumenty Vneshnei Politiki SSSR.* Sixteen vols. to date (Moscow, 1959–)

I.I. MINTS and E.N. GORODETSKII (eds.), *Dokumenty o Razgrome Germanskikh Okkupantov na Ukraine v 1918 g.* (Moscow, 1942)

Ofitsal'naia Perepiska Diplomaticheskago Korpusa v'' Vologde c'' Narodnym'' Komissariatom'' po Inostrannym'' Delam'' po Voprosu o Pereezde Pervago iz Vologdy v'' Moskvu (Vologda, 1918)

Partiinyi Arkhiv Murmanskogo Obkoma KPSS, Arkhivnyi Otdel UVD Murmanskogo Oblispolkoma, Gosudarstvennyi Arkhiv Murmanskoi Oblast, *Bor'ba za Ustanovlenie i Uprochenie Sovetskoi Vlasti na Murmane. Sbornik Dokumentov i Materialov* (Murmansk, 1960)

Piatyi Vserossiiskii S''ezd Sovetov Rabochikh, Krest'ianskikh, Soldatskikh i Kazach'ikh Deputatov. Stenograficheskii Otchet (Moscow, 1918)

KARL RADEK, *Die internationale Lage und die äussere Politik der Räteregierung* (Berlin, 1919)

GERHARD A. RITTER and SUSANNE MILLER (eds.), *Die Deutsche Revolution, 1918-1919. Dokumente* (Frankfurt am Main, 1968)

JOSEPH STALIN, *Works.* 13 vols. (Moscow, 1952-4)

IA.M. SVERDLOV, *Izbrannye Proizvedeniia.* Three vols. (Moscow, 1960)

Tretii Vserossiiskii S''ezd' Sovetov' Rabochikh', Soldatskikh i Krest'ianskikh Deputatov (Petrograd, 1918)

LEON TROTSKY, *Kak Vooruzhalas' Revoliutsiia.* Three vols. (Moscow, 1923-5)

– *Sochineniia* (Moscow, 1925)

'Un échange de notes diplomatiques sur la terreur blanche et la terreur rouge' (Zurich, 1918)

UNITED STATES OF AMERICA, Department of State. *Proceedings of the Brest-Litovsk Peace Conference: The Peace Negotiations between Russia and the Central Powers, 21 November 1917–3 March 1918* (Washington, 1918)

– *Bolshevik Propaganda Hearings before a Subcommittee of the Committee on the Judiciary, United States Senate, Sixty-Fifth Congress* (Washington, 1919)

– Department of State. *Papers Relating to the Foreign Relations of the United States, 1918, Russia.* Three vols. (Washington, 1931)

Das Werk des Untersuchungsausschusses der Deutschen Verfassunggebenden Nationalversammlung und des Deutschen Reichstag, 1919-1928. Vierte Reihe: *Die Ursachen des Deutschen Zusammenbruchs im Jahre 1918* (Berlin, 1927-9)

E.L. WOODWARD and R. BUTLER (eds.), *Documents on British Foreign Policy, 1919-1939.* Series I, vol. III (London, 1949)

Z.A.B. ZEMAN, *Germany and the Revolution in Russia: Documents of the German Foreign Ministry* (London, 1958)

G.E. ZINOVIEV, *Sochineniia* (Leningrad, 1925)

NEWSPAPERS

The Call (London)
The Weekly *Dispatch* (London)
Izvestiia (Petrograd and Moscow)
Pravda (Petrograd and Moscow)
The London *Times*
The New York *Times*

AUTOBIOGRAPHIES AND MEMOIRS

VLADIMIR A. ANTONOV-OVSEENKO, *Zapiski o Grazhdanskoi Voine.* Four vols. (Moscow, 1924-33)

MIKHAIL DMITRIEVICH BONCH-BRUEVICH, *From Tsarist General to Red Army Commander* (Moscow, 1966)

VLADIMIR DMITRIEVICH BONCH-BRUEVICH, *Izbrannye Sochineniia*. Three vols. (Moscow, 1963)

KARL BOTHMER, *Mit Graf Mirbach in Moskau* (Tübingen, 1922)

LOUIS BRYANT, *Six Red Months in Russia* (New York, 1918)

SIR GEORGE BUCHANAN, *My Mission to Russia and Other Diplomatic Memories*. Two vols. (London, 1923)

GEORGII CHICHERIN, 'Lenin i Vneshniaia Politika.' In *Mirovaia Politika v 1924 godu. (Sbornik Statei pod redaktseii F. Rotshteina)* (Moscow, 1925) 3-10. Reprinted in *Voprosi Istorii*, no. 3 (1957) 20-5 with significant omissions from original article

COUNT OTTOKAR CZERNIN, *In the World War* (London, 1919)

LOUIS FISCHER, *Men and Politics: An Autobiography* (New York, 1941)

D.G. FOKKE, 'Na Stsene i za Kulisami Brestkoi Tragikomedii,' *Arkhiv'' Russkoi Revoliutsii* XX, 5-207

DAVID R. FRANCIS, *Russia from the American Embassy: April 1916–November 1918* (New York, 1921)

GUSTAV GRATZ and RICHARD SCHÜLLER, *The Economic Policy of Austria-Hungary during the War* (New Haven, Connecticut, 1928)

KARL HELFFERICH, *Der Weltkrieg* (Berlin, 1919)

G. HILGER and A.G. MEYER, *The Incompatible Allies* (New York, 1953)

GENERAL MAX VON HOFFMANN, *War Diaries and Other Papers*. Two vols. (London, 1929)

A.A. IOFFE, 'Brest-Litovsk: Vospominaniia,' *Novy Mir* (June 1927) 137-46

THOMAS JONES, *Whitehall Diary*. Two vols. (Oxford, 1969)

MIKHAEL SERGEEVICH KEDROV, *Bez Bolshevistskogo Rukovodstva (iz Istorii Interventsii na Murmane)* (Leningrad, 1930)

VLADIMIR KOROSTOVETZ, *Seed and Harvest* (London, 1931)

NADEZHDA KRUPSKAIA, *Reminiscences of Lenin* (New York, 1970)

RICHARD VON KÜHLMANN, *Erinnerungen* (Heidelberg, 1948)

M.J. LARSONS, *Als Expert im Sowjetdienst* (Berlin, 1929)

DAVID LLOYD GEORGE, *War Memories of David Lloyd George*. Two vols. (London, 1938)

SIR ROBERT H. BRUCE LOCKHART, *British Agent* (Garden City, New York, 1933)

ERICH LUDENDORFF, *Meine Kriegserinnerungen* (Berlin, 1919)

– *The General Staff and its Problems* (London, 1920)

IVAN MAISKY, *Journey into the Past* (London, 1962)

PAVEL D. MALKOV, *Reminiscences of a Kremlin Commandant* (Moscow, n.d.)

MAXIMILIAN, PRINCE OF BADEN, *The Memoirs of Prince Max of Baden*. Two vols. (New York, 1928)

MAJOR-GENERAL SIR C. MAYNARD, *The Murmansk Venture* (London, 1928)

GEORGE ALEXANDER VON MÜLLER, *Regierte der Kaiser?* (Göttingen, 1959)

CONSTANTIN NABOKOFF, *The Ordeal of a Diplomat* (London, 1921)

RUDOLF NADOLNY, *Mein Beitrag* (Wiesbaden, 1955)

HENRI ALBERT NIESSEL, *Le triomphe des bolcheviks et la paix de Brest-Litovsk; souvenirs, 1917-1918* (Paris, 1940)

JOSEPH NOULENS, *Mon Ambassade en Russie Sovietique, 1917-1919.* Two vols. (Paris, 1933)

WILLIAM J. OUDENDIJK, *Ways and By-Ways in Diplomacy* (London, 1939)

ALFONS PAQUET, *Im kommunistischen Russland* (Jena, 1919)

G.I. PETROVSKII, *Nash Mudryi Vozhd'* (Moscow, 1970)

M. PHILIPS PRICE, *My Reminiscences of the Russian Revolution* (London, 1921)

KARL RADEK, 'Noiabr'. Stranichka iz vospominanii,' *Krasnaia Nov'*, no. 10 (1926) 139-75

F. RASKOLNIKOV, *Rasskazy Michmana Il'ina* (Moscow, 1936)

LOUIS DE ROBIEN, *Journal d'un diplomate en Russie, 1917-1918* (Paris, 1967)

JACQUES SADOUL, *Notes sur la révolution bolchévique* (Paris, 1920)

B.V. SAVINKOV, *Bor'ba s Bol'shevikami* (Warsaw, 1920)

PHILIPP SCHEIDEMANN, *The Making of New Germany. The Memoirs of Philipp Scheidemann.* Two vols. (New York, 1929)

VICTOR SERGE, *Year One of the Russian Revolution.* Translated and edited by Peter Sedgwick (London, 1972)

EDGAR SISSON, *One Hundred Red Days: A Personal Chronicle of the Bolshevik Revolution* (New Haven, Connecticut, 1931)

G. SOKOL'NIKOV, *Brestskii Mir* (Moscow, 1920)

L. TROTSKY, *Lenin* (London, 1925)

– *My Life* (New York, 1930)

I. VATSETIS, 'Vystuplenie levykh eserov v Moskve,' in *Etapy Bol'shogo Puti* (Moscow, 1963)

I. ZALKIND, 'Iz pervykh mestiatsev NKID,' *Mezhdunarodnaia Zhisn'*, no. 15 (133) (7 Nov. 1922) 55-61

– 'NKID v semnadtsam godu,' *Mezhdunarodnaia Zhisn'*, no. 10 (1927) 15-25

SECONDARY WORKS

RAFAEL ABRAMOVICH, *The Soviet Revolution, 1917-1939* (New York, 1962)

ARTHUR E. ADAMS, *Bolsheviks in the Ukraine: The Second Campaign, 1918-1919* (New Haven, Connecticut, 1963)

A.A. AKHTAMAZIAN, *Ot Bresta do Kila* (Moscow, 1963)

WINFRIED BAUMGART, *Deutsche Ostpolitik 1918* (Wien und München, 1966)

PETER BOROWSKY, *Deutsche Ukrainepolitik 1918* (Hamburg, 1970)

J.F.N. BRADLEY, *La légion tchécoslovaque en Russie, 1914-1920* (Paris, 1965)

- *Allied Intervention in Russia, 1917-1920* (London, 1968)

JULIUS BRAUNTHAL, *History of the International, 1914-1943* (London, 1967)

GEORGE A. BRINKLEY, *The Volunteer Army and Allied Intervention in South Russia, 1917-1921* (Notre Dame, Indiana, 1966)

ALAIN BROSSAT, *Aux origines de la révolution permanente: la pensée politique du jeune trotsky* (Paris, 1974)

EDWARD HALLETT CARR, *A History of Soviet Russia: The Bolshevik Revolution, 1917-1923.* Three vols. (New York, 1950-3)

F.L. CARSTEN, *The Reichswehr and Politics, 1918-1933* (Oxford, 1966)

WILLIAM HENRY CHAMBERLAIN, *The Russian Revolution, 1917-1921.* Two vols. (New York, 1935)

VICTOR CHERNOV, *The Great Russian Revolution* (New Haven, Connecticut, 1936)

A.O. CHUBAR'IAN, *V.I. Lenin i Formirovanne Sovetskoi Vneshnei Politiki* (Moscow, 1972)

- *Brestskii Mir* (Moscow, 1964)

W.P. COATES and ZELDA K. COATES, *Armed Intervention in Russia, 1918-1922* (London, 1935)

STEPHEN F. COHEN, *Bukharin and the Bolshevik Revolution: A Political Biography. 1888-1938* (New York, 1973)

ROBERT V. DANIELS, *The Conscience of the Revolution: Communist Opposition in Soviet Russia* (Cambridge, Massachusetts, 1960)

- *Red October* (New York, 1968)

ISAAC DEUTSCHER, *The Prophet Armed: Trotsky, 1879-1921* (New York, 1954)

BORIS DVINOV, 'Pervaia Mirovaia Voina i Rossiskaia Sotsialdemokratiia,' Inter-University Project on the History of the Menshevik Movement, Paper no. 10 (New York, 1961). Columbia University Library

C.H. ELLIS, *The British 'Intervention' in Transcaspia, 1918-1919* (Berkeley, California, 1963)

JOHN ERICKSON, *The Soviet High Command, 1918-1941* (New York, 1962)

MERLE FAINSOD, *International Socialism and the World War* (Cambridge, Massachusetts, 1935)

OLEH S. FEDYSHYN, *Germany's Drive to the East and the Ukrainian Revolution, 1917-1918* (New Brunswick, New Jersey, 1971)

FRITZ FISCHER, *Germany's Aims in the First World War* (New York, 1967)

LOUIS FISCHER, *The Soviets in World Affairs.* Two vols. (Princeton, New Jersey, 1951)

- *The Life of Lenin* (New York, 1964)

- *Russia's Road from Peace to War* (New York, 1969)

DAVID FOOTMAN, *Civil War in Russia* (London, 1961)

W.B. FOWLER, *British-American Relations, 1917-1918: The Role of Sir William Wiseman* (Princeton, New Jersey, 1969)

A.L. FRAIMAN, *Revoliutsionnaia Zaschita Petrograda v Fevrale – Marte 1918 g* (Moscow, 1964)

GERALD FREUND, *Unholy Alliance* (London, 1957)

R.SH. GANELIN, *Sovetsko-Amerikanskie Otnosheniia v Kontse 1917–Nachale 1918 g* (Leningrad, 1975)

D.L. GOLINKOV, *Krakh Vrazheskogo Podpol'ia* (Moscow, 1971)

I. GOROKHOV, L. ZAMIATIN, and I. ZEMSKOV, *G.V. Chicherin – Diplomat Leninskoi Shkoly* (Moscow, 1966)

S.R. GRAUBARD, *British Labour and the Russian Revolution, 1917-1924* (Cambridge, Massachusetts, 1956)

K. GUSEV, *Krakh Partii Levykh Eserov* (Moscow, 1963)

WERNER HAHLWEG, *Lenins Ruckkehr nach Russland 1917* (Leiden, 1957)

– *Der diktatfrieden von Brest-Litowsk 1918 und die bolschewistische Weltrevolution* (Münster, 1960)

WILLIAM HARD, *Raymond Robins' Own Story* (New York, 1920)

GEORGES HAUPT, *Socialism and the Great War: The Collapse of the Second International* (Oxford, 1972)

JULES HUMBERT-DROZ, *Der Krieg und die Internationale* (Vienna, 1964)

Institut für Deutsche Militärgeschichte, *Militarismus gegen Sowjetmacht 1917 bis 1919* (Berlin, 1967)

Iz Istorii Vserossiiskoi Chrezvychainoi Komissii, 1917-1921 gg. (Moscow, 1958)

MAUNO JÄÄSKELÄINEN, *Die ostkarelische Frage* (Helsinki, 1965)

WILHELM JOOST, *Botschafter bei den Roten Zaren* (Vienna, 1967)

PETER KENEZ, *Civil War in South Russia, 1918* (Berkeley, California, 1971)

GEORGE F. KENNAN, *Russia Leaves the War* (Princeton, New Jersey, 1956)

– *The Decision to Intervene* (Princeton, New Jersey, 1958)

I.K. KOBLIAKOV, *Ot Bresta do Rapallo* (Moscow, 1954)

N.E. KOROLEV, *Lenin i Mezhdunarodnoe Rabochee Dvizhenie, 1914-1918* (Moscow, 1968)

LIUBOV KRASIN, *Leonid Krassin: His Life and His Work* (London, 1929)

MARCEL LIEBMAN, *Le leninisme sous Lenine.* 2 vols. (Paris, 1973)

ARNO MAYER, *Political Origins of the New Diplomacy, 1917-1918* (New Haven, Connecticut, 1959)

– *Politics and Diplomacy of Peace Making* (New York, 1967)

R.N. MORDVINOV, *Kursom 'Avrory.' Formirovanie Sovetskogo Voenno-Morskogo Flota i Nachal ego Boevoi Deiatel'nosti (Noiabr' 1917-Mart 1919 gg)* (Moscow, 1962)

DAVID W. MORGAN, *The Socialist Left and the German Revolution: A History of the German Independent Social Democratic Party, 1917-1922* (Ithaca, 1975)

JAMES WILLIAM MORLEY, *The Japanese Thrust into Siberia, 1918* (New York, 1957)

WILLIAM PERRY MORSE, JR, 'Leonid Borisovich Krasin: Soviet Diplomat, 1918-1926.' University of Wisconsin doctoral dissertation (Madison, Wisconsin, 1971)

A.P. NENAROKOV, *Vostochnyi Front 1918* (Moscow, 1969)

D.V. OZNOBISHIN, *Ot Bresta do Iur'eva* (Moscow, 1966)

RICHARD PIPES, *The Formation of the Soviet Union: Communism and Nationalism, 1917-1923.* Rev. ed. (Cambridge, Massachusetts, 1964)

- (ed.), *Revolutionary Russia* (Cambridge, Massachusetts, 1968)

ALEXANDER RABINOWITCH, *Prelude to Revolution: The Petrograd Bolsheviks and the July 1917 Uprising* (Bloomington, Indiana, 1968)

OLIVER H. RADKEY, *The Agrarian Foes of Bolshevism* (New York, 1953)

- *The Sickle under the Hammer* (New York, 1963)

ARNOLD REISBERG, *Lenin und die Zimmerwalder Bewegung* (Berlin, 1966)

JOHN S. RESHETAR, JR, *The Ukrainian Revolution, 1917-1920* (Princeton, New Jersey, 1952)

LEONARD SCHAPIRO, *The Origin of the Communist Autocracy* (New York, 1965)

- and PETER REDDAWAY (eds.), *Lenin: The Man, the Theorist, the Leader* (New York, 1967)

GERHARD SCHULTZ, *Revolutions and Peace Treaties, 1917-1920* (London, 1972)

ALFRED ERICH SENN, *The Russian Revolution in Switzerland, 1914-1917* (Madison, Wisconsin, 1971)

JOHN SILVERLIGHT, *The Victors' Dilemma* (New York, 1970)

C. JAY SMITH, JR, *Finland and the Russian Revolution, 1917-1922* (Athens, Georgia, 1958)

P.G. SOFINOV, *Ocherki Istorii Vserossiiskoi Chrezvychainoi Komissii (1917-1922)* (Moscow, 1960)

M.E. SONKIN, *Okno vo Vneshnii Mir* (Moscow, 1964)

- *Kliuchi ot Bronirovannykh Komnat* (Moscow, 1966)

L.M. SPIRIN, *Krakh Odnoi Avantiury: Miatezh Levykh Eserov v Moskve 6-7 Iiulia 1918 g.* (Moscow, 1971)

WOLFGANG STEGLICH, *Die Friedenspolitik der Mittelmächte 1917/1918* (Wiesbaden, 1964)

ISAAC N. STEINBERG, *Spiridonova, Revolutionary Terrorist* (Freeport, New York, 1971)

GEORGE STEWART, *The White Armies of Russia* (New York, 1933)

LEONID I. STRAKHOVSKY, *The Origins of American Intervention in North Russia* (Princeton, New Jersey, 1937)

V.T. SUKHORUKOV, *XI Armiia v Boiakh na Severnom Kavkaze i Nizhnei Volge (1918-1920)* (Moscow, 1961)

RONALD G. SUNY, *The Baku Commune, 1917-1918* (Princeton, New Jersey, 1972)

N.I. SUPRUNENKO, *Ocherki Istorii Grazhdanskoi Voiny i Inostrannoi Interventsii na Ukraine* (Moscow, 1966)

IA.G. TEMKIN, *Tsimmerval'd-Kintal'* (Moscow, 1967)

– *Lenin i Mezhdunarodnaia Sotsial-Demokratiia, 1914-1917* (Moscow, 1968)

JOHN M. THOMPSON, *Russia, Bolshevism and the Versailles Peace* (Princeton, New Jersey, 1966)

GERBURG THUNIG-NITTNER, *Die tschechoslowakische Legion in Russland* (Wiesbaden, 1970)

LEON TROTSKY, *The History of the Russian Revolution.* Three vols. (Ann Arbor, Michigan, 1961)

ULRICH TRUMPENER, *Germany and the Ottoman Empire, 1914-1918* (Princeton, New Jersey, 1968)

M.I. TRUSH, *Vneshnepoliticheskaia Deiatel'nost' V.L. Lenina. 1917-1920* (Moscow, 1963)

ADAM B. ULAM, *The Bolsheviks* (New York, 1965)

RICHARD H. ULLMAN, *Intervention and the War* (Princeton, New Jersey, 1961)

BETTY MILLER UNTERBERGER, *America's Siberian Expedition, 1918-1920* (Durham, North Carolina, 1956)

AUSTIN VAN DER SLICE, *International Labour, Diplomacy and Peace, 1914-1919* (Philadelphia, Pennsylvania, 1941)

V.S. VASIUKOV, *Vneshnaia Politika Vremennogo Pravitelstva* (Moscow, 1966)

– *Predystoriia Interventsii* (Moscow, 1968)

S.IU. VYGODSKII, *Leninskii Dekret o Mire* (Leningrad, 1958)

– *U Istokov Sovetskoi Diplomatii* (Moscow, 1965)

REX A. WADE, *The Russian Search for Peace: February-October 1917* (Stanford, California, 1969)

ROBERT D. WARTH, *The Allies and the Russian Revolution: From the Fall of the Monarchy to the Peace of Brest-Litovsk* (Durham, North Carolina, 1954)

JOHN W. WHEELER-BENNETT, *Brest-Litovsk: the Forgotten Peace, March 1918* (London, 1938)

JOHN ALBERT WHITE, *The Siberian Intervention* (Princeton, New Jersey, 1950)

WILLIAM APPLEMAN WILLIAMS, *American-Russian Relations, 1781-1947* (New York, 1952)

JOHN G. WILLIAMSON, *Karl Helfferich, 1872-1924* (Princeton, New Jersey, 1971)

S. ZARNITSKII and A. SERGEEV, *Chicherin* (Moscow, 1968)

Z.A.B. ZEMAN, *The Gentleman Negotiators* (New York, 1971)

V.K. ZHUKOV, *Chernomorskii Flot v Revoliutsii 1917-1918 gg.* (Moscow, 1931)
N. ZUBOV, *F.E. Dzerzhinskii* (Moscow, 1965)

ARTICLES

A.A. AKHTAMAZIAN, 'O Brest-Litovskikh peregovorakh 1918 goda,' *Voprosi Istorii*, no. 11 (1966) 32-46
RODNEY BARFIELD, 'Lenin's Utopianism: State and Revolution,' *Slavic Review* XXX, no. 1 (March 1971) 45-56
WINFRIED BAUMGART, 'Die "Geschäftliche Behandlung" des Berliner Ergänzungsvertrags vom 27 August 1918,' *Historisches Jahrbuch* LXXXIX (1969) 116-52
– 'Das "Kaspi-Unternehmen" – Grössenwahn Ludendorffs oder Routineplanung des deutschen Generalstabs,' *Jahrbucher fur Geschichte Osteuropas* XVII (1970) 47-126; 231-78
– 'Brest-Litovsk und Versailles: Ein Vergleich zwier Friedensschlüsse,' *Historische Zeitschrift* CCX, no. 3 (June 1970) 583-619
S.I. BLINOV, 'V.I. Lenin i Nekotorye Voprosy Nachal'nogo Etapa Vneshnei Politiki Sovetskogo Gosudarstva,' *Vestnik Moskovskogo Universiteta – Istoriia*, no. 3 (1972) 3-22
MICHAEL J. CARLEY, 'The origins of the French intervention in the Russian civil war, January-May 1918: a reappraisal,' *Journal of Modern History* XLVIII, no. 3 (Sept. 1976) 413-39
RICHARD K. DEBO, 'The making of a Bolshevik: Georgii Chicherin in England, 1914-1918,' *Slavic Review* XXV, no. 4 (Dec. 1966) 651-62
– 'Dutch-Soviet Relations, 1917-1924: the role of finance and commerce in the foreign policy of Soviet Russia and the Netherlands,' *Canadian Slavic Studies* IV, no. 2 (Summer 1970) 199-217
– 'Lockhart plot or Dzerzhinskii plot?' *Journal of Modern History* XLIII, no. 3 (Sept. 1971) 413-39
– 'Litvinov and Kamenev – ambassadors extraordinary: the problem of Soviet representation abroad,' *Slavic Review* XXXIV, no. 3 (Sept. 1975) 463-82
FRITZ EPSTEIN, 'Forschungsberichte: Die Periode von Brest-Litovsk,' *Jahrbücher für Geschichte Osteuropas* XXI, no. 1 (1973) 61-75
ULDIS GERMANIS, 'Some observations on the Yaroslav revolt in July 1918,' *Journal of Baltic Studies* IV, no. 3 (1973) 236-43
E.N. GORODETSKII, 'Demobilizatsiia Armii v 1917-1918 gg,' *Istoriia SSSR*, no. 1 (1958) 3-31
B.P. GUREVICH, 'Vzaimootnosheniia Sovetskikh Respublik s provintsiei Sin'tszian v 1918-1921 godakh,' *Sovetskoe Kitaevedenie*, no. 2 (1958) 96-105

WERNER VON HAHLWEG, 'Lenin und Clausewitz. Ein Beitrag zur Politischen Idee-geschichte des 20. Jahrhunderts,' *Archiv für Kulturgeschichte* XXXVI (1954) 20-59, 357-87

HOLGER H. HERWIG, 'German policy in the Eastern Baltic Sea in 1918: expansion or anti-Bolshevik crusade?' *Slavic Review* XXXII, no. 2 (June 1973) 339-57

KONRAD H. JARAUSCH, 'Co-operation or intervention? Kurt Riezler and the failure of German Ostpolitik, 1918,' *Slavic Review* XXXI, no. 2 (June, 1972) 381-98

B. KANTAROVICH, 'Organizatsionnoe razvitie NKID,' *Mezhdunarodnaia Zhisn'*, no. 15 (133) (7 Nov. 1922) 51-5

GEORGE KATKOV, 'The assassination of Count Mirbach,' *St Antony's Papers* 12 (Soviet Studies 3) (1962) 53-93

J.L.H. KEEP, '1917: the tyranny of Paris over Petrograd,' *Soviet Studies* XX, no. 1 (July, 1968) 22-45

GEORGE F. KENNAN, 'The Sisson documents,' *Journal of Modern History* XXVIII, no. 2 (June 1958) 130-54

S.S. KHUSEINOV, 'Vmeshatel'stvo Imperialisticheskikh Derzhav v Sovetsko-'Vmeshatel'stvo Imperialisticheskikh Derzhav v Sovetsko-Kitaiskie Peregovory, 1917-1918 gg.' *Narody Azii i Afriki*, no. 5 (1962) 83-91

A.P. KLADT, 'S Mandatom Lenina,' *Voprosi Istorii*, no. 10 (1971) 120-37

I.K. KOBLIAKOV, 'Bor'ba Sovetskogo Gosudarstva za Sokhranenie Mira s Germaniei v Period Deistviia Brestskogo Dogovora. (Mart–Noiabr' 1918),' *Istoriia* SSSR, no. 4 (1958) 3-26

'Likvidatsiia Levoeserovskogo Miatezha v Moske v 1918 g.,' *Krasnyi Arkhiv*, no. 4 (1940)

H. SCHURER, 'Karl Moor: German Agent and Friend of Lenin,' *Journal of Contemporary History* V (1970) 131-52

KONSTANTIN L. SELESNJOW, 'Die Propaganda der bolschewistischen Partei unter den deutschen Soldaten an der deutschen Ostfront 1914-1918,' *Zeitschrift für Militärgeschichte*, nos. 1 and 2 (1970) 47-63, 148-65

P. SELIVANOV, 'Sozdanie Zapadnogo Uchastka Otriadov Zavesy,' *Voenno-Istoricheskii Zhurnal*, no. 1 (1972) 28-35

M.I. SVETACHEV, 'Kontseptsii burzhuaznoi istoriografii o vossozdanii vostochnogo fronta v Sibiri v 1918 godu,' *Voprosi Istorii*, no. 2 (1977) 20-37

L.I. TROFIMOVA, 'Pervye Shagi Sovetskoi Diplomatii,' *Novaia i Noveishaia Istoriia*, no. 6 (1971) 37-52; no. 1 (1972) 63-79

TEDDY J. ULDRICKS, 'The Soviet diplomatic corps in the Chicherin era,' *Jahrbücher für Geschichte Osteuropas* XXIII, no. 2 (1975) 213-24

V. VLADIMIROVA, 'Levye Esery v 1917-1918 gg,' *Proletarskaia Revoliutsiia*, no. 4 (63) (1927) 101-39

REX A. WADE, 'Argonauts of peace: the Soviet delegation to Western Europe in the summer of 1917,' *Slavic Review* XXVI, no. 3 (Sept. 1967) 453-67
- 'Irakli Tsereteli and Siberian Zimmerwaldism,' *Journal of Modern History* XXXIX, no. 4 (Dec. 1967) 425-31
- 'Why October? The search for peace in 1917,' *Soviet Studies* XX, no. 1 (July 1968) 36-45
DAVID R. WOODWARD, 'The British government and Japanese intervention in Russia during world war I,' *Journal of Modern History* XLVI, no. 4 (Dec. 1974) 663-85

Index

on *Realpolitik* 342-3; opposes protest against red terror 362; supports Operation Schlussstein 367; opposes occupation of Petrograd 367

Historians: soviet on compromise between Lenin and Trotsky 80-1, 107, 109; on Brest-Litovsk 157-8

Hoffmann, Max von (German general) 27, 30, 31, 66, 97; reluctantly accepts Kühlmann's policy in first phase of Brest-Litovsk 52-5; explains German policy to Ioffe 54; presents German demands to Trotsky 69; on Rada 98; refuses to evacuate occupied territories 101; on treaty with Rada 102; exclamation at meeting of 10 February 111; calls for resumption of war 113-15; considers resumed war to be comical 126; and offensive in central Russia 158-9; delays resumption of peace talks 129-30; launches general offensive 130-2; doubts Bolsheviks will ratify peace treaty 195; plans Operation Schlussstein, 367; halts operation 367

Höglund, Karl (Swedish Social Democrat) 95

Holtzendorff, Henning von (chief of the German naval staff) 116

Homburg, Crown Council of: 13 February 1918 116-20

House, Colonel Edward M. (adviser of American president Wilson): persuades Wilson to oppose Japanese intervention 235; and Wilson's message to All-Russian Congress of Soviets 242

Iaroslav: insurrection at 289-90
Ino, Fort 212-13, 228; abandoned 213

Ioffe, Adolf Abramovich (Soviet diplomat) 86, 143-4, 343, 348; heads Soviet armistice delegation 29-32; leaves for peace conference 49; heads Soviet peace delegation 50-5; lack of caution 52-3; surprised by Hoffmann 54; asks for recess 55; replaced by Trotsky 61; informs Petrograd that Soviet press is exaggerating events in Germany 107; required to go as far as Dvinsk with Soviet peace delegation 147-8; appointed Soviet ambassador to Germany 218; and problem of 'hanging weights' on feet of German generals 218, 309, 353; and problem of Black Sea Fleet 222-6; and negotiation of supplementary treaties 303-5, 309, 331, 332, 333, 334, 335, 336; and ambition to be *narkom* 309-11; and assassination of Mirbach 328, 329; and problem of concentrating Soviet armed forces 282, 341; protests German intention to sweep mines in Baltic Sea 369; appeals for continuation of policy of maneuver 344-5; signs supplementary treaties 346; on supplementary treaties 354; requests German aid against Ukraine 370; threatens to denounce supplementary treaties 371; and crisis with Turkey over Baku 371-2; on danger of sending propaganda to Germany 377; spreads propaganda in Germany 383; briefed on necessity of peace with allies 385; on aid to German revolution 391-2; and expulsion from Germany 394-6; exchanged for German diplomats 405

man military activity in Russia 223;
at Crown Council of Spa 307, 308;
and assassination of Mirbach 326-7
Wilson, Sir Henry (chief of the imperial general staff): favours seizure of
Russian north 265
Wilson, Woodrow (president of the
United States): withdraws objections
to Japanese intervention 235; rein-
states objections 235; sends message
to All-Russian Congress of Soviets
242-3; decision to send American
troops to Siberia 286; asked to initiate peace negotiations 386-9; policy
toward Russia 389

Zalkind, Ivan (deputy foreign commissar): takes charge of foreign commissariat 19-20; and Spanish minister 25n; refuses exit visas to British
subjects 35; proves unsatisfactory as
deputy foreign commissar 88-9
Zinoviev, Grigorii E. (Bolshevik
leader) 82, 140, 315, 325; elected to
Central Committee 180; receives
diplomatic protest against red terror
358; refuses to interfere with Cheka
358
Zvegintsev, Major-General Nikolai I.
(Murmansk Soviet leader) 281